ENGAGED BUDDHISM IN THE WEST

Engaged Buddhism in the West

EDITED BY

CHRISTOPHER S. QUEEN

WISDOM PUBLICATIONS
Boston

WISDOM PUBLICATIONS
199 ELM STREET
SOMERVILLE, MA 02144 USA

LIBRARY OF CONGRESS CATALOGING-IN-PUBLICATION DATA

Engaged Buddhism in the west / Christopher S. Queen, editor.
p. cm.
Includes bibliographical references and index.
ISBN 0-86171-159-9 (alk. paper)
1. Buddhism—Social aspects—North America—History.
2. Buddhism—Social aspects—United States—History.
3. Buddhism—Social aspects—Europe—History.
4. Religious life—Buddhism.
5. Religion and Politics.
I. Queen, Christopher S., 1945– .
BQ724.E64. 2000
294.3'37—DC21   99-36870

ISBN 0-86171-159-9

04 03 02 01 00
6   5   4   3   2

Cover photographs: Courtesy Paul Green (top), Franz-Johannes
Litsch (middle and lower right), Marcel Duval (lower left).

Designed by: Graciela Galup

Wisdom Publications' books are printed on acid-free paper and meet the
guidelines for the permanence and durability of the committee on production guidelines for book longevity of the council on library resources.

Printed in the United States of America

CONTENTS

ENGAGED BUDDHISM IN EUROPE, AFRICA, AND AUSTRALIA

LOOKING AHEAD

Reverend Kato Shonin and Venerable Bimal at the New England Peace Pagoda, Massachusetts, 1992. Courtesy Buddhist Peace Fellowship.

PREFACE

THIS COLLECTION OF ESSAYS was written by scholars and practitioners of socially engaged Buddhism. Unlike scholarly volumes that seek impartiality and critical distance, this book breathes a sense of appreciation for the persons, groups, and events that are shaping the new Buddhism. This is not to say that the contributors are dewy-eyed or uncritical. Most have risen to the challenge of defining "engaged Buddhism"—coming to widely different conclusions—and assessing its efficacy in prisons, shelters, hospices, the workplace, and the streets. It is rather to say that the essays gathered here are a labor of love, founded on a common perception that something important and unprecedented is happening in one of the world's ancient spiritual traditions.

Most of the contributors to *Engaged Buddhism in the West* have never met, yet the effect of reading their essays is similar to that of sitting around a seminar table, listening to a lively conversation. Patricia Hunt-Perry and Lyn Fine argue that, for members of Thich Nhat Hanh's Order of Interbeing, all Buddhism is engaged, while Sandra Bell reports that some of Britain's most socially engaged Buddhists reject the term altogether. These discussions point to a myriad of others going on in faraway places. Rod Bucknell, trained as a monk in Thailand, reports on the hospice services and overseas relief projects of fellow Australian Buddhists, while Franz-Johannes Litsch shares his experience as leader of the German Buddhist Union.

The sense of a close-knit community of discourse is reinforced by the fact that authors often cite other authors' roles as leaders of engaged Buddhism. Robert Goss cites Judith Simmer-Brown as director of the Naropa Institute masters degree program in engaged Buddhism. Judith Simmer-Brown cites Susan Moon, editor of the Buddhist Peace Fellowship's quarterly, *Turning Wheel*, in her chapter on the Buddhist Peace Fellowship, while Susan Moon, in her chapter on activist Buddhist women, features Paula Green, author of the Nipponzan Myohoji chapter, for her work in international conflict resolution—and so on. Meanwhile, major figures like Thich Nhat Hanh, Joanna Macy, and Bernard Glassman appear and reappear as the founders and role models for numerous engaged Buddhist organizations and projects throughout the world.

The need for this volume became apparent years ago as Sallie King and I discussed the scope of our earlier collection, *Engaged Buddhism: Buddhist Liberation Movements in Asia* (1996). In treating the global influence of figures like Thich Nhat Hanh and the Dalai Lama, it was difficult to resist the temptation to explore Buddhist peace and service groups in the developed countries of North America, Europe, and the Southern Hemisphere. Yet at the same time it seemed important to acknowledge the priority of Asian leaders and groups in addressing the collective, institutionalized sources of human suffering and ecological degradation. We admitted that a treatment of engaged Buddhism in the West would have to wait for another occasion.

Despite the broad scope of this book, which details scores of engaged Buddhist organizations and projects, I cannot guarantee exhaustive coverage of the field. During the three-year gestation of the book, I received numerous suggestions for inclusion. Typical was the scribbled note accompanying David Chappell's final draft chapter:

> I have been negligent in not promoting a local socially-engaged movement started in a Jodo Shinshu Temple here in Hawaii. Are you including Project Dana in your book? It is a voluntary project for the homebound that involves 19 temples in Hawaii and 2 in California with 600 volunteers serving 800 frail, elderly, and handicapped people. It was started in 1989. Its founder, Rose Nakamura, received the first Rosalyn Carter national award for caregiving, and they are the only Buddhist group in the National Association of Volunteer Interfaith Caregivers that includes 750 groups! Project Dana was inspired by Project Respect, a Christian group which has since folded, but now Christian groups are joining Project Dana—a real interfaith development!

I had not heard of Project Dana before, and none of the twenty contributors had mentioned it in their essays. I added the note to a file with many others. Some of these groups appeared in the chapters submitted later, but others remain in the file. I only wish I could have mentioned them all.

I would like to thank my students at Harvard for forcing me to defend my hypotheses about the emergence of a new Buddhism. I also thank Charles Prebish, Virginia Straus, Richard Seager, Steve Jenkins, John Dunne, Duncan Williams, and each of the contributors to this book for detailed e-mails, immoderate phone calls, voicemails, faxes, lunches at the Café of India, scribbled notes, and in-flight debates about the direction of contemporary Buddhism. I thank Tim McNeill, David Strom, Samantha Kent, Graciela

Galup, Paul Miller, Tony Grima, Peter Bermudes, and their skillful colleagues at Wisdom Publications; David Mumper for assistance preparing the manuscript; Friederike Baer-Wallis for her translation of the chapter on engaged Buddhism in German-speaking Europe; Stuart Chandler for preparing the bibliography and index; and Andrew Olendzki for opportunities to lecture and retreat at the Barre Center for Buddhist Studies. I thank my wife, Alys Terrien-Queen, and daughter, Laura, for their love and encouragement, and my parents, Dr. Merritt B. Queen and Dorothea Mitchell Queen, for demonstrating wisdom and compassion each day of their lives.

CHRISTOPHER S. QUEEN
Cambridge, June 1999

Nipponzan Myohoji peace march, New England, 1988.
Courtesy Paula Green.

Introduction: A New Buddhism

Christopher S. Queen

AT THE TURN OF THE THIRD MILLENNIUM, amid the triumphs of science and technology, the global competition for resources, markets, and loyalties, and the decay of many of the political and environmental systems that sustain human and biological life, people of religious faith are once again bringing ancient teachings and practices into a new era. Most acknowledge the profound transformation the world has undergone since the founding of their traditions, and many are engaged in refashioning their heritage to meet the challenges of the future.

For Buddhists and practitioners of the other world faiths, it is no longer possible to measure the quality of human life primarily in terms of an individual's observance of traditional rites, such as meditation, prayer, or temple ritual; or belief in dogmas such as "the law of karma," "buddha-nature," "the will of God," or "the Tao." Now there are widespread forces at work, many of them humanly created, that separate the world into sectors of relative safety and comfort, and much larger regions of poverty, oppression, and war. Even within the borders of "the West," as the comfort zone is called, the number of citizens who face poverty, marginalization, and the denial of human rights continues to increase.[1]

In this introduction, we shall consider the thesis that socially engaged Buddhism—the application of the Dharma, or Buddhist teachings, to the resolution of social problems—has emerged in the context of a global conversation on human rights, distributive justice, and social progress. Inasmuch as these concepts have had few parallels in the classical formulations of early Buddhism (later called Hinayana or "narrow vehicle"), reform Buddhism (Mahayana or "great vehicle"), and syncretic Buddhism (Vajrayana or "diamond vehicle"), I shall argue that the general pattern of belief and practice that has come to be called "engaged Buddhism" is unprecedented, and thus tantamount to a new chapter in the history of the tradition. As a style of ethical practice, engaged Buddhism may be seen as a new paradigm of Buddhist

I

liberation. Invoking traditional terminology, Buddhists might call it a "new vehicle"—or *Navayana*, as the Indian civil rights leader B. R. Ambedkar did on the eve of his conversion to Buddhism in 1956—or a *fourth yana* in the evolution of the Dharma.

In the following sections let us consider (1) the shift in religious orientation that is reflected in new Buddhist attitudes toward liberation and society, (2) the range of activities and interpretations offered by engaged Buddhists in this collection, (3) the nature of "engagement" in the context of earlier styles of Buddhist ethics: discipline, virtue, and altruism, and (4) the argument for regarding engaged Buddhism as a new turning of the wheel of Dharma—a new vehicle, or a fourth yana.

LIBERATION AND SOCIETY

All of the ancient spiritual traditions offer some form of relief from the reality of human suffering. These teachings and techniques typically comprise a *theodicy*, an explanation of the causes of evil and suffering in the world, and a *soteriology*, a complex of beliefs and practices to overcome and transcend the hardships of life, such as the action of natural and divine forces and the knowledge and rituals of the human community in relation to these forces. The fortunes and blessings of the individual and the group are sealed by their faithfulness to, or dissent from, the laws of God, the demands of the spirit world, or the impersonal workings of karma. Rewards and punishments result from actions performed in the past, while today's actions determine tomorrow's happiness, suffering, rebirth, or eternal life.[2]

The Buddha's unique manifesto for human liberation, the four noble truths, addresses the dynamics of psychological suffering, finding its cause in a craving for objects and relationships that are ultimately ephemeral, and prescribing relief through an eight-step program of re-education and self-cultivation. His religious order, the Sangha, offers intensive spiritual practice to those who renounce the obligations of family life and economic production, while a set of moral and practical teachings point the lay community toward harmonious and productive roles in society.

These liberation teachings remain as viable today as they were in the Bronze and Iron ages. But another set of ideas about the possibility of human fulfillment and happiness have emerged with the achievements of modernity. While they are rooted in ancient conceptions of individual striving, such as discipline, virtue, and altruism; and in ideas of tribal identity, covenant community, and monastic order; they owe their distinctive character to notions of human rights, social justice, political activism, and due process that have evolved in the "Western" cultural tradition, with contributions from

Judaism, Greek humanism, Christianity, Roman and Anglo-Saxon law, the scientific and social Enlightenment of seventeenth and eighteenth century Europe, and the pragmatism and progressivism of nineteenth and twentieth century America.[3]

The essence of the new outlook is a recognition of (1) the inalienable value of the human person, whatever his or her level of achievement or standing in the community, (2) the social and collective nature of experience, shaped in particular by cultural and political institutions that have the power to promote good or evil, fulfillment or suffering, progress or decline, and (3) the necessity of collective action to address the systemic causes of suffering and promote social advancement in the world. Despite the inalienable value of the person, it is no longer possible to see the individual as the sole "unit" of liberation or salvation—a solitary subject of divine or natural forces, or the prime beneficiary of self-cultivation—separate from the complex of roles and relationships that make up his or her life-world. Indeed, the very notion of an "individual" belies the multiplicity of roles, loyalties, and identities that comprise the modern "protean self."[4]

Now it is necessary to consider the effects of personal and social actions on others, particularly in the realms of speech and symbol manipulation in the Information Age, and in the policies, programs, and products of large and small institutions. "The others" affected by these actions must be understood not only as unit selves, but as significant collectivities: families, neighbors, and workplace teams; social, ethnic, and economic groups; national and international populations; and, not least, biological species and ecosystems.[5]

Collective consciousness is not new, of course. Tribal people have accounted for their destiny as a *totemic group* in relation to the spirit world and other groups; the Hindu caste system is a sacred *hierarchy of groups* defined by meticulous rules of occupation, marriage, and privilege; and the ancient Hebrews recorded their history as the biography of a *chosen people* before God. Yet these ancient conceptions bound members of the totem group, the endogamous caste, and the covenant community together in fealty to God, priesthood, economy, and king in ways that limited dissent.[6]

By contrast, the religious communities founded by the Buddha, Jesus, and Muhammad were more fluid and spontaneous, calling their converts away from old economic and tribal obligations to practice the holy life. Here the institutions of mainstream society—government, commerce, and temple—were at least partially abandoned in the fervent quest for an ethical-spiritual counterculture, in which converts were free to come and go in search of a spiritual home. In time, however, the countercultures of the sangha, the church, and the *umma* (Muslim community), like those of the tribe, the caste, and the people of Yahweh, imposed their own restrictions and boundaries upon members, while simultaneously reintegrating them into the structures of society at large.[7]

Today the dynamics of collective consciousness are more complex. While formerly the identity and mission of tribal, social, and religious groups evolved gradually in interaction with changes in the natural and political environment, today the identity and mission of organizations, including religious communities, are changing constantly and rapidly. Since the end of World War II, a state of permanent revolution has superseded the cultural and religious evolutions of the past—driven, among many factors, by the sheer number of organizations in the world, including businesses, governments, civic organizations, and social and religious groups.

Also significant in preparing the soil for the rapid growth of religiously inspired social activism in the late twentieth century have been the heightened, often desperate, competition for resources—water, food, employment, education, and healthcare, to name a few—in many parts of a shrinking planet, and the instantaneous global telecommunications made possible by satellite and computer technology. These conditions in combination fuel rising expectations and deepening disaffection among the have-nots, who can now see and hear the images of a forbidden world—one in which children are fed and schooled, illness is treated, and clear water flows from taps in the kitchen and bath.[8]

VARIETIES OF ENGAGED BUDDHISM

It is into such a world that socially engaged Buddhism began to make its appearance in the postwar period. The years from 1956 to 1966, for example, saw millions of India's ex-Untouchables take refuge in Buddhism as a tradition of equality and liberation that could guide their struggle against the Hindu caste system; the founding of the Sarvodaya Shramadana movement of volunteer work-camps in Sri Lanka, which applied traditional Buddhist principles to the alleviation of rural poverty; and the founding of the School of Youth for Social Service and the Tiep Hien Order (Order of Interbeing) by the Vietnamese Buddhist monk Thich Nhat Hanh and nun Chan Khong, who responded to the ravages of the war in their country by organizing volunteers in the rebuilding of bombed villages, starting farmers' cooperatives, establishing clinics, and lobbying in the West for an end to the war.

The study of engaged Buddhism in Asia alone must encompass liberation movements for the survival of the Tibetan people and culture; local movements for the rights of ordained and lay women in many Buddhist lands; the writings of engaged Buddhist thinkers and activists, such as Buddhadasa

Bhikkhu and Sulak Sivaraksa of Thailand; the social and peace work of the Soka Gakkai and other Nichiren-inspired movements in Japan, particularly the Rissho Kosei-kai and Nipponzan Myohoji sects; the peace work of Maha Ghosananda, "the Gandhi of Cambodia"; and the opposition leadership of Aung San Suu Kyi, the Nobel Peace laureate of Myanmar (Burma).[9]

As the twenty studies of the present volume reveal, the range of concerns that motivate Western Buddhists to public service and political activism encompass nearly every area of social experience, conflict, and suffering: war and violence, race, human rights, environmental destruction, gender relations, sexual orientation, ethnicity, health care, prisons, schools, and the workplace. Like informed and caring members in every religious culture, engaged Buddhists have seen, heard, and responded to the cries of fellow human beings—and of nonhuman living beings—who face abuse, injury, or violent death.

There is great unity among the engaged Buddhists profiled in this book on one point: that the existence of suffering in the world evokes in them a feeling of "universal responsibility," as the Dalai Lama has called it, and the traditional vow to "save all beings." More importantly, engaged Buddhists would agree that such a feeling impels them to act "in the world." In a time when those who speak of "saving the world" can expect snide derision, if not social ostracism, these Buddhists are uninhibited in their expression of universal compassion *(maha karuna)*:

> Once there is seeing, there must be acting....
> We must be aware of the real problems of the world.
> Then, with mindfulness, we will know what to do,
> And what not to do, to be of help.

Something had to be done, and specifically something political needed to be done by Buddhists. "Anyone, feeling compassion, seeing no boundary between self and others, would feel compelled to do something," observed Nelson Foster, reflecting on the occasion.

> I vow to listen to all others and to allow myself to be touched
>   by the joy and pain of life.
> I vow to invite all hungry spirits into the circle of my practice
>   and raise the mind of compassion as my offering of the Supreme
>   Meal.
> I vow to commit my energy and my love for the healing of myself,
>   the earth, humanity and all creations.[10]

These passages, taken from the first three chapters below, express in turn the social philosophy of Thich Nhat Hanh, who is credited with introducing the term "engaged Buddhism" in the 1960s; the sense of urgency of the founders of the Buddhist Peace Fellowship, sitting on the front porch of their teacher, Robert Aitken Roshi, in Maui in the late 1970s; and three vows of the Zen Peacemaker Order, founded by Roshi Bernard Glassman and the late Sandra Jishu Holmes in the 1990s.

Three characteristics of socially engaged Buddhism may be gleaned from these quotations. The first may be called *Awareness*. The metaphors of seeing and hearing, and the ancient Buddhist term "mindfulness" (Pali: *sati*) are familiar ways of expressing the essence of a *buddha*, an "Awakened One," whose deep wisdom (Pali: *pannya*) comes from seeing the true constituents and interdependence of oneself and the world. The term *sati* refers to a form of meditation, the simple but penetrating awareness of breathing and other bodily and mental states, and the conditions in and around the meditator, as they are happening. Mindfulness contains the additional meaning of "remembering"—one's previous condition or lives, and consequently the interrelatedness of all beings. Among the heroic savior figures in Mahayana Buddhism, the *bodhisattvas* ("enlightenment beings"), the most famous is the Indian Avalokiteshvara (Kuan-yin in China, and Kannon or Kanzeon in Japan), "He/she who sees/hears the cries of the world." All of these associations provide touchstones of understanding and inspiration for engaged Buddhists today.

The second characteristic of engaged Buddhism is a deep *Identification* of the self and the world—a sense of oneness, nondualism, interdependence, and empathy for all beings. First becoming aware of the sufferings of others by seeing, hearing, and acknowledging their experience, one then has "compassion," or "sym-pathy," a co-feeling or fellow-feeling that, unlike pity, dissolves the boundary between oneself and the other.[11] In the essays collected here, Thich Nhat Hanh identifies with the murderous pirate and the underworld arms dealer in his compassion for the plight of war refugees and victims, while Bernard Glassman observes that the "hungry ghosts" we invite to our table are no different than we, who serve the "supreme meal of compassion." We learn of the Nichiren Buddhist doctrine of *esho funi*, "the oneness of self and world," and the healing (or *wholing*) of mind, body, self, and society that engaged Buddhists have discovered in Mindfulness-Based Stress Reduction programs and the Gay Buddhist Fellowship in San Francisco.

The third characteristic of engaged Buddhism suggested by our quotations is the imperative of *action*. "Once there is seeing, there must be acting," writes Thich Nhat Hanh. "Something had to be done, and specifically something political needed to be done by Buddhists," writes Judith Simmer-Brown of the founding of the Buddhist Peace Fellowship. For Glassman, the identification of others' suffering as "my suffering" leads inexorably to action:

> If this is me, and it's bleeding, I take care of it. I don't join a discussion group or wait for the right equipment or wait until I am enlightened or go off to get trained. I immediately get some rags to stop the bleeding—because it's me that's bleeding![12]

One recalls the Buddha's advice to bystanders in the parable of the poison arrow—"Pull out the arrow and treat the wound; leave the questions for later!"—and the urgent sense of compulsion of the Hebrew prophets when confronted by social injustice: "The lion has roared; who will not fear? Lord Yahweh has spoken; who can but prophesy?" (Amos 3.8).

The essays collected here may be used as a mine for prospecting additional features of engaged Buddhism as it is practiced in the West at the end of the twentieth century. Indeed, certain themes and threads reappear throughout the book and suggest an emerging consensus. In addition to awareness, identification, and action, most engaged Buddhists view their practice as *nonviolent* (observant of the first Buddhist precept, not to harm others), *nonhierarchical* (believing in the equal dignity of all persons, if not all sentient beings), and *nonheroic* (believing that effective social change requires collective, "grass-roots" activity, not the charismatic leadership of high-profile individuals).[13]

Engaged Buddhists do not agree on all matters, however, and a most significant area of disagreement is their attitudes toward the term and notion of "engagement" itself. Our first essay, provocatively titled "All Buddhism is Engaged," surveys the teachings and activities of Thich Nhat Hanh and the Order of Interbeing. Early in the chapter we learn that Nhat Hanh's work was a "departure from the twentieth century traditional world of monastic Vietnamese Buddhism":

> A Buddhist collective action emerged which was aimed at directly influencing public policy and establishing new institutional forms. One form of collective action was noncooperation with government, such as strikes, mass resignations, the return of government licenses, and boycotts of classes by students. Another was the use of cultural forms such as fiction and non-fiction writing, and anti-war songs.

Thus it is clear that, "despite the presence in Vietnamese history of earlier roots of engaged Buddhist practice," the founding of the School of Youth for Social Service and the politicization of the Unified Buddhist Church (UBC) represented a new kind of Buddhist practice. But by the 1990s, some followers of Thich Nhat Hanh defined engaged Buddhism as "practicing mindfulness in daily life" and stressed that "socially engaged practice and social activism do not necessarily overlap." In the end, some critics regard Thich Nhat Hanh's teachings as "too engaged," while others believe they are "not engaged enough."

British Buddhists present a wide range of views on the meaning of "engagement." Venerable Khemadhammo, the founder and spiritual director of the Buddhist prison chaplaincy and aftercare service, Angulimala (discussed in chapters 13 and 15 below)—certainly an "engaged Buddhist" by any standard—is disturbed by the term:

> When people ask me, as they quite often do, What is an engaged Buddhist? I am embarrassed. The phrase seems to imply that there are, can be, disengaged Buddhists. That is not something I feel it is polite, or politic, to admit. This becomes clearer if we use the Dalai Lama's alternative expression, "universal responsibility." Would it sound okay to say, "We are the responsible Buddhists, they are the irresponsible ones?"

On the other hand, Ken Jones, author of *The Social Face of Buddhism: An Approach to Political and Social Activism* (1989) and *Beyond Optimism: A Buddhist Political Ecology* (1993), and a prominent member of the Network of Engaged Buddhists in Britain, is not at all shy about the term. Jones has proposed the use of the terms "soft" for Buddhists committed primarily to "mindfulness in daily life" and "hard" for those committed to "influencing public policy and establishing new institutional forms":

> At the soft end are individuals and organizations who see Engaged Buddhism as ranging from being kind to your neighbors to promoting a society based on the principles of the Dharma. The hard-enders do not deny the irrefutable logic of this, but claim that it robs Engaged Buddhism of a sufficiently clear definition....Hard-enders believe governments and other institutions should be included in the active concerns of Buddhist morality; soft-enders tend to urge only personal responsibility. Soft-enders tend to be less keen on Buddhist social analysis and more on personal experience and mindfulness.

If the continuum from personal experience (soft) to social analysis (hard) reflects one way of classifying, if not defining, engaged Buddhists, the continuum from *mindfulness-based practice* to *service-based practice* represents another. In his study of Jon Kabat-Zinn's Mindfulness-Based Stress

Reduction programs, Andrew Olendzki demonstrates their debt to the psychology of ancient Buddhism, in which health is defined as the absence of *dukkha*, the state of dissatisfaction that arises from craving for objects and relationships that are ultimately ephemeral. Thus *dukkha* is a form of self-imposed, cognitive-emotional stress that is subject to clinical treatment. Enter the Buddha, a great healer whose four noble truths are (1) the doctor's diagnosis of illness *(dukkha),* (2) its etiology *(tanha,* craving, and *moha,* ignorance), (3) a prescription for health *(nibbana,* the absence of illness), and (4) the treatment plan (the eightfold path).

In traditional Buddhism, as in modern science, the mind and the body are correlative and interactive, each causing effects and changes in the other. Yet in the Theravada Buddhist world view, only the mind—through meditation—can engage and overcome the dynamics of suffering. For suffering, like the whole phenomenal world, is a product of the mind. But what about society—is this not the realm in which engaged Buddhism operates? Olendzki writes,

> The fact that mindfulness practice involves the inner life rather than external manifestations does not necessarily make it any less a form of engaged Buddhism. When meditation practice is used in healing, with what is it really engaging? Unlike other forms of engaged Buddhism it is not interacting with oppressive social institutions, or with the makers of war or the breakers of peace, or with those who violate human rights or ravage the environment.

Only by overcoming the *disease* of suffering in the world at its root—the unwholesome psychological "secretions" *(ashravas)* of hatred, greed, and delusion—through mindfulness meditation, may engaged Buddhists address the external symptoms of social suffering. "It may be possible to engage the mind without significantly changing the larger world we all share," Olendzki concludes, "but it is not possible to engage the world except through engagement with the mind."

A further implication of *mindfulness-based engaged Buddhism* is that the Buddha's "comprehensive program for understanding and addressing...the deep craving that causes suffering...is almost entirely out of the reach of most contemporary Buddhists." According to Olendzki, it takes a "professional sage"—a full-time meditator—to recover fully from the disease of *dukkha*, while "the rest of us may employ an array of practices which can effectively mitigate its symptoms." This is the traditional position of the Theravada School of ancient Buddhism, which the Mahayana populists called the "elite" or "narrow" path, *Hinayana*, because of its emphasis on the holy life of the monk as the most effective prescription for the relief of suffering in the world.

Service-based engaged Buddhism is my term for the results-oriented practice of teachers like Bernard Glassman and many of the Buddhist environmentalists, prison chaplains, and peace activists profiled in this book. These practitioners may be rightly called "activists" as they work to create jobs, increase the participation of Blacks and Hispanics in the sangha, stop the violence in the maximum security unit, restore the Tibetans to their rightful land, and save the California redwoods.

Because all people are "hungry ghosts," suffering from the diseases of craving and ignorance, Roshi Glassman emphasizes the preparation and service of the Supreme Meal, his metaphor for the life of an engaged Buddhist, with his or her own unique "ingredients": talents, resources, motives, and opportunities. Unlike the holy meals in the Western religious traditions—the Passover Seder, the Christian Eucharist, and the evening feasts during the Muslim month of Ramadan—in which those who *consume* the food are nourished, healed, and liberated, the Zen meal is the spiritual practice of the *tenzo*, the Buddhist chef, a bodhisattva whose own spiritual goal of nourishment, healing, and liberation can only be achieved by *serving the meal to others*.

I asked Roshi Glassman whether he regarded *zazen*, sitting meditation, as indispensable to the practice of engaged Buddhism. Inasmuch as Zen is the Mahayana School that emphasizes meditation (*zen* being the Japanese mispronunciation of the Chinese *ch'an,* the mispronunciation of the Sanskrit *dhyana*, "meditation"), I was surprised by his answer:

> I'll be radical and say no. For me personally *zazen* has been very important, and I can't imagine not having a daily sitting practice, but I have met wonderful people who are considered great teachers, who have wonderful sitting practices, who I don't consider very enlightened. And I have met wonderful people who don't practice *zazen* who I think are enlightened. So I would say no. If you mean, like the Sixth Patriarch, that the elimination of subject-object is indispensable, I would agree. But simply sitting is not essential. There are many ways to actualize that state of oneness, of nonduality. I know Sufis and Jews who don't have a daily sitting practice. I know many Tibetans who don't sit everyday.

Can a meditator on retreat in a cave be an engaged Buddhist? Yes, says the Zen master, again confounding the visitor. The cave meditator may be just as engaged as someone who works with the homeless. "Our aim in meditation and spiritual practice is to find the wholeness of life." Before we can bring peace to the family, the community, the nation, or the world, we must bring peace to ourselves. The means might be meditation, chanting, or ritual, such as placing fresh flowers before the Buddha image or performing the Gate of Sweet Nectar ceremony with the Zen Peacemaker community—in the *zendo* or on the streets of lower Manhattan. On the other hand, the means to wholeness might be service or activism, practiced alone (writing a letter or a donation check) or with others (volunteering at a hospice or attending a public rally); accompanied by the other skillful means (meditation, chanting, ritual), or by itself, as the sole form of spiritual practice undertaken by an engaged Buddhist.

With Glassman Roshi, the continuum from mindfulness-based to service-based engaged Buddhism becomes a full circle.

FOUR STYLES OF BUDDHIST ETHICS

These reflections on the varieties of engaged Buddhism raise the larger question of the place of social engagement in the history of Buddhist ethics. Of course, Buddhism in Asia and the West is hardly a single, unbroken story. Indeed, some of the teachings and practices we have already sampled reflect the historical branching and broadening of the tradition as the Dharma was carried from India to China, Southeast Asia, Tibet, Korea, and Japan over two thousand five hundred years.

Despite these great spans of time and space, I believe it is possible to identify four distinctive styles of Buddhist ethics: *discipline, virtue, altruism,* and *engagement.* I prefer to describe them as "styles of practice" rather than "historical stages," for they may be seen as overlapping and cumulative. On the other hand, I think it is accurate to say that discipline and virtue are probably characteristic of the earlier centuries of Buddhist history, while altruism and engagement came to prominence later on. It may even be accurate to say that the fourth style, "engagement," has few precedents before the nineteenth century, as I have argued elsewhere.[14]

The ethics of discipline, virtue, and altruism will be familiar to those who study Buddhist literature. David Chappell writes, "Mahayana ethics has a threefold emphasis, avoiding evil, cultivating good, and saving all beings."[15] These objectives, enacted by observing monastic "discipline" *(vinaya)* and lay "morality" *(shila);* meditating on the "divine abodes" *(brahma viharas)* and "perfections" *(paramitas);* and vowing to serve others *(bodhisattvacarya)* became leitmotifs in the Mahayana commentarial literature, providing, for example, the basic structure of Asanga's *Chapter on Ethics* (India, fifth century C.E.) and Gyonen's compendium of ethics, *Risshu Koyo* (Japan, thirteenth century C.E.). The Japanese scholar Ono Hodo has found at least fourteen sets of terms to represent these three categories in Chinese literature.[16]

Another indication of the centrality of discipline, virtue, and altruism for Mahayana ethics is their role in Atisha's commentary, *The Lamp of the Path to Enlightenment and Its Explanation* (Tibet, eleventh century C.E.). According to Georges Dreyfus, this text

> became the model for a genre of Tibetan Buddhist literature, later known as *lam rim* (Gradual Stages of the Path), which represents a basic view of Buddhist practice...widely accepted in Tibet, both among [the] lay population and *virtuosi*. It is practiced by all the contemporary schools of Tibetan Buddhism...[and] its views resonate with the understanding of other Buddhist traditions, particularly Theravada, which share a similar gradualist approach.[17]

Let us examine briefly these three styles of practice, which, taken together, Mahayana philosophers and systematizers came to call *shila* or morality.

The Ethics of Discipline

This style of Buddhist practice takes us back to the primitive community of men and women who attempted to follow the Buddha's path to enlightenment. Like the Biblical Hebrews, the early Buddhists were committed to the disciplined observance of moral regulations. And like the Hebrews and Israelites, the Buddhists formulated their morality in memorable lists—the *pancha shila* or "five precepts" for laity, and the *vinaya* or "discipline" of some two hundred and fifty rules for monks and nuns—which were regularly recited at community rituals.

The ethics of discipline entails the avoidance of conduct that arises from the mental impurities of hatred, greed, and delusion. "I undertake to abstain from taking life...from taking what is not given...from sexual misconduct...from untruthful speech...from taking intoxicants." This is the chant of lay and ordained Buddhists of every practice lineage. Along with the *tisarana* or "three refuge" formula (reverence to the Buddha, the Dharma, and the Sangha), the pledge to observe the *pancha shila,* or *pansil*, is perhaps the most universal expression of Buddhist identity.

Early Buddhists often referred to their practice as *buddhasasana* or simply *sasana*, which means "instruction, admonition, message, order." This instruction was summed up in a well-known verse, found in such early texts as the *Dhammapada*, the *Mahapadanasutta*, and an early form of the *Patimokkha*, the disciplinary code of monastic rules. The verse reads,

> Refraining from all that is evil,
> Attaining what is wholesome,
> Purifying the mind:
> This is the instruction *[sasana]* of the Buddhas.[18]

The focus of the Buddhist ethics of discipline is the training of the solitary practitioner, although the effects of such observance are obviously beneficial to society as a whole. In its Mahayana formulation, the first level of *shila* concerns the avoidance of two types of faults: natural faults that directly harm others, such as killing; and conventional faults that abrogate ritual obligations, such as a monk's eating after the noon hour. While both failures of discipline engender negative karma for the practitioner, the lam rim tradition defines morality as the resolution to abstain from harming others, and thus takes the commission of natural faults more seriously.[19]

The Ethics of Virtue

Prefigured in the verse above, in which "refraining from what is detrimental" is linked to "attaining what is wholesome [and] purifying the mind," an ethics of virtue moves from a restrictive sensibility to a constructive one, in which the practitioner's relationship to other persons comes more clearly into view. It is difficult to imagine the practice of *metta bhavana* or "loving-kindness meditation," for example, without considering the projection of good wishes first to oneself and then, progressively, to loved ones, acquaintances, strangers, and enemies. Likewise, the *vipassana* or insight meditator may project feelings of compassion *(karuna)*, joy *(mudita)*, and equanimity *(upekkha)* toward others, thus cultivating these virtuous states of mind or "divine abodes" *(brahma viharas)* and, in the process, favorably dispose herself or himself to act in these ways in society—or "off the cushion," as we say today.

A great deal has been written about the return of Aristotle's "virtue ethics" in recent moral philosophy and Buddhist ethics. In his introduction to a scholarly discussion of Buddhist ethics in 1996, Charles Prebish noted what he called a "creative paradigm shift" among scholars from the study of *vinaya*, an externally enforced code concerned with self-purification, to *shila*, an internally enforced ethical framework around which any Buddhist practitioner might structure his or her life. *Shila*, he concluded, is an enormously rich concept for understanding individual ethical conduct.[20]

In *The Nature of Buddhist Ethics* (1992), Damien Keown argues that all Buddhist ethics are founded on self-cultivated virtue.[21] Dreyfus finds in Atisha's *Lamp of the Path*, for example, the Mahayana counterpart of ancient Buddhism's *brahma viharas*—namely, the bodhisattva practice of the six perfections *(paramitas)*: generosity, morality, courage, patience, contemplation, and wisdom. Called "the whole range of virtuous practices" undertaken by one who vows to reach buddhahood for the sake of all sentient beings, these practices, like the divine abodes, are forms of personal cultivation that do not entail specific behaviors in specific situations. Rather, they point to a quality of living that is inherently valuable, free from suffering, and conducive to good deeds.[22]

Virtuous "moods and motivations" (to use Clifford Geertz's phrase) are not necessarily virtuous deeds, however.[23] In *Love and Sympathy in Theravada Buddhism* (1980) and a companion article, "Motivations to Social Action in Theravada Buddhism," Harvey B. Aronson warned that the Theravada practice of meditation on the four abodes does not entail social action or service to others, but rather "personal, psychological, or soterio-logical benefits."[24] This is not to say that the Buddha and his community did not teach the Dharma "for the welfare and happiness of the multitude and out of sympathy for the world" (in the famous formula that punctuates the Pali texts), but rather that sympathy *(anukampa)* and service *(karunnya)* were less often mentioned as goals of the path. Modern authors, such as Walpola Rahula, who argue that the heritage of the Buddhist monk *(bhikkhu)* was public service based on compassion and love, have misread the tradition.[25]

Similarly, Dreyfus stresses the value of ethical cultivation for its own sake, outside of the domain of rules and injunctions and outside the utili-tarian calculus of "choosing the right course of action for the sake of the greater happiness of the greater number." While externalized, duty-based, deontological, or consequentialist ethics have dominated moral reflection since the time of Kant in the West, they miss the qualitative heart of Buddhist virtue, namely, the cultivation of character for its own sake, or to achieve final liberation from future rebirth in the world.[26]

The Ethics of Altruism

Service to others, or altruism, is the third style of Buddhist moral develop-ment recommended in the Mahayana treatises. This activity is spelled out by Atisha in ways that the Pali literature reserved for occasional advice to monarchs and the laity: "nursing the sick, leading the blind, helping the down-trodden, feeding those who are hungry, and providing lodging for those who are needy." "This dispels the misrepresentation of Buddhism as promoting self-involvement," writes Dreyfus. Unlike discipline and virtue, altruism is resolutely oriented toward others. In the lam rim tradition of Tibetan Buddhism, meditation on compassion is intended "not just to develop a healthy concern for others—but to actually help them."[27]

Altruism does not entail self-denial or ignore self-cultivation, however. It is a fulfillment of the practitioner's capacity for generosity, morality, courage, patience, mindfulness, and wisdom—the virtues of the bodhisattva path. Now service becomes, not the by-product of self-cultivation, but the means to it, the very manifestation of buddhahood.

David Chappell's exegesis of the *Upasaka Precept Sutra*, an early Mahayana text available only in Chinese until recently, shows the decisiveness of the shift from virtue to altruism.[28] In the first chapter, lay bodhisattvas are described as the highest practitioners of the Dharma, above desire-realm beings, non-Buddhist teachers, stream-enterers, once-returners, *arhats*, and *pratyekabuddhas*. The idea is that a lay person *(upasaka)* who has merely summoned "the thought of enlightenment" *(bodhichitta)* is in a superior position to help other beings. One example of what Chappell calls the "broadened perspective" of the *Upasaka Precept Sutra* is a scenario that recalls the Good Samaritan parable in the Christian gospel (Luke 10.30-35):

> If an upasaka who has taken the precepts comes across a sick person along the road and does not look after and arrange a place for him, but deserts him, he commits a fault. He cannot rise from degradation, nor can he purify his actions.[29]

Now compassion comes in two versions: ordinary compassion, which arises through a sympathetic response to the suffering others, and is thus ephemeral and limited to those present at any time; and "great compassion," *maha karuna*, which arises after enlightenment, is boundless, does not waver, can greatly save and help countless beings, and is practiced with wisdom.[30]

Chappell points out that compassion in pre-Mahayana Buddhism occurs in the *brahma viharas*, as we have seen, and as an attribute of the Buddha, whose primary activity is teaching. But for *arhats* (enlightened monks) and occasional lay people, it is recommended only as an antidote to hostile feelings, and is thus a kind of emotional fine-tuning or service-check for an otherwise well-running vehicle.

By contrast, the first of the Four Great Bodhisattva Vows introduced by Tientai-Zhiyi in tenth-century China is the grandiose proclamation, "Beings are infinite in number. I vow to save them all!"

The Ethics of Engagement

The reader may be wondering at this point how a final style of Buddhist ethics could improve upon the altruism of the Mahayana, as it was taught and practiced in Asia over the past two millennia. Or, if not improve upon, at least differ from the previous styles of morality. Indeed, some will ask, have we not been speaking of engaged Buddhism all along? Are the disciplined observance of *vinaya* regulations, lay precepts, and advice for daily living found in the Pali literature not productive of a better society—as Russell Sizemore, Donald

Swearer, and the contributors to *Ethics, Wealth, and Salvation* (1990) have shown?[31] And do we not see an intimate structural and developmental relationship between the virtue ethics of meditative goodwill, compassion, and generosity, and the skillful altruism of the bodhisattva path?

It would be wrong to argue that the first three styles of Buddhist morality are not productive of a more peaceful and prosperous society, as well as happier individuals. But one may wonder, in light of the widespread conditions of human misery in our world today, whether rule-based morality, mental cultivation, individualized good works, and generalized vows to save all beings will be enough to prevent the spread of political tyranny, economic injustice, and environmental degradation in the era to come. Such a question itself reflects a critical shift in thought and practice that distinguishes Buddhist leaders and communities today from their predecessors in traditional Asian societies.

A perfect illustration of this shift may be found in the contrast between the religious and political attitudes of Mahatma Gandhi and B. R. Ambedkar, the Indian Untouchable leader in the 1930s and 1940s. Gandhi advocated compassion and improved social services for India's Untouchables, while Ambedkar demanded the abolition of the caste system itself. As a devout Hindu, Gandhi believed that each person is limited or empowered by the cumulative effects of his or her own karma, and thus cannot be rescued by outside forces. Gandhi separated his political philosophy in this respect from his morality. India must struggle toward *swaraj*, independence from the British, which will benefit all Indians. But caste is a deeper issue, he held—indeed a cosmic law—that cannot be abrogated by human struggle or legislative fiat.

Gandhi's Hindu world view was deeply compatible with the altruism of the Mahayana bodhisattva tradition that we have discussed, while his ascetic "experiments with truth," such as fasting and celibacy, and his cultivation of *satyagraha*, "truth force," are reminiscent of the Buddhist ethics of discipline and virtue. His great compassion encompassed the *Harijans* ("God's Children," his name for Untouchables) along with the Brahmins and Banias (his own Vaishya caste, reserved for merchants and bankers). As a trained jurist, like Ambedkar, he could imagine a society transformed by legislation and the action of the courts. But Gandhi firmly rejected the idea that religious identities, beliefs, practices, and morality itself were negotiable or subject to reform.[32]

Ambedkar, a product of the slums of Maharashtra and the classrooms of Columbia University and the London School of Economics, saw karma from the other side. If the collective, institutionalized expression of greed, hatred, and delusion was India's legacy of colonialism, bureaucratic corruption, and the religious-based caste system, then all of these structures, fashioned by human hearts and minds, could be repaired, remodeled, or removed. The key was the notion of collective action—both in the genesis of human suffering, and in its relief.

Ambedkar was not a spiritual teacher in the mold of the Buddha or Gandhi, but a public intellectual in the mold of his American mentor, John Dewey. Dewey and Ambedkar believed that democratic bodies, courts, and schools were the proper tools of informed, engaged citizens. Such citizens speak out on community issues, vote their conscience, file legal suits if necessary, and, as a last resort, agitate for social change in the streets. Here we would seem to have a match with Gandhi, the father of nonviolent protest in the twentieth century. But Gandhi and his followers practiced satyagraha to restore a classical, precolonial India—symbolized by the spinning wheel and homespun clothing—while Ambedkar sought to build a new India on humanistic principles, embodied in the world's longest democratic Constitution, which he drafted.

As the fourth style of Buddhist ethics, engaged Buddhism is radically different from the Mahayana path of altruism because it is directed to the creation of new social institutions and relationships. There are indeed harbingers of socially engaged practice in the annals of Buddhist history, such as the public works projects of the Indian king Ashoka in the third century B.C.E., and the free dispensaries, hospitals, and bridge-building and tree-planting campaigns of Buddhist temples in the Sui and T'ang periods in China, but these are exceptions to the practices of individual discipline, virtue, and altruism advocated in the tradition.[33] Robert Aitken Roshi, one of the founders of the Buddhist Peace Fellowship, and a great innovator and commentator on the emergence of engaged Buddhism in the West, wrote in his book on Zen Buddhist Ethics, *The Mind of Clover,*

> Here and there in Buddhist history we find millenarian individuals devoting themselves to social welfare and social protest, but generally the practice of enlightenment, social or individual, was focused within the monastery and among monks. We do not find Buddhist social movements developing until the late nineteenth century, under the influence of Christianity and Western ideas generally.[34]

THE YANAS IN BUDDHIST HISTORY

Another way of understanding the emergence of engaged Buddhism is through the traditional metaphor of "vehicles." In Hindu mythology, the great gods were pictured riding on birds or animals that represented their peculiar power or domain (Shiva on the Bull Nandi, Vishnu on the bird Garuda, and Brahma on the swan Hamsa). In Buddhism the simile of the boat or raft was

17

associated with the practice of Dharma from early times: "Bhikkhus, I shall show you how the Dhamma is similar to a raft, being for the purpose of crossing over, not for the purpose of grasping."[35] After "crossing over" to the other shore of *nibbana* or final awakening, the practitioner should leave the vehicle of beliefs and practices behind. Vehicle imagery was reinforced by the image of the "wheel" (synecdoche for "cart" or "chariot") of Dhamma, which the Awakened One "turned" in his first sermon at the Deer Park at Sarnath.[36] Finally, we read in a famous passage of the *Saddharmapundarika Sutra* that a "rich man" (the Buddha) lured his children out of a "burning house" (cyclic existence) by offering them "ox-drawn carriages, goat-drawn carriages, and deer-drawn carriages" (the various practice traditions of Buddhism), only to give them "a single great ox-drawn carriage" (the *Ekayana* or "Single Vehicle" or *Mahayana* or "Great Vehicle" of bodhisattva practice) when they emerged safely from the house (entered upon the path to buddhahood).[37] Let us take a closer look at the evolution of the yanas in Buddhist history.

One of the textbook "facts" that students of comparative religion learn is that Christianity and Buddhism both underwent dramatic Reformations in which lay spirituality, openness to new ideas, outreach to the uninitiated, and service to the needy were featured. Although occurring only four hundred years after the death of the founder in the case of Buddhism (compared to fifteen hundred years after Christ for the Protestant Reformation in Europe), the emergence of "great vehicle" Mahayana Buddhism around the turn of the Common Era was defined by its apologists as a repudiation of the "narrow" or "elite" Hinayana Buddhism that went before. Although the anti-elitist polemics in Mahayana scriptures such as the *Saddarmapundarika Sutra* and the *Vimalakirtinirdesha Sutra* were couched in yana categories that highlighted old and new styles of leadership in Buddhism—for example, *sravakayana*, the "hearer [not doer] vehicle," and *pratyekabuddhayana*, the "solitary-buddha vehicle," of the early monastic orders; and *bodhisattvayana* for "enlightenment-bound vehicle" missionaries of the Mahayana's *ekayana* or "unified-practice vehicle" Reformation—the schismatic rancor and internal differentiation among practitioners within the Buddhist fold was unmistakable.[38]

Yet our picture of the history and sociology of ancient Buddhist sects remains obscure. Scholars are far from agreed on the attributes and events that separated practitioners of the Mahayana and Hinayana in ancient times. While early commentators such as Arya Asanga (*Mahayanasutralamkara*, fourth century) asserted that "the Sravakayana and Mahayana are mutually opposed," the precise boundaries of their opposition are impossible to map with confidence. Yet we find these two yanas laid out in stark opposition in most textbook accounts of Buddhist history, as Richard S. Cohen shows:

The Hinayana champions the arhat ideal, the Mahayana, the bodhisattva ideal; the Hinayana is centered on the sangha, the Mahayana, on the Buddha; the Hinayana is rationalist in its metaphysics, the Mahayana, mystical; Hinayana is ethical, Mahayana devotional; the Hinayana has closed its canon, the Mahayana allows for continuing "revelation."[39]

Against such artificial dichotomies, Cohen offers convincing evidence of the blurring of the Hinayana and Mahayana patterns in his study of selected textual and iconographic records from Buddhist caves at Gilgit in Afghanistan and Ajanta in Western India. In the case of the *Ajitasenavyakarananirdesa Sutra*, for example, found only at Gilgit, we find "an admixture of both the Hinayanic and Mahayanic ideal," extolling the supremacy of buddhahood and the availability of the bodhisattva path to monks and laity alike (Mahayana characteristics), but at the same time refraining from attacking *sravakas* ("hearer" monks), *arhats* ("worthy" senior monks), or the monastic tradition itself, as is the pattern in most Mahayana scriptures. However early such a "missing link" text may have been, Cohen comments, "the manuscript's colophon tells us that as late as the sixth century [c.e., or the tenth century after the Buddha] two lay Buddhists, Balosimha and his wife Jijadi, chose to have *this* sutra copied, perhaps at the behest of their spiritual benefactor Sthirabandhu."[40]

Cohen reports another, perhaps more definitive, example of the blurring of Hinayana and Mahayana characteristics from his year at the vast cave complex at Ajanta. Here, Cave 22 contains an image of seven buddhas and the bodhisattva Maitreya seated under separate bodhi trees—an image that suggests the Mahayana's multiplication of buddhas and bodhisattvas. But again the taxonomy of distinct yanas breaks down. The donor is identified as an *Aparasaila*, that is, a member of one of the eighteen Hinayana *nikayas*, or monastic orders, raising the question "Can a self-described member of a *nikaya* accept the bodhisattva vow and still be categorized as a Hinayanist?" Indeed, are the traditional yana categories dependable at all, if one insists upon their incommensurability? Can they be considered "natural taxonomies" based on social-historical patterns of ideological and institutional affiliation, or are they "artificial taxonomies," defined according to arbitrary and functional conventions? If we plan to continue using yana-language, Cohen concludes,

we must first decide whether we want this classificatory system to conform to, and describe, historical actualities on their own terms, reconstructed through available evidence; or whether it should be treated as a conventional construction, stipulatively defined so as to yield a useful analysis of whatever specific material is at hand. *There is no reason to believe that scholars of Buddhism have heretofore sought anything but a natural, historical understanding of the* yanas.[41]

In the end, Cohen votes for both of these options, admitting that, "of all the categories through which to reconstruct Indian Buddhism's history, Mahayana and Hinayana are the most productive," and then stipulating, "our approach to Buddhism's history in India must rely upon a hermeneutic sensitive to, and respectful of, the many divergent discursive, historical, institutional, psychological, practical, ideological, and social contexts within which we use these analytic categories."[42]

For our purposes, Cohen's position of problematizing, then endorsing, the continued use of the yana categories may be buttressed by suggesting that, even as *artificial taxonomies*, that is, as conventional, schematic summaries of historical patterns of practice and belief, the yanas may help us to trace the evolution of Buddhist spirituality. Here we may recall Max Weber's notion of the "ideal type":

> An ideal type is formed by the one-sided *accentuation* of one or more points of view and by the synthesis of a great many diffuse, discrete, more or less present and occasionally absent *concrete individual* phenomena, which are arranged according to those one-sidedly emphasized viewpoints into a unified analytical construct *(Gedandenbild)*. In its conceptual purity, this mental construct cannot be found empirically anywhere in reality.[43]

Like Thomas More's neologism, *utopia*, which, because it is a perfect "good place," (Greek *eu-topos*) is found exactly "no place" *(ou-topos)*, so, as Weber concludes, "Historical research faces the task of determining in each individual case, the extent to which this ideal-construct approximates to or diverges from reality."[44]

Weber illustrates the application of ideal typical constructions with reference to the history of Christianity. In the process he adds a dimension to the discussion that will help us to appreciate the impact of engaged Buddhism today:

> There is still another even more complicated significance implicit in such ideal-typical presentations. They regularly seek to be, or are unconsciously, ideal-types not only in the *logical* sense but also in the *practical* sense, i.e., they are *model types* which—in our illustration—contain what, from the point of view of the expositor, *should* be and what *to him* is "essential" in Christianity *because it is enduringly valuable....*[Here] the sphere of empirical science has been left behind and we are confronted with a profession of faith, not an ideal type construct.[45]

Like Clifford Geertz's notion of religious symbols as "models of" reality, at the same time that they are "models for" conduct—inasmuch as the activities of the gods or the saints are paradigmatic for human conduct, for example—so Weber's ideal types may be useful both as high-level observations of the patterns of thought and action in social history, and as normative value configurations for emulation in the future.[46]

The Swiss theologian Hans Küng offers further insights into the meaning and function of the Buddhist yanas, following a symposium at the University of Hawaii on "Paradigm Change in Buddhism and Christianity," which he attended in 1984. Participants adopted the notion of *paradigm* adumbrated by Thomas S. Kuhn in *The Structure of Scientific Revolutions* (1962), namely, the "total constellation of convictions, values, and patterns of behavior" that shape the religion, economics, law, politics, science, art, and culture of an era. The value of the paradigm concept is its application both to problems of structural change in the "total constellation" and to problems of periodization over time. Thus, in the case of Christianity, the dominant paradigms fall into the following familiar sequence: Jewish-Christian, Church-Hellenistic, Medieval-Roman Catholic, Reformation-Protestant, Modern-Enlightenment, and Postmodern. Meanwhile, Indian Buddhism may be seen to fall into "the old Buddhist Lesser Vehicle" (Hinayana), the subsequent Great Vehicle (Mahayana), and finally the Tantric Diamond Vehicle (Vajrayana). "As prevailing, wide-ranging, and deeply rooted total constellations of conscious-unconscious convictions, values, and patterns of behavior, these paradigms are…'more' than simply religion, more comprehensive than religion."[47]

According to Küng, identifying the yanas as paradigms, or "total constellations" of cultural habits and values encourages us to enter into dialogue with each one on its own terms, to compare and contrast the paradigms without prejudice, and finally "to measure critically every new form of Buddhism…against its source (Gautama, the Buddha)."[48] Furthermore, Thomas Kuhn's notion of paradigm, like Weber's ideal type, is genetic as well as structural: old paradigms in science are weakened, modified, discarded, or absorbed into emerging new paradigms, as discoveries that do not fit the reigning paradigm accumulate. In the classic example, the mathematical gymnastics required to support the stellar epicycles of the geocentric, Ptolemaic universe finally collapsed when a flood of new observations, made possible by better telescopes, tipped astronomers like Kepler and Galileo to the new, heliocentric paradigm.

In the history of Buddhism, the new yanas have not cancelled the old ones, as in the case of paradigms in the natural sciences. Rather the old have tended to be modified sufficiently to survive side-by-side with the new. This is precisely the situation that Cohen describes in the Gilgit text and the Ajanta art, which suggest the coexistence and interpenetration of Hinayana and Mahayana elements by the end of the first Buddhist millennium. And, bringing the *Vajrayana*, or tantric-practice-vehicle, into the discussion, Buddhist historian John Dunne adds,

> It is important to note that for both the Indian systematizers and Tibetan scholars, the Vajrayana is part of the Mahayana. This is even more strongly maintained than the inclusion of the Hinayana within the Mahayana. That is, the Hinayana is distinct from the Mahayana in the following sense: any Mahayanist necessarily has Hinayana vows, but a Hinayanist might choose to reject the Mahayana vows and practices. But anyone who practices tantra necessarily has Mahayana vows (and therefore also Hinayana vows, whether lay or monastic).
>
> The upshot is that the tantric practitioner is just a special kind of Mahayanist, and the Vajrayana is just a special branch of the Mahayana, just as the Pratyekabuddhayana is a special branch of the Hinayana. In Tibet, this [situation] is discussed in a type of literature called "Three Vows" *(sdom gsum)* literature, the three being lay/monastic, bodhisattva, and tantric.[49]

Today we are in a better position to see the results of this branching-coexisting pattern in the history of religions—as opposed to the linear, winner-take-all pattern in the history of science—as we witness the (not always peaceful) coexistence of Orthodox, Roman Catholic, and Protestant communions of Christianity, and the survival of Theravada Buddhism (the last of the eighteen Hinayana *nikayas* or orders), alongside Zen, Pure Land, and Nichiren Buddhism (all evolved under the banner of the great vehicle, "Mahayana"), and the various Tibetan monastic lineages—Gelukpa, Kagyupa, Nyingmapa, and Sakyapa—and the esoteric Shingon Buddhism of China and Japan (which evolved from the Tantric "Vajrayana" societies of India). What is more, all of these manifestations of the cultural history of Buddhism have been transplanted over the past century to the West, where they compete and coexist in relative harmony.

ENGAGED BUDDHISM AS THE FOURTH YANA

On the eve of the historic conversion on October 14, 1956, in Nagpur, India, when nearly a half-million ex-Untouchable Hindus embraced the Buddhist religion, Dr. Ambedkar, their leader, held a press conference to explain the event. Reporters wanted to know why a former cabinet minister and the architect of India's constitution would abandon the country's majority religion for a faith that had virtually disappeared from India eight hundred years before. Ambedkar parried the question. "Ask yourselves and your fathers, what self-respecting person could remain in a system that offers only token handouts and menial jobs to low-born citizens? Are you Brahmins prepared to change places with us Untouchables? Only by leaving Hinduism can we find a better life!"

"But why Buddhism, and not some other faith—such as Islam or Christianity—that has attracted low-caste people in the past?" Alluding to the murderous hatred dividing Hindus and Muslims and the antipathy most Indians felt for the vestiges of colonialism, including the Christian missions, Ambedkar answered carefully, "For all my differences with Gandhi, I agree with his nonviolent path. And this requires conversion to a religion that is part and parcel of Indian culture. I have taken care that my conversion will not harm the culture and history of this land."

"Well, then," the reporters pressed on, hoping to stump the ailing leader at last, "exactly what kind of Buddhism will you be embracing?"

"Our Buddhism will follow the tenets of the faith preached by Lord Buddha himself," Ambedkar replied, "without stirring up the old divisions of Hinayana and Mahayana. Our Buddhism will be a Neo-Buddhism—a *Navayana*."[50]

The twenty essays that comprise *Engaged Buddhism in the West* offer a rich fund of ideas and images with which to explore the implications of Ambedkar's "Navayana," Thich Nhat Hanh's "engaged Buddhism," Glassman's Supreme Meal, and the many other terms that practitioners and scholars have proposed for the new Buddhism. In the final chapter, Kenneth Kraft suggests another, *Terrayana*, the "Earth Vehicle," for a Buddhism focused on the pains and promises of this life, in this world. South Asians might translate this as *Lokayana*, the "World Vehicle" or "Global Vehicle." Certainly we can look forward to many more proposals as the direction and character of engaged Buddhism comes into ever clearer focus.

In this introduction I have argued that the direction of contemporary Buddhism, like that of other ancient faith traditions, has been deeply influenced both by the magnitude of social suffering in the world today, and by the globalization of cultural values and perspectives we associate with the Western cultural tradition, especially, the notions of human rights, economic justice, political due process, and social progress. I have identified some points of agreement and disagreement in the present discussion about and among engaged Buddhists, and suggested that engaged spirituality may be distinguished from other traditional styles of morality: discipline, virtue, and altruism.

Now I wish to propose that the ancient Buddhist notion of practice vehicles, or yanas, may be reanimated to identify and characterize the new Buddhism, and that engaged Buddhism be thought of as the fourth yana.

There are some clear liabilities in making such a proposal. The first comes from reviving yana-language itself, for, as we have seen, the first of the traditional yanas, Hinayana, was originally coined—and is still perceived by some practitioners of Theravada Buddhism—as a pejorative term. There is no doubt that the "narrow" or "elite" path meant the "small," "inferior" path to polemicists of the Mahayana. Some contemporaries have attempted to avoid the term altogether, calling it "the H-word," and coining alternatives, such as "Nikaya" or "Sectarian" Buddhism (referring to its eighteen orders) or "Mainstream," "Foundational," or "Background" Buddhism (alluding to its priority to the offshoot Mahayana).[51] On the other hand, Protestants, Quakers, and Methodists have survived such name-calling by embracing their tormenters' language.[52]

Another liability in proposing that engaged Buddhism (as opposed to some other permutation of the Dharma) is different and important enough to be called the Fourth Yana is the implication that Buddhists who are not socially and politically active are not fully evolved or "up to date." Worse, warned the Venerable Khemadhammo, would be the implication that those who are not socially and politically engaged are not concerned, compassionate, responsible, or perhaps, even in touch with reality—the "disengaged Buddhists." If engaged Buddhism is conceived as the "authentic" Buddhism of the future (until the Fifth Yana comes along), then traditional practitioners must be made to feel retrogressive, irresponsible, or obsolete.

There are two effective rejoinders to this concern, it seems to me, which we have already encountered in our discussion. One is the astonishing range of practices and attitudes that socially active Buddhists such as Khemadhammo have exemplified in their understanding of the Dharma. From "soft" to "hard," and from "mindfulness-based" to "service-based," there is no admissions test for engaged Buddhism: "All Buddhism is engaged" (Thich Nhat Hanh); "Buddhism has always been engaged" (Robert Thurman); "The private meditator is as engaged as the social worker when that practice embraces the wholeness of life, promotes healing, and reconnects him or her to a larger community of living beings" (Bernie Glassman).

Another reply to those who worry that a new Buddhist elite is attempting to commandeer the tradition is the history of the yanas themselves. As Richard Cohen as shown, the ancient yanas coexisted and intertwined at a very early stage. Since then none has discredited nor defeated another, but together they have absorbed and appropriated the values of the new host cultures to which they have been transmitted. This universal mutability and hybridity has given us the tasty selection—the Supreme Meal as potluck supper—of Buddhisms that we find in our cosmopolitan, pluralistic world. Anyone who claims or fears that engaged spirituality will edge out more traditional practices or beliefs is not familiar with the history of Buddhism.

Our proposal to consider engaged Buddhism as the Fourth Yana is based on more modest considerations. Taken together, the voices and actions of figures like Joanna Macy, Robert Aitken, Claude Thomas, Nichidatsu Fujii, Paula Green, Jon Kabat-Zinn, Franz-Johannes Litsch, Stephanie Kaza, Christopher Titmuss and many other authors and subjects of the chapters that follow display a world view and a praxis that is arguably fresh and unprecedented in the history of Buddhism. This Buddhism is endowed with many, if not all, of the themes and techniques from the past: interdependence, mindfulness, compassion, skillful means, chanting and walking meditation, community practice, right livelihood, and many, many more. But it is also endowed with a sensitivity to social injustice, institutional evil, and political oppression as sources of human suffering, that has not been central to Buddhist analysis in the past.

Winston King, a pioneer in the study of Buddhist ethics, has offered several reasons for traditional Buddhists' "seeming insensitivity to injustice." They include (1) the other-worldly "hope of *nibbana*," to escape future rebirths in this sad world, (2) an aversion to any notion of justice that creates whiney victims like the one at the beginning of the *Dhammapada:* "He abused me, he beat me, he defeated me, he robbed me," and, most importantly, and (3) the belief that injustice is a misconception, for "karmic justice, like the mills of the Greek gods, may grind very slowly, but grinds exceedingly fine." Universal karma, the complete system of justice, is already in place, is absolute, and is completely personalized. Thus it follows,

> Since society is perceived as only a collection of individual karmic characteristics, to talk about improving or reforming society in a collective way is futile. It is only by means of a one-by-one improvement of individual persons that any society can be changed.[53]

On the other hand, King shows, "there is no mystery as to the cultural origins of the much invoked concept of 'justice' in the Western world: it came directly out of the Judeo-Christian biblical tradition and teaching."[54]

Tracing the cultural origins and transformations of other beliefs and practices of engaged Buddhists, such as human rights, ecological sustainability, "collective karma," "Buddhist economics," and product boycotts, must await future study. Meanwhile, I believe that our discussion, and this book, will have served its purpose if the novelty, the significance, the cultural complexity, and the promise of the new Buddhism has been conveyed.

May the conversation we have joined continue into a new age, when the Buddhist vow to save all beings is universally shared.

NOTES

1. A dark vision of the future in both worlds—rich and poor—is offered in the works of Robert D. Kaplan, *Balkan Ghosts: A Journey Through History* (New York: Random House, 1993); "The Coming Anarchy," *The Atlantic Monthly* (February 1994); *The Ends of the Earth: A Journey at the Dawn of the Twenty-First Century* (New York: Random House, 1996); and *An Empire Wilderness: Travels into America's Future* (New York: Random House, 1998). In "The Coming Anarchy," Kaplan predicts a world of "environmental degradation, disease, over-population, unprovoked crime, scarcity of resources, refugee migrations, the increasing erosion of nation-states and international borders, and the empowerment of private armies, security firms, and international drug cartels...an ever-mutating representation of chaos."

2. A concise interpretation of the role and development of religious symbol systems in relation to social and cultural systems since the Neolithic period is offered in Robert Bellah's "Religious Evolution," *American Sociological Review* 29 (1964): 358–74; and in *Beyond Belief: Essays on Religion in a Post-Traditional World* (New York: Harper and Row, 1970), 20–50. In this important essay, Bellah compares changes in the theodicy and soteriology of Buddhism and other "historic religions" from the first millennium before the Common Era to the "post-traditional" period today.

3. In this essay, I use the terms "Western" and "the West" to represent the cultural traditions that derive from the Abrahamic religions, Judaism, Christianity, and Islam; the philosophical and social traditions of the classical Greeks and Romans; and the cultural experience of Europe and its former colonies, including North America, Australia, and South Africa. Other contributors to the volume may have other geographic or cultural parameters in mind.

4. See Robert Jay Lifton, *The Protean Self: Human Resilience in an Age of Fragmentation* (New York: Basic Books, 1993). Lifton writes, "Historical influences contributing to the protean self can be traced back to the Enlightenment and even the Renaissance in the West, and to at least the Meiji Restoration of the nineteenth century in Japan. These influences include the dislocation of rapid historical change, the mass media revolution, and the threat of human extinction. All have undergone an extraordinary acceleration during the last half of the twentieth century, causing a radical breakdown of prior communities and sources of authority. At the same time, ways of reconstituting the self in the midst of radical uncertainty have also evolved" (p. 3).

5. This conception is spelled out at the sociological level, for example, in Arthur Kleinman, Veena Das, and Margaret Lock, eds., *Social Suffering* (Berkeley: University of California Press, 1996). "Social suffering...brings into a single space an assemblage of human problems that have their origins and consequences in the devastating injuries that social force can inflict on human experience. Social suffering results from what political, economic, and institutional power does to people and, reciprocally, from how these forms of power themselves influence responses to social problems. Included under the category of social suffering are conditions that are usually divided among separate fields, conditions that simultaneously involve health, welfare, legal, moral, and religious issues. They destabilize established categories. For example, the trauma, pain, and disorders to which atrocity gives rise are health conditions; yet they are also political and cultural matters. Similarly, poverty is the major risk factor for ill health and death; yet this is only another way of saying that health is a social indicator and indeed a social process" (p. ix).

6. The involuntary nature of totem-group and caste membership is not exactly paralleled by the covenant relationships of the Hebrew tribes and the Israelite state to their god, Yahweh, in which the freedom of dissent is always implicit. Yet the consequences of apostasy—individual or collective execution—are graphically illustrated in the pan-Biblical image of God's punishing fire from the sky, as visited on the inhabitants of Sodom and Gomorrah in Genesis 19 and threatened in warnings of the late prophet Malachi, cf. 3.19–21. Such limits on dissent within the religious community also form the backdrop for Christianity (e.g. Mark 13 and the Apocalypse of John) and Islam (the Qur'an opens with homage to Allah, "King of the Day of Judgment").

7. The establishment and legitimation of Buddhism and Christianity in society is rightly associated with the conversions, respectively, of the monarchs Ashoka (ruled 270–232 B.C.E.) and Constantine (ruled 306–337 C.E.), approximately three centuries following the founders' careers. In the case of Islam, Muhammad, a successful businessman, integrated the ethical-spiritual impera-

tives of submission to Allah with the requirements of government and economics immediately following his emigration to Medina, only twelve years after the revelation of the Qur'an.

8. V. S. Naipaul's *India: A Million Mutinies Now* (New York: Viking, 1990), takes the reader into the homes of Indians who are being left behind in the high-tech revolution, as well as the entrepreneurs and movie moguls who are benefiting from the new prosperity. The mood of the book, like that of the author's earlier work, is one of despair—a stance that many of Naipaul's critics blame on his personality, not India.

9. See Christopher S. Queen and Sallie B. King, eds., *Engaged Buddhism: Buddhist Liberation Movements in Asia* (Albany: State University of New York Press, 1996).

10. Citations without annotation are from the present volume.

11. See Harvey B. Aronson, *Love and Sympathy in Theravada Buddhism* (Delhi: Motilal Banarsidass, 1980) for a discussion of the early Buddhist virtues of love *(metta)*, sympathy *(anukampa)*, compassion *(karuna)*, and equanimity *(upekkha)*; and Aronson's "Motivations to Social Action in Theravada Buddhism: Uses and Misuses of Traditional Doctrines," on the differences between *karuna*, "the heartfelt wish 'May all beings be free of suffering,'" *karunna* ("simple compassion"), and *anukampa*, which "motivated all the activities of the bodhisattva," in A. K. Narain, ed., *Studies in the History of Buddhism* (Delhi: B. R. Publishing Corp., 1980), pp. 1–12.

12. Bernard Glassman, Harvard Divinity School lecture, January 20, 1997.

13. These characteristics parallel the findings of recent studies in American Buddhism, namely "*Democratization*, a leveling of traditional spiritual and institutional hierarchies, entailing both *laicization* (the emphasis on lay practice and the de-emphasis of ordained and monastic vocations), and *feminization* (the rise of women in membership and leadership); *Pragmatism*, an emphasis on *ritual practice* or *observance* (particularly meditation, chanting, devotional and ethical activities) and its benefit to the practitioner, with a concomitant de-emphasis of beliefs, attitudes, or states of mind *(agnosticism)*; and *Engagement*, the broadening of spiritual practice to benefit not only the self, but also family and community *(domestication)*, and society and the world, including the social and environmental conditions that affect all people *(politicization)*." See Duncan Ryuken Williams and Christopher S. Queen, *American Buddhism: Methods and Findings in Recent Scholarship* (Surrey, U.K.: Curzon Press, 1999), p. xix.

14 Christopher S. Queen, "Introduction: The Shapes and Sources of Engaged Buddhism," in Queen and King, eds., *Engaged Buddhism: Buddhist Liberation Movements in Asia*, pp. 20–21.

15. David W. Chappell, "Searching for a Mahayana Social Ethic," *Journal of Religious Ethics* 24.2 (fall 1996): 351.

16. Ibid.

17. Georges Dreyfus, "Meditation as Ethical Activity," *Journal of Buddhist Ethics* 2 (1995): 31, referring to *byang chub lam gyi sgron ma dang de'i dka' 'grel* (Dharamsala: The Tibetan Publishing House, n.d.).

18. John Ross Carter, *On Understanding Buddhists: Essays on the Theravada Tradition in Sri Lanka* (Albany: State University of New York Press: 1993), p. 13.

19. Dreyfus, "Meditation," p. 40.

20. Charles S. Prebish, "Ambiguity and Conflict in the Study of Buddhist Ethics," *Journal of Religious Ethics* 24.2 (fall 1996): 298.

21. Damien Keown, *The Nature of Buddhist Ethics* (London: Macmillan, 1992).

22. Dreyfus, "Meditation," p. 40.

23. Clifford Geertz, in "Religion as a Cultural System," in *The Interpretations of Cultures* (New York: Basic Books, 1973), defines religion as "a system of symbols which acts to establish powerful, pervasive, and long-lasting moods and motivations...." (p. 90).

24. "To seek in the discourses on 'love' and 'compassion' for teachings on the motivation to social action is to seek in vain." Aronson, "Motivations to Social Action in Theravada Buddhism," pp. 6–7.

25. For a critique of Rahula's interpretation of engaged Buddhism, see Queen, "Introduction," in Queen and King, eds., *Engaged Buddhism: Buddhist Liberation Movements in Asia*, pp. 14–20.

26. Dreyfus, "Meditation," p. 40.

27. Ibid., p. 41.

28. David Chappell, "Searching," pp. 351–75, on the Upasaka Precept Sutra (T. 30. 1034–1075, no. 1488); see English translation by Shih Heng-ching, *The Sutra on Upasaka Precepts* (Berkeley, CA: Bukkyo Dendo Kyokai, 1991).

29. Chappell, p. 358, citing Shih Heng-ching, p. 75.

30. Ibid., pp. 366ff.

31. Russell F. Sizemore and Donald K. Swearer, eds., *Ethics, Wealth, and Salvation: A Study in Buddhist Social Ethics* (Columbia, SC: University of South Carolina Press, 1990).

32. See Eleanor Zelliot, "Gandhi and Ambedkar: A Study in Leadership," in *From Untouchable to Dalit: Essays on the Ambedkar Movement* (New Delhi: Manohar, 1992), pp. 150–78; and Asha Krishnan, *Ambedkar and Gandhi: Emancipators of Untouchables in Modern India* (Mumbai: Himalaya Publishing House, 1997).

33. Ashoka's Rock Edict II, for example, calls for medical treatment of men and animals, the import of medicines, well-digging, and tree-planting, all at state expense; see N. A. Nikam and Richard McKeon, eds. and trans., *The Edicts of Asoka* (Chicago: University of Chicago Press, 1959; Midway Reprint, 1978), p. 64. According to Arthur F. Wright, "The growth of Buddhism as a common

faith was accompanied by a great increase in charitable works of all kinds. Buddhist monks had been the first to open free dispensaries, and in time of epidemics the clergy ministered to thousands in the stricken areas. They established free or low cost hostels reported by Ennin, and such charitable enterprises as the building of bridges and the planting of shade trees along well-traveled roads." See *Buddhism in Chinese History* (Stanford, CA: Stanford University Press, 1959), p. 75.

34. Robert Aitken, *The Mind of Clover: Essays in Zen Buddhist Ethics* (San Francisco: North Point Press, 1984), p. 164. In a review of *Engaged Buddhism: Buddhist Liberation Movements in Asia*, Bardwell Smith objects to "the overly sharp distinction that is made between modern forms of Buddhist engagement, however unprecedented many of their features may be, and those that have occurred over the centuries, almost as if there were no prophetic or deeply engaged precursors in Buddhist history." His only counterexample is the life and teachings of Nichiren, which was treated in the book under review, and is again treated in the present volume (see chapters 5 and 20). In lieu of a concerted argument that engagement, as we have defined it, has co-evolved with the ethics of discipline, virtue, and altruism in Buddhist history, however, one must conclude, with Aitken Roshi and others, that it is the product of dialogue with the West over the past one hundred years or so. For Smith, see *Journal of the American Academy of Religion*, 67.2 (summer 1999): 500–502.

35. *Alagaddupama Sutta* (Sutta 22, The Simile of the Snake), *Majjhima Nikaya*. See Bhikku Nanamoli, trans. and ed., *The Middle Length Discourses of the Buddha* (Boston: Wisdom Publications, 1995), pp. 228–29.

36. See O. H. DeA. Wijesekera, "The Symbolism of the Wheel in the Cakravartin Concept," in *Buddhist and Vedic Studies* (Delhi: Motilal Banarsidass, 1994), pp. 267–73; and Christopher S. Queen, "The Peace Wheel: Nonviolent Activism in the Buddhist Tradition," in *Subverting Hatred: The Challenge of Nonviolence in Religious Traditions* (Boston: Boston Research Center for the 21st Century, 1998), pp. 49–66.

37. Leon Hurvitz, *Scripture of the Lotus Blossom of the Fine Dharma* (The Lotus Sutra) (New York: Columbia University Press, 1976), pp. 58–61.

38. See Paul Williams, *Mahayana Buddhism: The Doctrinal Foundations* (London and New York: Routledge, 1989), pp. 6–33, for a summary of the literature and emergence of the Mahayana movement.

39. Richard S. Cohen, "Discontented Categories: Hinayana and Mahayana in Indian Buddhist History," in *Journal of the American Academy of Religion* 63.1 (spring 1995): 2.

40. Ibid., pp. 4–5. Cohen explains that "the manuscripts discovered at Gilgit, of which the *[Ajitasenavyakarananirdesa]* is one, are the only cache of Buddhist man-

uscripts that have survived intact from ancient India, our single window onto the precise texts that held interest for an identifiable local Buddhist community. If in the first century [this text] was a text characteristic of 'Mahayana before "Mahayana"' (Paul Williams, *Mahayana Buddhism: The Doctrinal Foundations* [New York: Routledge, 1989], p. 26), *in the sixth century it was simply another Mahayana sutra to be copied and worshiped.*"

41. Ibid., p. 17 (emphasis added).

42. Ibid., pp. 20–21.

43. *Max Weber: Selections from His Work, with an Introduction by S. M. Miller* (New York: Thomas M. Crowell, 1963), p. 28 (emphasis in original). The selection on ideal types is taken from Max Weber, *The Methodology of the Social Sciences*, ed. Edward A. Shils and Henry A. Finch (New York: The Free Press of Glencoe, 1949), pp. 89–99, which was taken, in turn, from "'Objectivity' in Social Science and Social Policy," first published in 1904 in the *Archiv fur Sozialwissenschaft und Sozialpolitik*.

44. Ibid.

45. Ibid., pp. 30–31 (emphasis in original).

46. Clifford Geertz, "Religion as a Cultural System," p. 93.

47. Hans Küng, *Theology for the Third Millennium: An Ecumenical View* (New York: Doubleday, 1988), p. 211.

48. Ibid., pp. 223–24.

49. John Dunne, personal communication, July 15, 1997.

50. This paraphrase of Ambedkar's press conference is based on Dhananjay Keer's summary account in *Dr. Ambedkar Life and Mission*, 3d ed. (Bombay: Popular Prakashan, 1971), p. 498.

51. Donald S. Lopez, Jr., "The H Word," *Tricycle: The Buddhist Review* 5.1 (fall 1995): 84–85.

52. As one trained in the Theravada practice lineage that produced American Dharma teachers Jack Kornfield, Joseph Goldstein, and Sharon Salzberg, I imagine myself as a "hinayanist" (the small "h" seems appropriate), someone attempting something that few others know or care about—certainly narrow and small, if not elite, but in no way inferior to other Buddhisms or faith traditions.

53. Winston L. King, "Judeo-Christian and Buddhist Justice," *Journal of Buddhist Ethics* 2 (1995): 75.

54. Ibid., p. 67.

ENGAGED BUDDHISM
AS PEACEMAKING

Buddhist peacemakers at Auschwitz retreat, 1998.
Courtesy Franz-Johannes Litsch.

Thich Nhat Hanh leads walking meditation in memory of Holocaust victims, Oldenburg, Germany, 1993. Photo by Gert-Ulrich Rump, courtesy Franz-Johannes Litsch.

ALL BUDDHISM IS ENGAGED: THICH NHAT HANH AND THE ORDER OF INTERBEING

Patricia Hunt-Perry and Lyn Fine

THICH NHAT HANH'S TEACHINGS AND PRACTICES for practical peace-making, sometimes called engaged Buddhism, developed out of the crucible of the years of colonialism and war in Vietnam and in response to the needs of people from all over the world. Since 1982 he has offered these practices in Western countries, in Asia, in Israel, and at Plum Village, his monastic training and retreat center in southwestern France. Grounded in the Theravada and Mahayana teachings of Buddhism, as they have come through the Bamboo Forest School of Vietnamese Zen Buddhism, and informed by both Indian and Chinese Buddhism, these practices renew and re-articulate traditional Buddhist teachings in ways that have spoken to the hearts of people of all faiths and of no faith in countries around the world. Increasing numbers of people have been inspired by and are being attracted to Thich Nhat Hanh's retreats, touched by the power of his presence and by his transmission of the Buddha's wisdom and compassion. In North America in 1997 several thousand people attended each public lecture, day of mindfulness, and retreat he offered, and many more have come into contact with his teachings through books and tapes.

In this chapter we place Thich Nhat Hanh's approach to engaged Buddhism in historical context. We explore the specific engaged Buddhist peacemaking teachings and practices that Thich Nhat Hanh and his long-time associate Sister Chan Khong offer to Westerners. And we give examples of how Thich Nhat Hanh's teachings have been manifested in the lives of people inspired by his life and presence.

The fundamental premise of this chapter is that, for Thich Nhat Hanh and the Order of Interbeing, peacemaking and socially engaged Buddhism encompass all aspects of life, from family practice to public policy and culture. Socially engaged Buddhism arises from mindfulness practice and touches every aspect of life. The basic tenets of engaged Buddhism in the tradition of Thich Nhat Hanh that we have identified include: (1) "Buddhism is already engaged Buddhism. If it is not, it is not Buddhism."[1] (2) Insight into interbeing (nonseparate self, emptiness of a separate self) and impermanence is fundamental to engaged Buddhist practice and peacemaking. (3) Socially engaged Buddhist practice includes mindfulness practice, social service, and nonpartisan advocacy to reduce and stop injustice. (4) Engaged Buddhism is the way we live our lives. Peace is not only the absence of war; peace needs to be in each action of our daily life. (5) Teachings and practices must be appropriate for the time and place. (6) We continue to learn, and we can learn from everything.

ROOTS OF ENGAGED BUDDHISM IN VIETNAM

In the last hundred years, roots of socially engaged Buddhist practice in Vietnam can be found in the so-called "Monks' War" against the French colonial government, 1895-1898, and in the 1930s, when reforms made in China by a Chinese abbot, Tai Hsu, inspired a Vietnamese Buddhist revival movement. Discussion of the concept of engaged Buddhism—*nhap gian phat giao*—began at this time, and the idea of Buddhism as "the true national religion" of Vietnam was articulated.[2] The development of engaged Buddhist practice in Vietnam and the West by Thich Nhat Hanh and others is rooted in Vietnamese history and Vietnamese Buddhist traditions. "The thing that we called engaged Buddhism or Buddhism in daily life has been in existence for a long time in Vietnam," Thich Nhat Hanh reminded his students at his monastic training and retreat center at Plum Village, France, in 1996.[3] To understand engaged Buddhism as it is being expressed today in the worldwide Order of Interbeing, it is instructive to look at its historical roots.

Buddhist teachings are said to have come to Vietnam around the first century of the Christian era. Buddhist monks traveling by sea on their way to China from India and central Asia landed first in Vietnam to rest. There they founded the Luy Lau Center of Buddhist Studies. The Dhyana School of Buddhism was introduced into Vietnam in the third century by Tang Hoi, a Buddhist monk of central Asian descent. (*Dhyana* is Sanskrit for meditation, and is translated as *thien* in Vietnamese, *ch'an* in Chinese, *zen* in Japanese, and *son* in Korean.) In the fifth century, Dharmadeva, an Indian monk, came to Vietnam to teach Dhyana Buddhism. Between the sixth and the twelfth centuries, four to six important schools of Dhyana Buddhism were founded in Vietnam. In the early eighteenth century the Lieu Quan

Zen School was founded. This Dharma line, of which Thich Nhat Hanh is a member of the eighth generation, was especially important in the central and southern parts of Vietnam.[4]

Links between Buddhist teachers and political/social action and policy developed in Vietnam, especially in the eleventh through the thirteenth centuries. In 1010, for example, the Chinese were discouraged from invading Vietnam when a dispute among the members of the royal government was avoided through the intervention of the national Buddhist teacher, Van Hanh, who was well known for his nonviolent action.[5] In 1069, King Ly Tong became a student of Master Thao Duong, a monk of Chinese origin who had been taken to Vietnam as a prisoner of war. In 1299, King Tran Nhan Tong (1258-1308), a peacemaking king for fourteen years, abdicated his throne in favor of his son, King Anh Tong. He became a monk, a disciple of Buddhist Master Que Trung (1229-1291). With the Dharma name of Master Fragrant Cloud, he went on foot from village to village, giving teachings. Later named Master Truc Lam, he became the Dharma heir of Master Que Trung and the first ancestor of the Bamboo Forest School (Lam Te School) on Mount Yen Tu in northern Vietnam. This school, of which Thich Nhat Hanh is a member of the forty-second generation, is rooted in the teachings of the Chinese Ch'an master Lin-chi (Rinzai in Japanese).

"Bamboo Forest Buddhism is a kind of engaged Buddhism," Thich Nhat Hanh has said. "It can be applied in all aspects of life, political, social, and cultural."[6] Between 1300 and 1329, the Bamboo Forest School ordained more than fifteen thousand nuns and monks.[7] Thich Nhat Hanh described the situation at the time:

> We have the father king teaching the Dharma as he walks from village to village, and the son is sitting on the throne running the country according to Buddhist principles. So the whole country is being protected by the teachings of the Buddha. There was frequent danger of invasions from the North, and it was so important that the country be unified in their practice, because Dai Viet was a very small country lying to the south of a very big country, and that big country could have swallowed up the little country very easily. Many little countries like Dai Viet have already been swallowed up by big countries.[8]

THICH NHAT HANH AND ENGAGED BUDDHISM

Born October 11, 1926, in a village in central Vietnam, Thich Nhat Hanh (Nguyen Xuan Bao) entered a world of traditional Vietnamese monastic

Buddhism when, in 1942 at age sixteen, he joined Tu Hieu Monastery in Hue as a novice. His name, Nhat Hanh, means "one action," and recalls the eleventh-century national teacher Van Hanh mentioned above.[9] After attending Bao Quoc Buddhist Institute in Hue, Thich Nhat Hanh received full ordination in 1949.

As a student, Thich Nhat Hanh developed ideas that at the time were considered radical. He requested of his Buddhist elders, for example, that traditional Buddhist training be expanded to include foreign languages, literature, and philosophy. This suggestion was rejected. He and five others left monastic training and went to study at Saigon University. While studying there he wrote poetry and novels to support himself and the others. In 1950, he co-founded a temple in Saigon, which later became An Quang Buddhist Institute, a leading center of Buddhist Studies and activism. Six years later he established Phuong Boi, a new monastic community. He was appointed editor-in-chief of *Vietnamese Buddhism*, a magazine that gave public voice to his developing views of engaged Buddhism, encompassing both monastic and lay Buddhism.

Lotus in a Sea of Fire

The 1960s, which changed the lives of so many people worldwide, gave birth to new levels of Thich Nhat Hanh's work and influence. He first came to the United States in 1961, studying religion at Princeton and later lecturing on Buddhism at Columbia University. In 1963, however, one of the leaders of the Vietnamese Unified Buddhist Church, Tri Quang, convinced him to return to Vietnam because of the political situation. During the next several years in Vietnam, Thich Nhat Hanh co-founded a Buddhist university, Van Hanh, which would incorporate the broad curriculum he had advocated as a young student. He wrote *Engaged Buddhism,* coining a term that would gain increasing currency.[10] And, with others, he established the School of Youth for Social Service.

The founding of the School of Youth for Social Service was a major manifestation of engaged Buddhism during this period. Volunteers in the School of Youth for Social Service were trained to relieve the sufferings caused by the war and to extend their work to all Vietnamese people regardless of political orientation.[11] They were also trained "to prepare to die without hatred."[12] Thich Nhat Hanh wrote to his students:

> Our enemy is our anger, hatred, greed, fanaticism, and discrimination against people. If you die because of violence, you must meditate on compassion in order to forgive those who kill you. When you die realizing this state of compassion, you are truly a child of the Awakened One.

Even if you are dying in oppression, shame, and violence, if you can smile with forgiveness, you have great power.[13]

During these years Thich Nhat Hanh also made significant theoretical contributions to the developing Unified Buddhist Church (UBC), in particular his engaged Buddhist perspective. He expressed his views in *Vietnam: Lotus in a Sea of Fire* and in other books and poems, speaking out strongly against the continuation of the war and calling for the immediate cessation of the United States' bombing. He and others advocated a "third force" or "third way" approach, which emphasized Vietnamese self-determination: "Vietnam" was for the Vietnamese people to decide, without the intervention of any outside nation.[14]

Despite the presence in Vietnamese history of earlier roots of engaged Buddhist practice, the approach of Thich Nhat Hanh and the UBC was a departure from the twentieth-century traditional monastic Vietnamese Buddhism. A Buddhist collective action emerged which was aimed at directly influencing public policy and establishing new institutional forms. One form of collective action was noncooperation with government, such as strikes, mass resignations, the return of government licenses, and boycotts of classes by students. Another was the use of cultural forms such as fiction and nonfiction writing, and anti-war songs.

Anticipating what would happen in the West in the post-1970s era, Thich Nhat Hanh emphasized and encouraged the development of cultural forms. He also emphasized the establishment of communities as a conveyor and support of engaged practice. Reflecting on his work and especially on the establishment of monastic communities in Vietnam in the 1950s and 1960s, Thich Nhat Hanh observed, in dialogues with Catholic peace activist Daniel Berrigan, that

> both monks and nuns have made efforts to find a form of community that most fitted our need....It was successful because, I think, it grew out of the tradition, because most who came to the community had undergone some training in monasteries. But our community, well, we made it different....We also accepted non-monks—writers and artists—to be residents for months or years. That worked well, I think....Unfortunately, the war prevented us from continuing. But that too proved a blessing. Many of the young monks and nuns have cooperated with peasants to form new communities....*In our tradition, monasteries are only a kind of laboratory to spend time in, in order to discover something. They are not an end, they are a means. You get training and practice of the spiritual life so you can go elsewhere and be with other people.*"[15]

The Order of Interbeing

In 1966 Thich Nhat Hanh brought institutional expression to his conception of engaged Buddhism by founding the Tiep Hien Order (the Order of Interbeing). On the full moon in February three laymen and three lay-women, all of whom were board members of the School of Youth for Social Service, were ordained. They ranged in age from twenty-two to thirty-two years old. The charter of the order stated that the aim of the order would be to *actualize* Buddhism by "studying, experimenting with, and applying Buddhism in modern life, with a special emphasis on the bodhisattva ideal." The order was grounded in "four spirits": the spirit of nonattachment from views; the spirit of direct experimentation on the nature of interdependent origination through meditation; the spirit of appropriateness; and the spirit of skillful means. It would seek "to realize the spirit of the Dharma in early Buddhism, as well as in the development of that spirit through the history of the Sangha, and its life and teachings in all Buddhist traditions."

The Vietnamese word *tiep* means "continuing"—continuing the way of enlightening, of being awake—and "being in touch" with reality—the reality of the mind, "the process of our inner life, the wellspring of understanding and compassion," and the reality of the world, "the wonders of life and also the suffering." *Hien* means "realizing"—"transforming ourselves, manifesting the presence of understanding and compassion rather than talking about the idea of understanding and compassion." Hien also means "making it here and now"—the deep understanding that the means are the ends, that the present moment contains the future.

"Why a new order?" Professor Hyun-kyung Chung, a Christian feminist liberation theologian, asked Thich Nhat Hanh when he offered retreats in Korea in 1995. He responded by emphasizing continuity, first describing himself as a monk in the tradition of Lin-Chi Zen, and then characterizing the Order of Interbeing not as a new entity but as a "new branch of an ancient tree, a bridge between the lay and monastic communities, an important instrument for responding to difficulties and anguish of the world (that is, engaged Buddhism)." He emphasized what has become one of his themes, that "church leaders need to renew practice to respond to the needs of the young people, and help Buddhists [and others] make peace with their own tradition."[16]

The Order of Interbeing would also seek to end war and work for social justice "without taking sides." When, in 1995, Professor Chung commented to Thich Nhat Hanh that in liberation theology there is a tendency to think of God as "opting to side with the poor," he responded, "The rich suffer too. God operates with the highest understanding and embraces the rich and the poor. Work for social justice should be done without taking sides. You have to find the causes of oppression and do the right thing to help transform the situation. Dualistic ways only strengthen suffering. Love and understanding are our best 'weapons.'" [17]

The first ordinees in the Order of Interbeing committed themselves to the discipline of living by fourteen precepts based in the teachings of the Buddha, and practicing at least sixty days of mindfulness a year. They decided that they themselves would practice living deeply by the precepts and not add more members for at least fifteen years. [18] It has been said that these fourteen precepts, which are a set of guidelines or principles for engaged Buddhist understanding and action, issue a clarion call of Emptiness and Non-ego in action. Each precept is permeated with the understanding that concepts, thoughts, and actions are inherently impermanent and insubstantial. Each precept enjoins a form of moral action that is based on nonseparation and an unceasingly aware state of compassion. Not holding on to a notion of self, we are invited to engage ourselves courageously in the world, to see the nature of suffering clearly, and with discriminating awareness to undertake the task of liberating all sentient beings. [19]

Sister Chan Khong

One of the original six people ordained in the Tiep Hien Order was Cao Ngoc Phuong. Her Tiep Hien name, *Chan Khong*, means "true emptiness." She was an idealistic young university teacher who was devoted to working among the poor and those who were suffering. From the time of their meeting in 1959 until the present day, Sister Chan Khong and Thich Nhat Hanh have worked closely together, and she has taken major responsibility for implementing particular engaged Buddhist practices, such as helping to initiate projects that minister to ill and wounded people, providing medicine and food to people who are hungry, building communities, and starting schools. [20]

Although Sister Chan Khong did not then have a term for it, she had already been practicing engaged Buddhism when she met Thich Nhat Hanh. Deeply involved in working with the poor and those who were suffering, she faced a Buddhist tradition that saw the purpose of such work as gaining merit for a good rebirth. In her book *Learning True Love,* Sister Chan Khong writes,

> I wrote and told [Thich Nhat Hanh] about my work and my dream of
> social change in Vietnam. I also expressed concern that most Buddhists did
> not seem to care about poor people. I said I did not believe that helping
> poor people was merely merit work....He said that he was sure a person

could be enlightened by whatever work he or she liked most....He said that I was not alone, that he had seen many efforts by Buddhists to help the sick and poor in Vietnam. Thay [Thich Nhat Hanh] believed that Buddhism had much to contribute to real social change. He said he would find ways to support me in *a movement for social change according to the Buddhist spirit*. He would help bring together many good hearts who wanted to work together....He said he would help my friends and me with these social projects. From that day on I knew he was the teacher I had been looking for.[21]

Thich Nhat Hanh gave Sister Chan Khong a foundation in Buddhist practice from which she could continue her work of social service and social change, and in their subsequent years together they have forged a tradition of engaged Buddhism in theory and practice.

"How is everything [in Vietnam]?" the Trappist monk and scholar Thomas Merton asked Thich Nhat Hanh, whom he thought of as his brother. Thich Nhat Hanh responded with three words. "Everything," he said, "is destroyed."[22] The suffering caused by the war and by the divisions within the country was great. "Sometimes," Thich Nhat Hanh recalled on a video made by one of his students, "we had to *burn ourselves alive to get the message across*."[23] On June 11, 1963, Thich Quang Duc, an elderly monk, poured petrol over his body and immolated himself for peace, sitting calmly as the fires burned his body.[24] Four years later, on May 16, 1967, Nhat Chi Mai, one of the six people ordained into Thich Nhat Hanh's Order of Interbeing in February 1966, also immolated herself as "a torch for peace."

In *Learning True Love*, Sister Chan Khong devotes a full chapter to Sister Mai. "When you want something ordinary," she writes, "you can just go out and buy it, but when you want something extraordinary, like love, understanding, and peace for a whole nation, you have to pay for it with something much more precious than money. My sister, Nhat Chi Mai, did not commit suicide. She loved life....She sacrificed her life because, more than anything, she wanted the killing to stop."[25]

BRINGING ENGAGED BUDDHISM TO THE WEST

The message of Thich Nhat Hanh's engaged Buddhism in the 1960s had an increasing impact in the West as well as in Vietnam. Sponsored by the Fellowship of Reconciliation to travel to the United States in the mid-1960s, Thich Nhat Hanh spoke to public audiences, local and national media, and U.S. government officials, including members of the House and Senate and then Secretary of Defense Robert McNamara. Senators George McGovern, Claibourne Pell, and Birch Bayh invited him to speak to a large gathering of congressmen.[26] Catholic monk and theologian Thomas Merton, an intellectual and spiritual mentor of peace movement activists, spoke about and supported Thich Nhat Hanh in discussions and in his writings,[27] and peace activists such as Dorothy Day and Joan Baez became his associates.[28]

Not everyone, however, understood Thich Nhat Hanh's coming to the West to try to stop the bombing. "The anti-war movement was very violent, very angry," Thich Nhat Hanh remembers. "I came and advocated for a ceasefire, because I was under the bombs, and my friends, the majority of the Vietnamese people, were under the bombs....What we wanted was life....A very angry young American stood up at a meeting and shouted at me, 'Why are you here?! You should be home right now! The war is there, you should be fighting the American imperialists!' He was shouting at me like that. I saw the war in him, as a pacifist—because that kind of anger is war itself."[29] After taking a few moments to breathe deeply, Thich Nhat Hanh responded that he was speaking in the United States because the roots of the war were in the United States, and it was the roots of the war that needed attention.[30]

From this moment, Thich Nhat Hanh understood how much anger many United States peace activists at the time were bringing to their activism, and he began to emphasize *being* peace as an essential element for peacemakers and peacemaking. His influence on the American peace movement and especially on Martin Luther King, Jr., was significant. Known for his civil rights work, King's decision to speak out against the war required personal struggle and incited controversy in the civil rights movement. It was an important turning point for the peace movement to have Dr. King speak publicly on this topic.

In an interview, King's close associate, Andrew Young, recalled the impact: "I remember the spiritual inspiration of Thich Nhat Hanh on Martin," Young began, and then added, "his spiritual presence was something that he [Martin] talked about afterward." King gave Young a copy of *Lotus in a Sea of Fire* to read. "Third Force gave Martin an intellectual position," Young commented. "Third Force gave Martin a comfort, as it was Buddhist nationalism, to become involved in the war.... It didn't support either communist or anti-communist." Young went on to say that it was "clearly Thich Nhat Hanh's visit to Martin [and] King's chance meeting with [Dr. Benjamin] Spock on an airplane that changed King's views on speaking out on Vietnam."[31] Indeed, Martin Luther King, Jr., regarded Thich Nhat Hanh and his work so highly that he nominated him for the Nobel Peace Prize in 1967, saying, "This gentle Buddhist monk from Vietnam...is a scholar of immense intellectual capacity. His ideas for peace, if applied, would build a monument to ecumenism, to world brotherhood, to humanity."[32]

There were consequences to Thich Nhat Hanh's bold, nonpartisan, and outspoken activities in the West, however. During a speaking tour in 1966, his associates in Vietnam urged him not to return there, as they feared that he would be imprisoned or killed.[33] At this writing Thich Nhat Hanh has not yet been able to return to Vietnam.

Exile: A Time for Renewal

The decade of the 1970s was a time of coming to terms with the deep pain, trauma, and sorrow caused by the war. Unable to return to his homeland, Thich Nhat Hanh and his associates took refuge in Paris, France, and then established the Sweet Potato Farm community about 150 kilometers southeast of Paris.

Although Thich Nhat Hanh could not return to Vietnam, he and Sister Chan Khong continued to find ways to stay engaged in the relief of suffering. They worked to help the refugees ("boat people") who were leaving Vietnam during the 1970s.[34] Sister Chan Khong attempted social service relief work in Bangladesh and Thailand in addition to her work with the boat people. After six weeks, however, she decided to return to France, where she developed creative ways to continue helping to relieve suffering in Vietnam. Reflecting on her attempt to do social service work in a culture different from her own, Sister Chan Khong wrote that she came to realize the importance of doing social service work that was based in the expertise that one had in one's birth culture and traditions. As she and Thich Nhat Hanh continued to live in exile in the West, they also began to articulate, for themselves and others, the reality of our "multirooted" nature and the importance of giving nourishment to more than one root, so that if one were cut off, there would still be strong nourishment. They began to speak about being home anywhere on the planet, and to teach that "rooting is our practice."

In the 1980s and 1990s many new manifestations of Thich Nhat Hanh's and Sister Chan Khong's work flowered in the West. Modern communications technologies have made their work available in Vietnam as well. During this period Thich Nhat Hanh gave mindfulness retreats in the United States for environmental and peace activists, psychologists, writers, artists, and United States veterans of the war in Vietnam, while providing interfaith retreats and retreats for more general audiences. He also offered retreats in Western and Eastern Europe, Russia, Australia, New Zealand, India, China, Taiwan, Korea, Japan, and Israel. These retreats inspired the growth of more than 350 small practice groups (*sanghas* or "base communities"). His ideas and writings were translated into English by Anh Huong Nguyen, Mobi Warren, and Sister Annabel Laity, and into thirty other languages as well, and were introduced to a wider audience in the United States by the establishment of two presses, La Boi Press for publications in Vietnamese, and Parallax Press for publications in English. Parallax, founded by Arnold Kotler and Therese Fitzgerald, became a project of the Community of Mindful Living, also established by Kotler and Fitzgerald. The Community of Mindful Living coordinated Thich Nhat Hanh's biannual tours of the United States, published *The Mindfulness Bell* (the journal of the Order of Interbeing), and developed socially engaged action projects with veterans and prisoners in the United States and with poor children and families in Vietnam. Both Kotler, who had been a young American monk in a Japanese Zen tradition when he met Thich Nhat Hanh in 1982 at the Reverence for Life Conference, and Fitzgerald, also a student of Japanese Zen, had been active in the Buddhist Peace Fellowship, which had initiated Thich Nhat Hanh's visits to the United States.

In 1982, Thich Nhat Hanh and his associates established Plum Village in southwestern France. Refugee families of Vietnamese origin, Western Buddhist practitioners, United States veterans of the war in Vietnam, and people who had simply read one of Thich Nhat Hanh's books began to arrive from countries around the world.[35] By 1998, the Plum Village community had become a monastic training center of five "hamlets" and a community of monastics and lay persons numbering about one hundred residents, in addition to being a retreat center where lay people could learn meditation practice in the style of Thich Nhat Hanh. During these decades, Plum Village offered annual periods of "summer opening" from July 15 to August 15, three-month winter retreats, a twenty-one-day retreat every two years, and spring and fall retreats.

During the 1980s and 1990s, the Order of Interbeing grew to approximately five hundred monastic and lay core members. In 1981 Anh Huong Nguyen, the first new member since the founding of the order fifteen years earlier, was invited to join. This followed the intentional fifteen-year "period of experimentation" since the establishment of the order in 1966. Order of Interbeing members worldwide committed themselves to practicing the fourteen precepts/mindfulness trainings, reciting these trainings at least monthly with a sangha, and practicing at least sixty days of mindfulness a year. Organizationally, the order developed as an international community and spread to different regions. By 1998, approximately seventy-five *dharmacharyas* (monastic and lay Dharma teachers) had been ordained. About three hundred lay sanghas developed worldwide. The Second International Conference of the Order of Interbeing, held at Plum Village, France, from September 30 to October 2, 1996, brought together more than one hundred members from Australia, New Zealand, England, France, Germany, Switzerland, Holland, Italy, Russia, Sweden, Canada, the United States, Vietnam, and other countries.[36] A new administrative structure to coordinate organizational communications and maintenance, and international working groups in the areas of education and training, youth and family practice, sangha building, social action, and inclusiveness and special needs were established. Each committee was intentionally composed of both monastic and lay members from different countries.

Ecumenism, interfaith and "post-denominational" connections were another hallmark of Thich Nhat Hanh's engaged Buddhism in the West in the 1980s and 1990s. In 1987 he offered an interfaith retreat during which participants observed both Easter and Passover. In 1988, he and his associates organized an important "conference in a retreat setting," which they called "Watering the Seeds of American Buddhism." For the first time, American and other students of Buddhist contemplative traditions being seeded in North America (Vipassana, Zen, Tibetan, and other Buddhist traditions) came together to discuss the emerging face of Buddhism in the United States.[37] In 1995 Thich Nhat Hanh's book *Living Buddha, Living Christ* was published, inviting dialogue between faith traditions. In 1993 and 1995, at retreats in upper New York State during the Jewish high holidays, Rabbi Shefa Gold offered Rosh Hashanah and Yom Kippur services, and in September 1996, Jewish high holiday observances were co-created by retreatants during a three-week retreat at Plum Village, stimulating Dharma discussions and dialogue among many retreatants, and in particular between retreatants of German and of Jewish backgrounds.

Vietnam Veterans, Rodney King, War in the Gulf

Central to the engaged Buddhist perspective suggested by Thich Nhat Hanh's life and teachings is insight into interbeing and the understanding of co-responsibility that arises from this insight. "In each of us, there is a certain amount of violence and a certain amount of nonviolence," Thich Nhat Hanh writes in *Love in Action: Writings on Nonviolent Social Change*. "If we divide reality into two camps—the violent and the nonviolent—and stand in one camp while attacking the other, the world will never have peace. We will always blame and condemn those we feel are responsible for wars and social injustice, without recognizing the degree of violence in ourselves. We must work on ourselves and also work with those we condemn if we want to have a real impact. It never helps to draw a line and dismiss some people as enemies, even those who act violently."[38] Co-responsibility, rather than being a concept, idea, belief, or issue of morality is grounded in the realization of the nondual, interbeing nature of reality. "This is like this because that is like that."

During the 1980s and 1990s, Thich Nhat Hanh spoke explicitly, in the light of this insight, about three situations specific to societal suffering in the United States: the trauma of veterans who had served in Vietnam, the beating of Rodney King, and the 1991 Gulf War. His approach to engaged Buddhism can be seen clearly through his perspective on these three socio-political situations. In 1989 he led the first of several retreats in the United States for Vietnam veterans. At this retreat, he told the American veterans that they were the flame, the light at the tip of the candle. Their society sent them to Vietnam out of ignorance and misunderstanding to do exactly what it wanted. "You were sent there to fight, destroy, kill, and die. You were not the only one[s] responsible....Our individual consciousness is a product of our society, ancestors, education, and many other factors....You have to look deeply to understand what really happened. Your personal healing will be the healing of the whole nation, your children, and their children."[39] In 1990 he led a gathering of four hundred people in walking meditation to the Vietnam Veterans Memorial in Washington, D.C. In subsequent general retreats a "retreat within a retreat" was offered in which veterans met, spoke, and wrote in depth about their wartime experiences in the context of mindfulness practice, and then in a public forum they shared their writings with the so-called "nonveterans" attending the general retreat.

The realization of interbeing must be cultivated anew in each situation. Thich Nhat Hanh responded to the 1991 Persian Gulf War: "The night I heard President Bush give the order to attack Iraq, I could not sleep. I was angry and overwhelmed....But after breathing consciously and looking deeply, I saw myself as President Bush....In our collective consciousness there are some seeds of nonviolence, and President Bush did begin with sanctions. But we did not support and encourage him enough, so he switched to a more violent way. We cannot blame only him. The president acted the way he did because we acted the way we did."[40]

He spoke about the beating of Rodney King: "People everywhere saw the Los Angeles policemen beating Rodney King. When I first saw that video on French TV, I felt that I was the one being beaten, and I suffered a lot. I think you must have felt the same. All of us were beaten at the same time. We were all victims of violence, anger, misunderstanding, and the lack of respect for our human dignity. But as I looked more deeply, I saw that the policemen beating Rodney King were no different from myself. They were doing it because our society is filled with hatred and violence.

Everything is like a bomb ready to explode, and we are all a part of that bomb; we are all co-responsible. We are all the policemen and the victim."[41]

Engaged Buddhism for Thich Nhat Hanh and the Order of Interbeing means to be aware of what is going on within oneself and in the world. "Meditation is to be aware, and to try to help."[42] Understanding and compassion arise out of the deep realization of interbeing (nonself) and of impermanence, such that true peacemaking becomes possible. In these situations, as in his experiences with the suffering of the Vietnamese boat people, Thich Nhat Hanh offers a type of engaged Buddhism that does not stop at policy change and institutional, structural change but includes fundamental consciousness transformation. His clear realization of interbeing was the "fruit" of his own transformation of the outrage that arose in him in response to the rape of a twelve-year-old refugee girl on a boat escaping from Vietnam in the 1970s. This realization found expression in his well-known poem "Please Call Me By My True Names."[43] This poem reads in part:

> I am a frog swimming happily in the clear water of a pond
> And I am the grass-snake that silently feeds itself on the frog.
>
> I am the child in Uganda, all skin and bone, my legs as thin as
> bamboo sticks.
> And I am the arms merchant selling deadly weapons to Uganda.
>
> I am the twelve-year-old girl, refugee on a small boat,
> who throws herself into the ocean after being raped by a sea pirate
> And I am the pirate, my heart not yet capable of seeing and loving.

Some of the teachings and practices that Thich Nhat Hanh and his associates offered in the 1980s and 1990s to Westerners follow in the next section. These practices of engaged Buddhism were developed to help cultivate the capacity, as well as the willingness, to offer fresh, creative, nonviolent responses to injustice, bringing compassion and insight to the challenge of transforming culture from violence to mindfulness and nonviolence.

TEACHING SOCIAL ENGAGEMENT

In the Buddha's teachings as they are interpreted by Thich Nhat Hanh, the practice of socially engaged Buddhism can be understood as a radical practice—peacemaking at the root—of embodying peace that is itself a cultural transformation. There is no separation between "socially engaged" and "non-socially engaged" Buddhist practice. Choice-making in a consumer-focused society is socially engaged action, in the view of Thich Nhat Hanh. The way we live our daily lives is socially engaged action for peace. Thich Nhat Hanh writes:

> We think we need an enemy. It is not correct to believe that the world's situation is in the hands of the government and that if the president would only have the correct policies, there would be peace. Our daily lives have the most to do with the situation of the world. If we can change our daily lives, we can change our governments and we can change the world. Our presidents and our governments are us. They reflect our lifestyle and our way of thinking. The way we hold a cup of tea, pick up a newspaper, and even use toilet paper have to do with peace.[44]

Thich Nhat Hanh's teachings arise from traditional Buddhist sources, but they are frequently renewed in contemporary language to address the modern situation in the West. His commentaries on the precepts and the sutras include concrete reminders of contemporary societal concerns.

During the late 1980s and 1990s, the five and the fourteen precepts (mindfulness trainings) became key elements in Thich Nhat Hanh's engaged Buddhist practice in the West. Practitioners could commit themselves to the five wonderful precepts for a peaceful society and request a Dharma name at retreats with Thich Nhat Hanh or in a formal transmission ceremony led by a *dharmacharya* (lay teacher) ordained by Thich Nhat Hanh. Having formally received the five precepts, practitioners could state their aspiration to receive the fourteen precepts of the Order of Interbeing and join the core community of the order. Sponsorship by a sangha with whom they had practiced for at least a year, preferably several years, and by an Order of Interbeing member or a *dharmacharya* was generally required to receive the fourteen mindfulness trainings in a formal ceremony. Whereas the decision to receive the five mindfulness trainings was an individual one, more and more emphasis was placed on sponsorship by a sangha, a community of practitioners, in the decision to receive the fourteen.

"In the past, I was not very fond of ordaining people or having disciples," Thich Nhat Hanh wrote in 1990. "I tried to avoid that, especially when I saw that there were many other teachers. But during my visit [to the United States] last year, I changed my idea. We have to support each other, and the practice of the precepts is very important to help us." Furthermore, Thich Nhat Hanh said, "we do not practice meditation alone. We practice with a teacher and with friends. When you have a good *sangha*, your practice is easy, because you are supported by the *sangha*."[45] During the next eight years more than five thousand people worldwide received the five mindfulness trainings in a formal ceremony with Thich Nhat Hanh or a lay teacher ordained by him.

Five Wonderful Precepts for a Peaceful Society

During the 1990s, the wording of the precepts was "renewed" from time to time, in order to find words in English and other Western languages that would accurately reflect the true meaning of the precepts in the context of Buddhist understanding and in order to make them more easily accessible to Westerners, especially to young people.

In 1991, for example, the imperative form of the five precepts was reworded. Each one now began with a statement of *awareness of suffering* and continued with a *commitment*, arising out of that awareness, to cultivate beneficial qualities and refrain from actions harmful to oneself and society. With the new wording, the commitment or vow undertaken in receiving the five precepts was clearly understood as a determination one was making from one's own awareness and insight, rather than in obedience to an authority perceived to be external to oneself, as could be felt in the imperative form.

In 1996, the Pali word *sila* (Sanskrit: *shila*), which had usually been translated as "precepts" but which in some Buddhist traditions had been translated as "training," was translated as "mindfulness trainings." This change again focused practitioners' awareness on inner determination rather than external authority as the source of the intention to cultivate nonharming ways of acting and thinking. The change, Thich Nhat Hanh said, came in response to Westerners who "told me that the word 'precepts' evokes in them a strong feeling of good and evil; that if they 'break' the precepts, they feel great shame." It was especially intended that these ethical teachings would become more accessible to young people as the source of the intention to cultivate nonharmful ways of acting and thinking.[46]

The five mindfulness trainings include concrete examples of socially engaged practice in the body of each precept, as well as in Thich Nhat Hanh's commentary. The commitment is to the deepening of individual understanding and well-being, but also to taking action (or refraining from action) and cultivating ways of thinking that can contribute to reducing societal suffering. Child sexual abuse, alcoholism, the destruction of trees and the environment, exploitation and oppression, and war and other forms of violence are explicitly mentioned.

The Fourteen Precepts of the Order of Interbeing

For Thich Nhat Hanh and the Order of Interbeing, the fourteen mindfulness trainings are the essence of engaged Buddhism. These precepts, grounded in the Buddha's original teachings, were forged during wartime and aim "not only to help people develop serenity and learn to look more deeply into themselves, but also to look deeply into conditions in the world."[47] Based on the "ten wholesome things"—precepts taught by the Bamboo Forest master, Master Truc Lam, in the thirteenth century[48]—the fourteen mindfulness trainings of the Order of Interbeing are specific to twentieth- and twenty-first-century peacemaking. They have been called a "true expression of bodhisattva practice of socially engaged Buddhism," which "blend traditional Buddhist morality and contemporary social concerns."[49]

In 1996 the fourteen precepts of the Order of Interbeing were also reworded. The imperative form was changed into statements of awareness and commitment. The restatements explicitly include both societal (collective) and individual levels. For example, the ninth mindfulness training, "truthful and loving speech," states:

> Aware that words can create suffering or happiness, we are committed to learning to speak truthfully and constructively, using only words that inspire hope and confidence. We are determined not to say untruthful things for the sake of personal interest or to impress people, nor to utter words that might cause division or hatred. We will not spread news that we do not know to be certain nor criticize or condemn things of which we are not sure. We will do our best to speak out about situations of injustice, even when doing so may threaten our safety.[50]

The trainings start with the collective "we," reflecting the importance given to making a collective commitment to the cultivation of beneficial action and views, while refraining from nonbeneficial or harming actions and views, and emphasizing sangha, not only individual, practice. In Thich Nhat Hanh's view, it is essential that people practice collectively—as families, communities, and nations—as well as individually, for a truly peaceful future to be possible.

In the 1990s Thich Nhat Hanh and the Plum Village community continued to renew traditional Buddhist teachings and forms of practice, making them practical and appropriate for engaged practice in contemporary societies. These forms of practice assume the interbeing nature of so-called individual practice with family practice and societal practice. Instructions and commentaries for walking meditation, *gathas* (short verses for practicing mindfulness in daily life), guided meditations, and the new form of "hugging meditation" all include reminders of contemporary societal concerns, planting and watering "seeds" in the storehouse of consciousness.

Other traditional practices that have been renewed or reworded in Thich Nhat Hanh's tradition are bowing, reconciliation practices like "beginning anew," verses for eating meditation, *metta* or loving-kindness meditation, and mantra practice. "Touching the earth," for example, is a prostration or bowing practice developed by Thich Nhat Hanh, Sister Chan Khong, Sister Annabel Laity, and others at Plum Village when they observed that people raised in Western countries were sometimes reluctant to engage in traditional Buddhist prostration or bowing practices. The focus on touching the earth gave an accessible universal meaning to bowing (prostrations) while being deeply grounded in Buddhist tradition. The touching the earth guided meditation practice fosters connection and reconciliation with one's blood family; gratitude to and connection with spiritual teachers, one's land ancestors, and one's loved ones; and finally reconciliation with enemies. It offers deepening realization of interbeing in the historical dimension—through time and space—and also in the ultimate dimension, beyond the human-made categories of time and space. Organizing and conducting collective, socially engaged action in the public arena can be more fruitful when it is grounded in the insight into interbeing and in the experience of individual and community wholeness and stability that these practices nourish.[51]

Sutra Teachings on Impermanence and Interbeing

The foundation of Thich Nhat Hanh's work with environmentalists and other peace and social change activists are the traditional Buddhist teachings on interbeing and impermanence. In his book of guided meditations, *Blooming of a Lotus*, Thich Nhat Hanh offers a teaching on impermanence that explicitly addresses the public arena. "It is precisely because of its impermanence that we value life so dearly. Therefore we must know how to live each moment deeply and use it in a responsible way."[52]

For Thich Nhat Hanh, it is clear that the "responsible way" includes societal levels, such as governments. In a traditional guided meditation to deepen the realization of impermanence, the first instructions establish mindfulness of the parts of the body and their impermanence, as is traditional in *vipassana* practice. "Aware of the hair on my head, I breathe in. Seeing the impermanence of the hair on my head, I breathe out." Subsequent instructions, however, direct awareness to impermanence and change in the political world. "Aware of my nation, I breathe in. Seeing the impermanence of my nation, I breathe out. Aware of governments, I breathe in. Seeing the impermanence of governments, I breathe out."[53]

Thich Nhat Hanh's teachings based in the *Diamond Sutra* offer a foundation for environmental activism that he calls "universal ecology," which is essential for peacemaking. If people who work to protect the environment contemplate and can break through four "notions"—the four "erroneous perceptions" identified in the *Diamond Sutra* as the notion of a separate "self," the notion of a person or human being, the notion of a living being; and the notion of a life span—they will know how to be and how to act, he observes with characteristic simplicity.[54] To truly protect the environment, Thich Nhat Hanh says, "we have to remember that our body is not limited to what lies within the boundary of our skin....There is no phenomenon in the universe that does not intimately concern us....To save our planet is to save ourselves, our children, and grandchildren....We protect the Earth because we are motivated by compassion and respect for all things, animate and inanimate."[55] Most fundamentally, "when we realize our nature of *interbeing*, we will stop blaming and killing, because we know that we *inter-are*."[56]

The arenas of public policy, social structure and global institutions, as well as consciousness, are included in Thich Nhat Hanh's teachings related to what is going on in the world. In his poetic narrative of the Buddha's life and teachings, we hear the teaching on interbeing and the wisdom of the Buddha as he advises King Pasenadi, "The prosperity and security of one nation should not depend on the poverty and insecurity of other nations. Majesty, lasting peace and prosperity are only possible when nations join together in a common commitment to seek the welfare of all. Foreign and economic policies must follow the way of compassion for true peace to be possible."[57]

The Paramitas

Engaged Buddhist practice is clearly articulated in Thich Nhat Hanh's teachings on the six paramitas—*dana*, generosity; *shila*, morality; *virya*, energy or diligence; *kshanti*, patience, forbearance, and inclusiveness; *dhyana*, meditation, including *shamatha* (stopping, calming, concentrating) and *vipassana* (looking deeply, seeing and understanding); and *prajna*, wisdom or understanding. "We are on the shore of ill-being, anger, fear, hatred, and we know that these are killing us," said Thich Nhat Hanh as he introduced a discussion of the paramitas at a retreat in 1997. "We don't want to be the victim of anger, fear, hatred, and we want to cross over to the other shore. There are six ways to cross over. It is our business every day to cross to the other shore. We don't want to be victim to these afflictions. If we know the practice, we can cross to the other shore many times a day."[58]

In the context of Thich Nhat Hanh's engaged Buddhism, his teachings on *kshanti* are of particular interest. Usually translated as "patience," "forbearance," "acceptance," or "tolerance," Thich Nhat Hanh in 1997 proposed "inclusiveness" as a better translation for the contemporary situation. Speaking from his own experience during the war in Vietnam, he addressed directly the suffering caused by racial and other discrimination in the United States. "I myself am not a white person. [In Vietnam], I felt that I was discriminated against. But I didn't suffer, I didn't suffer at all. Gays, lesbians, Hispanics, black people—they have understood what discrimination is. Many of them have suffered from discrimination. But if they know how to practice the *paramitas*, they will stop suffering and they will get resource [from within], *in order to help the people who discriminate against them.*" With the practice of the *kshanti paramita* and the other *paramitas,* Thich Nhat Hanh taught, "what has made you suffer in the past is no longer capable of making you suffer anymore, and that is why the word *inclusiveness* is used. You embrace everyone...."[59]

THE SOCIALLY ENGAGED SANGHA

In Buddhist practice over the centuries, the Sangha or "spiritual community" jewel has been emphasized less than the jewels of the Buddha and the Dharma. Thich Nhat Hanh has suggested however that the next buddha, *Maitreya*, will come not as a single person but as a sangha, or community. By 1998, about three hundred sanghas in the tradition of Thich Nhat Hanh had been established in many parts of the Western world, and in the late 1980s and 1990s in the West, Thich Nhat Hanh was giving increasing attention to the importance of sangha and to the practice of sangha-building.

A sangha is essential for socially engaged practice. In *Touching Peace*, Thich Nhat Hanh writes, "Even if we are a skilled meditator and well versed in the sutras, if we don't know how to build a sangha, we cannot help others."[60] It functions as a community of resistance countering and transforming the individualism, isolation, and greed fostered in modern Western societies. It is a base community of spiritual friends who are living in ways that nourish a culture of mindfulness, compassion, and understanding. In this way, transformation of the culture of materialism, alienation, consumerism, and violence gradually occurs. In Thich Nhat Hanh's emerging tradition, the development of communities of mindfulness and mindful living that are grounded in the teachings of the Buddha and that do not succumb to unwholesome individual and societal practices is itself seen as socially engaged Buddhism.

In order to give support to and develop the art of sangha-building, Thich Nhat Hanh and the hundred or so resident monks, nuns, and lay people at Plum Village have developed sangha-building practices based on the Buddha's teachings and their own experience of developing an international community. Practices such as "beginning anew," "the peace treaty," and "seven steps to reconciliation"[61] offer a foundation for socially engaged practitioners and peace and social change activists who wish to develop effective organizational and community relationships with colleagues and co-workers. These practices are intended to transform anger, jealousy, and conflicts when they arise, sustain commitment and prevent burnout, and maintain a beneficial balance of activism and solitude in their lives. As such, these practices are part of the foundation of a socially engaged Buddhism.[62]

Members of the Order of Interbeing and of the wider sangha—anyone inspired by the teachings and practices of Thich Nhat Hanh—have developed diverse forms of socially engaged practice. These include relatively large-scale collective actions and projects, sangha practice, family and workplace practice, and individual practice. These fall generally into the categories of embodying or *being* peace, awareness-raising about a particular public issue, engaging in social service, engaging in action to shift public policies in a more wholesome direction, and offering mindfulness practice itself in various arenas. Only a few examples from telephone and in-person interviews and responses to questionnaires can be highlighted here.

Large-Scale Ongoing Projects

In France, Partage, an organization to assist children worldwide, was founded by an Order of Interbeing member, Pierre Marchand. In 1972 Marchand, who was then seventeen, organized with Sister Chan Khong the first benefit concert in Paris for orphans in Vietnam.[63] In 1997 he initiated the Nobel Peace Laureates Campaign for the Children of the World, with Nobel Peace Prize recipient Mairead McGuire. The aim of the campaign was for the United Nations to declare the year 2000 as a year of education for nonviolence, and the decade 2000–2010 as the decade for a culture of peace and nonviolence. The general assembly approved this initiative in 1998.

In the Netherlands, Order of Interbeing members Françoise Pottier and Shelley Anderson publish *Reconciliation International*, the journal of the International Fellowship of Reconciliation, "an international, spiritually-based movement of people committed to active nonviolence as a way of life and as a means of personal, social, economic and political transformation."

In England, the Amida Trust was founded by Order of Interbeing members David and Caroline Brazier to support people interested in socially engaged Buddhism. Order members in England and elsewhere are active with the International Network of Engaged Buddhists founded by the Thai teacher of engaged Buddhism and student of Thich Nhat Hanh, Sulak Sivaraksa.[64]

In the United States, the Community of Mindful Living founded by lay Dharma teachers Arnie Kotler and Therese Fitzgerald has, among other projects, organized ongoing correspondence with prisoners and a Vietnam veterans writing project, guided by author Maxine Hong Kingston.[65] A project on "being with dying" was started by Joan Halifax, ordained as a lay Dharma teacher by Thich Nhat Hanh in 1990. The Being with Dying project "is a training and support program for health care professionals, people with severe illnesses, and others who are working with issues related to death and dying," and trains people to bring engaged mindfulness practice into the dying process.[66] Wendy Johnson, also a lay Dharma teacher ordained by Thich Nhat Hanh in 1990, has led major protests of the clearcutting of the redwood trees in California.[67] A third Dharma teacher, Cynthia Jurs, has founded Animal Alliance "to ensure the survival of endangered species and reduce animal suffering."[68]

In the United States and Europe, Claude AnShin Thomas, a Vietnam veteran and student of Thich Nhat Hanh, has led many retreats with veterans and nonveterans. In the mid-1990s, Thomas founded the Zaltho Foundation "to promote peace and nonviolence in and among individuals, families, societies and countries...through whatever peaceful and nonviolent means are available," including the "creation of Dharma centers for the study and practice of engaged Buddhism as well as other socially active projects." Thomas has also participated in street retreats, retreats at Auschwitz, and pilgrimage walks from Auschwitz to Hiroshima (1995) and across the United States (1998).[69] Daphne White, a parent inspired by Thich Nhat Hanh's teachings, started the national Lion and Lamb Project to end violence on children's television and the production and buying of war toys.[70] National nursing summits and roundtables that bring together leaders in nursing from around the United States to reflect on the state of health care in the country and the state of the nursing profession have been organized by Order of Interbeing member Jeanne Anselm.

Since the 1980s, musician Betsy Rose has reached many Western practitioners through their own cultural forms. As previously mentioned, the use of cultural forms has been emphasized in Thich Nhat Hanh's work since the 1950s. Rose has transformed traditional Buddhist teachings such as the three refuges and some of Thich Nhat Hanh's peace poetry into a folk music format. Performed at numerous retreats, Rose's inspirational music is also widely available on cassette and CD through Paper Crane Music.[71]

Sangha Practice

Sanghas have undertaken engaged practice in two ways. Sanghas have engaged in particular projects as a group. Alternatively, individual sangha members have launched or joined social/political projects in which no one else in the sangha actively participated, but with the sangha's support. Such support might include financial assistance, helpful discussions of issues and concerns related to members' socially engaged actions, and group mindfulness practice in relation to the project.

Sanghas in Maine, Montana, North Carolina, and Pennsylvania, for example, provided ongoing prison projects, offering mindfulness practice in prisons. Other sanghas have organized or helped organize neighborhood unity rallies, multiethnic citywide observances of Martin Luther King's life and work, peacemaking demonstrations to protest ongoing nuclear arms research, and vigils and town meetings in connection with the 1991 Gulf War and the possibility of bombing in Iraq in 1998. Some sanghas practice engaged mindfulness by cleaning up a beach,[72] collecting food for hungry people, participating in projects to end hunger, sponsoring benefit concerts to raise money for local or international programs to help children and families, and sponsoring speakers or videos to raise awareness of important social issues. Others distribute information related to abolishing the death penalty, and ensuring animal and human rights.

Individuals frame their socially engaged practice in different ways. These include sharing their mindfulness practice both systematically and in everyday encounters with others who are not familiar with the practice. Socially engaged practice has also included working with social change or peacemaking organizations, leading workshops to end racism, social service work, organizing neighborhood rallies, participating in pilgrimage walks, living in countries other than their own to assist in social service or political projects, making financial contributions, and engaging in local government affairs. In the deepest sense, all of these actions can be considered peacework.

Family and Practice in Relationships

"My most important socially engaged practice is in my family relationships, which have benefited tremendously from the equanimity and wisdom I have begun to develop through mindfulness practice" wrote one Order of Interbeing member.[73] In writing this, he gives expression to Thich Nhat Hanh's more recent emphasis on the importance of nonviolent communication within families and in relationships, as a key element in the cultural transformation of the roots of violence. In this view, mindfulness in interpersonal relationships is a foundation for effective socially engaged action.

The relationship between children and the larger sangha is a central focus for Thich Nhat Hanh and the Order of Interbeing. A children's program is offered simultaneously at most adult retreats given by Thich Nhat Hanh. The children are taught peacemaking activities and ways to foster peacefulness in their family settings. Often the children produce art or music about peace. Each morning, after all retreatants gather in the meditation hall, the children come in as a group. Thich Nhat Hanh speaks directly to them before the Dharma talk, with the whole adult sangha present. Sometimes the children share their peacemaking activity with the adult sangha before leaving for their own program. Thich Nhat Hanh has also encouraged teens and young adults to share with him what practices have been beneficial to them, so that he can offer practices uniquely suitable to young people to other groups.

Right Livelihood and Workplace Practice

A sampling of responses to our survey indicates the diversity of socially engaged participation. Some people chose their livelihood because through it they could be, or had the intention to be, engaged in the political, social, or cultural transformation of society. Many others found their socially engaged practice in sharing mindfulness practice in their work environments, either explicitly teaching mindfulness to their co-workers, or being socially engaged, in their view, simply by "being mindful." Practicing mindfulness and teaching the way of awareness, whether explicitly stated or invisibly embodied, was seen as the key to socially engaged workplace practice and the transformation of these institutions.

A sampling of responses to our survey follows. Several practitioners have written professional journal articles that specifically incorporate mindfulness practice.[74] Organizational development consultants and stress-reduction workshop leaders infused mindfulness training into their professional workshops. There was a lawyer who worked for an environmental protection agency and another who did mediation work. Practitioners led meditation groups and retreats at alcoholism rehabilitation centers and homeless shelters and prisons. Others led mindfulness-based conflict resolution and workshops to end racism for the public and for social activists. One high school teacher wrote about generally supporting the growth of spiritual awareness in students, while another explicitly taught her students mindfulness-based conflict resolution skills in an inner-city public school, including using the "breathing bell" as it is used in Thich Nhat Hanh's tradition. One nurse taught walking meditation in the hospital where she worked, while another, who worked in an intensive care unit, wrote about "seeing patient, doctor, coworker as me." Thus, without the icongraphy of Buddhism, mindfulness was brought into the workplace and, in the view of our respondents, constituted socially engaged action and practice.

Volunteer and Pro Bono Work

Several people practiced socially engaged action through their volunteer work. Some worked with social change organizations such as Amnesty International, East Bay Sanctuary, Interfaith Voices Against Hunger, and action against human rights abuses in Vietnam. Others wrote about their volunteering in a soup kitchen, an agency for runaway teens, a teen suicide hotline, an alternative high school, a hospice, a children's nursing home for the severely disabled, and doing volunteer work as a wildlife rehabilitator. And still others highlighted their contact with individuals: writing letters to or sharing resources of time and energy with a prison inmate or a dying person. A lawyer wrote of his pro bono work and his work with the Buddhist Peace Fellowship.

Social Activism

Our survey included people who defined themselves as having been social activists earlier in their lives. Their responses reflect a shift in their understanding of socially engaged action. In general, they focused less on social activism, as traditionally defined, and more on "practicing mindfulness in daily life." How widespread this shift is and its implications are as yet unclear. The example of Jill (not her real name) is indicative of the self-reflection of people who responded from this historical experience. "I was active but not at peace," Jill wrote. "Socially engaged practice and social activism do not necessarily overlap."

Jill's description of the evolution of her thinking from the period of her life when she was an activist, as a "child of the 1960s," to her current view of socially engaged practice, offers an insight into how Thich Nhat Hanh's teachings and practices have contributed to a deeper and broader understanding of socially engaged action—one that includes such socially engaged practices as peacemaking and cultural transformation, as distinct from only social activism in the public arena. Jill had embraced feminism and helped to establish a women's center and family planning services. She had been part of the anti-war movement against the Vietnam war, but not, as she put it, the peace movement. Indeed, she wrote, she had seen the distinction between these movements only after attending a retreat with Thich Nhat Hanh. Jill emphasized how Thich Nhat Hanh's insight into interbeing had influenced and deepened her understanding of socially engaged practice and social activism. "Thay [Thich Nhat Hanh] asked us, on the eve of the Gulf War, to stop this war. He told us also, many times, to cultivate peace in ourselves. All too often we forgo the war within to protest the one without. This is, I think, futile."

CONCLUDING REFLECTIONS

For the students of Thich Nhat Hanh we interviewed, the term "socially engaged practice" is essentially a term integrating mindfulness and love, and including by definition an awareness of and commitment to the world "off the cushion." Socially engaged practice is characterized by being grounded in the establishment of mindfulness throughout one's everyday life, and by the general aim and commitment to relieve and reduce suffering.

Beyond these elements, however, the "map" of socially engaged action and practice offered by those we heard from was varied and inclusive. Socially engaged practice could be expressed through volunteerism or paid work. It could equally take the form of social service, of advocacy to change public policies perceived as harmful, and of action intended to transform social structure. Socially engaged practice could occur in public arenas and institutions. It could equally refer to mindful interactions in the interpersonal arenas of family, workplace, and random encounters. It could be large-scale or small-scale, collective (for example, by a practice community) or individual, explicitly "Buddhist" or "invisibly Buddhist"— informed by Buddhist teachings but formless, nonsectarian, and transdenominational. Practitioners in Thich Nhat Hanh's tradition of socially engaged Buddhist practice are in all these ways manifesting three of the phases identified by Norwegian peace theorist Johan Galtung (the "father" of peace research/peace studies), as necessary for social change, peacemaking, and peacebuilding: consciousness formation, organization, and solidarity/mobilization.[75]

Many people are attracted to Thich Nhat Hanh's teachings and practice because of his explicit inclusion of social issues and in particular his attentiveness to young people. The teachings and practices he offers also address four key challenges confronting practitioners who are involved in socially engaged action in the public arena and who are committed to deep cultural and social as well as political transformation.

One of these challenges (or forms of suffering) concerns intention and motivation: how to cultivate true love, compassion, and joy as a source of motivation for socially engaged action rather than anger and fear? A second is the question of real connection: how to go beyond the alienation, anomie, numbness, isolation, and sense of meaninglessness that may be present in oneself and in others in modern societies, and to deepen and sustain true connection, "being deeply in touch" with both the suffering and the joy of oneself and others? A third challenge is the divisiveness and attachment to views within political organizations and peace movements and a tendency to view political adversaries as an "enemy." The fourth is burnout, so prevalent in the traditional movements for peace and social justice and other social action projects. Thich Nhat Hanh's teachings expressly emphasize practices that sustain a mindful life. From this foundation, it is possible for people to engage social concerns for decades without suffering burnout.

Critics of Thich Nhat Hanh's form of socially engaged Buddhism suggest that his teachings are either too engaged with the world and do not give enough emphasis to traditional notions in Buddhist practice such as enlightenment; that he is not engaged enough with Buddhist collective action in the public arena; or that he does not address fundamental issues of class and power, institutional and structural violence. Several people we heard from and interviewed suggested (and lamented) what they see as a shift in emphasis in Thich Nhat Hanh's teachings in the later 1990s from the more politically engaged and collective Buddhist activism of the 1960s in Vietnam to a more individual- and sangha-based engaged practice in the West. The assumption that individual transformation and even small sanghas functioning as base communities can effect real social transformation is naive and idealistic, according to some critics. Also, with the donation of land in 1997 for the establishment of Maple Forest Monastery in Vermont, concern was expressed by some that increasing attention to developing monastic communities in Plum Village, France, and in Vermont meant a withdrawal or diminishing of support for the lay practice and for socially engaged action.

As we have surveyed the teachings and practices of Thich Nhat Hanh both historically and in the most recent period, and from our interviews with practitioners who have been inspired by these teachings and practices, it appears to us that Thich Nhat Hanh—in looking deeply at the roots of violence, loneliness, materialism, and sorrow in Western society—has correctly seen that individual and family healing is a necessary link to cultural and political transformation. We believe that changes in public policy can indeed be advanced as socially engaged activists strengthen their individual and collective practice of mindfulness as a foundation for their activism. Peacemaking from this perspective is an all-inclusive, living activity that enters all levels of existence from the so-called internal, to family interactions, to movement-building in order to forge beneficial public policy and transform consciousness.

The perception among some that Thich Nhat Hanh's current emphasis on nonviolent communication in sanghas, families, and workplaces encourages a "quietism" with respect to socially engaged practice in the public arena appears not to be borne out by our (admittedly limited) sampling. His focus on monastic training at Plum Village in France, and at the newly established Maple Forest Monastery in Vermont, appears to be balanced by the development of the Green Mountain Dharma Center in Vermont for lay and monastic practitioners and by the encouragement of mindfulness practice centers in every city. These mindfulness practice centers in the tradition of Thich Nhat Hanh are envisioned as places where mindfulness practice may be widely shared in a nonreligious, nonsectarian form, without the iconography of Buddhism, and from which the teaching of mindfulness practice in public institutions may be supported.

As of this writing, the Green Mountain Dharma Center near Woodstock, Vermont, is seen as the home of Thich Nhat Hanh's teaching in North America. It offers retreats for lay people and is the home of approximately twenty-five monks and nuns, as well as lay people, until monastery buildings at nearby Maple Forest Monastery are completed. In May and again in October 1998 the center was the site for gatherings of Order of Interbeing members living in the United States, Canada, and other countries. A recent emphasis on the importance of the "fourfold sangha" appears to be an attempt to clarify that each element of the developing community in the tradition of Thich Nhat Hanh is essential: monks, nuns, laymen, and laywomen. In early 1999, however, it is still too early to say how the embryonic institutional forms now being manifested will develop with respect to socially engaged action and practice, and what the implications are for the Order of Interbeing as a peacemaking and socially engaged sangha in the United States and worldwide.

Perhaps the key, as Thich Nhat Hanh continues to remind us, is that

Mindfulness must be engaged.
Once there is seeing, there must be acting....
We must be aware of the real problems of the world.
Then, with mindfulness, we will know what to do, and what not to
    do, to be of help.[76]

NOTES

1. See Thich Nhat Hanh, *Love in Action: Writings on Nonviolent Social Change* (Berkeley: Parallax Press, 1993).

2. Stephen Batchelor, *The Awakening of the West* (Berkeley: Parallax Press, 1994), p. 355.

3. Thich Nhat Hanh, "Dharma Talk."

4. See Arnie Kotler, "The Life of a 'Lazy Monk,'" *Shambhala Sun* (March 1998), p. 49; Thich Nhat Hanh, "Dharma Talk"; Stephen Batchelor, *The Awakening of the West*.

5. Thich Nhat Hanh, *The History of Buddhism in Vietnam*, trans. Sister Annabel Laity; synopsis, "A Special Section: Buddhism in Vietnam," in *The Mindfulness Bell* 5 (autumn 1991): 32.

6. Thich Nhat Hanh, "Dharma Talk."

7. See Rick Fields, *Taking Refuge in L.A.: Life in a Vietnamese Buddhist Temple* (New York: Aperture, 1987), pp. 26–36.

8. Thich Nhat Hanh, "Dharma Talk"; synopsis, "History of Buddhism," *The Mindfulness Bell* 5, p. 35. Thich Nhat Hanh's novel *Hermitage Among the Clouds* records some of the stories of the life of the Bamboo Forest master and his daughter, Princess Amazing Jewel—later ordained as Fragrant Garland—as they tried to make peace with the kingdom of Cham. The novel is based on the historical records of the three Bamboo Forest patriarchs.

9. Catherine Ingram, *In the Footsteps of Gandhi* (Berkeley: Parallax Press, 1990), p. 76.

10. Ibid., p. 77.

11. Chan Khong, *Learning True Love* (Berkeley: Parallax Press, 1993), p. 70ff.

12. Thich Nhat Hanh, *Call Me By My True Names* (Berkeley: Parallax Press, 1993), p. 19.

13. Ibid., p. 19.

14. For an in-depth analysis of Thich Nhat Hanh's relationship to the Unified Buddhist Church, see Sallie B. King, "Thich Nhat Hanh and the Unified Buddhist Church," in *Engaged Buddhism: Liberation Movements in Asia*, ed. Christopher S. Queen and Sallie B. King (Albany: State University of New York Press, 1996), pp. 321–64.

15. Thich Nhat Hanh, *The Raft Is Not the Shore: Conversations Toward a Buddhist-Christian Awareness* (New York: Beacon Press, 1975), p. 119 (emphasis added).

16. Therese Fitzgerald, "Four Springs in Asia," *The Mindfulness Bell* 14 (autumn 1995): 24–25.

17. Ibid.

18. Thich Nhat Hanh, *Interbeing* (Berkeley: Parallax Press, 1998), p. viii. See also

Chan Khong, *Learning True Love.*

19. Fred Eppsteiner, ed., *The Path of Compassion* (Buffalo: White Pine Press, 1985), p. 101.

20. Maxine Hong Kingston, foreword to *Learning True Love*, pp. vii–viii.

21. Chan Khong, *Learning True Love*, pp. 25–26. Italics added.

22. Thomas Merton, talk at Gethsemane Abbey, Kentucky, 1967. Audiotape available from Credence Communities, 6314 Brookside Plaza, POB 22582, Kansas City, MO 64113, tel: 888-595-8273.

23. *Peace Is Every Step*, videotape, Gaetano Maida, producer for Legacy Media, Inc., distributed by Mystic Fire, 1997.

24. Stephen Batchelor, *The Awakening of the West*, p. 353.

25. Chan Khong, *Learning True Love*, p. 105ff.

26. Ibid., p. 156.

27. Thomas Merton, *The Non-Violent Alternative* (NY: Farrar, Straus, Giroux, 1980).

28. Chan Khong, *Learning True Love*, p. 156.

29. *Peace Is Every Step*, videotape.

30. Thich Nhat Hanh, *Peace Is Every Step* (New York: Bantam, 1991), pp. 114–15. See also *Being Peace* (Berkeley: Parallax Press, 1987), chapter 5, "Working for Peace."

31. Interview with Andrew Young by Patricia Hunt-Perry, American Political Science Association Meeting, Atlanta, Georgia, Sept. 1, 1989. For further sources, see *The New York Times,* August 14, 1965, p. 13.

32. Dr. Martin Luther King, Jr., nomination letter, 1967. Unpublished, available from Parallax Press, Box 7355, Berkeley, CA 94707.

33. Chan Khong, *Learning True Love*, p. 88.

34. Interview with Mobi Warren by Patricia Hunt-Perry, June 1998. See also Chan Khong, *Learning True Love*, pp. 187–200; *The Awakening Bell*, videotape available from Parallax Press, Box 7355, Berkeley, CA 94707.

35. See Thich Nhat Hanh, ed., *A Joyful Path: Community, Transformation and Peace* (Berkeley: Parallax Press, 1994). See also *The Mindfulness Bell*, passim; and videotapes *The Awakening Bell; Peace Is Every Step.*

36. "Being Wonderfully Together: Report from the Order of Interbeing Second International Conference," *The Mindfulness Bell* 18 (Jan.–April 1997): 18–20.

37. Watering the Seeds of American Buddhism Conference, Mt. Madonna Conference Center, California, June 1988. Attended by both authors.

38. Thich Nhat Hanh, *Love in Action*, pp. 65–66.

39. Ibid., p. 87. The 1989 conference/retreat was co-sponsored by the Buddhist Peace Fellowship and Fellowship of Reconciliation, April 1989, and was attended by Patricia Hunt-Perry. A 1991 retreat for veterans at the Omega Institute in Rhinebeck, NY was attended by both authors.

40. Ibid., p. 82.

41. Ibid., p. 84.

42. Thich Nhat Hanh, *Being Peace*, pp. 11, 45.

43. Ibid., p. 63. See also Thich Nhat Hanh, *Please Call Me By My True Names*, pp. 72–73; "A Lone Pink Fish" in Thich Nhat Hanh, *The Stone Boy and Other Stories* (Berkeley: Parallax Press, 1996); and Thich Nhat Hanh, *A Taste of Earth and Other Legends of Vietnam* (Berkeley: Parallax Press, 1993).

44. Thich Nhat Hanh, *Love in Action*, p. 109.

45. Thich Nhat Hanh, "Five Wonderful Precepts," *The Mindfulness Bell* 1.2 (spring/summer 1990), p. 1.

46. Thich Nhat Hanh, *Teachings on Love* (Berkeley, CA: Parallax Press, 1997), p. 125.

47. Thich Nhat Hanh, introduction to *Interbeing*.

48. Thich Nhat Hanh, "Dharma Talk."

49. Thich Nhat Hanh, introduction to *Interbeing*.

50. Ibid., p. 41.

51. Thich Nhat Hanh, *Teachings on Love*, chap. 13, "Touching the Earth"; and chap. 14, "The Three Prostrations."

52. Thich Nhat Hanh, *The Blooming of a Lotus* (Berkeley, CA: Parallax Press, 1993), pp. 51–52.

53. Ibid., pp. 51–52.

54. Thich Nhat Hanh, *Love in Action,* pp. 132–33. See also Thich Nhat Hanh, *The Diamond That Cuts Through Illusion* (Berkeley, CA: Parallax Press, 1995), p. 41; *Cultivating the Mind of Love* (Berkeley, CA: Parallax Press, 1996), and Allan Hunt-Badiner, ed., *Dharma Gaia: A Harvest of Essays in Buddhism and Ecology* (Berkeley, CA: Parallax Press, 1990).

55. Thich Nhat Hanh, *Cultivating the Mind of Love*, pp. 88–89.

56. Thich Nhat Hanh, *Love in Action*, p. 137.

57. Thich Nhat Hanh, *Old Path, White Clouds* (Berkeley, CA: Parallax Press, 1991), p. 274.

58. Thich Nhat Hanh, "Dharma Talk No. 5," October 23, 1997, Omega Institute, Rhinebeck, New York.

59. Ibid.

60. Jack Lawlor, *Sangha Building*, 1992 (available from Jack Lawlor, PO Box 7067, Evanston, IL 60201).

61. Thich Nhat Hanh, *Teachings on Love*. See also Thich Nhat Hanh, *Touching Peace* (Berkeley, CA: Parallax Press, 1992); *Being Peace*, pp. 74–79.

62. Thich Nhat Hanh, *Teachings on Love*. See also Thich Nhat Hanh, ed., *A Joyful Path*.

63. Chan Khong, *Learning True Love*, pp. 137–38.

64. See Sulak Sivaraksa, *Seeds of Peace* (Berkeley, CA: Parallax Press, 1992). See also *Loyalty Demands Dissent: Autobiography of an Engaged Buddhist* (Berkeley, CA:

Parallax Press, 1998) by the same author, and Donald K. Swearer, "Sulak Sivaraksa's Buddhist Vision for Renewing Society," in *Engaged Buddhism: Buddhist Liberation Movements in Asia*, Christopher S. Queen and Sallie B. King, eds. (Albany: State University of New York Press, 1996).

65. See Therese Fitzgerald, "Writing Out the War," *The Mindfulness Bell* 9 (autumn 1993): 26; and Maxine Hong Kingston, "Writing in Community," *The Mindfulness Bell* 10 (winter 1994): 28; Michael Gardner and Therese Fitzgerald, "Healing Through Writing," *The Mindfulness Bell* 12 (winter 1994): 29; Maxine Hong Kingston, "Writing Peace," *The Mindfulness Bell* 18 (Jan.–April 1997): 6.

66. See Joan Halifax, "Being with Dying," *The Mindfulness Bell* 14 (autumn 1995): 6. See also Bernard Glassman, *Bearing Witness* (New York: Riverhead, 1998); and the newsletter of the Upaya Foundation, 1404 Cerro Gordo Road, Santa Fe, NM 87501, tel: 505-986-8518.

67. Wendy Johnson, "Redwood Sangha," *The Mindfulness Bell* 18 (Jan.–April 1997): 7. See also the ongoing column "On Gardening" in *Tricycle: A Buddhist Review*.

68. Cynthia Jurs, "Turtle Visions," newsletter of the Animal Alliance, Sterling Institute, 402 Don Gaspar, Santa Fe, NM 87501 (winter 1998).

69. Claude Thomas, "Finding Peace After a Lifetime of War," in *A Joyful Path*, ed. Thich Nhat Hanh; and *Peace Is Every Step*, videotape.

70. See Daphne White, "Stopping Violent Play," *Mindfulness Bell* 14 (autumn 1995): 7. Also, newsletter of the Lion and Lamb Project, 4300 Montgomery Avenue, Suite 104, Bethesda, MD 20814-4413.

71. See "In My Two Hands," audiotape, Betsy Rose Paper Crane Music, Box 9538, Berkeley, CA 94709.

72. Thompson, Penelope, "Beach Cleaning Meditation," *Mindfulness Bell* 9 (autumn 1993): 11.

73. Survey of Order of Interbeing members by Lyn Fine and Patricia Hunt-Perry, 1997–1998.

74. See, for example, Fred Allendorf, "The Conservation Biologist as Zen Student," in *Conservation Biology* 11.5 (October 1997), pp. 1045–46.

75. Johan Galtung, *The True Worlds: A Transnational Perspective* (New York: The Free Press, 1980), p. 140.

76. Thich Nhat Hanh, *Peace Is Every Step*, p. 91. For additional references on the work of Thich Nhat Hanh and the Tiep Hien Order, see the following websites: www.plumvillage.org (Plum Village, France); www.parallax.org (Parallax Press).

SPEAKING TRUTH TO POWER: THE BUDDHIST PEACE FELLOWSHIP

Judith Simmer-Brown

IN THE DEVELOPMENT OF ENGAGED BUDDHISM IN AMERICA, there is probably no force more important than the alliance that calls itself the Buddhist Peace Fellowship (BPF).[1] Structured as a nonprofit organization, an affiliate of the international peace consortium Fellowship of Reconciliation, BPF is an association of four thousand independent Buddhists from a variety of lineages, traditions, and communities who hold a common allegiance to Buddhist practice and to social engagement. For the last two decades it has provided the venue for the discussions that have shaped the American engaged Buddhist identity. In the pages of its journal, *Turning Wheel*, and in its chapters and town meetings, BPF has traced the foundations of social and political concern in the Asian Buddhist traditions, forged a language of social engagement in Buddhist terms, and reported and commented upon the myriad forms of institutionalized suffering in the world. Through the Buddhist Peace Fellowship's influence, a broad range of Buddhist teachers, communities, and practice centers now actively contemplate and participate in social action.

In the context of American engaged Buddhism, BPF's journey has been largely a grassroots movement. Though there have been influential Asian and American Buddhist teachers who have advised and guided the organization, the vision and identity of BPF have been held by the collective of members, staff, and board, who have been for the most part Euro-American lay people, heavily representing West Coast Zen and Vipassana practitioners. They have, from the beginning, carried out the charter's intention to remain a nonsectarian, nonaligned Buddhist organization.

This commitment has been both a blessing and a challenge. It has been a blessing in that the organization has exhibited a truly American flavor— populist, diverse, with great value placed on direct and tangible action and upon championing the oppressed. The Buddhist Peace Fellowship has also been able to appeal directly to unaffiliated Buddhists and to non-Buddhist, especially Christian, organizations. Its challenge has been the criticism that its social action agenda has suffered from purely conventional thinking, polarizing the oppressor and oppressed, and that its actions have no distinctly Buddhist analysis or strategy behind them. What is Buddhist about BPF? Observers comment that some BPF activities seem sometimes randomly chosen, without discrimination or direction. Also, the distinctively American flavor has put off ethnic Asians and American Buddhists with a stronger devotion to and identification with their Asian teachers and traditions.

The Buddhist Peace Fellowship as an organization has been responsive to these criticisms, and has begun to look carefully at what composes a spiritually based social activism that is Buddhist in orientation. In doing so, BPF is not diverting its energy from its initial vision: rather, it is expressing a new maturity in understanding the importance of a cohesive vision, a clearly focused mission, and a finely honed strategy. This has produced new initiatives and projects that will shape BPF's identity into the next millennium.

BPF continues its leadership in American engaged Buddhism, recognizing the interdependence of all things, that the suffering of others is also one's own suffering, and that the violence of others is also one's own violence. As a result of this maturity, BPF is putting its energies into addressing structural violence in the United States and throughout the world. At the same time, the BPF leadership recognizes the fundamental, guiding principle of engaged Buddhism, in which "social work entails inner work, and social change and inner change are inseparable."[2]

AITKEN ROSHI AND THE FOUNDING OF BPF

On a tropical afternoon in 1977, a group of friends gathered in the balmy air on the front porch of the old Maui *zendo*. "Two-Twenty," the old *zendo's* nickname drawn from its rural-route address, was a small, green-shingled former plantation house shaded by banana and mango trees, and had been the original site of the Maui Zen community founded by Robert Aitken Roshi.[3] Now it had finally become the private "retirement" dwelling of Roshi and his wife, Anne, the purpose for which it was intended upon its purchase in 1967. Aitken Roshi and Anne and their friends gathered on the partially enclosed shaded porch, around a round table. The conversation centered on nuclear weapons and the massive buildup of the American military following the Vietnam war. They felt that compassion required that they become involved, that they do something. How could they best engage practicing Buddhists in the issues of the day? How could discussion, and hopefully action, arise in Buddhist practice centers?

This particular meeting was the culmination of several years of general discussion and reflection. Present were Robert and Anne Aitken, Nelson Foster, Stephen Gockley, W. S. (William) Merwin, and Dana Naone. Aitken Roshi had a highly developed social conscience dating back to his internment in Japan during the Second World War, and his subsequent years of peace activities. He was the driving force of the meeting, without wanting to be. For Aitken Roshi, social and political activism had been woven into his Zen practice from the beginning, and his particular style of expression of the relationship between the two had been forged in the crucible of his Zen training.

The others present were younger or less practiced, both in Zen and in political activities. As a young woman, Anne Aitken had worked in settlement houses in Chicago and for the Red Cross during the Second World War, and joined her husband in Zen practice and political activities after their marriage in 1957. Nelson Foster had engaged in peace issues in the way many college students of the 1960s did, but his political awareness had deepened in the three years of service to Aitken Roshi as secretary, assistant, and eventually Dharma heir. By the time he received Dharma transmission sometime later, Foster had spent a decade working closely with the Quakers, and his activities and outlook continued to evolve in directions somewhat different than Aitken Roshi's. Stephen Gockley had been a conscientious objector before coming to the Maui *zendo*, laying the foundations for a life of service. W. S. Merwin, a Pulitzer prize winning poet, had a well-established social conscience long before meeting Aitken Roshi; while Merwin hesitated to identify himself as a Buddhist, his strong concern over nuclear proliferation brought him to this gathering. Dana Naone was also reluctant to identify herself as Buddhist, and was at that time inexperienced in activism.

The group was concerned that Buddhist practice centers and groups had become entirely removed from the social and political issues of the day: some teachers and organizations were even actively discouraging political involvement. The Maui group envisioned an organization which would attract a wide range of Buddhists, fomenting political discussion and action. Something had to be done, and specifically something political needed to be done by Buddhists. "Anyone, feeling compassion, seeing no boundary between self and others, would feel compelled to do something," observed Nelson Foster, reflecting on the occasion.

After some discussion, the group decided to found a chapter of the Fellowship of Reconciliation (FOR), an ecumenical organization dedicated to world peace, which was founded in England in 1916 and spread to the United States just after the First World War.[4] Foster had visited FOR headquarters in Nyack, New York the previous year, and found it a receptive and sympathetic organization for a Buddhist affiliation. FOR had been a central force in investigating peace possibilities during the Vietnam war, and in 1966, had sponsored Thich Nhat Hanh's landmark lecture tour in the United States, on which he entreated Americans to bring an end to war in his country. Later, the FOR invited Thay (as he is known) to serve as vice-chairman of the fellowship, and published Thay's first book in English, *Miracle of Being Awake*, based on his U.S. tour.[5] During decades of pacifist activity, Aitken Roshi had followed the FOR activities closely and had become a member in 1967. In his years of involvement, he had found it to be a broadly ecumenical, effective peace organization whose mission the rest of the Maui group could admire.

Their design, which followed Fellowship of Reconciliation's style, was to draw a wide variety of Buddhist organizations into a network of activities and discussions. It was to be a nonsectarian Buddhist network, not allied with any particular Buddhist tradition or teacher, ecumenical as a matter of principle. This became BPF's hallmark, its most distinguishing feature, at times its most difficult commitment. In later years, several luminaries influenced BPF's development, and its greatest crises have revolved around the appropriateness of this influence. Still, in its first twenty years, the Buddhist Peace Fellowship has managed to retain its independent profile, its nonsectarian identity, and its ecumenical stance.

As engaged Buddhism in America has emerged as a movement, it must be acknowledged that Aitken Roshi has served as dean, mentor, as well as the strongest supporter. His strongly moral, almost righteous approach has influenced many people in both the Buddhist and peace movements. He served as first president of BPF's board, and was the featured guest speaker at its first two institutes. Yet, Aitken Roshi has never been comfortable with pyramidic hierarchies, so his leadership of BPF, like that of the Diamond Sangha in Hawaii, has taken different forms. He sowed seeds at the inception of Buddhist Peace Fellowship that definitively shaped its development.

Robert Aitken, son of a military enthusiast, grew up in Hawaii a loner and rebel against the war-fever of the 30s and 40s. At the outbreak of the war, while working as a civilian construction worker on Guam, he was captured by the Japanese, and was held for three years in an internment camp near Kobe. There, under the tutelage of fellow prisoner R. H. Blyth, and with the support of an idiosyncratic English library, he was introduced to Zen and anarchism. This first of several important apprenticeships honed his temperament and proclivities. In the years after the war, he simultaneously pursued Zen practice and political discussions of peace and labor issues. In the Cold War atmosphere of the late 40s and 50s, this earned him the dubious honor of being investigated by the FBI.

With his dual interests, Robert Aitken deviated from Zen's Japanese and Chinese past in which teachers and their communities, with scant exception, refrained from overt political involvement of any kind. This cultural fact was essential to Zen's survival in East Asia, in which the dominion of the emperor was supreme. In fact, Zen was repeatedly used to further imperial ambitions throughout Japanese history. For Aitken, this was merely a dangerous cultural artifact, having nothing to do with the essence of Zen, and he cultivated the "diplomacy of discretion" in refraining from exploring politics with his Zen teachers.[6] For his Western students, he clearly distinguished between personal insight and compassion stemming from practice and conventional society's political and material demands. As he wrote,

> Treating our Bodhisattva vows seriously, we must respond to America's stockpiling of nuclear weapons, its materialism, its profligate consumption of energy, its destruction of forests and animals, and its depersonalization of life....We can learn...to maintain our integrity as Buddhists, seeking good public relations as far as integrity permits but standing fast and saying No! to our country's rush toward nuclear war and biological holocaust.[7]

Throughout his Zen training, Aitken never abandoned his social conscience as a pacifist. In the fifties he demonstrated against nuclear testing. In the sixties, he opposed the war in Vietnam, and, following the guidelines of the American Friends Service Committee, he counseled draft resisters. After Vietnam, he opposed the proliferation of nuclear weapons and the military buildup that followed. He was one of the first American religious leaders to champion the "deep ecology" movement, and he manifested his feminist sympathies by encouraging his women students in the publication of the first American nonsectarian Buddhist women's magazine, *Kahawai: The Journal of Women and Zen*.

For Aitken, issues of authority were central to his personal reflections in the Hawaii Zen community. While he was diffident in his growing authority in the *zendo*, he did not back down from keeping traditional discipline. Always, he was committed to the complete discipline of Zen training, with its full practice and work *(samu)* schedule. During his years of working with counterculture populations, he enforced a "no drugs" rule and encouraged his students to follow right livelihood. In turn, his hippie community found itself respecting him even while they continued to question authority in whatever guise it appeared. So, even while Aitken had anarchist political tendencies, he followed the traditional Zen practice of bowing deeply to his teachers. Walking this delicate line, Robert Aitken both received Dharma transmission from Yamada Roshi in Japan in 1974 and remained a layman, declining the monastic trappings that often accompany a *roshi's* status.

Some of this concern can be seen in Aitken Roshi's writings on the role of the teacher in Zen Buddhism. It is important to distinguish between the *roshi* and the *guru*, he writes. The *roshi*, literally "old teacher," is a guide through unknown lands who stands to one side at the crucial moments of a student's practice, encouraging him or her to understand the experience and to present it in all circumstances.

> The *guru* encourages falling away, but in the act of identifying with the guru. The *guru* is omnipotent, and though he or she may try to encourage the student to find independence, the Dharma will have a specific name and face and the student cannot truly be free....The *roshi* is not interested in being deified and will refuse to be placed in such a position.[8]

While this may have been written in response to the Hindu *gurus* of the 1970s, Aitken has often remained critical of Buddhist traditions such as the Tibetan, which place strong emphasis upon personal relationship with the *guru*, feeling such a relationship to be less conducive to enlightenment, especially for American students.

This anti-authoritarian tendency of Aitken Roshi's helped shape the Buddhist Peace Fellowship as a nonaligned organization, unaligned even with him. Another factor was the timing of the chartering of the Buddhist Peace Fellowship. In 1977, Aitken Roshi had received Dharma transmission just three years before, and his first book, *Zen Wave*, had just appeared. At that point in his career, he had not yet emerged as a prominent Western teacher. He was not accustomed to being a "personality" around whom such an organization might form.

In any case, as Nelson Foster now explains, "it just never occurred to us to do it any other way." If Buddhists were to engage socially and politically, such engagement would require a large amount of resources, both human and financial, in order to succeed. Comparable Christian organizations had generous financial backing and hoards of involved people. If Buddhists were to do the same, the organization would need broad-based support. And this ecumenical approach was endemic to the Fellowship of Reconciliation.

After the Maui meeting, Aitken Roshi wrote the Fellowship of Reconciliation, officially asking to form a Buddhist chapter, and FOR warmly responded.[9] The group established itself as Buddhist Peace Fellowship in 1978, under the direction of Nelson Foster, the first corresponding secretary. Foster sent an initial letter proposing the creation of BPF to one hundred people whose names were drawn mainly from Aitken Roshi's personal files and from FOR membership files. When the responses arrived in the little BPF post office box in Makawao, Maui, there were thirty-three charter members. Among them were Jack Kornfield and Joanna Macy of the Theravada tradition; Richard Baker Roshi and Gary Snyder from Zen Buddhism; and Al Bloom, Tai Unno, and Ryo Imamura from the Japanese-American Pure Land School (Buddhist Churches of America).

While the founding membership was composed primarily of Euro-American Zen practitioners, especially from Roshi's Diamond Sangha in Hawaii, its representation from the American Vipassana and ethnic Japanese Jodo Shinshu communities was significant. And while these founding members were clustered in Hawaii and the Bay Area, they quickly began to invite membership from across the United States. Conspicuous in its absence in the charter membership was strong representation from Tibetan Buddhism and from ethnic Asians other than Japanese-Americans. This reflected the kinds of contacts the founding circle had, and their sense, accurate or not, that there was limited interest within these communities.

For the first several years, the BPF was primarily a network linked by Buddhist practice and personal friendship, held together by the publication of a newsletter in 1979 and the dedicated correspondence of its editor, Nelson Foster. Foster was at that time an English teacher at a private boarding school on Maui, writing for the newsletter and getting out mailings between classes and soccer practice sessions. For some time, it remained an organization in a drawer. But, because of the chords it struck, the conversation grew.

The FOR gave moral support to this new network, encouraging its articulation of a Buddhist approach to peace parallel with the traditions of Christ, Mahatma Gandhi, Thomas Merton, and the Reverend Martin Luther King, Jr. In the early years, the newsletter took up Thich Nhat Hanh's terminology of "engaged Buddhism," articulated in the forest monasteries and temples of Vietnam during the war. When Zen monks and nuns there confronted with the injured and dying villagers at the gates of their monastery asked whether they should continue meditating or care for their people, Thay responded that they must do both. This he called "engaged Buddhism," commenting that "the object of our mind is the world. When we see clearly and know what is going on, we will do something to help the situation."[10]

In its early days, the BPF took responsibility for establishing the historical and doctrinal basis of this American engaged Buddhism, citing traditional texts from the Theravada, Tibetan, Zen, and Pure Land canons as precedents. Samples of such essays appear in BPF's only book, edited by Fred Eppsteiner, called *The Path of Compassion*.[11] In these formative years, members of the network fortuitously shaped a Buddhist–activist identity, creating a theoretical foundation and sealing their role as the key leaders in American engaged Buddhism. As first-generation American Buddhist practitioners, they endeavored to envision themselves in the Asian tradition of meditation, realization, and action to develop a genuinely Buddhist approach to activism and nonviolence. But they needed to join their own activist interests, strongly rooted in American soil, to their traditional Asian Buddhist meditation practice. As Kenneth Kraft noted retrospectively in his introduction to the second edition of the BPF book,

> Because Buddhism has been seen as passive, otherworldly, or escapist, an "engaged Buddhism" may initially appear to be a self-contradiction. Isn't one of the distinguishing features of Buddhism its focus on the solitary quest for enlightenment? The contributors to this volume reply that no enlightenment can be complete as long as others remain trapped in delusion, that genuine wisdom is manifested in compassionate action. When they re-examine Buddhism's 2,500-year-old heritage, these authors find that the principles and even some of the techniques of an engaged Buddhism have been latent in the tradition since the time of the founder. Qualities that were inhibited in pre-modern Asian settings, they argue, can now be actualized through Buddhism's exposure to the West, where ethical sensitivity, social activism, and egalitarianism are emphasized.[12]

By the end of the first year, fifty people counted themselves members of the network. While it was the newsletter that linked them, clusters of members joined in activities such as anti-nuclear protest and Nuclear Freeze advocacy. By 1981, the network had grown to several hundred members and had established an office in Berkeley with one part-time staff member, Patrick McMahon. Chapters had formed in several cities across the country, and meetings brought members together for lively debate. A board of directors was formed to guide the organization, composed of Aitken Roshi, Nelson Foster, and Michael Roche. When Roche resigned, the board expanded to five members with Joanna Macy, Gary Snyder, and Ryo Imamura joining the remaining pair. A year or two later, Aitken Roshi and Foster rotated off the board, reflecting the movement of BPF beyond the direct guidance of its founding circle.

As the Berkeley chapter of BPF became a strong and vital organization, they developed their own newsletter entitled *No Need to Kill*, eclipsing the national newsletter, and so it was decided that the Berkeley chapter would produce a newsletter on behalf of the national organization. The newsletter was edited successively by Andy Cooper, Steve Walker, Fred Eppsteiner, Arnie Kotler, and David Schneider, becoming more professional in appearance and expanding circulation to document the growing interest in a Buddhist approach to peace. Fred Eppsteiner published *The Path of Compassion* in 1985, and its rich array of essays brought so much interest that it has been reissued twice.

As the BPF developed, certain problems arose, indicating the need for a more effective, broadly based, and inclusive organizational structure. BPF started with a volunteer staff with little organizational or political experience, a limited mailing list, and no money; it eventually became clear that this was a weak foundation for the kind of Fellowship the charter members had envisioned. These problems were reflected in the Zen-flavored language in the statement of purpose, in the format of the early newsletter, and in an organizational style that simply did not appeal to a broad segment of American Buddhist communities.

All of this changed with the U.S. tours of Venerable Thich Nhat Hanh. Thay had been living in France since the era of his heading the Vietnamese Buddhist Peace Delegation at the Paris Peace talks during the war, after which he was advised not to return to Vietnam. During his years there, he settled into the life of an exile, taught at the Sorbonne and headed the Vietnamese Buddhist Peace Delegation, an organization advocating peace in Vietnam and the welfare of Vietnamese refugees. After the accords were signed, Thay retreated to rural France with other Vietnamese exiles, eventually establishing a practice center called Plum Village. In the early 1980s he was still refusing invitations to teach the Dharma in America, replying that he was not ready to return to the United States, as he still had some remaining bitterness regarding the war.[13] In 1983, Richard Baker Roshi organized Thay's first retreat for Western Buddhists at Tassajara, San Francisco Zen Center's monastery in the Los Padres National Forest south of San Francisco. That retreat included BPF's entire board and only staff member, as well as a number of other invited guests. By 1985, Thay was ready to tour the U.S. as a Dharma teacher, and his tours were sponsored by the Buddhist Peace Fellowship.

By that time, Arnold (Arnie) Kotler and Therese Fitzgerald were the guiding staff of the BPF. This married couple admired Thich Nhat Hanh and were in the process of founding Parallax Press, a small press in Berkeley, which was to publish most of Thay's English-language books. While Kotler took on the editing of the newsletter and directing several projects, Therese became the half-time coordinator of Buddhist Peace Fellowship, its most senior executive position, and the two together worked devotedly on the details of his tours and all the other work of BPF.

In his American tours of 1985, 1987, and 1989 Thich Nhat Hanh stepped from relative obscurity into the forefront of American Buddhism. He was gentle, unassuming, and personally accessible; his message was direct, compassionate, and riveting. His meditation instruction drew no distinction between time on the cushion and life in the world, an approach that directly addressed American lay Buddhist practice. He saw political and social involvement as a completely organic extension of meditation practice. Embracing American Vietnam veterans, whom he called "the light at the tip of the candle," the bearers of the guilt of a nation for a brutal war on the other side of the world, he sought reconciliation with them, and with the entire nation, for the destruction of his country.

With Thay's first tour, the BPF also stepped out of obscurity. Everywhere Thay went, his audiences were being introduced to BPF, and new members flocked to join the fledgling organization. Christopher Reed, a *vipassana* teacher in Los Angeles and the L.A. chapter head, remembered,

> I had been frustrated by the subtle but pervasive airline-ticket view of Buddhism, that you stand in line and then you're out of here via personal enlightenment. With Thich Nhat Hanh, I got the sense that sympathy and compassion were the prime movers. That really inspired me.[14]

During these years, BPF became identified in the minds of many with Thay, and his vision, pragmatism, and compassion gave new impetus to BPF's identity. Membership grew to six hundred in 1986, and by 1988 that membership had doubled.

With this rapid expansion, a difference of opinion developed concerning BPF's chartered commitment to remain a nonaligned organization. Some in the leadership, especially Arnie and Therese, naturally gravitated toward Thay, so that for them there was no boundary between BPF and Thay's American student community. Others felt loyal to BPF's original charter, and while they deeply respected Thay's teachings, they viewed him as only one of several important mentors and teachers.

This difference of opinion continued for some years, but erupted in 1989 during Thay's third American tour. Therese Fitzgerald, then the BPF coordinator, and her husband Arnold Kotler went on tour for six months with Thay, leaving the organization under the leadership of an acting director. With the burgeoning membership, the board of directors had been feeling they needed a more professional organization, but they responded to this situation hastily, replacing Therese with the acting director without notifying her. Therese's return precipitated a painful split, which could not fully be healed. Therese and Arnie eventually took the lead in creating a separate organization devoted to Thay's activities, the Community of Mindful Living, and broke off all official connections with BPF. As the years have passed CML and BPF have developed a "very friendly relationship"—cosponsoring Thay's events—but they remain careful in working together, reflecting a painful chapter in their histories. Everyone concerned agreed that they needed to develop greater skills in mediation, conflict resolution, and governance, and the result was perhaps, in the final analysis, positive.

The next period of explosive growth in the Buddhist Peace Fellowship membership occurred in 1991 during the Gulf War, when so many American Buddhists simply could not accept U.S. aggression in the Middle East. BPF opposed the war, and thought it particularly important to sponsor "town meetings" at their chapter centers, generating contemplation of the ramifications of the war. Scores, even hundreds of new people attended these meetings at various chapter centers, and many new members joined, bringing with them new concerns and issues for the organization to address.

The Gulf War period also brought BPF its current director, Alan Senauke. Alan had been an activist in the civil rights and peace movements in the 60s and 70s, but by the time he became an active Zen practitioner at the Berkeley Zen Center in the early 80s, his activism had become dormant. While he joined BPF in the 80s, read the newsletter regularly, and thought carefully about the things he read, he did not actively engage in BPF activities. In livelihood, Alan was a musician and poet, and worked at a variety of jobs to support his art and practice, including jobs at Parallax Press and the Buddhist bookstore at Jodo Shinshu headquarters in Berkeley. At the time of the Gulf War, Alan, like so many others, wanted to get involved. He applied for the directorship of BPF, and was delighted when he was hired because now he could join all the parts of his practice, community, and life.

Tova Green joined the board in 1994 and became board president in 1996. A longtime *vipassana* practitioner trained at the Insight Meditation Society in Barre, Massachusetts, Tova was an MSW psychotherapist and teacher with a vigorous activist background in the civil rights and the gay-lesbian rights movements in the 60s and 70s. She became attracted to Joanna Macy's programs in despair and empowerment in the anti-nuclear movement, and became a trainer for InterHelp on the East Coast and in Japan and Australia. She has co-authored, with Peter Woodrow, a book on contemplative social activism called *Insight and Action* (New Society Publishing, 1993). She and her activist-partner, Fran Peavey, founded Crabgrass, a social change organization with projects in India and the former Yugoslavia. She brought interest and experience in strategic planning, organizational development, and process skills to the BPF board.

Under Alan Senauke's and Tova Green's leadership, BPF has entered a more considered and strategic phase of its development, moving from an eager, outward-turning, slightly parochial activism to an activism that contemplates the sources of the violence in our society and the world. The board of directors has flourished as an engaged body. With two-thirds of its membership in the Bay Area, the local board meets monthly, and all board members are directly involved in special committee work. Twice a year the entire board meets to set budget and strategy for the year. In addition, several board members and other affiliated members have engaged in a "futures process" designed to refine strategies concerning institutional and "structural *dukkha*" (suffering), its sources, and the actions and realizations that might lead to its relief.

THE BUDDHIST PEACE FELLOWSHIP TODAY

The Buddhist Peace Fellowship is a network of people throughout the United States who are linked by their common concerns with bringing about peace in the world and by Buddhist meditation practice of a variety of traditions. Because Buddhist Peace Fellowship has not been led by a single, charismatic spiritual leader and has not been affiliated with a single school of Asian Buddhist practice, it is at times difficult to identify a coherent and consistent philosophy. Rather, it is important to study the materials disseminated by the board and executive staff regarding BPF's identity, its mission, and its strategies for action. According to its current literature, Buddhist Peace Fellowship has a five-point mission, expressed in this way:

1. To make a clear public witness to Buddhist practice and interdependence as a way of peace and protection for all beings;

2. To raise peace, environmental, feminist, and social justice concerns among North American Buddhists;

3. To bring a Buddhist perspective of nonduality to contemporary social action and environmental movements;

4. To encourage the practice of nonviolence based on the rich resources of traditional Buddhist and Western spiritual teachings;

5. To offer avenues for dialogue and exchange among the diverse North American and world sanghas.[15]

If we examine the underlying principles and approaches of Buddhist Peace Fellowship, we can recognize the following features in its charter, its goals, and its actions.

Inclusiveness

The Buddhist Peace Fellowship is not just for Buddhists, and is "unaffiliated with any particular school or lineage, open to anyone who agrees with our purpose, vision, and path." Its association with Buddhism has to do with its being guided by the compassionate vow to save all beings, defined not as just other Buddhists, but "all people, animals, plants, the earth itself." In this presentation, BPF goes beyond the classical Indian Buddhist definition of sentience as having four categories: beings produced from eggs, wombs, moisture, and miracles. This statement expresses the desire to save plants and the earth itself, following the direction of the "deep ecology" movement.

How successful has BPF been in fulfilling this portion of their mission? Nelson Foster has acknowledged the founding group's naivete in chartering the organization and designing a mission and goals without creating a broadly based network, one crossing the lines of many Buddhist schools and lineages. As he observes now, if the organization had been done differently, "engaging the stakeholders," a stronger and more inclusive organization would have existed from the beginning.

As it is, while representative Tibetan Buddhist practitioners and ethnically Asian Buddhists in America can be seen in the membership, the strongest representation continues to be West Coast Vipassana and Zen communities. To be truly inclusive, much greater partnership with Asian Buddhists is needed—monastics, activists, and the very poor. Another problem of inclusiveness has to do with the geographical concentration of the fifteen chapters listed in 1997 copies of *Turning Wheel*: five are in California, and an additional four are on the West Coast or in Hawaii. Affiliates are much more broadly represented, though Europe appears to be an underdeveloped territory.

With regard to ethnic Asians in America and Asian Buddhists, there are aspects of BPF's organization that are uncomfortable for potential members. The American consensus model and its informality are difficult for Asians who are accustomed to a different style of communication. As Ryo Imamura, a Jodo Shinshu priest and professor at Evergreen College in Olympia, Washington, observed, "Asian and American Buddhists are very different in reason and practice. When I was president [of the BPF board], some Asians signed on for a year or two, because of the personal connection. When I left, most of those people left too, because the new members didn't understand the etiquette that Asians require."[16] Students in some Tibetan Buddhist communities have also become accustomed to this kind of decorum, and have difficulties at times with BPF's anti-hierarchical bias.

To their credit, the BPF staff and board members understand the limitations of their own scope, and have developed admirable clarity concerning their needs for growth and expansion. In order to expand their base beyond the West Coast, they have organized training sessions on community and ethics in Chicago, Boston, and other metropolitan centers in the United States. BPF staff have met the leaders as well as the rank and file of the major liberation movements in Asia, and know a great deal about their work and needs. They have become "painfully aware of [their] own insensitivity and cultural chauvinism,"[17] which has helped them a great deal in the U.S. This will continue to be a challenge in the next century.

Analysis of Suffering

"Saving beings" seems especially to suggest relieving suffering, and while there is no in-depth analysis of suffering itself, it is clear from BPF literature that this understanding is derived from classical Buddhist understandings of *dukkha*, or emotional and physical suffering, which pervades human life. But suffering that exists in the world is not merely individual, personal suffering, says BPF literature:

> We feel our particular responsibility is to address structural and social forms of suffering, oppression, and violence. These are not abstractions— war, racism, sexism, economic oppression, denial of human rights and social justice, and so many other ills cause great fear and suffering for all beings. These social forces are simply the workings of individual greed, anger, and delusion made social and multiplied in ways that often hide its roots and hide our own relationship to and for that suffering.[18]

In this analysis, BPF is expressing the core of its most current theoretical contribution to engaged Buddhism in America: that meditation practice and training the mind directly relate to diminishing our personal suffering, but that practitioners will not have fully addressed the suffering of the world if they do not address the social, economic, and political structures that legitimize violence and suffering. This legitimized violence, this structural *dukkha*, is "so diffuse that it becomes very hard to identify the source of suffering," says Alan Senauke. "No one seems to be directly responsible, because it is moved ahead by governments, corporations, and is seemingly anonymous."[19]

But, says the BPF, these structures are not anonymous; they have only the appearance of anonymity, and protect those in power from taking responsibility for their own actions and the effects of the systems they have in place. In order to recognize this legitimized violence, it is important first to become educated in the way in which structural violence works in the institutions in society and globally. For the Buddhist, this entails understanding interdependence in specific ways. What is the impact on the world of purchasing nectarines grown in Mexico during February? Of buying toys for our children that were assembled in Asian factories by child labor? Of trekking to Mount Everest? It is necessary to understand, with all these acts, how one is implicated in a global system of exploitation and of privilege feeding off the poor of the world. How can a meditator respond with wisdom and compassion to this insight?

The Buddhist Peace Fellowship does not routinely engage in formal education in these matters, though it sponsored three summer institutes in the Bay Area in the 90s, which spawned in-depth discussion of interdependence and social and political activism. It has also sponsored workshops and training programs in other major cities on peacemaking and conflict resolution, Buddhist social analysis, and mindfulness and community building. These activities seem likely to grow in the coming years.

The primary educational venue of BPF can be found in the analyses and commentary in its journal, *Turning Wheel*. In issue after issue, contributors reflect on aspects of suffering, especially suffering caused by social, economic, and political structures. There is no way one could follow these articles without developing a deeper reflection on the nature of suffering in the world. This analysis goes beyond the Buddha's. As Aitken Roshi observed,

> The Buddha did not live in a time like ours, when dangerous competition between nations threatens to blow up the world. He was not faced with the probability of biological holocaust....I wonder what he would say today.[20]

In the early years, the newsletter talked about issues far from our front doorsteps, with a strong international emphasis on oppression in Asia, nuclear weapons, and warfare in various trouble spots in the world. In recent years, these interests have continued but there has been a greater emphasis upon the suffering that surrounds us daily. In the spring of 1995, an issue devoted to the topic of suffering had articles on insomnia, mothers-in-law, and chronic pain, interspersed with poems on Vietnam, prisoners' accounts from death row, and memoirs of Germans and Jews at Auschwitz.[21] Ongoing domestic topics in the journal have been prisons, homelessness, consumerism, and ecology.

Turning Wheel's current editor, Susan Moon, has served for the last eight years, steadily refining the quality, scope, and diversity of articles presented. Susan worked in the civil rights movement in Mississippi in the 60s, was active in the women's movement of the 70s, and protested against nuclear testing in the 80s. She also had extensive editorial and writing experience. After years of Zen practice in Berkeley, she welcomed the opportunity to join these three aspects of her life at the *Turning Wheel.* Quarterly circulation now stands at six thousand, one thousand of which are distributed through bookstores.

The guiding principle of the journal, its mission statement reads, is to "work for peace, to reveal and address the causes of suffering in the world, and to that end, to publish writing which develops a theory and practice of engaged Buddhism."[22] A recent issue on hatred[23] treated issues of rage in the skinhead movement and in prison as well as hatred in divorce, between siblings, and in domestic violence. These articles were interwoven with meditations on "composting hatred" and other narrative accounts of how practitioners have broken open the heart of anger and transformed its intensity and richness into care for the world. For many BPF members, *Turning Wheel* is the Buddhist Peace Fellowship. Through the journal, members are able to keep informed about violence and war far from their doorsteps as well as to bring reflections on violence into their everyday lives. The consistent presentation of distilled information, deep reflection, hands-on narrative and just plain good writing has made *Turning Wheel* a journalistic jewel.

In the search for a penetrating social analysis that is truly Buddhist, BPF has turned for inspiration to a variety of visionary teachers, each of whom has made a genuine contribution to its understanding. However, say the BPF staff and board, none has been able to provide a single model of a truly Dharmic society, because of the many complexities involved in global societies. Proposals for such models appear in part in the pages of the journal, in the board's "futures process," and in the imaginations of members of the network. From this point of view, the BPF vision remains, fittingly, a work-in-progress.

Social visionaries like Joanna Macy have been a constant source of support and creativity in the area of social analysis for the Buddhist Peace Fellowship. Macy is an activist and scholar who stepped outside the confines of either discipline in an attempt to bring her insight to bear very practically on the question of how to relieve the suffering of the world. She has authored books on causality, activism, and engaged Buddhism. Her most innovative work has been in the area of despair and empowerment, working with the natural rhythms of activism as a practice to expand caring for the world. Throughout BPF's history she has been an unfailing friend, mentor, and advisor; she has shared her decades-long contemplation of interdependence with the BPF community, and it has greatly enriched their understanding of the nature of suffering.

Another important influence in the area of social analysis and an understanding of structural violence has been the Thai journalist, activist, and intellectual Sulak Sivaraksa. After years of open criticism of the military dictatorships of Thailand, several dangerous imprisonments on the charge of *lèse majesté*—for which he has suffered threats, trials, and several imprisonments—the irrepressible Sivaraksa has devoted his recent work to the issues of structural violence and consumerism. A student of the renowned Theravada philosopher-monk Buddhadasa Bhikkhu, Sivaraksa has developed an articulate analysis of global interdependence propagated by multinational corporations and militarism. He has been an important international advisor to BPF, and founded the International Network of Engaged Buddhists (INEB) in Asia to carry on similar activities in Asia. BPF continues to be deeply influenced by Sulak, and often turns to his articulate, practical understanding of structural violence in its analysis of suffering.

Strategic Approach

Several years ago Donald Rothberg, associate professor of philosophy at Saybrook Institute and a current board member, observed, "I have the sense that many chapters are groping for appropriate activities. That's partly due to the decentralized nature of the organization, the idea that people know what to do in their local situations. But I also think we need a more centralized approach, to provide some more leadership."[24] In the last several years, BPF's board of directors has put increasing emphasis upon the development of strategy appropriate to the mission statement. With so much suffering in the world, where must one begin? Which actions are most effective, and how well informed are they? BPF has been besieged with ideas, concerns, and information, but how can the board assign priorities and develop initiatives?

This conundrum has often forced the staff into networking as its primary activity. Through the *Turning Wheel* and personal contacts, they have collected an enormous amount of information regarding violence in the world, and they have constantly communicated that information in a variety of ways. Alan Senauke calls his task that of the "journeyman weaver"[25] who weaves together the jewels of Indra's net, the complex interdependent factors that comprise every situation. But he also admits to frustration; while networking has been important, it does not fulfill BPF's commitment for effective and direct action in the world. More clear strategy is needed.

On the other hand, BPF has had many international projects that have sustained its involvements in Asia. With grants from the Kaiser Foundation, BPF has for several years sponsored mobile medical teams for displaced Burmese on both sides of the Thai-Burmese border. Their revolving loan program has distributed over $60,000 in low interest loans to right livelihood projects in Tibetan exile communities in Nepal and India, and the East Bay chapter has a long-standing program that provides thousands of meals to Tibetan children in the settlements. BPF has sponsored Dharma Walks in Cambodia led by Maha Ghosananda ("the Gandhi of Cambodia"), and has consistently petitioned for the release of Unified Buddhist Church leaders imprisoned in Vietnam. And BPF has served as organizational and financial support for the International Network of Engaged Buddhists (INEB) based in Thailand.

Domestically, the group has long been involved with disarmament actions, such as the August Desert Witness at the Nevada Nuclear Test Site and Abolition 2000. It also has ties to the Anti-Land Mines Campaign in the United States and Cambodia, and has worked assiduously for the banning of cheap weapons of mass destruction produced in the U.S. and Europe. The largest domestic activity of BPF has been focused on prison work, and this commitment is being intensified. There are 150 BPF members in prison (membership is free to prisoners), and members on the outside carry on active correspondence with them, providing Dharma books as they are made available.

In its work within American Buddhism, BPF formed a network focused on issues of ethics of teachers and on healing the sexual abuse of power in a variety of Buddhist communities. In these activities, BPF has been asked to track issues of abuse against women students and to coordinate support for Buddhist communities to raise issues of abuse for discussion and response. Some of this information appears in the pages of the journal.[26] Closely supported by Aitken Roshi, Jan Chozen Bays Sensei, Marie Fortune, and Yvonne Rand, BPF has written a book of ethical guidelines for Buddhist teachers that is being distributed throughout Buddhist centers in America. In addition, it has co-sponsored training and support for survivors of sexual abuse by teachers and plans to continue this work into the next decade, as appropriate.

These many projects appear as a patchwork with strengths and weaknesses. As Alan Senauke wrote,

> The main strength is our ability to act quickly and flexibly as we learn of suffering through friends in our network. We respond to what is right in

front of us, as our training in mindfulness teaches us to do. Another strength is that we are consistent. Over the years, the key issues we have raised…are always in our sight.…The principal weakness is lack of strategy. Why do we choose to do the work we do, and what approach do we take? Are we about service or social transformation—is there a clear distinction?[27]

As a result of this conundrum, the board has spent an increasing amount of time in recent years developing strategies in such a way that BPF's mission is being focused on more specific forms of action. In 1994, the board began a series of training sessions on strategy and planning through "strategic questioning."[28] Out of those workshops developed a committee that generated a strategic analysis project called the "futures process," eventually involving the entire staff as well. This project has systematically asked what BPF's goals are, what constitutes "engaged Buddhist" activities, and what fundamental institutional issues must be examined. At the foundation of their efforts has been a mutual embrace of the analysis of suffering described above—Buddhist Peace Fellowship focuses on issues of structural violence. How is it that structural *dukkha*, seemingly anonymous in its institutionalized forms, oppresses everyone involved in it, the exploiter and the exploited.

The board has begun to exert leadership about appropriate strategies, and they have begun to identify the development of "community-based social change" as a priority for the organization. This statement, issued in 1997, reveals the developing maturity of understanding of the board.

> Individual responsibility is critically important, but it is naive and counterproductive to think that social forces, nations, corporations, etc. can be challenged by lone individuals. This is the cowboy theory of history and it doesn't work. What we believe and are trying to develop is the recognition and reality of community-based social change. This means the community where one lives, works, and practices. And it means the vast interdependent world community. It means creating social forms to enact social change.[29]

BPF has taken these explorations into its training and education programs, promoting community building and the creation of enlightened society on a local scale in a variety of settings. Its workshops have been held in Chicago, Santa Rosa, Seattle, Barre, Santa Cruz, and Berkeley, and more are planned throughout the United States.

From this commitment has come a new project at the cutting edge of the Buddhist Peace Fellowship's activities, the BASE project. BASE, Buddhist

Alliance for Social Engagement, is a new paradigm for BPF and expresses the board's commitment to more directly guide the strategy of the organization while at the same time honoring the locally based, grassroots chapter approach. This new paradigm is consistent with BPF's interest in the problems of structural violence. This project carries peace work into local communities, developing models of practice and action that are attempting to construct a society based upon mutuality, personal reflection, and compassionate action.

BUDDHIST ALLIANCE FOR SOCIAL ENGAGEMENT (BASE)

It was Aitken Roshi who initially suggested the idea for BASE in discussions at one of BPF's summer institutes in Oakland in 1992. But it was Diana Winston, an energetic young woman in the new generation of BPF leadership, who developed its paradigm and format, and who implemented the first programs. Winston trained in *vipassana* meditation with Joseph Goldstein and Venerable U Pandita Sayadaw, and throughout her *vipassana* training sustained an interest in social engagement. However, she was frustrated to discover that

Walking meditation at the first retreat of the Buddhist Alliance for Social Engagement (BASE), sponsored by the Buddhist Peace Fellowship, at Vajrapani, near Santa Cruz, California. Courtesy Buddhist Peace Fellowship.

most Buddhist activists didn't actually practice meditation, and her fellow retreatants showed little interest in social engagement. She welcomed the chance to form a training program that would integrate Buddhist practice, social engagement, and community life into one organic whole. BPF's director, Margaret Howe, and the board, intrigued with Winston's intense commitment and creative vision, commissioned her in 1994 to develop a pilot program.

Winston began researching similar "volunteer corps" type programs found in faith-based (predominantly Christian) service communities, such as the Jesuit Volunteer Corps, and the Catholic Workers movement. The six-month pilot program opened in the Bay Area in 1995 with a structured curriculum of study, a service volunteer internship placement, and regular community meditation practice and process sessions. The initial group of students worked with mentors who were local Buddhist activists and fostered a greater connection between their community life, their practice, and their social work. The experience of this first group was profound; they organized urban community gardens, mediated conflicts in high schools, cooked at homeless shelters, and cared for the dying. And daily they processed this work together with their mentors, developing a deeper understanding of social service and action. At the end of the program, Henry Hon Yan Wai of Toronto, Canada, wrote:

> My experience with BASE has deepened my understanding of how sangha fellowships of like-spirited people can provide the support to continue on difficult journeys. For me, spiritual practice and social activism are like axle and wheel on a rocky road. As the wheel turns easier when each part fits and supports the others, so it has been easier for me to maintain spiritual practice and social activism when the elements of my life are more integrated. The experience of fellowship and of a more integrated life has renewed my enthusiasm and encourages me to seek similar conditions back in Canada.[30]

Winston was involved in every aspect, working under BPF staff supervision and with the local mentors; she immediately began envisioning how the program design could be effective in other geographic locations. Soon, six-month BASE programs began in three other areas, with five more groups forming in the Bay Area, each slightly different in design and organization. In 1997, Diana Winston and mentor Donald Rothberg wrote a handbook describing how other BASE programs could be organized in a variety of locations, self-governing and responsive to local needs and concerns.

BASE is now billed by BPF as "North America's first Buddhist volunteer corps," serving needy populations in a variety of settings. The BASE paradigm is grounded in the principle that "social service and social change work is facilitated by an on-going community of like-minded people."[31] Its program design has five component parts, as described in its handbook:

1. Service/Social Action *(seva)*: The day-to-day experience of engaging with suffering is the heart of BASE. BASE participants work either in service or in social action jobs. Some participants have volunteer positions, others have regular employment. Participants work in diverse jobs such as hospices, community organizing, homeless chaplaincy outreach work, and social change organizations.[32]

2. Wisdom/Training *(pannya)*: BASE provides an opportunity to explore political, social, and environmental problems through group training in "Buddhist activism." As a group, participants explore the multitude of questions arising from service or social action work and their relation to Buddhist teaching and practice.

3. Dharma Practice *(samadhi)*: In BASE there is a commitment to deepening Buddhist practice while deepening one's social change work. These two are not separable. The insight that arises through practice can lead to deeper understanding as one works to address the suffering on the planet.

4. Community *(sangha)*: Ongoing work for change cannot happen without support. BASE is rooted in a community of shared purpose. Our hope is to create a growing national and international network of Buddhist-based activists working for change who are connected with each other and with local support communities.

5. Commitment *(adhitthana)*: To be part of BASE, one must take on BASE as a primary commitment for the allotted period of time, typically six months, much in the same way one commits to a spiritual practice. A commitment of time and intention provides spaciousness for the ups and downs of learning.[33]

While the basic component parts are presented in this way, the specific model to be implemented can differ, says the handbook, depending on local needs and circumstances. Five possibilities are presented, from all BASE members living together in the same house and working together on the same project ("Catholic worker model") to a training and support program for those already employed in social service or social action work. Other proposed models are invited—BPF gives the impression that there is no real boundary in how this paradigm may be applied. The Berkeley office offers help in advising the set-up and structure of the BASE program, in helping find internship placements, in creation of a job contract for internships, designing the study curriculum, and dealing with nonsectarian Buddhist practice forms. In general, BPF encourages "bottom-up, non-hierarchical" structures in the variety of BASE programs, but offers advice on the process involved in conducting evening meetings that are sensitive to group dynamics and in conducting retreats that are focused without being biased toward one particular Buddhist tradition. After one and a half years of BASE programs Diana Winston took a one-year sabbatical to do retreat and travel in Asia, and was replaced by acting coordinator Tova Green, who is also president of BPF board.

BASE's openness to innovation has produced responses that are somewhat different than the Bay Area groups, stretching the limits of the BASE paradigm. For example, the Boulder, Colorado BASE program has taken the form of a loose alliance of roughly thirty people from a variety of sangha and nonsangha environments meeting every four to six weeks for meditation practice, community, and social service. This group, organized in the autumn of 1996 by Roger Dorris, an engaged Buddhism instructor at the Naropa Institute, has developed its own interpretation of the BASE paradigm, using a flexible, intermittent format to fulfill several goals that are different from BPF's formulation. Probably the most divergent goal is that of creating an alliance not only of people, but of existing Buddhist sanghas or communities, engaging its membership in social action and mutual meditation practice sessions. This project has also made a special effort to involve the resident Buddhist teachers of each of these communities, referring to them as *kalyana mitra*, spiritual friends. Sample service projects have been making Christmas ornaments for the disabled, preparing and serving food at homeless shelters, and building a deck for a women and children's center.

Tova Green, president of BPF board, helped lay the groundwork for a BASE project in Boston in the latter half of 1997. An organizing group catalyzed by Diana Gregorio, an Oxfam worker and activist straight out of a three-month *vipassana* retreat, met for months until a core of interested practitioners coalesced. By June, eleven members committed to BASE for the six-month period. This group lived and worked separately, taking their service-based employment as placements: three members added appropriate volunteer work for placements. During the six months, they met weekly and held a day-long group retreat each month. Like several of the earlier BASE projects, they remained a leaderless group, rotating facilitation and study responsibilities among their membership. Members ranged in age from their twenties to their fifties, and came primarily from Vipassana and Zen communities in Boston. Even after the conclusion of their BASE commitment, they continue to meet monthly and are revitalizing the Boston chapter of BPF.

BASE reflects a new direction for BPF, slightly changing the other priorities of the organization. Certainly, international work will continue to be important but less dominant in BPF's mission and actions. Its accompanying activities of raising funds, deciding on projects, and overseeing the implementation of the projects will continue to be supervised by the International Committee of the Board. But the board and staff feel there is more balance with BASE taking such a central role in the activities of the organization. BPF's current budget reflects its current priorities: about one-third of its budget is devoted to *Turning Wheel* and BASE, and an additional third pays administrative salaries and service to the membership. The remaining third is spread over BPF's other international and domestic projects and training programs.

The BASE experiment has also influenced BPF's thinking about chapter structure and support. In recent years, chapters were beginning to lose momentum and potency, with several closing down altogether. Under Tova Green's care, chapters are receiving regular phone check-ins, mailings, suggestions for programming and activities, and personal visits. As a result, new chapters are emerging in Boston and Minneapolis, and several ailing chapters from New York to Los Angeles are reviving. The BASE model suggests that regular study, community-building, practice programs, and joint activities can nurture the development of communities in the chapter format as well.

CONCLUSION

Buddhist Peace Fellowship, in its history, identity, and activities, reflects one characteristic paradigm of Buddhism in America. That paradigm is the American populist one of "grassroots" organization, direct and effective action, nonhierarchical decision-making structures, and ecumenical, nonsectarian religious identity. Its committed group of members, volunteers, board members, and staff have brought "a Buddhist perspective to the peace movement, and...the peace movement to the Buddhist community," as their mission statement puts it. In so doing, they have avoided certain elements of some Asian Buddhist traditions, such as spiritual hierarchy, privilege, and political conservatism, substituting activist American elements.

BPF has influenced diverse American Buddhist communities to extend their compassion to the oppressed, the disinherited, the forgotten, and the poor throughout the world. But some wonder if BPF may have gone too far. Is BPF truly Buddhist? For example, is there genuine respect for realized Asian teachers and their Dharma heirs, no matter how out-of-step with contemporary American culture they may appear to be? What commitment to Buddhist meditation practice is held by its leadership and members? Is there compassion for the oppressor as well as for the oppressed, as is characteristic in the most profound Buddhist teachings on engaged Buddhism? Can BPF properly lead its membership to give up merely political stances and to take the courageous stance of compassion at whatever cost, in every situation?

If BPF is to remain in the forefront of American Buddhism, it must cultivate close relationships with diverse Buddhist communities of all kinds. The nonsectarian, nonaligned nature of BPF is firmly established; now, in order to remain compatible with American Buddhism, it needs to draw on the developing American traditions that might nurture it. If political concern surpasses contemplative depth, spiritual peril lies near. BPF might benefit from closer exchange with Asian Buddhist teachers and their American Dharma heirs, even with those who may disagree with what they might perceive as an excessively political focus of BPF interest. While it is true that Dharma teachers do not have a monopoly on truth, the truth they propagate could serve to nurture the depth of BPF's spiritual development.

BPF must also explore the unevenness of commitment to meditation practice among its membership. If BPF's mission is to be fulfilled, it is important that members, staff, and board look for the enrichment of individual and group practice opportunities. Especially beneficial would be the cultivation and propagation of specific practices from various meditation traditions (*metta* and *lojong* practices, for example) that transform anger into patience, or change depression and disempowerment into inspiration. Supporting these practices might enable the Buddhist Peace Fellowship as an organization to excel in its desire to relieve suffering on the planet in a way consistent with Buddhist teachings. The cutting edge of activism and the heart of profound meditation practice must be yoked together if BPF is to effectively transform suffering into joy.

Finally, it seems the greatest current contribution that BPF might make to American Buddhism is insight gained from community-building based upon loving-kindness and caring concern. Of course, BPF's contributions to engagement with international issues and with the violence in American society have been significant, and hopefully these contributions will continue. Carrying Buddhist practice into the practice of daily life in a way that is attuned to the pain of structural violence, the recognition of interdependence, and the importance of community is the only way in which peace can truly be cultivated in the world. American Buddhist communities, no matter how reticent, would benefit from this conversation.

In sum, it can be seen that the issues that face Buddhist Peace Fellowship are those that face the whole of American Buddhism, and the creative solutions that BPF is forging provide one paradigm for the shape of American Buddhism in the new millennium.

ACKNOWLEDGMENT

I am indebted to a number of individuals for their invaluable help in providing unrecorded information and in shaping this chapter: Alan Senauke, current director of Buddhist Peace Fellowship in Berkeley; BPF staff members Diana Winston, Susan Moon, Tova Green; Nelson Foster from Ring-of-Bone Zendo in San Juan, California; David Schneider of Shambhala International in Marburg, Germany; Arnie Kotler and Therese Fitzgerald of Parallax Press in Berkeley; and Roger Dorris, Engaged Buddhism track of the M.A. Buddhist Studies Program, The Naropa Institute, Boulder, Colorado. All interpretations and errors in understanding, of course, are my own.

It is difficult to fully account for all of the activities and figures who shaped the development of a broadly based organization like BPF, for its identity and power have drawn from the efforts of many talented and committed people from a variety of backgrounds, Buddhist communities, and levels of experience. While this chapter may feature a few in cameo portraits, countless others are also important, some of whom are briefly named here. But there are also those who remain nameless, and they are no less important in the development of the network known as Buddhist Peace Fellowship. I regret not being able to include more of them in this article.

NOTES

1. The chapter title, "Speaking Truth to Power," is a Quaker saying, quoted by Robert Aitken, Roshi, as applying to BPF activities in a fundraising letter, November 1, 1996.
2. Kenneth Kraft, "Prospects of a Socially Engaged Buddhism," in *Inner Peace, World Peace: Essays on Buddhism and Nonviolence* (Albany: State University of New York Press, 1992), p. 12.
3. Helen Tworkov, *Zen in America: Five Teachers and the Search for an American Buddhism* (New York: Kodansha International, 1989, 1994), p. 43. Tworkov

describes the evolution of the Maui Zen community from an undisciplined band of hippies to a fully developed Zen training center headquartered at "Two Twenty."

4. There was some disagreement about founding a new, Buddhist-based organization. Merwin and Naone wished instead to work through and with existing organizations. The two of them never joined Buddhist Peace Fellowship.

5. This book was later published under the title *Miracle of Mindfulness* (New York: Beacon Press, 1976). In it, James Forest of FOR described Thay's 1968 tour, pp. 101–8.

6. Tworkov, p. 42.

7. Robert Aitken, "Three Lessons from Shaku Soen," in *The Path of Compassion: Writings on Socially Engaged Buddhism*, ed. Fred Eppsteiner (Berkeley, CA: Parallax Press, 1985, 1988), p. 148.

8. Robert Aitken, *Taking the Path of Zen* (San Francisco: North Point Press, 1982), pp. 89–90.

9. At first, BPF was a chapter of FOR, with dual membership; eventually, BPF became an independent organization under the umbrella of FOR.

10. Quoted in Arnie Kotler, "Buddhism Must Be Engaged," in Sulak Sivaraksa, ed., *Radical Conservatism: Buddhism in the Contemporary World* (Bangkok: International Network of Engaged Buddhists, 1990), p. 135.

11. Eppsteiner, *The Path of Compassion*.

12. Kenneth Kraft, "Engaged Buddhism: An Introduction," from Eppsteiner, *The Path of Compassion: Writings on Socially Engaged Buddhism*, pp. xii–xiii.

13. From a letter to the author in 1982 from Thay's secretary.

14. Quoted in Susan Davis, "Working with Compassion: The Evolution of the Buddhist Peace Fellowship," *Tricycle: The Buddhist Review* (spring 1993): 60.

15. From BPF mailing and fundraising request, February 11, 1997. Additional quotes in the paragraphs to follow are extracted from the "Questions of Analysis and Strategy" document, also in this mailing.

16. Quoted in Susan Davis, "Working with Compassion," p. 61.

17. Alan Senauke, "Buddhist Peace Fellowship: The Work and the Network of Engaged Buddhism," unpublished ms. prepared for the Numata Lecture Series, Institute of Buddhist Studies, Berkeley, California, November 1995, p. 7.

18. "Questions of Analysis and Strategy," February 11, 1997.

19. Interview, April 1997.

20. Tworkov, *Zen in America,* p. 52.

21. *Turning Wheel* (spring 1995).

22. *Turning Wheel* Mission Statement (January 1998).

23. *Turning Wheel* (summer 1997).

24. Quoted in Susan Davis, "Working with Compassion," p. 61.

25. Senauke, "Buddhist Peace Fellowship."

26. See *Turning Wheel* (spring 1996), "Sexual Misconduct: Who's Hurting Whom?" and articles that appear regularly in its pages.

27. Ibid., pp. 9–10.

28. This is a specialty of Fran Peaby of Crabgrass, who led these workshops.

29. "Questions of Analysis and Strategy," February 11, 1997.

30. Henry Hon Yan Wai, "The Gift of Encouragement," unpublished ms., p. 5.

31. Diana Winston and Donald Rothberg, *A Handbook for the Creation of the Buddhist Alliance for Social Engagement* (BASE) (Berkeley: Buddhist Peace Fellowship, August 1997), p. 4.

32. The Pali terminology reflects Diana's *vipassana* training. (Their publication has errors in Pali spellings, which the author has corrected.) It has been difficult for BPF to find a common Asian terminology for its work, alternately using Japanese, Pali, and Sanskrit terms. Mostly, it has relied on English.

33. Winston and Rothberg, *Handbook*, p. 4

GLASSMAN ROSHI AND THE PEACEMAKER
ORDER: THREE ENCOUNTERS

Christopher S. Queen

AS ONE OF THE MOST INVENTIVE FIGURES IN ENGAGED BUDDHISM,
Roshi Bernard Tetsugen Glassman, born in Brooklyn in 1939, has taken his
place as a leading preceptor of the movement. Since the 1980s Glassman has
become familiar to readers of American Buddhist journals like *Tricycle* and
Shambhala Sun, in which he is often pictured in rumpled clothes and griz-
zled beard, with members of the Zen Peacemaker Order on week-long
"street retreats" in the alleyways and subways of lower Manhattan, or sitting
in meditation on the snow-covered tracks that lead to the crematoriums at
Auschwitz-Birkenau in Poland, "bearing witness to the pain of the world."
Mainstream media such as the *Wall Street Journal*, the *New York Times*, and
the TV networks have covered Glassman's Greyston Mandala, a network of
for-profit businesses and not-for-profit agencies that serve the poor in the
rundown neighborhoods of Yonkers, New York. In Bernie Glassman's
Buddhism, a vision of human reclamation and social change only imagined
by New Deal liberals and sixties radicals—and surely unimagined in traditional Asian versions of human liberation—is realized in job training programs, full-time employment, permanent housing, nursery and toddler care,
and drug treatment and hospice centers for the destitute and dying.

Bernard Glassman is the protean man of engaged Buddhism, rivaled
only, in his many roles and guises, by the late Dr. Ambedkar, leader of India's
Untouchables. Like Ambedkar, Glassman was a bright child born in a poor
family who earned advanced academic degrees, displayed extraordinary
prowess in professional life, and then chose Buddhism as a vehicle to address
the injustice and violence in society. For Ambedkar, the story involved out-
caste status in Hindu India, degrees in the social sciences and law from
Western universities, a front-page career in national politics, and leadership
of a mass Buddhist conversion movement for India's lowliest people.[1] For

Glassman, it was childhood in a Jewish immigrant section of Brooklyn, a Ph.D. in applied mathematics from UCLA, leadership of the Earth-Mars Shuttle team at the McDonnell-Douglas aerospace corporation, and ordination as the first American-born lineage-holder in the Soto Zen sect of Japan—"number eighty-one in a line that claims direct descent from the historical Shakyamuni Buddha."[2]

Glassman's restless energy, like Ambedkar's, is not driven by raw ambition or a hunger for experience and attention, though these elements are present. Both men adopted Buddhism in later life because it gave expression to thoughts and feelings they already had: a fierce compassion for discarded people, belief in the potential for wholeness in life, and a vision of society founded on human dignity and interdependence. Glassman likes to tell about his pizza parlor vow to a college friend in 1960, as both shared their dreams for the future. "First, I wanted to study Zen in a monastery. Second, I wanted to experience communal living on a kibbutz. And third, I wanted to live as a bum on the Bowery."[3] At a time when people were reading D. T. Suzuki, Alan Watts, and *The Dharma Bums*, and idealistic Jewish youths imagined a sojourn with Israeli communards, Glassman's fantasy was not exceptional. Nor was it exceptional when he took his family to live in a kibbutz years later. But when Bernie from Brighton Beach became the first American Buddhist to complete *koan* study and priestly training under Asian Zen masters, to experience two *dai kensho* or "great spiritual openings," to be recognized as a Dharma-holder in formal ceremonies at the Soto head temples of Eihei-ji and Soji-ji in Japan, and to count among his many friends Bernard Isaacs, "king of the mole people"—an estimated seven thousand "mole people" live in the tunnels under New York City—this was exceptional.

In his two books, *Instructions to the Cook* (1996, with Rick Fields), and *Bearing Witness* (1998), Glassman tells the stories that grow out of his work with the homeless and with religious activists who have joined the Peacemaker Order. He offers reflections on the meaning of engaged Buddhism—as the fulfillment of the Buddhadharma, and as a new departure for the ancient tradition.[4] There is an intimate quality in the writing, sometimes fatherly, sometimes playful, always probing, as if the author had taken the reader on as a valued student. At the same time there is an unmistakable note of challenge:

> When we live our life fully, our life becomes what Zen Buddhists call "the supreme meal." We make this supreme meal by using the ingredients at hand to make the best meal possible, and then by offering it to others. This book is about how to cook the supreme meal of life.[5]

Roshi Bernard Tetsugen Glassman with Sensei Claude AnShin Thomas and the late Roshi Sandra Jishu Holmes. Courtesy Franz-Johannes Litsch.

The Supreme Meal prepared by the Zen cook or *tenzo* consists of five courses: spirituality, study and learning, livelihood, social action, and relationships and community. These emphases can be found in all religious traditions. But Glassman's metaphor of the Holy Meal sets his Buddhism apart, both from the New Age religions of self-healing, self-cultivation, and low-stress-for-success, and from the Holy Meal symbolism of the Western religious traditions. The Jewish Passover Seder, the Christian Eucharist, and the nightly feasts of the Muslim month of Ramadan offer liberation, salvation, and redemption to those who consume the Holy Meal. In Roshi Bernie's Zen Meal, the focus is on those who prepare the Supreme Meal of their lives for the nourishment of others. Glassman's feast is not something to eat, but something to serve: a call to altruism and sacrifice.

The challenge of service to others is issued again at the beginning of Glassman's second book, *Bearing Witness*.

> On January 18, 1994, I celebrated my fifty-fifth birthday by throwing myself a party. I held my party outdoors in the snow on the steps of the U.S. Capitol. There, wrapped in a coat and a blanket, I sat the entire day with one question in mind: What can I do about homelessness, AIDS, and violence in this country?[6]

Glassman's answer was to start the Peacemaker Order, a community of social workers, activists, and religious leaders from many countries and religious traditions who embrace three tenets: not knowing, the renunciation of fixed ideas and prejudices; bearing witness to the pains and joys of the world; and healing oneself and all beings in the universe. One is struck again by the other-directedness of Glassman's Buddhism, particularly in contrast to the self-involvement of the Beat, Square, and Cool Zen he first encountered in the 1950s and to the religious consumerism of the counterculture that swept the West in following decades.

In this chapter I will try to picture Glassman Roshi's achievements and the texture of his movement from close range, drawing on our private conversations and his informal remarks and the give-and-take with audiences following his public Dharma talks. I first met "Bernie"—as he prefers to be called—at a dinner in his honor at Harvard University in 1994. Since then we have met for interviews in New York, Boston, Connecticut, and California. While it is true that one of the marks of engaged Buddhism as a worldwide movement has been its grassroots collectivism, an emphasis on the social action of committed groups, and not on the personal style or pronouncements of charismatic individuals, it is also true that Asian Buddhist leaders like Dr. Ambedkar, the Dalai Lama, Thich Nhat Hanh, A. T. Ariyaratna, Sulak Sivaraksa, Buddhadasa Bhikkhu, Maha Ghosananda, Aung San Suu Kyi, and Daisaku Ikeda have personally shaped the direction of the Dharma in our time. It is for this reason, and because I believe that Bernie and a few other Westerners have made as significant contributions to the new Buddhism as have the Asian leaders, I will try to portray Bernie and the Peacemaker Order from a personal perspective.

I have organized my reflections around three series of encounters. My first meetings with Glassman and his late wife, Sensei Sandra Jishu Holmes, were held in Yonkers, New York, in September 1996 and continued in January 1997, during Bernie's speaking engagements at the Buddhism in America conference at the Boston Park Plaza Hotel, and at the Harvard Divinity School in Cambridge, Massachusetts. These conversations explore the roots of Glassman's engaged Buddhism, the creative use of traditional Buddhist metaphors and images in his teaching, and the emergence of a distinctive new Dharma of social service. A second set of interviews took place during my three-day visit with the Peacemaker Order and Greyston Mandala in Yonkers in July 1997. This visit focused on the institutional shape of Glassman's Zen and the challenges of community life—in essence, the coming of a new vision of sangha. My most recent encounter took place at the Peacemaker Order's Year Beginning Retreat at Wisdom House in Litchfield,

Connecticut, in January 1999, and in a seaside cottage on Half Moon Bay, south of San Francisco, two weeks later. In this section I will focus on the question of Buddhist identity: how can social activism and engagement manifest the spirit of a buddha, an awakened one, in the kind of world we face today? In the three encounters, thus, we shall use the rubrics of the ancient Buddhist commitment formula—"I take refuge in the Buddha, the Dharma, and the Sangha"—to examine the personal, ideological, and institutional features of the new Buddhism.

FIRST ENCOUNTER: THE ROOTS OF PEACEMAKER DHARMA

When Bernie Glassman gives public lectures on his experiments in engaged spirituality and inner-city entrepreneurship, he is often grandly introduced as Dr. Bernard Tetsugen Glassman, Roshi, former aeronautical engineer, Lineage-holder and Spiritual Leader of the White Plum Sangha of Soto Zen Buddhism, Abbot of the Zen Community of New York and the Zen Center of Los Angeles, Founder of the Greyston Mandala of social services agencies, and co-founder of the Zen Peacemaker Order. But when he begins to speak, he seems tentative, as if feeling his way, searching for words, asking the audience to help out with questions, using self-deprecation and gentle humor. At the Boston Park Plaza Hotel on January 18, 1997, he began, "My name is Bernie and I'm an addict. I'm addicted to myself—as I think all of us in this room are. About forty years ago I fell upon a recovery program called Zen that has helped me to deal with my addiction to myself. It took a lot more years before I realized that that addiction wasn't going to go away."[7]

Two days later at Harvard Divinity School, addressing a room of students and faculty who came out on Martin Luther King Day to hear a Buddhist version of "I Have a Dream," Glassman began by describing the record-setting cold that he and his companions endured on the U. S. Capital steps during the weeklong street retreat in 1994 that led to his vow to found the Peacemaker Order. The unspoken allusion to the famous civil rights speech on the Washington Mall nearby was ironic. King had been thunderously applauded by tens of thousands for his grand vision of America, where little black and white children would some day play together. In contrast, Glassman and his ragtag followers, pondering an America of homelessness, AIDS, and violence, were ignored by the media and by Congress, who were out of town on recess.

In both talks Glassman offered his own experience to make a personal connection with his audience. But soon he was talking about Shakyamuni, the historical Buddha: "When Gautama saw old age, illness, and death outside the palace grounds, he had to act. Out of wisdom comes compassion. Just sitting allows us to see the wholeness of life. Out of seeing comes action."[8] Someone asked how you could listen to pain when there are no answers. Now the *roshi* invokes the bodhisattva of compassion, variously known as Avalokiteshvara, Kuan-yin, Kannon, and Kanzeon.

> Kanzeon, "the listener of the sufferings," means fully *embodying* listening, not with the ears, but listening with the pores of the body, with the hairs on the head, with the feet, listening and fully becoming the pains of the world....So Avalokiteshvara—Kanzeon—takes a vow to bring an end to all the sufferings, but he/she/it was put into the position of listening to all this stuff and having no answers.
>
> Do you know what happened? She burst into millions of pieces! Then all those pieces came back together—now we have thousand-armed Kanzeons—and each hand held a different implement. One had a pen, one had a sword, one had a hoe, and one had a flower.
>
> Now Kanzeon is doing the work. He's listening, still having no answers, but is doing everything in every sphere where she/he appears, doing the things that need to be done in that sphere.

Glassman speaks of his beloved teachers, Taizan Maezumi Roshi (1931–1995), Haku'un Yasutani Roshi (1885–1973), and Osaka Koryo Roshi (1901–1985), from whom he received Dharma transmission and authorization to teach.[9] The point of these references in the public talks of January 1997 was not to burnish his reputation as the *wunderkind* of American Zen, but to make the connection between the fiendish difficulty and rewards of the traditional *koan* study systems Glassman mastered under these teachers, and the spiritual challenges and benefits that will come from social activism and service. In *koan* study "you fully become the situation, and present the answer by *being, not by saying.*" So the work of the Peacemaker Order involves "going into situations our society ignores and working with them as a *koan.*" This involves letting go of all presuppositions, "penetrating the unknown," and "bearing witness." For Glassman, "bearing witness" is a way of translating the Japanese *shikan taza,* "just sitting," which is the central practice of the Zen School of Buddhism (*zen* being the Japanese mispronunciation of the Chinese *ch'an,* which is a mispronunciation of the Sanskrit *dhyana,* "meditation"). Bearing witness, or opening the mind to "the wholeness of life," automatically generates the impulse "to heal oneself and others" or to "make peace." So, the tenets of the Peacemaker Order, not knowing, bearing witness, and healing, are presented as the marrow of Zen training—both of the Rinzai School, which emphasizes *koan* study, and the Soto School, which emphasizes just sitting.[10]

As the constant touchstones of Glassman Roshi's teaching, and the foundation of his commitment to social engagement, the three Peacemaker tenets deserve a closer look.

Not Knowing

The Peacemaker tenet of not knowing is a kind of methodological agnosticism—not a total renunciation of cognition and understanding, but a strategic bracketing of formal knowledge and prejudgment. Tellingly, the first ingredient in Glassman's recipe for social change in his *Instructions to the Cook* is doubt: "Doubt is a state of openness and unknowing. It's a willingness to not be in charge, to not know what is going to happen next. The state of doubt allows us to explore things in an open and fresh way."[11] In a similar passage in *Bearing Witness*, Glassman asks, "What is peacemaking?"

> It's about living a questioning life, a life of unknowing. If we're ready to live such a life, without fixed ideas or answers, then we are ready to bear witness to every situation, no matter how difficult, offensive, or painful it is. Out of that process of bearing witness, the right action of making peace, of healing, arises.[12]

Glassman Roshi, whose Dharma name, Tetsugen, means "to penetrate mystery," is not the only contemporary Buddhist teacher to stress the renunciation of fixed opinions.[13] Thich Nhat Hanh's warning against any belief in "changeless, absolute truth" and "narrow-minded[ness]...bound to present views" is the second of his fourteen precepts for members of the Order of Interbeing (Tiep Hien Order), founded during the Vietnam War and now reporting thousands of members in Asia and the West. What is remarkable is not the existence of such a warning near the top of his list, but the fact that Nhat Hanh's first and third precepts also parallel Glassman's *Not Knowing*. The first one reads, "Do not be idolatrous about or bound to any doctrine, theory, or ideology, even Buddhist ones. All systems of thought are guiding means; they are not absolute truth." And the third one reads, "Do not force others, including children, by any means whatsoever, to adopt your views, whether by authority, threat, money, propaganda, or even education. However, through compassionate dialogue, help others to renounce fanaticism and narrowness." In Nhat Hanh's manual for peacemakers, Being Peace, each precept is followed by a commentary that links it to traditional Buddhist teachings, to the crisis of the Vietnam War, and to circumstances likely faced by readers in less perilous times.[14]

Glassman's theme of Zen agnosticism is prefigured in two books that have appeared since the American Zen boom of the 50s and 60s. In *Zen Mind, Beginner's Mind* (1970), the Japanese Soto master Shunryu Suzuki begins with the aphorism "In the beginner's [Japanese: *shoshin*] mind there are many possibilities, but in the expert's there are few."[15] Later in the book he writes, "I discovered that it is necessary, absolutely necessary, to believe in nothing....No matter what god or doctrine you believe in, if you become attached to it, your belief will be based more or less on a self-centered idea."[16] Likewise, the Korean master Seung Sahn titles his book of teaching letters *Only Don't Know* (1982). In the preface, two of his students explain

> "Only don't know" means choosing to pay attention. When we choose to just pay attention, confusion is dispelled; just seeing, just hearing, or just perceiving the needs of others is the turning point for clarity and compassion.[17]

More recently, Buddhist agnosticism has surfaced again in the writings of the British teacher, Stephen Batchelor, whose 1992 volume, *The Faith to Doubt, Glimpses of Buddhist Uncertainty*, and 1997 volume, *Buddhism Without Beliefs: A Contemporary Guide to Awakening*, advocate what we might call cognitive renunciation. Batchelor begins the latter book by citing the most often-quoted Buddhist text among users of the Buddhist websites on the Internet (according to Richard Hayes of McGill University),[18] namely the Buddha's advice to the Kalamas (*Anguttara Nikaya* 1:187):

> Do not be satisfied with hearsay or with tradition or with legendary lore or with what has come down in scriptures or with conjecture or with logical inference or with weighing evidence or with someone else's ability or with the thought "The monk is our teacher." When you know in yourselves, "These things are wholesome, blameless, commended by the wise, and, being adopted and put into effect, they lead to welfare and happiness," then you should practice and abide in them.[19]

In his commentary, Batchelor warns the reader not to confuse Buddhist agnosticism with a refusal to know or to investigate, or with the intellectual passivity that "legitimizes indulgent consumerism and the unreflective conformism dictated by mass media." Instead, he invokes T. H. Huxley, who coined the term "agnosticism" in 1869 to signify the rigorous testing of all propositions by reason and experience. The Dharma, for Batchelor, is thus "something to do," a consistent, liberating orthopraxy in a world of superficial belief.[20]

In my first interview with Roshi Glassman in September 1996, I wanted to know why a teacher with a Ph.D. in applied mathematics and recent successes in business management, finance, and community development would insist on unknowing. "In Zen," he replied, "the words *source* and *essence* are equivalent to Unknowing, and they come up again and again. We have the absolute and the relative perspectives about life, and Unknowing is the one source of both of these."[21] I was reminded of the opening verses of the sixth-century Chinese text the *Hsin Hsin Ming*, the sutra of Seng-ts'an, the third Zen patriarch (d. 606): "The Great Way is not difficult for those who have no preferences....If you wish to see the truth, then hold no opinions for or against anything."[22] The interview continued:

Queen: "Early Buddhism in India was very comfortable with notions of knowledge, wisdom, and technique. Yoga, meditation, and philosophy were all developed by experts, the virtuoso monks. But in China a mistrust of words and concepts and intellectualism came into the early Zen tradition from Taoism, and we hear about book-burning and Zen masters who do wild, irrational things to break their students' dependency on logic and learning. Is this part of Not Knowing for you?"

Glassman: "Yes, and for me it fits in with my Jewish background. In contrast to the whole rabbinical tradition of Talmudic learning and scholarship comes the mystical tradition of Kabbalah and Hasidism, where all the earthly qualities and emanations come from the infinite *Ein Sof*. And the Sufis have some of the same ideas. But the important thing is that Not Knowing was emphasized by my teacher Maezumi Roshi, and it fits my temperament. It just makes so much sense to start from Not Knowing."

Queen: "But how does this work when you are dealing with people with no educational opportunities, who have a desperate need for knowledge and expertise? Ambedkar was just as jealous for education as he was for economic opportunities for the Untouchables who converted to Buddhism in 1956."

Glassman: "Yeah. But the other side must be stressed. At every moment one starts from unknowing *so that* all the acquired knowledge will arise spontaneously and be used in a new, creative way. It's like the old monk Hotei's totebag—everything comes out when the time is right."

Bearing Witness

The second tenet, bearing witness to the pains and joys of the world, has seemingly propelled Roshi Glassman to investigate—or "plunge into"— some of the most desperate communities and dismal places in the Western world. He has not visited India, Latin America, or other third world countries at this writing, but he has become intimate with the homeless communities of New York, with the death camp at Auschwitz-Birkenau, and with the Letten, a vast outdoor area once cordoned off by the city of Zurich, Switzerland, for use by drug addicts and their dealers. Glassman's instincts as a Zen master are not unlike those of Thich Nhat Hanh, whose fourth precept is "find ways to be with those who are suffering by all means, including personal contact and visits, images, sound. By such means, awaken yourself and others to the reality of suffering in the world."[23] But Glassman appears to have made a career of going where other Buddhist teachers are seldom found—and identifying the encounter with suffering as the most powerful incentive to spiritual awakening.

Glassman associates bearing witness with meditation and mindfulness. But he also sees it as a form of engagement with the world.

Queen: "What is engaged Buddhism, anyway? The Nipponzan Myohoji monks stage peace marches and build peace pagodas all over the world, but they don't work with the poor. Some people say your street retreats are just consciousness-raising for the rich—you don't hand out blankets or food—in fact you seem to soak up some of the limited good will that still exists on the streets of New York."

Glassman: "The same question could be raised about the Buddha. How did he benefit mankind by sitting in meditation? This is a problem with the term 'engaged Buddhism' in a broad sense. Anything anyone is doing to make themselves whole in their own life, or realizing the Way, or becoming enlightened—whatever term you would use—these are all involved in service, because if we realize the oneness of life, then each person is serving every other person and is reducing suffering."

Queen: "You and Thich Nhat Hanh are very nondualistic about this: not separating your own suffering and its relief from that of others. But Ambedkar, contrasting the voluntary homelessness of sadhus and mendicants in India with the desperate homelessness of the Untouchables, came to feel that no religion should romanticize poverty. Aren't you doing that by spending a week on the street and then coming home to a hot shower?"

Glassman: "I think that the person who has lived with the Untouchables can work with the Untouchables in a way that others cannot. You can't *become* Untouchable in this way, of course. At the same time I believe that those who came out of that experience have a deeper understanding of it, and we should learn from them. I want to figure out how to learn from those who have suffered in a certain way, even though I can't fully enter that realm. So we go on the streets. I know we aren't homeless and I make that quite clear. At the same time those who come will experience something that is closer to that world than those who haven't been there. This is the meaning of 'bearing witness.' It's like entering a church knowing you're not God or the priest. But you will experience something different from someone who stays out of the church or someone who is just hired to fix the roof."

Queen: "Why are you attracted to places of such great suffering—the inner city, Auschwitz, and the park in Zurich where thousands of junkies buy, sell, and shoot up in broad daylight?"

Glassman: "I don't know. The words that come to me are *the desire to learn.* I don't know what it is, but it happens a lot to me when I encounter a situation I don't understand. It generally involves suffering. Like Wall Street—I don't know what's happening there, but I don't particularly care. When I enter a situation that is too much for me and I don't understand—I have a desire to sit there, to stay a while."

Queen: "You talk about an energy that surrounds such places."

Glassman: "Yeah. There's a magnet that pulls me so that I want to stay there. I haven't figured it out, but I'm not sure it's so unusual."

Queen: "Is it possible to imagine a twisted individual who derives some kind of sadistic pleasure from being near human pain and suffering?"

Glassman: "Sure. But the people and situations I'm talking about are a metaphor for our whole society—all the attachments and addictions. In the drug zone in Zurich the metaphor is so naked you couldn't miss it unless you ran away. But if you stayed and looked, the human condition is laid more bare than it is in a bank lobby."

Healing

The third Peacemaker tenet, healing oneself and the world, grows out of an intense experience of the earlier two tenets, as we have seen. Yet here Glassman consistently points to two central teachings in the Buddhist tradition: the oneness of life and universal interdependence. Today the idea of interdependence is widely associated with Buddhism because of the popular perception that Buddhism is the religion of ecology and vegetarianism. While neither of these perceptions is accurate (few Buddhists in China and East Asia have been vegetarians, and the tradition as a whole is not concerned primarily with nonhuman nature),[24] the metaphysical and soteriological teachings of moral causation *(karma)*, dependent co-origination *(pratityasamutpada)*, nondualism or emptiness *(shunyata)*, and the interpenetration of all things *(shih shih wu-ai)* have indeed occupied a central place at various stages in the history of Buddhist thought.[25]

Parallels with the teaching of Thich Nhat Hahn are useful again. The third precept of the Order of Interbeing invites contact, indeed *intimacy*, with "suffering in the life of the world," meaning both one's own suffering and that of others. Nhat Hanh recalls the Buddha's first sermon, focusing on the reality, origin, cessation, and remedy of suffering, and then he reflects on the isolation of Americans:

> America is somehow a closed society. Americans are not very aware of what is going on outside of America. Life here is so busy that even if you watch television and read the newspaper, and the images from outside flash by, there is no real contact....[But] if we get in touch with the suffering in the world and are moved by that suffering, we may come forward to help the people who are suffering, and our own suffering may just vanish.[26]

For Thich Nhat Hanh the relationship between the suffering of others and one's own suffering is one aspect of their *interbeing*. He coined this expression to translate the Vietnamese *tiep hien* ("to continuously be in touch [with others] in the present moment") and to capture the notion of cumulative interpenetration found in the *Avatamsaka* (Chinese *Hua-Yen*, Korean *Hwaom*, Japanese *Kegon*) *Sutra*. Interbeing represents the co-arising and co-existence of all beings, sentient and nonsentient. "In one sheet of paper," he says, "we see everything else, the cloud, the forest, the logger. I am, therefore you are. You are, therefore I am. This is the meaning of the word 'interbeing.' We interare."[27]

For Bernie Glassman the first step in healing the world is to go where the wounding is. He chose Yonkers for his social activism in the early eighties because it was the dumping ground for the homeless of affluent Westchester

County—an ideal place to develop some of his Zen-based institutions for economic development: a for-profit bakery and a construction company to provide job training and employment, tenant-operated coop housing in rehabbed slum buildings, and drug treatment clinics and AIDS hospices, to name only a few.[28]

Healing the world reminds Bernie of the imperative in Jewish social ethics of "repairing the world" *(tikkun olam)* and of the meaning of the Hebrew *shalom*, "peace," "to make whole." But, like the Buddha, who asked if the doctor would waste time analyzing the poison arrow lodged in his patient or pull it out and give emergency treatment, Glassman also employs similes of injury and medical treatment to convey his idea of engaged Buddhism:

> We all have the illusion that "something is not part of me." If I cut my hand and it starts to bleed, I could get angry at it—it's messing up my new clothes. But this is a metaphor for life. It's easy to get angry at those people who are screwing me up and messing me up. But if this is me, and it's bleeding, I take care of it. I don't join a discussion group or wait for the right equipment or wait until I am enlightened or go off to get trained. I immediately get some rags to stop the bleeding—because it's me that's bleeding![29]

SECOND ENCOUNTER: THE SOCIALLY ENGAGED SANGHA

Entering the city of Yonkers from the north, where the landscaped suburbs of Westchester County meet the abandoned buildings and homeless people of Ashburton Avenue, offers a stark reminder of the material extremes that divide America from itself and from much of the world. As a second-time visitor to Bernie Glassman's adopted neighborhood on a balmy July evening in 1997, I try to open myself to these realities by concentrating on the first Peacemaker precept, "to plunge into the Unknown, the source of all manifestations."

The Zen Peacemaker Order (ZPO) headquarters occupy two buildings on a tiny cul-de-sac. One building served, at the time of my visit, as home to Bernie, Jishu, and the business offices of the order, while the other was a guest house and Dharma hall where elaborate ordination ceremonies were staged and communal meals prepared. At one end of the street stands a Hispanic holiness church that comes alive with Gospel singing and preaching several nights a week, while the other end, across Ashburton Avenue, is dominated by the abandoned carcass of Public School 6, until recently surrounded by tall weeds, broken glass, and used hypodermic needles. Now the weeds are gone and the trash is removed, thanks to months of toil by ZPO members. In the schoolyard, a circle of flat gray stones provides open-air seats for twenty meditators at morning and afternoon services: the Greyston *zendo*.

The Peacemaker community is sitting down to a picnic supper on tables in the backyard. I feel at home here, recalling the commune of seminarians, poets, and activists I joined thirty years ago on a street of brownstones in Brooklyn. The dress is jeans and work shirts, and the talk is a Creole of the exotic and the mundane. I run into the freshly tonsured Joan Halifax, the Zen teacher, hospice movement leader, and environmentalist who has just been quoted in Sunday's *New York Times* for her work with dying patients at the Upaya Foundation in Santa Fe. As a guest speaker in my engaged Buddhism class at Harvard some years earlier, Joan had fallen silent for the five minutes that the Memorial Church bell chimed the hour, a practice of Thich Nhat Hanh's order, in which she is already an ordained member—hearing all bells as a call to mindfulness. The class members sat in silence too, surmising that Zen masters sometimes lapse into spontaneous states of grace.

Some order members speak of their plans to return to Oswiecim, Poland, for a second Thanksgiving retreat, to sit again on railroad tracks leading to the crematoriums and to pray with Holocaust survivors, former Nazis, and their children, and with Catholics, Protestants, Jews, Buddhists, and atheists from several countries. They explain that to "bear witness to the pains and the joys" of Auschwitz—the second tenet of Zen Peacemaking—was the most powerful experience of their lives.

Bernie is chatting affably with tablemates and working on a plate of beans, rice, and salad. He is beginning to let his hair and beard grow out in preparation for an upcoming street retreat. He introduces me to the people at the table and then listens as others pick up the conversation. It occurs to me that the reason people want to be around him is that he is basically shy—like the corporate CEOs who score "introvert" and "intuitive" on personality tests, and unlike the extroverts and pragmatists who end up working at the front desk and in the sales department. At the same time he seems to know exactly what needs to happen next and who should be involved.

After supper the community gathers in the parlor for a Dharma talk by Joan, who has formalized her long-standing commitment to engaged Buddhism by taking the vows of the Peacemaker Order. The community repeats the vows:

> I vow to be unity. I vow to be diversity. I vow to be harmony.
>
> I vow to penetrate the unknown, I vow to bear witness. I vow to heal myself and others.
>
> I vow not to kill. I vow not to steal. I vow not to be greedy.

I vow not to tell lies. I vow not to be ignorant.

I vow not to talk about others' errors and faults.

I vow not to elevate myself by blaming others.

I vow not to be stingy. I vow not to be angry.

I vow not to speak ill of myself and others.

I vow to listen to all others and to allow myself to be touched
by the joy and pain of life.

I vow to encounter each creation with respect for the dignity
inherent in that creation.

I vow to invite all hungry spirits into the circle of my practice and
raise the mind of compassion as my offering of the Supreme Meal.

I vow to commit my energy and my love for the healing of myself,
the earth, humanity, and all creations.

I vow to commit myself to a daily practice of meditation.[30]

Gazing around the room at the thirty order members, candidates, students, and visitors, I am reminded of the 50s and 60s, when small gatherings of spiritual seekers and social misfits sat on the floor in city apartments and rural farmhouses, sharing their vision of a new America and a world at peace. Then the politics and religion were inchoate and raw, like the drunken ravings of Kerouac's Ray Smith and Japhy Ryder and the angry memoirs of Malcolm X. Today's group is infinitely more evolved—Buddhists with a sense of history stretching back two thousand five hundred years, a feeling for the potential mystery and misery of life, and a deep yearning to heal themselves and everyone else.

Joan tells the story of a young woman whose restless spirit drove her across the Sahara Desert in a VW bus, to several universities in quest of a Ph.D. in medical anthropology, and from one Zen teacher to another to find a Buddhism that takes society and service as seriously as it takes selftransformation. All these journeys have converged in this room on Ashburton Place, in the person of this freshly minted priest in the Peacemaker Order. Glassman sits quietly in the circle, a faint smile on his face, as if warming himself in the reflected glow of his newest senior colleague.

The next day begins with early breakfast in a small diner with Claude AnShin Thomas, a thrice-decorated Vietnam veteran whose life is featured in Glassman's *Bearing Witness*. An intense man who carries deep sadness, Thomas survived multiple combat wounds and the further injuries of homelessness and substance addiction when he returned from the war. As an international anti-war activist and Zen Peacemaker priest, Claude tells me about the peace walk he joined in 1994 that began in Auschwitz, proceeded south through the war-torn Balkan states, across the Mediterranean to the Middle East, down through Pakistan and India, though Southeast Asia to Vietnam, and finally to Hiroshima, on the fiftieth anniversary of its bombing by Americans. Like the first Auschwitz retreat that Bernie attended, the march was organized by the Nippanzan Myohoji sect of Nichiren Buddhists from Japan. Thomas met Glassman at the outset of this journey and joined the Peacemaker Order at its end. Since then he has walked across America, wearing Buddhist robes, engaging anyone who would listen in conversations about peacemaking, and begging for food and lodging from strangers in the ancient Buddhist way.[31]

After breakfast, Claude shows me two abandoned apartment buildings that were slated for renovation by the Greyston Mandala. Further down the street we come to the Greyston Family Inn, with twenty-eight units of permanent housing and a freshly painted, fully accredited daycare center serving fifty children. As described in *Instructions to the Cook*, the Greyston Mandala comprises a network of companies and agencies committed to community development: the Greyston Bakery, a million-dollar gourmet confectioner providing job training and employment to the homeless and formerly homeless men and women; Greyston Builders, specializing in the renovation of affordable housing; Maitri House, an AIDS hospice and walk-in clinic; Pumsala, a handicrafts company that recycles used and discarded clothing, providing employment for low-income women; and the Greyston Family Inn.

Most of these thriving operations were fragile start-ups in the 1980s that quickly attracted generous public and private funding as word spread of their sound management and sincere commitment to the local community. By January 2, 1992, the *Wall Street Journal* was converted: "Blending Zen and the Art of Philanthropic Pastry Chefs, Buddhist Monk Puts the Poor to Work, and Houses Them with the Profit," blared a headline in the Enterprise section. The story, by staff reporter Udayan Gupta, has mythic overtones:

Yonkers, N.Y.—A systems engineer-turned-Buddhist monk is feeding the poor by feeding the rich with gourmet pastries. He's also housing the poor, counseling their teen-age children and providing day care for their toddlers. But in trying to build a better world, he has learned to keep a close eye on the bottom line...."I am trying to build a world that is all interconnected." Says Mr. Glassman, a 52-year-old sensei, or Zen teacher, who once worked at McDonnell-Douglas Corp.

Occupying a corner of the living room in the Glassman–Holmes apartment is a space-age chiropractic, massage, and vibrating lounger chair with NASA-style controls. An electrically heated, liquid-filled toilet seat graces the bathroom. I tease the "*roshi* of the streets" about these Sharper Image catalogue items. "Jishu gave me the toilet seat for my birthday," he proudly replies. We settle down on couches for an interview. I turn up the recording volume on my tape machine, wondering if the din of heavy trucks on Ashburton Avenue and a noisy pack of neighborhood dogs will drown out Glassman's soft-spoken reflections.

Queen: "I guess you spend a lot of time doing interviews."

Glassman: "Yeah, we get about one documentary film crew asking to come every month, and print media people about once a week. There are plenty of others who are doing this work without the spotlight. When the "News of the Week in Review" [Sunday *New York Times*, July 6, 1997] covers Joan's work, it says to people that a Buddhist perspective is worth considering. But it takes a lot of time."

Queen: "Are you criticized in the media?"

Glassman: "The *L. A. Times* carried a piece that talks about the people who say I am moving too much to social action and leaving Zen behind. Then it quotes the president of the Buddhist Association of L. A., Venerable Ratnasara, who said that Buddhism always moves into the streets when it comes to a new culture and that Glassman is doing what has to be done. Of course, if someone thinks I'm leaving Zen behind, that's fine with me. I'm just doing what I'm doing."

Queen: "During this development phase of the Zen Peacemaker Order you seem to be spending a lot of time in business meetings, paying attention to group process. You even have a consultant to keep the planning on track and make sure everybody is heard. Yet some former students call you as a despot, however benevolent."

Glassman: "Many *koans* in the Zen tradition are group *koans. Uman addressed the assembly and said, 'There is a snake in the mountains. What do you say about that!'* And different novices respond to the question. In a sense that is what we are doing with the Peacemaker Order. The group work that we're doing, with a theme, or just in the moment, is like working on a group *koan* about the issues and about ourselves. I'm finding that very powerful. There is now a history accumulating in all the meeting minutes and business reports and brainstorming exercises, but each time we start, it feels like we start from scratch.

"Some people rebel because they want to be going forward. But we keep coming back to Unknowing. Of course, everything that's happened in the past is still part of you, so even when you start from scratch it all unfolds. I think this will be one of the things the Zen Peacemaker Order offers to the world.

"One of our teachers, Grover Genro Gauntt, who is also our executive director, told us of a bank closing he attended recently. The loan officer had just lost both his parents, so everybody stopped to process that for a while before dealing with the money. This is the same kind of process we are developing. This is peacemaking, and I have a feeling that we are not unique in this. We are borrowing a lot from the Council methods of the Ojai Foundation that Joan Halifax brought to us, which is based on Native American group process and the ancient Buddhist traditions of Shakyamuni's sangha meetings in India."

Queen: "You must have a lot of confidence in your consultant."

Glassman: "I have a lot of confidence in Jishu, who hired the consultant, and we learned a lot from Joan. I couldn't have imagined doing this two years ago. It's not my format, it's not my history, but I've learned a lot."

Queen: "Gender and sangha. Do men and women bring different qualities to decision-making?"

Glassman: "We're experimenting with forms of gender partnership in our organization. Jishu and I are co-founders, and we have male and female co-chairs for our board committees and co-leaders for the staff. I'm not sure how it will turn out. Sometimes we meet all together, and then sometimes we meet apart—men and women. Then we will have the women's group in a circle with the men listening outside as observers, and then we switch, with the men in the fishbowl and the women observing around the outside."

In the afternoon I join order members for *zazen*, sitting meditation, outdoors in the Greyston *zendo*. We are separated from the traffic on Ashburton Avenue by a chainlink fence, and each passing pedestrian and driver sneaks a peek through the fence at the silent figures on stone cushions in the old

Peacemaker Order members meditate in abandoned schoolyard, Yonkers, New York.
Photo by Peter Cunningham.

schoolyard. One by one, Bernie's regular students are summoned from the circle for *dokusan*, a private interview with the *roshi*. When they return, it is hard not to look into their faces for signs of enlightenment. But Zen students have mastered the deadpan, and vicarious dokusan is not possible.

After *zazen*, Sensei Jishu Holmes, a strikingly focused and kindly person, shows me around the business offices of the Peacemaker Order, which occupy three floors of the house she shares with Bernie. Each time I have seen her since the big Buddhism conference in Boston, I recall the dramatic end to Glassman's two-hour seminar with an overflow crowd in the Park Plaza Hotel. The last question to the *roshi* was "What are you afraid of?"—at which the man with answers for everything fell silent. This silence was particularly deep because the session had run overtime and people were aware of being late for the next meetings. Then a woman's voice rang out from the back of the room, "His wife!" Everybody joined the Zen master in a good laugh.

Going from room to room, Jishu showed me the voluminous notebooks outlining the scope of the Zen Peacemaker Order: mission and vision statements, business plans, and endless board minutes and reports. Taped to the walls are giant newsprint sheets with the minutes from the week's committee and focus group meetings. One emerging project is the Interfaith Peacemaker Assembly and its home sanctuary, the House of One People. Housed in a refurbished Roman Catholic chapel on a hill nearby, the House of One People is "An interfaith center where the expressions of spiritual traditions can be encountered, studied, and celebrated." "Joining hands across religious and cultural differences," its mission statement reads, "we will work together for justice, peace, and the integrity of the earth." Clergy from several faiths, who are also senior Zen students of Glassman Roshi, are actively involved in establishing the Assembly: The Very Reverend James Morton, emeritus dean of the Episcopal Cathedral of St. John the Divine and spiritual director of the House of One People (Protestant), Father Robert Kennedy, S.J., Reverend Pat Enkyo O'Hara, and Sister Janet Richardson (Roman Catholic), Rabbi Don Singer (Reform Jewish), and Sheik Fariha Friedrich (Muslim).

I read about the growing network of Peacemaker villages, local groups from the United States and abroad, engaged in service and activism and affiliated with the Peacemaker Order through publications, funding arrangements, training, and planning: Upaya in New Mexico (death and dying hospice work, environmental activism), Tara Mandala in Colorado (meditation, ecology, healing), Metta Vihara in New York (homelessness, multiple-diagnoses/AIDS), Latino Pastoral Action Center in the Bronx (inner city community development), Zaltho Foundation in Massachusetts (international peacemaking communities), Village Community in Manhattan (AIDS and gender issues), Prison Peacemakers in Missouri (Dharma and hospice network in prisons), Arts (using arts to promote peace), Stress Reduction Center in Massachusetts (clinical applications of mindfulness meditation), Buddhist Relief Committee in Japan (refugee relief in Southeast Asia), and Greyston Mandala in Yonkers (urban renewal, jobs, housing, health care).

I learn of plans for a Peacemaker institute, which will offer practical training in peace activism, mediation, community development; academic study of peacemaking traditions; conferences and internships for practitioners; a peace library, a website, and publications; and a children's peace school. The institute will seek academic accreditation and a suitable campus location.

In the late afternoon I join a men's group of ten senior students for discussion of personal and spiritual concerns. This would seem to be a traditional therapy group, except that no one takes charge. In the Native American council tradition, a "talking stick" is passed around, assuring that only one person may speak at a time. Some members share deeply painful experiences, while others offer advice and encouragement. Glassman Roshi listens sympathetically, but says very little. When the session is over, the members linger, savoring the sense of empathy the group has achieved. There is some curiosity and speculation about the women's group, which had been meeting with Jishu in the other building at the same time.

After supper and kitchen cleanup, the Peacemaker community again retires to the parlor for evening exercises. Tonight the program is a full-dress rehearsal of the *Kan Ro Mon*, "The Gate of Sweet Nectar," a traditional Zen ceremony of dedication, chanted partly in Japanese and partly in English. Roshi Tetsugen, Sensei Jishu, and several senior order members don full priestly regalia, while others wear the Zen student's bib or *kesa*. Designated members play an ensemble of gongs, bells, and wood blocks to accompany the formal procession, liturgical movements, and frequent *gassho*, or bowing. Choreography is everything, but the blocking, movements, and sequences are still being worked out, as Roshi frequently stops the whole thing to correct the woodblock person or the person rounding the corner slightly late.

Bernard Glassman seems to be fully in his element now, teaching a motley but earnest assembly of middle-aged Americans how to bow and play the gong, to invoke the buddhas and bodhisattvas, and to appropriate and internalize the tenets and precepts of engaged Buddhism for the twenty-first century of the Common Era and the twenty-sixth century of the Shakyamuni Buddha Era.

Attention! Attention!

Raising the bodhi mind, the Supreme Meal is offered
to all the hungry spirits in the ten directions throughout
    space and time,
filling the smallest particle to the largest space.

All you hungry spirits in the ten directions, please gather here.
Sharing your distress, I offer you this food,
hoping it will resolve your thirsts and hungers.

I pray that all who receive this offering will return its merits
to all buddhas and to all creations throughout space and time;
in this way they will be thoroughly satisfied.

I further pray that in receiving this meal
all your sufferings will be eliminated, and that you will be liberated,

so that being joyously reborn you will play freely in the fields of
the Pure Land.

Raising the bodhi mind and practicing the enlightened way,
you become the future buddhas without any further regress.
Those who realize the way first, please vow to liberate all others
throughout all space and time.[32]

THIRD ENCOUNTER: HUNGRY GHOSTS
AND FUTURE BUDDHAS

Glassman Roshi's Buddhism is always practiced in dialogue with other faiths:
Judaism, Islam, and especially Roman Catholic Christianity. His deep com-
mitment to ecumenical collaboration was evident at the recent Year
Beginning Retreat of the Zen Peacemaker Order, held each January at
Wisdom House, the Catholic retreat center in Litchfield, Connecticut. In
addition to new Buddhists and practitioners of other faiths, ordained Roman
Catholic members of the Peacemaker Order were much in evidence: Father
Robert Kennedy and Sister Janet Richardson, both *roshis,* or senior precep-
tors of Zen Buddhism, and Father Niklaus Brantschen and Sister Pia Gyger,
Zen masters and co-directors of the Lassalle-Haus spiritual training center in
Bad Schonbrunn, Switzerland.

The Lassalle-Haus connection has special significance for engaged
Buddhism, as it was named for Hugo Enomiya Lassalle (1898-1990), the
Jesuit priest and Zen teacher known for his work among the poor of Tokyo
and for founding the Church of World Peace in Hiroshima. On the last day
of a week of *zazen* meditation, the Connecticut retreatants rose at daybreak
to attend a Catholic Mass. Glassman and the Buddhists looked on as the elements of the Eucharist were consecrated by Father Kennedy and offered by
the nuns of Lassalle-Haus to Christian members of the Peacemaker Order:
"This is my body, given for you.... This is the blood of the new covenant...."

The Wisdom House retreat in January 1999 was a week of monastic-
style meditation, spiritual direction, brainstorming and strategy sessions, business meetings, spiritual sharing groups, formal Zen instruction, leadership
training, and daily performances of the *Kan Ro Mon,* now the signature ceremony of the order, impeccably mounted in full regalia and instrumentation.
Again the centrality of the Holy Meal in the Christian and Zen traditions—
and their contrasting motivations—challenged the comparative religious historian in me. *In Instructions to the Cook,* Glassman writes:

> In Buddhism, the hungry ghosts are pictured as miserable creatures who have
> huge, swollen bellies and needle-thin necks. Even though they are surround-

ed by food, they can never satisfy their hunger or thirst because they can eat or drink only one drop of food at a time....Actually, we are all hungry ghosts.

Hungry ghosts manifest themselves in all sorts of ways. I myself experienced the immense hunger that we all have one morning while I was riding in my car pool to work. I had been practicing meditation intensively during the early mornings when I suddenly realized the universality of hunger.

I felt this great hunger all around me. I saw that even though there is enough food in our society to feed everyone, many, many people hunger for food. I saw that even though some people have more than enough food, they hunger for power. I saw that some of us thirst for appreciation or fame. Others are starved for love. And spiritual seekers, including Zen students, crave enlightenment.[33]

Glassman was recalling the powerful *kensho* or spiritual opening he experienced in 1971 while working at McDonnell-Douglas and studying the *koan MU* with Maezumi Roshi. "I couldn't stop laughing or crying, both at once, and the people in the car were very upset and concerned, they didn't have any idea what was happening, and I kept telling them there was nothing to worry about! Luckily I was an executive and had my own office, but I just couldn't stop laughing and crying, and finally I had to go home."[34] An earlier *kensho*, under the stern Koryu Roshi the previous year, had resulted in a deep sense of oneness with all beings ("Tears were pouring down my face as I served Koryu Roshi, and afterwards, when I went out of the zendo, there was a tree there, and looking at the tree....I felt the wind on me, I felt the birds on me, all separation was completely gone").[35]

But the great carpool *kensho* of 1971 took Glassman to a new level of realization, one that helps to explain the future direction of his career as an engaged Buddhist master.

That opening brought with it a tremendous feeling about the suffering in the world; it was a much more compassionate opening than the first. I saw the importance of spreading the Dharma, the necessity to develop a Dharma training in America that would help many people. Until then, I had believed in strong zazen, in "forcing" people, using the kyosaku [discipline stick]. That method encourages kensho, but the effects are not so deep and lasting, and anyway, it doesn't work for everybody. I wanted to work with greater numbers because I saw the "crying out" of all of us, even those who do not feel they are crying out. And that second opening had nothing to do with the zendo atmosphere, or working on a koan. The major opening can occur anywhere, we never know when it's going to happen.[36]

The Litchfield Year Beginning Retreat offered the rare opportunity for Peacemaker Order members and leaders to gather for spiritual revival, planning, and celebration. In addition to the daily celebration of religious liturgy (and, on the last morning, of Roshi Bernie's sixtieth birthday, in which a great white cake was ritually consumed), another kind of celebration—a rite of remembrance, sober and unsettling—pervaded the gathering throughout the week. On the Buddha altar, opposite a picture of the late Maezumi Roshi, a new photo of order co-founder, Sandra Jishu Holmes, reminded everyone of her quiet intelligence, strength, and beauty—and of her sudden death by heart attack only twelve days after she and Bernie moved all their worldly belongings to Santa Fe, New Mexico in March 1998.

Sandra Jishu Holmes had been a Zen student of Glassman's since the early 80s. As his wife she became the co-founder and co-director of many projects, including the Greyston Family Inn, Pumsala Handicrafts, and the Zen Peacemaker Order. As Greyston Family Inn director, she would scour the welfare motels in Westchester County, inviting single mothers with young children to become tenants at GFI and to work toward economic self-sufficiency.[37] A former medical researcher with a Ph.D. in biochemistry, Jishu became the principal judge, executor, and quality-control officer for the flood of ideas and schemes that emanated from her husband's overactive imagination. And significantly, she also became a role model and inspiration for scores of talented and outspoken women who are now leaders in the Peacemaker Order.

In the months following Jishu's death, Bernie cancelled all outside appointments and devoted himself full-time to grieving. "I went into personal oblivion for about five months," he told me. But with the support of Joan Halifax—no stranger to death and dying, as the hospice movement leader whose own beloved father had passed away months earlier—and other senior order members and Dharma brothers, like John Daido Loori Roshi, abbot to the Zen Mountain Monastery in New York, and a fellow heir of Maezumi Roshi's White Plum lineage, Glassman gradually resumed his place as spiritual head of the Zen Peacemakers.

When I visited Glassman in California two weeks after Wisdom House retreat, in a cottage on Half Moon Bay, he was working on his third book with the assistance of Eve Myonen Marko, his collaborator on *Bearing Witness*. He told me the book is "a love story for Jishu."

> It's about our life and work together, and more importantly, what we taught each other. Many spiritual communities, Buddhist and non-Buddhist alike, are built around one particular teacher, one personality. Often he or she is

charismatic, with qualities we admire, such as leadership, power, and confidence. But we don't honor people working together, bringing to a mutual endeavor more qualities and strengths than one person could possibly bring. And we give even less respect to the person who stands in the back, always ready to fade into the background, who publicly expresses self-doubt and shows little concern for the public persona. I represented the first personality, Jishu the second. The book is about partnership and integration—without these there can't be peacemaking.

Bernie talked about his feeling that Jishu's personality had begun to transform, and even to merge with, his own in the long months since her passing, giving birth in him to a new kind personality he calls "Jishu-Bernie" or "Bernie-Jishu," depending on the context.

I asked Bernie to evaluate this year's Wisdom House retreat.

Glassman: "The empowerment ceremonies were my main focus. It will probably take another two years to complete the transmissions. There are always new people who pop up—like Joan and Father Nicholas. But for me there is a feeling of closure."

Queen: "How has this movement ripened since last year's retreat?"

Glassman: "One of the things we realized is that so many seeds have been planted and things are happening—in Poland and Germany and all over Europe. They are developing ZPO sanghas on their own with no guidance from us. This year we need to work on communication and making sure everyone knows each other. Heinz Jürgen will coordinate the European villages. We need to decide on leadership and structure: centralization or decentralization?"

Queen: "The structure of the organization still seems very complicated."

Glassman: "All the answers are on the website, which I produce. But we still have a lot of loose ends. There is the umbrella organization, the Peacemaker Community, with its four aspects: the school, the House of All People, the villages, and the orders. When people call in they want to get connected to the spirit of the thing—they don't care about the structure. They want to be connected to the Peacemaker Community and affiliate with the works that are going on. Some want the training that goes along with the order. There is the Zen Peacemaker Order and the Peacemaker Order. We're having our first meeting of elders of the Peacemaker Order, for people who aren't into Zen or even Buddhist—Jews and Christians. Rabbi Zalman Schechter wants to be an elder, Father Theophane [from the Trappist monastery in Spencer, Massachusetts] wants to be an elder, Father Keeting is too old and ill to start a new thing. But Jim Morton will be an elder. And the rector of All Saints Church in Pasadena—like St. John's Cathedral in New York—wants to get involved.

"We're not quite there yet, but it's opening up. Someday we'll formalize our training paths. Pat O'Hara well help with that. Jishu was our key person for developing the organization. Now Pat and Joan both have the inclination. They are both teacher types. Pat has just retired from New York University, where she ran the film program; she had been teaching for a long time. Nancy and Eve will work with Pat on the four lay paths: Novice, Apprentice, Mentor, and Senior. To bring Pat on as training director has been very important."

Queen: "Why is there such emphasis on ritual in ZPO? How does this relate to social action?"

Glassman: "Shingon Buddhism in Japan is the most highly ritualized school, yet the founder of Shingon, Kobo Daishi [Kukai, 774-835], was a social activist. I read the main Shingon manual that lays out their precepts, deities, principles, founding; it clearly states that the leading principle is that *you recognize a buddha by their activities in service to others.* Maezumi Roshi once told me to study Shingon because Kukai was the Japanese Buddhist social activist. He said that Kukai was the leading philosopher of Japanese Buddhism—even greater than Dogen! Quite a statement for a Soto teacher. Building dams and great social works—this was his own predilection, not something he picked up with esoteric Buddhism from China. So from his time at least, engagement and ritual have played complementary roles."

Queen: "In Nancy Baker's group on social service, some people quoted you as saying that a meditator in a cave was just as engaged as someone who worked with the homeless. What about a woman who stays home and cares for her family? Does one have to be involved in politics?"

Glassman: "Our aim in meditation and spiritual practice is to find the wholeness of life. If we forget those high-falutin ideas like *kensho* and talk in terms of family, if we are working toward the wholeness of the family structure, then I would say that is peacemaking. I can't divorce it from the spiritual—the realization of this wholeness. It's not just anything you do—it must have that whole-making quality. But the particular activity could be almost anything. If you see the possibility of wholeness in a situation, you can't just stand by and witness the suffering."

Queen: "Many people who are drawn to Buddhism in the West appear to me to be alienated at some level. Often, their priority is their own wholeness. No study has shown that American Buddhism is attracting activists. The Vipassana scene, for example, that I know best, is focused on self-cultivation, not social action. They are affiliating with Sarvodaya now, according to Dr. Ariyaratna, but this is new. I am not convinced that self-cultivators are inclined or able to extend their concerns to society at large."

Eve Marko: "We have a problem. As teachers meeting in May, we looked at what people joining the order would need for beginning practices. They listed a whole bunch, meditation, etc. They pointed out that people have family and jobs, and they argued that just living one's life is social action. So the question came up, Can we demand that people do more? It went back and forth, and finally we said yes, you have to do more. Even if you have full work and a family, and the sangha, and retreats, you have to do something in the community—I think we put in some demand for hours. But there was a real argument on that."

Glassman: "I still want to stick with what I said. The question for me is, whatever the state of clarity we have about the oneness of life, we each have a boundary separating my life and that of 'the other.' I keep trying to push at those boundaries with people who train with me. For someone the family is the other, but for another person at a later stage of practice, it may be the community. Ariyaratna does that in his [Sarvodaya] work camps, a little exercise. People get together and sit quietly for a while and then he asks them to wish for something to bring peace to themselves, then to wish for something that would bring peace to their families, then to their village, then to their country, then to the world. And he says that when he first started this, the poor villagers had no concept of anything outside the village—that there was a world out there.

"I would say the same thing was true in our bakery. Many of the people that started to work at first could only think of themselves. The problems going on in the rainforest in South America was not something they would think about. But when we started making Rainforest Cookies they did start to think about it and talk about it. So I would push it in that direction. I've talked to Sharon [Salzberg at the Insight Meditation Society] and she is moving more in the direction of social action."

Eve Marko: "There were people working in the bakery who were spiritual types, right there in Yonkers. It was so raw in that bakery—more so than the Zendo, which is such a cocoon. You have the pressures, and the collection of people. It is very hard to learn in a silent Zendo where everyone is quiet."

Glassman: "I still feel—maybe it's wrong—that if you keep on practicing, even in the cave, there is no way of not working on social issues, only the method might be different. The person who hasn't grown in that way is the person who says you are only doing one thing at a time—the practice is only one thing. If you have been to the Bowery, that becomes who you are, it becomes part of your work."

Queen: "What issues are most important to you now?"

Glassman: "I am interested in the movement of Buddhism into the larger cultural context in this country—through lay participation and families. Social action is established now. It was always amazing to me how people could think it wasn't an element of Buddhism, but I don't hear that anymore. Maybe there are still some fanatics left! But we didn't import monastic Buddhism to the West. Everybody knows that, so we have been working to adapt those models to the lay context, starting afresh, from a state of unknowing, from a clean slate. I'm still not sure it will work."

Queen: "Do you think that *zazen* is fundamental?"

Glassman: "I'll be radical and say 'no.' For me personally it has been very important, and I can't imagine not having a daily sitting practice, but I have met wonderful people who are considered great teachers, who have wonderful sitting practices, who I don't consider very enlightened. And I have met wonderful people who don't practice *zazen* who I think are enlightened. So I would say no. If you mean, like the Sixth Patriarch, that the elimination of subject-object is indispensable, I would agree. But as simply sitting, it is not essential. There are many ways to actualize that state of oneness, of nonduality. I know Sufis and Jews who don't have a daily sitting practice. I know many Tibetans who don't sit everyday."

Queen: "You don't see a God-based practice as problematic?"

Glassman: "No. In some sense Pure Land or Shin Buddhism is a good example of that. Almost any practice, whether devotion or physical yoga, can lead to awakening. The only problem comes from creating dualism. I don't see anything wrong with these other practices."

Queen: "What would Maezumi Roshi have said about this year's retreat?"

Glassman: "There is a Yiddish expression that says, 'He would be a proud parent.' He was proud that I was friends with [the Asian engaged Buddhists] Maha Ghosananda and Ariyaratna, and he would have appreciated the presence of so many strong teachers in the Peacemaker Order today. Maezumi allowed each of us to go in our own direction in establishing American Zen. This is an amazing aspect of his transmission—it was so open. Toward the end Maezumi began to return to the old conceptions. But I studied with him during his more creative open years. The bodhisattva path goes in all directions. There are a number of my students who are not interested in social action, and that's okay."

Queen: "Is there a distinctive handicap for Americans in approaching the Dharma?"

Glassman: "I would say that the problem is not so much culture, but the newness. For some teachers the experience of Buddhism is so small, but there is an arrogance in thinking that they have the whole thing. Since I was pushing envelopes I would always run into resistance. In L. A. we started off with one house. I traveled to Japan in 1970. In New York we bought this much bigger place—the Greyston Mansion. I made the zendo in a separate place from the service hall. But some people were very resistant to the separation of the two halls—this was not kosher! They didn't realize that the halls were together in the L. A. house *because it was so small*, not because it was traditional. I saw that same thing time and again: clinging to something as true Buddhism that was simply an improvisation. So I think we can look at *upayas* [skillful means] that arise in the quest of enlightened experience, as long as we don't become attached to any of them."

Queen: "Are shifts in the belief system—the falling away of such massive beliefs as rebirth and spirits—inevitable?"

Glassman: "These issues are ahead of us. We are now working on our own versions of these cultural aspects. The role of the family is important in Jewish and Catholic culture, for example, so we are not completely in the dark in appreciating the Asian outlook on the sacredness of the family."

Queen: "The mainstream religious groups have a political side to them: the Anti-Defamation League, the pro-life and anti-war lobbies, the Moral Majority, and so forth. They are also practical, providing childcare and parking for weekend services. But the Buddhism of American converts is still a counterculture. People—mostly single people—like to sit on bare floors and go on meditation retreats. You sold the Greyston Mansion to start a bakery, and Joseph Goldstein is building cottages in the woods at Barre for long-term solitary practice—these aren't mainstream activities. So which direction do you think American Buddhism should go: to the mainstream or the margins?"

Glassman: "As it grows there will be people in both aspects. I was still in an active phase last year, moving in a more mainstream direction—the National Council of Churches [NCC], being on the board of some national organizations to deal with AIDS, the housing crisis, where Catholic Charities used to be the only interested group. We presented new models—Andrew Cuomo, secretary of housing, is a good friend—and I was a keynote speaker at a state-level conference on housing. People were interested in 'the Buddhist approach' to the problem. I thought we should have a voice even though there aren't many Buddhists who are interested in these issues. If Sulak [Sivaraksa, the Thai Buddhist activist] were in this country, that would be his place. I have an e-mail from Jay Rock, who heads the interfaith committee at the NCC. He wants to invite the Buddhists into the council. He wants to meet with me."

Queen: "You said you *had* been going in this direction—you mean before Jishu's death?"

Glassman: "I am operating in the spirit of Steven Levine's book, *You Only Have One Year to Go.* I want to spend time writing and spend time cultivating the ZPO teachers. I'm the main ZPO webmaster now. There has been pressure to settle down more in the past, but I was too busy with activism. I am very interested in the concept of family practice. I know my history has been to always move in new directions, but now I want to consolidate."

Queen: "From Zen master to webmaster?"

Glassman: "Yeah, that's it. But I can't forget the hungry ghosts. I was talking with a homeless guy in Berkeley the other day about the number of people who die on the streets in the Bay Area. I've been thinking of doing a fast about this."

ACKNOWLEDGMENT

I thank Bernie Glassman and members of the Peacemaker Order for taking time to reflect on the meaning and direction of engaged Buddhism in the West. I also thank Tony Stultz for helping to arrange my first visit to Yonkers, Eve Marko for providing useful documentary materials, and *Tikkun* magazine for permission to use passages from my article, "Buddhism, Activism, and Unknowing: A Day With Bernie Glassman," 13.1 (January–February 1998). This chapter is dedicated to the memory of Sandra Jishu Angyo Holmes Roshi.

NOTES

1. For an account of Ambedkar's Buddhism, and that of other engaged Buddhists in Asia, see Christopher S. Queen and Sallie B. King, eds., *Engaged Buddhism: Buddhist Liberation Movements in Asia* (Albany: State University of New York Press, 1996).
2. For a critical profile of Glassman's early development and leadership of the Zen Community of New York and the Greyston businesses in the 1980s, see Helen Tworkov, *Zen in America: Profiles of Five Teachers* (San Francisco: North Point Press, 1989), pp. 111–51. Reference to Glassman's place in the Soto lineage, page 112.
3. Bernard Glassman and Rick Fields, *Instructions to the Cook: A Zen Master's Lessons in Living a Life That Matters* (New York: Bell Tower, 1996), p. 12.
4. Bernard Glassman, *Bearing Witness: A Zen Master's Lessons in Making Peace* (New York: Bell Tower, 1998).
5. Glassman and Fields, *Instructions to the Cook*, p. 1.
6. Glassman, *Bearing Witness,* p. 1.
7. Bernard Tetsugen Glassman, "Instructions to the Cook: Zen Lessons in Living a Life That Matters," public talk, transcribed in *Buddhism in America: Proceedings of the First Buddhism in America Conference,* compiled by Al Rapaport and edited by Brian D. Hotchkiss (Rutland, VT: Charles E. Tuttle, 1998), p. 428.
8. Bernard Glassman, "Buddhism, Peacemaking, and Social Change," lecture at Harvard Divinity School, January 20, 1997 (unpublished).

9. For a narrative account of Glassman Roshi's teachers and his own development as a teacher, see Peter Matthiessen, *Nine-Headed Dragon River: Zen Journals 1969–1982* (Boston: Shambhala Publications, 1986). Matthiessen, the noted travel writer and novelist, is Glassman's first Dharma heir.

10. These associations were spelled out in the Harvard Divinity School talk of January 20, 1997. For a parallel analysis, using the famous *koan* "Why does the Western barbarian have no beard?" as his example, see Glassman in Rapaport, *Buddhism in America,* pp. 433–34.

11. Glassman and Fields, *Instructions to the Cook,* p. 51.

12. Glassman, *Bearing Witness,* p. xiv.

13. Tworkov, *Zen in America,* p. 113.

14. Thich Nhat Hanh, *Being Peace* (Berkeley, CA: Parallax Press, 1987), pp. 89–91.

15. Shunryu Suzuki, Zen Mind, *Beginner's Mind: Informal Talks on Zen Meditation and Practice* (New York: Weatherhill, 1970), p. 21.

16. Ibid., p. 116.

17. Seung Sahn, *Only Don't Know: The Teaching Letters of Zen Master Seung Sahn* (San Francisco: Four Seasons Foundation, 1982), p. x.

18. Richard P. Hayes, "The Internet as Window onto American Buddhism," in Duncan Williams and Christopher S. Queen, eds., *American Buddhism: Methods and Findings in Recent Scholarship* (Surrey, U.K.: Curzon Press, 1999), p. 170.

19. Stephen Batchelor, *Buddhism Without Beliefs: A Contemporary Guide to Awakening* (New York: Riverhead Books, 1997), p. xiii.

20. Ibid., pp. 17–18.

21. Christopher Queen, "Buddhism, Activism, and Unknowing: A Day with Bernie Glassman," *Tikkun* 13.1 (January/February 1998): 66.

22. Seng-tsan, *Hsin Hsin Ming: Verses on the Faith-Mind,* trans. and ed. Richard B. Clarke (Buffalo: White Pine Press, 1984), p. 5. These verses further recall the Taoist wisdom of Chuang-tzu (third century B.C.E.): "Tao is obscured when men understand only one of a pair of opposites, or concentrate only on a partial aspect of being. Then clear expression also becomes muddled by mere wordplay, affirming this one aspect and denying all the rest. Hence the wrangling of Confucians and Mohists; each denies what the other affirms and affirms what the other denies. What use is this struggle to set up 'No' against 'Yes,' and 'Yes' against 'No'? Better to abandon this hopeless effort and seek true light!" From Thomas Merton, ed., *The Way of Chuang Tzu* (New York: New Directions, 1965), p. 42. And these verses further recall the opening of the Tao Te Ching of Lao-tzu (sixth century B.C.E.): "Existence is beyond the power of words to define: terms may be used but are none of them absolute. In the beginning of heaven and earth there were no words. Words came out of the womb of matter; and whether a man dispassionately sees to the core of life or

passionately sees the surface, the core and the surface are essentially the same, words making them seem different only to express appearance. If name be needed, wonder names them both: from wonder to wonder existence opens." From Witter Bynner, trans., *The Way of Life According to Lao Tzu* (New York: Capricorn, 1942), p. 25.

23. Thich Nhat Hanh, *Being Peace*, pp. 90–91.

24. For a comprehensive collection of scholarly articles on Buddhism and ecology, see Mary Evelyn Tucker and Duncan Ryuken Williams, eds., *Buddhism and Ecology: The Interconnection of Dharma and Deeds* (Cambridge, MA: Harvard Center for the Study of World Religions, 1998).

25. A comprehensive yet succinct presentation of Buddhist philosophy is that of Junjiro Takakusu, *The Essentials of Buddhist Philosophy* (Delhi: Motilal Banarsidass, 1975).

26. Thich Nhat Hanh, p. 92.

27. Ibid., p. 87. For thorough accounts of the philosophy of Hua-Yen Buddhism, see Garma C. C. Chang, *The Buddhist Teaching of Totality: The Philosophy of Hwa Yen Buddhism* (University Park: The Pennsylvania State University Press, 1974); Francis H. Cook, *Hua-yen Buddhism: The Jewel Net of Indra* (University Park: The Pennsylvania State University Press, 1977); and Steve Odin, *Process Metaphysics and Hua-yen Buddhism* (Albany: State University of New York Press, 1982).

28. See Glassman and Fields, *Instructions to the Cook,* for the story of the Greyston Mandala of for-profit and not-for-profit companies, and their emergence from a Zen-based vision of public/private/social/political/spiritual interdependence.

29. Bernard Glassman, Harvard Divinity School lecture, January 20, 1997.

30. From the unpublished liturgy booklet of the Zen Peacemaker Order.

31. An account of Thomas's American peace walk may be found on the website for his Zaltho Foundation: <http://www.access.ch/spuren/Claude Thomas.html>.

32. "Gate of Sweet Nectar: Kan Ro Mon," unpublished liturgy used by the Zen Peacemaker Order, 1997.

33. Glassman and Fields, *Instructions to the Cook*, pp. 15–16.

34. Matthiessen, *Nine-Headed Dragon River*, pp. 125–26.

35. Ibid., p. 125.

36. Ibid., p. 126.

37. See the Peacemaker community tribute to its co-founder at <http://www.peacemakercommunity.org/jishu.htm>.

WALKING FOR PEACE: NIPPONZAN MYOHOJI

Paula Green

At the age of ninety-eight
I attend the disarmament session
Beating the drum,
Proclaiming to the world
That all military, all nuclear weapons
Must disappear.
One sky, four oceans
Entirely at peace.

NICHIDATSU FUJII, 1983

IN JAPAN, ONE'S SIXTIETH BIRTHDAY is honored as a significant milestone, marking a passage toward the respected elder years. August 6, 1945, the day the United States unleashed the devastating fires of nuclear weapons on Hiroshima, the Venerable Nichidatsu Fujii, founder of the Nipponzan Myohoji order of Japanese Buddhism, turned sixty. From that day of conflagration, Venerable Fujii determined to devote his life to the abolition of nuclear weapons and the construction of peace pagodas. A monk since 1916, a disciple of the thirteenth-century prophet Nichiren and a Japanese Buddhist with a profound spiritual tie to Mahatma Gandhi, Venerable Fujii held an unwavering commitment to nonviolence and peace. His catastrophic sixtieth birthday intensified and reinforced his certainty that human survival depends on the ability to turn away from materialistic civilizations that have caused so much destruction, war and misery:

> Civilization has nothing to do with having electric lights, airplanes, or manufacturing nuclear bombs. It has nothing to do with killing human beings, destroying things or waging war. Civilization is to hold one another in mutual affection and respect. What constitutes its foundation is not the establishment of a judicial system but religious faith that seeks gentleness, peace, simplicity and righteousness.[1]

NICHIREN BUDDHISM

Nichidatsu Fujii's spiritual ancestor and mentor was Nichiren, who lived under the Japanese Kamakura Shogunate six hundred years before Fujii's birth. Fujii and Nichiren each perceived their own era as a time of *mappo*, or "Dharma in decline." They shared a belief that only true spiritual teachings could "release all sentient beings from the evil forces of the prevailing order"[2] and overcome the rampant chaos and terror characteristic of *mappo*. Nichiren and Fujii's unique Buddhism and ardent social Dharma evolved from the *Lotus Sutra,* which inspired in both monks an unfaltering mission to lead society from aggression and militarism to spiritual harmony. In the twentieth century, Fujii would bring the *Lotus Sutra* to India, honoring his mentor's prediction. Fujii believed that the acceptance of the *Lotus Sutra* chant by Gandhi fulfilled the prediction of Nichiren that the *Lotus Sutra* would root itself once again in Indian soil. The phrase *namu myoho renge kyo* (rhythmically chanted *Na Mu Myo Ho Ren Ge Kyo*) means "Homage to the *Lotus Sutra*" or "Praise to the wonderful Dharma of the *Lotus Sutra*." But followers of Nipponzan Myohoji say that the chant cannot be fully translated—its ineffable meaning reveals itself to devotees only through time.[3]

Recitation of the chant *Na Mu Myo Ho Ren Ge Kyo* forms the core daily practice of the Nipponzan Myohoji order of Japanese Buddhism. Nichiren's fervent social conscience and the chant of the *Lotus Sutra* would come alive again in the person of Nichidatsu Fujii, and later spring forth in the United States through the lineage of Nipponzan Myohoji monks and nuns ordained by Fujii. In the United States today, the chant can be heard at anti-nuclear demonstrations, at vigils for social justice and on walks for peace across the length and breadth of the land. The chant unites Nipponzan Myohoji, from Nichiren to Nichidatsu Fujii to the disciples in the United States.

Japan in the thirteenth century, the time of Nichiren, was a period of political instability and natural disasters. Born to a family of fishermen in 1222, the young boy who would become Nichiren revealed an unusual childhood zest for spiritual learning and at twelve prayed to the bodhisattva Kokuzo, asking to become the wisest man in Japan.[4] Drawn to the study of Buddhism, Nichiren entered the temple at Mt. Kiyosumi and was ordained there at age sixteen. In order to ascertain the crucial teachings of the Buddha, he immersed himself in systematic study of all ten schools of Buddhism then existing in Japan: Tendai, Shingon, Pure Land, Zen, and the six schools of the Nara Period. Known as an exceptional young monk, Nichiren yearned for the pure essence of Buddhism, its central and ethical truth. Experiencing grave doubts about all the Buddhist schools, Nichiren persisted in his quest to encounter a devotional practice that would engage his heart, uplift his countrymen, and unify his vision.

Nichiren believed that the true teachings of the Buddha should address both the purification of the mind and the purification of society, which for him were inseparable. Religious teachings, Nichiren proclaimed, must respond to society as a whole and to people trapped in the raging violence of man and nature. He struggled over the paucity of relevant teachings available to help the suffering people. He blamed Pure Land Buddhism for promising happiness in the next life rather than offering meaningful answers to the political strife and natural disasters of this life. As he labored to grasp a unifying doctrine for a Buddhist spiritual life that would dispel his doubts, conditions worsened in medieval Japan:

> There were problems to vex the wisest philosopher-king confusing 13th century Japan. The imperial regime had broken down, its divided remnants fought each other while the new feudal organization really ruled the country from the north; the civilian population besides enduring a civil war suffered from fires and plagues and all sorts of natural and unnatural calamities; while the nobles sought escape from responsibility in the aestheticism of a degenerate court life and a ritualistic cult of Buddhism.[5]

Prolonged anguish and deep quest brought Nichiren to the *Lotus Sutra,* which revealed itself to him as the scripture appropriate for this time of decline and ruin. In 1253 he returned to Mt. Kiyosumi and there, facing the rising sun, Nichiren first chanted *Na Mu Myo Ho Ren Ge Kyo,* devoting himself to the entire *Lotus Sutra.* He changed his name to Nichiren; *nichi* means the sun, which eliminates darkness, and *ren* is the lotus, which brings forth a pure white blossom from the mire of the swamp.[6] Embracing the sutra that culminated his search for a Buddhist truth that responded to his grave concerns, Nichiren took *Na Mu Myo Ho Ren Ge Kyo* to the people. Nichiren described himself as a lone individual sent by the Buddha "to bring peace to this land that has been laid waste by continual warfare."[7] Nichiren challenged the state, the religious establishment and the mighty Shogunate with his faith and zeal. He believed absolutely that only adherence to the teachings of the *Lotus Sutra* would prevent adversity. He predicted further disasters, and as calamities such as the wars of rebellion appeared, Nichiren grew even more tenacious and demanding.

Nichiren developed a missionary fire: persistent, determined, driven and uncompromising. He implored the state and the Buddhist leaders to adopt what he ardently believed were the only correct teachings. He suffered moral anguish at the misguided direction of those who governed and attempted to awaken them to righteousness and deeper understanding. His extreme criticisms of the regime and harsh judgments of Pure Land Buddhism infuriated the ruling class, earning him several extended periods of punishment by exile and an attempted beheading. Despite his perilous circumstances, Nichiren persevered without reservation in his efforts to reform the corrupt political administrations, establish a righteous way among the people and promote the ascendancy of the *Lotus Sutra*.

Rissho Ankoku Ron (Establishing Righteousness to Secure the Peace of Nations), a treatise written by Nichiren urging the government to follow a true moral and ethical path, was three times rebuked by the Kamakura Shogunate. *Rissho Ankoku Ron* asserted that misguided religion turned the human mind and the entire nation in a chaotic and destructive direction.[8] Those who resort to violence, he wrote, will be destroyed by violence. Corrupt politics must be abandoned, Nichiren predicted, or internal contention and foreign invasion will further ruin the country. The text preached that "when those who disparage the Dharma are dismissed and those who follow the right way are honored, there will be tranquillity in the entire land."[9] With characteristic fervor, this treatise and Nichiren's five other texts implored the populace and those who ruled to follow a life of righteousness. Only through righteousness and the elimination of a debased realm, Nichiren believed, would people experience a spiritual and true state of security and peace. He longed for redemption in the hearts and minds of people, but instead received rebuke, persecution, and banishment.

Nichiren felt that his duty as a faithful Buddhist was to confront evil and protest against unjust laws that contradict the Dharma. To fulfill one's obligation to the rulers required that he and other believers admonish the leaders, present them with the authentic Buddhist laws, and sacrifice everything, including one's life, if necessary, to propagate the true Dharma:

> If you would be free from the offense committed by the country as a whole, make remonstrance to the rulers and be yourself prepared for death or exile. Is it not said in the Scripture, 'never shrink from sacrificing the body for the sake of the Incomparable Way'...That we have, from the remotest past down to the present, not attained Buddhahood is simply due to our cowardice, in that we have always been afraid of these perils and have not dared to stand up publicly for the Truth. The future will never be otherwise so long as we remain cowards.[10]

The Lotus Sutra

It was in the *Lotus Sutra* that Nichiren found unqualified inspiration. Nichiren asserted that the *Lotus Sutra* is the sole source of human salvation: the only religious expression capable of responding to *mappo*, the one truth, and the singular prevention of further strife and calamity. To bring forth the true teachings of the *Lotus Sutra* for the salvation of all people, and to protect the leaders and the population from what he experienced as their own blindness, he pleaded, implored and harangued them to adhere to the sutra.

The twenty-eight chapters of the *Hokekyo*, the Chinese translation of the *Lotus Sutra*, are divided into two parts. The first fourteen chapters describe the path and the laws of the historical Buddha Shakyamuni, while the latter half of the sutra concerns itself with the eternal buddha who exists in all time. Aware of the complexity of the *Lotus Sutra*, Nichiren declared that wholeheartedly chanting *Na Mu Myo Ho Ren Ge Kyo* would develop faith and purify the mind of the devotee, because the chant itself contains the essence of the sutra. Chanting with devotion and respect, he believed, would bring spiritual benefit to the believer.

When the entire nation converted to accept the *Lotus Sutra*, Nichiren proclaimed, the suffering of the *mappo* age would be replaced with the realization of our true nature and would usher in a realm of peace and tranquillity. The heavenly paradise would then exist on earth.[11] The sutra includes passages praising those who, like Nichiren, live its truths and fulfill its prophecies. Nichiren ardently embraced these passages, which he devotedly chanted and which sustained his difficult life:[12]

> This sutra is so difficult to keep.
> If anyone keeps it a short time, I shall be pleased,
> And so will all the Buddhas.
> Such a one as this will be praised by all the Buddhas;
> Such a one is brave; such a one is zealous;
> Such a one is named precept-keeper and dhuta-observer;
> Speedily shall one attain the supreme Buddha-way.
> One who, in coming generations,
> Can read and keep this sutra
> Is truly a child of the Buddha.
> Dwelling in the stage of pure goodness,
> After the Buddha's extinction,
> One who can expound its meaning
> Will be the eye of the world

For Gods and humans.
One who, in the final age of fear,
Can preach it even for a moment,
By all Gods and humans
Will be worshipped.[13]

Nichiren the Prophet

In his later years Nichiren came to identify himself, with characteristic zeal, with the bodhisattva Eminent Conduct (Vishishtacharitra) prophesied by Shakyamuni Buddha in the *Lotus Sutra*. Nichiren himself believed, but did not insist, that he was the spiritual reincarnation of the bodhisattva Eminent Conduct and thus had received the transmission of the *Lotus Sutra* directly from Shakyamuni Buddha. In chapter 21 of the *Lotus Sutra* there is reference to a messenger from the Tathagata. Nichiren felt himself to be this messenger and a servant of the Buddha, and this produced in him unbounded joy, which he described as "tears of ambrosia."[14] Nichiren wrote of his destiny: "Common mortal that I am, I am not well aware of the past, yet in the present I am unmistakably the one who is realizing the Lotus of Truth....I, Nichiren, a native of Awa, am most probably the man whose mission it is...to propagate the doctrines of the Lotus of Truth."[15]

Modern followers of Nichiren in the traditional Nichiren Schools consider him a prophet and the reincarnation of the bodhisattva Eminent Conduct. In Nipponzan Myohoji, the likeness of Maha (Great) Bodhisattva Nichiren occupies a prominent place on the altar, just beneath the Buddha. Persecuted and criminalized by the state, Nichiren was clearly a visionary. His concern for the common welfare and the promotion of spiritual righteousness, his vocal opposition to militarism and warfare, and his unremitting attempts to awaken the populace to the social and political causes of suffering place him as a singular figure in Japanese Buddhist history:

> If Japan ever produced a prophet or a religious man of prophetic zeal, Nichiren was the man. He stands as almost a unique figure in the history of Buddhism, not alone because of his persistence through hardship and persecution, but for his unshaken conviction that he himself was the messenger of Buddha....Not only one of the most learned men of his time, but most earnest in his prophetic aspirations, he was a strong man, a powerful writer, and a man of tender heart. He was born in 1222, the son of a fisherman, and died in 1282, a saint and a prophet.[16]

NICHIDATSU FUJII

A young Japanese monk named Gyosho Fujii, himself living in an age of declining Dharma and catastrophe, revived the teachings of Nichiren for the twentieth century and became the founder and preceptor of Nipponzan Myohoji. Fujii found inspiration in the passionate spiritual yearnings and radical social vision of Nichiren. Echoing Nichiren's devotion to the penetrating wisdom of the *Lotus Sutra*, Fujii brought the teachings forward for our own time.

Like his mentor, Fujii began life in rural Japan, where he was born in 1885. In 1903, when he was nineteen, Fujii was ordained as a monk in the Nichiren tradition. Spending his twenties exploring the many streams of thought and practice in Japanese Buddhism, Fujii studied in the various schools of Buddhism investigated by Nichiren six centuries earlier. Legendary stories describe Fujii's genius as a student and meditator, including a two-year practice period with Rinzai Zen monks and masters, who urged him to remain with them.[17] Many offers of scholarship and temple leadership were bestowed on this gifted young man. Fujii realized, however, that his teachers and mentors could neither anticipate nor describe the meaning of his life. He would have to find guidance and determine the journey for himself. Thus Fujii left monastic study to strengthen his own Buddhist path and ascertain his relationship to Nichiren and the *Lotus Sutra*. As Nichiren had been thirty-two when he began his true teaching, Fujii waited until he was thirty-three to begin his own mission, thereby demonstrating his respect and humility.[18]

Fujii's studies of Nichiren, a prophetic dream about Nichiren, and experiments with long periods of fasting and severe self-discipline confirmed Fujii's decision to follow the teachings of Nichiren and to propagate the chant *Na Mu Myo Ho Ren Ge Kyo* to the accompaniment of a handheld prayer drum. A rather extraordinary experience clarified his mind. The second time Fujii fasted under a freezing waterfall near the ancient Buddhist city of Nara he was thirty-three years old and undertaking a final effort to determine his destiny. In search of resolution for his spiritual questions, for seven days he took neither food nor drink, slept little, and endured the intense cold of a winter waterfall. At the completion of his fast, Fujii heard a drum and then watched as a figure of an old man wearing shabby clothes appeared, beating a prayer drum and carrying a baby on his back. The stranger climbed the hill near the waterfall. Fujii, astounded by the apparition, inquired about the identity of the man, who announced himself as the bodhisattva Eminent Conduct and identified the baby as Shakyamuni Buddha. Fujii insisted the encounter was not a dream or a metaphor, but a physical experience mani-

fested from the "total openness, spiritual vulnerability, and intense consciousness which placed him on a different realm."[19] Because this encounter
confirmed a prophecy of chapter 15 in the *Lotus Sutra*, at that moment Fujii
realized the completion of his search and knew irrevocably that his path
would be to bring the *Lotus Sutra* and *Na Mu Myo Ho Ren Ge Kyo* to the
world. He ordained himself as a direct disciple of Shakyamuni Buddha and
Nichiren.

Fujii understood the *Rissho Ankoku Ron* written by Nichiren to be a
book of prophecy that would establish true enlightened Dharma for all peoples. He also believed that escaping from the tasks of this world through
focusing attention on rebirth in the Pure Land is an erroneous interpretation
of Buddhism. Nichiren observed that Buddhism in Japan had become "isolated from and indifferent to the happenings in the world because it tends to
be occupied in seeking solutions of one's own spiritual matters, such as one's
own anxiety, suffering and grief."[20] Fujii noted that "if we fail to prevent
[war], one's desire to secure himself is nothing but a dream."[21] The ethical
and social dimensions of *Rissho Ankoku Ron* further affirmed Fujii's
discipleship:

> *Rissho Ankoku Ron* is a great book of prophecy of the world....Nichiren
> applied the words expounded by the Buddha to a larger unit of human life,
> the nation....He urged the nation to profess faith in the genuine and cor-
> rect teachings of Shakyamuni Buddha...who is the Preceptor of this actu-
> al world rather than the world to come.[22]

Nichidatsu Fujii adapted, expanded, and developed *Rissho Ankoku Ron*
for international application, clarifying the connections between religion
and society and amplifying the relationships between thought and deed. He
wrote: "It is thought that religion is a question of an individual's mind and
that there is no harm for him to believe whatever he likes. This is wrong.
What a person believes and thinks is manifested in society. A mistaken
thought will become a social problem."[23]

Nichidatsu Fujii began to practice the *Lotus Sutra* publicly in 1918, traveling first in remote and austere regions of Manchuria, Korea, and China.
Identified by some scholars as an "Asianist" rather than a pacifist, the young
monk harbored grave doubts about the European and U.S. presence in Asia,
which he feared would spread dominant values of materialism, colonialism,
and secular life. He hoped that Japan and other Asian countries would preserve their more spiritually oriented civilizations. However, as he observed
Japan's behavior toward its neighbors, he recognized the evils of dominance
and colonial exploitation by his own government, and criticized Japanese

ambitions for war against China. Walking and beating the prayer drum while chanting *Na Mu Myo Ho Ren Ge Kyo* throughout Japan, he warned of the dangers of the growing militancy of Japanese thinking. As a monk, Fujii took responsibility and made efforts to subdue Japanese aggression toward its neighbors, feeling that warfare would harm victims and warriors alike. "Earnest devotion to killing and depriving of life is the accepted glory. When our country comes to admire soldiers and find pleasure in killing people, the country will immediately lose Buddha's love and become vanquished and ruined."[24] Commencing with these experiences in his youth and lasting throughout his extraordinarily long life, Fujii consistently focused his concerns on militarism and the devastation of warfare, balancing these passions with an equally committed spiritual and moral discipline. His conversion to absolute pacifism came to its maturity after World War II, but in the years building up to the war, Fujii increased his denunciation of the Japanese authorities and their military ambitions. He attempted to convert as well as criticize, to "awaken the submerged mind away from killing."[25]

Attracted by his strength of character and radical ethical views, followers and devotees began to gather around Nichidatsu Fujii. He and the disciples whom he ordained opened several temples in Japan in the 1920s, after which Fujii left for India. His decision to go to India, which would bring him to Gandhi and thus profoundly influence him and the moral direction of Nipponzan Myohoji, arose to fulfill a prophecy made by Nichiren. Fujii wrote: "Seven hundred years have elapsed and not a single one has propagated the chant of *Na Mu Myo Ho Ren Ge Kyo* to India. If this Dharma does not return to the Western Heaven (India), the prediction of our great master Maha Bodhisattva Nichiren will not be realized. Therefore I decided to go to India, even alone, to walk about chanting."[26]

India and the War Years

During his extensive travels in India (1931–1938) to regenerate Buddhism there in the land of its birth, he met and soon became closely associated with Mahatma Gandhi. It was Gandhi who first called him Guruji (spiritual teacher), a title by which his disciples and the lay public have affectionately called him ever since. Guruji joined Gandhi at his ashram in Wardha, where Gandhi actively took up the practice of the chant and drum as part of his daily prayer. A deep recognition transpired between these two spiritual seekers who were so nourished by their Hindu or Buddhist faiths. Guruji delighted at Gandhi's embrace of the drum and his attempts to learn the chant of *Na Mu Myo Ho Ren Ge Kyo*, which is still used at the Gandhi

Ashram in Wardha during daily prayer. Gandhi later wrote to Guruji that "the subtle and profound sound of your drum resonates in my ear."[27] Guruji, much discouraged by the Japanese consuls in India, celebrated Gandhi's acceptance: "Ah, my long and cherished desire…has finally found its time. The voice of the 30 million people rejoicing in the sound of Dharma was now heard through the melting voice of joy that passed Gandhi-ji's lips here at the Ashram of Wardha."[28]

Already committed to the realization of a spiritually based civilization, Guruji's deep ties with Gandhi further developed his mind and enlarged his vision. Through the inspiration of Gandhi and his remarkable social, political, and spiritual experiments, Guruji extended active spiritual support toward the nonviolent independence movement of the Indian people. Profoundly moved and influenced by Gandhi, Guruji later reflected that "Nonviolent resistance, a gentle movement through which people are spiritually united and raise their voices of protest, is the only way to extinguish the violent fire that would result in human annihilation."[29] Fujii Guruji did propagate *Na Mu Myo Ho Ren Ge Kyo* in India, establishing temples, making pilgrimages to Buddhist holy sites, and firming a commitment to re-establish Buddhism in Rajgir, where the Buddha had first preached the *Lotus Sutra* on Vulture Peak.

Deeply concerned during his India years about Japan's expansion of military power, Guruji returned from India in 1938. He presented the defense ministers with ashes of the Buddha, which he had received in Sri Lanka, and proposed the adoption of peaceful national and international policies. Guruji suffered as he watched the false gods of militarism dominate the Japanese people. During the war years of 1939-1945, Guruji and his followers moved actively within and beyond Japan, chanting and beating the prayer drum, crying out for the early termination of war and the establishment of righteousness. Preaching Nichiren's *Rissho Ankoku Ron* for Japan and for the world, Guruji called for "a radical change in man's religious consciousness and at the same time a new kind of human community and civilization." He condemned "modern Western civilization itself, in as much as it is materialistic—as devoid of moral and religious faith…. True civilization," he wrote, "is necessarily spiritual."[30]

In the waning days of World War II, on the sixtieth birthday of Nichidatsu Fujii, the atomic bomb fell on Hiroshima and the United States launched the world into the nuclear age. For forty more years, until his death in 1985 at age one hundred, Guruji and his disciples would build peace pagodas, initiate long peace walks, and seek to rid the human community of the scourge of nuclear weapons.

PEACE PAGODAS

The history of peace pagodas, known as *shanti stupas* in India and much of Asia, stretches back two thousand five hundred years to the first stupas, which enshrined the relics of Shakyamuni Buddha. However, according to Nipponzan Myohoji, a previous history of stupas and buddhas prefigure the historical records.[31] Chapter 11 of the *Lotus Sutra*, preached by the Buddha, already mentioned the stupa of the Buddha of Abundant Treasures, who existed since "no beginning," eons ago, in time beyond our comprehension. The Buddha of Abundant Treasures appears wherever the *Lotus Sutra* is taught and is depicted by the Nichiren School alongside Shakyamuni Buddha, with a stupa arising between them. The manifestation of these two buddhas and the stupa represent a vast span of time and universality, both encompassing and exceeding the historical Shakyamuni Buddha of two thousand five hundred years ago.

Na Mu Myo Ho Ren Ge Kyo is also understood as the name of the eternal buddha. Thus the construction of peace pagodas is directly related to the *Lotus Sutra* and is intimately connected to the practice of Nichiren and Nichidatsu Fujii. The arising of the stupa was predicted by Nichiren and foretold in the *Lotus Sutra*, whose eleventh chapter title is translated from the Chinese as "Beholding the Precious Stupa." The chapter depicts an exquisite stupa that sprang up in front of the Buddha:

> It was decorated with all kinds of precious things, splendidly adorned with 5000 parapets...countless banners and flags; hung with jeweled garlands...gem bells...fragrance of sandalwood...streamers of gold, silver, lapis lazuli...flowers...perfumes...reaching up to the palaces of the four heavenly kings.[32]

After the cremation of the body of Shakyamuni Buddha, his ashes were distributed to his closest disciples. All who had obtained a portion of the relics created stupas in their respective villages, each stupa to be venerated as a symbol of the living Buddha. Legend records that in the third century B.C.E., Emperor Ashoka further divided the relics of the Buddha, causing eighty-four thousand stupas to be built in India and beyond. Over time additional subdivisions were made and relics taken to various lands, where additional stupas arose. When visiting the holy mountain of Sri Pada in Sri Lanka, Guruji had unexpectedly received the gift of Buddha relics from the head monk of a Sri Lankan temple. "I considered it to be a result of the grace of the Buddha and graciously accepted his favor."[33] Taking this offering as an auspicious sign for the future arising of peace pagodas, Guruji wore the relics in a silver box around his neck while in India. When he returned to Japan in 1938-1939, he presented this treasure to the Japanese government.

Nichidatsu Fujii revived the ancient tradition of stupas after the bombings of Hiroshima and Nagasaki, building the order's first peace pagoda in Japan. Fujii believed that out of the ravages of World War II, people's pure desire for peace could be awakened:

> The appearing of a Pagoda touches the hearts and minds of all people. Those who venerate this Pagoda absolutely reject nuclear warfare and firmly believe that a peaceful world will be manifested. The vision of a Pagoda has the power to bring about a spiritual transformation. It illumines the dawn of a spiritual civilization.[34]

Today there are approximately eighty Nipponzan Myohoji peace pagodas worldwide, in Asian countries as well as Europe and the United States, with construction currently underway for Africa's first peace pagoda, in Zambia. Striking in form and design, usually constructed with a large concrete dome as much as one hundred feet high, the gleaming white peace pagodas often contain niches with carvings depicting the life of Shakyamuni Buddha, decorative concrete lotus petals, carved walkways, and elaborate pinnacles. Sacred Buddha relics are enshrined within each pagoda. Many are surrounded by lovingly crafted Japanese gardens, presenting altogether a tranquil and prayerful environment. "It appears to rise, as a prayer, from the very elements surrounding it—the earth, air, water and sky. All people, regardless of their creed, may feel its appeal to the inviolable sacredness of life."[35]

Developing Fortitude and Virtue

As a child in late nineteenth century Japan, Nichidatsu Fujii suffered from weakness, for which his mother prescribed long walks; as her son's strength increased, she made offerings in thankfulness. This provided the future monk with warm memories of both walking and spiritual practice, each of which would become pivotal in his life. Guruji adapted the custom of long walks for peace early in his career as a monk, taking his inspiration from Nichiren, who walked the streets of Kamakura chanting for righteousness and peace. Shakyamuni Buddha walked through what is now the Indian state of Bihar in order to expound the Dharma, making pilgrimages, mingling freely with the populace, teaching and meditating. Nipponzan Myohoji monks consider walking with spiritual intention as natural medicine that yields patience, fortitude, and virtue.[36] Walking is nonexploitive, preserves natural resources and allows contemplation of an entire materialistic and mechanical way of life. From his earliest positive experiences with walking in Manchuria and Korea, through his observation of Gandhi's walks with tens of thousands of disciples, and until his life ended, Guruji advocated and participated in walks.

Guruji also felt that "At a time when all sentient beings are about to fall into the abyss of unrelievable suffering, recitation of sutras in temples or sitting on mountains in meditation is of no use."[37] He believed that in times of *mappo*, minds and hearts are too crude to benefit from refined practices such as sitting meditation, and that perhaps walking would be better "medicine." For as long as he could walk, Guruji led his disciples in walking practice throughout Japan, India, Sri Lanka, and later the West. Each year on the August anniversary of the nuclear bombing, Guruji and members of the order walked from Tokyo to Hiroshima and Nagasaki. Confined to a wheel chair in his nineties, Guruji still participated in walks, believing deeply in the power of visible prayer among the people. He reminded his monks and nuns not to be concerned about their own comfort or welfare, but to sacrifice themselves for the sake of chanting *Na Mu Myo Ho Ren Ge Kyo* and "uniting the minds and hearts of all people."[38]

One Hundred Years of Life

Two significant and intertwined practices most deeply convey the Dharma teachings of the Venerable Nichidatsu Fujii. Guruji disciplined his life in faithfulness to *Rissho Ankoku Ron*, wanting to establish among the populace the "true law of righteousness to secure the peace of nations." He devoted himself to the realization of a spiritual civilization and to raising awareness about the delusions of militarism and materialism, first in his native Japan and later as a world citizen. Guruji called for a radical change in religious consciousness and a human community based on fundamental spiritual truths. He called for this social transformation now, not in eternal life but in the midst of our soiled human condition and decaying circumstances. He believed that the work of religion included the purification of the debased minds and occluded views of human beings, who fail to see the essential bodhisattva nature in each other, thus causing undue harm and suffering.

This practice complements the spiritual discipline of *tangyo raihai*, which translates the Japanese "practice only reverence to others."[39] *Tangyo raihai* is expressed through the custom of humble bowing and genuine obeisance that Guruji showed to each and every person without exception. Guruji felt that if all people embraced the practice of putting palms together and bowing deeply in authentic respect, the consciousness of reverence would develop and thoughts of violence would cease to arise in the human mind, thus purifying both the individual and the society. Guruji also believed that chanting *Na Mu Myo Ho Ren Ge Kyo* in all greeting and parting demonstrates profound reverence to others. The bowing gesture as a sign of humility and an acknowledgment of the buddha-nature within each being originated with a bodhisattva described in the *Lotus Sutra* as Sadaparibhuta, "the bodhisattva who never despises." The discipline of "never despising" requires "absolute nonresistance and absolute nonviolence."[40] Taken together, *Rissho Ankoku Ron* and *tangyo raihai* demonstrate Guruji's consistency between reflection and action, weaving the inner refinement of self-transformation of Venerable Fujii: the peace of nations secured through the practice of respect and mutual veneration.

The contributions of Venerable Fujii toward the abolition of nuclear weapons and the awakening of humankind to a new civilization span his extraordinarily long life. In addition to the construction of peace pagodas and the undertaking of peace walks, Guruji faithfully nurtured his vision of a harmonious and nonviolent world community. His energy unflinching and his spirit strong until the very end, Guruji traveled worldwide to participate in the great events of the times, including the United Nations Second Special Session on Disarmament, world conferences on religion and peace, ceremonies, pilgrimages and other gatherings where his chanting and drumming the *Odaimoku* (O-, "honored," *daimoku*, "title," the chant *Na Mu Myo Ho Ren Ge Kyo*), his eloquent speeches and his humble practice of bowing with palms together touched a deep spiritual longing for peace in a war-weary world. Among his special honors, the Venerable Nichidatsu Fujii received the renowned Jawaharlal Nehru Award for International Understanding in 1979 for his "untiring struggle against violence and for the establishment of peace in the world."[41]

Before his death, land was consecrated for the first peace pagoda in the United States, and three peace pagodas were dedicated in Europe. Guruji had unified the fractured disarmament movement in Japan, spoken out against the United States' war in Vietnam, established connections with Native Americans and African Americans struggling for justice, and left a small order of monks and nuns dedicated to carrying forth his vision.

In January of 1985, at the age of one hundred, the Venerable Nichidatsu Fujii died in Japan.

Head and eyebrows white with snowy age,
A monk of ninety-nine years
Worships the power of the great mercy of Buddha
Entreating the conversion of the world—
When everyone feels the terror of final conflagrations—
To peace and tranquillity.

Nichidatsu Fujii, 1984

NIPPONZAN MYOHOJI IN AMERICA

By the 1970s, when the sangha first established itself in the United States, there were approximately 250 monks and nuns ordained by Guruji in the Nipponzan Myohoji order, disciplined in the strict and self-sacrificing practices of the order and committed to the bodhisattva path of liberating all beings. In addition to the more traditional monastic vows of obedience, poverty, and celibacy, these monks and nuns undertook a further commitment to rid the world of nuclear weapons. Guruji was demanding of his disciples, admonishing them not to grow lazy or self-satisfied, never to wear "gold brocaded satin damask"[42] and always to place the needs of others before their own. Guruji taught them to be tolerant regarding the beliefs of others but uncompromising in the maintenance of their own. Like their mentor, the monks and nuns follow the teaching of *Rissho Ankoku Ron* and the discipline of bowing humbly to all persons. He encouraged "these young disciples who depart on a journey to unknown lands, chanting the *Odaimoku*, where they have nothing to depend on, where people speak tongues unknown to them. These young disciples are spreading the Buddhadharma in Europe and the United States."[43]

Nipponzan Myohoji practices differ from the rituals of Dharma common to most American practitioners. Nipponzan Myohoji monks and nuns do not engage in the silent meditation familiar to American Buddhists. The chanting of *Na Mu Myo Ho Ren Ge Kyo* is their daily practice, both while walking and while seated at the altar. Their temples, quite elaborate in Japan and generally less embellished in the United States and Europe, contain altars with images of the Buddha and Nichiren, loving photos of their Guruji, incense pots, flowers, miniature peace pagodas and whatever gifts of food have been offered to the temple. The altar is abundant, and the temple decorative and colorful, all in rather startling contrast to the severe austerity of the more well-known Japanese Zen temples. In their daily practice in America or Japan, the monks and nuns chant with a hand drum or a large floor drum, recite chapters of the *Lotus Sutra*, light incense, offer food to the Buddha on the altar, bow to each other and to the images of their teachers, and leave the temple to circumambulate the peace pagoda, chanting and bowing to the statues of the Buddha. Each ritual aspect of their worship is precisely choreographed and carefully obeyed. Every month the monks and nuns fast, chant, and pray steadily for three days. To commemorate the enlightenment of Shakyamuni Buddha, they fast for eight days in December, observing a tradition borrowed from Japanese Zen.[44]

A significant aspect of Nipponzan Myohoji Buddhism in the United States involves walking practice that often extends for months, covering fifteen to twenty miles daily in all conditions of weather. The disciples work laboriously under challenging circumstances building peace pagodas and temples, maintain strict discipline, practice faithfully, and seem to sleep little. On the other hand, they maintain solid friendships within and beyond the order, celebrate intensely, laugh, joke, and enjoy life zestfully. Ordination in Nipponzan Myohoji requires heartiness of body and spirit.

Important decisions are taken by members of the worldwide order with respectful consultation among the hierarchy of elder monks in Japan. Spiritual inspiration to undertake a yearlong walk, practice in a particular region of the world, or manifest a peace pagoda, arises within the heart and mind of the individual disciple. To clearly discern a spiritual calling, the disciple seeks advice from the elders and guidance from the sangha. Guruji taught the monks and nuns to "avoid the arrogance" of solitary decision making and to seek collective wisdom. Following Buddha's teaching, he encouraged harmony, respect, and veneration within the ordained sangha, especially toward the elders. Nipponzan Myohoji monks remain in dialogue with each other across the continents, supporting and guiding each vision.[45]

Neither a successor to Venerable Fujii nor a head temple in Japan exists in the order. A senior monk, who is honored and who will intervene if necessary, holds special status but has no formally empowered authority. Monks or nuns in their early years of ordination receive guidance and nurturance by a senior member of the order. Within this understanding of consultation and collaboration, each monk and nun discerns direction and obeys inner faith.

Financial decisions, like spiritual direction, are made in consultation. Guruji forbade his monks and nuns to raise money through direct requests or solicitations. He believed that lay devotees would support the sangha if the monks and nuns remained pure and practiced faithfully. Members of the order survive on whatever donations are offered, living simply as renunciates. Peace pagodas, temples, and walks arise as funds manifest spontaneously, without request, through the attraction of lay people to the spiritual values and social commitments of Nipponzan Myohoji.

In the order today, there are approximately 150 monks and nuns world-wide, including approximately ten in the United States and ten in Europe. Mostly Japanese, there are currently two American and two European ordained nuns in the order, and two South Asian monks. The monks, nuns, and lay sangha who support this very small order both in Japan and throughout the world are Guruji's legacy and serve as a living tribute to his leadership.

Early Years in the U.S.

Although Guruji had been in the United States as early as 1968, when he denounced United States involvement in Vietnam, the first established sangha in the United States arose in Washington, D.C., where a Nipponzan Myohoji temple opened its doors in 1974. The monk Shiomi Shonin (*shonin* is a Japanese honorific for monks, equivalent to Reverend or Brother) selected Washington, D.C., in order to bring the spirit of *Rissho Ankoku Ron* to the nation's rulers. Then in 1976 the War Resisters League planned "The Continental Walk for Disarmament and Social Justice." From their connections in Japan through the annual Hiroshima anti-nuclear conference, members of WRL had met Nipponzan Myohoji and invited them to participate in this United States cross-country walk. Among those who arrived was Kato Shonin, who would later create the first peace pagoda in the United States. Two years later, Guruji sent sangha members to support a walk initiated by Native Americans, "The Longest Walk: From Alcatraz to Washington, D.C." A Japanese nun named Jun Yasuda joined this walk, developing a lasting spiritual bond with Native Americans. The second peace pagoda in the U.S. would later arise under the direction of Sister Jun Yasuda and with the blessing and support of the Native peoples.

These early connections with the U.S. peace movement and with Native Americans became sustaining and mutually nourishing relationships. The great faith that Nipponzan Myohoji placed in the value of walks bestowed new life on this long-established form of advocacy in the U.S. With their prayer drums and chants, yellow robes, and shaved heads, these first Nipponzan Myohoji monks in the U.S. gained favor especially with anti-nuclear activists, who recognized them as allies despite their national and religious differences. The monks and nuns added a deep spiritual and calming presence to demonstrations, and offered firm commitments to nonviolence, a clear social analysis of injustice, and consistent self-discipline and stamina. The friendships later became pivotal to Nipponzan Myohoji, when a few

Sister Clare Carter (left) and Reverend Kato Shonin (center) in Nipponzan Myohoji
peace march, Washington, D.C., 1988. Courtesy Paula Green.

intrepid monks and nuns began to establish themselves in the United States.
Their relationships with the newly emerging American Buddhist communities remain friendly but more marginal, as different agendas provide less
opportunity for interface and collaboration.

With the Native American community, the connection to Nipponzan
Myohoji began during The Longest Walk, in 1978. From his earliest years in
the United States, Guruji recognized the Native Americans as "people with
whom we can unite through our religious beliefs of peace…as they lead
their daily life in religious prayers and hearts of thankfulness and gratitude."[46]
Guruji felt that the native peoples of the United States had a special mission
to heal the "defilements" in America and to "mend the mistaken ways of the
United States."[47] He resonated with the Native American emphasis on a
spiritual society, which did not rely on materialism or consumerism, and
encouraged his monks and nuns to nurture these friendships.

After participating in the Boston-to-Washington, D.C., branch of the
"Continental Walk for Disarmament and Social Justice" in 1976, Kato
Shonin, a Nipponzan Myohoji monk, returned to Boston to bring *Na Mu Myo
Ho Ren Ge Kyo* and the teachings of Guruji to the region. Then thirty-six

years old, with few possessions other than a prayer drum and a copy of the *Lotus Sutra*, the monk spent several years chanting the *Odaimoku* on the streets of Boston and Cambridge. In 1978 he walked the twenty-mile route from Boston to Walden Pond consecutively for fifty days in the New England winter, in honor of Thoreau. For Kato Shonin, Thoreau's exemplary life of simplicity, nonviolence, and resistance to unjust laws made Walden Pond a perfect pilgrimage spot to affirm this direction in the American spirit. Additionally, Kato Shonin felt intrigued by the history of Concord, not only the site of Walden Pond but also a village noted for its involvement in the Revolutionary War. On his daily pilgrimage, Kato Shonin contemplated the contrast between Thoreau's nonviolence and the firepower of the War of Independence, expressing his concern about the necessity of force and its continued use in United States history.[48] Kato Shonin participated in vigils and anti-nuclear actions with the peace and justice communities of Boston. He maintained his strict vows and daily Buddhist practices: chanting in his small temple (a room in the well-known Arlington Street Church), walking, fasting, venerating his teachers, and living very simply.

Resonating to the sound of the prayer drum, an American woman named Clare Carter, whose roots were in the Boston peace movement, experienced a profound spiritual call to join Kato Shonin in walking and chanting *Na Mu Myo Ho Ren Ge Kyo*. After several years of intense practice and study with Kato Shonin in the United States, Clare left for Japan to deepen her understanding of Nipponzan Myohoji, where she was ordained as a Buddhist nun in 1981, before returning to Boston. She re-joined Kato Shonin, who by late 1983 had moved to western Massachusetts.

The New England Peace Pagoda

Kato Shonin felt that a peace pagoda would benefit Americans, but that the desire essentially had to manifest from the wishes and intentions of the American people. Although Kato Shonin moved to western Massachusetts in the hopes that land for a peace pagoda would appear, he later discovered an important karmic tie to Amherst. Dr. William S. Clark, the first president of the former Massachusetts Agricultural School in Amherst (now the University of Massachusetts), had founded a famous agricultural school in Japan. His student Dr. Kanzu Chimura, an eminent Christian thinker, wrote a biography of Nichiren as a prophetic figure, which had strongly motivated Guruji to study Nichiren when he was a young man exploring his spiritual path. Learning this history, Kato Shonin felt affirmed in his commitment to the region.

Kato Shonin and Sister Clare continued their prayers for land and made contacts with the peace community in western Massachusetts. In 1984 a young follower who had walked with the monks on the 1982 World Peace March donated a thirty-five-acre hilltop in nearby Leverett, Massachusetts, to the order. Slow Turtle, the supreme medicine man of the Wampanoag nation, blessed its presence on former Indian land. The first peace pagoda in America would soon rise on that hill, to be dedicated ten months after the death of Venerable Nichidatsu Fujii.

The town of Leverett, with a population of approximately two thousand, is home to both progressive newcomers and more traditional, longtime resident Yankees. As befits New England democracy, Leverett citizens organized a town meeting to present the Nipponzan Myohoji order to the townspeople, who found themselves divided in opinion over the desirability of a strange Buddhist order in their midst. Kato Shonin, speaking for Nipponzan, presented his case with great dignity, compassion, and characteristic equanimity, revealing his long years of spiritual discipline. Through his presence and that of Sister Clare and another remarkable monk named Sasamori Shonin, Leverett agreed to grant a building permit to the order, and a lay sangha gathered in Leverett to erect the peace pagoda. This fluid community attracted participants from other areas of the United States and throughout the world, including young Japanese lay people, European peace activists, American Buddhist practitioners, students and faculty from the nearby academic institutions, an assortment of dedicated peace pagoda builders, and onlookers. Many Nipponzan monks joined the community during the year and a half of land clearing and construction. This interface and fusion of cultures, beliefs, practices, and social norms created a brew of learning, challenge, and change for all who participated.

For the lay community, the practice of chanting the *Odaimoku* both as formal meditation and as generic greeting, the *tangyo raihai* custom of bowing with palms together, the respect for elders, the apparent hierarchy, the traditional Japanese gender relations, the *Lotus Sutra* recitations, the altar and incense, the strict rituals and etiquette of practice in a Japanese temple, the veneration of Guruji, and much more, challenged the established behaviors of many of the Western participants. And for the Japanese monks and nuns, the Western sangha and its mix of Christians and Jews, New Age spiritual seekers, Buddhist explorers, feminists, hippies, lesbians and gays, and so many others in various nontraditional life styles and living arrangements must have been not only challenging but often overwhelming. Nonetheless, a warm, congenial, and happy atmosphere ensued, and the New England Peace Pagoda was erected in an astounding eighteen months by this highly eclectic, constantly changing sangha. For the inauguration of the peace pagoda in 1985, an event attended by more than three thousand people on a cold and rainy October Sunday, the American friends and supporters wrote to the monks and nuns of Nipponzan Myohoji:

> Your lives are an inspiration for us. You represent the highest ideals of spiritual service, loving devotion and unfailing dedication to the realization of true peace, both within the self and in the world. Your presence in the West, and most especially in this community, is a gift of enormous magnitude....We bow reverently and wholeheartedly to each of you.

And the monks and nuns of Nipponzan Myohoji wrote to the American sangha:

> We are astounded by your response [to] the Peace Pagoda. We never dreamed of your generosity, dedication and faith....Only because the potential seed of the Peace Pagoda has been within you has it blossomed so quickly....When people come together and are tuned in truthful work, the divine power of the universe immediately cooperates....We monks and nuns bow down a thousand times before you, deeply and with reverence.[49]

Following the inauguration of the New England Peace Pagoda, which is a sealed dome that cannot be entered, the monks and lay community erected a temple on the same grounds to be used for daily chanting and prayer. Unfortunately a fire of unknown origin destroyed the beautiful structure just a month after its 1987 dedication. Another temple is currently under construction on the site, this one made of concrete after the style of temples in India. Kato Shonin and Sister Clare maintain close connections with local people, residing and practicing in a modest structure on the grounds. Each October a larger community gathers for a commemoration of the inauguration of the peace pagoda, listening to Americans and international speakers rooted in their own faiths and in the movements for peace and justice. As the years progress, increasing numbers of people visit the peace pagoda and the Japanese gardens surrounding the pagoda, appreciating the tranquillity and the pervasive spirit of peace. The land, now shared by a Cambodian temple built by followers of Maha Ghosananda, has affectionately become known as Buddha Hill.

The Nipponzan Myohoji sangha has grown in other areas of the United States as well. The second peace pagoda in America arose in Grafton, New York, a small town near Albany, under the guidance of Sister Jun Yasuda. The only Japanese nun of the order living in the United States to undertake the development of her own community, peace pagoda, and temple, Sister Jun transcends the traditional gender norms embedded in Japanese society and reflected in Nipponzan Myohoji. She has attracted a loyal following and developed significant relationships with Native American communities, with whom she participates in arduous peace walks and engages in movements for Native American rights. At the same time she upholds her commitment to the abolition of militarism and nuclear weapons through long pilgrimages, vigils, and public witness.

In Atlanta, Georgia, another Nipponzan Myohoji sangha is emerging, this time in connection with a newly developing relationship with the African-American community of Atlanta and with strong ongoing ties to the peace constituency of the southeast United States. The monk Utsumi Shonin and the only other American nun, Sister Denise, renovated an old crack house in an African-American neighborhood of Atlanta and converted it into a Nipponzan temple. Through their connection with the Reverend Timothy McDonald, an African-American Baptist Church leader whose life was touched by Guruji, Utsumi Shonin, and Sister Denise offer themselves to a community not usually associated with American Buddhism, encouraging new alliances and bringing their own strengths as Mahayana Buddhists concerned with social liberation. Their presence in Atlanta has the potential to invigorate local movements for justice and cross-fertilize African-American activists with anti-nuclear peace movement constituencies who might not otherwise create partnerships. Utsumi Shonin and Sister Denise enjoy a warm relationship with the African-American Baptist congregation who housed them for many years; the Buddhist monk and nun attend Sunday church services and participate in the life of the community.

In the western United States, Jungi Shonin moved to Big Mountain to bear witness with Navajo and Hopi Native Americans struggling for land and human rights. In keeping with the community, he built a small temple in the fashion of the Navajo hogan. And in Washington State in the 1980s, a community of anti-nuclear activists known as Ground Zero welcomed the Nipponzan Myohoji monks to join them in protesting the trident submarine at the naval base and to establish a temple on nearby land. A leader of that community writes:

> Their chants are the backdrop for many conversions to peace; their drums help to keep people centered in times of danger; their smiles and gassho open many hearts closed to the messages of peace. All this happens now because Guruji refused to quit when he was one person praying by himself. That teaches me that we must continue in spite of adversity, and that we must never underestimate the power of prayer....Guruji's face teaches me not to be afraid to pray and to love and to suffer, because on the other side of prayer and love and suffering he has found joy.[50]

WALKING FOR PEACE

There are probably few Buddhist groups in America experiencing the diverse level of acceptance afforded to Nipponzan Myohoji. As engaged Buddhists, they are connected to circles of progressive political and social change, which include Native Americans and African Americans as well as many of the major movements for peace and justice in the United States. Their presence offers a spiritual perspective and discipline to lay activist groups, and an activist passion and commitment to Buddhists and others unfamiliar with the worlds of social activists. Their absolute commitment to nonviolence and to the abolition of war and militarism, and their personal disciplines of simplicity and spiritual steadfastness, inspires and uplifts those whose lives they touch.

Sasamori Shonin, who dedicated himself to the construction of the Leverett peace pagoda and first temple, moved to Managua, Nicaragua to support the efforts of the Nicaraguan people to freely develop their society. Sasamori Shonin was attracted both by the liberation theology developed in Latin America and by the spirit of the North Americans assisting the Nicaraguan liberation movement, who guided and supported his Nicaraguan witness. In cooperation with the United States movements for justice in Central America, Sasamori Shonin lived among the poor and, with the support of the local churches in Managua, prayed and fasted for peace. He went to Nicaragua as he had come to Leverett, with language skills not yet acquired, with neither protection nor possessions, but with enormous faith in the power of his prayer drum and chant. Sasamori Shonin remained in Nicaragua for several years, developing very significant contacts with the grassroots and religious leadership in Managua, with North American activists and with the movement for liberation theology. To pray for peace and for the Nicaraguan movement for self-determination, he undertook a forty-day fast and prayer vigil in front of the church on the main plaza in Managua. Slight in stature under normal circumstances, his body was skeletal after forty days of fasting and chanting

Undertaking pilgrimages for peace, an ancient and honored tradition, acquired new life under the guidance of contemporary spiritual leaders. Gandhi marched throughout India with tens of thousands of followers in a campaign to declare independence from Britain. Martin Luther King, Jr. walked with his followers throughout the southern United States protesting the laws of segregation. Nichidatsu Fujii established walking practice to bear witness for a spiritual civilization, both in Japan and abroad. The monks and nuns of Nipponzan Myohoji residing in the United States continue that tradition, walking ceaselessly across the length and breadth of the United States and beyond, walking for peace, to end nuclearism, to support justice and minority rights, to end violence, and to proclaim the need for a new relationship to each other and to the earth. In every year since their arrival in the United States there have been walks led by or accompanied by Nipponzan Myohoji, to military bases or weapons production facilities, to seats of government or the United Nations, or on behalf of particular communities or individuals suffering discrimination and injustice.

The 1982 World Peace March exemplified the logistical and physical efforts made by Nipponzan Myohoji to awaken the public to the issues of nuclear war. Simultaneous walks were organized by the monks and nuns in Europe, Asia, and North America, all to convene on the United Nations in June 1982 for the beginning of the Second Special Session on Disarmament. Walks in the United States began both from San Francisco and Los Angeles to New York, with other walks originating in New Orleans, Maine, and Canada. Religious leaders invited by Nipponzan Myohoji arrived in New York to lend their moral authority to the New York gathering of one million people, including walkers and demonstrators. Guruji, then aged ninety-seven, spoke at this public event, where over one million people, plus a televised audience, convening to protest the manufacture and proliferation of nuclear weapons, heard the aged monk Guruji chant *Na Mu Myo Ho Ren Ge Kyo*.

Sasamori Shonin organized the Quincentennial Peace Walk in 1992 from Panama City through Central America and the south of the United States to Washington, D.C., to chronicle the history of the European conquest and the 500 years of oppression of the indigenous and marginalized poor of the Americas. Sister Clare helped organize the international outreach for a pilgrimage in Sri Lanka. The purpose of that pilgrimage was "to seek a way for neighboring groups divided by fear and strife to live together in trust and amity, transcending differences of thought and creed."[51] Thus while a small group of Nipponzan Myohoji nuns and monks live and practice Buddhism in the United States, their reach is global and their focus encompasses interfaith commitments to world peace. Each walk arises from very strong vision, prayer, and spiritual guidance, initiated only after deep searching and collaborative advise from the sangha.

In 1980 Sasamori Shonin prayed and fasted at the Auschwitz-Birkenau concentration camps in Oswiecim, Poland, profoundly experiencing the horrors of the Holocaust. These memories remained in his heart and provided the inspiration for the Convocation at Auschwitz and the Interfaith Pilgrimage for Peace and Life 1995.

From 1994-1995 Sasamori Shonin organized and led an eight-month peace walk from Auschwitz to Hiroshima in commemoration of the fiftieth anniversary of the bombings of Hiroshima and Nagasaki, the termination of the Second World War, and the liberation of the concentration camps. He wanted to encourage moral reflection on the crimes against humanity committed during and since World War II, to offer repentance, especially as a Japanese in those Asian countries occupied by his own government, and to contemplate the current ethical and moral issues facing the world community. Two hundred people gathered in Auschwitz for a week-long convocation and prayer vigil, during which Sasamori Shonin and many other Nipponzan monks and nuns chanted and fasted on the platform of the railroad tracks at Birkenau, at the final destination point for prisoners fated for the gas ovens. For a week in Poland's December weather they endured cold and hunger while praying for the victims of the camps, the sound of their prayer drum echoing in the vast and eerie emptiness of Birkenau. While the monks and devotees prayed on the tracks, most of the two hundred international participants plumbed the depths of their own grief and rage, reflecting on the rise of intolerance and hatred and its ultimate manifestation in Auschwitz. Mixing intercommunal dialogue with vigils at the two concentration camps, sharing sorrow and tears, meditation and prayer, the interfaith gathering allowed people from many nations to bridge their differences, express their compassion, and intensify their commitment to ethnic healing.

At the close of the Convocation at Auschwitz, Sasamori Shonin took his place before the long line of peace marchers, lifted his drum, and chanted *Na Mu Myo Ho Ren Ge Kyo*. With this, more than one hundred peace pilgrims took the first step of the walk to Hiroshima that would take them through Bosnia, the Middle East, Iraq, Cambodia, and many other countries that have suffered the effects of war and ethnic hatred. The Interfaith Pilgrimage for Peace and Life 1995 included daily interfaith prayers and dialogues on peace with citizens in cities and villages visited by the walkers. A peace pilgrim who walked the entire eight months of this journey wrote that "Sasamori helped shape the pilgrimage into an event that would touch thousands of lives through contact and prayer and would change the lives of the pilgrims forever."[52] In August 1995, the walkers arrived in Hiroshima for the solemn fiftieth anniversary commemoration of the destruction of Hiroshima by nuclear bomb. Sasamori Shonin reflected on their eight-month pilgrimage and the lessons of compassion and understanding learned by the walkers:

> I believe that if we face the painful facts of history unflinchingly and convey the lessons drawn from them to future generations, we will be able to bring peace to the souls of those who died in anguish in time of war. From the loss of their precious lives, we can establish new values today and for the future.[53]

In 1998 and 1999 Sister Clare will walk for justice and an end to racism as she undertakes a pilgrimage that she has envisioned for years and has worked steadily to organize. An American of European heritage concerned with issues of injustice and discrimination toward Americans of African descent, Sister Clare's contribution to heal the wounds of slavery and racism takes the form of the Interfaith Pilgrimage of the Middle Passage, a twelve-month peace walk that will retrace the journey of slavery through the United States, the Caribbean, and West Africa. Sister Clare believes that "the pilgrimage will be a living prayer of the heart, mind and body for the sons and daughters of the African diaspora....It is hoped the journey will be...a purification of the heart of all those connected, intimately or distantly, with this history."[54]

> When we walk together, our feet touch the same earth, we walk beneath the same sun and soak the same rain. As we journey together with a common purpose, we realize that joys and difficulties need not stop us walking, we begin to restore the spiritual strength of humanity, the strength to reverse the vicious repercussions of our history and to move onwards a genuinely peaceful society nourished by the innate generosity of human beings and the natural world.[55]

INFLUENCE IN THE WEST

In the annals of engaged Buddhism in the West, the voice of Nipponzan Myohoji is unique. Beloved by the United States peace community, the religious left, and many Native Americans, African Americans, Central Americans and others, Nipponzan Myohoji has established itself as a faithful and serious partner in the process of building a new civilization based on spiritual values. Kato Shonin serves as an Advisory Board member of the Buddhist Peace Fellowship; Sister Clare contributes as a member of the Amherst Interfaith Council. All of them lead interfaith walks and participate in the development of multi-religious dialogues in this country and abroad. They embrace people of all faiths and no faith, carrying their own disciplines and beliefs while accepting all others without contradiction or any instincts toward proselytizing. Their commitment to Nichidatsu Fujii and their own spiritual path remains profound and unwavering; despite the years since Guruji's death they are connected to him every day of their lives. They experience no discrepancy between activism for the sake of changing the world and a life of devotion and prayer. The life of each monk and nun, firmly grounded in their world peace work, is anchored in many hours of daily chanting practice.

In reflecting on Buddhism and social engagement, Kato Shonin believes that since the Buddha turned the Wheel of Dharma on this earth, this earth is where we obtain his teachings and reach enlightenment. "The Buddha expounds the Dharma eternally because of the yearning in people's minds." If individuals practice the *Lotus Sutra* correctly, Kato Shonin says, "life itself is engagement and we do not need to separate into engaged or not-engaged Buddhism. The Buddha's teaching is not a tool or an ornament, but exists to bring peace to the world. We follow the teaching because it leads to peace."[56] Like his mentor and preceptor Guruji, Kato Shonin disciplines and purifies his mind through the practices of *Rissho Ankoku Ron* and *tangyo raihai*, bowing reverently to all beings and bringing righteousness into prayer, work and relationships. Every moment of life is engagement; every moment of life is Buddhist.

The Nipponzan Myohoji order may not survive beyond the lives of this current sangha, as there are few young monks and nuns. The arduous path of Nipponzan Myohoji and the prevailing values of materialism in Japan and the United States discourage ordination. However, it may be too early to predict the future of Nipponzan Myohoji. For the present, the approximately 150 ordained members of the sangha throughout the world uphold the traditions, spreading their light and ethical concerns with influence and visibility beyond their small numbers. Nipponzan Myohoji monks and nuns living in the United States have certainly been changed by their contacts with this culture, evidence of which appears in their greater understanding of feminist issues and the empowerment of women, increased tolerance for participatory decision-making and ever-increasing interfaith and intercommunal engagement with America's moral dilemmas.

But the real beneficiaries may be the Americans who are touched by the reverence, generosity, and kindness that the monks and nuns of Nipponzan Myohoji bestow on all people, by their radical social vision, and by their inspiring and dedicated lives as Buddhists committed to bring forth a world filled with peace, compassion, and spiritual harmony. Through their peace walks, building of peace pagodas, and religious practices, they steadfastly continue their "...single task to deliver humanity from its present suffering,"[57] planting seeds of peace with every step and messages of love and consciousness, tolerance and respect, courage and hope, with every bow.

ACKNOWLEDGMENT

I wish to express my enduring appreciation to Kato Shonin and Sister Clare of the Leverett peace pagoda, not only for their essential contributions to this chapter and for their patient readings of the text in progress, but for the blessings of their presence in my life, their years in the community of Leverett,

Massachusetts, which is my home, and their commitment to the ethical issues in the United States. I bow deeply with thanks and gratitude for the moral vision of all the monks and nuns of Nipponzan Myohoji, both in the United States and abroad.

NOTES

1. Nichidatsu Fujii, in brochure of the Interfaith Pilgrimage of the Middle Passage, Leverett, MA, 1998. Booklets and commemorative volumes are available from: New England Peace Pagoda, 100 Cave Hill Road, Leverett, MA 01054.
2. Nichidatsu Fujii, *The Wonderful Law: Universal Refuge* (Tokyo: Japan-Bharat Sarvodaya Mitrata Sangha, 1984), p. 285. (This book is also published in Japanese as *Itten Shikai Kaiki Myoho,* 1984.)
3. Nichidatsu Fujii, *Buddhism for World Peace,* trans. Yumiko Miyazaki (Tokyo: Japan-Bharat Sarvodaya Mitrata Sangha, 1980), p. 12.
4. Teresina Rowell in *The Open Court* 45, no. 907 (Dec. 1931): 756.
5. Ibid., p. 755.
6. Tsuyoshi Kuniyoshi, *Shakyamuni Buddha and the Stupa* (Tokyo: O-busshari-to Hosan kai, 1981), p. 23.
7. Ibid., p. 22.
8. Fujii, *Buddhism for World Peace*, p. 17.
9. Fujii, *The Wonderful Law,* p. 287
10. Rowell, p. 766
11. Private conversation with Sister Clare Carter, Leverett, MA, 1998.
12. Private conversation with Kato Shonin, Leverett, MA, 1998.
13. Chapter 11 of the *Lotus Sutra of Wonderful Law,* "Beholding the Precious Stupa," in the commemoration booklet of the New England Peace Pagoda (Leverett, MA, 1985).
14. Masaharu Anesaki, *Nichiren the Buddhist Prophet* (Cambridge, MA: Harvard University Press, 1916), p. 84.
15. Ibid., pp. 85–87.
16. Ibid., p. 3.
17. Nichidatsu Fujii, *Itten Shikai Kaiki Myoho* (Tokyo: Japan-Bharat Sarvodaya Mitrata Sangha, 1984), p. 243.
18. Private conversation with Kato Shonin, Leverett, MA, 1998.
19. Ibid.
20. Nichidatsu Fujii, *The Time Has Come* (Tokyo: Japan-Bharat Sarvodaya Mitrata Sangha), p. 15.
21. Ibid.
22. Fujii, *Buddhism for World Peace*, pp. 15–23.

23. Ibid.

24. Talk by Nichidatsu Fujii, Atami Dojo, Japan, 1976.

25. Private conversation with Sister Clare Carter, Leverett, MA, 1998.

26. Talk by Nichidatsu Fujii, 1930 (Tokyo: Bharat Sarvodaya Mitrata Sangha, n.d.).

27. Fujii, *Buddhism for World Peace*, p. 62.

28. Ibid., p. 61.

29. Nichidatsu Fujii commemoration booklet for the inauguration of the Leverett Peace Pagoda, 1985.

30. Fujii, *Itten Shikai Kaiki Myoho*, pp. 290–91

31. Private conversation with Kato Shonin, Leverett, MA, 1998.

32. Commemoration booklet of the New England Peace Pagoda, Leverett, MA, 1985.

33. Fujii, *Buddhism for World Peace*, p. 43.

34. Commemoration booklet of the New England Peace Pagoda, 1985.

35. Ibid.

36. Private conversation with Kato Shonin, Leverett, MA, 1998.

37. Talk by Nichidatsu Fujii (Tokyo: Bharat Sarvodaya Mitrata Sangha, n.d.).

38. Ibid.

39. Private conversation with Kato Shonin, Leverett, MA, 1998.

40. Fujii, *The Wonderful Law*, p. 297.

41. Written communication by Venerable Bakula Rinpoche (Tokyo: Bharat Sarvodaya Mitrata Sangha).

42. Nichidatsu Fujii, "The Meaning of Monkhood" (Tokyo: Bharat Sarvodaya Mitrata Sangha, 1984).

43. Ibid.

44. Fujii, *Buddhism for World Peace*, p. 248.

45. Private conversation with Sister Clare Carter, Leverett, MA, 1998.

46. Fujii, *Buddhism for World Peace*, p. 164.

47. Ibid., p. 166.

48. Private conversation with Kato Shonin, Leverett, MA, 1998.

49. Commemoration booklet of the New England Peace Pagoda, 1985.

50. Fujii, *The Wonderful Law*, p. 132.

51. Booklet from South India Interfaith Pilgrimage for Peace and Life, Sri Lanka, 1993.

52. Lisa Roche and Dan Turner, *Ashes and Light: Auschwitz to Hiroshima Interfaith Pilgrimage for Peace and Life*, 1995 (Amherst, MA: H. Newell Printing, 1996).

53. Sasamori Shonin quoted in Roche and Turner, *Ashes and Light*.

54. "The Interfaith Pilgrimage of the Middle Passage," pamphlet of the New England Peace Pagoda, 1998.

55. Ibid.

56. Private conversation with Kato Shonin, Leverett, MA, 1998.

57. Fujii, *Buddhism for World Peace*, p. 23.

ENGAGING THE ISSUES:
ENVIRONMENT, RACE,
HUMAN RIGHTS

Author John Powers with His Holiness the Dalai Lama and Cindy Powers, Dharamsala, India, 1988. Courtesy John Powers.

To Save All Beings: Buddhist Environmental Activism

Stephanie Kaza

MEDITATORS FORM A CIRCLE at the base camp of the Headwaters Forest. All are invited to join the Buddhists sitting still in the flurry of activity. While others drum, talk, dance, and discuss strategy, the small group of ecosattvas—Buddhist environmental activists—focus on their breathing and intention amidst the towering trees. They chant the *Metta Sutta* to generate a field of loving-kindness. Here in volatile timber country they renew their pledges to the most challenging task of Buddhist practice—to save all beings.

In this action, old-growth redwoods are the beings at risk, slated for harvest on the Maxxam company property in northern California. Until recently the sixty-thousand-acre ecosystem was logged slowly and sustainably by a small family company. Then in 1985 logging accelerated dramatically following a hostile corporate buyout. Alarmed by the loss of irreplaceable giants, forest defenders have fought tirelessly to halt clear-cutting and preserve these ancient stands of redwoods. They have been joined by Hollywood stars, rock singers, and Jewish rabbis, many willing to practice civil disobedience in protest. How is it that Buddhists have become involved with this effort?

Motivated by ecological concerns, the ecosattvas formed as an affinity group at Green Gulch Zen Center in Marin County, California. As part of their practice they began exploring the relationship between Zen training and environmental activism. They wanted to know: What does it mean to take the bodhisattva vow as a call to save endangered species, decimated forests, and polluted rivers? What does it mean to engage in environmental activism from a Buddhist perspective?[1] The ecosattvas are part of an emerging movement of ecospiritual activism, backed by a parallel academic development which has become the field of Religion and Ecology.[2] Christian scholars, Jewish social justice groups, Hindu tree-planting projects, and

Islamic resistance to usurious capitalism are all part of this movement. Buddhist efforts in the United States like those of the ecosattvas are matched by monks in Thailand protesting the oil pipeline from Burma and Tibetans teaching environmental education in Dharamsala.[3]

Activist scholar Joanna Macy suggests these actions are all part of the "third turning of the wheel [of Dharma]," her sense that Buddhism is undergoing a major evolutionary shift at the turn of the millennium.[4] In today's context, one of the oldest teachings of the Buddha—*paticca samuppada* or dependent co-arising—is finding new form in the ecology movement. If ecosystem relationships are the manifestation of interdependence, then protecting ecosystems is a way to protect the Dharma: "with the Third Turning of the Wheel, we see that everything we do impinges on all beings."[5] Acting with compassion in response to the rapidly accelerating environmental crisis can be seen as a natural fruit of Buddhist practice.

Is there a Buddhist ecospiritual movement in North America? Not in any obvious sense, at least not yet. No organizations have been formed to promote Buddhist environmentalism; no clearly defined environmental agenda has been agreed upon by a group of self-identified American Buddhists. However, teachers are emerging, and Buddhist students of all ages are drawn to their writings and ideas. Writers Joanna Macy and Gary Snyder have made ecological concerns the center of their Buddhist practice. Teachers Thich Nhat Hanh and His Holiness the Dalai Lama have frequently urged mindful action on behalf of the environment. Activists John Seed, Nanao Sakaki, and others are beginning to define a Buddhist approach to environmental activism. There is a strong conversation developing among Western and Eastern Buddhists, asking both practical and philosophical questions from this emerging perspective. With environmental issues a mounting global concern, Buddhists of many traditions are creatively adapting their religious heritage to confront these difficult issues.

In this chapter I begin the preliminary work of documenting the scope of Buddhist environmentalism in the late 1990s, gathering together the historical and philosophical dimensions of what has been called "green Buddhism." This study will be necessarily limited to Western Buddhism, in keeping with the focus of this volume. However, it is important to note the strong relationship with other global initiatives. Buddhist tree-ordaining in Thailand, for example, has inspired similar ceremonies in California.[6] Environmental destruction by logging and uranium mining in Tibet has prompted the formation of the U.S.-based Eco-Tibet group.[7] Environmental issues in Buddhist countries have been a natural magnet for Buddhist activists in the West. But Western Buddhists have taken other initiatives locally, bringing their Buddhist and environmental sensibilities to bear on nuclear waste, consumerism, animal rights, and forest defense.[8] Out of these impulses Buddhist environmental activism is taking shape, based on distinct principles and practices.

One of the most challenging aspects of documenting these developments is finding the hidden stories. In the United States today, environmentalism has grown so strong as a political and cultural force that it is suffering the impact of "brownlash," as biologists Paul and Anne Ehrlich call it. Christian fundamentalism is often allied with the wing of the conservative right that promulgates anti-environmental views. Taking a strong environmental position as a self-proclaimed Buddhist can be doubly threatening. My personal experience is that the environmental arena is a place to act as a small "b" Buddhist. This means concentrating on the message of the Buddha by cultivating awareness, tolerance, and understanding, and acting from a loving presence. "In Buddhism, we say that the presence of one mindful person can have great influence on society and is thus very important."[9] Mindful Buddhist practitioners engaging difficult environmental issues may not proclaim their Buddhism to help solve the problem at hand. Yet they can bring inner strength and moral courage to the task at hand, drawing on the teachings of the Buddha as a basic framework for effective action.

LOOKING BACK

When Buddhism arrived in the West in the mid-1800s, there was little that could be called an environmental movement. Although Henry David Thoreau had written *Walden* in 1854, it was not until the end of the century that a serious land conservation movement coalesced. Advocates recognizing the unique heritage of such landforms as Yellowstone, Yosemite, and the Grand Canyon pressed for the establishment of the National Park system. Conservationists alert to the ravaging of eastern forests and the rush to cut the West spurred the formation of the National Forest Service. But serious concern about overpopulation, air and water pollution, and endangered species did not ignite until the 1960s. Since then the list of dangerous threats has only increased—toxic wastes, ozone depletion, global climate change, genetic engineering, endocrine disrupters—fires are burning on all fronts.

The most recent Western wave of interest in Buddhism coincides almost exactly with the expansion of the environmental movement.[10] Young people breaking out of the constrictions of the 1950s took their curiosity and spiritual seeking to India, Southeast Asia, and Japan; some discovered Buddhist meditation and brought it back to the United States.[11] During this period,

Gary Snyder was probably the most vocal in spelling out the links between Buddhist practice and ecological activism. His books of poetry, *Turtle Island* (1974) and *Axe Handles* (1983), expressed a strong feeling for the land, influenced by his seven years of Zen training in Japan. His 1974 essay "Four Changes" laid out the current conditions of the world in terms of population, pollution, consumption, and the need for social transformation. Core to his analysis was the Buddhist perspective "that we are interdependent energy fields of great potential wisdom and compassion."[12] Snyder's ideas were adopted by the counterculture through his affiliation with beat writers Jack Kerouac and Allen Ginsberg and then further refined in his landmark collection of essays, *The Practice of the Wild*.[13]

Interest in Buddhism increased steadily through the 1970s along with the swelling environmental, civil rights, and women's movements. While Congress passed such landmark environmental laws as the Marine Mammal Protection Act, the Endangered Species Act, and the National Environmental Protection Act, Buddhist centers and teachers were becoming established on both coasts. San Francisco Zen Center, for example, expanded to two additional sites—a wilderness monastery at Tassajara, Big Sur, and a rural farm and garden temple in Marin County. By the 1980s the Buddhist Peace Fellowship was well along in its activist agenda and a number of Buddhist teachers were beginning to address the environmental crisis in their talks. In his 1989 Nobel Peace Prize acceptance speech His Holiness the Dalai Lama proposed making Tibet an international ecological reserve.[14] Thich Nhat Hanh, the influential Buddhist peace activist and Vietnamese Zen monk, referred often to ecological principles in his writings and talks on "interbeing," the Buddhist teaching of interdependence.[15]

The theme was picked up by Buddhist publications, conferences, and retreat centers. Buddhist Peace Fellowship featured the environment in *Turning Wheel* and produced a substantial packet and poster for Earth Day 1990.[16] The first popular anthology of Buddhism and ecology writings, *Dharma Gaia*, was published by Parallax Press that same year, following the more scholarly collection, *Nature in Asian Traditions of Thought*.[17] World Wide Fund for Nature brought out a series of books on five world religions, including *Buddhism and Ecology*.[18] *Tricycle* magazine examined green Buddhism and vegetarianism in 1994;[19] *Shambhala Sun* interviewed Gary Snyder and Japanese anti-nuclear poet-activist Nanao Sakaki.[20] The Vipassana newsletter *Inquiring Mind* produced an issue on "coming home"; *Ten Directions* of Zen Center Los Angeles, *Mountain Record* of Zen

Mountain Monastery, and *Blind Donkey* of Honolulu Diamond Sangha also took up the question of environmental practice.

Some retreat centers confronted ecological issues head on. Green Gulch Zen Center in northern California had to work out water use agreements with its farming neighbors and the Golden Gate National Recreation Area. Zen Mountain Monastery in New York faced off with the Department of Environmental Conservation over a beaver dam and forestry issues. In earlier days when vegetarianism was not such a popular and commercially viable choice, most Buddhist centers went against the social grain by refraining from meat-eating, often with an awareness of the associated environmental problems. Several Buddhist centers made some effort to grow their own organic food.[21] Outdoor walking meditation gained new stature through backpacking and canoeing retreats on both coasts.

By the 1990s, spirituality and the environment had become a hot topic. The first "Earth and Spirit" Conference was held in Seattle in 1990, and Buddhist workshops were part of the program. Middlebury College in Vermont hosted a "Spirit and Nature" conference that same year with the Dalai Lama as keynote speaker, sharing his Buddhist message for protection of the environment.[22] More interfaith conferences followed and Buddhism was always represented at the table. By 1993, human rights, social justice, and the environment were top agenda items at the Parliament of the World's Religions in Chicago. Buddhists from all over the world gathered with Christians, Hindus, pagans, Jews, Jains, and Muslims to consider the role of religion in responding to the environmental crisis.

Parallel sparks of interest were ignited in the academic community. Though both environmental studies and religious studies programs were well established in the academy, very few addressed the overlap between the two fields. In 1992 religion and ecology scholars formed a new group in the American Academy of Religion and began soliciting papers on environmental philosophy, animal rights, Gaian cosmology, and other environmental topics. Out of this initiative, colleagues generated campus interreligious dialogues and new religion and ecology courses. In the spring of 1997, Mary Evelyn Tucker and John Grimm of Bucknell University convened the first of a series of academic conferences with the aim of defining the field of religion and ecology.[23] The first of these addressed Buddhism and Ecology; the volume of collected papers was the first publication in the series.[24] The spring 1998 meeting of the International Buddhist-Christian Theological Encounter also focused on the environment, looking deeply at the impacts of consumerism.[25]

For the most part, the academic community did not address the *practice* of Buddhist environmentalism. This was explored more by socially engaged Buddhist teachers such as Thich Nhat Hanh, Bernie Glassman, the Dalai Lama, Sulak Sivaraksa, Christopher Titmuss, John Daido Loori, and Philip Kapleau.[26] One leader in developing a Buddhist ecological perspective for activists was Joanna Macy. Her doctoral research explored the significant parallels and distinctions between Western general systems theory and Buddhist philosophy.[27] In her sought-after classes and workshops, Macy developed a transformative model of experiential teaching designed to cultivate motivation, presence, and authenticity.[28] Her methods were strongly based in Buddhist meditation techniques and the Buddhist law of dependent co-arising. She called this "deep ecology work," challenging participants to take their insights into direct action. Working with John Seed, a Buddhist Australian rainforest activist, she developed a ritual "Council of All Beings" and other guided meditations to engage the attention and imagination on behalf of all beings.[29] Thousands of councils have now taken place in Australia, New Zealand, the United States, Germany, Russia, and other parts of the Western world.

Following in the footsteps of these visionary thinkers, a number of Buddhist activists organized groups to address specific issues—nuclear guardianship, factory farming, and forest protection. Each initiative has had its own history of start-up, strategizing, attracting interest, and, in some cases, fading enthusiasm. When these groups work with well-established environmental groups, they seem to be more successful in accomplishing their goals. Some Buddhist environmental activists have been effective in helping shape the orientation of an existing environmental group. The Institute for Deep Ecology, for example, which offers summer training for activists, has had many Buddhists among its faculty, especially on the West Coast.

Though the history of Buddhist environmentalism is short, it has substance: bright minds suggesting new ways to look at things, teachers and writers inspiring others to address the challenges, and fledgling attempts to practice ecospiritual activism based in Buddhist principles. As Western interest in Buddhism grows, it affects wider social and political circles. As other Buddhist activists take up the task of defining the principles and practices of socially engaged Buddhism, environmental Buddhism can play a vital role. As Buddhist teachers come to see the "ecosattva" possibilities in the bodhisattva vows, they can encourage such practice-based engagement. The seeds for all this are well planted; the next ten years of environmental disasters and activist responses will indicate whether

Buddhist environmental activism will take its place among other parallel initiatives.

PHILOSOPHICAL GROUND

During its two-thousand-year-old history, Buddhism has evolved across a wide range of physical and cultural geographies. From the Theravada traditions in tropical South and Southeast Asia, to the Mahayana Schools in temperate and climatically diverse China and Japan, to the Vajrayana lineages in mountainous Tibet—Buddhist teachings have been received, modified, and elaborated in many ecological contexts. Across this history the range of Buddhist understandings about nature and human–nature relations has been based on different teachings, texts, and cultural views. These have not been consistent by any means; in fact, some views directly contradict each other.

Malcolm David Eckel, for example, contrasts the Indian view with the Japanese view of nature.[30] Indian Buddhist literature shows relatively little respect for wild nature, preferring tamed nature instead; Japanese Buddhism reveres the wild but engages it symbolically through highly developed art forms. Tellenbach and Kimura take this up in their investigation of the Japanese concept of nature, "what-is-so-of-itself"; Ian Harris discusses the difficulties in comparing the meaning of the word "nature" in different Asian languages.[31] When Harris reviews traditional Buddhist texts, he does not find any consistent philosophical orientation toward environmental ethics. He also challenges claims that Buddhist philosophies of nature led to any recognizable ecological awareness among early Buddhist societies, citing some evidence to the contrary. Lambert Schmithausen points out that according to early Buddhist sources, most members of Buddhist societies, including many monks, preferred the comforts of village life over the threats of the wild.[32] Images of Buddhist paradises are generally quite tame, not at all untrammeled wilderness. Only forest ascetics chose the hermitage path with its immersion in wild nature.

Even with these distinctions, Buddhist texts do contain many references to the natural world, both as inspiration for teachings and as source for ethical behavior. For Westerners tasting the Dharma in the context of the environmental crisis, all the Buddhist traditions are potential sources for philosophical and behavioral guidelines toward nature. The newest cultural form of Buddhism in the West will be different from what evolved in India, Thailand, China, and Japan. In seeking wisdom to address the world as it is now, Westerners are eagerly, if sometimes clumsily, looking for whatever may be helpful. From the earliest guidelines for forest monks to the hermitage songs of Milarepa, from the Jataka tales of compassion to Zen teachings on mountains and rivers, the inheritance is rich and diverse.[33] In this section, I lay out the principal teachings identified by leading Buddhist environmental thinkers in the late twentieth century as most relevant to addressing the current environmental situation.

Interdependence

In the canonical story of the Buddha's enlightenment, the culminating insight comes in the last hours of his long night of deep meditation. According to the story, he first perceived his previous lives in a continuous cycle of birth and death, then saw the vast universe of birth and death for all beings, gaining understanding of the workings of karma. Finally he realized the driving force behind birth and death, and the path to release from it. Each piece of the Buddha's experience added to a progressive unfolding of a single truth about existence—the law of mutual causality or dependent origination (in Sanskrit *pratityasamutpada*, in Pali *paticca samuppada*). According to this law, all phenomena, that is, all of nature, arise from complex sets of causes and conditions, each set unique to the specific situations. Thus, the simple but penetrating Pali verse:

> This being, that becomes;
> from the arising of this, that arises;
> this not being, that becomes not;
> from the ceasing of this, that ceases.[34]

Ecological understanding of natural systems fits very well within the Buddhist description of interdependence. This law has been the subject of much attention in the Buddhism and Ecology literature because of its overlapping with ecological principles.[35] Throughout all cultural forms of Buddhism, nature is perceived as relational, each phenomenon dependent on a multitude of causes and conditions. From a Buddhist perspective these causes include not only physical and biological factors but also historical and cultural factors, that is, human thought forms and values.

The Hua-Yen School of Buddhism, developed in seventh-century China, placed particular emphasis on this principle, using the jewel net of Indra as a teaching metaphor. This cosmic net contains a multifaceted jewel at each of its nodes. "Because the jewels are clear, they reflect each other's images, appearing in each other's reflections upon reflections, ad infinitum, all appearing at once in one jewel."[36] To extend the metaphor, if you tug on any one of the lines of the net—for example, through loss of species or habitat—it affects all the other lines. Or, if any of the jewels become cloudy (toxic or polluted), they reflect the others less clearly. Likewise, if clouded jewels are cleared up (rivers cleaned, wetlands restored), life across the web is enhanced. Because the web of interdependence includes not only the actions of all beings but also their thoughts, the intention of the actor becomes a critical factor in determining what happens. This, then, provides a principle of both explanation for the way things are, and a path for positive action.

Modern eco-Buddhists working with this principle have taken various paths. Using the term "interbeing," Thich Nhat Hanh emphasizes nonduality of view, encouraging students to "look at reality as a whole rather than to cut it into separate entities."[37] Gary Snyder takes up the interdependence of eater and eaten, acknowledging the "simultaneous path of pain and beauty of this complexly interrelated world."[38] Feminist theologian Rita Gross looks at the darker implications of cause and effect in the growing human population crisis.[39] Activist Joanna Macy leads people through their environmental despair by steadily reinforcing ways to work together and build more functional and healing relationships with the natural world.[40]

The law of interdependence suggests a powerful corollary, sometimes noted as "emptiness of separate self." If all phenomena are dependent on interacting causes and conditions, nothing exists by itself, autonomous and self-supporting. This Buddhist understanding (and experience) of self directly contradicts the traditional Western sense of self as a discrete individual. Alan Watts called this assumption of separateness the "skin-encapsulated ego"—the very delusion that Buddhist practices seek to cut through. Based on the work of Gregory Bateson and other systems theorists, Macy describes a more ecological view of the self as part of a larger flow-through.[41] She ties this to Arne Naess's deep ecology philosophy, derived from a felt shift of identification to a wider, more inclusive view of self. Buddhist rainforest activist John Seed described his experience of no-self in an interview with *Inquiring Mind*: "All of a sudden, the forest was inside me and was calling to me, and it was the most powerful thing I have ever felt."[42] Gary Snyder suggests this emptiness of self provides a link to "wild mind," or access to the energetic forces that determine wilderness. These forces act outside of human influence, setting the historical, ecological, and even cosmological context for all life. Thus "emptiness" is dynamic, shape-shifting, energy in motion—"wild" and beyond human imagination.[43]

The Path of Liberation

The Buddhist image of the Wheel of Life contains various realms of beings; at the center are three figures representing greed, hate, and delusion. They chase each other around, generating endless suffering, perpetrating a false sense of self or ego. Liberation from attachment to this false self is the central goal in Buddhist practice. The first and second of the four noble truths describe the very nature of existence as suffering, due to our instincts to protect our own individual lives and views. The third and fourth noble truths lay out a path to liberation from this suffering of self-attachment, the eight-fold path of morality, awareness, and wisdom.

Buddhist scholar Alan Sponberg argues that green Buddhism has overemphasized interdependence or the relational dimension almost to the exclusion of the developmental aspect of practice.[44] By working to overcome ego-based attachments and socially conditioned desires, students cultivate the capacity for insight and compassion. This effort, he says, is crucial to displacing the hierarchy of oppression that undermines the vision of an ecologically healthy world. Sponberg suggests that a Buddhist environmenal ethic is a virtue ethic, based fundamentally on development of consciousness and a sense of responsibility to act compassionately for the benefit of all forms of life. This is the basis for the Mahayana archetype of the bodhisattva, committed to serving others until suffering is extinguished. Macy argues that this responsibility need not be some morally imposed self-righteous action (often characteristic of environmentalists) but rather an action that "springs naturally from the ground of being."[45]

The path of liberation includes the practice of physical, emotional, and mental awareness. Such practice can increase one's appreciation for the natural world; it can also reveal hidden cultural assumptions about privilege, comfort, consumption, and the abuse of nature. When one sees one's self as part of a mutually causal web, it becomes obvious that there is no such thing as an action without effect. Through the practice of green virtue ethics, students are encouraged to be accountable for all of their actions, from eating food to using a car to buying new clothes. Likewise, they can investigate the reigning economic paradigm and see how deeply it determines their choices. Through following the fundamental precepts, environmentally oriented Buddhists can practice moderation and restraint, simplifying needs and desires to reduce suffering for others. For Westerners this may mean withdrawal from consumer addictions to products with large ecological impacts, such as coffee, cotton, computers, and cars.

Practice in Action

Buddhist environmental teachers and writers point to three primary arenas of practice that can serve the environment: compassion, mindfulness, and nonharming. In the Theravada tradition, one practices loving-kindness, wishing that all beings be free from harm and blessed by physical and mental well-being. In the Mahayana tradition one takes up the bodhisattva path, vowing

Buddhist Peace Fellowship members make offerings prior to an anti-nuclear demonstration
and civil disobedience, Easter Sunday, 1993, U.S. Government test site, Nevada.
Courtesy Buddhist Peace Fellowship.

to return again and again to relieve the suffering of all sentient beings—the
life work of an environmentalist! Both practices are impossible challenges if
interpreted literally; the environmental implications of these prayers or vows
can be overwhelming. Yet the strength of intention offers a substantial foundation for Buddhist environmental activism. Budding eco-Buddhists struggle with the application of these spiritual vows in the very real contexts of
factory farms, pesticide abuse, genetic engineering, and loss of endangered
species habitat.

Mindfulness practice, a natural support to Buddhist environmentalism,
can take a range of forms. Thich Nhat Hanh teaches the basic principles of
the *Satipatthana Sutta* or the mindfulness text, practicing awareness of breath,
body, feelings, and mind. Walking and sitting meditation generate a sense of
grounded presence and alertness to where one actually is. Environmental
educators stress mindfulness through nature appreciation exercises and rules
of respect toward the natural world. Environmental strategists use promotional campaigns to generate awareness of threatened species and places.
These efforts take mindfulness practice off the cushion and out into the
world where alarming situations of great suffering require strong attention.

The practice of *ahimsa* or non-harming derives naturally from a true
experience of compassion. All the Buddhist precepts are based fundamentally on non-harming or reducing the suffering of others. Practicing the first
precept, not killing, raises ethical dilemmas around food, land use, pesticides,
pollution, and cultural economic invasion. The second precept, not stealing,

suggests considering the implications of global trade and corporate exploitation of resources. Not lying brings up issues in advertising and consumerism. Not engaging in abusive relations covers a broad realm of cruelty and disrespect for nonhuman others. As Gary Snyder says, "The whole planet groans under the massive disregard of ahimsa by the highly organized societies and corporate economies of the world."[46] Thich Nhat Hanh interprets the precept prohibiting drugs and alcohol to include the toxic addictions of television, video games, and junk magazines.[47] Practicing restraint and non-harming is a way to make Buddhist philosophy manifest in the context of rapidly deteriorating global ecosystems. Zen teacher Robert Aitken offers this vow:

> With resources scarcer and scarcer, I vow with all beings—
> To reduce my gear in proportion even to candles and carts.[48]

BUDDHIST ENVIRONMENTAL ACTIVISM

How is green Buddhism being practiced? What is the evidence of green Buddhism on the front lines? Macy suggests three types of activism that characterize environmentalism today: 1) holding-actions of resistance, 2) analysis of social structures and creation of new alternatives, and 3) cultural transformation.[49] Some of the best examples of Buddhist environmentalism come from outside the West, but here I report only on local efforts in North America.

Holding-actions aim primarily to stop or reduce destructive activity, buying time for more effective long-term strategies. The small group of ecosattvas protesting the logging of old growth redwood groves is part of the holding-actions in northern California. They draw on local support from Buddhist deep ecologist Bill Devall and his eco-sangha in Humboldt County as well as support from the Green Gulch Zen community and the Buddhist Peace Fellowship. For the big 1997 demonstration, the ecosattvas invited others to join them in creating a large prayer flag covered with human handprints of mud. This then served as visual testimony of solidarity for all those participating in Headwaters actions. Six months after the protest, several ecosattvas made a special pilgrimage deep into the heart of the Headwaters, carrying a Tibetan treasure vase. Activists used the vase to bring attention to the threatened trees at various Bay Area sangha meetings. People were invited to offer their gifts and prayers on behalf of the redwoods. On a rainy winter's day, the vase was ceremonially buried beneath one of the giants to strengthen spiritual protection for the trees.[50]

Resistance actions by Buddhists Concerned for Animals were initiated by Brad Miller and Vanya Palmers, two Zen students in the San Francisco area. Moved by the suffering of animals in cages, on factory farms, and in export houses, they joined the animal rights movement, educating other Buddhists about the plight of monkeys, beef cattle, and endangered parrots. Vanya has continued this work in Europe, where he now lives, focusing on the cruelty in large-scale hog farming.[51]

When the federal government proposed burial of nuclear waste deep under Yucca Mountain, a group of Buddhists and others gathered together under Joanna Macy's leadership and met as a study group for several years. They took the position that nuclear waste was safer above ground where it could be monitored, and they developed an alternate vision of nuclear guardianship based in Buddhist spiritual practices.[52] At about the same time, Japan arranged for several shipments of plutonium to be reprocessed in France and then shipped back to Japan. Zen student and artist Mayumi Oda helped to organize Plutonium-Free Future and the Rainbow Serpents to stop these shipments of deadly nuclear material. One ship was temporarily stopped, and although shipments resumed, the actions raised awareness in Japan and the United States, affecting Japanese government policies.[53]

The second type of activism, undertaking structural analysis and creating alternative green visions, has also engaged twentieth-century Buddhists. Small "b" Buddhist Rick Klugston directs the Washington, D.C.-based Center for Respect of Life and the Environment, an affiliate of the Humane Society of the United States. He and his staff work on sustainability criteria for humane farming, basing their work in religious principles of nonharming. In 1997 the Soka Gakkai-affiliated group, Boston Research Center for the 21st Century, held a series of workshops addressing the people's earth charter, an internationally negotiated list of ethical guidelines for human-earth relations. The center published a booklet of Buddhist views on the charter's principles for us in discussions leading up to United Nations adoption.[54] A subgroup of the International Network of Engaged Buddhists and the Buddhist Peace Fellowship, called the "Think Sangha," is engaged in structural analysis of global consumerism. Collaborating between the United States and Southeast Asia, they have held conferences in Thailand on alternatives to consumerism, pressing for moderation and lifestyle simplification.[55] One of the boldest visions is the Dalai Lama's proposal that the entire province of Tibet be declared an ecological reserve. Sadly, this vision, put forth in his Nobel Peace Prize acceptance speech, is nowhere close to actualization.[56]

Scholars have offered structural analyses using Buddhist principles to shed light on environmental problems. Rita Gross, Buddhist feminist scholar, has laid out a Buddhist framework for considering global population issues.[57] I have compared eco-feminist principles of activism with Buddhist philosophy, showing a strong compatibility between the two.[58] Through Buddhist-Christian dialogue, process theologian and meditator Jay McDaniel has developed spiritual arguments for compassionate treatment of animals as a serious human responsibility.[59] Sociologist Bill Devall integrated Buddhist principles into his elaboration of Arne Naess's Deep Ecology philosophy urging simplification of needs and wants.[60] Joanna Macy likewise draws on Buddhist philosophy and practices to analyze the paralyzing states of grief, despair, and fear that prevent people from acting on behalf of the environment.

As for the third type of activism, transforming culture, these projects are very much in progress and sometimes met with resistance. Two Buddhist centers in rural northern California, Green Gulch Zen Center and Spirit Rock, already demonstrate a serious commitment to the environment through vegetarian dining, land and water stewardship efforts, an organic farm and garden at Green Gulch, and ceremonies that include the natural world.[61] On Earth Day 1990, the abbot led a tree-ordaining precepts ceremony and an animal memorial service. Other environmental rituals include special dedications at the solstices and equinoxes, a Buddha's birthday celebration of local wildflowers, Thanksgiving altars from the farm harvest, and participation in the United Nations Environmental Sabbath in June. The ecosattvas meet regularly to plan restoration projects that are now part of daily work practice. When people visit Green Gulch, they can see ecological action as part of a Buddhist way of life. Similar initiatives have been undertaken at Spirit Rock Meditation Center, also in the San Francisco Bay area.

In the Sierra foothills, Gary Snyder has been a leader in establishing the Yuba River Institute, a bioregional watershed organization working in cooperation with the Bureau of Land Management. They have done ground survey work, controlled burns, and creek restoration projects, engaging the local community in the process. "To restore the land one must live and work in a place. To work in a place is to work with others. People who work together in a place become a community, and a community, in time, grows a culture."[62] Snyder models the level of commitment necessary to reinhabit a place and build community that might eventually span generations. Zen Mountain Center in Southern California is beginning similar work, carrying out resource management practices such as thinning for fire breaks, restoring degraded forest, and limiting human access to some preserve areas.[63] Applying Buddhist principles in an urban setting, Zen teacher Bernard Glassman has developed environmentally oriented small businesses that employ local street people, sending products to socially responsible companies such as Ben and Jerry's.[64]

As the educational element of cultural transformation, several Buddhist centers have developed lecture series, classes, and retreats based on environmental themes. Zen Mountain Monastery in the Catskills of New York offers "Mountains and Rivers" retreats based on the center's commitment to environmental conservation. These feature backpacking, canoeing, nature photography, and haiku as gateways to Buddhist insight. Ring of Bone Zendo at Kitkitdizze, Gary Snyder's community, has offered backpacking *sesshins* in the Sierra Mountains since its inception. Green Gulch Zen Center co-hosts a "Voice of the Watershed" series each year with Muir Woods National Monument, including talks and walks across the landscape of the two valleys. At Manzanita Village in southern California, Caitriona Reed and Michele Benzamin-Masuda include deep ecology practices, gardening, and nature observation as part of their Thich Nhat Hanh-style mindfulness retreats.

Most of these examples represent social change agents working within Buddhist or non-Buddhist institutions to promote environmental interests. But what about isolated practitioners, struggling to consider the implications of their lifestyles in consumer America and other parts of the West? Independent of established groups, a number of Buddhists are taking small steps of activism as they try to align their actions with their Buddhist practice. One growing area of interest is ethical choices in food consumption, prompted both by health and environmental concerns. Many people, Buddhists included, are turning to vegetarianism and veganism as more compassionate choices for animals and ecosystems. Others are committing to eat only organically grown food, in order to support pesticide-free soil and healthy farming. Thich Nhat Hanh has strongly encouraged his students to examine their consumption habits, not only around food and alcohol, but also television, music, books, and magazines. His radical stance is echoed by Sulak Sivaraksa in Thailand, who insists the Western standard of consumption is untenable if extended throughout the world. Some Buddhists have participated in "International Buy Nothing" Day, targeted for the busiest shopping day right after Thanksgiving. Others have joined support groups for reducing credit card debt, giving up car dependence, and creating work cooperatives. Because Buddhism is still so new in the Western world, the extent of Buddhist lifestyle activism is very hard to gauge. But for many students, environmental awareness and personal change flow naturally from a Buddhist practice commitment.

ELEMENTS OF GREEN BUDDHIST ACTIVISM

What makes Buddhist environmentalism different from other environmental activism or from other eco-religious activism? The answer in both cases lies in the distinctive orientation of Buddhist philosophy and practice. Buddhist environmentalists turn to principles of nonharming, compassion, and interdependence as core ethics in choosing activism strategies. They aim to serve all beings through equanimity and loving-kindness. Though activists may not fulfill the highest ideals of their Buddhist training, they at least struggle to place their actions in a spiritual context. This reflects an underlying premise that good environmental work should also be good spiritual work, restoring both place and person to wholeness.

To be sure, there are significant challenges. Engaged Buddhist scholar Kenneth Kraft outlines four dilemmas a generic American Buddhist environmentalist ("Gabe") might encounter.[65] First, he or she would likely encounter some gaps between the traditional teachings and current political realities. Most of the Buddha's advice to students deals with individual morality and action; but today's environmental problems require *collective* action and a conscious sense of group responsibility. It is not so easy to find guidelines for global structural change within these ancient teachings. Second, Gabe must make some tough decisions about how to use his or her time. Meditate or organize a protest? When political decisions are moving at a rapid rate, activists must respond very quickly for effective holding action. Yet cultivating equanimity, patience, and loving-kindness requires regular hours of practice on the cushion. The yearning for time dedicated to Buddhist retreats can compete with time needed for soul-renewing wilderness. Third, Gabe may question the effectiveness of identifying his or her efforts as specifically Buddhist. It may be easier just to "blend in" with others working on the same issue. Fourth, Gabe may also begin to wonder about the effectiveness of some forms of practice forms in combatting environmental destruction. How can meditation or ceremony stop clear-cut logging? Can spiritually oriented activists make a difference in the high pressure political world? Given these and other challenges, green Buddhists nonetheless try to carry out their work in a manner consistent with Buddhist practice and philosophy.

Characteristic ideals for green Buddhism can be described in terms of the Three Jewels: the Buddha, Dharma, and Sangha. The Buddha exemplified a way of life based on spiritual practice, including meditation, study, questioning and debate, ceremony and ritual. Each Buddhist lineage has its own highly evolved traditional practice forms that encourage the student to "act like Buddha." At the heart of the Buddha's path is reflective inquiry into the nature of reality. Applying this practice in today's environmental context, eco-activists undertake rigorous examination of conditioned beliefs and thought patterns regarding the natural world. This may include deconstructing the objectification of plants and animals, the stereotyping of environmentalists, dualistic thinking of enemy-ism, the impacts of materialism, and environmental racism.

In addition, the green Buddhist would keep his or her activist work grounded in regular engagement with practice forms—for example, saying the precepts with other activists, as Thich Nhat Hanh has encouraged, or reciting sutras that inspire courage and loving-kindness (that is, the *Metta Sutta* for example, or the Zen chant to Kanzeon). Ring of Bone Zen students chant Dogen's "Mountains and Rivers" treatise on their backpacking retreats. Mindfulness practice with the breath can help sustain an activist under pressure, during direct political action or in the workplace. Green Buddhist ceremonies are evolving, often as variations on standard rituals—for example, the Earth Day precepts at Green Gulch, and the earth relief ceremony at Rochester Zen Center.[66] If the Buddha's path is foundational to Buddhist environmental activism, it means each engaged person undertakes some form of spiritual journey toward insight and awakening. Activism is the context in which this happens, but the Buddha's way serves as the model.

Of the Buddha's teachings, or Dharma, several core principles contribute to a green Buddhist approach. First, it is based on a relational understanding of interdependence and no-self. This may mean, for example, assessing the relationships of the players in an environmental conflict from a context of historical and geographical causes and conditions. It may also mean acknowledging the distribution of power across the human political relationships, as well as learning about the ecological relationships that are under siege. Second, green Buddhist activism could reflect the teachings of ahimsa, nonharming, with compassion for the suffering of others. For the Buddhist environmentalist this may extend to oppression based on race, class, or gender discrimination as well as to environmental oppression of plants, animals, rivers, rocks, and mountains. This recognition of suffering in the non-human world is rarely acknowledged by the capitalist economy. Voicing it as a religious point of view may open some doors to more humane policies. This green Buddhist teaching is congruent with many schools of ecophilosophy that respect the intrinsic value and capacity for experience of each being.

A third Buddhist teaching applicable to activism is the *nondualistic* view of reality. Most political battles play out as confrontations between sworn enemies: loggers vs. spotted owl defenders, housewives vs. toxic polluters, birdlovers vs. pesticide producers. From a Buddhist perspective, this kind of hatred destroys spiritual equanimity; thus, it is much better to work from an inclusive perspective, offering kindness to all parties involved, even while setting firm moral boundaries against harmful actions. This approach is quite rare among struggling, discouraged, battle-weary environmentalists who, in fact, are being attacked by government officials, sheriffs, or the media. A Buddhist commitment to nondualism can help to stabilize a volatile situation and establish new grounds for negotiation.

A fourth Buddhist teaching reinforces the role of *intention*. Buddhist texts emphasize a strong relationship between intention, action, and karmic effects of an action. If a campaign is undertaken out of spite, revenge, or rage, that emotional tone will carry forth into all the ripening of the fruits of that action (and likely cause a similar reaction in response). However, if an action is grounded in understanding that the other party is also part of Indra's jewel net, then things unfold with a little less shoving and pushing.

Perhaps the most significant teaching of the Dharma relevant to Buddhist activism is the practice of detachment from the ego-generating self. Thus, a green Buddhist approach is not motivated primarily by the need for ego identity or satisfaction. Strong intention with less orientation to the self relieves the activist from focusing so strongly on results.[67] One does what is necessary in the situation, not bound by the need for it to reinforce one's ideas or to turn out a certain way. By leaning into the creative energies moving through the wider web but holding to a strong intention, surprising collaborative actions take place. Small 'b' Buddhists have been able to act as bridge-builders in hostile or reactive situations by toning down the need for personal recognition.

Sangha, the third of the Three Jewels, is often the least recognized or appreciated by American Buddhists. As newcomers to the practice in a speedy, product-driven society, most students are drawn to the calming effects of meditation practice and the personal depth of student-teacher relationships. Practicing with community can be difficult for students living away from Buddhist centers. Building community among environmental Buddhists is even harder, since they are even more isolated geographically from each other and sometimes marginalized even by their own peers in Buddhist centers. From a green Buddhist perspective, sangha work presents not only the challenges of personal and institutional relations, but also ecological relations. Some of the leading green Buddhist thinkers have suggested ways to move toward this work in an integrated way.

Gary Snyder brings his sangha work home through the framework of bioregional thinking and organizing. His foundation for this is more than ecological; it is aesthetic, economic, and practice-based. He suggests that "by being in place, we get the largest sense of community." The bioregional community "does not end at the human boundaries; we are in a community with certain trees, plants, birds, animals. The conversation is with the whole thing."[68] He models and encourages others to take up the practice of *rein-habitation*, learning to live on the land with the same respect and understanding as the original indigenous people. He expects this will take a number of generations, so the wisdom gathered now must be passed along to the young ones. Spiritual community on the land offers one place to do this.

Others can participate in eco-sangha through supporting and lobbying for ecological practices at their local Buddhist centers. The hundreds of people who come to Green Gulch Zen Center or Spirit Rock Meditation Center, for example, follow the centers' customs regarding water conservation, recycling, vegetarianism, and land protection. With each step toward greater ecological sustainability, local community culture takes on a greener cast. These actions need not be only a painful commitment to restraint, rather they can become a celebration of environmental awareness. Printed materials such as the booklet on environmental practices at Green Gulch can help to educate visitors about institutional commitments.

Joanna Macy recommends sangha-building as central to deep ecology work. Through trust-building exercises, brainstorming, and contract-making, Macy helps people find ways to support each other in their activist efforts. Learning networks of Buddhists and non-Buddhists often stay together after her workshops for mutual support and prevention of activist burnout. Macy helps people taste the power of *kalyana mitta*, or spiritual friendship—acting together in the web to help others practice the Dharma and take care of this world.

CONCLUSION

How might Buddhist environmentalism affect the larger environmental movement and how might it influence Western Buddhism in general? Will Buddhist environmentalism turn out to be more environmental than Buddhist?[69] The answers to these questions must be largely speculative at this time, since green Buddhism is just finding its voice. It is possible that this fledgling voice will be drowned in the brownlash against environmentalists, or in the Western resistance to engaged Buddhism. Environmental disasters of survival proportions may overwhelm anyone's capacity to act effectively. The synergistic combination of millennialism and economic collapse may flatten green Buddhism as well as many other constructive social forces.

But if one takes a more hopeful view, it seems possible to imagine that green Buddhism will grow and take hold in the minds and hearts of young people who are creating the future. Perhaps some day there will be ecosattva chapters across the world affiliated with various practice centers. Perhaps Buddhist eco-activists will be sought out for their spiritual stability and compassion in the face of extremely destructive forces. Buddhist centers might become models of ecological sustainability, showing other religious institutions ways to encourage ecological culture. More Buddhist teachers may become informed about environmental issues and raise these concerns in their teachings, calling for moderation and restraint. Perhaps the next century will see Buddhist practice centers forming around specific ecological commitments.

Making an educated guess from the perspective of the late 1990s, I predict that the influence of green Buddhism may be small in numbers, but great in impact. Gary Snyder, for example, is now widely read by college students in both literature and environmental studies classes. Joanna Macy has led workshops for staff at the White House and the Hanford nuclear reactor in Washington State. Thich Nhat Hanh has shared his commentaries on the interbeing of paper, clouds, trees, and farmers with thousands of listeners on lecture tours throughout the West. Some practicing Buddhists already hold influential positions in major environmental groups such as the Natural Resources Defense Council, Rainforest Action Network, and Greenpeace. Perhaps in the near future they will also hold cabinet positions or Congressional committee chairs or serve as staff for environmental think tanks.

Buddhist centers and thinkers will not drive the religious conversation in the West for quite some time, if ever. The Judeo-Christian heritage of the West is still a prominent force in Western thinking, laws, and religious customs. However, Buddhists are already significant participants in interfaith dialogue regarding the environment. This could have an increasing impact on public conversations by raising ethical questions in a serious way. Right now, decisions that affect the health and well-being of the environment are often made behind closed doors. To challenge these in a public way from a religious perspective could shed some much needed light on ecologically unethical ways of doing business.

What happens next lies in the hands of those who are nurturing this wave of enthusiasm for green Buddhism and those who will follow. It may be religious leaders, writers, teachers, or elders; it may be the younger generations, full of energy and passion for protecting the home they love. Because the rate of destruction is so great now, with major life systems threatened, any and all green activism is sorely needed. Buddhists have much to offer the assaulted world. It is my hope that many more step forward boldly into the melee of environmental conflict. Side by side with other bodhisattvas, may they join the global effort to stop the cruelty and help create a more respect-ful and compassionate future for all beings.

NOTES

1. For information on ecosattva activity, see "Universal Chainsaw, Universal Forest," *Turning Wheel* (winter 1998): 31–33.
2. See, for example, such recent volumes as Steven C. Rockefeller and John C. Elder, *Spirit and Nature: Why the Environment Is a Religious Issue* (Boston: Beacon Press, 1992); Mary Evelyn Tucker and John A. Grim, eds., *Worldviews and Ecology* (Lewisburg, PA: Bucknell University Press, 1993); Fritz Hull, ed., *Earth and Spirit: The Spiritual Dimensions of the Environmental Crisis* (New York: Continuum, 1993); David Kinsley, *Ecology and Religion: Ecological Spirituality in Cross-Cultural Perspective* (Englewood Cliffs, NJ: Prentice Hall, 1995); Dieter T. Hessel, ed., *Theology for Earth Community: A Field Guide* (Maryknoll, NY: Orbis Books, 1996); Roger Gottlieb, ed., *This Sacred Earth: Religion, Nature, and Environment* (New York: Routledge, 1996).
3. Parvel Gmuzdek, "Kalayanamitra's Action on the Yadana Pipeline," *Seeds of Peace* 13.3 (September–December 1997): 23–26.
4. Joanna Macy, "The Third Turning of the Wheel," *Inquiring Mind* 5.2 (winter 1989): 10–12.
5. Ibid., p.11.
6. Wendy Johnson and Stephanie Kaza, "Earth Day at Green Gulch," *Journal of the Buddhist Peace Fellowship* (summer 1990): 30–33.
7. See reports on their activities in Bay Area Friends of Tibet newsletters.
8. Stephanie Kaza and Kenneth Kraft, eds., *Dharma Rain: Sources of Buddhist Environmentalism* (Boston: Shambhala Publications, 1999).
9. Sulak Sivaraksa, "Buddhism with a Small 'b,'" *Seeds of Peace* (Berkeley, CA: Parallax Press, 1992), p. 69.
10. Peter Timmerman, "It Is Dark Outside: Western Buddhism from the Enlightenment to the Global Crisis," in Martine Batchelor and Kerry Brown, eds., *Buddhism and Ecology* (London: Cassell, 1992), pp. 65–76.
11. See Rick Fields, *How the Swans Came to the Lake: A Narrative History of Buddhism in America* (Boston: Shambhala Publications, 1986), for a thorough history of these and earlier forays to the East by Westerners.
12. Gary Snyder, *A Place in Space* (Washington, D.C.: Counterpoint Press, 1995), p. 41.
13. Gary Snyder, *The Practice of the Wild* (San Francisco: North Point Press, 1990).
14. "The Nobel Peace Prize Lecture," in Sidney Piburn, ed., *The Dalai Lama: A Policy of Kindness* (Ithaca, New York: Snow Lion Publications, 1990), pp. 15–27.

15. Thich Nhat Hanh, *Love in Action* (Berkeley, CA: Parallax Press, 1993).

16. Issues on the theme of environmental activism were published in spring 1990, spring 1994, and spring 1997.

17. Alan Hunt-Badiner, ed., *Dharma Gaia* (Berkeley, CA: Parallax Press, 1990); J. Baird Callicott and Roger T. Ames, eds., *Nature in Asian Traditions of Thought* (Albany: State University of New York Press, 1989).

18. The other four books in the series address Christianity, Hinduism, Islam, Judaism, and Ecology.

19. See *Tricycle* 4.2 (winter 1994): 2, 49–63.

20. For Gary Snyder interviews, see "Not Here Yet" 2.4 (March 1994): 19–25; "The Mind of Gary Snyder" 4.5 (May 1996): 19–26; for Nanao Sakaki, see "Somewhere on the Water Planet" 4.2 (November 1995): 45–47.

21. For a detailed study of two Buddhist centers see Stephanie Kaza, "American Buddhist Response to the Land: Ecological Practice at Two West Coast Retreat Centers," in Mary Evelyn Tucker and Duncan Ryuken Williams, eds., *Buddhism and Ecology: The Interconnectedness of Dharma and Deeds* (Cambridge: Harvard University Press, 1997), pp. 219–48.

22. See conference talks in Rockefeller and Elder, eds., *Spirit and Nature*.

23. Mary Evelyn Tucker, "The Emerging Alliance of Ecology and Religion," *Worldviews: Environment, Culture, and Religion* 1.1 (1997): 3–24.

24. Tucker and Williams, eds., *Buddhism and Ecology*.

25. See one of the lead papers from the meeting: Stephanie Kaza, "Overcoming the Grip of Consumerism," forthcoming in *Journal of Buddhist-Christian Studies.*

26. See, for example, such works as Thich Nhat Hanh, "The Individual, Society, and Nature," in Fred Eppsteiner, ed., *The Path of Compassion* (Berkeley, CA: Parallax Press, 1988), pp. 40–46; Dalai Lama, "The Ethical Approach to Environmental Protection," in Piburn, ed., *The Dalai Lama: A Policy of Kindness* (Ithaca, NY: Snow Lion Publications, 1990), pp. 118–28; Sulak Sivaraksa, *Seeds of Peace* (Berkeley, CA: Parallax Press, 1992); Christopher Titmuss, "A Passion for the Dharma," *Turning Wheel* (fall 1991): 19–20; John Daido Loori, "River Seeing River," in *Mountain Record* 14.3 (spring 1996): 2–10; and Philip Kapleau, *To Cherish All Life: A Buddhist Case for Becoming Vegetarian* (San Francisco: Harper and Row, 1982).

27. Joanna Macy, *Mutual Causality in Buddhism and General Systems Theory: The Dharma of Natural Systems* (Albany: State University of New York Press, 1991).

28. Joanna Macy, *Despair and Personal Power in the Nuclear Age* (Philadelphia: New Society Publishers, 1983).

29. John Seed, Joanna Macy, Pat Fleming, and Arne Naess, *Thinking Like a Mountain: Towards a Council of All Beings* (Philadelphia: New Society Publishers, 1988).

30. Malcolm David Eckel, "Is There a Buddhist Philosophy of Nature?" in Tucker and Williams, eds., *Buddhism and Ecology,* pp. 327–50.

31. Ian Harris, "Buddhism and the Discourse of Environmental Concern: Some Methodological Problems Considered," in Tucker and Williams, eds., *Buddhism and Ecology,* pp. 377–402; and Hubertus Tellenbach and Bin Kimura, "The Japanese Concept of 'Nature,'" in *Nature in Asian Traditions of Thought*, ed. J. Baird Callicott and Roger T. Ames (Albany: State University of New York Press, 1989).

32. Lambert Schmidthausen, "The Early Buddhist Tradition and Ecological Ethics," *Journal of Buddhist Ethics* 4 (1997): 1–42.

33. Represented in Stephanie Kaza and Kenneth Kraft, eds., *Dharma Rain.*

34. *Samyutta Nikaya* II.28,65; *Majjhima Nikaya* II.32.

35. See, for example, Francis H. Cook, "The Jewel Net of Indra," in Callicott and Ames, eds., *Nature in Asian Traditions of Thought,* pp. 213–30; Bill Devall, "Ecocentric Sangha," in Hunt-Badiner, ed., *Dharma Gaia*, pp. 155–64; Paul O. Ingram, "Nature's Jeweled Net: Kukai's Ecological Buddhism," *The Pacific World* 6 (1990): 50–64; Joanna Macy, *Mutual Causality in Buddhism*; and Gary Snyder, *A Place in Space.*

36. Tu Shun, in Thomas Cleary, *Entry into the Inconceivable: An Introduction to Hua-Yen Buddhism* (Honolulu: University of Hawaii Press, 1983) p. 66.

37. Thich Nhat Hanh, "The Individual, Society, and Nature," in Eppsteiner, ed., *The Path of Compassion,* p. 40.

38. Snyder, *A Place in Space,* p. 70.

39. Rita Gross, "Buddhist Resources for Issues of Population, Consumption, and the Environment," in Tucker and Williams, eds., *Buddhism and Ecology*, pp. 291–312.

40. Joanna Macy and Molly Young Brown, *Coming Back to Life: Practices to Reconnect Our Lives, Our World* (Gabriola Island, British Columbia: New Society Publishers, 1998).

41. Macy, *Mutual Causality in Buddhism.*

42. Interview with John Seed, "The Rain Forest as Teacher," *Inquiring Mind* 8.2 (spring 1992): 1.

43. Gary Snyder, "The Etiquette of Freedom," in *The Practice of the Wild*, p. 10.

44. Alan Sponberg, "Green Buddhism and the Hierarchy of Compassion," in Tucker and Williams, eds., *Buddhism and Ecology*, pp. 351–76.

45. Joanna Macy, "Third Turning of the Wheel," *Inquiring Mind* 5.2 (winter 1989): 10–12.

46. Snyder, *A Place in Space*, p. 73.

47. See his discussion of the fifth precept in Thich Nhat Hanh, *For a Future to Be Possible* (Berkeley, CA: Parallax Press, 1993).

48. Robert Aitken, *The Dragon Who Never Sleeps* (Berkeley, CA: Parallax Press, 1992), p. 62.

49. Macy and Brown, *Coming Back to Life.*

50. Wendy Johnson, "A Prayer for the Forest," *Tricycle* 8.1 (fall 1998): 84–85.

51. Vanya Palmers, "What Can I Do," *Turning Wheel* (winter 1993): 15–17.

52. Joanna Macy, "Guarding the Earth," *Inquiring Mind* 7.2 (spring 1991): 1, 4–5, 12.

53. Kenneth Kraft, "Nuclear Ecology and Engaged Buddhism," in Tucker and Williams, eds., *Buddhism and Ecology*, pp. 269–90.

54. Amy Morgante, ed., *Buddhist Perspectives on the Earth Charter* (Cambridge, MA: Buddhist Research Center for the 21st Century, November 1997).

55. See 1998–1999 issues of *Seeds of Peace* for reports and announcements of these events.

56. Tenzin Gyatso, "The Nobel Peace Prize Lecture," in Piburn, ed., *The Dalai Lama: A Policy of Kindness*, pp. 15–27.

57. Gross, "Buddhist Resources for Issues of Population, Consumption, and the Environment," in Tucker and Williams, eds., *Buddhism and Ecology*, pp. 291–312.

58. Stephanie Kaza, "Acting with Compassion: Buddhism, Feminism, and the Environmental Crisis," in Carol Adams, ed., *Ecofeminism and the Sacred* (New York: Continuum, 1993).

59. Jay B. McDaniel, *Earth, Sky, Gods, and Mortals: Developing an Ecological Spirituality* (Mystic, CT: Twenty-Third Publications, 1990).

60. Bill Devall, *Simple in Means, Rich in Ends: Practicing Deep Ecology* (Salt Lake City: Peregrine Smith Books, 1988).

61. Stephanie Kaza, "American Buddhist Response to the Land: Ecological Practice at Two West Coast Retreat Centers," in Tucker and Williams, eds., *Buddhism and Ecology*, pp. 219–48.

62. Snyder, *A Place in Space*, p. 250. See also David Barnhill, "Great Earth Sangha: Gary Snyder's View of Nature as Community," in Tucker and Williams, *Buddhism and Ecology*, pp. 187–217.

63. Jeff Yamauchi, "The Greening of Zen Mountain Center: A Case Study," in Tucker and Williams, eds., *Buddhism and Ecology*, pp. 249–65.

64. Interviewed by Alan Senauke and Sue Moon, "Monastery in the Streets: A Talk with Tetsugen Glassman," *Turning Wheel* (fall 1996): 22–25.

65. Kenneth Kraft, "Nuclear Ecology and Engaged Buddhism," in Tucker and Williams, eds., *Buddhism and Ecology*, pp. 280–83.

66. A selection of such evolving practice forms are presented in the forthcoming anthology by Kaza and Kraft, *Dharma Rain.*

67. See Christopher Titmuss, "A Passion for the Dharma," *Turning Wheel* (fall 1991): 19–20; also Chogyam Trungpa, *Shambhala: The Sacred Path of the Warrior* (Boston: Shambhala Publications, 1988).

68. David Barnhill, "Great Earth Sangha: Gary Snyder's View of Nature as Community," in Tucker and Williams, *Buddhism and Ecology*, p. 192.

69. As Ian Harris suggests in "Buddhism and the Discourse of Environmental Concern: Some Methodological Problems Considered," in Tucker and Williams, eds., *Buddhism and Ecology*, pp. 377–402.

Racial Diversity in the Soka Gakkai

David W. Chappell

THE LARGEST AND MOST RACIALLY DIVERSE Buddhist organization in America is Soka Gakkai International—USA.[1] All Buddhist groups affirm racial harmony in theory, but in practice they are usually ethnic enclaves. The recent book *A Complete Guide to Buddhist America* lists over one thousand centers and includes all white American groups, but omits Soka Gakkai and Jodo Shinshu, the two largest Buddhist organizations in America.[2] In a country of immigrants like America, religion often reflects and reinforces the distinctive ethnic heritage of its members, and Sunday morning is said to be the most segregated time in America. In contrast, Soka Gakkai came to the United States in 1960 and attracted a greater diversity of races and classes of people in its first three decades than any other Buddhist organization. Since its diversity has not been precisely documented and analyzed, this chapter seeks to establish how racially diverse American Soka Gakkai is, and to ask what policies and practices have brought this about.

Soka Gakkai began in 1930 as a lay Buddhist educational movement in Japan. Founded by a school principal, Tsunesaburo Makiguchi, who later affiliated himself with Nichiren Shoshu, the tiny sect had only seventy-five temples by 1939.[3] Since its formal introduction to the United States in 1960, Soka Gakkai has undergone many changes, including a name change. From 1966 to 1991 it was called NSA (Nichiren Shoshu of America), a lay movement ratified by the Japanese Nichiren Shoshu priesthood,[4] but in November 1991 most lay Soka Gakkai members broke away from NSA to become SGI-USA (Soka Gakkai International in the United States of America).[5] Although it mentions Soka Gakkai in Japan and NSA (which still continues under Nichiren Shoshu priests), this article analyzes the racial diversity of only the Soka Gakkai lay movement in America, now known as SGI-USA.

Studies of Soka Gakkai usually focus on Japan, but even those centering on America have not focused on racial diversity, nor do they include the major changes of SGI-USA in the 1990s.[6] The specific task of this study is to explore racial diversity in SGI-USA in 1997, and then—since racial integration is still a problem in the United States[7] and with an eye to the theme of this book—to ask in what ways Soka Gakkai might be understood as socially engaged. To develop national statistics on racial diversity in SGI-USA, I have analyzed the racial composition of district leaders in nine cities,[8] which totaled 2,449 leaders in 1997. Before the racial breakdown is presented, however, I shall describe the methodology used in the research and briefly outline Soka Gakkai's history in America.

METHODOLOGY

This study began with the cooperation and support of SGI-USA. The editor, Christopher Queen, first proposed the topic to Rob Eppsteiner, director of academic affairs, SGI-USA, and they contacted me to do the study. I am not a member of Soka Gakkai, but I have had friendly relations in the past few years.[9] Rob Eppsteiner arranged for me to study major urban centers of SGI-USA in the summer of 1997 to analyze their racial composition, and SGI-USA agreed to pay for my travel, accommodations, and food during my fieldwork of forty-five days: April 25-27, May 19–June 17, and August 10-21, 1997. Also, the national staff of SGI-USA and the regional staff in the selected urban centers arranged meetings and provided information. Their help has been enormous: I am deeply grateful for the kindness of many individuals too numerous to mention, and it is clear that I could not have done this study without their active support.[10] In each city I visited,[11] the members were exceptionally kind and thoughtful, but also candid, open, and accommodating to my interests. Publications and records were made available to me, meetings and travel arranged, surveys collected, the ethnic identity of district leaders compiled, and often special histories and videotapes were made to facilitate accuracy and clarity in my analysis. Never has any SGI-USA member sought to censor or limit my inquiry, and at my request leaders have even provided materials to me that were critical of Soka Gakkai. I cannot thank these leaders and members enough for their exceptional cooperation and goodwill, and wish to begin this article by citing their cooperation as strong evidence for the new emphasis on openness and dialogue of present-day SGI-USA.

In order to gather information on the racial diversity of SGI-USA, I looked at the heart of the organization where the vast majority of the people focus their practice, namely, the district level.[12] Even though it was impractical for me to survey all members within SGI-USA, it was possible to identify and analyze the racial identity of the district leaders in major cities. Since a district has between fifteen and forty people, and each district has three or more leaders (men's chief, women's chief, young men's chief, young women's chief, and guidance leader), and since leaders are nominated locally and approved at the regional level, my working assumption has been that the racial identity of district leaders should be a fair reflection of the racial makeup of local SGI groups in each city.

Specifically, in each city I audiotaped and/or videotaped interviews with members from four groups: current regional leaders, founding members, or pioneers, to learn how Soka Gakkai grew in that area, a few district leaders who would distribute questionnaires for me, and members of the Culture Department. As a result, my fieldnotes are supported by a total of seventy-three ninety-minute audiotapes, nineteen four-hour videotapes, plus lists of district leaders from each city. During my trips, much more was learned than can be included in this report, such as the distinctive histories in each area, and when, how, and why the early Japanese group began to include non-Japanese members.[13]

TWO PERIODS OF SGI-USA

The history of Soka Gakkai in the United States must be divided into two periods: the period of aggressive evangelism *(shakubuku)* in the 1960s, 1970s, and 1980s, and the period of dialogue *(taiwa)* in the 1990s. The sudden growth of a racially diverse membership and its fusion into a tightly organized religion took place during the first period when Soka Gakkai became famous for its aggressive evangelism, and it is this period that has been the focus of most scholarship on Soka Gakkai in the United States. This article, however, looks at SGI-USA in 1997, long after the rapid expansion and street evangelism had disappeared, and six years after the separation from the exclusive and triumphalist Nichiren Shoshu priestly control. Instead, 1997 is a time when a second generation of community centers were being established not to recruit hippies but to serve their members in suburbia and the inner city; not focused on converting others but on improving their neighborhoods and entering into dialogue with local institutions.

The period of evangelism produced a racially integrated religious movement that was remarkable, especially since the main goal was not to change society but to convert individuals (called the "human revolution" in Soka Gakkai terminology). The unique convergence of Soka Gakkai street campaigns with the openness of the counterculture generation and the African-American civil rights generation in the 1960s and 1970s meant Soka Gakkai was flooded with new people eager to try this strange but alluring Asian religion. But the racial diversity occurred only as a by-product of converting as many individuals as possible, not as a deliberate policy. Measured against the values of socially engaged Buddhism, the racial diversity in Soka Gakkai (NSA) in the 1960s, 70s, and 80s was a major achievement, but this is not a study of the events and methods of those times of radical evangelism, which produced racial diversity, but a study of what has remained. In the period of dialogue in the 1990s, new socially engaged activities are sponsored nationally and locally that are explicitly aimed at supporting diversity within SGI-USA, as well as meeting other social needs. Our task is to evaluate how racially diverse SGI-USA is today and to ask how this diversity is sustained.

In the 1950s various Japanese Soka Gakkai members moved to the United States either on business or as wives of American servicemen who had been part of the occupation forces in Japan after the Second World War. The main point of contact for these individuals was with the overseas office of Soka Gakkai in Japan, which sometimes had names of other members in an area. Whether members met accidentally or learned of each other through correspondence from Japan, their meetings were always in Japanese and their focus on Japan.

The Period of Evangelism[14]

Soka Gakkai formally began in America in October 1960 with the visit to America by the young new president, Daisaku Ikeda. At each stop on his way he organized a Soka Gakkai group by appointing a leader and urging members to do three things: learn English, get a driver's license, and become a citizen. This is the official beginning of Soka Gakkai outside of Japan. Ikeda's trip took him to Hawaii on October 1, then to San Francisco, Seattle, Chicago, Toronto, New York, Washington, Sao Paulo, and Los Angeles, before returning to Japan on October 24. From this beginning, Soka Gakkai in the United States underwent phenomenal growth unmatched by any other Buddhist group in the West: in a period of three decades it expanded from a membership of five-hundred Japanese to over three hundred thousand members of mostly non-Japanese ancestry (although today two-thirds of these members are no longer active).[15]

A major reason for this remarkable growth was the dynamic leadership of Masayasu Sadanaga (since 1972, a.k.a. George M. Williams), who had practiced with Ikeda in Japan for four years before coming to the United States in May 1957. He accompanied Ikeda on his trips to America and became the national director in 1963, with headquarters established in the Los Angeles area. To encourage the American husbands of these Japanese members and a few American converts, meetings began being held in English from 1963 to 1965. When thousands of young hippies began wandering the streets seeking for truth in new places, Williams instructed members in 1965 to seek them out. The usual method was for young Japanese warbrides to invite people from the streets to attend a meeting on oriental philosophy or simply to "chant and be happy."[16] As young people responded to Soka Gakkai practice, Williams directed their energy into musical bands (started by Ikeda when he was youth leader in Japan), parades, and traffic control duties, and unleashed their talents in cultural and musical extravaganzas celebrating idealistic themes that integrated their diversity into a new community.[17]

Among the relatives, friends, and strangers from the streets who joined Soka Gakkai were a few black members, whose numbers increased dramatically beginning in 1971. After the civil rights movement many African Americans were seeking ways out of poverty and new spiritual alternatives to the racism that they had found in Christianity. Large groups began to emerge in cities like Chicago, New York, and Los Angeles; then members radiated outward to other areas like Boston, Philadelphia, Atlanta, Detroit, Cleveland, and San Francisco.

In spite of Korean[18] and Chinese hostility toward Japan following World War II, Soka Gakkai membership among Chinese and Korean immi-

Tri-Valley District discussion meeting, San Francisco area, June 1999. Photo by Mike Mullen, courtesy Soka Gakkai International—USA.

grants to the U.S. is large enough to allow them to hold meetings in their own languages. As a result, in most major cities there are regular monthly meetings of SGI-USA held in Spanish, Chinese, Korean, and Japanese, as well as in English. Separate language publications have appeared and separate meetings of these language groups are now held annually in the national conference facilities at the Florida Nature and Culture Center.

The Period of Dialogue

A new period began in February 1990 during a visit by Ikeda when Soka Gakkai was reorganized, prior to the break with the Nichiren Shoshu priesthood in November 1991. By asserting the *Lotus Sutra* doctrine whereby each person is a bodhisattva or saint-for-others, SGI gave "power to the people" in place of the priests, and thereby legitimated their new SGI organization. By 1997 the SGI leaders often invoked the Protestant Reformation to express this "priesthood of all believers," and substituted dialogue for authority as the new operating principle: both among members and leaders, and with other groups in society. The new importance given to local leaders was expressed immediately in 1990 by forming culture departments of the professionals in each region (lawyers, artists, educators, doctors, and health practitioners), by enlarging the national Central Executive Committee to make it more representative, and by preferring a more low-key leadership style by choosing a new general director in 1992, Fred Zaitsu.

ANALYSIS OF SGI-USA DISTRICT LEADERS

In October 1997 the SGI-USA website stated that "the American organization has grown to a multi-ethnic membership of 330,000" in more than sixty community centers around the country.[19] Although this is a reasonable estimate of how many people joined Soka Gakkai at one time or another (that is, received a Nichiren scroll called *gohonzon*), subscriptions in October 1996 to the SGI-USA weekly newspaper, the *World Tribune*, were listed as 38,550. Accordingly, a more conservative figure would be about 100,000 people who would identify themselves as belonging to SGI-USA, with about 50,000 members regularly practicing and attending meetings. Although not large by Christian standards, in the Buddhist world SGI-USA is much bigger than the next largest Buddhist group in the United States, the Honganji Branch of Jodo-Shinshu (Buddhist Churches of America).[20]

Based on the information provided from the SGI leadership in nine major urban areas in the United States, I was given the racial identity of

2,449 district leaders. To assist in tabulation, abbreviations are as follows: W for white Caucasian, B for African-American, J for Japanese, K for Korean, Ch for Chinese, H for Spanish or Hispanic, Br for Brazilian, and Car for Caribbean (mostly black, but possibly white anglo, hispanic, or creole). For those who are mixed half and half, a slash was used, such as J/W for Japanese/Caucasian, whereas a hyphen was used to indicate a combination of mixed racial and cultural identity, such as J-A for Japanese American or K-A for Korean American. The racial composition of the district leaders in nine cities in 1997 was:

Atlanta: 12W, 43B, 6J, 4K, 1J/W, 1Car = 67
Boston: 123W, 24B, 18J, 1H, 1Ch, 1K, 3J/W, 1J/B, 1Ch-A, 3Br,
    4 other = 180
Chicago: 56W, 75B, 26J, 1K, 1 half-J, 1 other = 160
Los Angeles: 156W, 101B, 140J, 13H, 36 Asian (15K, 14Ch, 7SEAsia),
    12 other = 458
Miami: 21W, 5B, 7J, 24H, 1Ch, 2J/B, 4 other = 64
New York: 142W, 141B, 56J, 53H, 25 Asian, 13Ch, 31Car, 4 other = 465
Philadelphia:[21] 44W, 60B, 10J, 6 other = 120
San Francisco: 280W, 103B, 127J, 44H, 15 Asian,
    30 Asian-American = 599
Washington: 113W, 103B, 67J, 4H, 22 Asian, 17 Asian Ancestry, 2Car,
    8 other = 336

If these 2,449 district leaders from nine cities are arranged by race, the percentages are:

947W (European-American) = 38.67%
655B (African-American) = 26.74%
457J (Japanese) = 18.66%
139H (Hispanic) = 5.68%
119 Other Asian = 4.86%
56 Asian ancestry = 2.29%
34 Caribbean = 1.39%
42 other or unkown = 1.71%

TOTAL: 2,449 district leaders = 100%

To what degree do these statistics of the ethnicity of district leaders reflect the composition of the membership? Stephen Bonnell surveyed the total membership in the Miami area and found about 795 members compared to 64 district leaders (based on names supplied by Tony Sugano), making the ratio of 12.4 members for each district leader. However, different areas had different ratios. For example, New York apparently has more members than San Francisco,[22] but fewer district leaders, 465 to 599. Accordingly, I conservatively estimate that there are 10 members for each district leader, which means that our total of 2,449 district leaders could represent over 24,000 members, more than half of the active SGI-USA membership.

Stephen Bonnell's data for Miami shows the following information with regard to the degree to which the ethnicity of district leaders reflects that of the members.

	District Leaders	Percent	Members	Percent
W	21	32.81	234	29.4
B	7	10.94	112	14.1
J	7	10.94	59	7.4
H	24	37.5	208	26.2
Other	5	7.81	182	22.9
TOTAL	64	100	795	100

Based on these figures, Hispanics, Japanese, and whites have a larger percentage of district leaders than their actual membership (37.5% versus 26.2%; 10.94% versus 7.4%; and 32.81% versus 29.4%, respectively), whereas black membership has a slightly smaller percentage of district leaders in relation to their membership (10.94% to 14.1%). Only in the Hispanic case does the leadership exceed the membership by more than 5%, which is probably due to the dominance of Hispanics in Miami politics. Based on the Miami figures for ethnic groups other than Hispanic, I should add a ±5% margin of error in using the ethnicity of district leaders to reflect the composition of local membership. Until further study is done, therefore, we may assume that the district leadership profile in these nine cities is fairly representative of the ethnicity of SGI-USA membership.

How does SGI-USA membership compare to the overall American population? The estimated total population of the United States in June 1996 was 265,089,998, with blacks estimated at 33,618,000 or 12.7% of the population. Hispanics (Spanish-speaking people of any racial origin) were estimated at 27,937,000 or 10.5% of the population. If one adds the Caribbean leaders to the total of African-American leaders, then black leadership of 689 consists of 28.1% of the total, which is considerably higher than the percentage in the total population. If we remove the Japanese leaders from our totals (since they largely represent a past generation), then the proportions become even more revealing: out of 1,992 non-Japanese district leaders, whites represent 47.5%, blacks 32.8 (or 34.6%), and Hispanics 7%. These figures still mean that SGI-USA, relative to the general population, has a higher percentage of blacks, whereas whites and Hispanics are underrepresented. Given the failure of other Buddhist groups to attract black membership, the most striking achievement of SGI-USA is its success in breaking down the color barrier. What is even more unusual is that this breakthrough has been made not just against American prejudices, but also against Japanese tradition, where light-colored skin has been valued.

By comparison with SGI-USA success among black Americans, even based on adjusted figures (with Japanese leaders omitted), the major group that has not yet produced as many SGI practitioners as their national ratio is the Hispanic (namely, Spanish-speaking members from Spain, Puerto Rico, Mexico, or Latin America, not including Portuguese-speaking Brazil). New York has the largest group, with 53 Hispanic leaders, or 11% of its 465 district leaders. The other major concentration is in Miami, but even there the numbers are limited, with the active Hispanic members being a little over 200 or 26% of the south Florida membership, as analyzed by Stephen Bonnell,[23] and these members are represented by 24 Hispanic district leaders. Because of the increasing presence of Hispanics within the United States, the Hispanic role within SGI-USA requires more discussion.

Based on these totals, it is clear that at the local leadership level, SGI-USA cannot be called a Japanese Buddhist group without serious qualification. What is remarkable is the massive change that has taken place since 1960 when President Ikeda visited small enclaves of Japanese members with their American husbands. Today, Japanese members constitute less than one-fifth of the leadership at the local level, and one must assume that their percentage of the actual membership is even lower than this. Also, it is clear that the membership of SGI-USA has twice the percentage of black Americans found in the population as a whole. Since this is a major achievement and contrasts with all other Buddhist groups in America, where black Americans are severely underrepresented, it also requires further analysis.

WHY HAVE MINORITIES JOINED SGI-USA?

Racial diversity in each city has its own distinctive story,[24] but there are some common patterns. In the Washington, D.C., area, for example, the leadership of Ted Osaki played a key role in building a practice where district leaders are one-third black. But I also heard many reports from people that echoed stories from other cities: people had joined because some individual Soka Gakkai members had maintained contact with them, cared about them, and helped them believe in themselves, and through this support they found a practice that enabled them to improve their attitude and circumstances, that gave them a purpose that was larger than themselves, and that involved them in working with and helping others. These three elements—people, practice, and purpose—are echoed by many across SGI-USA.

Ronnie Smith, an African-American leader in Washington who joined in 1972, asserted that when there were difficulties at home, or in the group, or with members of the same race, the teachings of Soka Gakkai made it clear that he had a choice: he could be stuck and miserable, or he could be positive and change the situation. Being positive was not just an attitude, but an activity. While Ted Osaki's leadership had attracted many into the Washington SGI-USA group, the program that he taught is not unique but is found across SGI-USA, and Ronnie Smith has remained for twenty-five years after the departure of Ted Osaki from the Washington area.

While the stories of practical benefits that resulted from chanting the *daimoku* (*namu myoho renge kyo,* devotion to the *Lotus Sutra*) are often heard, what was more impressive was the process of handling life when things did not go favorably, when bad things happened even after a commitment to what is good. For example, from Los Angeles to New York, from Chicago to Miami, I have heard the same remarkable method with which SGI-USA members are taught to respond to people who hurt them. The process that they outlined involved taking their problem into their daily devotions before the *gohonzon* (a scroll designed by Nichiren), squarely facing the pain and owning it by acknowledging that any difficulties they might experience were part of their own karma, then affirming their participation in a universal source by chanting the *gongyo* (scripture selections) and *daimoku*, and then transforming the situation from negative to positive by chanting for the well-being of the person who was the source of their pain.

Members and leaders of SGI-USA, like all people everywhere, are not always balanced and fair. But those members who have been hurt not only by outsiders but also by SGI leaders and members, and who still continue with Soka Gakkai, invariably say that the reason for staying is because Soka Gakkai teaching gives each member a tool to acknowledge, deal with, and transform personal hurt: namely, their chanting practice before the *gohonzon*—the teaching of Nichiren—and the encouragement of SGI president, Daisaku Ikeda. This is an abiding core in the hearts of members that maintains the sense of a caring community and belief in their own empowerment even when other individuals do not live up to their commitments. Members understand that other members, like themselves, live their lives in the tension between the ideal and the actual, and, like themselves, others sometimes fail. But there is an abiding faith in being empowered by the *daimoku* to meet and overcome any obstacle.

President Ikeda on Racial Diversity

Beyond their experience within the local community of SGI-USA and their personal practice, American members have stressed their respect for President Daisaku Ikeda. Beside each *gohonzon*, a picture of Ikeda can usually be found hanging on the wall. His influence on the thought and practice of SGI-USA members as they chant cannot be underestimated, especially for minority members. African-American members in Chicago remember how he was angered during his first visit to America in 1960 by seeing the hurt in a little black boy's eyes when he was kept out of a baseball game in Lincoln Park by a white adult.[25] It is well known across SGI-USA that although Nelson Mandela was neglected by the Japanese media and political leaders when he first visited Japan before he was the head of South Africa, Ikeda gave him a special welcome as a champion of human rights. African-Americans also often quote the remark by Ikeda that Africa is the continent for the twenty-first century.

It is well known across SGI-USA that Ikeda specially honored Rosa Parks, the southern black woman who refused to give up her seat on the bus and was arrested on December 1, 1955, thereby sparking the bus boycott and the civil rights movement. It is also well known across SGI-USA that when Rosa Parks was asked to choose a single picture to represent her life, she chose a picture not of her arrests or civil rights demonstrations, but a picture of her shaking hands with Ikeda in 1993, because it was "about the future." She went on to write about how she was often seen as a troublemaker by racists, but was amazed that someone from such a different, faraway culture would find kinship with her. She saw this as a model for the world, and wrote:

> I can't think of a more important moment in my life. It shows an unprecedented private meeting I had in 1993 with Daisaku Ikeda, and it reminds us how people of very varied opinions and unique personalities from two different cultures have an opportunity to work together on a mission of world peace.[26]

As recently as September 5, 1997, in a speech to a leaders' conference in Japan, Ikeda honored and described in detail the achievements of Sojourner Truth (1797-1883), an African-American woman born into slavery who became a champion for equal rights during the presidency of Abraham Lincoln. This speech, which described how NASA chose her name, Sojourner, as the name for its roving vehicle that sent such spectacular pictures of Mars to earth in 1997, was printed in the November 14 1997 issue of the *World Tribune*. As a result it is well known across SGI-USA that Ikeda champions Sojourner Truth. Since no other Buddhist leader in the world has upheld civil rights activists as consistently as Ikeda, it should come as no surprise that minority members feel that their struggles are particularly recognized and honored. It should come as no surprise that people such as Joe Parks of Washington, D.C., a member for almost three decades, would not emphasize material benefits from SGI-USA membership, but would write: "as an African-American young man, this organization of people is the only group aside from my family where I have felt fully accepted, and acknowledged. This is the only place in society I have found this to be true. I am 47 years old."[27]

Since George Williams was not only the pioneer leader of Soka Gakkai in America but also had known Ikeda from their youth and had accompanied Ikeda on his first trips around the world, I asked him how Ikeda had developed his internationalism. He replied that based on his experience with Ikeda from the 1950s, it was always there. Williams remembered that during Ikeda's first travels outside of Japan, such as his first speech in Italy, Ikeda threw his arms above his head and shouted: "I am Italian!" And when he first went to Brazil, the scene was repeated: "I am Brazilian!"[28] This sense of kinship and support that members of other races feel from Ikeda pervades SGI-USA. For example, Ken Levy of Los Angeles wrote:

In 1981, I met Daisaku Ikeda in Japan. I was impressed with his consideration for the common man, a man like me. I saw him again in 1984 and he
remembered me. He showed his sincerity, he was not a phony. Being a black
man raised in America, I was suspicious of leaders. They seemed generally
concerned with their own welfare. I realized from my encounter with Mr.
Ikeda that I was in the correct organization. I wanted to be treated with
dignity and respect. Through my practice I realized that I am a capable
human being. I have observed prejudice in some of the leaders of SGI, [but]
I realize they were a mirror of me because I was intolerant also. I know I
can change a negative situation into a positive one through chanting and
practicing Nichiren Dai Shonin Buddhism. I have seen people of different
race, color, economic status, age, etc. work together to accomplish a common goal for world peace. SGI has taught me not to blame anyone for my
problems. As a 59 year old man, I have won over every obstacle, now I have
set higher goals to attain. I can thank President Ikeda and SGI for that.[29]

The other side of this affirmation of all humanity is Ikeda's consistent
criticism of the perniciousness and falseness of the very idea of race:
"Concepts of race and ethnicity are in large part fictitious, and ethnic iden-
tifications have been artificially constructed by one means or another."[30]
Consistent with Ikeda's conviction that race is an artificially constructed idea,
several Soka Gakkai members refused to give any ethnic or racial identification on the questionnaire that I distributed in 1997. Others asserted that one
of the reasons they were members was because SGI-USA ignored issues of
race, but affirmed the solidarity of all humans as equally bodhisattvas of the
earth, each with a buddha-nature. For example, one district leader who had
practiced since 1972 identified her race as the "human race," but her culture
as "Black, Native American, Japanese," and her social role as "bodhisattva,"
which she claimed as central in her life. When asked for another factor
important in her identity, she listed "character."[31] Another example was a
twenty-six year old African-American woman who described her life before
Soka Gakkai as "hell" and "darkness," herself as a "lost little girl in Harlem"
who "was racist." "I was raised to hate white people," she said, but now she
could write that "I have cleaned this hate out of my life. I don't see
color...much now....I am not a black girl. With all my heart, I am a person—
I am just 'me.'"

The Appeal of Nichiren Buddhism

Outsiders often say that Soka Gakkai tricks people to join by bribing them
with the promise that you can get whatever you want if you just chant for it,

especially material objects such as money and cars. This claim that you can get whatever you want by chanting is certainly part of the core teaching of Soka Gakkai. However, this expectation has been a part of the Buddhist tradition since its beginning. Practicing Buddhism for practical benefits is not a distinctive feature of Soka Gakkai, but pervades Japanese Buddhism.[32] On the other hand, contrary to the stereotype about Soka Gakkai, in a recent study of Soka Gakkai members in Britain the main reason for joining for eighty percent of the members was not in order to obtain more material benefits that make life easier.[33] My experience of SGI-USA is similar to the British report: peace of mind, integrity, social justice, and commitment to world peace were important reasons for chanting.

While recognizing that Soka Gakkai invites people to chant for whatever they wish, it is also important to notice what members should not chant against: namely, they should not chant against their problems or their enemies. Rather, based on the Soka Gakkai interpretation of karma and as reflected in the comment by the woman from Harlem, each person is responsible for their own situation: no one should indulge in self-pity or blame others for their difficulties.

A major failure of previous research on SGI has been the way in which scholars have pictured Soka Gakkai as exploiting the weak with false promises. It has often been true that Soka Gakkai has attracted those who have problems—the poor and the sick and the troubled—but that is true for many religions. In SGI-USA, as in other religions, there are also many stories of miraculous cures of fatal illnesses. Scholars are prone to dismiss "faith healing" as something for the deluded who first created their own problems and then were cured of them. But I have also heard equally numerous stories of how people have transformed their interpersonal relations in their family, work, or school. In 1997 I did not see SGI-USA squeezing money out of the gullible, since appeals for money were notable by their muted tone. Instead, what was emphasized were the tools and friendships that SGI-USA gave that enabled people to discover their own capacities for empowerment, improvement, and service. Members can be described not as the needy, but as those who are also working to improve themselves. Yes, there are needs, but there are also dreams and ideals, and constant daily practice to overcome difficulties to achieve these ideals.

In sum, SGI-USA has attracted many people, including African-Americans, through its attention and care to the needs of members, its concrete practices, and visionary purposes that reach across color barriers to support those who are seeking to improve themselves and change the world. SGI and President Ikeda have championed heroes of racial equality like

Nelson Mandela, Rosa Parks, and Sojourner Truth, and African-Americans have responded to them in large numbers, in contrast to other American Buddhist groups.

Hispanic Membership in SGI-USA

While African-Americans are represented in SGI-USA in greater proportion than in the general U.S. population, Hispanics are underrepresented. Especially after the liberalization of the immigration law in 1965, Hispanics from Mexico and Latin America increasingly migrated to American cities and began to join Soka Gakkai. However, Hispanic membership in Soka Gakkai has remained low in more settled Hispanic communities like New Mexico, probably because of the strength of the Roman Catholic church. The largest number of Hispanic members seems to be in Puerto Rican neighborhoods in New York, but in recent years Hispanic members have also begun to emerge in other cities such as Miami.

Although Hispanics are not prominent, they occupy a place in SGI-USA that is not found in other Buddhist groups. First, SGI-USA is the only Buddhist group in the United States which regularly holds monthly meetings in Spanish in major cities such as New York, Boston, Miami, Los Angeles, Chicago, and San Francisco. Second, SGI-USA is the only Buddhist group that sponsors a national Buddhist meeting in Spanish (held in 1998 in the Florida Nature and Culture Center on May 14-17). Third, SGI-USA is the only Buddhist group in the United States that regularly sponsors annual Latino Festivals (in New York, San Francisco, Chicago, and Los Angeles) to develop better understanding and appreciation of Hispanic culture. While there are several Hispanic scholars in Buddhist studies in the United States,[34] and various groups scattered throughout Latin America, SGI-USA is the only Buddhist group to develop committees that systematically seek representation from each Latin American country.[35] Of course, this is facilitated by the fact that SGI is the only Buddhist group with branches in every South American country and with a widespread and established network to nurture and support the development of Hispanic Buddhism in the future. Fifth, and finally, SGI-USA is the only Buddhist group in the United States that publishes a regular Spanish language newsletter, namely, the *Arco Iris de Miami: Boletín de la SGI Miami, Estados Unidos*.[36] Therefore, it is safe to predict that SGI-USA will continue to expand its Hispanic membership and is the only Buddhist group in America prepared for the emergence of Hispanic culture as a dominant feature of the United States in the twenty-first century.

THE SOCIAL IMPACT OF SGI-USA

American Soka Gakkai in the 1960s and 1970s (when it was NSA) evangelized anyone and everyone. In 1997 a San Francisco pioneer, Marge Richards, described how she and other members recruited everyone on the street without trying to guess who might or might not be receptive, calling it the "scorched earth" method. This all-inclusive approach was most successful not on the streets, however, but among friends and families of members, who have always been the major source of membership.[37] In the 1980s when its growth began to slow, NSA already had become the most racially diversified form of Buddhism in America.

Not only did NSA recruit everyone, it believed in the value of everyone. NSA taught a view of buddha-nature in each person, which functioned regardless of conditions. Williams wrote: "The principle of enlightenment as we are (soku shin jobutsu) teaches that each and every human being can reveal his or her inherent buddha-nature without changing any outward circumstances." Then he quoted Nichiren: "Cherry, peach, plum, and damson blossoms all have their own qualities, and they manifest the three properties of the life of the original Buddha without changing their own character."[38] This universal affirmation of the value of every human being is found in Buddhism, Christianity, and Islam, but the way Soka Gakkai applied this principle to all strata of society without demanding a change in their lifestyle was exceptional and represents a second distinctive feature. For example, I have heard longtime members from the East Coast to the West Coast recall their amazement in the 1960s when, as young hippies, they had asked NSA leaders if they could chant namu myoho renge kyo to get girls or drugs, and were told that it was okay.

This unconditional openness of Soka Gakkai did not result in a loose organization featuring drugs and sex, but a in remarkably tight and caring group, which nurtured supportive friendships. In the end it was these supportive social groups that became the real benefit for new recruits, and it was these new support groups that then enabled new members to discover more positive goals in life. The role of Soka Gakkai in providing a surrogate family and committed friends is a recurring theme that is a third crucial element in their success at breaking down social barriers. While the constant contact made with potential members is sometimes a source of irritation for people who wish to be independent and who have complained about being hounded by Soka Gakkai members, for others this attention from members is an answer to a deep need. Williams noted that NSA had attracted a higher percentage of minorities than were present in the general population:

In addition to blacks and Asians, there are a significant number of American Indians, Hawaiians, Eskimos, Aleuts, Asian Indians, and other ethnic groups in NSA. The overrepresentation of various minority groups in NSA may, on the one hand, derive from their attraction to a religious practice that enables them to overcome their disadvantages in a still race-conscious society. It also reflects the fact that NSA is concentrated in America's major cities.[39]

Many other religious groups that teach nondiscrimination are also found in the inner city, but NSA added the crucial third element of personal caring. The minorities who populate America's inner cities often have relocated from their rural backgrounds and are frequently without friends or family. As a result, the attention and support from a group filled with positive encouragement can fill an important need in their life. The active energy in a Soka Gakkai meeting is qualitatively different from the quiet of a Zen or Vipassana group because of this constant, interpersonal engagement.

A fourth element that is often neglected in explaining the success of Soka Gakkai is an idealism that inspires and guides members into constructive new activities. Many outsiders have implied that Soka Gakkai preys on the weak and needy with false promises of personal gain, but these critics often miss the positive vision of a new society that Soka Gakkai emphasizes in the phrase *kosen rufu*. While this phrase literally means the widespread propagation of Buddhism, Ikeda and American Soka Gakkai members expand the phrase to mean bringing about a humanistic world of peace and happiness.[40] By asserting that individual happiness could not be complete without the happiness of others, Soka Gakkai became inherently socially engaged.

There are a number of levels in this effort. First is the individual sphere where negative energy is to be turned positive, where broken and bitter relationships are healed, and bad karma is transformed into good. Almeda Bailey of Chicago affirmed that "One of the reasons people are so victimized is because they are taught to look outside of themselves for solutions....In Buddhism each individual has the potential and the ability to become absolutely happy; we do that by empowering our own lives through our daily practice."[41] The idea of karma is used to urge members to accept responsibility for any bad situation they may be in, but also to be confident that they can create positive, new karma through chanting whereby "poison is turned into medicine" *(hendoku iyaku)* and "heavy karma is changed to light" *(tenju kyoju)*.

Individuals are changed through their chanting and study, but also through sharing of personal struggles and experiences in small discussion groups, and their social collaboration in a variety of musical activities, parades, and recruitment drives. Even the high-spirited competition among groups to see who can recruit the most members each month creates bonds of friendship across race lines.[42] The result is social change. When George Williams, the national director of NSA, discussed the social role of NSA activities in overcoming racial barriers, he quoted the following testimony:

> If I were not an NSA member, I might have voted for the white candidate. However, because I have a lot of opportunities within NSA to practice together with many black people, I've been able to observe them without any prejudice. So from an impartial standpoint, I checked the contents of the two candidates' policies and decided to vote for [black mayorial candidate] Harold Washington.[43]

In its emphasis on local meetings, American Soka Gakkai has provided an organized and deliberate way for bringing about both individual transformation and social change. The group and district meetings consist of chanting and interpersonal sharing of experiences in which racially diverse people are mixed together in a positive and supportive atmosphere that is usually lacking in conventional society.

IS SGI-USA SOCIALLY ENGAGED?

The phrase "engaged Buddhism" was coined in the 1960s by Thich Nhat Hanh, the Vietnamese monk who was nominated for the Nobel Peace Prize by Martin Luther King, Jr. because of his social activism during the Vietnam War. Sulak Sivaraksa, the founder of the International Network of Engaged Buddhists, says that the phrase means that "Buddhism is for social as well as personal liberation."[44] While Soka Gakkai liberates individual members from racism, does SGI-USA aim to liberate society?

In the 60s, 70s, and 80s, SGI's recruitment of a diverse membership was not aimed at directly challenging the social structure, but of fulfilling its own promise.[45] In his 1985 book, *Freedom and Influence: The Role of Religion in American Society*, George Williams supported the separation of church and state. But he also argued that, unlike other religious practitioners, Soka Gakkai/NSA members "help both themselves and society" since they are "based on the principle of *esho funi*, the inseparability of the individual and his or her environment...according to the principle of *shiki shin funi*, the inseparability of matter and spirit, or body and mind. In other words, human beings cannot achieve true happiness in the spiritual realm alone."[46] This means that members must change not only their inner spirit, but also their personal relations, their physical surroundings, and the conditions of others. True happiness is social and material, and involves the happiness of others.

In his book, Williams presents America as "an immigrant nation…a microcosm of the world's population," and he believes that this "pluralism is precisely what gives America a special mission in the world."[47] Based on the profile of Soka Gakkai members who cut across class and race barriers (chapters 9 and 10), he argues that Soka Gakkai actualizes the values of America better than anyone else and is the religion of the future. Williams argues for Nichiren Buddhism as the message for humanity based on social analysis, in striking contrast to other American Buddhist leaders such as Philip Kapleau, Robert Aitken, Chogyam Trungpa, Sogyal Rinpoche, Joseph Goldstein, or Taitetsu Unno, who appeal to individual personal experience.[48] The Zen master Bernard Glassman is one of the few Buddhist leaders in America who appeals to social action to demonstrate the value of Buddhist life.[49] This emphasis on social change to demonstrate the effectiveness of Nichiren Buddhism reveals the primacy of social engagement for Soka Gakkai.

It is equally significant that in the early 1970s Ikeda developed an extensive dialogue with Arnold Toynbee, the greatest historian of his era, to provide a framework to evaluate Soka Gakkai's social impact. Ikeda noted that the "most pressing problem facing the United States on the home front is that of racial discrimination,"[50] and throughout the dialogue proposed inner change, education, and culture as ways to move politics beyond conflict to harmony and peace. Since racial inclusiveness is an essential element of Soka Gakkai philosophy and practice, and since social integration is a crucial test of its claims, we must conclude that Soka Gakkai is inherently "socially engaged."

Whereas Soka Gakkai in Japan formed a political reform party (Komeito) to change society, in America it maintained the separation of church and state while emphasizing the importance of individual change. Nevertheless, today's practice is also deliberately linked to the transformation of the social surroundings of members. In 1997 in San Francisco, a district leader from the Mission area, Jackie Henderson, reported how much safer her neighborhood was after a year or two of practice, with the assumption that her practice had lessened the negativity in her area. Near the projects in Chicago, another district leader, Joanne Brewster, worked in 1997 to make her neighborhood safe through her practice. This connection between the improvement of an individual and the transformation of local social conditions became an institutional strategy in 1994 when a national campaign was started to reorganize district meetings so that their members were from the local neighborhood, rather than a gathering of familiar, established friendships from distant areas. Not only was this reorganization designed to ease travel distance, but also to make an impact on local neighborhoods. Accordingly, in the 1990s the role of the local district was not limited to individual transformation, but included local social responsibility.[51]

During dinner on May 23, 1997, the present general director of SGI-USA, Fred Zaitsu, kept emphasizing the theme of dialogue *(taiwa)*. Six months earlier he had explained the formation of a national diversity committee to ensure a voice for minority viewpoints by saying:

> Respect for others lies at the heart of Buddhism. Bodhisattva Never Despising [in the *Lotus Sutra*] is our eternal model. Leaders, of course, should never scold the members. But this idea, I believe, can be expanded to all human relationships. A spirit of generosity and forbearance to all people—member or not—is crucial if our humanistic organization is to make a greater impact on society.
>
> Our organization has one of the greatest mixes of races, backgrounds, educational levels, tax brackets and lifestyles of any other religious group. This is both our strength and our challenge. Learning to live and prosper in this diverse organization should be one of our highest priorities, for when we can find the solution to living harmoniously and justly, we'll be looked to ever more seriously by society at large.
>
> Toward this end, a historical step was taken this year with the formation of a special committee on diversity...this is only the first step....Nevertheless, the dialogue has been started and I'm determined that the effects will be felt throughout the SGI-USA.[52]

No other American Buddhist organization has made a similar commitment to diversity within itself. And yet, the formation of a national Diversity Committee within SGI-USA was also a recognition that the top leadership positions have been shaped by Japan and that now the organization needs to better respond to and reflect the diverse American membership. Before 1990, the executive committee of NSA had always been a small group of Japanese males, but after SGI-USA was formed the executive committee was greatly enlarged and became more gender balanced. Finally, in 1997 with the appointment of Sheilah Edwards as a vice-general director, an African-American cracked the top leadership circle, while in 1998 Ronnie Smith became the first male African-American vice-general director and the only appointee in 1998.[53]

American Soka Gakkai in the 1990s has also become more engaged with the work of changing outer society. Although the Santa Monica national office does not directly initiate efforts to change external social structures, it encourages social engagement under local leadership, especially in the areas of "peace, education, and culture." For example, each region has its own Culture Department consisting of professionals in healing, law, art, and education. A local diversity committee emerged in Chicago in 1997. Several Youth Peace Conferences (which were founded in Japan) were organized by the New York-SGI and have supported the work of the United Nations. Other local initiatives include ethnic festivals (Latin, African, Chinese, Korean, etc.), ecology exhibits, AIDS awareness projects, anti-nuclear arms exhibits, and diversity workshops.

Another change in the 1990s has been the development of affiliated SGI organizations on American soil that are not directly under SGI-USA but which enrich it: the Boston Research Center for the 21st Century founded in 1993,[54] the Toda Institute for Global Peace and Policy Research begun in 1996, and Soka University of America, scheduled to open its Aliso Viejo campus in 2001.[55] While collaborating with SGI-USA, the management and funding of these institutions are separate. Unlike the religious organization of SGI-USA, these institutes are clearly designed to change social attitudes and structures, but are specialized groups not needing or requiring all Soka Gakkai members to participate or even to agree with all their actions.[56] In five years, the Boston Research Center has sponsored many conferences, has collaborated with academics, and published several books.[57] The aim of these institutes is to build a civil society and a culture of peace, instead of direct social action such as helping the homeless or supporting civil disobedience. Nevertheless, SGI is the only Buddhist group not serving the United Nations as a Religious NGO, but instead as a cultural agency supporting the practical work of refugee relief and UNESCO.[58] For the fiftieth anniversary of the United Nations in 1995, SGI-USA recommended that each region arrange some activity to reflect SGI's "long-standing support,"[59] and a United Nations liaison office was opened in New York in 1997.[60]

The SGI sponsorship of peace, education, and culture has come to balance the religious activities of SGI-USA. Concretely, then, SGI in America now has two structures: the religious institution is SGI-USA, with its national headquarters in Santa Monica, and its district-region model not unlike the Parish-Diocese model of Christianity; and a group of institutions that are affiliated with, but independent of, SGI-USA and funded from Japan. These institutions (Boston Research Center, Toda Peace Institute, United Nations office, and Soka University) are directly sponsored by SGI but, unlike Catholic orders (such as the Jesuits,

Dominicans, and Maryknolls), are educational and nonsectarian. This pattern is clearly illustrated by the Toda Peace Institute, whose first director is Majid Tehranian, an Iranian Muslim.

CONCLUSION

What is the source of racial diversity in SGI-USA? If the major reason is the value placed on each individual by the *Lotus Sutra* and by the social activism of Nichiren (1222-1282), Japan's most socially engaged Buddhist prophet, then why are other Nichiren Buddhist groups not as socially active and racially diverse? SGI's leaders have prepared the way. The founder of Soka Gakkai in the 1930s, a geography teacher named Tsunesaburo Makiguchi (1871-1944), emphasized the importance of education that inspires value and purpose in life.[61] After wartime imprisonment, the second president, Josei Toda (1900-1958), challenged military and political policies and aggressively evangelized individuals *(shakubuku)* to Nichiren Buddhist faith in the *Lotus Sutra*. When Daisaku Ikeda became president in 1960, he traveled to America to meet members who were largely Japanese war brides. Rather than preserving Japanese customs, he urged them to learn English and become useful citizens, while encouraging their American husbands in the organization. Since then Ikeda has travelled constantly and widely, often engaging in dialogues with historians and statesmen about world trends and global problems. The internationalism and value education of Makiguchi, the geography teacher, has been restored by Ikeda and become his signature. Certainly this global vision and emphasis on value-education (ecology, peace, culture, and human rights) has made Soka Gakkai socially relevant far beyond its religious base.

Pivotal to the successful growth of Soka Gakkai in America was the brilliant and charismatic national leadership of George Williams (a.k.a. Masayasu Sadanaga), who practiced with Ikeda from 1953 to 1957. After studying political science in America, Williams accompanied Ikeda on his foreign travels in the early 1960s and began the energetic recruiting campaigns in the 60s and 70s that produced the large and racially diverse membership of today. Soka Gakkai was successful in America partially because it emphasized outreach at the right time, it offered a transforming practice and enthusiastic personal support to its new members, and it fostered an idealistic world vision. Soka Gakkai diversified in the 1960s when young people in the counterculture movement were looking for new alternatives beyond Western religions, and black Americans after the civil rights movement were looking for positive alternatives beyond race. But its popularity has endured in the conservative 1980s and 1990s, even after the split from the Nichiren Shoshu priesthood, by providing a method for personal transformation that includes a commitment to the happiness of others and an inspirational vision. Then and now, young people seem willing to surrender to discipline and responsibility in Soka Gakkai not because they are abandoning their ideals of freedom, but because they are fulfilling them by working together to show the world a better way to happiness and to lead the world to peace.

Early in the 1960s Ikeda declared that world peace did not require everyone to follow Nichiren, only one-third. Also, he began several initiatives that were aimed at changing society, such as the Soka school system and the Komeito political party.[62] At the same time Ikeda was furthering his own education by traveling around the world and engaging the best minds of the planet in dialogue. As a result, Ikeda balanced Toda's emphasis on religious conversion with a new focus on education and a civil society that facilitated diversity and dialogue. The more Ikeda traveled and learned, the more the topic of world peace changed from being an idealistic dream and turned into a practical problem.[63] In the mid-70s Soka Gakkai International was formed, and Ikeda began supporting the relief and cultural work of the United Nations. However, only after Soka Gakkai formally broke away from the authoritarian exclusivity of the Nichiren Shoshu priesthood in 1991 did Ikeda's vision for America become fully expressed.

Racial diversity has never been a goal of Soka Gakkai, and Ikeda has attacked the very concept of race as a false social construct. Instead, Soka Gakkai affirms the value of everyone just as they are, and the capacity of each individual to improve, as well as the joy and responsibility everyone has for the happiness of others. Unlike the intolerant *shakubuku* in the postwar period, it is clear that SGI-USA in the 1990s supports friendly cooperation with other religions and a concern for diversity at most levels of its organization. Also, Soka Gakkai in America has committed more resources to applying these values in a wider range of socially engaged ways (sponsoring civil society, peace education, internationalism, ecology, racial diversity, and multicultural cooperation) than any other American Buddhist group.[64] However, its primary mediums of work are twofold: personal transformation through religious practice and educational programs. The political fight for equal rights and economic justice, or practical relief for the dying, homeless, imprisoned, or sick, is encouraged among its members but is not institutionalized within SGI-USA. It is fair to say in 1998, however, that with its large diversity of local leaders, its emphasis on dialogue by its national director, Fred Zaitsu, and the socially engaged educational institutions established by its international leader, Daisaku Ikeda, Soka

Gakkai in America has committed more resources, has impacted more lives, and has created more substantial institutions to implement programs for social and cultural improvement than any other American Buddhist organization.[65]

NOTES

1. This claim is based on comparing Buddhist institutions that have active members who can be listed and counted. Although there are many Americans who now sympathize with and privately practice various kinds of Buddhism to some degree, the number who are active members of a particular Buddhist group—namely, who are officially listed, financially supportive, and who regularly attend meetings—is much smaller. I believe that the largest Buddhist organization in America outside of Soka Gakkai is the Buddhist Churches of America, but after a century of work in America, it remains almost entirely Japanese: the national board of directors has only three non-Japanese lay directors out of forty-one, and only five European-American ministers out of sixty-two. See Kenneth Tanaka, "Issues of Ethnicity in the Buddhist Church of America," in Duncan Ryuken Williams and Christopher S. Queen, eds., *American Buddhism: Methods and Findings in Recent Scholarship* (Surrey, U.K.: Curzon Press, 1999): 3–19. Among the almost one hundred Buddhist temples in Hawaii representing twenty-five different Buddhist organizations, each one has a clear ethnic identity except for Soka Gakkai. See *Unity in Diversity: Hawaii's Buddhist Communities* (Honolulu: Hawaii Association of International Buddhists, 46–150 Hilinama Street, Kaneohe, HI 96744, 1997).

2. See Don Morreale, *The Complete Guide to Buddhist America* (Boston: Shambhala Publications, 1998). Although most immigrant Buddhist groups in the United States have remained cultural enclaves as support groups for the culture of their country of origin—whether China, Japan, Korea, Vietnam, Laos, Sri Lanka, or Thailand—the three exceptions have been Vipassana, Zen, and Tibetan Buddhism. While the leadership of these two latter groups are often Japanese and Tibetan respectively, the membership of all three largely consists of educated middle-class European-Americans, while their leadership and their membership contain few African-Americans, Latin Americans, or Asian-Americans from other parts of Asia. The so-called *Complete Guide* lists over one thousand groups, mainly Zen, Vipassana, and Tibetan with a sprinkling of Asian groups.

3. Murata, Kiyoaki, *Japan's New Buddhism: An Objective Account of Soka Gakkai* (Tokyo: Weatherhill, 1969), p. 71.

4. The name of "Soka Gakkai of America" was changed to "Nichiren Shoshu of America" (NSA) in December 1966. "NSA's History," *NSA Quarterly* (spring

1974): 127, quoted in Jane Hurst, *Nichiren Shoshu Buddhism and the Soka Gakkai in America* (New York: Garland, 1992), p. 145.

5. Although the lay membership of Soka Gakkai was incorporated under the Nichiren Shoshu of America (NSA) in the 70s and 80s, since the split with the Nichiren Shoshu priesthood on November 29, 1991, Soka Gakkai in America has dropped the name NSA and only used the name of Soka Gakkai International (SGI)—an umbrella organization for the lay Soka Gakkai members formed in 1975—which in America was incorporated as SGI-USA. Those American lay members who chose to stay under the Nichiren Shoshu priesthood after 1991 have continued under the name of Hokkeko, which refers to all the laity who have formally joined Nichiren Shoshu through the ceremony of *gojukai*. See "Fundamentals of the Hokkeko (1)" and "Fundamentals of the Hokkeko (2)," *Shinyo* 2 (spring 1993): 23–28, published by the *Shinyo* Publishing Committee, Myokoji Temple, 1-6-26 Nishi Shinagawa, Shinagawa-ku, Tokyo 141.

6. Histories of Soka Gakkai in America include Jane Hurst, *Nichiren Shoshu Buddhism*; David Allen Snow, *Shakubuku: A Study of the Nichiren Shoshu Buddhist Movement in America* (Carbondale: Southern Illinois University Press, 1993); and George M. Williams, *Freedom and Influence: The Role of Religion in American Society* (Santa Monica, CA: World Tribune Press, 1985). Cf. Daniel A. Metraux, *The Lotus and the Maple Leaf* (New York: University Press of America, 1996), a recent study of Soka Gakkai in Canada. James Dator has a useful study of the American members in Japan during the 1960s in his *Soka Gakkai: Builders of the Third Civilization* (Seattle: University of Washington Press, 1969), pp. 29–82; David Snow has a helpful analysis of "who joined and why" during the 1960s and 1970s in America in his *Shakubuku*, pp. 193–26; and Jane Hurst clearly documents the shift that was emerging in 1992 in contrast to the 1970s in her *Nichiren Shoshu Buddhism*, pp. 139–74.

7. In early 1997 President Bill Clinton announced an initiative to improve race relations in the United States. In a press release on November 6, 1997, the President's Initiative on Race listed the first set of Promising Practices, which were described as "efforts that are successfully bridging racial divides in communities across America," to provide models for other groups to participate in or replicate. For more information, the public can contact the One America website at <www.whitehouse.gov/Initiatives/OneAmerica>.

8. In my research, I visited and conducted interviews in the cities of Los Angeles, San Francisco, Chicago, Atlanta, Miami, Boston, New York, Honolulu, and Washington. In addition, I was given data on the district leaders from Philadelphia that I substituted for the data from Hawaii in order to focus on mainland U.S.A.

9. I had some brief acquaintance with Soka Gakkai in 1977 when I took my University of Toronto undergraduate class to visit their center, but because of the exclusivism of Soka Gakkai I had no other contact until 1993 when I invited Soka Gakkai to send representatives to edit a volume on Buddhist groups in Hawaii. The SGI representatives were Joanne Tachibana and Heather Carver, and the book *Unity and Diversity: Hawaii's Buddhist Communities* (Honolulu: Hawaii Association of International Buddhists, 1997) can be ordered from Richard Paw U at 808-247-1150. Then in 1995 the SGI Hawaii Cultural Center agreed to participate in a community project that I was organizing entitled "Living and Dying in Buddhist Cultures" by hosting one of our Saturday workshops on June 24 and sending a national representative (Gerry Hall) to speak. Gerry Hall is director of the Culture Department, SGI-USA, and he reports that this meeting in Hawaii was the first time that he had spoken about SGI to a group outside SGI, which reveals that in 1995 SGI was just beginning to abandon their isolation to participate with other community groups. The development of a Public Relations Department at the national headquarters and the Boston Research Center for the 21st Century were early ways of institutionalizing contact outside SGI, and their participation in the annual meetings of the Society for Buddhist-Christian Studies also began about 1994, and saw concrete expressions through a resolution by the Society that raised caution about the increasing Japanese government regulations on religious freedom. The culminating event, however, was the co-sponsorship of the fifth international conference of the Society on the topic Socially Engaged Buddhist-Christian Conference held in Chicago in the summer of 1996. Since I happened to be President of the Society in 1994–1996, I was invited to Soka University in Tokyo and to the Institute of Oriental Philosophy to give talks in 1994 and 1996, and met with President Ikeda in April 1996.

10. Rob Eppsteiner was joined by a senior vice-general director, Guy McCloskey, in seeking SGI-USA support for the project. In addition, the Public Relations Committee under Al Albergate and the Organization Department under Greg Martin and Ann Miks at the Santa Monica national headquarters followed through to develop cooperation at each step of my journey. For example, they formed a Support Committee in Santa Monica that met me in late April to discuss my plans to focus on the district level and to meet with local Pioneers and the Culture Department of each area to discover how Soka Gakkai had developed and is now evolving. At my request, the Support Committee helped revise the two questionnaires that I had written for the districts and Pioneers in each urban center to provide more information on local experience. Copies of these questionnaires and the SGI-USA Memo #ORG-011 circulated by

Greg Martin on May 2, 1997 to the local areas asking for their cooperation can be obtained by contacting the author. After my regional visits, Ann Miks led me through the national archives and was endlessly helpful in clarifying information and explaining developments of SGI-USA history. In Hawaii, Joanne Tachibana and Bert Kawamoto of the SGI Culture Center, as well as Majid Tehranian and the staff of the Toda Peace Institute, have continued to keep me apprised of recent developments.

11. The one city whose statistics are included that I did not visit was Philadelphia district. However, their information was kindly provided by a longtime Philadelphia staff member, Stefanie Kaplan, whom I met at the Florida Nature and Cultural Center.

12. In December 1994 it was announced that 1995 would be the Year of the District. A year later the SGI-USA headquarters declared in its reorganization document that "The district is the frontline organization which should possess all the functions necessary to support the members' practice including study, propagation activities, publications (promotion and administration), guidance, planning, discussion meetings, home visitation, communication and encouragement in the basics of faith" ("SGI-USA Organizational Development Guidelines," Dec. 28, 1995, p. 1).

13. This anecdotal material is being prepared for publication in a collection to be compiled and edited by Phillip Hammond and Bryan Wilson on Soka Gakkai around the world.

14. David Snow has done the most thorough study of this period in *Shakubuku*. Whereas he uses the term "propagation and recruitment" for *shakubuku*, I am grateful to Jan Nattier for suggesting "evangelism" as an apt translation, as well as for her numerous other helpful suggestions for improving this article.

15. In October 1960, President Ikeda visited the United States and appointed leaders for Soka Gakkai groups in seven cities, thus marking the beginning of Soka Gakkai as an organization in the United States. According to James Dator, *Soka Gakkai,* p. 16, the *Seikyo Shimbun* (July 15, 1960) reported 466 members in North America. By May 1962, a membership of three thousand families in the United States was reported in the Seikyo News 1.1 (May 15, 1962): 2.

16. A parallel evangelistic method was practiced in Japan when female hostesses in Japanese bars invited American servicemen to meetings. See James Dator, *Soka Gakkai,* pp. 29–58. In his summary of the typical American convert in Japan, James Dator concluded: "We discovered that almost all of the Americans were lower-class, poorly educated, alienated American servicemen who—most importantly—were married to Japanese female members of the Soka Gakkai who were older than their husbands. We doubt that the Soka Gakkai will spread much beyond people like these, at least for the time being, because of its

Japanese culture-bound forms, language, and administration" (p. 135). It is a tribute to George Williams and the Soka Gakkai program that this prediction was wrong, that Americans of every social and racial class have joined, that the Japanese language has been replaced by English except in rituals, and that non-Japanese leaders are prominent at the national level, except in the highest leadership group of vice-general directors.

17. A vivid record of the extravaganzas created by Soka Gakkai in the cities of America under the direction of Williams can be found in George Williams, *Arise the Sun of the Century: Thirty Years of NSA* (Santa Monica, CA: World Tribune Press, 1989). The most thorough study of the early years of evangelism of NSA is by David A. Snow in *Shakubuku*. Also of great importance are the internal reports by NSA leader George M. Williams in *Freedom and Influence* and his *Arise, the Sun of the Century*; the first is analytical and the second is a pictorial account of NSA in America. For a discussion by the current General Director, Fred Zaitsu, on the purposes of these cultural festivals, see *World Tribune* (July 24, 1998): 7.

18. The phenomenal growth of Soka Gakkai in Korea into an organization with 220 cultural centers (compared to 64 in the United States) is briefly told in *SGI Quarterly* 14 (October 1998): 10–11.

19. The website address is: <http://sgi-usa.org/aboutsgi-usa.html>.

20. See Kenneth K. Tanaka, "Issues of Ethnicity in the Buddhist Churches of America," in Christopher Queen, ed., *American Buddhism Transformed* (forthcoming).

21. I am indebted to Stefanie Kaplan, former staff member of SGI in Philadelphia, who asked for a list of the district leaders from Carmela Menchaca (who was appointed Joint Territory chief in 1995) and who identified their ethnicity for me.

22. This claim was made by Rob Eppsteiner in a private conversation in Hawaii on March 5, 1998.

23. I am indebted to Stephen Bonnell, the territory chief for Miami #1 Territory, who personally contacted and compiled statistics on all the active members of the various districts in the three Territories of South Florida, namely, Miami #1 and #2 and Palm Beach Territory. This is the only region of the country where I was able to learn the ethnic identity of active members rather than just data on district leaders. Private correspondence of July 17, 1997.

24. A fuller account of the growth of Soka Gakkai in the Washington, D.C., area is given in my article in a forthcoming collection being compiled and edited by Phillip Hammond and Bryan Wilson on Soka Gakkai around the world.

25. Vividly retold by Daisaku Ikeda in his novel, *The Human Revolution*, vol. 1 (Santa Monica, CA: SGI-USA, 1995), pp. 146–48.

26. Marvin Heiferman and Carole Kismaric, *Talking Pictures: People Speak about the Photographs that Speak to Them* (San Francisco: Chronicle Books, 1994), pp. 198–99. I am indebted to Richard Yoshimachi, head of the San Francisco SGI Joint Territory (now Region), for bringing this picture to my attention.

27. Joe Parks joined Soka Gakkai in 1970 as a young hippie when he was hitch-hiking and was picked up by Mike Brown, another young hippie member. His statement was written as part of a packet kindly prepared by Kathy Geisler and the SGI-USA Community Center of Washington for my visit on August 17–19, 1997.

28. Taped interview in Santa Monica on May 21, 1997.

29. Taped interview in Santa Monica SGI-USA Headquarters (May 20, 1997), plus an Individual History Survey and a typed statement.

30. *Seikyo Times* (July 1995): 56.

31. A survey form returned from the Pyramid district, New York. Cf. Shelby Steele, *Content of our Character: A New Vision of Race in America* (New York: Harper, 1990).

32. See George Tanabe and Ian Reader, *Practically Religious: Worldly Benefits and the Common Religion of Japan* (Honolulu: University of Hawaii Press, 1998).

33. Bryan Wilson and Karel Dobbelaere, *A Time to Chant: The Soka Gakkai Buddhists in Britain* (Oxford: Oxford University Press, 1994), p. 63. The main reason for joining was the quality of the members for 37%, the character of the organization for 16%, and personal happiness and confidence for 14%, where-as practical benefits were the main reason for joining for only 19%. For those who remained members, the quality of the other members was decreasingly important, about the same number remained because of practical benefits, but more remained because of the character of the organization, even more for per-sonal happiness and intellectual satisfaction, and more still for ethical motives.

34. Luis Gomez and Donald Lopez at the University of Michigan and José Ignacio Cabezón at Iliff School of Theology, for example.

35. Miami Joint Territory (Region) and San Francisco Joint Territory (Region) have formed such committees in the 1990s. One reason has been that each Latin American country has its own unique cultural heritage and could ideal-ly present a booth or performance at the annual Latino festivals. Another rea-son is to facilitate contacts and support between immigrants to the United States and their homelands. In Miami, the Liaison/Exchange Committee in Miami has been headed by Monica Lema from Colombia.

36. Information on *Arco Iris de Miami* can be obtained through the Florida Nature and Culture Center, 20,000 SW 36th Street, Ft. Lauderdale, FL 33332-1929 (phone: 954-349-5000, fax: 954-349-5001), or the Florida Nature and Culture Center (phone: 954-349-5200, fax: 954-349-5201).

37. David A. Snow has done the most careful work analyzing channels of recruitment, especially from the mid-60s to the mid-70s, when NSA experienced its largest membership increases. He found that social relationships (friends and family) always accounted for at least three-quarters of the membership. See Snow, *Shakubuku*, pp. 193–246, especially Table 8.

38. Williams, *Freedom and Influence: The Role of Religion in American Society*, p. 190.

39. Ibid.

40. For the traditional meaning of the term, see *The Dictionary of Buddhist Terms and Concepts* (Tokyo: Nichiren Shoshu International Center, 1983), pp. 235–36, but in the mid-1960s Ikeda transformed the term to mean a vision of world happiness and peace, while softening aggressive *shakubuku* to be more non-confrontational (Murata, pp. 129–32), whereby a "third civilization" can be built. This utopian ideal of world peace and human happiness permeates American Soka Gakkai (Snow, *Shakubuku,* pp. 57–60).

41. Denver Long, "The Soka Gakkai International Towards the 21st Century, Nichiren Daishonin's Buddhism in Chicago's African-American Community: Reflections on Twenty Five Years of Socialization (1970–1995)" (Chicago: DePaul University M.A. thesis, 1994), p. 40.

42. The bonding of white and black is exemplified by Daniel Liebowitz and Richard Brown, who presently collaborate as a public health professional and a lawyer to resolve social problems in Atlanta, but who became friends as leaders of NSA teams competing to bring in the most members each month back in the 1970s.

43. Williams, *Freedom and Influence,* p. 188.

44. Sulak Sivaraksa, *Loyalty Demands Dissent: Autobiography of an Engaged Buddhist* (Berkeley, CA: Parallax Press, 1998), chapter 18.

45. Hurst, *Nichiren Shoshu Buddhism*, pp. 161–62.

46. Williams, *Freedom and Influence*, p. 218.

47. Ibid., p. 221.

48. See books such as Philip Kapleau, *The Three Pillars of Zen* (New York: Weatherhill, 1965), Robert Aitken, *Taking the Path of Zen* (San Francisco: North Point Press, 1982), Chogyam Trungpa, *Cutting Through Spiritual Materialism* (Berkeley: Shambhala, 1973) and *The Myth of Freedom and the Way of Meditation* (Boulder: Shambhala, 1976), Sogyal Rinpoche, *The Tibetan Book of Living and Dying* (San Francisco: Harper, 1994), Joseph Goldstein, *The Experience of Insight: A Natural Unfolding* (Santa Cruz: Unity Press, 1976), and Taitetsu Unno, *River of Fire, River of Water* (New York: Doubleday, 1998). Certainly Robert Aitken, founder of the Buddhist Peace Fellowship, has many books on Buddhist ethics, such as *The Mind of Clover* (San Francisco: North Point Press, 1984) and *The Practice of Perfection* (New York: Pantheon, 1994), but

he does not appeal to examples of successful social change as a way to legitimate his "encouraging words." Instead, his guidance is persuasive, and his books successful, because they strike a chord that is both true to his spiritual heritage and to the minds of his readers.

49. Bernard Glassman and Rick Fields, *Instructions for the Cook: A Zen Master's Lessons in Living a Life that Matters* (New York: Bell Tower, 1996).

50. Arnold Toynbee and Daisaku Ikeda, *Choose Life: A Dialogue* (Oxford: Oxford University Press, 1976), p. 177.

51. For details on this reorganization work throughout SGI-USA, contact the Organization Department headed by George Kataoka.

52. Minutes of the SGI-USA Central Executive Committee for December 7, 1996, dealing with the creation of a national Executive Committee on Race and Ethnic Diversity.

53. In 1997 the members of the board of directors with fiduciary responsibility were still all male (Fred Zaitsu, George Williams, James Kato, David Kasahara, Richard Sasaki, Guy McCloskey, and Danny Nagashima) and only Guy McCloskey was not ethnically Japanese. Among the seventeen vice-general directors, four were women: Kazue Elliot and Wendy Clark are ethnically Japanese, Matilda Buck is white American, and Sheilah Edwards. I am indebted to Guy McCloskey for supplying me with the information about Ronnie Smith and for making other valuable editorial corrections.

54. The threefold purpose of the Boston Research Center is explicitly aimed at social transformation: "(1) the prevention of violent confrontation through enhanced mutual understanding; (2) the evolution of a widespread consensus in favor of life-affirming human values; and (3) the development of a philosophical basis for appreciating differences and fostering harmony among the world's peoples, cultures and religions." *Newsletter* 1 (spring 1994).

55. In 2001, Soka University of America will open its doors in Orange County, California, designed for a student body of about 1200 undergraduates and 200 graduate students. It is incorporated separately from SGI-USA and has an academic purpose rather than a religious one. One way in which it will work to develop a culture of peace is by instituting a unique foreign language/internship abroad program that will require three years of a foreign language to prepare the students in the third or fourth year of instruction to be placed in an internship abroad. This internship will be different from just study abroad since it will require students to use their language in a real-life work situation. Students who enroll in this program must be dedicated to working in the international arena. Information can be obtained from Dr. Eric Hauber, Vice President for Academic Affairs, Soka University of

America, 85 Argonaut, Suite 200, Aliso Viejo, CA 92656 (phone: 949-472-3050, fax: 949-472-3063, and e-mail: <wwharder@soka.edu>). See *World Tribune* (December 5, 1997).

56. In some ways, these new institutes parallel the system of Catholic Orders (such as the Jesuits, Franciscans, and Maryknoll, as well as Catholic Social Services), whereas the districts-territory system parallels the Catholic parish-diocese system, except that the new SGI institutes are educational nonprofit organizations, not religious organizations.

57. The many symposia sponsored by the Boston Research Center are reported in their quarterly Newsletter. Recent books that have resulted from direct sponsorship include, in 1997, *Women's Views on the Earth Charter,* edited by Helen Marie Casey and Amy Morgante; and *Buddhist Perspectives on the Earth Charter,* edited by Amy Morgante; and, in 1998, *Subverting Hatred: The Challenge of Nonviolence in Religious Traditions,* edited by Daniel Smith-Christopher; *Abolishing War: Dialogue with Peace Scholar,s* edited by Elise Boulding and Randall Forsberg; and *Human Rights, Environmental Law, and the Earth Charter,* edited by Helen Marie Casey and Amy Morgante; all published by Boston Research Center for the 21st Century, 396 Harvard Street, Cambridge, MA 02138-3924.

58. See the *Survey of Activities of Religious NGOs at the United Nations 1995–1996* (no place or date of publication) published by The Committee of Religious NGOs at the United Nations and available through its President, Rev. Chung Ok Lee, Won Buddhist United Nations Representative, 431 East 57th Street, New York, N.Y. 10022. There are three Buddhist members (Won Buddhism, Rissho Koseikai, and the Association of American Buddhists). For two decades SGI has worked with the United Nations to provide over $5 million (U.S.) in refugee aid and has worked with UNESCO for cultural and educational exchange. That is to say, instead of focusing on religious practice at the United Nations, which emphasizes prayer and/or meditation, SGI has given both financial and educational support. The serious and sustained work of SGI with the United Nations was recognized on December 7, 1997, when the World Federation of United Nations Associations (which has seventy-seven member associations worldwide) accepted SGI as a member association in recognition of its longtime support for United Nations activities. See *World Tribune* (January 9, 1998): 5.

59. This recommendation was included in the 25th Central Executive Committee Documents, May 19–22, 1994: 25–27.

60. The SGI United Nations Liaison Office is directed by Rob Eppsteiner and staffed by Andrew Gebert and Hiroyuki Sakurai (phone: 212-727-7018, fax: 212-727-7020, and e-mail: <sgiunny@pop.net>) and is located in the SGI-

New York Culture Center. Its purpose is to facilitate the involvement of SGI-USA members with the United Nations and to encourage more SGI-USA projects to support United Nations work.

61. The founder of Soka Gakkai was the educator. Makiguchi Tsunesaburo, born June 6, 1871, four years after the Meiji government began its dramatic modernization reforms. His early interest was in geography, which gave him a worldwide vision of humanity. His first book was called *Jinsei Chirigaku* (Human-life Geography), published in 1903, and his second book was *Kyoju no Togo Chushin to shite no Kyodoka Kenkyu* (A Study of the Places of Origin as the Core of All Lessons), published in 1912, but his work as a principal of six elementary schools in Tokyo from 1913 to 1932 directed his attention away from the past and toward developing young lives in the modern world. The result of his new focus was his most influential work, *Soka Kyoikugaku Taikei* (A Value-creating Educational System), published on November 18, 1930, which Soka Gakkai takes as the date of its establishment. Already while working on this book, Makiguchi became a Nichiren Shoshu practitioner in 1928 when he was fifty-seven years old. During the next decade, a small discussion group led by Makiguchi became the Value-creating Educational Society and gradually took on more religious dimensions. When Makiguchi refused to support government thinking during the war, he was arrested in 1943 and died in prison on November 18, 1944 at the age of seventy-three. Although Makiguchi was firm in not compromising his principles, the primary focus of Makiguchi's reformist ideas was not to change society but to bring creative fulfillment to the individual. Helpful studies of Makiguchi that evaluate his teachings within their educational context are: Koichi Mori, *Study of Makiguchi Tsunesaburo: The Founder of Soka Gakkai* (Th.D. diss., Graduate Theological Union, 1977, available from University Microfilms International, Ann Arbor, as #78-5457); Dayle M. Bethel, *Makiguchi the Value Creator* (Tokyo: Weatherhill, 1973), and Dayle M. Bethel, *Education for Creative Living: Ideas and Proposals of Tsunesaburo Makiguchi* (Ames, IA: Iowa State University Press, 1989).

62. Kiyoaki Murata, *Japan's New Buddhism: An Objective Account of Soka Gakkai* (Tokyo: Weatherhill, 1969), pp. 129–32, 137. Even though the Komeito is now the second largest opposition party in Japan, today it is legally separated from Soka Gakkai, and no direct political involvement was ever attempted in America; instead the separation of church and state has always been emphasized.

63. Each year on the anniversary of the founding of the Soka Gakkai International on January 26, 1975, Ikeda has presented major policy statements on global peace that are permeated with ideas drawn from Mahayana Buddhism, the United Nations, the Club of Rome, and various statesmen and peace policy

advocates around the world such as Linus Pauling, Mikhail Gorbachev, Aurelio Peccei, and Boutros Boutros-Ghali.

64. The other forms of socially engaged Buddhism in America are discussed in detail in other chapters of this book.

65. Again, it is important to emphasize that this article analyzes a Buddhist institution, SGI-USA, but is not claiming that SGI-USA has more influence than various Buddhist cultural movements such as Zen, or has made more impact in America than certain Buddhist individuals such as the exiled Tibetan Buddhist political leader, the Dalai Lama, or the exiled Vietnamese social activist and poet, Thich Nhat Hanh.

THE FREE TIBET MOVEMENT:
A SELECTIVE NARRATIVE

John Powers

AT DAWN OF MARCH 10, 1959, crowds of Tibetans began to gather outside the Norbulingka, the Dalai Lama's summer palace, a short distance from the capital city of Lhasa. Their aim was to protest an order from Tan Guansan, Political Commissar for the Peoples' Republic of China (PRC), that the Dalai Lama attend a theatrical performance, and that he arrive alone, with no bodyguards or retainers. The Tibetan crowd feared that the order was a pretext for arresting their spiritual and temporal leader.[1]

By noon there were over thirty thousand Tibetans around the Norbulingka, and many were shouting anti-Chinese slogans and demanding that China leave Tibet. The populace had become increasingly restive under Chinese rule, and the March 10 demonstrations became the occasion for a public venting of anger. When troops of the People's Liberation Army (PLA) first began to enter Tibet in 1950 they told the people they met that their aim was only to help, and that they would bring modernization and economic prosperity to the backward region. They further promised that Tibet's unique culture and religion would not be harmed, and that the Dalai Lama would retain his authority over domestic affairs.[2]

After gaining control of the country, however, the Chinese authorities began to remake Tibet in accordance with Mao Zedong's vision of Marxism-Leninism. As it became more and more apparent that the invaders intended to completely eradicate the traditional institutions of the country, Tibetans became restive. The March 10 demonstrations proved to be the flashpoint, and as crowds took to the streets to protest the Chinese occupation of their country, the new rulers decided to act decisively. Reinforcements were brought to Tibet from all over China, while the authorities sent out broadcasts urging the populace to remain calm.

On the following day a public meeting was held at the government printing press at Shöl, below the Potala (the Dalai Lama's winter palace). The meeting, attended by Tibetans from all segments of society, unanimously issued a formal declaration of Tibetan independence that called for the Chinese to leave Tibet. More demonstrations were held during the next several days, and monks, nuns, and villagers from surrounding areas poured into the city to join the growing anti-Chinese movement.

On March 17 two mortar shells were fired from a Chinese army camp into the Norbulingka, prompting the Tibetan Cabinet to urge the Dalai Lama to flee the country. At dusk the Dalai Lama, disguised as a soldier, slipped from the palace through a door in a remote part of the compound and joined a small group of relatives and retainers. The band traveled to the banks of the Kyichu River, where they were met by thirty Tibetan resistance fighters, who had brought horses and provisions for the Dalai Lama's flight into exile.

On March 20, unaware that the Dalai Lama had slipped away, the Chinese army began shelling the Norbulingka, sparking more fighting and demonstrations among the Tibetan populace. On March 31, just one day ahead of Chinese patrols that had been sent to intercept and capture him, the Dalai Lama arrived at the Indian check post of Chuthangmo and was granted political sanctuary by Jawaharlal Nehru, the Indian prime minister.

In the following months PRC authorities embarked on a massive show of force to crush the growing dissent. In the aftermath of the demonstrations, an estimated 87,000 Tibetans were killed by Chinese forces and another 25,000 imprisoned. The demonstrations and subsequent massacres have become the focal symbols of the Free Tibet movement, which has steadily gained momentum in the decades since China first annexed the country, ostensibly to reunite it with the "motherland" and free it from foreign "imperialists." Despite China's claims, Tibet had been officially independent since 1912, and China had never actually ruled the country as part of China prior to its invasion.[3] Also, at the time when PLA troops crossed the border, there were only six foreigners in the entire country, none of whom had significant influence with the Tibetan government.

TIBET IN EXILE

Once in India, the Dalai Lama sent messages to governments and political organizations around the world pleading for help, but none cared to listen. Tibet had been isolated from the rest of the world for centuries, and even though it had been treated as an independent state on several occasions in international negotiations,[4] no government was prepared to give it recognition as an independent state or to intercede on its behalf. After months of fruitless attempts to garner international support for his cause, the Dalai

Lama began to turn his attention to making a home in India for himself and the estimated one hundred thousand Tibetans who followed him into exile.

Shortly after the establishment of a Tibetan government-in-exile in 1960, the Dalai Lama issued a statement outlining the goals of the government:

1. Representation of Tibetan refugees;

2. Guardianship of Tibetan culture, religion, and language;

3. Care and education of Tibetan children;

4. Preservation of national and cultural identity in exile;

5. Defense of the national sovereignty of the Tibetan people on the basis of a democratic form of state;

6. Continuing the nonviolent Tibetan struggle for freedom in the name of the five million Tibetans in Tibet and in exile.[5]

Since that time, the Tibetan government-in-exile, under the Dalai Lama's direction, has established fifty-three refugee communities in India and Nepal and has provided the administrative basis for a form of self-government in exile. It has also set up several educational facilities for Tibetan children, called "Tibetan children's villages," as well as institutes to preserve Tibet's traditional performing arts, scriptures, and medical traditions. In addition, the exile government has become increasingly effective at gathering and disseminating information regarding the situation in Tibet and the plight of the refugee community.

The efforts of the Dalai Lama and his fellow refugees mark the beginning of the Free Tibet movement, which in recent decades has become a global phenomenon. The movement has taken some surprising turns and attracted a diverse cast of characters, including the Tibetan refugees, Western students of Buddhism, the American CIA, conservative Republicans and liberal Democrats in the U.S. Congress, and more recently high-profile movie stars and rock musicians. The story of the movement is now told all over the world, and the Dalai Lama has become one of the most widely recognized people on the planet. Because of the diversity of the movement and the large number of people who have played an important role in it, it will only be possible in this article to highlight some of the significant events of the past four decades and to provide vignettes of the backgrounds and motivations of a select group who have played major roles or whose ideas and activities are representative of important segments of the movement.

Unlike most of the other movements discussed in this book, the Free Tibet cause is not primarily an explicitly Buddhist movement, although many of its most active members have been Buddhists. During the research for this article, I spoke to a number of pro-Tibet activists, both Westerners and Tibetans living in Western countries, and the dominant theme in their accounts was diversity. The Tibet cause has attracted an exceptionally diverse group of people, some of whom see their activities on behalf of the cause as connected with Buddhist belief and practice, while others are concerned with human rights, opposing communism, and a range of other motivations.[6]

THE BEGINNINGS OF THE FREE TIBET MOVEMENT

Although there is now widespread international support for the cause, when the Tibetan exiles first arrived in India, there was little awareness of their situation in other countries, and world leaders were generally unwilling to help them. The most important exception to this was the government of India, which agreed to accept the Dalai Lama and his fellow refugees, and also offered to give them land in South India for farming and a headquarters in the almost abandoned British hill station of Dharamsala in Himachal Pradesh. But India was also wary of angering China, and it played a key role in stifling debate in the United Nations in 1950, when moves were made by some member nations to investigate China's invasion and annexation of Tibet. The Indian action was a result of Nehru's policy of "India-China Mutual Affection" *(hindi chini bhai bhai)*, which he believed would serve as a model for peaceful cooperation for other nations. It lasted until 1962, when China invaded India, claiming that large tracts of Indian territory rightfully belonged to China.

Meanwhile, the Dalai Lama and the Tibetan exile government continued to plead their case at the United Nations and other international organizations. Despite the indifference of the world's governments, there was some interest in, and sympathy for, the Tibetans in the early 1960s. Following the Dalai Lama's flight to India, media outlets around the world carried front-page articles on the "god-king's" exile, and Tibet's case was heard by the International Commission of Jurists, which concluded that prior to the Chinese invasion Tibet had met all the requisite criteria for an independent state, and that the invasion was illegal under international law.[7] Not surprisingly, China rejected the decision, declaring that it had a centuries-old claim on Tibet. Despite China's assertions, the United Nations General Assembly in 1961 and 1965 passed resolutions endorsing the Tibetan peoples' right to self-determination.[8]

After the initial flurry of interest in the early 1960s, however, the world largely lost interest in Tibet. China closed the country to foreign visitors, and for decades little reliable information was able to find its way out. During the Cultural Revolution of the 1960s Chinese repression was increased significantly, and the society was radically restructured along Marxist-Leninist lines. Private property was confiscated, and most of the population forced into communes and work units. Members of the aristocracy and religious figures were subjected to "struggle sessions" *(thamzing)*, during which they were physically and verbally assaulted and accused of "crimes against the people." Many died during these sessions, and many more Tibetans were killed and tortured in Chinese prisons. In addition, hundreds of thousands died as a result of famines caused by confiscation of crops by Chinese authorities, who sent them to feed people starving in China. Ironically, this was a time of bumper crops in Tibet, but the Cultural Revolution had produced catastrophic famines in China, largely as a result of mismanagement.[9] According to the Tibetan government in exile, over 1.2 million Tibetans died during this time.[10]

Interestingly, during the 1960s the American CIA was the international organization that provided the most tangible support to the Free Tibet movement. Even prior to the Dalai Lama's flight into exile, the CIA was covertly arming and training resistance fighters, and it also established a clandestine base in Nepal.[11] During the mid-1950s groups of Tibetans from border regions that were particularly affected by the Chinese encroachment began to form resistance units. They conducted a guerrilla campaign against the numerically superior and better-armed People's Liberation Army, and because of their superior knowledge of the landscape and their acclimatization to the harsh environment they were able to successfully harass the Chinese troops. Recently declassified documents reveal that the CIA played a crucial role behind the scenes, secretly arming the rebels and even training some in remote bases in Colorado, in terrain that was thought to resemble the mountains and valleys of Tibet. This support continued until 1971, when President Nixon and his Secretary of State, Henry Kissinger, embarked on a policy of rapprochement with China.

Nixon's courting of China was based entirely on pragmatic considerations. An avowed anti-communist, Nixon also realized that China represented a huge emerging market and that nations which treated it as an enemy were likely to be shut out of the coming economic opportunities. Other nations followed suit, and as more and more Western leaders followed Nixon and Kissinger in paying court to the new rulers of China, the voices of Tibetan exiles and their few supporters were almost entirely ignored.

After the first spate of resolutions from the United Nations and various governments, following the enactment of United Nations Resolution 1723

(xvi) in 1965, Tibet was not even mentioned again in the United Nations until 1985. The Tibetan exile community had initially expected that their cause would galvanize the rest of the world to action, and there was widespread resentment when this proved not to be the case. As Hugh Richardson notes,

> Until too late, the Tibetans showed no proper understanding of the power of publicity and expressed the ingenuous hope that the truth would surely make itself known. Partly from inexperience and partly from anxiety not to provoke the Chinese...they relied on others to put their case for them, but there were few people to attempt that.[12]

Their forced entry into the modern world proved to be a shock for many Tibetans. But as it became clear that the rest of the world had its own concerns, the refugee community began to develop activist organizations. One such organization is the Tibetan Youth Congress, which began in the early 1970s. The formation of the TYC followed a meeting in Dharamsala in October 1970, during which the Dalai Lama addressed the assembled delegates, drawn from various sections of the exile community:

> Having held this youth conference during the past few days, let us ask ourselves what is the most essential task for the young people. The answer is: service to the people. In order to serve the people one must learn the difficulties and the sufferings of the people by keeping close touch with them.[13]

The organization grew quickly, attracting mainly young Tibetans who were dissatisfied with the government-in-exile, which it characterized as being too polite and nonconfrontational. Often at odds with the exile government, its stated aim is "a free and independent Tibet and the restoration of His Holiness the Dalai Lama to his rightful position as the sole religious and temporal leader of all Tibet."[14] The TYC has mainly worked at grass roots activities designed to help the Tibetan exile community, but has also engaged in a number of high-profile campaigns designed to put pressure on China and to convince the United Nations and other international organizations to press the Tibet cause.

Another activist organization was the Tibetan People's Freedom Movement, which held a demonstration in Delhi in 1977. This marked the first time that Tibetan demonstrators had taken such direct action to force the world to take notice of their cause. A group of young Tibetans began a hunger strike outside the United Nations Information Centre, vowing to fast until death if necessary in order to force the United Nations to enforce its earlier resolutions on Tibet. The press release issued on March 20 indicates the sense of frustration felt by Tibetans during this time, as the rest of the world appeared to them to be ignoring the ongoing human rights abuses in Tibet:

> We Tibetans are treated as political lepers by the international community and our cause as an embarrassing and contagious disease. We the victims are ignored and shunned while our oppressors are courted and feted by a world gone mad. We are a peaceful people and we have nowhere to turn to for justice except the United Nations. We do not ask for charity. We only demand what is ours, what was assured to us by the U.N. in its three resolutions. The United Nations in those days claimed impotence, as Red China was not a member of that international body. But now Red China is not only a member, but also sits in the Security Council. Hence, we urge the United Nations to implement your resolutions passed on Tibet.[15]

The 1970s and 1980s were a time of growing frustration within the Tibetan exile community, and many of its members began to adopt increasingly militant stances. The Dalai Lama's policy of negotiation rather than confrontation with China had produced few if any tangible results, and reports of human rights abuses continued to filter out of Tibet, often carried by new refugees seeking to escape the oppressive conditions there.

Despite the exile community's despair, however, this was a time in which significant grass roots work was being done in Western countries, and this would lay the groundwork for a growing awareness of the Tibet cause. Tibet support organizations were formed all over the world at this time, and information about Tibet's human rights situation—as well as books and articles on its traditional culture and religion—were being made available to the international community. Some of the leading figures in this growing movement were political activists, and others who played significant roles included academics who traveled to India and Tibet, studied with Tibetan scholars, and returned to the West to publish their research. These early academic pioneers included Jeffrey Hopkins, who became fluent in colloquial and literary Tibetan and who served as the Dalai Lama's chief interpreter for ten years. After spending several years in India studying with the Dalai Lama and other Tibetan scholars, he returned to the United States, received a Ph.D. in Tibetan Buddhist Studies from the University of Wisconsin–Madison, and later began a program in Tibetan Buddhism at the University of Virginia. An avowed Buddhist, Hopkins became involved in political activism in the early 1970s and was one of the key players in arranging for the Dalai Lama's first visit to the United States in 1979. Regarding his decision to become involved in political activism, Hopkins says,

> Tibet has been the prime source for the teachings that constitute my own practice of Buddhism, so I think that I'm obligated to help [Tibet] in whatever way I can. I do not think that aside from the Tibetan community there are groups of people who maintain these [religious and philosophical] traditions at the level that it was maintained in Tibet. It takes a whole infrastructure that we don't have here [in the West].[16]

As the Dalai Lama's chief English-language interpreter, Hopkins played a key role in the 1980s, both as a translator for public lectures and as a collaborator on several books, including some that have become best sellers.[17]

When academics like Hopkins began to publish their research, many mainstream academic presses considered Tibetan studies to be a field that was too obscure for successful commercial publications, and many of their books appeared in presses devoted primarily to Tibetan religion and culture that were founded in the 1970s and 1980s. Two of the most prominent of these were Snow Lion Publications and Wisdom Publications, which have extensive catalogues of titles on a wide range of topics in Tibetan Buddhism.

Like many other Western Buddhists involved in the Tibet movement, Tim McNeill, president of Wisdom Publications, first encountered Tibetan religion and culture during a trip to Asia following his graduation from college. In 1972 he visited Dharamsala and was immediately impressed by the Dalai Lama and his fellow Tibetan exiles. He began attending lectures on Buddhist philosophy and practice at the Library of Tibetan Works and Archives. After some time in Dharamsala he traveled to Nepal and was among the first Western students to complete a one-month retreat course at Kopan Monastery with Lama Zopa Rinpoche and Lama Yeshe. This experience provided the inspiration for the founding of Wisdom Publications.

After several years in the Himalayan region, primarily with the Peace Corps in Afghanistan, McNeill returned to the United States to complete a graduate degree in Public Policy at Harvard University. After several years as a senior executive with a major commercial publishing house he turned his political avocation into a full-time role, as associate issues director of the 1988 Dukakis presidential campaign. Following the Democrats' defeat, McNeill accepted his teacher Lama Zopa Rinpoche's request to assume the directorship of Wisdom, which was struggling for survival in London. In the following years, Wisdom benefited from the growing interest in Buddhism, especially Tibetan Buddhism, in the West.

McNeill, like so many others working to support Tibet and its culture, happily trades off more lucrative career pursuits for the opportunity to practice Buddhist *right livelihood* in his daily life. As he points out, the current success of the Tibet movement and of publishers of Tibet-related books is not an anomaly but the result of almost two decades of hard work. During that time, interest in Tibet has grown slowly. Teachers such as the Dalai Lama have become increasingly known in the West as researchers, translators, and publishers have helped bring their ideas to Western audiences. At the same time political activism has made people aware of the human rights situation in Tibet and put pressure on international bodies like the United Nations to take action.

THE LHASA RIOTS

When China began to emerge as a major economic and military power, other nations became increasingly reluctant to risk angering its leaders and thus losing access to the world's largest market. During the 1970s and early 1980s most countries strove to improve ties with China, and there was a hiatus in resolutions by governments and the United Nations regarding Tibet and the human rights situation in China in general. Reports of human rights abuses continued to filter out of the country, but it appeared that no one had the will to act on them.

This situation changed in 1987 when riots erupted in Lhasa on the anniversary of the 1959 March 10 uprising. Large crowds, led by monks and nuns, gathered in the Barkhor square of Lhasa and denounced the Chinese occupation of their country. The authorities were initially surprised by this public show of defiance after decades of Chinese rule, but they soon moved armed troops into Lhasa to suppress the demonstrations. In the weeks that followed, a brutal crackdown was carried out in Lhasa and the surrounding area, but unlike previous shows of force by China, the rest of the world took notice this time.

Believing that the country was secure, China had begun allowing tourists to visit, proclaiming that Tibet had benefitted greatly under Chinese rule and that the populace was prosperous and happy. The riots demonstrated that this was not the case, and the brutality of the Chinese security forces was witnessed by a number of foreign tourists, some of whom became pro-Tibet activists upon their return to their home countries. One such person was John Ackerly, who happened to be in Lhasa at the time of the riots with his friend Blake Kerr, who wrote a vivid first-hand account of the riots and their suppression by Chinese security forces.[18] Ackerly traveled to Tibet with the intention of climbing mountains, but instead became caught in the middle of the fighting. After witnessing the brutality of the Chinese crackdown, he resolved to form a lobby group to put pressure on the U.S. government and media in order to get China to negotiate with the Dalai Lama and the government-in-exile.

Upon his return to the United States, Ackerly, a lawyer with a background in human rights, began to develop plans to create an organization to lobby for Tibet. In 1988 the International Campaign for Tibet was established as an umbrella organization for people with an interest in the Tibet cause. In the intervening decades it has grown into the world's largest such organization, and it now has branches all over the world. Many of its members are Western Buddhists, primarily belonging to Tibetan traditions, who feel a particular kinship with the Tibetan cause due to their religious beliefs. Others, like Ackerly, are not Buddhists, but have a deep commitment to human rights. Ackerly reported that in the early years of the campaign there was an average membership of two thousand, a large percentage of whom were Buddhists, and that many of the most active members identified themselves in this way. Ackerly also indicated in a phone interview that much of their successful recruiting has come from contacting people in lists of Buddhist organizations, but the International Campaign is a nonreligious political organization whose main commitment is to addressing the human rights situation in Tibet.

The organization currently has forty thousand people on its membership lists, and the number is growing steadily. As John Avedon (author of *In Exile from the Land of Snows*) pointed out during a telephone interview, the groundwork for the current interest in the Tibet cause was laid in the 1970s, when people like Ackerly and Avedon traveled to Asia and encountered Tibetans. Like Ackerly, Avedon came to the movement almost by accident. He traveled to Nepal in 1973 and wrote an article on the trip for *Rolling Stone*. During that time, as he developed an interest in Buddhist practice, he grew increasingly concerned that the Tibetan Buddhist tradition was under threat and needed to be defended.

In the late 1970s he began to involve himself in political activism and was one of the key players in making arrangements for the Dalai Lama's first visit to the U.S. in 1979. This proved to be a breakthrough for the movement, because it provided the Dalai Lama with a larger international forum, and China's protests of the visit served to focus attention on its human rights record. During the next several years Avedon traveled extensively with the Dalai Lama and gathered information for *In Exile from the Land of Snows*. A beautifully written and impassioned account of the Dalai Lama's life in exile, the book became a best seller and drew many of its readers to the Tibet cause.

Meanwhile, Avedon was involved in lobbying efforts in conjunction with the International Campaign for Tibet, mainly aimed at the U.S. media and Congress. The first major initiative began with hearings in the House Foreign Relations Committee in 1987, which led to several resolutions, the first being a Senate Foreign Relations Authorization in 1988, which was the first Congressional resolution specifically targeting human rights issues in Tibet.[19] Another bill affirmed Tibet's statehood under international law, and a Senate resolution declared that Tibet was an occupied country under international law and that the Dalai Lama and the government-in-exile were its legitimate representatives.[20] These resolutions were not binding on the president or the State Department—which chose to ignore them—but they demonstrated a growing awareness of the Tibet cause and a willingness on the part of some U.S. lawmakers to raise the issue of human rights in China.

Like many Tibet activists, Avedon is an avowed Buddhist, who sees his activism as being connected with his religious convictions and practice. He described his motivation to engage in political activism as being based on "a profound desire to save and make the Dharma available to those who are interested," and further stated that he sees Tibetan Buddhism as "a treasure of humankind that is in danger."[21] Like others whom I interviewed for this article, he stated that his decision to become politically active in the Tibet cause arose from a sense of dedication to Tibetan Buddhism, and he also indicated that he feels a sense of personal fulfillment in being able to make a contribution to the movement.

THE FOURTEENTH DALAI LAMA

In the decades following his flight into exile, the fourteenth Dalai Lama, Tenzin Gyatso, has emerged as the most prominent spokesperson for the Free Tibet movement. Born in a small village in eastern Tibet on July 6, 1935, he was officially recognized at the age of six as the reincarnation of Tupden Gyatso (1876-1933), the thirteenth Dalai Lama. After his recognition, he was brought to Lhasa to begin a rigorous program of studies in traditional Buddhist subjects such as logic, epistemology, and monastic discipline. He is reported to have excelled at both memorizing and debating the volumes of technical literature that are required reading for scholars of the Gelukpa order, the largest and most powerful sect in Tibet. His studies were cut short, however, following the Chinese invasion in 1950. For the next few years he continued to study with his tutors, but as events reached a crisis point in

1959, the Tibetan Cabinet hastily decided to invest him with full temporal authority, two years before the traditional age of eighteen. The decision was reached shortly after a ceremony in which the Gadong oracle went into trance and urged the Tibetan officials in the audience to "make him king."[22]

Following his investiture, the young Dalai Lama sought to negotiate with the Chinese authorities, but they were committed to radical Marxist reorganization of the country, and had no intention of sharing any real power with the Dalai Lama. After the events of March 10 demonstrated that there was no possibility of rapprochement, the Dalai Lama fled into exile in India. Once settled in Dharamsala, he began to work for Tibet's independence. In recent years he has become one of the most widely recognized religious figures on the planet, and as he travels the world he meets with many powerful and famous figures, as well as with ordinary people. His warmth and charm, coupled with his humility and sincerity, win him followers and supporters wherever he travels.

The charismatically challenged Chinese leaders, however, take a very different view of the Dalai Lama. In the early years of the invasion, they were reluctant to publicly criticize someone who enjoyed broad support among Tibetans. The turning point came in 1995, when President Bill Clinton officially unlinked human rights in China with United States trade. He had threatened to revoke China's Most Favored Nation (MFN) trading status, which would have subjected Chinese imports to heavy tariffs. At the time the U.S. had a $30 billion trade deficit with the PRC, and so had far less to lose than China, but a group of Chinese leaders had recently gone on a high-tech buying spree in the United States, and corporate leaders of several major companies lobbied the president to maintain the favorable trade relations. Clinton subsequently reversed his campaign promise to revoke MFN unless China made substantial progress in human rights.

Human Rights Watch Asia has argued that this move demonstrated to China's authorities that they can safely ignore human rights concerns.[23] Since that time, they have dramatically increased repressive measures in Tibet and have also begun a public vilification campaign against the Dalai Lama. Regularly branding him as "a political corpse" and "a wolf in monk's clothing," China's propaganda apparatus describes him as the leader of "the cruelest serfdom the world has ever known" and as a monster who delighted in torturing and exploiting his miserable subjects. Tibetans are forced to publicly denounce him, and possession of a picture of the Dalai Lama has been declared a criminal offense.[24] Despite these efforts, support for him remains strong in Tibet, and it continues to grow in the rest of the world. As Pico Iyer writes,

It is, in fact, the peculiar misfortune of the Chinese to be up against one of those rare souls it is all but impossible to dislike....Everyone who meets the Dalai Lama is thoroughly disarmed by his good-natured warmth and by a charisma that is all the stronger for being so gentle.[25]

His position as the leader of an exile community has forced him to come to terms with a world that is very different from the traditional Buddhist society in which he was born. He is viewed by his followers as a physical manifestation of Avalokiteshvara, Buddha of Compassion, and they look to him as the key player in their struggle for freedom. He has risen to the challenge, and has become not only the most prominent advocate of the Tibet cause, but also its main theoretician. As a Buddhist leader, he believes that he has a responsibility to all sentient beings, but states that much of his energy is focused on the cause of Tibet. In an interview in which he discussed his life, he declared, "My motivation is directed towards all sentient beings. There is no question, though, that on a second level, I am directed towards helping Tibetans."[26]

In his public speeches and his writings, he stresses the interdependence of national interests and universal human goals, and he links these notions with a Buddhist rejection of military conflict.

It is quite clear that everyone needs peace of mind. The question, then, is how to achieve it. Through anger we cannot; through kindness, through love, through compassion we can achieve one individual's peace of mind. The result of this is a peaceful family....Extended to the national level, this attitude can bring unity, harmony, and cooperation with genuine motivation. On the international level, we need mutual trust, mutual respect, frank and friendly discussion with sincere motivation, and joint efforts to solve world problems. All these are possible. But first we must change within ourselves.[27]

The only way to bring about lasting peace between nations, he contends, is through internal transformation that works at controlling anger and other negative emotions. He argues that this is not an idealistic notion, but rather one that it is based on simple pragmatism. He points out that everyone is equally committed to achieving his or her own happiness, and that the generation of negative emotions leads to suffering and discontent.

Hatred, anger, and greed simply produce uneasiness and always more dissatisfaction. Even nations need to control and minimize anger and hatred; it is the only way they can avoid suffering and bring their people happiness....Goodness is finally the most practical, the most realistic solution.[28]

He contends that his philosophy of developing a "good heart" is based on core Buddhist principles, but also believes that it is in accordance with the best principles of all religions.[29] In his talks to Buddhist organizations, he often stresses the notion that compassion is basic to all Buddhist practice, and he further insists that direct engagement with other people and their problems is necessary in the development of genuine compassion. Too many Buddhists, he believes, withdraw from the world and cultivate their own minds, and although this is an important first step for many, he also urges Buddhists to become involved in the world.

> In the first stage, sometimes we need isolation while pursuing our own inner development; however, after you have some confidence, some strength, you must remain with, contact, and serve society in any field— health, education, politics, or whatever. There are people who call themselves religious-minded, trying to show this by dressing in a peculiar manner, maintaining a peculiar way of life, and isolating themselves from the rest of society. This is wrong. A scripture of mind-purification says, "Transform your inner viewpoint, but leave your external appearance as it is." This is important. Because the very purpose of practicing the Great Vehicle is service to others, you should not isolate yourselves from society. In order to serve, in order to help, you must remain in society.[30]

Some people, he admits, have a special predilection for isolated meditative practice, but he believes that they are a small exception. He insists that most Buddhists should strive to achieve a balance between contemplation and social activism. Both are essential components of a healthy spiritual life, and for most people no amount of contemplative activity can take the place of engagement in the world. On the other hand, he cautions that activism alone tends to become sterile and can lead to negative emotions such as frustration, anger, and hatred.

A basic tenet of his teachings is that Buddhism is essentially activist. He asserts that Buddhism teaches people to renounce the world, but in his view this does not mean physically separating oneself from worldly activities, but rather cultivating an attitude of cognitive detachment while still working for others. This, he asserts, is the proper attitude of a bodhisattva,[31] who is able to work within the world for the benefit of others without becoming dragged down by its negative elements.

In practical terms, he teaches that one should engage in meditative practice early in the morning and then consciously remain mindful throughout the day of the motivation of the practice (genuine compassion for all sentient beings). During the day one should regularly consider whether or not one's actions are of real benefit to others, and before going to sleep one should review the day's activities to evaluate what one has done for others. In *Kindness, Clarity, and Insight* he writes:

> We must promote compassion and love; this is our real duty. Government has too much business to have time for these things. As private persons we have more time to think along these lines—how to make a contribution to human society by promoting the development of compassion and a real sense of community.[32]

The Dalai Lama's vision of Buddhist practice has had a profound impact on many of his followers. An example is Robert Thurman of Columbia University, who in recent years has emerged as one of the most effective spokespeople for the Free Tibet movement. Thurman first developed an interest in Tibetan Buddhism while traveling in India in 1961, and later became the first Westerner to receive ordination as a Tibetan Buddhist monk. After returning to the United States in 1962, he began studying with Geshe Wangyal, a Kalmyk Mongolian who founded the first Tibetan Buddhist monastery in North America.[33]

During the 1960s, Thurman was primarily interested in meditation practice and study, and had little interest in the Tibet cause. He believed that it was hopeless and that Tibetan culture in Tibet was doomed,[34] and so he concluded that the only rational course of action was to avoid the issue. In the early 1970s, however, he began to study Buddhist ethics and Tibetan society, and as a result became convinced that he had a moral obligation to become involved with the Free Tibet cause. By the late 1970s he had decided that there was reason to hope that Tibetan culture might survive and that activism was essential in order to put pressure on China to change its ways.

In 1992 he assumed administrative leadership of Tibet House in New York, which has been particularly effective in bringing celebrities to the Free Tibet cause. In the 1990s Thurman has become one of the highest-profile activists in the movement, and was chosen by *Time* magazine in 1997 as one of the "twenty-five most influential men in America."

Thurman believes, contrary to the opinions of a number of other scholars of Buddhism, that Buddhism has always been socially engaged. He contends that the Buddha was a *kshatriya* (the ruling class in ancient India) and that as such he was raised to rule people and to benefit his subjects. As he contemplated his situation, however, he realized that a king's abilities to truly help his subjects are limited, and that as a worldly ruler he would be unable to cure the fundamental problems facing humanity. Thus the Buddha resolved to form a monastic order, which Thurman terms a "radical social intervention" that was devised as "the only social institution that has the ability to truly protect people." It provides an opportunity to opt out of society, but in Thurman's vision it simultaneously challenges that society and presents it with a model group founded on the values of compassion and wisdom.

Like the Dalai Lama, Thurman sees his social activism on behalf of the Tibet cause as being intimately linked with his Buddhist practice, a sentiment that was echoed by several of the people I interviewed for this article. A number of Buddhists who are involved in the Free Tibet movement indicated that their activism interferes with Buddhist practice, but this sentiment appears to be the exception rather than the rule. In most cases activist Buddhists have developed cognitive strategies for integrating social activity and religious practice. Jeffrey Hopkins' statement on this issue expressed ideas held in common with many other Buddhists working for the Free Tibet movement:

> There's no question that activism is religious practice, and it's a way of putting into deeds attitudes like compassion for others that otherwise are just verbal. It gives me plenty of opportunities for acting together with other people and, through acting, seeking to counteract what some other people have done. [35]

HOLLYWOOD ADOPTS TIBET, AND TIBET ADOPTS HOLLYWOOD

As recently as 1979 the Dalai Lama was not able to get a visa to enter the United States. Because the U.S. government was eagerly courting China, the government wished to avoid conflict with its newfound trading partner, and State Department staff were forbidden from even speaking to his representatives. The grass roots activism of the 1970s and 1980s gradually eroded the resistance of United States leaders to confront the Tibet issue, but the key turning point came after the Tiananmen Square massacre in 1988. For the first time foreign media were present to record a brutal crackdown by Chinese security forces against their own citizens, who were peacefully calling for democracy and basic human rights. Images of the crackdown were broadcast all over the world, and many governments officially denounced China's actions.

A further boost to the Tibet movement came in 1989, when the Dalai Lama was awarded the Nobel Peace Prize for his nonviolent efforts on behalf of his people. [36] This had the effect of dramatically increasing his public profile and made it more difficult for the PRC's leaders to simply ignore him.

It also gave him a wider international forum for his cause, and as a result he was increasingly sought out for interviews by the media.

Since then he has also been asked to speak in the United States Congress on several occasions, and his public lectures regularly draw huge crowds. When he visited Australia in 1996 to officiate at a Kalachakra initiation ceremony, the interest was so great that the ceremony was held at a pavilion often used for rock concerts. The Dalai Lama sold out the Horden Pavilion in Sydney for seven straight days, but when Michael Jackson came the next month he only sold out two shows. The event carried the paraphernalia of a rock concert, and there were bouncers at the entrances with Dalai Lama T-shirts, souvenir stands displaying Dalai Lama memorabilia, and stalls selling his books and tapes of his public lectures. Responding to the massive public interest and to Chinese denunciations of the event, the media gave saturation coverage to the Dalai Lama's visit.[37]

A key moment in the current surge of interest in the Tibet cause was Richard Gere's impassioned speech at the 1993 Academy Awards, during which he called for Deng Xiaoping, then China's paramount leader, to stop oppressing the Tibetans. Gere, a devout Tibetan Buddhist, asked the audience to mentally send a message to Deng asking him to bring "a little sanity" to the Tibet situation. Gere was subsequently banned by the academy for bringing politics into the award ceremony, but in subsequent interviews he has indicated that this is of little concern to him and that he is pleased that his speech was able to reach a large audience and make more people aware of the Tibet situation.

Gere was the first major celebrity to become active in the Tibet cause, but he has been followed by a number of others, including film star Harrison Ford, his wife Melissa Mathiesson, a movie script writer, and rock musician Adam Yauch of the Beastie Boys.

Yauch has been particularly active in bringing the Tibet cause to younger audiences, mainly through his efforts in organizing a series of "Tibetan Freedom Concerts," which have drawn a veritable who's who of contemporary music, including such bands as the Foo Fighters, REM, and U2. At the time this article is being written, Yauch is organizing the fourth such concert, which will be held simultaneously on June 12 and 13, 1999 in four cities: Sydney, Chicago, Tokyo, and Amsterdam.[38]

With the growing interest in Tibet among Hollywood stars, rock musicians, and other celebrities, the Free Tibet movement is enjoying unprecedented publicity. Once the plight of the Tibetans was portrayed only in documentaries on public television, but in 1998 two big-budget Hollywood films were released. The first was *Seven Years in Tibet,* a $70 million Sony Tristar production directed by Jean-Jacques Annaud and starring Brad Pitt. Pitt played Heinrich Harrer, an Austrian mountaineer who was interned in a British prisoner of war camp during World War II but managed to escape and make his way to Tibet along with his climbing partner Peter Auschneiter.

The other major film was *Kundun*, written by Melissa Mathiesson and directed by Martin Scorcese. It tells the story of the Dalai Lama's early life and ends with powerful images of the Chinese invasion of Tibet. According to John Ackerly, since these films were released membership in the International Campaign for Tibet has tripled.

The Chinese government has responded with a public relations effort of its own. Following the release of *Seven Years in Tibet*, Chinese authorities denounced the film's portrayal of the Chinese invasion as "a pack of lies" that unfairly and inaccurately demonized China's "peaceful liberation" of the country. Sony Tristar executives responded by publicly distancing themselves from the film, hoping by this to preserve their future plans of expansion into the huge Chinese market. Similarly, during the filming of *Kundun*, the Chinese government publicly threatened Disney, stating that it could lose access to China's huge market if the film were released. Disney initially adopted a principled stance, defending the film on the grounds of freedom of speech and refusing to censor *Kundun* or its director, but later Disney CEO Michael Eisner strove to put as much distance between his company and the film as possible.

Scorcese was hired by Disney's Touchstone Pictures with the intention of initiating a long-term relationship, but after China threatened Disney's projects in China the company decided to pull back on advertising. A major Scorcese film would ordinarily open in three thousand theaters in the U.S., but Disney decided to release *Kundun* in only four hundred venues. Despite this, the film did well at the box office, and China backed up its threats by freezing Disney projects in China for almost a year.

As more and more Hollywood stars adopt the Tibet cause, it seems somehow fitting that the Tibetan community should respond by adopting one of Hollywood's major stars. In 1997 Penor Rinpoche, supreme head of the Nyingma order, officially recognized Steven Seagal—star of such ultraviolent movies as *Under Siege* and *Hard to Kill*—as a reincarnate Tibetan lama *(tulku)*. Seagal has been practicing Buddhism for over twenty years, and he claims that his Tibetan teachers identified him as a reincarnation long ago, although the recognition has only recently been made public. In an interview in the *Shambhala Sun*, Seagal said of the recognition:

What I have consistently said is that I don't believe it is very important who I was in my last lives. I think it is important who I am in this life. And what I do in this life is only important if I can ease the suffering of others. If I can somehow make the world a better place, if I somehow serve Buddha and mankind.[39]

His Buddhist spirituality is on display in his movie *The Glimmer Man*, in which he wears Tibetan prayer beads around his neck and speaks of cultivating inner peace. In the following scene, however, someone insults his sissy beads and he kicks him through a glass door, indicating that he may still need to put in more quality time on the meditation cushion.

TIBET AT THE MILLENNIUM'S END

As worldwide interest in the Tibet cause grows, so does the pressure on world leaders to confront China on its human rights record. For example, John Avedon believes that Bill Clinton—despite his retreat from his election promise to revoke China's MFN status unless it made significant improvements in this area—has done more for Tibet than any previous U.S. president. He points out that Clinton's linkage of human rights and trade was the first time that any U.S. administration had done so.[40] Clinton has also raised Tibet as an issue in several meetings with Chinese leaders, most prominently in a June 1998 visit to China, during which he publicly debated Chinese premier Jiang Zemin on Chinese television, pointedly challenging China's human rights record and urging Jiang to talk with the Dalai Lama. In 1997 he also appointed a special assistant for Tibet affairs, a move that China heatedly denounced as "interference in China's internal affairs."

Clinton is a politician who responds to public sentiment, and he clearly understands that the Tibet cause is gaining increasing support in the U.S. and the rest of the world. China has done a remarkably poor job of presenting its case, and it has few supporters outside of the areas that it controls. For most people, as John Hocevar of Students for a Free Tibet says, Tibet is one of the few causes in which "there's relatively little grey."[41] The Dalai Lama's nonviolent struggle contrasts sharply with the authoritarian rule China has imposed on Tibet, which is maintained by an estimated 300,000 troops on the "Roof of the World."

The most important focal symbol of the growing movement is the March 10 demonstrations, which are commemorated every year all over the world, and which in recent years have drawn ever-increasing numbers of protesters. These demonstrations explicitly recall the events of 1959. Typically, crowds of demonstrators gather in a conspicuous public place, often in front

Save Tibet rally, Washington, D.C., March 10, 1989. Courtesy John Powers.

of a Chinese embassy. Generally speeches are made and slogans chanted, and Tibetans and their supporters don traditional Tibetan dress and wave Tibetan flags and pictures of the Dalai Lama. Mention is always made of the fact that such activities are illegal in Tibet and result in long prison sentences and physical torture. The speeches outline the Tibetan case against China, and the demonstrators often march from one place to another.

This yearly event has become a major symbolic drama for Tibet supporters. A typical March 10 demonstration was held in Canberra in 1999, marking the fortieth anniversary of the first March 10 demonstrations in Lhasa. Organized by Gerry Virtue of the Australia Tibet Council and Zatul Rinpoche, a *tulku* who emigrated to Australia in 1997, a group of about one hundred demonstrators gathered in the morning outside of the Chinese embassy, listened to speeches by several Tibetans, and shouted slogans like "China Out of Tibet!" "Tibet for Tibetans!" "Free the Panchen Lama!"[42] and "Long Live the Dalai Lama!" Both the speeches and placards were in English, rather than Tibetan, as the rally was intended to garner public support within Australia.

The speeches and slogans stressed themes common to other March 10 demonstrations I have witnessed: Tibet's historical independence from

China, the differences between Tibetan and Chinese culture, and warnings that Tibetan culture is being eradicated in its homeland. As Margaret Nowak has observed, this dramatic sequence of events is characteristic of March 10 demonstrations all over the world, which she describes as:

> a ritual that publicly dramatizes both an ideal goal (proudly affirmed national identity) and the strategy for achieving it (self-conscious proclamation of "Tibetanness" to and in the midst of others who are not Tibetan).[43]

As often happens in March 10 demonstrations, a march followed the rally outside the Chinese embassy. About thirty people embarked on a fourteen-day trek from Canberra to Sydney, stopping at rural townships along the way. When I interviewed Zatul Rinpoche in Canberra about the march, he remarked at the widespread support the marchers received. At every rural township along the route, they were given a mayoral reception, during which speeches by local politicians were made and the Tibetan flag was flown. He was struck by the fact that all the politicians they approached already knew of the Tibet cause, and all were willing to lend their public support. The Australian media also provided coverage, and although the marchers spent several days trudging in rain, they were pleased at the support and publicity they received.

Zatul Rinpoche expressed a deep reverence for the Dalai Lama, stating that "he gives me hope and moral courage,"[44] but he opposes the Dalai Lama's "middle way" approach to China, in which he has publicly renounced his earlier commitment to full independence for Tibet and has agreed to be content with genuine autonomy within the PRC.[45] This is also the official position of the Tibetan government-in-exile, but Zatul Rinpoche is one of a growing number of Tibetans who feel that their leaders have given away too much before negotiations have even begun. At present the PRC has refused steadfastly even to discuss the Tibet situation with the Dalai Lama or his representatives, but he continues to make conciliatory gestures toward China. Rejecting the exile government's position, Zatul Rinpoche states that "the Tibetan people will never be happy as long as we have an association with China."

Since emigrating to Australia, Zatul Rinpoche has worked to organize Australia's small Tibetan community and to promote activism, particularly among Tibetan youths. He believes that the Tibetan Youth Congress is the only Tibetan organization that is fighting for independence, and contends that this approach is finally the only viable one for Tibetans: "they need to have a fire in their hearts, and wherever we live, we must live as Tibetans."

Such sentiments are being heard increasingly within the Tibetan refugee community, many of whom are questioning the Dalai Lama's approach in increasingly public ways. In its meeting in August 1998, the TYC pointed out the total lack of results of the nonviolent path. It also noted that Tibetans are now a minority in Tibet, their culture is being steadily eradicated, religious persecution is becoming increasingly severe, monks and nuns are imprisoned, and parents send their children on hazardous treks over the mountains to reach freedom in India.[46]

In recent years the TYC has adopted an increasingly aggressive stance and has engaged in more confrontational activism, even though this puts it at odds with the exile government. An example of this was a demonstration held in Delhi in 1997, during which a group of mostly young Tibetans embarked on a "fast unto death" reminiscent of the earlier fast described in this article. This time the fast was broken up by Indian security forces, and in the resulting clashes between Tibetan hunger strikers and Indian police a Tibetan man named Thupten Ngodup set himself alight in protest against the police action.

He was rushed to the hospital but died of his burns several days later. In the aftermath he has become a symbol of courage to many Tibetans who are dissatisfied with the Dalai Lama's nonviolent approach. His stance has gained him widespread admiration around world, but it has had little if any positive effect on China's policies toward Tibet. A growing number of Tibetan exiles have publicly called for a change of tactics, pointing out that violent resistance movements have often succeeded in gaining independence.

Even the exile leadership admits that its current approach has produced little in the way of concrete results. When I spoke to Samdhong Rinpoche, chairman of the Assembly of People's Deputies in June 1998, he stated that he had met with the hunger strikers, but was unable to dissuade them from what he considered to be a violent approach because "we have been unable to present them with an effective alternative."

The Dalai Lama must be aware of the irony of the situation. He enjoys widespread reverence all over the world for his nonviolent campaign, he has an international forum for his cause, but he is unable to soften the PRC's intransigence, and so at a time when his cause is gathering adherents around the world he is steadily losing the support of his own people. In spite of these factors, he still remains committed to dialogue. He points out that it would be suicidal for five million Tibetans to adopt violent methods in confronting China, a nation of 1.2 billion people with an army of five million.

Despite these factors, the Dalai Lama remains hopeful. He is encouraged by the growing grass roots support for him and his cause and hopes that it will eventually lead to a softening of China's position as a result of international pressure. In any event, he feels that as a Buddhist the nonviolent approach is the only one open to him. In his March 10, 1999 speech he stated:

> Now it's forty years since the Chinese invasion and we are beginning a new decade....Now in this fourth decade, again it's human will—the truth—which is all we have in dealing with China. Despite their brainwashing, despite their using every atrocity and propaganda, and despite all of the resources they have utilized, still the truth remains the truth. Our side has no money, no propaganda, nothing except weak, feeble voices. Yet now most people have lost faith in the strong voices of the Chinese. Their strong voices have lost credibility. Our weak voices have more credibility. The history of this century is confirming the nonviolence what Mahatma Gandhi and Martin Luther King, Jr., spoke of. Even when it is against a superpower who has all these awful weapons, the reality of the situation can compel the hostile nation to come to terms with nonviolence.

In spite of the Dalai Lama's hopeful words, his increasingly restive followers are looking for some concrete signs of progress. After the initial hope raised by Clinton's 1998 call for Jiang Zemin to negotiate with the Dalai Lama and Jiang's off-the-cuff agreement to do so, China actually broke off all contacts, and so at the time that this article is being written there is no dialogue—either official or unofficial—between the Tibetan exile government and the PRC. China has apparently decided that it holds all the cards and that there is no reason for it to negotiate. Even though Hollywood has thrown its considerable public relations weight behind the Tibet cause, there is currently little basis for hope that a happy ending will be written to this story.

NOTES

1. For more information on these events, see Hugh E, Richardson, *Tibet and Its History* (Boston: Shambhala Publications, 1984), pp. 206ff.
2. See John F. Avedon, *In Exile from the Land of Snows* (New York: Vintage Books, 1979), pp. 34ff, and David Patt, *A Strange Liberation: Tibetan Lives in Chinese Hands* (Ithaca, NY: Snow Lion Publications, 1992), pp. 20–36.
3. There were several occasions when China stepped in to put an end to political unrest, and on at least three occasions Chinese troops were involved. But prior to the twentieth century Tibet was mainly viewed as a remote border area by China, and it had its own autonomous government, language, and culture.

For an account of Tibetan society prior to the invasion, see Melvyn C. Goldstein, *A History of Modern Tibet, 1913–1951* (Berkeley: University of California Press, 1989), and C.W. Cassinelli and Robert B. Ekvall, *A Tibetan Principality: The Political System of Sa sKya* (Ithaca: Cornell University Press, 1969).

4. An example is the Simla Convention in 1914, at which Britain, Tibet, and China negotiated as independent states. See Richardson, *Tibet and Its History*, pp. 107ff.

5. Cited in Gyaltsen Gyaltag, "From Monarchy to Democracy: An Historical Overview," in *The Anguish of Tibet*, ed. Petra K. Kelly, Gert Bastian, and Pat Aiello (Berkeley, CA: Parallax Press, 1991), p. 13.

6. I am grateful to the people who generously agreed to be interviewed for this article, including Zatul Rinpoche, John Avedon, Robert Thurman, Jeffrey Hopkins, Rita Gross, Daniel Cozort, Tim McNeill, Chope Tsering, Tenzin Tethong, John Hocevar, and Samdhong Rinpoche. Some of them are mentioned explicitly in the article, but all contributed to my understanding of the history and activities of the movement, even though some of them do not perceive themselves as being directly involved in it. I am also grateful to Chris Queen for making arrangements for most of the interviews.

7. See International Commission of Jurists, *The Question of Tibet and the Rule of the Law*, Geneva, 1959.

8. United Nations General Assembly Resolution 1353 (XIV) (New York, 1959) called for respect for the fundamental human rights of the Tibetan people and for respect for their distinctive cultural and religious life. United Nations General Assembly Resolution 1723 (XVI) (New York, 1961) renewed the United Nation's call for the cessation of practices that deprive the Tibetan people of their fundamental human rights and freedoms, including their right to self-determination. United Nations General Assembly Resolution 2079 (xx) (New York, 1965) stated that the United Nations "solemnly renews its call for the cessation of all practices which deprive the Tibetan people of the human rights and fundamental freedoms which they have always enjoyed."

9. See Avedon, *In Exile from the Land of Snows*, pp. 83ff.

10. These figures are based on reports by Tibetan escapees compiled by the exile government in Dharamsala, India. They have been disputed by both the Chinese government and by Western scholars such as Tom Grunfeld of Empire State University. Unlike the Nazis during the Holocaust, the Chinese authorities in Tibet have not been concerned with keeping accurate figures of deaths, tortures, and imprisonments. As a result, most estimates are based on eyewitness accounts, but as Grunfeld has pointed out, given the number of Tibetan refugees each would have had to report approximately twenty deaths, which

he considers to be excessive. While I share his concern with the uncertainty of the sources, I think that in a preindustrial village society like pre-invasion Tibet most people in villages and neighborhoods would have known each other, and so they would be more aware of what happened to neighbors, relatives, and friends than would people in modern Western society. In addition, I have heard no convincing counter-evidence suggesting that the figures have been artificially inflated.

In any event, even the Chinese government agrees that many thousands of people have died and been imprisoned since their invasion (which they refer to as a "peaceful liberation"), and even if only a handful have been killed or tortured, this undermines the Chinese claims for legitimacy of their occupation of Tibet.

11. A good short overview of the program may be found in the article "CIA Gave Aid to Tibetan Exiles in '60s, Files Show," in the *Los Angeles Times*, September 15, 1998. For an account of the CIA's role from the point of view of some Tibetan resistance fighters, see "How the CIA Helped Tibet Fight their Chinese Leaders," by Paul Salopek, in *Chicago Tribune*, Tuesday, January 25, 1997.

12. Hugh Richardson, "The Independence of Tibet," in *The Anguish of Tibet*, p. 35.

13. Margaret Nowak, *Tibetan Refugees: Youth and the New Generation of Meaning* (New Brunswick, NJ: Rutgers University Press, 1984), p. 143.

14. This message appears on the back cover of *Rangzen* ("Independence"), a magazine published by the TYC.

15. Cited in Nowak, *Tibetan Refugees*, p. 147.

16. Phone interview, January 22, 1999.

17. The most popular of these is Tenzin Gyatso, *Kindness, Clarity, and Insight,* trans. Jeffrey Hopkins (Ithaca, NY: Snow Lion Publications, 1984), which has sold over sixty thousand copies worldwide, according to Snow Lion Publications.

18. Blake Kerr, *Sky Burial: An Eyewitness Account of China's Brutal Crackdown in Tibet* (Chicago: The Noble Press, 1993).

19. United States Congress, S. Con. Res. 129, Washington, D.C., September 16, 1988, expressed the support of the Congress for the Dalai Lama and his proposal to promote peace, protect the environment, and gain democracy for the people of Tibet.

20. United States Congress, S. Con. Res. 82, Washington, D.C., March 15, 1989, expressed the concern of the Senate for the ongoing human rights abuses in Tibet.

United States Congress, H. Con. Res. 63, Washington, D.C., May 16, 1989, declared that Tibetans engaged in peaceful demonstrations in Lhasa were fired on by Chinese authorities, reportedly killing thirty to sixty persons and injuring hundreds.

United States Congress, S. Con. Res. 79, Washington, D.C., October 5, 1989, congratulated His Holiness the XIV Dalai Lama of Tibet for being awarded the 1989 Nobel Peace Prize. Details of these resolutions are available on the Tibetan government-in-exile's website (<http://www.tibet.com/>).

21. Phone interview, January 18, 1999.

22. See Avedon, *In Exile from the Land of Snows*, pp. 32–33.

23. See Tibet Information Network and Human Rights Watch Asia, *Cutting Off the Serpent's Head: Tightening Control in Tibet*, 1994–1995 (New York: Human Rights Watch, 1996), pp. 13ff, which documents the changes in China's public stances prior to and following Clinton's decision to unlink trade and human rights.

24. Early in February of 1999 he issued a public statement to the people of Tibet in which he urged them to "denounce me without hesitation" rather than be subjected to torture. Reported in *TIN News*, February 8, 1999.

25. Pico Iyer, "Tibet's Living Buddha," in Sidney Piburn, ed., *The Dalai Lama: A Policy of Kindness* (Ithaca, NY: Snow Lion Publications, 1993), p. 31.

26. Tenzin Gyatso, "His Life: An Interview with John Avedon," in Piburn, ed., *The Dalai Lama: A Policy of Kindness,* p. 40.

27. Tenzin Gyatso, "Kindness and Compassion," in Piburn, ed., *The Dalai Lama: A Policy of Kindness*, p. 49.

28. Tenzin Gyatso, *Snow Lion Newsletter*, spring 1993.

29. See Tenzin Gyatso, *Kindness, Clarity, and Insight*, pp. 9–17 and 45–50.

30. Tenzin Gyatso, "A Talk to Western Buddhists," in Piburn, ed., *The Dalai Lama: A Policy of Kindness*, p. 82.

31. The bodhisattva is a Buddhist practitioner who is committed to achieving buddhahood in order to benefit others. This is the ideal of Mahayana Buddhism.

32. Tenzin Gyatso, *Kindness, Clarity, and Insight*, p. 64.

33. It was established in Freewood Acres, New Jersey, in 1955 and named the "Lamaist Buddhist Monastery of America."

34. Phone interview, January 25, 1999.

35. Phone interview, January 22, 1999.

36. His acceptance speech is reprinted in *The Dalai Lama: A Policy of Kindness*, pp. 15–25.

37. Ironically, much of the credit for the media interest was due to China's stance regarding the visit, which it vigorously denounced. Chinese officials even went so far as to warn John Howard, the prime minister, and Alexander Downer, the foreign minister, against meeting with him. Realizing the fallout from appearing to bow to pressure not to meet a highly respected visitor on Australian soil, both men decided to have meetings with the Dalai Lama, and when I spoke

to Mr. Downer at a reception he indicated that the Chinese government's threats were key reasons behind his decision.

38. The first concert, in 1996, was held in San Francisco. The next was in New York in 1997, and a third was held in Washington in 1998.

39. *Shambhala Sun*, December 1997, p. 54.

40. Phone interview, January 25, 1999.

41. Phone interview, January 21, 1999.

42. This refers to one of the most emotional current disputes between the Tibetan exile government and the PRC. Several years ago, the Dalai Lama announced his official recognition of a six-year-old boy named Gendün Chökyi Nyima as the reincarnation of the tenth Panchen Lama. The Panchen Lama is the second most powerful reincarnate lama after the Dalai Lama and plays a key role in the selection of the Dalai Lama. China subsequently declared the Dalai Lama's choice "illegal and invalid," placed the boy and his parents under house arrest, and installed its own candidate. Gendün Chökyi Nyima is now the European Parliament's youngest ever prisoner of conscience. See John Powers, "Opiate of the Atheists? The Panchen Lama Controversy," *Asia Pacific Magazine* 1.1 (1996): 4–11.

43. Nowak, *Tibetan Refugees*, p. 35.

44. Interview, Canberra, March 11, 1999.

45. In the early 1970s, the Dalai Lama introduced the "middle way approach," which means that he does not demand total Tibetan independence, but rather autonomy within the framework of Chinese domination. In 1978, a dialogue was initiated with the Chinese leader Deng Xiaoping, but all formal contacts ceased five years later, in 1983. Since then, messages have been exchanged only through informal channels. But now, this contact too is broken by the Chinese leadership.

46. In 1998 an estimated four thousand Tibetans made the hazardous journey to escape to India or Nepal.

IDENTITY POLITICS:
GENDER, SEXUAL ORIENTATION,
ETHNICITY

Public celebration of Wesak, Toronto, 1990.
Courtesy Buddhist Communities of Greater Toronto.

Susan Moon, editor of *Turning Wheel*, the journal of the Buddhist
Peace Fellowship. Courtesy Buddhist Peace Fellowship.

Activist Women in
American Buddhism

Susan Moon

I HAVE BEEN A BUDDHIST, OFFICIALLY SPEAKING, SINCE 1976, when I became a member of the Berkeley Zen Center. As to when I became an activist, I suppose I could point to the summer of 1959, when I went to a high school work camp organized by the American Friends Service Committee, on the Fort Berthold Indian Reservation in North Dakota, to "help" some Mandan Indians build an earth lodge. I've been female at least from the beginning of this life, and I've been a feminist since the fifth grade, when the school rules decreed that I had to start wearing a dress to school, just because I was a girl, even though I was a girl who liked to climb trees and hang by my knees.

I have thought a lot about the relationship between these three jewels: Buddhism, activism, and feminism. How do they strengthen one another? How do they challenge one another?

I will examine this trinity of concerns through the work of four contemporary Buddhist women activists: Joanna Macy, Paula Green, Sala Steinbach, and Melody Ermachild Chavis. In different ways, their lives exemplify what it means to be a Buddhist, an activist, and a feminist, whether they call themselves by these labels or not. These women are extraordinary, and at the same time they are just like the rest of us.

Like me, all four were activists before they were Buddhists. I asked them how becoming a Buddhist had changed their activism, how their social concerns showed up in their Buddhist practice, and what, if anything, does being a woman have to do with all this?

As we talked, certain themes emerged. Several aspects of the Buddhist teachings were mentioned repeatedly, because of the way they support a life involved in making social change. The two most central were the following. First, there's no "enemy" out there. No "us" and no "them." This is the teaching of interconnectedness, of the jeweled net of Indra. Second, we can't necessarily measure our progress, and we may not reach our explicit goals; still, we act in the faith that beneficial actions produce beneficial results, whether we see it in our lifetime or not. This is the law of karma. Other Buddhist teachings were also mentioned, such as the importance of kindness, or the equanimity we can find through meditation, that helps us avoid the activists' occupational disease—burnout.

How does feminism fit in? Because we are women, we know what it is to be marginalized, and this knowledge can help us to be truly inclusive. We have a leg up, as women, at recognizing the patriarchal structure that is so often embedded in our Buddhist institutions, and knowing it is not the ultimate truth. So we tend to be flexible in terms of doctrine. As women we also know something about the suffering caused by oppression, and we feel a moral imperative to redress this.

In the very particular examples of their lives these women inspire me. They walk their talk, and in this chapter I want to demonstrate some of that walking, not just the talking.

JOANNA MACY

One of the elders of "engaged Buddhism" in the West, Joanna Macy was one of the first board members of the Buddhist Peace Fellowship. The "despair and empowerment" work she developed in response to the nuclear crisis has helped a generation of activists to work without burning out. Her pioneering work in "deep ecology" has brought together spiritual, environmental, and social concerns under one roof. She has consistently modeled the understanding that the life of the spirit and the life of the activist are one life. She has taught us that when we bring our most vulnerable human selves forward, the work that we do in the world will be strengthened.

Joanna was born in 1929 and grew up in New York City. Her grandfather was a Congregational minister, and her father was an unsuccessful businessman, always short of money, and tyrannical with his wife and children. Because her father was a Francophile, she went to a French lycée, where she got a classical French education, and a double lesson in what it's like to be marginalized. In school she was one of the few Americans, and out of school, among her American peers, she was an oddball because she went to a French school.

Joanna got an early start on public speaking. While she was still in high school, she was part of a Presbyterian youth caravan that traveled around preaching the gospel, and there's something of the evangelist's drama, timing, and persuasiveness in her public voice even now. She studied religion at

Dr. Joanna Macy. Photo by Catherine Allport.

Wellesley College, but when she graduated and went to France on a Fullbright, her interest turned from religion to politics and economics. When she returned to the U.S., she worked briefly for the C.I.A., and later for the State Department.

She married Fran Macy in 1953, and they started a family. After a painful period in which Joanna was a full-time suburban housewife and mother, waiting for Fran to come home from his New York City office so she'd have an adult to talk to, Fran began working overseas in cultural affairs and then with the Peace Corps. For ten of the next fourteen years they lived in and raised their three children in Germany, India, and Africa.

Wherever they lived, Joanna became involved in the social issues of the place and made lifelong friends. She was introduced to Buddhism through Tibetan refugee lamas she met while the family was living in India.

When the Macy family returned to the U.S., Joanna went to graduate school and got a doctorate in religion from Syracuse University, specializing in Buddhist Studies. There she became fascinated with general systems theory, a nonlinear view of reality emerging from the life sciences, and she was struck by the way systems theory sheds fresh light on the Buddha's central doctrine of causality. The interplay between these two bodies of thought, explored in her dissertation and later books, has provided, she says, the intellectual backbone of all her subsequent work and teaching. In 1974, she took the Buddhist precepts from her first Buddhist teacher, Sister Palmo, a Tibetan nun from India.

It was thanks to her college-age children that Joanna became an anti-nuclear activist. Her son Jack wrote a freshman college paper on pollution from the nuclear power industry that alarmed her profoundly, so she took her tent and joined him at the Clamshell Alliance "occupation" of the nuclear reactor in Seabrook, New Hampshire.

It was her children, too, who got her to a conference in Boston about critical threats to the biosphere, in 1977. During that weekend, she had one of the visionary moments that are the characteristic turning points of her journey. While riding the subway over the Charles River, she felt overwhelmed by the real possibility that life on this planet might not survive. The crippling despair that came over her then, and continued for days, was also what gave birth to her despair work. She knew she had to find a way to acknowledge the despair, to admit it, and to keep on going. And believing that other people might have a similar need, she wrote her first piece, "How to Deal with Despair," which was published in *New Age Journal* in June 1979.

In 1979 Joanna went back to Asia for a year to live with the Sarvodaya movement, a village self-help and training model developed in Sri Lanka by a man named Ari Ariyaratne, and to study the many ways that Sarvodaya integrated Buddhism with social action.

Gradually, Joanna's work as an organizer, activist, public speaker, teacher, and workshop leader/trainer began to take more and more of a front row seat in their family life. In 1987, Fran and Joanna moved to Berkeley, California, and this has been their base of operations ever since. Joanna now teaches at the California Institute of Integral Studies in San Francisco, the Graduate Theological Union in Berkeley, and the University of Creation Spirituality in Oakland. She travels all over the world, leading trainings and workshops in anti-nuclear and deep ecology work.

The teachings of the Buddha and the insights of the sangha have taught Joanna that social action is the natural expression of being alive and awake. As we talked in her living room, she flipped through a pile of magazines— mostly environmental—beside the couch.

"Pick up any one of these magazines," she said. "Look at what's happening to our oceans, to our agriculture. Look what jerks we have in government. I think I'd go numb without Buddhism. The huge and boundless heart of the Buddha holds it all. In the vision of the Dharma, it's okay. It's just *samsara*. We're *all* driven by ignorance, hatred, and greed. And we're *all* jewels in the net. Buddhism saves us not only from numbness, but also from cynicism.

"I was a woman before I was a Buddhist or an activist, and a woman aware of oppression. I'm enormously grateful to the women's movement for naming that oppression. It's one of the great revolutions of our times. It's a great advantage to be a woman, because, even if you come from privilege, you are linked with animals, children, the aged, people of color, people in poverty. We women, too, have been treated as extraneous by the patriarchy.

"When I was growing up, I had no models of strong women, except for Eleanor Roosevelt, but I couldn't sit down and have a cup of tea with her. There was nobody *in my life*. So I felt very lonely as a young woman, and crazy. In the second half of my life I found wonderful older women like Sister Palmo, who were my mentors, and they helped me become a mentor to younger women.

"I've been lucky enough to live seven decades. I have the blessing of being able to be there for younger women, and give them the kind of confidence that an older woman can give a younger woman. And I want to say that young men need help, too. It's hard to be a man in a dying patriarchy.

"Buddhist institutions still have a lot to learn from women. In the last couple of years I've been meeting with a group of Buddhist women teachers, and that's been very helpful. I'm knocked out by our wisdom, by the wedding of brain and heart, the readiness to be with pain. It's good to explore together: Where do we find our authority? How important it is to stand confidently. Gratitude is the basis for a kind of confidence. A mother bear defends her cubs out of gratitude for their existence."

Joanna described to me a process she has developed in the last year that she is now using in her trainings and workshops. She calls it "the bodhisattva check-in."

"We imagine ourselves back to the point just before this birth. We imagine we are sitting around together taking our ease; we've been through so many incarnations. It feels so good to kick back for a while. Then the word comes of what's happening on Earth in the middle of the twentieth century, how the dominant species has released the power in the center of the atom. Humans are so undeveloped spiritually and morally that they have taken the greatest power in the universe and put it in canisters and dropped it on whole cities. And they're using it to boil water! And the wars—if you back away a little bit, it's incredible what we expect ourselves to get used to. And then the thought occurs to us, although we try to push it aside: 'Should I go back to that world? What good would it do? They have these huge systems in place.' But the thought won't leave us alone.

"Then I say to everyone, 'When you've decided you really want to go back, stand up.' One by one, people stand up. We don't know what faces or forms we will take. We won't even be able to recognize each other. So it's like jumping off a cliff, diving into isolation and loneliness, and getting swept up into the madness of the twentieth century.

"But you don't just come back as a general being—you have to be particular. People walk around the room, and they walk into their own particularity. What is the date you choose to be born? Into what culture? What class? What ethnicity? What gender? And as they are walking around the room, I invite people to look at each other with recognition. It relieves them of a sense of victimhood. It's useful to have the feeling: *I want to be here.*"

I asked Joanna what work she still wants to do in her life. "The work I want to do now is threefold. First, to take out into the world the work that has grown up—this blend of Buddhadharma and the fires of activism—through leading trainings." She will continue to do intensive trainings in Germany, Australia, Israel, England, and Japan, to share the insights and practices she has developed, like the "bodhisattva check-in." She has done trainings at a Buddhist retreat center in the Santa Cruz Mountains, and is booked there through the year 2000, to do periodic twelve-day retreats, for thirty people at a time.

The second thing she wants to do is to return to activism about nuclear waste, and to the nuclear guardianship project. "The nuclear mafia is strong, not only in Russia now, with the economic collapse, but everywhere. We need to create ways for citizens to be trained to oversee nuclear sites. It's got to be a spiritual passion that no money can buy, because money is not going to tide us over. I want to go back to that work, and the mysteries of time that it unfolds."

The third thing is a book she wants to do with Molly Brown, with whom she wrote *Coming Back to Life*. She sees the need for an anthology of readings on systems theory and social change, as nothing like that has yet been published.

And on a more personal note, she wants to spend time with her children and grandchildren. All three of her children and both of her grandchildren live in Berkeley. Julien, almost two, lives in the flat downstairs, and makes frequent trips upstairs to see his grandma. Babysitting is an important part of Joanna's life these days, and she relishes her grandchildren in a way she didn't her own children.

The balance between Joanna's personal and career life is working out well. She's moving at a slower pace, physically and mentally, at least she says so, though I found this difficult to observe. The slowing down banishes the old restlessness.

Dr. Paula Green, Karuna Center, Leverett,
Massachusetts. Courtesy Karuna Center.

"My appetite to be outdoors is huge. I've had two decades of a lot of jetting around, airports and conference rooms, classroom, auditoriums, talking heads. The living body of the earth is magical. I am enraptured by it. Last night I said to Fran, 'Let's go swimming!' So we went up to Lake Anza at seven o'clock, and I swam with my eyes just above the level of the water, and watched the fading sun on the ripples of the water, and the frogs were croaking. There's an enormous sufficiency to that."

PAULA GREEN

"For me, to commit to the spiritual realm and ignore the social realities is an incomplete spirituality....As I understand it, spirituality brought to earth is justice." [1]

The work Paula Green has done so far in this life in the fields of psychology, spirituality, and peace activism would take several lifetimes for most of us to accomplish. It would also take far more space than I have here to speak with any depth about all the realms in which she has traveled. So I will touch only briefly on what I think of as her first several lives, and focus on the last ten years of her work in international nonviolent peacebuilding.

Paula was born in 1937, a second-generation Jewish American whose grandparents had fled the pogroms of Eastern Europe. She grew up in New Jersey, with secular, progressive parents. As a young woman in the 1960s, Paula taught school for a few years, married, and adopted two sons. She was active in the burgeoning civil rights and anti-war movements, got a graduate degree in Human Relations, and worked on the integration of public schools and facilities in New York City. This was an exciting time for her, but something was missing: her life was out of balance, her marriage strained.

Changes do not come without internal fears and doubts. After years of stress, guilt, and sadness, Paula divorced and moved to rural New Hampshire, seeking greater peace and a more balanced life, and she has lived in the country ever since. She shared the custody of her growing sons with her ex-husband, who lived in New Jersey.

In the 1970s, she threw herself into the women's movement. She taught women's studies at a local college and later at Lesley College in Cambridge, Massachusetts. She co-founded and worked in Womankind, one of the first feminist therapy collectives. And she began to practice Buddhism at the Insight Meditation Society (IMS) in Barre, Massachusetts. She started going to *vipassana* ("insight") meditation retreats regularly, and questioning her work as a psychotherapist. Meditation touched the depths of her being in a new way, and she wondered if it was a better tool for healing and transformation than psychotherapy.

To investigate this question further, Paula went back to school at Boston University for a doctorate in psychology and religion, and wrote her dissertation on the relationship between psychotherapy and Buddhist meditation.

In a cabin on a tranquil pond, with her typewriter on a sawhorse, surrounded by all the books she could find on Buddhism (there weren't so many then) and on humanistic psychology, Paula tried to understand the similarities and differences of these two paths. The underlying question for her was: "What should I be doing with my life?" She realized that both therapy and meditation are useful and not in conflict.

By the 1980s, the little town of Henniker, New Hampshire, came to feel too small, and she moved to the university town of Amherst in Western Massachusetts, a kind of Cambridge in the country, near IMS. She continued her teaching, her work as a therapist, and her *vipassana* practice. She also joined the newly formed Buddhist Peace Fellowship, and started the Western Massachusetts chapter.

Paula formed another Buddhist connection in 1983, when the Nipponzan Myohoji Japanese Buddhist order of monks and nuns, famous for their commitment to world peace, were offered a piece of land in Leverett,

Massachusetts, just two miles from her newly purchased house, to build a peace pagoda. She had seen the monks with their yellow robes and hand drums chanting at peace demonstrations. At a town meeting in Leverett that would decide whether or not to welcome these Japanese Buddhists to the town, Paula was deeply moved when she saw the head monk respond to an angry speaker with a silent bow. She introduced herself and offered support, and the monks and nuns ended up sleeping on her living room floor while they were clearing the land to build the pagoda. She has had a close association with the group ever since.

Paula met her second husband Jim Perkins at IMS. He was out on parole after serving a prison sentence for a nonviolent Ploughshares action against nuclear weapons. Their *vipassana* romance blossomed after a retreat; they soon became a couple and planned to marry.

But first, Paula went to the Burma border on a trip that would change her life, again. Her international peace work had begun a couple of years before, and now, in 1990, as a member of the newly created International Network of Engaged Buddhists (INEB), she traveled to the Thai-Burma border with Quaker activist George Willoughby to investigate conditions.

In 1988 there had been a brutal military crackdown of the democracy movement in Rangoon, and thousands of Burmese students had fled to the jungle along the border. Paula and George traveled by jeep, boat, and foot through the dense and uncharted jungle to the village of Manerplaw, just inside the Burma border. Here, unknown to the world, students, monks, and indigenous Karen people were organizing nonviolently against Burma's military dictatorship. Food and medicine were in short supply, and hundreds of students were dying of malaria for lack of medicine. Government soldiers were closing in on the dissident students and their indigenous hosts in the jungle.

Paula and George met with a group of student leaders for strategic planning and nonviolence training. They were in the middle of an introductory go-around when a runner came to warn them of a bombing attack. The circle dispersed. There were no shelters or trenches of any kind in Manerplaw, and they were told to go sit against the wall of a house. The shelling began soon after, from the other side of the mountain ridge behind the town. Paula and George leaned against a wall. George, who was in his seventies, said this would be a good way to die. Paula, who was planning to marry Jim on her return home, said she wasn't ready yet; it would be a rotten trick to play on Jim. So, at the first break in the shelling, and at the urging of their hosts, Paula and George made the dangerous journey by boat from Manerplaw to the safety of Thailand.

Someone else might have responded to that experience by deciding to stay away from trouble spots from then on. But not Paula. That trip got her hooked on international peace work. Back in the United States she went into high gear as an international peace activist. And she married Jim Perkins.

Never afraid to start things, Paula created the Karuna Center for Peacebuilding, a vehicle for the international work that had become the central focus of her life. Karuna means compassion in Pali. At Karuna, Paula developed training programs in nonviolent social change based on Buddhist teachings.

As her international activism increased, it became difficult for Paula to continue her work as a therapist. Paula and Jim wanted to spend some extended time in Buddhist countries in Asia. So in 1993, Paula closed her therapy practice, and she and Jim sold their car, rented out their house, and went to Asia for a year, on a pilgrimage that was at once spiritual and political. They traveled simply; they studied with Buddhist teachers and attended retreats; they conducted nonviolence trainings; they learned from their Asian hosts and colleagues.

The year in Asia was profoundly life-changing for Paula. It increased her awareness of the privilege of her life, and also of its impermanence. When they returned to the woods of Leverett, the house seemed cluttered, the appliances and extra clothes superfluous. They checked their initial impulse to give away the refrigerator, but they gave other things away and simplified their lives.

Karuna Center now became Paula's full-time occupation. Thus far she has worked in Europe, Asia, Africa, and North America, in such diverse regions as Bosnia, Sri Lanka, Rwanda, and Israel/Palestine. At the invitation (and only at the invitation) of existing organizations in war-torn or war-threatened countries, Paula and her Karuna Center associates lead workshops and trainings, usually with partners from the host country. She has no illusions about the pace of change, but sees her organization as planting seeds of peace for the future.

One of the more remarkable experiences she had was in Zaire, where she conducted nonviolence trainings in a refugee camp on the Rwanda border. Here 200,000 Hutus lived, each family in a tent fashioned from a blue plastic sheet supplied by the U.N. Paula wrote, "I looked around, and as far as I could see in all directions there were these little blue plastic tents. And I thought, 'Here I am, with three other trainers, teaching for a few weeks in the world's largest refugee camp, with people whose lives have reached a state of unimaginable misery because they or their kinsmen have recently used machetes to kill their Tutsi neighbors. This task is as absurd as scratching at a mountain with a toothpick.' But we taught every day, all day, under our own blue-sheeted tent."[2] They were invited back a year later, and found to their amazement that participants had translated into French all the materials they had brought the year before. And there were seventeen tents in the camp with a sign in front of each saying, "Center for the Study of Nonviolence."

Paula's feminism, like the Dharma, is by now deeply internalized, and always present. Much of the work she does is for women's groups. "In the refugee camp in Zaire, a woman wanted to talk about the problem of rape in the camp itself. The men said, 'We have more pressing problems. We can't talk about rape.' So the women organized themselves with our support, overcame their silence, and worked constructively in the camps on issues of rape, domestic violence, and AIDS."

Paula stepped into the role of mentor some years ago. She trains young women (and men, too) as dialogue facilitators and community leaders, using the Dharma to guide her work. She teaches at the School for International Training in Vermont, and at the new International Fellowship Program in Coexistence at Brandeis University. As Joanna Macy has been a role model for Paula, of a "gifted and inspired Buddhist activist," so Paula sees that it is essential that she in turn make herself available to younger women as a mentor. There are so few older women actively engaged in developing skills for reconciliation.

Paula has a full extended family: husband, children, stepchildren, grandchildren. Jim especially supports and encourages Paula's work, tolerating her absences and distractions with great generosity of heart, in the context of a marriage based not on self, but on a shared vision of social justice.

In 1998 Paula co-facilitated a five-day workshop in Bosnia for Muslim and Serb educators who had not seen each other since 1992, when their lives were ripped apart by ethnic hatred and the Muslims were expelled from their teaching positions. As these former colleagues entered the room to face each other after six years of separation, Paula breathed deeply. "I've been on many winding paths, and I realized, with great gratitude, that in that moment in Sanski Most, I was using, and being, everything that had contributed to my life up to that point. I saw that my life is a seamless whole." Now, if she had to name her career, she would say she was a "peace builder."

"One needs to balance action with reflection, and I could do with a little more on the side of reflection. But even though I'm terribly busy, I feel guided. I'm being led by a golden thread that is pulling me forward. This is the most productive and joyous period of my life, the time to give of myself most fully."

SALA STEINBACH

"Every time a person of color walks into a Zen center, they [the white people in the Zen center] should treat that person as *the* most precious jewel, because he or she holds a truth that they just don't have. They're missing a huge part of the world and they just don't know it." This is what Sala Steinbach said, as we talked about the lack of diversity in the Zen centers we both practice in.

Sala is a nurse/midwife and a Zen practitioner. She and her husband Alan, a physician, moved from Berkeley to Muir Beach, California, in 1996, to be near Green Gulch Farm Zen Center where Sala practices. They are the parents of two grown children. Besides her midwifery work, Sala leads workshops in diversity training and "unlearning racism," usually working with her partner Yeshi Neuman.

Sala is African-American; she was born in the forties, and grew up in a middle-class family in the racially integrated Hyde Park neighborhood of Chicago. Sala's parents taught her that a lot of poor people worked very hard for them to be middle class, and that they should never take that for granted.

Sala was young when she started working for social change. She went to Mississippi in the summer of 1964 to work on voter registration, and after that she became involved in the anti-war movement. The young black men she had gone to high school with were being drafted, and she was horrified that the leaders of the country were sending black people from America to kill brown people in Vietnam.

Sala came to California in 1970, continued to work in the anti-war movement, and became involved in prison work. She saw the massacre and the imprisonment of the Black Panthers as coming out of a denial of black history: rather than understanding what it means that black children in this country are the great-grandchildren of slaves, the government was following what amounted to a deliberate policy of putting black men, especially Black Panthers, in prison, in order to break the back of the movement.

Then, for the first time, Sala joined some black support groups. Before this, she had never been in a group with only black people. She had never been able to just sit down and talk about what it was like to be black, without having to defend her position, without being challenged.

Sala Steinback, Berkeley, California. Courtesy Susan Moon.

She learned in that context that we are each the authority on our own stories. Each one of us knows better than anyone else what is true for us.

At that time there was still a competition of oppressions. For example, people argued about who had been more oppressed—Blacks or Jews. Sala believes that one of the things Buddhism later gave to the left in this country was the understanding that all oppression is horrible, that we do not ever have to compete with our suffering.

Sala was employed in an HMO that was very diverse in its staffing, and the staff members worked together well, but they did not talk honestly to each other across racial barriers, so when there was racial tension, staff unity fell apart in a big way. This motivated Sala to carry the processes she had learned in the black support group into racially mixed groups.

Sala began attending workshops led by Ricky Sherover Marcuse, widow of the Marxist theorist Howard Marcuse, who was developing a model of diversity training in Oakland in the 70s. She was excited by the work. "There are such barriers between groups. We don't know what other people's stories are until we hear them. Under normal circumstances, there's no way of getting information about what it's like to live as a member of another group except from TV, and that's not real information. But when we listen to each other's stories, we come to understand: every time I hear a story it becomes my story, too. For each of us to be able to say what's genuinely true for us seemed to me the only hope we had for any honest political work. We had to begin there."

After training with Ricky Sherover Marcuse, Sala began leading "unlearning racism" groups herself. "We all have to ask ourselves: *What am I willing to give up in order for racism to end*? We may have to give up some sense of ourselves—our shyness, for example, or our habit of letting the other person speak out first.

"We've internalized the messages of the society so thoroughly that we don't even realize how deeply racism affects us and our interactions with each other. We've been trained in racism, so that we don't have to be told what to do. In the same way, as women, we didn't have to be *told* to be quiet, we just *were* quiet."

One of the primary teachings of Zen is to know ourselves. Dogen says, "To study the way is to study the self. To study the self is to forget the self. To forget the self is to be enlightened by all things." Sala says, "When Buddhism tells me to look at myself, I take that seriously. I assume the teaching means look at *everything*, including the hard stuff, including the stuff that's total habit."

Buddhist practitioners generally go to their Buddhist centers to meditate, to hear a Dharma talk, to chant, or bow, or even weed the garden, but not to deal with race. "And yet," Sala says, "how can one practice Buddhism and not look at racism, sexism, and homophobia? It was in the air we breathed as we grew up. And Buddhism encourages us to see things as they are."

San Francisco Zen Center is in the heart of San Francisco. There used to be a large public housing project just a block away, occupied by hundreds of people, most of them poor and black. There was a lot of drug dealing in the vicinity. And there was a lot of fear of "the projects" at Zen Center. If you were leaving Zen Center alone, a resident would offer to walk you to your car. But Sala always turned down the offer. One day, as she walked to her car which was parked next to the projects, she passed a group of young people standing on the corner. She fumbled in her purse for her car keys. She had just been to the ATM, and suddenly there were $20 bills flying all over, and the young men on the corner all started running after the money, laughing, helping her. This was not the response most people at Zen Center would expect. Sala points out that even with a good heart, people make assumptions they do not know they are making.

Rita Gross has been using the language of Buddhism to talk about ecology and feminism. Sala would like to see someone start using the language of Buddhism to talk about diversity. It needs to be a person of color who will really develop the vocabulary, but more and more work is being done in this regard.

Jack Kornfield, one of the leading Vipassana teachers at Spirit Rock, in Fairfax, California, has been working on it. He's white, and he's made mistakes, but Sala feels he deserves credit for being willing to make those mistakes and to learn from them. The teachers at Spirit Rock have gone out of their way to train people of color as leaders. Quite a few people of color go to Spirit Rock now, and there are regular sittings for people of color.

Diversity doesn't just happen. On the contrary, Sala points out, sanghas that are all white tend to stay that way. Or all male, or all old. Whoever is on the margin tends to stay on the margin or to retreat even further, unless explicitly invited in. So now there's somebody at San Francisco Zen Center whose job it is to greet new people, with a particular awareness of the importance of making people of color feel welcome. And when you start welcoming one person, you realize that lots of other people need to be welcomed, too, and the whole community benefits. So, by celebrating diversity, Buddhists become more compassionate to everybody. If you're going to be inclusive, that means being inclusive of *everybody*.

At the public lecture at Green Gulch on a Sunday, there are usually one or two people of color. Sala makes a point of talking to them; it's important not to ignore them. "Sometime in the not-too-distant future there may be ten," Sala says. "There may be enough people of color that they feel comfortable and safe. But in order for them to feel welcome in a sangha that is overwhelmingly white, there has to be a genuine and consistent effort over time. Many white people feel that it's too hard to make this effort, or they think they don't know how, or that it won't do any good, or that 'they' [the people of color] won't like it. Everyone has tried to reach across a barrier and been rebuffed, and we don't want to have that happen again, especially at a place we come to to feel safe. But Buddhism asks us to give up picking and choosing, and not just to accept what's in front of us passively, but to meet it with our *whole selves*.

"Feminism and diversity are completely connected. You can't have one without the other. Diversity includes the full humanity of women. It's important for women to see other women around them in their sanghas, to see women in positions of leadership, to see other female bodies sitting up on the cushion. And as more women have been practicing and taking leadership roles, the centers have been changing, necessarily. The language has been changing.

"Likewise, Buddhist centers will naturally change when they are more racially diverse. Right now they seem very safe for white middle class folks.

But every time a person of color walks in, that person should be treated as the most precious jewel. We all come with our warts. We don't come any other way.

"It's tiring to be black in a predominantly white sangha, and to keep pushing for diversity. It's tiring to be the authority, to be the one who is always called on to support the white people who are working against racism. It wears me out, but the alternative is to put a whole part of me aside when I go to Zen Center. People ask me to lead workshops, but I'm so tired of one-shot efforts. There's a tendency for well-meaning white people to do a day of diversity training and then to stop thinking about it. Having a workshop on unlearning racism is not the completion of diversity training; it's just the beginning. It's so important to follow through.

"Still, even though I'm one of the very few people of color in a white sangha, and even though I get tired and mad, this Buddhist practice is precious. I think this practice can be so valuable to people of color. How wonderful to have a practice that says, 'With this breath I can be perfect. With this breath I can wake up. With this breath I can take myself seriously. Knowing myself is the most interesting thing that can possibly happen.'"

MELODY ERMACHILD CHAVIS

Melody was born in 1943, and grew up as an "army brat," mostly in Texas. She left home at seventeen, after a traumatic childhood, and she has made a number of choices that have taken her close to the edge of danger. Her experiences include helping deserters and draft dodgers during the Vietnam War, taking up rock climbing in her forties, and, for the last twenty years, being a private detective. She now works exclusively on death penalty cases, gathering evidence for the defense.

Melody is a writer as well as an investigator. She's the author of the memoir *Altars in the Street* and of many magazine articles and essays. She organized Strong Roots, a community gardening project for "high risk" young people in Berkeley; and she remains active in the community-gardening movement—she digs in the ground with the kids and also writes grants for them. She has been active on the Board of the Buddhist Peace Fellowship and has helped organize BPF's prison project. Besides all this, she is a "tent-pole person," a central support of a large extended family, and she spends a lot of time taking care of her grandchildren, celebrating birthdays, visiting sick relatives. She's busy.

About ten years ago Melody began practicing Buddhism—first Tibetan, at the Nyingma Institute in Berkeley, and then Zen, at the Berkeley Zen Center. Melody says her Buddhist practice sustains her work in the world,

Melody Ermachild Chavis raising funds for Strong Roots Garden Project, Berkeley, California. Courtesy Melody Chavis.

and that without Buddhism she would have "burned out" on her Death Row work long ago.

"Buddhism calmed me down, though you'd never know it from being around me! I often feel despairing, and I'm way too busy. But Buddhism reminds me to take a longer view, and not to be so attached to results. What I'm doing is good enough right now. Buddhism is like a floor under me. Without a spiritual practice, you could just go into a kind of free fall, which I think is what happens to a lot of people. It comes of frustration and cynicism. All my life I've actually feared cynicism. Cynicism is a deadly disease."

In 1998, a man named Thomas Thompson was executed at San Quentin Prison, in Northern California. He had been convicted of raping and murdering a woman, but there were serious questions about the case, as to whether the sex had been consensual, and whether another man actually committed the murder. He was not Melody's client, but his execution was discouraging to her. He had so many advantages to his appeal—more than most of her clients—and yet he was executed without a hearing.

Melody told me, "I used to see him all the time at San Quentin. He and his wife used to walk arm in arm around the little visiting room. He was there one day, and the next day he was killed by lethal injection by the government. His execution made me feel like I was wasting my time and my life. How could I possibly hope to save the lives of any of my clients, when Thomas Thompson's life couldn't be saved? His execution made me feel useless."

The next time Melody went to the Zen Center, there on the altar was a card with Thomas Thompson's name on it, next to the cards of others who had died and were being remembered. "I was surprised. And I thought: *Here's a place where people care about this person's life, even though he was a criminal.* Nobody said anything to me about it, but just the idea that the card was there changed something for me. It gave me back some confidence in my work.

"You can't always win. It's not as if the death penalty will be abolished because I drive around interviewing jurors. It might not be abolished while I'm alive. But the feeling that what I'm doing is completely worthless changed into a desire to work even harder, because I realized that what I'm doing is part of the larger scheme of things. When I saw that card I remembered that one life is worth honoring.

"Any struggle for justice is long; it's going to last your whole life, or longer. You can get lost in it. It's as if you were trying to save a forest and all you were thinking about was logging companies and lawsuits, and you forgot to go out in the forest and sit down under a tree. So Buddhist practice wakes me up to what's around me. And everything's actually okay right now, on a certain level."

Buddhism has given Melody a more measured view of what she's doing. "I used to think I was a *very good person* for doing this work. But when I became a Buddhist I was shocked to see my baser motives: I was trying to compensate for low self-esteem. I was drawn to working with abused people because I was one myself. There's a joke that severely abused people become either psychotherapists or criminals."

Melody is a feminist committed to nonviolence, and yet her clients are almost exclusively young men, often very violent ones. In fact, most of the violent crime in this country is committed by young men. Concerned about the violence done to women, she realizes that she can help women by working with men. By investigating the roots of violence in her clients' lives, she can help others understand its causes.

Buddhist practice has helped her to be compassionate with all sorts of people, including people who are seen as monsters by the society at large, people who have been convicted of heinous crimes, who are not stable psychologically. This is where the teaching of interconnectedness comes in. This is the message of Thich Nhat Hanh's oft-quoted poem, "Call Me By My True Names," in which he sees that he is both the child raped by the pirate and the pirate who commits the rape.

The teaching of karma helps here, too. Each man on death row is there as a result of a complicated set of causes and conditions. Where would you or I be if we had been so abused as children? How free from paranoia would we be if we grew to adulthood in a high security prison?

Melody often interviews the family of death row inmates. As an investigator, her purpose in these interviews is usually to get affidavits that will provide mitigating evidence for her clients. As a Buddhist, she has another job to do, whether she gets her signed statements or not. The Dalai Lama reminds us that the essence of Buddhist practice is kindness. And Melody has noticed she can do quite a lot of good by just being kind to people. People who have a child on death row, for example, need someone to listen to them with compassion.

As a child Melody knew the shame of family violence and alcoholism, and as an adult she has sat with this pain and explored it. So now she is better able to connect to the people she meets in her work, and to anyone else who feels shame—about family secrets, substance abuse, their own nature. She is a bridge person, who helps people connect across the chasms of race and class. She says, "I'm white, but like many so-called white people, I'm mixed. I have African-American ancestors on my father's side, and Cherokee ancestors on my mother's side. But I've always been socially perceived to be white, and gotten all the privileges of that, so I'm white. The big secret is that we Americans actually have mixed together so much. I hope someday we have the real family reunion in this country. But before we can have that party, a lot of facing-our-history will have to happen." She grew up working class; so, too, she makes a bridge between her clients on death row, who are usually poor, and the defense lawyers she works with, who are usually middle class.

Melody and her husband Stan Dewey, a lawyer, practice at the Berkeley Zen Center, which is tucked away in one of Berkeley's poorer neighborhoods. The Zen Center functions as an oasis of serenity in Melody's busy life. The place runs smoothly, thanks to the hard work of sangha members—it's clean and quiet and orderly and beautiful. There's a grassy courtyard and a flower garden. Bells are rung, paths are swept, tea is served. Birds sing in the plum trees beside the zendo. Melody feels grateful for the fact that others keep the Zen Center going; she goes there and is sustained by the place, and is able to go out into the world and sustain others, to do her community work, her youth gardens, her death penalty appeals, and take care of her grandchildren. All the parts of her life are sustained by the practice. She says it's the only part of her life where she doesn't take responsibility for running things. "I consciously let myself receive that gift."

The Zen tradition is highly patriarchal. The names on the lineage chart at Berkeley Zen Center, from Buddha down to Melody's teacher, Mel Weitsman, are men. But now, thanks to a growing feminist sensibility, of which Melody is a vocal part, the morning service includes homage to "all the female ancestors whose names have been forgotten or left unsung throughout history."

And in the ongoing process of discovering her own lineage, Melody is grateful to women role models like Maylie Scott, a priest at the Berkeley Zen Center. Maylie is very much an engaged Buddhist, involved in homeless advocacy, nonviolent civil disobedience, AIDS work, and prison work, as well as being a teacher within the Zen tradition.

Another woman in Melody's informal lineage who has inspired her in her community gardening work is Catherine Sneed, an African-American Sheriff's Deputy at San Francisco County Jail. Believing in the healing power of digging the earth and making things grow, Catherine created a garden for prisoners. It was such a positive, life-changing experience for the prisoners who worked in it that it made them reluctant to get out of jail!

Catherine had an impossible idea and she just did it. Her example was part of what gave Melody the confidence to start a gardening project for the teenagers in her south Berkeley neighborhood—a neighborhood ravaged by crack, where drug dealing was the best employment opportunity the teenagers could see, followed by arrest and prison or early death in a shooting. "I wanted the young people I knew to skip the going-to-jail part, and just start growing vegetables."

Melody learned that Catherine Sneed was inspired by a woman in Kenya named Wangari Matthai, who organized thousands of women in Kenya to plant trees in a major reforestation project. Thus Melody has become part of a lineage that goes from Wangari Matthai to Catherine Sneed to herself, and she becomes, in turn, a role model for those who will come after.

One of Melody's clients is a young black man named Jarvis Masters, a prisoner on San Quentin's death row, who has become a Buddhist and a writer, partly through Melody's support and encouragement. In 1991, Jarvis took his refuge vows from Chagdud Tulku Rinpoche through a glass window in the visiting room at San Quentin. He has become a courageous voice for nonviolence within the prison, and is respected by both guards and fellow prisoners. Jarvis's first articles about life on death row were published in *Turning Wheel*, and in 1997, his book, *Finding Freedom*, was published. Melody has organized a number of readings of the book, and now Jarvis's voice reaches far beyond San Quentin.

Jarvis, too, belongs in Melody's lineage, as both teacher and student. Her relationship with him is just one example of her wholehearted effort to express herself and at the same time enable others to be heard. Her Buddhist activism continually demonstrates the understanding that there is no us-and-them.

CONCLUSION

It's easy to see that these four women are bright jewels in Indra's net. They express the Dharma in four different ways, unique to each of them, and yet reflective of what the others are doing. All of them say that the Dharma supports them in their work, helping them to avoid burnout and cynicism.

There are unexpected commonalities, perhaps of no particular significance, but interesting to note. All four have been adventurous counterculture rebels. All have struggled to be taken seriously as women. Now, all four are over fifty, in long-term marriages, and all are grandmothers. So in one sense, they have become a very straight bunch.

There are, of course, other Buddhist women activists who are lesbians, or single, or childless, or otherwise not following the prescribed stages of a contemporary Western woman's life, and their lives are woven together with the lives of these four women, as friends, relatives, Dharma sisters. But the point I want to make is that one can be an engaged Buddhist and be living a surprisingly traditional life.

The Dharma tells us that there is no separation between self and other. We are taught to let go of our belief in a separate self. But I believe that another difficulty has been ignored; that women (and some men) just as often err on the side of identifying with *other*, whether it be children, husband, clients, or people on the other side of the world. We need to find and trust ourselves as well as lose ourselves.

So these four women are balancing both Kuan-yin and Manjushri, both compassion and wisdom. As they have gained confidence in themselves and their buddha-nature, they have strengthened their sense of being connected to others. Sala is still delivering babies and still urging San Francisco Zen Center to follow through on a commitment to diversity. Melody has gotten $70,000 in grants for urban gardens this past year, so that while other people are paid to do the work she used to do as a volunteer, she'll have a little more time for her family. Some days Joanna works on her autobiography in the morning, telling her story as an elder, to encourage us, and in the afternoon she takes care of her grandchildren. Paula is in high gear, traveling all over doing trainings, and still ready to take a weekend off to go to a friend's wedding. They all know the importance of following their own intuition, creating their own lives and their own practice within the Dharma, without judging others.

All of them were angry when they were young. Some have been angry more recently than that. But they have learned to transform their anger and to ask, "Who am I, and what I am producing here? What karma am I creating?"

As activists they are totally committed, living their personal lives in a way that reflects their beliefs. They search for community beyond the nuclear family, and support the lives of other activists around them. They are all seeking that elusive balance between work in the world and contemplation.

As women they have something to offer that enriches the practice of engaged Buddhism. Whether it is due to nature or nurture, these women have lived their lives close to tears, their own and other people's. So now they go right to the heart of suffering. To Chernobyl, to Bosnia, to death row, to the hidden pockets of racism and fear in our own institutions. They work there to alleviate suffering, to save all sentient beings, including themselves, without standing apart from the rest of us. Just being regular people, they help us to see that we can do it—indeed, that we are already doing it.

NOTES

1. *Insight*, Newsletter of the Insight Meditation Society and the Barre Center for Buddhist Studies (spring 1998): 31.
2. Ibid., p. 32.

GAY BUDDHIST FELLOWSHIP

Roger Corless

WHEREVER THERE HAVE BEEN HUMANS, there has been homosexual as well as heterosexual conduct, and we can be sure that there have always been followers of the Buddhadharma who have engaged in same-sex affectional, homoerotic, or genital behavior. What appears to be new to the Western scene is the social and political visibility of persons who identify themselves as gay and who wish to practice Buddhism in the conscious acceptance of their gayness. Whether or not this produces a gay Buddhism, or even a group of humans who can be called, or who call themselves, gay Buddhists, the phenomenon focuses simultaneously on Buddhism and gayness and thereby cuts across the lineage and cultural lines that Buddhism has established in Asia. Because of this, it is producing a new form of Buddhism that we can say is distinctively Western.

This chapter will discuss the emerging phenomenon of the practice of Buddhism in the gay community, and what it means for Buddhism in the West, by focusing on a particular case, the Gay Buddhist Fellowship (GBF) of San Francisco, California, which I have studied, as a participant-observer, for over three years.[1]

The mission statement of the Gay Buddhist Fellowship is a lucid and comprehensive statement of why gay men choose to practice together, and sets the theme for our discussion. The Gay Buddhist Fellowship exists to support Buddhist practice in the gay community. Our understanding of practice includes, but is not limited to, traditional Buddhist practices such as meditation and mindfulness, individual forms of practice, compassionate service to the community, and relationships with teachers and spiritual friends. The GBF is a forum in which all of the distinct Buddhist traditions can be brought together to address the spiritual concerns of gay men.

We respect and care for each other in a compassionate way as an expression of the full realization of the Dharma. We recognize that every aspect of our lives is practice. We cultivate a social environment that is accepting, open, inclusive, and caring. We acknowledge and support the growing network of gay practitioners in the United States and around the world. In addition, we intend to create programs that contribute to the well-being of the larger community.

The Gay Buddhist Fellowship Newsletter is published monthly by the Gay Buddhist Fellowship. It provides news of interest to GBF members, as well as writings by living Buddhist teachers covering a broad cross-section of current Buddhist thought. It also serves as a forum where gay Buddhist practitioners can address spiritual concerns regardless of their form of practice or tradition.[2]

It is clear from this statement that the GBF does not see itself as a new lineage of Buddhism but as a service to all existing Buddhist lineages, and a service to the gay community at large. Many of those who attend the GBF meetings, even many of those who attend regularly, do not consider themselves Buddhist. Nevertheless, GBF can be regarded as a new form of Buddhism, simply because of its explicit connection with gayness.

By *gayness* I mean the identification of oneself as a human whose erotically charged affections are largely or exclusively directed at other humans of the same sex. The distinction between "homosexual" and "gay" was made clear by John Boswell, who identified "homosexual" as referring to the broad category of same-sex genital activity and "gay" as referring to "persons who are conscious of erotic inclination toward their own gender as a distinguishing characteristic."[3] Homosexual activity is certainly as old as humanity, and it is observed to occur in many other species. Gayness is somewhat more restricted, since it is a self-identification. It is thus an exclusively human phenomenon and it can only occur under certain rather particular sociocultural conditions. The gay community has attempted to show that gayness is a phenomenon of hoary antiquity, but the evidence that has been collected only supports, in my opinion, homoeroticism, which is not the same thing.[4]

Gayness as I understand it is a comparatively recent phenomenon. It is not merely the sense that "I am different," experienced by any individual who, down the ages, has discovered that his or her erotic physiology does not react in the same way as that of their heterosexual peers, but the sense that "we are different," experienced by a collection of people who begin to think of themselves as a "tribe." The emergence of the gay "tribe," the self-aware, politicized, socially visible community of "out" men and women was part of the sexual revolution in the West in the 1960s. Once the tribe had found itself, and could say "we," it could ask itself "what is our spirituality?" The answer most often given was that there was none. The dominant Christian, or rather quasi-Christian culture of the West could not make a distinction between gayness and homosexuality, found Biblical support for homophobia, and declared gays to be grievous sinners. To discover that one was gay, apparently, meant that one could not have a spiritual life. One could only have sex. The question on everyone's mind at the time of the founding of what was to become the GBF was "Is it possible to be gay and a good Buddhist?"[5] The members of GBF believe that it is. Thus, it is forming a new Buddhism, a new understanding of the Dharma.

GBF AS ENGAGED BUDDHISM

When we think of engaged Buddhism we usually think of socially active Buddhism, a kind of Buddhist version of the understanding of Christianity preached by figures such as Walter Rauschenbusch[6] and Gustavo Gutiérrez.[7] The GBF mission statement mentions "compassionate service to the community" but that is not, in practice, a major part of its activities. Some members occasionally help out at the Hamilton Family Center, a shelter for homeless families, but in general, GBF's involvement in such projects is minimal.[8] Some members, when I suggested to them that GBF might be regarded as engaged Buddhism, rejected the idea outright.[9] Nevertheless, I argue that GBF is very much engaged Buddhism, but its engagement is not with social injustice directly; it is more subtly "engaged" by its involvement in the healing of homophobia, especially the internalized homophobia of its members. When their internalized homophobia is healed, the members can be happier, more effective members of the gay community, helping to heal both it and society at large.

External homophobia is easy to spot: the battle against it, spearheaded by political and legal action groups such as the National Gay and Lesbian Task Force, the Lambda Legal Defense and Education Fund, and the Human Rights Campaign, is ongoing and highly visible. Internalized homophobia is much more difficult to recognize. It is not an attack on the gay community from without, it is a sapping of strength from within. Just as women, having been told over the centuries that they are inadequate, failed males, may start to believe the lie, so gays often carry around in themselves a hatred of who they are. This self-hatred, which is said to be a leading cause of suicide among gay teenagers in the United States, is often so deeply hidden that it takes professional psychotherapeutic help to uncover and heal it. The problem of healing internalized homophobia in the gay community was one of the chief factors motivating the Insight Meditation teacher Eric Kolvig to start giving retreats for gays.[10]

The deep woundedness of the gay community is something that was, until recently, unrecognized even by the gay community itself. It was so common that it was regarded as normal and inevitable. Healing it by focus-ing the Buddhist message of liberation from suffering upon it is a significant change in the gay community, in gay consciousness, and in Buddhism. The gay community has been much assisted in its approach to the issue by the pioneering work of African Americans and feminists. Not that long ago, it was argued, often on Biblical grounds, that Africans and their descendants were subhuman. It was "natural" for them to be slaves and "unnatural" for them to be in positions of power and responsibility. Similarly, it was argued that women should keep their place in the home, doing the housework and praying for their menfolk. It was also "unnatural" for them to be in positions of power and responsibility.[11] African-American and feminist activists and scholars have put a considerable amount of energy into protesting this view of themselves and forcing a rereading of the tradition in their favor. Gays are similarly re-interpreting the tradition. With regard to Buddhism, they are proposing something genuinely new. With some notable exceptions, Buddhism has been silent on the subject of homosexuality[12] and has not been culturally aware of the category "gay." It is not unusual to hear Buddhist teachers who have come from Asia to the U.S.A. claim that there are no gays in their country of origin.

GBF, therefore, is making the path as it treads it. A central issue, discussed at many meetings and the subject of many articles in the *Newsletter*, is gay relationships. Given that GBF members are not monks vowed to celibacy, we ask ourselves, what is the place of gay sex in Buddhism? How might those of us in committed relationships behave in a dharmically wholesome way? Is it acceptable to continue, after deciding to practice the Dharma, a lifestyle of cruising and tricking, going to sex clubs, and having a massage with "some-thing extra"? There are no guidelines in traditional Buddhism as to how the third precept (abstention from sexual misconduct) should be applied to twen-tieth century gay life in America.

In fact, the whole question of what to do about ethical conduct *(shila)* and the precepts is put in suspension by GBF. Many members have been so hurt by homophobic authority figures that they rebel against any and all rules and will not be told how to live their lives ethically. The question of obser-vance of the precepts is brought up now and again and is either shelved or relegated to private choice. Some members have expressed their fear that GBF is merely rationalizing existing behavior as Buddhist. Others are more confident that the precepts are recommending themselves. David Holmes, who is regarded by many members as an "elder" or informal teacher, said, "We trust each other, we trust that people know when they are approaching their center."[13] My experience attending the weekday meetings at members' homes, which are less formal than the Sunday sittings, is that, when a point of ethical conduct is raised, there is apparently random discussion, but it settles down into a consensus about how to act that is almost always clearly in line with traditional Buddhist morality *(shila)*. The precepts, somehow, as Holmes says, do seem to arise naturally.

GBF AS QUEER SANGHA

Healing internalized homophobia is, in my view, the soul of GBF. Its body is the community or fellowship that is part of its name. Community is a prominent element in the GBF mission statement: "We respect and care for each other in a compassionate way as an expression of the full realization of the Dharma. We cultivate a social environment that is accepting, open, inclusive, and caring."

This is a definition of sangha, but it is nontraditional. In Asia, we would expect to see a temple at the heart of the sangha, staffed by monastics and led by a Dharma teacher who was also a monastic. Around the monastic

Issan Dorsey, founder of the Hartford Street Zen Center,
San Francisco. Courtesy David Schneider.

community there would be a loosely defined outer circle of lay people, some of whom, having taken refuge and precepts, would be closer to the monastics, a kind of inner circle of the outer circle, and most of whom would be more or less occasional members or visitors. There would be no clearly defined boundary to the community.

Observers of American Buddhism have noticed that it tends to have "centers" rather than temples or monasteries. This is said to be a defining characteristic of American Buddhism, distinguishing it from the Buddhism of immigrant communities (what Jan Nattier calls "baggage Buddhism" but which I prefer to call "ethnic Buddhism"), which tends to transplant the temple and monastic structure to American soil. GBF is like this, only more so. There is, in January 1998, no "GBF Center." It met for some years on Sundays in the downstairs living room of the Zen Hospice Project, on Page Street, kitty-corner from Zen Center. On May 11, 1997, it changed its Sunday location to the shrine room of the San Francisco Buddhist Center, 37 Bartlett Street, in the Mission District, the local home of the FWBO (Friends of the Western Buddhist Order). On Thursdays, in San Francisco, it meets in the home of any member who wishes to host it. There are also sittings at members' homes in the East Bay and in the Sonoma area.

Not only is there no physical center to GBF, there is no formal membership, even of a core group. There is a mailing list for the *Newsletter*, and when membership numbers are called for by researchers like myself, the number of names on the list is usually quoted. However, nobody pays dues,[14] and nobody checks to see if the persons on the mailing list ever attend any meetings, although the mailing list is updated and purged periodically. A number of members are regulars and become known to each other. Amongst the regulars some are respected as "elders" and, by common consent, recognized as teachers. Only one member, who is prominent but not a regular, has received formal ordination, being in the "lineage" of Issan Dorsey, the notorious drag queen turned Zen master who founded the Hartford Street Zen Center.[15] Many members reported having a connection with a nationally known Buddhist teacher and/or group. For some, this connection was merely an introduction to the Dharma, which they left behind when they joined GBF. For others, the connection is so valuable that they maintain it simultaneously with their attendance at GBF meetings. The presence, at every GBF meeting, of some members who are practicing with independently certified teachers helps to preserve a link with the traditional Buddhist Dharma.

The process of silent election by consensus is reminiscent of how leaders come to the fore in the Society of Friends. In fact, there is a very Quaker feel to the organization of the GBF sangha. Since there are no monastics (apart from the single exception just noted) there is no distinction between lay people and monastics, and there is no formal hierarchy. Volunteers open and close the meeting space and mark the beginning and end of the sitting period by ringing the bell. There is no sutra chanting, or even lighting of incense and bowing, so formal liturgical skills are not required of the facilitator *pro tem*. Attendees sit on *zafus* in the FWBO shrine room and, in members' homes, bring their own *zafus*, use whatever chairs are available, or just sit on the floor. There is no formal sitting posture and no-one goes round with a *kyosaku* checking on who is alert and who is not. Sitting is done in silence. At the end of the session, usually after the discussion, a formula somewhat recognizable as a distribution of merit or a radiation of loving-kindness *(metta)* may be said by the facilitator. However, following traditional Buddhist practice, and contrary to most Quaker practice, the sitting sessions are carefully timed, rather than being allowed to go on until the spirit prompts the meeting to stop.

Decision making also has a Quaker feel. Steering Committee meetings are held at a member's home, and the committee forms itself from whoever shows up. Once again, certain members are regulars and an informal core group manifests itself. One man volunteers, or is chosen, as editor of the *Newsletter*, holding the post for an indefinite period. He is the only member with anything approaching an officially recognized position. I attended a Steering Committee meeting on Tuesday, January 7, 1997, at a member's home, and was told that it was typical.

People began to assemble shortly before 7 P.M. Ten members (eleven, including myself as participant-observer or, as one member called me, "the worst fly-on-the-wall I've ever seen") were present at the start of the meeting, with one more member arriving later. The meeting began with members proposing agenda items, which were noted in order by the host, who acted as Chair. Then followed five minutes of silent meditation, with the participants seated mostly on chairs and couches, and some on the floor when there were insufficient chairs. The sitting began and ended without any chanting or other ceremony. Discussion of the agenda items began, with a volunteer acting as secretary and taking notes for the minutes. The format was free discussion with the chair, or someone else, occasionally proposing that an issue was too complex, or tangential to the matter at hand, and recommending that it be tabled. Decisions were made by consensus. About halfway through, the minutes of the last meeting were passed around for inspection and approval. Topics discussed included a book project, Sunday speaker invitations, the availability of tapes of previous talks, the newsletter, a year-end financial report, and engaged Buddhism projects (especially the

Hamilton Family Center dinners). Discussion ended at 9:10 P.M. and the meeting concluded with five minutes of silent meditation, again without ceremony.

The GBF sangha is a living example of self-organization by interdependent arising. It was formed by gay Buddhist men who felt the need for it. Having been formed, there are gay Buddhist (and quasi-Buddhist) men who value its support. GBF and its members came/come into existence simultaneously. It is a sangha with no center and no periphery. It is empty of inherent existence—it exists, yet it cannot be found. Organizationally, GBF is pre-eminently Buddhist and contrasts strongly with the rigid and complex institutions of traditional Buddhism.

QUEER DHARMA?

Even the Dharma, which is taught, or which teaches itself, in GBF, arises interdependently with the membership, that is, with whoever happens to be attending a particular GBF meeting. The "elders" who are accorded an honor of *primus inter pares* teach by suggestion and in the context of dialogue, often a pseudo-psychotherapeutic dialogue ("What I think I'm hearing from you is...."; "What I'm feeling, myself personally, about that is...."). Tom Moon, a GBF member and a psychotherapist with a regular column in the San Francisco edition of *Frontiers*, a free gay glossy magazine, says that the movement between Dharma and psycho-babble in GBF is something he also finds when he practices with Vipassana groups. He claims that there is something uniquely American about it.[16]

But the question remains, is there anything uniquely *gay* about the Dharma that self-arises in GBF meetings? Are they (we) queering the Dharma?

Most members, when asked directly "Is there a gay Buddhism?" responded in the negative. And yet they continued to attend GBF meetings. When asked why, most referred to the sense of community, or tribe, that they got at GBF meetings and did not get at the meetings of other Buddhist groups they had tried or with which they continued to practice.

Kobai Scott Whitney, a Zen teacher attached to the Diamond Sangha in Hawaii, near Honolulu, answers the question "is there a gay Buddhism?" by saying:

> Yes and no. There is no Buddha that is only gay, just as there is no dharma, no teaching, that is for gay people alone. Compassion is an imperative for all Buddhists. Generosity is not gay or straight. But there may be such a thing as a gay sangha.[17]

Whitney also says, "For gay people to sit together is to enact the exact opposite of the furtive, self-destructive bar scene that was so much a part of our 'coming out.'"[18]

So we come back to the notion of Sangha, which is, after all, one of the Three Jewels, and thus interdependent with the Dharma.

The answer to the question that Whitney proposes has, I suggest, more to do with gayness than with Buddhism. Heterosexual persons in a heterosexual society need not be aware that they are heterosexual. They are like Molière's middle-class gentleman who is unaware that he is speaking prose. Traditional Buddhist groups do not bring up the issue of homosexuality and *by that very fact* they support the status quo of heterosexism. A gay man who encounters, for the first time in his life, a community such as the Castro where homosexuality is the norm and heterosexuality is unusual is at first disoriented and confused, wondering who he is. Then, if he is out, or is able to come out even a little, and especially if he is able to come out to himself, there is an almost religious feeling of liberation and of presence here and now. What has always been normal for him is now seen and felt to be normal for all around him. He has found his own people, his family, his tribe, his home, his place in the scheme of things. This, surely, he thinks, is how heterosexuals must feel all the time. Accepted fully, with no need to hide what is essential about how he relates to other humans.

The cloud that such a man rides is pink in more ways than one. Eventually he must get off, and awaken to the reality of oppression not only of heterosexuals by heterosexuals, and of course of homosexuals by heterosexuals, but of homosexuals by homosexuals. Yet the experience is never quite forgotten. We still know where to find our true (albeit dysfunctional) family, our tribe, and our community. To be human is to be sexed. We can choose to be celibate, but we cannot choose to be asexual.

This being so, if we are gay, we cannot fully practice Buddhism, or even life, in a context that denies our gayness. To be fully Buddhist, we must be fully gay. And so we practice together as gay men.

What this means for the Dharma itself is as yet unclear. The feminists have gone before us in suggesting that there might be a post-patriarchal Buddhism in which we meet, not manfully endured suffering, but the *jouissance* of the Great Bliss Queen.[19] As gays, we are still fighting for recognition as full citizens, and sometimes it seems that we suffer as many reversals as successes in the courts and at the polls. But we can still move on to propose the restructuring of the status quo symbolism along other than heterosexist lines. Such a move may even pre-empt the legal and electoral reversals. By challenging the universality of sexual bifurcation, the image of the Other, and suggesting a symbology of Another Me, the nonduality that Buddhism preaches but too often does not practice may be strengthened. That is for the future. GBF has not done that, but it provides a context, or a community and a forum, as its mission statement says, for developing such a vision of the Dharma.

NOTES

1. See my "Coming Out in the Sangha: Queer Community in American Buddhism" in *Faces of Buddhism in America*, ed. Kenneth Tanaka and Charles Prebish (Berkeley: University of California Press, forthcoming,) for a general account of gay and lesbian Buddhist groups in the San Francisco Bay area. The present article attempts to use my material to ask more profoundly Dharmological questions than are addressed in that somewhat sociological study. My limited contact with the Dharma Sisters (in San Francisco) and the East Bay Lesbian Sangha (in Berkeley) causes me to suspect that the Dharmology of Buddhism in the lesbian community is significantly different from the Dharmology of Buddhism in the gay men's community. However, I have insufficient data to support this assertion and I postpone its discussion to another time.

2. *Gay Buddhist Fellowship Newsletter* (December 1997/January 1998).

3. John Boswell, *Christianity, Social Tolerance, and Homosexuality: Gay People in Western Europe from the Beginning of the Christian Era to the Fourteenth Century* (Chicago: University of Chicago Press, 1980), p. 44.

4. The antiquity of gayness has been argued in Judy Grahn, *Another Mother Tongue: Gay Words, Gay Worlds* (Boston: Beacon Press, 1984), and its ancient connection with spirituality in Randy P. Conner, *Blossom of Bone: Reclaiming the Connection between Homoeroticism and the Sacred* (San Francisco: Harper, 1993).

5. Interview with Steve Peskind (who was at the organizational meeting of what was then called the Gay Buddhist Group on April 6, 1980), San Francisco, Friday, January 3, 1997.

6. *Walter Rauschenbusch: Selected Writings*, ed. Winthrop S. Hudson (New York and Mahwah: Paulist Press, 1984).

7. Selections in *Third World Liberation Theologies: A Reader*, ed. Deane William Ferm (Maryknoll, NY: Orbis Books, 1986).

8. A feature on the Hamilton Family Center Project appeared in the January 1996 issue of the *GBF Newsletter*, where it is explicitly called "engaged Buddhist practice." An update was printed in the September 1997 issue, appealing for funds to allow GBF members to continue to provide meals at the center once a month.

9. The sentence in the mission statement that begins "In addition, we intend to cre-

ate programs…" originally read "As engaged Buddhists, we intend to create programs…" (*GBF Newsletter*, March 1996), but the phrase was unpopular and was dropped.

10. Eric Kolvig, "Gay in the Dharma: Wisdom and Love," *GBF Newsletter* (March 1993). Eric came to the Bay Area to teach Buddhist meditation to gay men in the context of the AIDS crisis. Now that medical advances have converted HIV/AIDS from a sentence of death to a chronic condition, the pandemic, while certainly not insignificant, is somewhat less in the forefront of the consciousness of the gay community. For the importance of AIDS in stimulating initial interest in Buddhism in the gay community, see my "Coming Out in the Sangha."

11. Kathy Rudy, in *Sex and the Church: Gender, Homosexuality, and the Transformation of Christian Ethics* (Boston: Beacon Press, 1997), has argued that this view of women is still active in the theology of the Christian right and its defense of family values.

12. For an overview, see José Ignacio Cabezón, "Homosexuality and Buddhism," in *Homosexuality and World Religions*, ed. Arlene Swidler (Valley Forge, PA: Trinity Press International, 1993), pp. 81–101.

13. Interview, San Francisco, Tuesday, December 31, 1996.

14. In December 1996 it was decided to request a $15 per annum donation for receiving the *Newsletter*, but in November 1997 the practice was abandoned when mailing costs were reduced due to GBF obtaining nonprofit status and therefore becoming eligible for a bulk mailing permit.

15. David Schneider, *Street Zen: The Life and Work of Issan Dorsey* (Boston and London: Shambhala Publications, 1993).

16. Interview, San Francisco, Friday, December 27, 1996.

17. Kobai Scott Whitney, "Vast Sky and White Clouds: Is There a Gay Buddhism?" in *Queer Dharma: Voices of Gay Buddhism,* ed. Winston Leyland (San Francisco: Gay Sunshine Press, 1998), pp. 15–26. The quotation is from p. 25. (*Queer Dharma* is a collection of scholarly essays, stories, poems, and personal accounts. It has many valuable pieces but is quite uneven; the reader is advised to approach it with caution.)

18. Whitney, "Vast Sky and White Clouds," p. 16.

19. Anne C. Klein, *Meeting the Great Bliss Queen: Buddhists, Feminists, and the Art of the Self* (Boston: Beacon Press, 1995).

Social Action among Toronto's Asian Buddhists

Janet McLellan

Since 1967, approximately five hundred thousand Asian immigrants and refugees have settled in the greater Toronto area. Similar to other ethnic groups, they have turned to religious institutions for support in their adjustment and adaptation to Canadian life. In 1965, the Toronto Buddhist Church was the only Buddhist group in Toronto. Within thirty years, over sixty-five new temples and Buddhist associations were established, with several undergoing expansion or developing sister branches within the city. The dramatic growth of Buddhism reflects sociocultural dynamics of ethnic, national, and linguistic diversity as well as disparate immigration patterns. Buddhist institutions and personnel are not only recreating traditional religious belief and practice but are also actively engaged in providing new systems of social support ranging from mental health intervention, counselling, assistance in employment, refugee sponsorship, or family reunification, to activities that sacralize individual action.

This paper explores the numerous ways in which Asian Buddhists in Toronto participate in both social and political activism. These engaged Buddhist practices reflect three different spheres of action: an ethnic community orientation; a homeland orientation; and an external orientation, beyond ethnic or national identities.

BUDDHISM IN MULTICULTURAL TORONTO

The greater metropolitan Toronto area, with over four million people, includes the cities of Toronto, Scarborough, North York, Mississauga, East York, and the regions of Markham, Thornhill, Peel, and Durham. It is the largest and most multi-ethnic urban center in Canada, with significant recent migrations from East and Southeast Asia, Africa, the West Indies, the Middle East, India, Pakistan, and Eastern Europe adding to the long-established United

Kingdom and European populations.[1] Since 1991, more than 441,000 new immigrants have settled in Toronto, raising the immigrant population to 1.8 million, nearly half of the area's total population (*Toronto Star*, November 5, 1997). The diversity of over sixty-five Buddhist groups and associations throughout the Toronto area, representing an enormous range of Buddhist beliefs, practices, and institutions, is reflective of this recent migration.[2] See the appendix for a partial list of Buddhist groups in Toronto.

Buddhist temples and organizations have grown at a remarkable rate within recent years. Toronto's first Buddhist institution was the Toronto Buddhist Church, founded in the late 1940s by Japanese Canadians who were forced to resettle in Eastern Canada. Following four years of wartime internment in British Columbia in which they were subject to massive human rights violations—seizure without compensation of monies, property, businesses, assets—Japanese Canadians (immigrants as well as citizens born and raised in Canada) had to choose between either leaving British Columbia or being repatriated to Japan.[3] In 1966, the first non-Asian Buddhist group, the Dharma Centre of Canada, began under the leadership of a non-Asian Canadian man trained as a monk in Burma. Following the 1967 change in Canadian immigration law—which introduced the point system and removed specific country restrictions—individuals from Asian countries such as Korea, Hong Kong, Sri Lanka, Burma, Tibet, India, and Thailand began to emigrate to Canada and eventually formed Buddhist groups and institutions in Toronto. By 1979 the number of Asian and non-Asian Buddhist groups had increased to approximately fifteen. The influx of large numbers of Indochinese refugees in the early 1980s contributed significantly to the growth of Buddhism in Toronto, with approximately twenty-one groups active by 1987. It is within the last ten years, however, that over thirty more Buddhist groups have become established. The steady immigration flow from Hong Kong, coupled with ongoing family sponsorship and reunification programs, has resulted in Chinese Buddhists representing one-third of all Buddhist groups in Toronto. Sangha estimates indicate that over 300,000 individuals in Toronto maintain some degree of Buddhist identity and/or participate in a wide range of Buddhist (or Buddhist affiliated) beliefs and practices.[4]

The diversity of Buddhists in Toronto is evident in the variety of teachings, approaches, styles of practice, and traditions. Asian Buddhist groups in Toronto include Theravada Buddhists (from Burma, Cambodia, Laos, Sri Lanka, Thailand); Ambedkar Buddhists from India; and Mahayana Buddhists (from Canada, Hong Kong, Taiwan, China, Japan, Korea, Vietnam, and Tibet). Non-Asian Buddhists (primarily Caucasians from a Judeo-Christian background), most of whom are in groups led by or affiliated with an Asian teacher, also pursue a variety of types of Buddhist meditation and practice. The majority of non-Asian Buddhists are involved with Tibetan Vajrayana and Japanese and Korean Zen lineages, with smaller numbers committed to Theravada practice.

Toronto Buddhist communities and groups vary in size. Small groups, with less than 500 members, include ethnic communities such as the Tibetans and most non-Asian Buddhist organizations. Midsize groups of up to 5,000 members are identified with larger ethnic communities such as the Cambodian, Laotian, Burmese, or Japanese Canadians. The largest Buddhist communities in Toronto consist of the Chinese (immigrants from Hong Kong, Taiwan, Malaysia, and Singapore, and refugees from Southeast Asia and China) and Vietnamese (primarily refugees), each with low estimates of over 200,000 and 70,000, respectively. Both are comprised of numerous Buddhist groups ranging from small (fifteen members to over 250), midsize (one to two thousand members), to large temple institutions (some with over 15,000 members).[5]

There are basically two types of Asian Buddhist organizations in Toronto. The first type can be characterized as "temple-focused organizations," comprising a recognized Buddhist temple with both a sangha (ordained monks and/or nuns) and a congregation (lay members). The function of the temple is to maintain particularistic Buddhist beliefs and practices; to facilitate communication between the sangha and lay members; and to coordinate a number of activities that involve religious endeavors (sutra readings, Buddhist rituals/ceremonies, and lectures), secular events (youth circles, educational classes, social meetings), and cultural celebrations (New Years, poetry readings, music and dance). Institutional and leadership roles of sanghas differ from temple to temple. In some Buddhist organizations, such as the Cham Shan temple complex, the sangha is comprised of the clerical administrators and primary authority in all temple affairs. In others, such as the Toronto Buddhist Church or Toronto Mahavihara, the sangha is relegated to the role of religious specialist, leaving temple administration and organization of activities to selected lay members. The relationship between sangha and laity may also comprise a unique blend of participatory democracy and individual authority, patterns identified with the Taiwanese Buddhist Light International Association or the Vietnamese Hoa Nghiem Temple when it was under the leadership of Thich Quang Luong.[6]

In contrast to the temple, focused organization is that of the "lay organization," a term generally indicating a Buddhist group with no resident sangha or where their primary meeting area is not recognized as a temple.

Lay organizations tend not to be affiliated with specific temples in Toronto— although they may represent a branch of an overseas temple or lineage. Sangha leadership is limited by intermittent visits, and lay members are totally responsible for the groups' administration, continuing Buddhist teaching, and regular practice. Lay organizations are especially evident among Chinese Buddhists and non-Asian Theravada practitioners.[7]

Most ethnic Buddhist traditions in Toronto have remained doctrinally conventional as well as culturally expressive, being clearly identifiable with communities from particular countries such as Thailand, Korea, and Tibet. The particularistic tendencies within the various Buddhist groups create boundaries that continue to delineate Buddhist identities along ethnic, national, linguistic, and doctrinal lines. Buddhist immigrants and refugees tend to re-create familiar ritual practices, culturally constructed ideas about Dharma, personalized versions of karma, various images of Buddha—including all the accompanying embodiments—socially specific interpretations and terms for explicit doctrine, and culturally appropriate attitudes toward the sangha (monks, nuns, priests, gurus, and teachers), especially in their expectations of strictness or continuity of the monastic tradition.[8]

Each Buddhist group, however, also provides distinct examples of the extent to which continuities and transformations of their respective traditions have occurred. Examples of religious transformation include new and/or modified rituals, invented traditions, changing roles of religious leadership, revised presentation of services and sermons, and innovative extensions of monastic rules and lay disciplines.[9] The particular parts of religious practice that are emphasized, the role and choice of symbols, the focus on renunciation or worldly affirmation, and the transformed structural arrangements within religious organizations reflect numerous determinants—pre- and post-migration experiences, availability of sanghas in Canada, connections to the homeland, exposure to and/or effectiveness of Christian conversion (in refugee camps or through sponsorship), systemic accommodation changes, and so forth. In many cases, sanghas are not only required to accommodate Buddhist beliefs and practices to the complex social and political ideals of Canadian society, but also to meet social and psychological needs of lay members. Expectations of the sangha have therefore grown to incorporate enhanced ministerial/counselling roles, gender egalitarianism (in theory at least), and increased involvement in social activities—ranging from cultural presentations to political protests to interfaith forums. New modes of communication and technology within and beyond the group (for example, newsletters, magazines, videos, fax, websites), place further demands on the sangha, and an increasing reliance on lay participation in temple affairs.

ENGAGED BUDDHISM

The enhanced ministerial/counselling roles and increased involvement in social activities most clearly indicate engaged Asian Buddhist action on the part of the sangha. Ordained leaders recognize that great suffering arises through the process of migration and refugee resettlement, intensified by poverty (or at least downward mobility), cultural alienation, adaptive difficulties, an enormous sense of loss (homeland, status, possessions, loved ones), excessive grief manifesting in physiological ailments, and exposure (as well as increasing attachment) to a social ethos of greed and consumption. Clergy view their endeavors to improve people's lives through intervention and counselling as an attempt to alleviate this suffering and enhance the well-being of their community. Even though many of these activities—counselling, home/hospital visits to the sick or dying, funeral home services—may be attributed to Protestant models of ministerial roles, Buddhist sangha members firmly ground their activities in traditional notions of Buddhist cosmology and soteriology.[10] Concepts of "right action"—*karuna, metta,* and *karma*—are employed to invoke compassionate action, as are examples from the canonical tradition such as Buddha charging his disciples to be responsible and care for one another, or Vimalakirti's illness. The extensive healing practices found within ethnic Buddhist lineages also provide well-established, culturally appropriate mechanisms for sangha involvement with the health care of laity.

The traditional Buddhist stance on integrative harmony and adaptive flexibility is especially applicable to adaptive and integrative strategies within Toronto's multicultural context. Lay Buddhists also participate in engaged activities, such as charity and social work, as a social manifestation of their own inner commitment and aspiration to Buddhist ideals. Mahayana practitioners view their forms of social activism as a manifestation of skilful means *(upaya)*, combining wisdom *(prajna)* and compassion *(karuna)*. Buddhists do not become Protestants (or even Protestant Buddhists) when they embrace engaged practices. Instead, within a Buddhist form of religious expression, they combine inner worldly asceticism with rationalized action—similar to that which the Protestant Max Weber (1930) idealized in his study on asceticism and the spirit of capitalism. The focus of Buddhist social engagement is to direct spiritual aspiration and efforts to a "mundane awakening," a liberation that may be achieved and recognized in this lifetime and in this world.[11] From a sociological perspective, engaged Buddhist activity can be seen as an attempt to "re-sacralize" the individual, which is necessary in order to counteract the de-sacralization of the world, that is, the inherent secularized nature of our global, postmodern, consumer-driven social environment.[12] The re-sacralized individual overrides the sacred/profane distinction inherent in modernity, and becomes an instrumental force and locus for actively resolving inequities and injustices in local or global contexts. The engaged Buddhist assumes personal responsibility as a self-reflective agent whose individual actions (or nonaction) have renewed spiritual meaning as well as social consequences. Among Asian Buddhists in Toronto, there is a range of engaged practices that actively attempt to alleviate or identify conditions that cause suffering in both social and natural environments. These practices to promote peace, equality, and justice, or to restore a sense of harmony within individuals and groups, reflect three spheres of action that can be identified as having an ethnic community orientation, a homeland orientation, and an external orientation.

ETHNIC COMMUNITY ORIENTATION

Within local Buddhist communities, engaged activities attempt to combine positive theological teachings with compassionate action geared to alleviate the suffering of everyday life. Ethnic Buddhist temples are more than just a religious center for immigrants and refugees. Buddhist temples serve as the nucleus for community networks and systems of support, concerned with both individual and community health and the perpetuation and transmission of cultural identity. Among those Asian groups whose belief and practice of Buddhism is closely linked with national and ethnic identity (Burmese, Cambodian, Lao, Thai, Sinhalese, and Tibetan), the Buddhist temple and sangha become tangible affirmations of these relationships. As such, when Buddhist institutions are re-created in the Canadian social context, often with little contact or support from homeland lineage temples, they tend to develop unique characteristics, ranging from structural and institutional alterations, to innovative strategies employed by sangha to meet the complex demands placed on them by the laity. The necessity of meeting distinct spiritual and social needs of immigrants was recognized as early as 1880 by the Japanese Jodo Shinshu Nishi Honganji.[13] The response by the then abbot Myonyo was to create a new category of overseas clergy *(kai kyoshi)* who would undergo demanding ordination qualifications in preparation for their extensive social and political engagement with migrant Japanese communities. Kai kyoshi were expected to prepare and conduct all religious and ritual services; organize English classes; create young adult Buddhist associations *(bukkyo seinen kai)* and Buddhist women's associations *(fujinkai)*; intervene in exploitive, racist, or discriminatory situations; counsel financial difficulties or marital problems; as well as mediate their own employment position with lay-controlled congregations.[14] Limited institutional power and authority in the temple resulted in a considerable loss of status to *kai kyoshi*, which, when combined with enormous work loads, resulted in a significant return rate to Japan, a situation that still impacts on the clergy situation at the Toronto Buddhist Church today. Among other Asian Buddhist groups as well, the request for sangha from specific temples in the homeland is often accompanied by an appeal that the sangha member be willing to undertake additional responsibilities to the laity, as well as their own extended language and educational training.

Through the process of immigration and resettlement, the centrality of family and kinship to social functions—involving political, financial, educational, recreational, and/or social relations—frequently declines. In response, religious institutions increasingly become the basis for new systems of social support. A variety of nonreligious activities at Buddhist temples and lay organizations are provided to members by both sangha and lay leaders. All of these activities are geared toward adaptive success, lessening the difficulties of resettlement, and supporting family and community networks. Temple activities focus on self-reliance (cultural mediation, employment advice, lessening dependency on government support, citizenship classes, advice for family reunification); learning new skills (sewing, language and literacy in English or a first language, finance/investment, real estate, temple administration); and community-based resources (senior citizen activities, nursing homes, home care support, day care facilities, youth groups, resettlement services, food and clothing, material assistance, and transportation to doctors, schools, and shopping).

Sangha members also recognize that within the multicultural context of Toronto there is not only increasing pressure to identify oneself along religious lines, but also a need to justify religious identity to oneself and others, especially when non-Buddhists ask "What is Buddhism?" or "Why are you not a Christian?" As such, several Buddhist temples have developed religious educational services (sutra studies, applying basic Buddhist precepts to the Canadian context, explaining the reasons for taking refuge) that require a much more active role and participation of the laity. Laity increasingly request traditional meditation teachings from sangha and lay leaders, especially on the cultivation of inner equilibrium and spiritual harmony. In many Asian temples and centers meditation instruction is provided during weekly classes by sangha and/or lay leaders, and some temples—such as the Burmese, Thai, Chinese, Korean, Sinhalese, and Vietnamese—offer extended meditation retreats during Christmas vacation time or full moon weekends.

Psychological needs arising from personal bereavement, feelings of insecurity or adaptive anxieties, loss of social status, family, possessions, or loss of country are especially prominent among refugees.[15] Severe and extensive family separation and loss enhance mental health risks such as debilitating, unresolved grief, or "survivorship syndrome." [16] Refugee identities and social consciousness are so tied to recent traumas of war, loss, and difficult survival experiences that innovative forms of religious worship have been developed within the temples to provide psychological comfort and to facilitate individual and communal healing. To counteract the loss of extended family, several Vietnamese temples in Toronto have introduced the *gia dinh phat tu* (Buddhist family) in which codes of kinship behavior, values of obligations toward one another, terminology, and rules of extended family hierarchy are reproduced among members not related to one another.[17] The Zen Vietnamese Meditation Group has also initiated a family-based therapy program (part of the Tiep Hien belief and practice) to protect fragile family relationships, enhance generational communication, and reinforce Vietnamese cultural identity. Another significant innovation on the part of Vietnamese Buddhist temples has been the development of abridged memorial practices. Sanghas at the Hoa Nghiem Temple, for example, include memorial chanting and traditional healing ceremonies within the weekly ritual service, reading out the names of the deceased on memorial anniversaries, and directing attention toward the huge Ban Vong memorial board, with pictures and names of the deceased. Through the weekly memorial services and the visual focus of the Ban Vong, Vietnamese suffering from profound and personal loss of family members can retrieve and face memories in a supportive and encouraging environment. The recovery and acceptance of past losses enhances positive mental health and reduces the risk for long-term suffering.[18]

In contrast to Vietnamese refugees, the suffering of Cambodian refugees in Toronto has been exacerbated by the scarcity of Buddhist monks in their early years of resettlement and the lack of supportive social services by governmental and NGO agencies.[19] Numerous studies detail that, in comparison with other Southeast Asian refugees, Cambodians continue to suffer extraordinarily high rates of emotional disorder ranging from protracted cultural and family bereavement to post-traumatic stress disorder to severe psychiatric impairment.[20] Yet, unlike other countries (Switzerland, United States, Australia, and New Zealand) where effective systems of mental health treatment for Khmer refugees have been developed, there are no medical clinics in Canada prepared to acknowledge or provide therapeutic intervention. Apart from one Cambodian medical doctor in Ontario, most medical and mental health personnel do not recognize somatic presentations of psychological difficulties among Khmer, nor do they understand culturally appropriate Khmer concepts of personal and social distress. They do not recognize or diagnose spiritual afflictions such as *neak ta, sramay* (visitation and/or possession by the ghosts of people who were murdered or not given proper burial rites), and *toah* (depression or extensive grief). The suffering of Cambodians has compounded since their initial resettlement in the early 1980s, manifesting in widespread mental health difficulties, ever increasing family breakdown and violence, rising unemployment, upwards of eighty percent of youth dropping out of school, and escalating dependency on public support.[21]

The small numbers of Khmer *kru* (ritual specialists) and Khmer Buddhist monks now present in Toronto play the crucial role in recognizing, mediating, and treating symptoms of spirit possession, bereavement, guilt, and other psychological ailments. At the same time, monks are looked upon as symbols of Khmer cultural identity and are expected to be role models, activists, and authority figures for the community. In addition to preparing and implementing weekly and annual religious observances, the Khmer monks (two from Cambodia and one Kampuchea Krom from Vietnam) provide an enormous range of ritual services for thousands of Cambodian refugees in Toronto and surrounding cities (London, Hamilton, and Windsor). Specialized services include performing protection rites from physical and spiritual harm; facilitating merit-making and honoring the deaths of loved ones; conducting exorcism rituals to get rid of an afflicting ghost or spirit; engaging in crisis intervention with families and/or service agencies; conducting bereavement and atonement rituals; instructing individuals in a variety of meditation techniques (to calm the mind or feelings, to let go of trauma, to take refuge in Buddha, Dharma, and Sangha); and counselling marital or intergenerational difficulties. Some unsettled individuals (often isolated elderly women) are given temporary residence in the temple, where they receive training to adhere to a structured schedule of daily meditation and provide service to the temple.[22] Monks also work with Khmer youth groups to provide them with a Buddhist perspective on the causes of the Cambodian crisis and on dealing with the continuing aftermath of violence and suffering in their lives. The monks' engagement with the Khmer community goes far beyond traditional monastic involvement with lay members and occurs at the expense of their own meditational practices, educational opportunities, and overall health.

HOMELAND ORIENTATION

Numerous Asian Buddhist temples and lay organizations also commit to social justice and support activities in their homeland. Among immigrants, these activities tend to be ad hoc responses to environmental disasters rather than enduring responses to social or political inequities. Chinese Buddhist temples, for example, respond generously to floods in China, while the Toronto Buddhist Church quickly mobilizes support for Japanese victims of earthquakes. Activism for homeland concerns among Asian Buddhist immigrants is more focused on individual activity, rather than as part of an identifiable Buddhist group effort. At the Han Shan Sih Buddhist Society, for example, Venerable Chan Ding Fa Shi is a highly committed, socially engaged advocate for health concerns in Taiwan, organizing several fundraising strategies. As an individual she also participates in annual protests against Chinese human rights violations and violence, unusual conduct for a Chinese sangha member in Toronto.

Members of the Ambedkar Mission in Toronto collectively engage in social and political activism. Most have immigrated from India within the last thirty years and identify themselves as Buddhists who follow Ambedkar's social advocacy agenda. The Ambedkar Mission publishes the magazine *Outcry: Voice of the Oppressed*, primarily concerned with Dalits (Untouchables) in India, but regularly including articles on the violation of human and Buddhist rights elsewhere, for example in Vietnam, Tibet, or Burma. Although initiated by first generation immigrants, those children born and raised in Canada carry on the commitment, writing articles and participating in community events that raise awareness of continuing oppression. In addition to the Ambedkar Mission, an individual activist, Yogesh Varhade, has formed the Toronto-based Ambedkar Centre for Justice and Peace, continuing his twenty-five-year struggle against India's caste system. Varhade's activities include documentation, research, and international presentation of his findings. During the August 1995 meeting of the U.N. Committee on the Elimination of Racial Discrimination, for example, Varhade cited numerous instances of violence and oppression against the Dalits.

Homeland-oriented social and political activism in Toronto, however, tends to be identified with refugee communities. Social and political advocacy among Buddhist refugees takes numerous forms. Individuals such as Khanh Le-kim may pursue their own activist agendas. Le-kim founded the Vietnamese Buddhist Association (Hoi Phat Giao Viet-Nam) in 1981 to raise awareness of the social abuse, persecution, beatings, imprisonment, and executions of sangha members in Vietnam. He has written letters to, and twice visited, the United Nations office in New York, and regularly attends Toronto-based sessions on human rights to focus attention on continuing violations in Vietnam. Bilateral forms of cooperation among refugee

Buddhist groups may also arise. During the 1980s and the early part of the 1990s, several Vietnamese temples came together in different committees to advocate against the Canadian government's unwillingness to allow sangha sponsorship from refugee camps, to advocate for further family reunification opportunities, to address resettlement difficulties, and to raise funds for specific concerns in Vietnam (supporting imprisoned sangha members or providing relief efforts). One Vietnamese Buddhist umbrella group actively sponsored over twenty monks and nuns from refugee camps and organized numerous protests against the forced repatriation of Vietnamese in Hong Kong, Malaysia, and Indonesian refugee camps. Vietnamese sangha members from most Vietnamese temples and groups also participate in locally organized political marches and annual "remembrance day" ceremonies, such as the commemoration of the 1975 Fall of Saigon, held on or near April 30. In a cohesive demonstration of political activism, sangha members carry wreaths and placards, perform ritual prayers and blessings, and speak out against continuing human rights violations in Vietnam, especially religious persecution. The Toronto Vietnamese sangha regularly takes part in international forums, such as the Vietnamese Buddhist Association, coordinating activities to address social and political issues in Vietnam, and remind potential financial investors of outstanding human rights violations.

Specific refugee groups, such as the Vietnamese Zen Meditation Group (part of Thich Nhat Hanh's Tiep Hien Order), engage in a continuous and well structured program of homeland social activism. Much of the Vietnamese Zen Meditation Group's activity is to support individuals in Vietnam (clergy, the elderly, school children, medical students, lepers, the homeless) through specific sponsorship programs. The group also contributes to a number of social services in Vietnam that include food and medical donations, medical clinics, trade and skills training, and orphanages. Several fund-raising dinners are held each year to profile and contribute to ongoing needs among Vietnamese people. In addition, monies are collected regularly through attendance at bi-monthly meditation sessions and periodic retreats.

The most visible form of homeland-oriented social and political activism among Toronto Buddhists occurs within the Tibetan community. Every year during the March 10 protest, several hundred Tibetans (from Toronto, Lindsay, Peterborough, and Belleville) demonstrate, outside either the Chinese consulate in Toronto or the federal parliament buildings in Ottawa. March 10 commemorates the 1959 uprising in Lhasa against Tibet's occupation by Chinese communist soldiers and subsequent events, which resulted in the massive refugee flow of over one million Tibetans, including the Dalai

Lama. Since that time, hundreds of thousands of Tibetans have died from execution, imprisonment, repression, and environmental devastation. Subversive resistance continues in Tibet, aided by overt criticism of China from exiled Tibetans and Tibetan supporters. The Toronto demonstration coincides with others throughout the world, all geared to bring attention to China's continuing genocidal colonization of Tibet. Usually the demonstration in Toronto is given good media coverage, featuring prayers and mantra recitations liberally mixed with loud cries and emotional appeals for Tibet's freedom.

Tibetans also take every opportunity to protest against Chinese leaders visiting Toronto. Over two hundred Tibetans (from Toronto, Peterborough, Lindsay, Belleville, and Alliston) recently protested against the 1997 visit of Chinese premier Jiang Zemin. As he dined inside the Metro Convention Centre with more than one thousand Chinese Canadians and Ontario politicians (all eager for increased trade with China), the Tibetans outside continuously shouted slogans such as "China out of Tibet" and "Tibet for

Toronto Buddhists protest the Chinese occupation of Tibet in commemoration of the March 10 1959 uprising of Tibetans against the Chinese invasion. Courtesy Rinchen Dakpa.

Tibetans," carrying numerous placards calling attention to the imprisonment of the six-year-old Panchen Lama, the forced sterilization and abortion programs, the migration of over nine million Chinese into Tibet (making the three million Tibetans a minority in their own country), and widespread environmental degradation.[23]

In recognition of the non-Asian support given to Tibet, the Tibetan community sponsors an annual New Year's celebration providing food, entertainment, and political commentary to non-Tibetan guests. Following a traditional religious ceremony in which prayers are offered to His Holiness and the principles of wisdom and compassion are invoked, slide presentations or talks are given to raise awareness of continued ethnic and religious genocide in Tibet. With assistance from Tibetans living in the nearby cities of Lindsay, Peterborough, and Belleville, the Toronto Tibetan community provides a traditional Tibetan dinner and performs Tibetan music and folk dances. During this event, raffle tickets are often sold to support individual sanghas and/or monasteries in India, or to facilitate health and educational programs in the large refugee communities in India and Nepal. The 1997 New Year's dinner and dance held on February 15 had a specific agenda to raise monies to support a "Walk for Tibet's Independence," marking the thirty-eighth anniversary of the March 10, 1959 uprising. This six-hundred-mile walk, from the Chinese consulate in Toronto to the United Nations Building in New York, was undertaken by local Tibetans under the leadership of Professor Thubten Jigme Norbu, the eldest brother of the Dalai Lama.

Other annual communal celebrations, such as honoring the birthday of His Holiness the Dalai Lama, provide a similar forum to raise awareness and support for Tibet, as well as to enhance intra-Buddhist goodwill. During community meetings that follow these celebrations, Tibetans actively debate various strategies to restore Tibet's freedom—ranging from the worth of the Dalai Lama's efforts to arrange peaceful negotiations to implementing *satyagraha* (truth-insistence) activism—thereby informing and gaining the interest and support of both Canadian-born Tibetan youth and non-Asians. The Toronto Tibetan community remains instrumental in inviting the Dalai Lama and other Tibetan monks to visit, thus raising awareness and funds for Tibet and Tibetan refugees in India. During these visits, the non-Tibetan support for Tibetan social and political activism is increased. Visiting Tibetan monks from India represent Drepung Loseling Monastery (performing devotional music to alleviate world suffering), Sera Je Monastery (performing the healing ceremony of the Medicine Buddha), and the Ganden Jangtse Monastery monks (profiled at the Royal Ontario Museum as they created a sand mandala of Chenrezig, Buddha of Compassion).

EXTERNAL ORIENTATION

Apart from ethnic community and homeland concerns, sangha and lay members from a variety of immigrant and refugee groups (Vietnamese, Chinese, Lao, Thai, and Burmese) support Toronto-based activist organizations such as Karuna Community Services and Across Boundaries, an ethnic mental health center. Both these groups were developed through the efforts of a local non-Asian Buddhist, Michael Kerr, to enhance generalized social activist concerns among Asian Buddhists and provide culturally appropriate health services, which are especially lacking among smaller Buddhist communities. Unfortunately, both organizations have curtailed activities due to lack of financial support from municipal, provincial, and federal funding agencies. Simultaneously, however, Asian Buddhist involvement in interfaith groups has grown. Interfaith forums provide an avenue for both sangha and lay to actively protest against current social policies that are causing increased suffering among those who are most vulnerable and disadvantaged.[24] Asian Buddhist sanghas join other Toronto faith leaders (for example, the Ontario Religious Leaders Forum comprised of Christian, Jain, and Jewish members), to denounce these policies as an abandonment of compassion and an increasing moral crisis. Asian Buddhists also belong to groups such as the Inter-Faith Social Reform Commission, the Multi-Faith Anti-Racism Committee, Amnesty International, and Inter-faith Witness for Social Justice and Compassion.

The Toronto-based Sangha Council, which represents several Buddhist temples and centers—Chinese, Vietnamese, Korean, Japanese, Burmese, Cambodian, Laotian, Sri Lankan, Thai, and Tibetan—is another means to raise general Buddhist awareness of social needs. The June 1995 lantern parade through downtown Toronto, repeated in 1996, in which over two thousand people participated, many in national dress, was to proclaim the Buddhist message of tolerance and peace. Unfortunately, the multi-Buddhist peace service and parade provides little more than an ideological statement of support for social justice, with little concrete action. Further, the event gained little media recognition and over the last three years the number of temples and centers participating has declined. Asian temples and centers are, however, increasing their own participation in annual mainstream fund-raising campaigns oriented toward specific ends for Toronto's disadvantaged. Campaigns include various United Way activities, community marches or group money collection, donating to Project Warmth, providing sleeping bags and winter clothing for the homeless, and collecting food to replenish food banks. To date, no Buddhist temple has organized itself as an overnight hostel for the homeless or participated in the Out of the Cold Program, which serves lunch or dinner to those in need of a meal. Temples may also provide donations to organizations whose mandate is to respond to global concerns. Hong Fa Temple and the Buddhist Association of Canada, for example, regularly donate to World Vision, despite its emphasis on Christian evangelism. Only two Asian Buddhist groups in Toronto, the Tzu Chi and Buddha's Light International Association (BLIA), are actively committed to encouraging ongoing engagement in social activism beyond local community or homeland needs.

The Tzu Chi and BLIA each belong to a Taiwanese-based Buddhist institution, whose focus is on providing aid to countries in need, regardless of race, ethnicity, politics, or religion. BLIA pamphlets advocate "humanistic Buddhism" and encourage members to provide "alms for the poor, medicine for the sick, protection for the weak, shelter for the homeless and assistance for the desperate." Guidelines for compassionate acts of charity in both local and global contexts are detailed. Throughout the world, BLIA members engage in providing meals for the homeless, distributing food baskets for low income families, and providing a variety of support services for seniors, orphans, hospital patients, and prison inmates. In Toronto, BLIA members are the most active Buddhist participants in United Way fund-raising, Project Warmth, and interfaith forums. The Tzu Chi group in Toronto, as part of the Buddhist Compassion Relief Tzu Chi Foundation, also contributes to medical relief projects throughout the world. Although it is relatively small and inactive in Toronto, their sister branch in Vancouver recently facilitated the donation of $6.2 million to open the Tzu Chi Institute for Complementary and Alternative Medicine in a Vancouver hospital, which is geared to providing Western, traditional Asian, and First Nations medicine and therapies.

CONCLUSION

Within most Toronto Asian Buddhist communities, flexible Buddhist beliefs and practices enhance the ability for effective social practices. Both Theravada and Mahayana sanghas adapt traditional theological tenets and institutional expressions to reflect the changing social circumstances of migration, integration, and opportunity; or develop innovative strategies to alleviate suffering among the laity. Although most of these new practices remain oriented to first-generation resettlement needs, they will undoubtedly change further as second- and third-generation members require fresh Buddhist responses to meet their particular requirements—spiritual, emotional, cultural, or social. In the short term, however, rising unemployment and reduced availability of social, medical, and educational services within Toronto specifically, and Ontario in general, will continue to demonstrate the importance of ethnic community engagement and increased social activism. The role of sangha and laity in addressing and meeting a variety of resettlement needs and social justice concerns will of necessity be expanded, especially as they continue to highlight the importance of the health and well-being of individuals and families.

In addition to an ethnic orientation, Asian Buddhist temples and groups are involved in a variety of activities oriented toward their homelands that encompass both social and political engagement—providing health and educational services, calling attention to human rights abuses, protesting against religious and cultural repression. A similar spirit of compassion and loving-kindness among sangha members and laity is also evident when they actively participate in activities to ease the suffering of those with different ethnic or national identities, either within Toronto or extended throughout the globe. Whatever the orientation, the focus on "this worldly" causes and the alleviation of suffering is a significant component of Asian Buddhist belief and practice in Toronto, and can be recognized as an integral form of engaged Buddhism.

NOTES

1. For details on Toronto's ethnocultural and racial diversity see Raymond Breton, Wsevolod Isajiw, Warren Kalbach, and Jeffrey Reitz, *Ethnic Identity and Equality: Varieties of Experience in a Canadian City* (Toronto: University of Toronto Press, 1990).

2. General sociological distinctions among Buddhists reflect different historical waves of arrival and migration identity status (i.e., refugee status or as an immigration category: independent class, business class, family reunification, and so forth); a variety of languages and dialects representing different national and ethnic identities; distinct socioeconomic classes (wealthy entrepreneurs, middle class professionals, manufacturing/service workers, impoverished); a wide range of educational attainments (university educated to illiterate); different political ideologies and values (democratic, communist, nationalist); and diverse pre-migration conditions (planned departure from a stable homeland, horrific experiences of genocide, long-term languishing in refugee camps). All these distinctions effect differential rates of adaptation and integration into Canadian society, including identifying and dealing with particularistic needs of specific communities, or developing subsequent practices that could be identified as engaged Buddhism. The integration of Asian Buddhist immigrants and

refugees within the last thirty years has also been facilitated by the federal policy of multiculturalism and the increasing ethnocultural diversity of Toronto. The Canadian Multiculturalism Act, for example, states that cultural diversity is an integral part of Canadian society and ensures individuals and groups the right to maintain and express cultural and religious heritage while participating fully and equally. This relatively receptive social context is vastly different from the Toronto of the 1940s in which the Japanese Canadian Buddhists, as the first Buddhist group, experienced widespread racism and discrimination as both a religious and a racial minority.

3. For further details on Japanese Canadian Buddhism, see Terry Watada, *Bukkyo Tozen: A History of Jodo Shinshu Buddhism in Canada 1905–1995* (Toronto: HPF and Toronto Buddhist Church, 1996), and Toyo Takata, *Nikkei Legacy: The Story of Japanese Canadians from Settlement to Today* (Toronto: NC Press, 1983).

4. Janet McLellan, *Many Petals of the Lotus: Five Asian Buddhist Communities in Toronto* (Toronto: University of Toronto Press, 1999), pp. 12–15.

5. Compared to smaller, ethnically heterogeneous Asian Buddhist communities (such as the Tibetans, Laotians, Sinhalese, Khmer, or Burmese), the larger Vietnamese and Chinese Buddhist communities incorporate numerous "sub-ethnicities" (arising from different ethnic or national origins) as well as overlapping multiple identities, thereby ensuring several distinct underpinnings for affiliation. Specific Chinese Buddhist organizations in Toronto such as Po Chai Temple or Tai Bay Buddhist Temple may be comprised of ethnic Chinese from Southeast Asia, while others may reflect an ongoing connection to an international community of faith arising from Hong Kong or Taiwan. Examples of transnational linkages include the Taiwanese Fo Kwan Shan movement founded by Venerable Hsing Yun (in Toronto, the Buddhist Progress Society of Toronto); the Taiwanese Tzu Chi movement founded by Venerable Cheng Yen; and the Hong Kong influenced Chan Shan Temple complex (McLellan, *Many Petals of the Lotus*). Vietnamese Buddhist identities in Toronto also reflect larger transnational and global religious linkages. The Chan Giac Vietnamese Buddhist Association, for example, is spread across Canada under the leadership of Thich Thien Nghi who maintains institutional religious connections with organizations in the United States, Europe, Australia, and Vietnam. Similarly, Amida Temple under the spiritual authority of Thich Tam Chau (based in France) and the Zen Vietnamese Meditation Group (part of the Tiep Hien Order under Thich Nhat Hanh) are also part of global religious networks, each with numerous sister temples and practice groups. Membership in these umbrella networks and alliances influence attitudes toward Vietnamese nationalism, to resettlement issues, to engaged practices, and to the degree of identification with Canadian life (ibid.).

6. Temple-focused organizations may be recognized as "traditional," i.e., following a standard established in the homeland, or they may reflect "new" types of Buddhist organization. New Buddhist organizations develop distinct structural patterns that reflect changing social and religious roles of sangha and lay members, especially regarding social activism or "engaged" Buddhist activities. Re-created traditional temples are, however, most common within Toronto's Asian Buddhist communities.

7. The absence of a formal Buddhist temple or adherence to a specific monk does not necessarily indicate a loss of Buddhist identity or practice. Although fewer than five hundred Tibetan refugees and their children live in Toronto and nearby cities, their sense of purpose in Canada, their successful adaptation and integration, their retention of a strong ethnic identity, and their continuing allegiance to the Tibetan government-in-exile, reflect an intensive commitment to Buddhism and His Holiness the Dalai Lama. Tibetans do not have their own temple but utilize non-Asian Buddhist temples under the leadership of Tibetan monks for monthly religious observances. Tibetan monks (local or those on the international circuit) are regularly invited to community gatherings or individual houses to perform ceremonial and ritual services. In comparison, numerous years without a functional temple and the absence of permanent sangha has had enormous negative impact among Cambodian refugees. The lack of traditional religious rituals, ceremonies, and socio/cultural support has not only exacerbated Cambodian resettlement difficulties, including mental health conditions such as post-traumatic stress disorder, but also enhanced difficulties in inculcating Buddhist and/or Khmer identities and practices among the children born or raised in Canada. For further detail, see McLellan, *Many Petals of the Lotus*, chapters 3 and 5.

8. As ethnically identifiable beliefs and customs are reinforced through particularistic traditions and attachments, a sense of a shared universal religious culture is undermined. In Toronto, each Buddhist group operates separately and differently in its own particular framework, continuing to view the others through unfamiliar practices, and confirmed prejudices. Indeed, migration to Canada often provides Asian Buddhists with their first exposure to Buddhists of different nationalities, practices, and identities. After thirty years, the majority of Toronto Buddhists still have no routinized way of dealing either with each other or with the Christian majority, nor do the majority of Buddhist groups welcome or work toward an institution that could do so. There is no common religious institution concerned with cohesion and unification among different Buddhist groups or with issues of power, authority, legitimation, or authenticity of tradition. Several Toronto temples that have shown an impressive capacity to build both facilities and membership, focus only on their own

individual Buddhist programs and activities. Their organizational networks tend not to be with other temples or associations in Toronto, but with overseas sangha members, lineages, temples, or headquarters. In certain contexts, such as the celebration of Wesak (the birth, enlightenment, and *parinirvana* of Shakyamuni Buddha), or in situations that may be advantageous in legitimating status or establishing presence in Toronto (Interfaith meetings or peace days), syncretisms and inter-Buddhist gatherings have been attempted. Yet, even within the limited circumstances of co-religious activity, participation remains within the boundaries of specific Buddhist communities and often reflects underlying agendas of particular Buddhist leaders. Overall, intergroup differences and disparate interests are perpetuated in Toronto, suppressing a more universalistic mode of Buddhist expression or sense of identity (ibid., pp.17–34).

9. McLellan, *Many Petals of the Lotus,* pp. 119–23, 197–219.

10. The influence of Christianity is noticeable in many Buddhist groups in Toronto. Certain groups such as the Toronto Buddhist Church (Japanese Canadian Jodo Shinshu) have incorporated numerous Christian institutional models such as pews, organs, notice boards, hymnbooks, choirs, weekly Sunday gatherings, and Sunday Dharma schools for children, as an adaptive mechanism against the excessive racism and discrimination they encountered in Toronto. Other Buddhist groups, such as the Vietnamese Hoa Nghiem or the Chinese Cham Shan, remain structurally traditional but also include Christian aspects that they feel are conducive to social networking and interaction (such as choirs, youth groups, weekly sutra discussion gatherings, Sunday school). Patterns of social activism beyond the ethnic group, which in this paper are included as an external orientation of engaged Buddhist practice, are also influenced by the Christian models of charity work (local and global), interfaith dialogue, and meeting social as well as spiritual needs among the disadvantaged, as seen among Tzu Chi Buddhists or those adhering to the Fo Kuang Shan Humanistic Buddhism.

11. Christopher Queen and Sallie King, eds., *Engaged Buddhism: Buddhist Liberation Movements in Asia* (Albany: State University of New York Press, 1996), p. 9.

12. John Simpson, "'The Great Reversal': Selves, Communities, and the Global System," *Sociology of Religion* 57.2 (1996): 117. In an attempt to re-sacralize the self, individuals become part of what Peter Beyer refers to in *Religion and Globalization* (London: Sage Publications, 1997), p. 97, as a liberalized religious response to the "residual" problems of globalizing systems, i.e., concern with social injustice, local and global conflict, environmental destruction, global inequalities, and the egalitarian inclusion of those marginalized from the benefits of modern institutions. The liberal response (as a contrast to other modern forms of religious expression such as fundamentalism or absolutism) is found in a variety of new religious movements ranging from Catholic-based

liberation theology to World Christian Churches to Wiccan revivals to engaged Buddhist organizations such as the Sinhalese Sarvodaya movement, Vietnamese-based Tiep Hien Order, and Taiwanese Tzu Chi or Fo Kuang Shan.

13. Donald Tuck, *Buddhist Churches of America: Jodo Shinshu* (Lewiston, NY: Edwin Mellen Press, 1987).

14. See Tetsuden Kashima, *The Social Organization of an Ethnic Religious Institution* (London: Greenwood Press, 1997), and Mark Mullins, *Religious Minorities in Canada: A Sociological Analysis of the Japanese Experience* (Lewiston, NY: Edwin Mellen Press, 1989).

15. See Edward Canda and Thitiya Phaobtong's article "Buddhism as a Support System for Southeast Asian Refugees" *Social Work* 37.1 (1992): 61–66.

16. See Morton Beiser's articles "Catastrophic Stress and Factors Affecting Its Consequences Among Southeast Asian Refugees," *Social Science Medicine* 28.3 (1989): 183–95; and "Migration: Opportunity or Mental Health Risk?" *Triangle* 29.2/3 (1990): 83–90; James Boehnlein, "Clinical Relevance of Grief and Mourning Among Cambodian Refugees," *Social Science Medicine Journal* 25.7 (1997): 765–72; Richard Mollica, Grace Wyshak, and James Lavelle, "The Psychological and Social Impact of War Trauma and Torture on Southeast Asian Refugees," *American Journal of Psychiatry* 144.12 (1987): 1567–72; Lenore Terr, "Family Anxiety After Traumatic Events," in *Journal of Clinical Psychiatry* 50.11 (1989): 15–19; and David Haines, Dorthy Rutherford, and Patrick Thomas, "Family and Communities among Refugees," *International Migration Review* 15 (1981): 310–19.

17. See Janet McLellan, "Hermit Crabs and Refugees: Adaptive Strategies of Vietnamese Buddhists in Toronto," in Bruce Matthews, ed., *The Quality of Life in Southeast Asia*, CCSEAS xx.1 (1992): 203–19.

18. Beiser, "Migration: Opportunity or Mental Health Risk," p. 85.

19. See Janet McLellan, *An Evaluation of the Resettlement, Adaptation and Integration of Cambodian Refugees in Ontario* (Toronto: York Lanes Press, 1994), pp. 49–76.

20. See J.D. Kinzie, "The Psychiatric Effects of Massive Trauma on Cambodian Refugees," in John Wilson, Zev Harel, and Boaz Kahana, eds., *Human Adaptation to Extreme Stress* (New York: Plenum Press, 1988); and David Kinzie, R.H. Fredickson, Ben Rath, et al., "Post Traumatic Stress Disorder Among Survivors of Cambodian Concentration Camps," *American Journal of Psychiatry* 141.5 (1984): 645–50.

21. See McLellan, *An Evaluation of the Resettlement.*

22. See McLellan, *Many Petals of the Lotus,* p. 158.

23. The Tibetan protesters were joined by several hundred others representing numerous Chinese groups (from China, Hong Kong, and Taiwan) and Amnesty International, drawing attention to Tiananmen Square (carrying photographs

of slain students), continuing human rights abuses in China, and the immorality of separating trade issues from the issue of China's human rights record. Earlier in the week when Jiang visited Edmonton, about one hundred placard-waving Tibetans also demonstrated, carrying signs that read "Free Tibet," "How many political prisoners have you executed? Stop the Slaughter," and "Human rights are everybody's business" (*Toronto Star,* November 27, 1997).

24. Since the election of Ontario's Tory (Conservative) government in 1995, new legislation concerned with welfare, unemployment, workers' compensation, and health care restructuring have been particularly harsh on immigrants and refugees, social assistance recipients, the unemployed, the homeless, and those with mental health ailments. Municipal downloading, in which local taxes are required to cover health and social services as well as subsidized housing costs, will exacerbate the situation by a dramatic reduction of assistance to those most in need, and increased polarization of the have and have-nots (especially as wealthier municipal areas restrict costly services such as English as Second Language programs, immigrant women's shelters, counselling and resettlement agencies, and nonprofit housing).

APPENDIX

Partial list of Buddhist groups in Toronto

MAHAYANA BUDDHIST GROUPS

Asian Mahayana Buddhists

Chinese Traditions (combination of Pure Land/Zen):

Anata Kuan-Yin Zen Buddhist Institute

Buddhist Association of Canada★

Buddhist Dharmalaksana Society

Buddhist Progress Society of Toronto (Toronto node of Buddha's Light International—BLIA, also known as Fo Kuang San)

Canada Po Chai Temple (Sino-Vietnamese)

Canadian Chinese Buddhist Ming-Yuet Society

Cham Shan Buddhist Gallery★

Cham Shan Temple★

Ching Fa Temple★

Chuen Te Buddhist Society

Fu Sien Tong Buddhist Temple

Han Shan Sih Buddhist Society

Hong Fa Temple★

Ling Shen Ching Tze Temple (three branches in Toronto)

Manshu Yuen

Nam Shan Temple★

Providence Maitreya Buddha Missionary Institute

Siu-Ping Chin

Tara Vihara

Tai Bay Temple (Sino-Vietnamese)

Toronto Buddhist Society★

Transnational Buddhist Youth Association (Toronto chapter)

Vajrayana Buddhist Association (Mi Shing Fo Shen Hui)

★All italicized entries are members of the Toronto-based Cham Shan Temple organization, which has also expanded to Niagara Falls, Hamilton, and Whitby.

Vietnamese Traditions (combination of Pure Land/Zen):

Amida Temple of Toronto (several groups across Canada)

Hoa Nghiem Temple (Toronto base of Chanh Giac Vietnamese Buddhist Association, with several temples across Canada)

Hue Lam Bhikkhuni Buddhist Association

Linh-Son Temple

Pho Hien Temple

Vietnam Temple (formerly Van Duc Temple)

Vietnamese Zen Meditation Group (Toronto base of transnational Tiep Hien Order)

Xaloi Temple

Japanese Traditions (Pure Land—Jodo Shinshu and Nichiren):

Nichiren Buddhist Church of Toronto

Toronto Buddhist Church

Korean Traditions (Zen):

Bul Kwang Sa
Daekak Sa (Nine Mountains Zen Gate Society)

Tibetan Tradition (Vajrayana/tantric):

Manjushri Buddhist Centre (large Chinese membership—
ethnic Tibetan lama)

Non-Asian Mahayana Buddhists

Tibetan Lineages (Vajrayana/tantric):

Dharmadhatu (Kagyupa)
Dharma Centre of Canada (Kagyupa)
Chandrakirti Buddhist Centre
Gaden Choling (Gelukpa—ethnic Tibetan leader)
Kampo Gangra Drubgyud Ling (Nyingmapa/Kagyupa—ethnic
Tibetan lama)
Karma Kagyu Buddhist Centre (Kagyupa—ethnic Tibetan lama)
Rigpa
Riwoche Pemavajra Temple of Toronto (Nyingmapa—ethnic
Tibetan lama)
Tengye Ling Tibetan Buddhist Centre (Gelukpa)
Toronto Shambhala Centre (Kagyupa)
Sakya Thubten Namgyal Ling (Sakyapa)

Japanese Traditions:

Mountain Moon Sangha (Soto/Rinzai Zen)
Toronto Zen Centre (Rinzai Zen)

Korean Zen:

Dharma Light Son Centre (ethnic Korean monk leader)
Jong-Hae Zen Centre
Ontario Zen Centre
Zen Buddhist Temple (ethnic Korean monk leader)

THERAVADA BUDDHIST GROUPS

Asian Theravada Buddhists

Bangladesh:

Buddhist Meditation Hermitage

Burmese:

Maha Dammika Temple
Buddha Sasana Yeiktha Ontario

Cambodian:

Khmer Buddhist and Cultural Community of Ontario

Laotian:

Wat Lao

Indian:

Ambedkar Mission

Sri Lankan:

Toronto Maha Vihara
West End Buddhist Centre (Halton-Peel Buddhist Society)

Thai:

Yanviriya Buddhist Temple II

Non-Asian Theravada Buddhists

Theravada Buddhist Community
Toronto Vipassana Community
Insight Meditation Retreats

ENGAGING THE INSTITUTIONS: HEALTH, EDUCATION, PRISONS, COMMERCE

John Daido Loori Roshi giving *jukai* to inmates of the Green Haven Correctional
Institution, New York, 1998. Courtesy Zen Mountain Monastery.

MEDITATION, HEALING, AND STRESS REDUCTION

Andrew Olendzki

Whatever medicines are found
In the world, many and varied—
None is equal to the Dhamma.
Drink of this, monks! And having drunk
The medicine of the Dhamma,
You'll be untouched by age and death.
Having meditated and seen—
[You'll be] healed by ceasing to cling.

—MILINDAPANHO[1]

GEORGE MUMFORD IS CONSULTING WITH THE CHICAGO BULLS, the National Basketball Association champion basketball team, guiding the players and coaches through basic meditation practice. Joseph Goldstein is talking to lawyers in training at Yale Law School about mindfulness and leading the students in simple meditation practices. Steven Smith is teaching meditation to officers and directors of some of the country's largest corporations, such as the Monsanto pharmaceutical company, while Daeja Napier teaches meditation to high school students at Phillips Exeter Academy in Massachusetts. Arnold Clayton uses mindfulness principles to structure learning environments in Cambridge Rindge and Latin high school, and Ted Slovin applies general mindfulness techniques at the University of Massachusetts during training workshops for undergraduates in the Department of Counseling and Assessment Services.

Rodney Smith, an insight meditation teacher, is bringing the skills of mindfulness to terminally ill patients in a series of hospices around the country. Gavin Harrison offers the insights of mindfulness to patients with HIV and AIDS and to survivors of sexual abuse. Sylvia Boorstein and Sheila Weinberg lead silent meditation retreats for Jewish Buddhists and rabbis, often culminating in mindful Sabbath observances; Grove Burnett hosts mindfulness retreats at the Vallecitos Mountain Refuge near Taos, New Mexico, for environmental and social activists; Jack Engler and other mental health professionals of the Cambridge Institute for Meditation and Psychotherapy integrate mindfulness training in their clinical practices; Paula Green leads her colleagues from the Karuna Center and the Buddhist Peace Fellowship on peacemaking missions to the Balkans, the Middle East, and central Africa. Mirabai Bush explores the social effects of mindfulness and meditation at the Contemplative Mind In Society Project, while teenage and young adult retreats grow steadily in popularity at established meditation centers like the Insight Meditation Society in Barre, Massachusetts, and Spirit Rock Meditation Center in Marin County, California.

More and more people have been participating in prison meditation and mindfulness projects, both in the U.S. and around the world. The popular Buddhist magazine *Tricycle* hosts huge events of collective meditation in Central Park in New York and on the West Coast. Urban meditation centers like the Cambridge Insight Meditation Center in Massachusetts are springing up across the country, helping busy householders and professionals integrate mindfulness practice with the complexities of daily life. Substance abuse recovery groups around the country are incorporating mindfulness techniques in their therapeutic programs, while the Harvard Divinity School offers courses that integrate mindfulness practice into the curriculum, not only as a tool for Buddhist studies but also as a means of directly investigating the nature of consciousness.

These are only a few examples—by no means a comprehensive survey—of how the Buddhist principles and practices of mindfulness *(sati)* and insight meditation *(vipassana)* are being applied to many of the complex aspects of contemporary life. The interaction and dialogue between the ancient meditative traditions of Asia and the melting pot of Western civilization is well under way, and questions about how each will transform the other grow ever more intriguing. Nowhere is this interaction more apparent than in the arts and sciences of healing. The American medical profession is in the midst of an important transformation, and the adaptation of Buddhist meditation practices to a growing range of clinical and therapeutic settings is a significant part of this process. At first glance it may seem an unusual combination—monastic mind-training and materialistic biological science. But a closer look at some of the attitudes toward illness and health on each side reveals their deep compatibility. New ways of viewing the relationship between mind and body are emerging, along with new models of health and wellness. The interface between meditation and healing is worthy of further exploration.

The theme of healing in Buddhist literature is too pervasive to survey in this brief chapter. Instead, let us focus on the earliest healing teachings attributed to the Buddha and preserved by the Theravada tradition of South Asia in the Pali language. Following our discussion of the metaphor and practice of healing in traditional Buddhism, let us turn to the influence of Buddhist meditative traditions on modern medical practice, specifically, the application of mindfulness meditation techniques to a variety of medical and nonmedical settings in the work of Jon Kabat-Zinn, founder and director of the Stress Reduction Clinic at the University of Massachusetts Medical Center.

Jon Kabat-Zinn was trained as a molecular biologist, and has long pursued a personal interest in Buddhist meditation, in both the Zen and Vipassana traditions. Since opening the Stress Reduction Clinic in Worcester, Massachusetts, in 1979, he has endeavored to bring these perspectives together in his work with patients in a mainstream medical context. The best source for understanding his program is his 1990 book, *Full Catastrophe Living: Using the Wisdom of Your Body and Mind to Face Stress, Pain, and Illness.*[2] The author makes two important points at the outset. The first is that he has no intention of introducing Buddhism or any explicitly religious perspectives to his patients and clients. In fact, it is quite crucial to the success of his work that "Buddhism" not distract his patients from the basic meditative techniques of tranquillity and insight. The second point is that Jon Kabat-Zinn is joined by many other clinicians and educators in similar work throughout the country.

In conclusion, I shall argue that insight meditation and mindfulness-based stress reduction of the kind taught by Jon Kabat-Zinn and his colleagues is an important expression of engaged Buddhism in the West.

HEALING AS METAPHOR IN ANCIENT BUDDHISM

If we allow ourselves to peruse the literature of the Buddhist tradition, even the fraction of that literature found in the Pali scriptures, or Nikayas, we find the metaphor of healing emerging again and again in ways that are creatively applied to many different situations. This is no mere embellishment, I would argue, but is indicative of the fact that healing is an intrinsic paradigm of the entire Buddhist enterprise. If we look at these texts in light of the work undertaken today in Kabat-Zinn's Stress Reduction Clinic, we begin to appreciate both the extent to which this work is embedded in the classical Buddhist tradition of healing, and the extent to which this healing can occur quite independently of the religious context so often associated with classical forms of Buddhism.

Let us begin by acknowledging the centrality of the healing metaphor in the Buddha's message. The Buddha is viewed as a great physician who, motivated by compassion for the welfare of all beings, sought, discovered, and shared a cure for the basic illness of human existence. As this chapter's epigram proclaims, the Buddha's teaching, or Dhamma, is the medicine that can effect this cure. More precisely, it is the prescription for a cure that can only be filled by the appropriate undertaking of each individual patient. At the same time, the Buddhist Sangha, or community of ordained and lay people, is a society of mutual help along the road to recovery.

Many writers have pointed out that the formula of the four noble truths is based upon a pre-Buddhist medical tradition, and deliberately employs the symbolism of curing. The first truth (illness) points to the presenting symptoms of an underlying affliction. The presence of aging and death, grief, lamentation, and despair all point toward and derive from the same fundamental condition: *dukkha*, "illness," "suffering," or the inherent "unsatisfactoriness" of the human condition. A healer cannot even begin his or her work, nor can a patient begin the healing process unless and until the illness has been diagnosed. The second truth (causes of illness) suggests the physician's role as diagnostician. Only when one understands the etiology of disease can one approach its cure. The Buddha's analysis of the human mind and body culminates in the conclusion that all our suffering and its symptoms are ultimately caused by desire or craving *(tanha)*. The third truth (absence of illness) is a hopeful prognosis: the elimination of craving will result in the elimination of suffering, as demonstrated by the Buddha's own physical and mental recovery under the bodhi tree, his robust good health over the next forty-five years of his teaching and healing career.

The healing regime presented in the Buddha's fourth noble truth (the eightfold path [to health]) entails the prescription of various treatments or therapies. There are great individual variations in the symptoms of a single illness: each patient will display somewhat different symptoms at different stages of the disease's progress, display varying strength or weakness of constitution, have dissimilar attitudes toward recovery, and be situated in diverse environments. The effective physician will be sensitive to a host of specific conditions and adjust the therapeutic strategy creatively, though he or she will usually draw upon a well-proven set of principles, flexibly applied. The tremendous diversity one finds in the twenty-five-hundred-year Buddhist tradition is anchored by a universal agreement on the first three truths about illness, its cause and its cessation, but afforded great variety and innovation in the practice of the fourth truth—the art of healing itself.

An interesting discussion is reported in the *Magandiya Sutta*[3] between the Buddha and the wanderer Magandiya regarding the nature of health. The case is presented of a leper whose affliction is such that pain in his extremities can only be assuaged by cauterizing his limbs in a charcoal fire. In fact, he might continue to scratch and burn his body for the sake of some temporary relief, even if such actions were making his condition progressively worse and more serious. Though all others would construe the fire to be painful, the unique malady of the leper so influences his perception that he experiences the fire as the source of some relief. At a later time he becomes cured, thanks to the medicines administered by a doctor procured for him by his friends, at which point he no longer welcomes the experience of burning his limbs over a fire. In fact, if strong men were to seize him and force him close to the fire he would vehemently resist, because he would now experience that fire as unremittingly painful.

All this is presented in the context of the Buddha's former life as a prince, wherein he sought relief from life's troubles in the pursuit of sensual pleasures. From the perspective of his awakening and subsequent renunciate life, however, he later realizes that such pursuits can never offer relief and actually make our condition worse. One of the important lessons learned by these experiences is a more subtle understanding of what is meant by "health," and this is pertinent to our discussion of the application of Buddhist perspectives to the field of modern medicine.

The advice to Magandiya centers on the following verse: "The greatest of all gains is health, *nibbana* [the cessation of *dukkha*] is the greatest bliss." The wanderer Magandiya praises this verse as making good sense, but the Buddha goes on to inquire what Magandiya thinks he means by his use of the word "health." The wanderer then "rubbed his limbs with his hands and said: 'This is that health…for I am now healthy and happy and nothing afflicts me.'" Through another series of stories and metaphors involving a blind man eventually healed of his blindness by a physician, the Buddha carefully leads Magandiya to a more profound understanding of what can be meant by health. It is not just the lack of physical affliction in the body at any particular time, but is rather a deeper experience of well-being that is accessed when the mind no longer clings in the presence of pleasure or pain.

Physical pain itself is not the sole determinant of whether or not a person is healthy, any more than the experience of pleasure, by nature transitory, can ensure well-being. In its fullest meaning, health encompasses a sense of wholeness that embraces both pleasure and pain, and is not dependent upon the presence or absence of either of these. It is just as common to find someone who may be in chronic pain but is fundamentally healthy, as it is to find someone who successfully pursues pleasure but is fundamentally ill. An example of the former might be a contented, well-adjusted person with a rich and fulfilling life who happens to have a chronic back problem; and an example of the latter might be a drug addict who succeeds in staying high most of the time but at tremendous cost to his body and to his human dignity. The presence of pain in the former case is not in itself sufficient to qualify the patient as unhealthy; nor is the experience of pleasure adequate to qualify the latter patient as healthy. This is precisely because "health," as the Buddha eventually helps Magandiya to realize—and as Jon Kabat-Zinn often helps his patients realize—is a larger concept than we ordinarily take it to be. What exactly is the prescription given by the Buddha to Magandiya at the end of the discourse to restore his health? It is to "practice in accordance with the true Dhamma," a phrase that flexibly accesses the entire range of ethical, meditational, and insightful trainings found in the Buddhist pharmacopoeia. Lying at the heart of the healing regimen is not a particular ointment or elixir, but an understanding that many of the things formerly taken as soothing are in reality functioning as "diseases, tumors, and darts" to worsen the affliction. It is essential that Magandiya come to this realization himself, for only then will he be able to loosen the clinging that is the root cause of his suffering. As the text puts it:

> When you practice in accordance with the true dhamma, you will know and see for yourself thus: "These are diseases, tumors, and darts; but here these diseases, tumors and darts cease without remainder. With the cessation of my clinging...sorrow, lamentation, pain, grief and despair cease. Such is the cessation of this whole mass of suffering."[4]

Just as the Buddha here identifies *clinging*, our habitual response to desire or craving, as the cause of our dis-ease, so also does Jon Kabat-Zinn posit stress as a factor contributing significantly to our lack of health. The identification of stress with clinging might be one of the pivotal points of connection between these two ways of looking at the workings of the mind-body organism.

In Buddhist thought clinging *(upadana)* is not the same as craving *(tanha)* or as suffering *(dukkha)*, but it is the factor that binds the two together. In the causal series of interdependent origination *(paticca samuppada)*, as well as in other miscellaneous formulations of the doctrine, craving is said to arise habitually from our experience of pleasure and pain—we want the pleasure to persist, and we want the pain to stop. As such, craving, in both its positive and negative manifestations, is a motivating factor. Clinging, on the other hand, is our response to this motivation, and it is the same basic response whether we are clinging to the continuance of pleasure or clinging to the cessation or avoidance of pain. We cling as much (or even more) to what we hate as to what we like. The outcome of such a response is inevitably suffering. According to the Buddha, the clinging response to the craving motivation always leads to suffering, because the objects of all this attachment are intrinsically changeable, unsatisfying, and ultimately not something that we can really possess.

The remarkable thing about this analysis of experience is that it reveals with some precision the point at which natural human psycho-physical activity turns pathological. The content of our experience is entirely benign—the sights and sounds, flavors, odors, and physical contacts that make up the data of our experienced world are never, in themselves, causes of suffering. Similarly, our thoughts and perceptions merely convey cognitive information, which in each case may then be experienced as either pleasurable or painful (or sometimes neither of these) in affective tone. All this is normal (yes, even the experience of pain). But how we then respond to this experience, to what extent we succumb to the motivation to pursue pleasure and avoid pain by clinging in various ways—this is the crucial point at which it is determined whether we suffer, or claim our freedom to simply be aware of our experience in all its natural diversity. It is in this sense that the expression is used by a number of modern meditation teachers, "Pain is inevitable, but suffering is optional."[5]

Another story in the Pali texts compares the experience of pleasure or pain to being pierced by an arrow.[6] Such experience is unavoidable for all sentient beings, since affective tone is a crucial part of the rich texture of sentience. But the text suggests that we stab ourselves again with a second arrow when we either resist the pain or revel in the pleasure. In the case of pain this doubles our suffering, an unskillful response eliminated by those who learn a better response through the practice of insight and awareness training. Traditionally it is said that how one responds to experience (painful or pleasant, strong or weak) is determined by the relative presence—in each moment—of the mutually exclusive factors of ignorance and wisdom. Buddhist practice is all about the many ways we can learn to overcome or circumvent the force of our latent ignorance and gradually build up the minor insights and awakenings that contribute to the development of wisdom. (The opposite metaphor is just as often used in the Buddhist tradition: practice is a matter of recognizing the almost irresistible force of our innate wisdom, by gradually peeling away the many layers of ignorance that obstruct it.) As this process progresses, we incrementally become more skillful at the challenging enterprise of learning to live free of suffering.

STRESS AND HEALING

Let us compare all of this with the way Jon Kabat-Zinn speaks about stress and healing in *Full Catastrophe Living*. He begins by agreeing with the pioneer researcher Hans Selye that stress is best viewed as a response, and he quotes him as defining stress as "the nonspecific response of the organism to any pressure or demand."[7] The two also agree that stress is largely if not entirely caused by the organism itself (rather than by an outside source) in its attempts to adapt to environmental changes. As Kabat-Zinn puts it, "our actual attempts to respond to change and to pressure, no matter what their particular source, might in themselves lead to breakdown and disease if they are inadequate or disregulated."[8] Furthermore, Kabat-Zinn draws upon research by Seligman showing that "it is not the potential stressor itself but how you perceive it and then how you handle it that will determine whether or not it will lead to stress."[9] In other words, the world is not nec-

Mindfulness practice at the Stress Reduction Clinic, University of Massachusetts Medical Center, Worcester, Massachusetts. Courtesy Andrew Olendzki.

essarily a stressful place, but there are various unhealthy ways of being in the world through which our interaction with it leads us to develop stress within ourselves.

Another distinction made by both the ancient tradition and the modern work with stress reduction is the difference between physical and mental suffering. As one Pali text puts it, "There are these two diseases…disease of body and disease of mind. There are beings who can achieve freedom from suffering from bodily disease for a year, two years…for even a hundred years. But it is hard to find beings who can admit freedom from mental disease even for one moment."[10]

From the Buddha's perspective, as demonstrated by the Magandiya story, we all suffer from a series of basic misconceptions about ourselves, the world, and the nature of happiness or health. It is in this sense that we can be construed as having a "mental disease," even if we have the good fortune to enjoy robust physical health for an entire lifetime. The mental disease, of course, is again the presence of clinging (provoked by desire) as it is manifested in each moment of consciousness.

The Stress Reduction Clinic often faces just the opposite situation— that of trying to help patients with irreversible physical problems, like the loss of a limb or a terminal prognosis, to discover in themselves the experience of wholeness that will enable them to be healthy of mind. As Jon Kabat-Zinn puts it, "Someone who has had an arm amputated…or who faces death from an incurable disease is still fundamentally whole.…It is the process of coming to terms with things as they are that embodies the process of healing."[11] We are so accustomed to the notion that our well-being is entirely dependent upon our physical state, that it often requires being reduced to the drastic condition of many of these patients in order to begin to imagine that this is not entirely the case. Physical health is indeed a blessing, but if it is no longer an option, freedom can still be claimed by the "coming to terms with things as they are" that constitutes mental health. What these two points of view have in common is not merely that they distinguish between the physical and the mental dimension of experience, but the more profound idea that there need not be a causal connection between the two.

This is not to say, we must be careful to note, that either system of thought would subscribe to a rigorous mind/body dualism; in fact both ways of viewing a person insist upon the close interdependence of mind and body. Body and mind continue to influence one another in various ways, but just because the body is healthy does not mean the mind is healthy (in the former case), and just because the body is afflicted does not mean the mind must be also afflicted (as in the latter case). Both of these declarations are counterintuitive to the cultures in which they are articulated, and in each instance some significant work is required to transform the conditioning of the patient. The discourse from which the above passage is quoted even goes so far as to give as an example of mental health the willingness and ability to "submit to painful bodily feelings, grievous, sharp, racking, distracting and discomforting, that drain the life away."

Pressing the matter of body and mind still further, there is another exchange registered in the Pali texts that is similarly echoed in Jon Kabat-Zinn's work with mindfulness training and stress reduction. A village elder named Nakulapitar is said to have approached the Buddha on one occasion saying, "Master, I am a broken-down old man, aged, far-gone in years, I have reached life's end, I am sick and always ailing."[12] To which the Buddha replied, "It is true, sir, that your body is weak and afflicted. For one carrying such a body about, to claim but a moment's health would be sheer foolishness. Therefore, sir, you should train yourself: 'Though my body is sick, my mind shall not be sick.'" One can almost imagine this conversation occurring at the University of Massachusetts Medical Center in Worcester.

The Buddha's chief disciple Sariputta has a chance to explain to Nakulapitar more fully how to go about doing this. First he identifies why people suffer mentally from physical affliction, explaining that untrained people have a tendency to think "I am the body" or "the body is mine." "And so, possessed by this idea, when body alters and changes, owing to the unstable and changeful nature of body, then sorrow and grief, woe, lamentation and despair arise in them." The same habit of identification is noted in regard to the other aggregates of experience, one's feelings, perceptions, dispositions, and consciousness—this, explains Sariputta, is what happens when a person is sick in both body and mind.

The way to heal the mind, therefore, even in the face of an afflicted body, is simply to dis-identify from these aggregates of experience, to regard them not as "mine," but as "not-mine." Without this possessiveness, this attachment, this clinging (once again), one is not so profoundly affected by the inevitable changes that our physical and mental experience undergoes. If we cling to the content of our experience—this or that particular painful sensation, for example—we will suffer because of its relentlessness and changeability; but if we can learn to abide rather in awareness of the process of experience, noticing with interest and some detachment the play of arising, changing, and passing phenomena, then a healthy mind is rising above the affliction of an unhealthy body. Jon Kabat-Zinn expresses such a similar sentiment, in the context of working with patients with chronic pain:

When practicing the body scan or any of the other mindfulness techniques, you may come to notice that when you identify with your thoughts or feelings or with the sensations in your body or with the body itself for that matter, there is much greater turmoil and suffering than when you dwell as the non-judgmental observer of it all....In the letting go of all this, you may come to a point at which all concepts dissolve into stillness and there is just awareness....In this stillness, you might come to know that whatever you are, "you" are definitely not your body, although it is yours to work with and to take care of and make use of....If you are not your body, then you cannot possibly be your body's pain....As you learn [this] your relationship to pain in your body can undergo profound changes.[13]

MINDFULNESS AS MEDICINE

The story from the Pali texts that most poignantly brings together the connection between illness, meditation, and nonclinging concerns a great lay supporter of the Buddha named Anathapindika.[14] After a lifetime of loyal support of the Buddha and his followers, including a major gift of land upon which the early Buddhist community lived, Anathapindika lay dying of a serious disease. He describes his symptoms to Sariputta, who comes to comfort him: "I am not getting better, I am sinking, not rising up; my head feels as if a strong man were crushing it; my bowels feel as though being ripped by a sharp sword."

Sariputta's compassionate response to this suffering is to teach him the basic techniques of mindfulness meditation: "You must train yourself [to think], 'I will not cling to body, I will not cling to feelings, I will not cling to...anything whatsoever in my experience.'" Upon hearing this instruction Anathapindika bursts into tears, not, as Sariputta at first presumes, because of a flare-up of his symptoms, but out of gratitude and recognition for the profoundly healing effect of this practice. No physical cure ensues, of course, and Anathapindika passes away shortly after this exchange; but we cannot help but think that he died with a greater sense of wholeness and ease as a result of this brief training in mindfulness.

In addition to all that has been said here about meditation working to heal the mental suffering that emerges in response to physical affliction, it is also, remarkably, the case that the physical healing process itself seems to be positively influenced by the practice of mindful awareness. Considerable attention is drawn these days to studies of healing that compare groups of people who actively engage their minds in the healing process in one way or another, and control groups who rely more traditionally on the medicines and therapies to do their work upon a more passive patient.[15] It appears to be more or less consistently the case that the former group heals more rapidly or more completely. What could explain this?

By removing meditation practice from its traditional religious context we can presumably rule out the intervention of a benign spiritual entity (although this may not be the case with studies of prayer and healing, for example, in the Western cultural context). It seems, at least in the case of mindfulness meditation, not to matter one bit whether or not the patient believes any of the traditional tenets of Buddhism, or, for that matter, whether they remain a faithful Jew, Catholic, Protestant, atheist, or secular humanist. This issue may well have nuances we fail yet to recognize, but let us presume for a moment that we were to try to explain the healing power of awareness as a scientific phenomenon. How might we account for the fact that mindful awareness is often a contributing factor to successful physical healing?

One explanation is the view that stress is a strong suppresser of the body's natural healing mechanisms, so that anything done to reduce its influence on the body will help allow the body to heal itself naturally. Certainly if stress impairs the immune system it will make us more likely to become ill, and perhaps also the removal of stress will render it easier for the body to repair itself once damaged. Jon Kabat-Zinn discusses this view in his book, much of which has to do with training his patients to respond to stress with some awareness rather than reacting, often habitually, to stress. This is an exciting field in modern medicine now, and there is still much to be learned about the mechanisms of immune system stimulation or inhibition. There is nothing particularly mysterious about this process, insofar as it is rooted in conventional biological theory (except perhaps the philosophical issue of the mind's ability to influence the physical system as much as it often seems to do).

The model for explaining mind's transformation of body preferred by Jon Kabat-Zinn in *Full Catastrophe Living* seems to rely heavily upon the notion of wholeness and connectedness. As he puts it,

> When we use the word healing to describe the experiences of people in the stress clinic, what we mean above all is that they are undergoing a profound transformation of view....It is a perceptual shift away from fragmentation and isolation toward wholeness and connectedness.[16]

> In moments of stillness you come to realize that you are already whole, already complete in your being, even if your body [is afflicted].[17]

It is the practice of meditation that allows us to get in touch with these positive perspectives. Quieting the mind and body reduces the forces of fragmentation and allows us to experience the lack of conflict that characterizes the subjective manifestation of wholeness. Meditation also offers access to various conscious and subconscious feedback mechanisms, which lets us feel more directly connected to all the processes of the mind and body. Kabat-Zinn regards the experiences of wholeness and connectedness that can be accessed through mindfulness meditation as inherently healing. Perhaps in part influenced by his Zen background, he seems to view the natural state of the human being as a state of fundamental wellness. The forces of disease and illness arise when we depart from this natural wellness, and meditation offers us a way of returning to it.

It might be mentioned that much of the explanation of the mind's apparent transformative influence upon the body, at least in the Buddhist tradition, is to be found in the mind-body connection itself. In ancient India the Buddha argued against the dominant view that the body was inhabited by the soul, and eventually rejected many of the yogic and ascetic practices that endeavored to separate the two. Fundamentally, says the Buddha of the Pali texts, mind and body are two aspects of the same phenomenon. It is more accurate to view the person as a single psycho-physical organism *(nama-rupa)*, consisting of an aggregate of materiality *(rupa)* that cannot in principle be separated from four other aggregates of mentality: feeling, perception, thought, and consciousness *(vedana, sanna, sankhara, vinnana)*. From this perspective the mind's transformation of the body becomes less enigmatic, for by nature the mental and physical dimensions of a person are thoroughly interdependent.

The central nervous system is, after all, distributed throughout the entire "fathom-long" body. We can easily verify with simple exercises that the mere act of directing attention to a specific part of the body will result in an almost immediate change in how that part of the body is experienced subjectively, and various measurements can be made of some changes of physical characteristics (temperature, blood pressure, etc.). We can similarly notice the many ways in which environmental impact upon the body corresponds to numerous mental changes. We may well be better off, therefore, by dispensing entirely with the whole dualist lexicon of mind-body relationship, replacing it with some manner of speaking that treats the psycho-physical entity as a single organism. Then perhaps we can speak less about how mind changes body or body changes mind, and see instead an integrated process of co-transformation.

In the Buddhist tradition it is taken for granted that all five aggregates are interdependent and inseparable, and hence the teaching often addresses all five aspects of personhood equally. Jon Kabat-Zinn routinely recognizes this mind-body interconnection, pointing out, for example, that

> our physical health is intimately connected with our patterns of thinking and feeling about ourselves and also with the quality of our relationships with other people and the world....Certain patterns of thinking and certain ways of relating to our feelings can predispose us to illness....On the other hand, other patterns of thinking, feeling and relating appear to be associated with robustness of health.[18]

A traditionally Buddhist explanation of why meditation can be useful in healing the body would begin by making the distinction between the two kinds of meditation, tranquillity (shamatha) and insight (vipassana), insofar as a different dynamic is at work in each of these. Tranquillity meditation involves concentrating the mind on a single object of attention, to the exclusion of all other objects. As the mind becomes increasingly able to hold attention steadily on a particular object with fewer and fewer interruptions, it can eventually remain very stable, very focused, and settle upon ever more rarefied states of absorption. Fairly early in this process the body is experienced as bathed in pleasant, blissful sensations; but as even more rarefied states of absorption evolve, all experience of the body ceases and the pleasure is transformed into profound states of equanimity.

OVERCOMING PAIN

One of the consequences of this sort of tranquillity meditation, as one might imagine, is that painful physical experiences can be temporarily overcome. Indeed we are told that the Buddha himself, when experiencing the painful bodily sensations accompanying his own terminal illness, could only know any physical comfort when entering into similar types of meditative states.[19] And yet this sort of attainment is regularly characterized as merely a "pleasant abiding here and now" (ditthe va dhamme sukhaviharam), and as such it falls far short of a more enduring solution to the problem of suffering. Drawing on contemporary medical language, we might say that tranquillity meditation temporarily relieves many of the symptoms of human suffering, but does not significantly address its fundamental causes.

Insight meditation strikes at the heart of the basic etiology of suffering—the dual factors of craving and ignorance—and as such points toward the very cure itself. Here the mind is also focused on a particular aspect of experience (a physical sensation, a feeling, a thought, etc.), but the objects of this focus are allowed to change naturally with the unfolding of experience in its entirely. For example, full attention is brought to bear in the moment on a physical sensation, but immediately following this attention may be focused on a feeling, and then a thought—and so on through the full range of experience as it is lived in any set of natural circumstances. Insight meditation seeks to strengthen the mental factor of mindfulness *(sati),* by means of which we fully attend to the nuanced presentation of any object to subjective experience. The effect of this habit of mindfulness is more subtle than concentration practice, and works to illuminate and eventually undermine the very processes by which we construct suffering as each moment of experience arises. Mindfulness itself is not the cure for suffering, but it is a powerful tool with which to access the cure.

Learning how to pay close attention to the moment-to-moment experience of the body and the mind eventually reveals many secrets of psychophysical dynamics. We actually begin to see for ourselves how feelings of pleasure give rise to the desire for continuing these or achieving even greater levels of satisfaction; how feelings of pain evoke automatic reflexes of contraction, avoidance, denial, and repression; how the mind creates illusions of continuity out of momentary presentations of sensory data; how much we want and conspire to believe in a self that is more coherent, substantial and significant than closer inspection warrants; how much our projections and expectations of ourselves and our world distort our ability to perceive anything clearly; how our bodies contain whole universes of diverse sensations and our minds throw up one thought after another, one memory after another, one fantasy after another, write one story after another, with very little order and even less control. All and all, it can be a very humbling encounter.

But as our understanding of ourselves changes, some of our habits of responding begin also to transform. Seeing the inherent changeability of experience, we hold on somewhat less tightly to each moment of it. Seeing the variability and insubstantiality of what we are accustomed to calling "myself," we are able to take ourselves less seriously and everything that happens to us somewhat less personally. Seeing that all satisfaction of desire is inevitably only temporary, we gradually expect less from our continual acts of gratification. The Buddha of the Pali texts tells us that if we look closely into our direct experience we will be able to recognize its impermanence *(anicca),* its selflessness *(anatta),* and its unsatisfactoriness *(dukkha),* and prescribed *vipassana* meditation as the tool for accessing these insights.

The result of seeing these characteristics of our experiences for ourselves will in fact loosen the influence of grasping, which causes the suffering in our lives. This, I believe, is essentially the agenda of contemporary stress reduction as taught and practiced in programs like the one at the University of Massachusetts Medical Center by Jon Kabat-Zinn and his colleagues. Mindfulness-Based Stress Reduction is effective in the secular American medical setting because it is training patients with various afflictions to discover some very fundamental truths about the human construction of suffering. By helping people expose this information, each in their own way, it also provides the tools by means of which they can begin to transform their relationship to their own suffering. And because of the fundamental interdependence of the mental and the physical, any transformation of viewpoint, attitude, or understanding will be attended by potentially significant transformations of the physical body. In a word, wellness has its roots in understanding, and the cure that penetrates to these very roots is wisdom.

It is useful that the Buddha pointed this out and provided a detailed program for gaining the tools and applying them appropriately to solve the problem, but insofar as the situation he was addressing is shared by all people at all times and in all cultures, there is nothing inherently Buddhist in the entire process of healing. In this particular area at least, Buddhism is playing the role not of a religion gaining converts or losing itself in syncretic forces, as much as a medical manifesto offering a unique perspective on the human condition that has to do with suffering and healing. It highlights certain features of the mind-body organism, sketches out a program for research and further investigation of its equilibrium, and suggests the use of the powerful tool of mindfulness meditation to access the deeper wisdom of wellness. As Jon Kabat-Zinn concludes,

> The challenge is whether you can see…and live in accordance with the way things are, to come into harmony with all things and all moments. This is the path of insight, of wisdom, and of healing.…It is the path of the mind-body looking deeply into itself and knowing itself.[20]

MEDITATION AS ENGAGED BUDDHISM

To what extent, if any, does the influence of mindfulness practice on contemporary behavioral medicine represent a new American form of engaged Buddhism? Much would depend, of course, on how one construes the label. As already noted, the work of the Stress Reduction Clinic is certainly not intentionally Buddhist, and is concerned rather with keeping the Buddhist dimensions of mindfulness meditation to a minimum (or even eliminate them entirely). It is certainly *engaged*, however, in the traditional Buddhist role of the alleviation of suffering. So, is this definition so broad that any physician or hospital is, in effect, practicing Buddhism when it endeavors to relieve suffering? No, because stress reduction programs define suffering in a different way: as a remediable attitude that affects all aspects of human existence.

The mindfulness method of treatment focuses upon changing our relationship to our *experience* of suffering, rather than changing the nature of the physical suffering itself. There is essential similarity between today's Mindfulness-Based Stress Reduction and the techniques of mind-training developed in the ancient cultures of north India. Meditation is part of a subjective science, the science of personal and universal phenomenology, and as such its realm is inherently psychological. Because of the thorough interactivity of body and mind, the body is also influenced, although this can only happen through the medium of personal experience. The world view of Buddhism might even require that *nothing but* the phenomenal realm can really be engaged, insofar as the world is essentially a construction of the individual mind. A collective world is also constructed out of the total karmic and intentional effects of individual minds, but the construction process in one's own mind *in this present moment* is the fundamental unit in the Buddhist view of reality. It may be possible to engage the mind without significantly changing the larger world we all share, but it is not possible to engage the world except through engagement with the mind.

The fact that mindfulness practice involves the inner life rather than external manifestations does not necessarily make it any less a form of engaged Buddhism. When meditation practice is used in healing, with what is it actually engaging? Unlike other forms of engaged Buddhism it is not interacting with oppressive social institutions, or with the makers of war or the breakers of peace, or with those who violate human rights or ravage the environment. Contemporary behavioral medicine is training people to engage not only their illness but, more profoundly, to engage themselves—their own deeply seated attitudes and conditioning. Let us not underestimate the heroic nature of this struggle. Just as the Buddha himself confronted and overcame the armies of Mara—the multitude of unconscious unwholesome impulses rooted in greed, hatred, and delusion that populate the subterranean reaches of the psyche—so also do the patients who show up at the doorstep of the Stress Reduction Clinic come to grips with their own frightening demons. The fear of pain, the terror of impending death, the loss of control over their lives, and so many other manifestations of suffering—all are merely accessed by the meditation practice. It remains for each in their own way to grapple with the forces within themselves that strengthen or weaken the power of the suffering in their lives.

It is interesting to think of what the classical Buddhist tradition might make of the modern application of its practices in our hospitals and clinics. It has become common to refer to a distinction in modern medicine between treating the symptoms of an affliction and treating its underlying causes, and perhaps this view can be helpful in conceptualizing such a response. The basic point is that the ultimate causes of suffering in the human condition lie in deeply held attitudes to self and the roles these play in the construction of every moment's experience. The Buddha laid out a comprehensive program for understanding and addressing these issues at a level of intensity sufficient for uprooting the deep craving that causes suffering. But this program is almost entirely out of the reach of most contemporary Buddhists, and surely beyond the reach of Jon Kabat-Zinn's usual patients. It is not that it is beyond their capability, for we are told it is accessible to all (from the impoverished peasant woman Kisagotami to the mass murderer Angulimala). But what is required to accomplish the task of full awakening—a radical re-orientation of almost every aspect of one's life and priorities—is more than all but a few handfuls of Western citizens seem interested in pursuing. The path to awakening in this lifetime is not for everybody, and the Buddhist tradition has outlined numerous ways in which one can practice the path of a householder or lay person with great dignity and effectiveness.

If the *professional sage* is bent upon the thorough uprooting of the fundamental causes of suffering (the cessation without remainder of all greed, hatred, and delusion), the rest of us may employ an array of practices that can effectively mitigate its symptoms. Both methods are addressing the agenda of alleviating suffering by understanding and treating its underlying foundations, but one path does so on a very deep level by withering the very roots of those causes, while the other more modestly aims to recognize the basis of their general symptoms and to neutralize them for temporary relief. For example, when an impulse rooted in selfishness or aversion arises in our mind in the course of our lives, we can use the tools of mindfulness meditation to first of all notice it, recognize its nature both as an afflictive thought and also as a transitory phenomenon, and thereby gain the extra space necessary to respond to it with some wisdom rather than to merely act it out or suppress it following the established patterns of our conditioning. With its roots still deeply imbedded in the psyche we can be sure such an impulse will arise again and even again, but we and all those around us are nevertheless immeasurably better off by noticing this and working with it in the moment, than if we were oblivious or uncaring about it. In a similar way there may be a physical condition with deep roots in an incurable disease that cannot be thoroughly eradicated, but it still makes all the difference in the world to the patient in the moment of suffering that his or her symptoms can be effectively treated.

There may well be the impulse in Americans to rebel against the apparently two-tiered approach this model suggests, suspecting the layman's path to be second rate and the monastic's role to be unacceptably privileged. But we don't consider it unfair or demeaning to recognize that we can't all be Olympic gold medal winners. We may all be capable of being the best in the world at *something* (if not sprinting or swimming, then perhaps chess or driving or wood carving or something else), but that is not to say we are willing to undertake the rigorous single-minded training we know is necessary to excel at anything. Perhaps the recognition of two approaches to the path of liberation, the professional and the amateur, is intended to relieve in the lay practitioner any feeling of obligation to join a monastery and to valorize the householder's life and path. Yet this function has the opposite effect if we respond to the word "amateur" as diminishing and condescending. For the suffering patient who visits the physician in search of some relief, I suspect the issue of practical means for immediate treatment is of more importance than the medically more ambitious ideal of eradicating the affliction forever. So if the classical Buddhist tradition would consider the applications of mindfulness meditation to contemporary healing protocols as something short of the goal of final liberation, it would presumably be quite consistent with and uncritical of the notion that the medicine of Dhamma is capable of relieving suffering wherever it is found.

The Mindfulness-Based Stress Reduction movement is presently caught between two paradigms. A modern physician might say that mindfulness is in no way addressing the fundamental causes of illness (which might be rapidly duplicating cancer cells or deficiencies in the immune system, for example). As an approach that is primarily psychological, it can never do more than treat certain presenting symptoms. Similarly, a traditional Buddhist might say that mindfulness is not reaching the deeper causes of suffering unless one takes on the rigorous path to full awakening in this lifetime. Relieving stress and gaining some insight into mind-body interactivity are relatively modest steps along a profound and lengthy path culminating in something much more extraordinary than freedom from the symptoms of physical affliction. But if the introduction of mindfulness practice to contemporary medical settings is satisfying neither of the traditionalists, it is undeniably helping people in ways that would gratify both the physician and the Buddhist sage. Perhaps, among other things, engagement involves the courage to displease one constituency in order to serve another.

NOTES

1. *Ye keci osadha loke vijjanti vividha bahu,/ dhammosadhasamam na-tthi; etam pivatha bhikkhavo./ Dhammosadham pivitvana ajaramarana siyum,/ bhavayitva ca passitva nibbuta upadhikkhaye ti.* Milindapanho, Pali Text Society (London: Routledge & Kegan Paul, 1964), p. 335. (All Pali references are given either in the tradition- al format of the canonical volume, chapter, and section, or to the volume and page number of the Pali Text Society editions.) The final phrase should perhaps be rendered more literally something like "one's suffering would become extinguished in the destruction of the substrates of clinging." I think the con- text gives license to make a closer connection between "the extinguishing of suffering" and "healing," and I follow I. B. Horner (*Milinda's Questions*, Pali Text Society, 1969) in emphasizing the "clinging" aspect of *upadhi* rather than the "substrate" aspect in my translation of this passage. I take similar liberties with "untouched by aging and death" insofar as the Pali merely puts the compound term in the negative. Some explanation is required of the *arahant's* special rela- tionship to these factors, since in the conventional sense of the word aging, for example, is not literally arrested by awakening.

   For ease of publishing, no diacritical marks are used when Pali or Sanskrit terms are given. Most of the terms are common, and those who want to inves- tigate them further can find the proper equivalents in many glossaries or stan- dard reference works such as A. P. Buddhadatta Mahathera's *Concise Pali-English Dictionary* (Colombo, 1968) or Bhikkhu Nanamoli's *A Pali-English Glossary of Buddhist Technical Terms* (Kandy, 1994).

2. Jon Kabat-Zinn, *Full Catastrophe Living: Using the Wisdom of Your Body and Mind to Face Stress, Pain, and Illness; The Program of the Stress Reduction Clinic at the University of Massachusetts Medical Center* (New York: Delta, 1990).

3. *Majjhima Nikaya*, 75, edited by V. Trenckner (Pali Text Society, 1979). For all *Majjhima* references, see also: Bhikkhu Nanamoli and Bhikkhu Bodhi, *The Middle Length Discourses of the Buddha: A New Translation of the Majjhima Nikaya* (Boston: Wisdom Publications, 1995).

4. *Majjhima Nikaya*, vol. 1, p. 512. Nanamoli, p. 616.

5. As with many of the expressions used in the contemporary oral tradition of Dharma teaching, it is difficult to say who first coined this phrase. It is used reg- ularly by teachers at the Insight Meditation Society such as Joseph Goldstein, Larry Rosenberg, Christina Feldman, etc.

6. *Samyutta Nikaya*, 36.6.

7. Kabat-Zinn, *Full Catastrophe Living*, p. 236.

8. Ibid., p. 237.

9. Ibid.

10. *Anguttara Nikaya*, 4.157.

11. Jon Kabat-Zinn, *Full Catastrophe Living*, p. 163.

12. *Samyutta Nikaya*, 22.1.

13. Kabat-Zinn, *Full Catastrophe Living*, pp. 297–98.

14. This entire exchange occurs in the *Anathapindikovada Sutta*, no. 143 in the *Majjhima Nikaya* (Nanamoli, pp. 1109–13).

15. Kabat-Zinn, *Full Catastrophe Living*, chapters 14, 15, etc. One example of such a study undertaken by Jon Kabat-Zinn and his colleagues is "Influences of a Mindfulness Meditation-Based Stress Reduction Intervention on Rates of Skin Clearing in Patients With Moderate to Severe Psoriasis Undergoing Phototherapy (UVB) and Photochemotherapy (PUVA)," published in *Psychosomatic Medicine: Journal of the American Psychosomatic Society* 60 (1998): 625–32. Although the study involved a relatively small population of patients, the results clearly indicated the beneficial effects of the mindfulness practice on the process of physical healing.

16. Kabat-Zinn, *Full Catastrophe Living*, p. 168.

17. Ibid., p. 173.

18. Ibid., p. 216.

19. *Mahaparinibbana Sutta,* 2.25. *Digha Nikaya,* vol. 1, p. 101. Translated by Maurice Walshe as *The Long Discourses of the Buddha* (Boston: Wisdom Publications, 1995), p. 245.

20. Kabat-Zinn, *Full Catastrophe Living*, p. 440.

Naropa Institute:
The Engaged Academy

Robert E. Goss

Engaged Buddhism is an international movement that brings together
Buddhists of many different traditions, cultural settings, and political
approaches. A response to global political and economic problems, engaged
Buddhism applies Buddhist principles of discipline, meditation, and insight
to contemporary challenges.[1]

Ever since Gautama arose from the bodhi tree, enlightened teachers in the Buddhist tradition have engaged the world with an alternative
set of religious values. The Buddha taught a way to liberation from suffering and demonstrated that liberation with the example of his life. For
two thousand five hundred years Buddhists have focused on a recognition
of suffering as the beginning of the religious path. At the same time,
Buddhism has addressed the social causes of suffering from the very
beginning. Throughout its history, Buddhism has found expression in a
wide variety of social institutions and cultures. Today "engaged Buddhism"
suggests not only Buddhism's historical interaction with cultural and
social institutions, but also its critique and transformation of them.[2]

The first disciples of Gautama formed a learning community dedicated to freeing themselves from ego-centeredness and other causes of suffering. They formed an alternative educational community (the sangha),
a casteless society with egalitarian structures.[3] The Buddha offered educational strategies for liberation through his mentoring relationship with
countless disciples. Gautama's message spread throughout Asia, transmitted
from teacher to disciple in unbroken lineages. Education was at the heart
of the Buddha's method of liberation. For millennia Buddhist teachers
have guided their students in the teachings of the Dharma and contemplative practice; they have exemplified a vision of peace, compassion,
and freedom and have attempted to construct a social world based on
these values.

Contemporary engaged Buddhism is an international movement crossing the denominational lines of Theravada, Mahayana, and Vajrayana Buddhism—responding to global political, economic, and social problems.[4] It has taken on the form of socio-political liberation movements actively involved in changing society and relieving human suffering. Contemporary engaged Buddhism teaches the application of the Buddhist principles of compassion and wisdom, interdependence, and emptiness. It uses Buddhist contemplative practices, educational strategies, social compassion, and the building of grassroots networks for active involvement and participation in society.

Engaged Buddhists, like all Buddhists, have formed educational networks such as the Spirit in Educational Movement, the International Network of Engaged Buddhists (INEB), Buddhist Peace Fellowship (BPF), Dharma centers, publishing houses, educational institutes, monasteries, and accredited universities.[5] Engaged Buddhist educational practice has a social edge, for it not only instructs students in how the mind shapes experience, how emotions are understood and transformed, and how to awaken to the potentialities of enlightenment, but also teaches them how to live in the world as an agent of change.

This chapter will examine a specific form of American engaged Buddhist educational theory and practice at the Naropa Institute. Naropa is a fully accredited Buddhist university that confers a masters degree in engaged Buddhism. To my knowledge, this is the first Buddhist university to confer such a degree. Naropa strives to combine a liberal arts curriculum with contemplative practice, to awaken in students selfless understanding and active social compassion.[6]

TRUNGPA RINPOCHE AND THE FOUNDING OF NAROPA

In his introduction to *Engaged Buddhism: Buddhist Liberation Movements in Asia*, Christopher Queen notes two significant features of a contemporary engaged Buddhist: "First, the engaged Buddhists were high-profile personalities whose careers straddled and blended East and West.…Second, the engaged Buddhists were dauntless activists for cultural renewal, social change, and an ecumenical World Buddhism."[7] Chogyam Trungpa, the eleventh *tulku* of Surmang Monastery and an important teacher in the Kagyu lineage, fits the two criteria articulated by Queen. He blended Asian and American religious traditions and educational practices, becoming the charismatic spirit behind the development of Naropa's educational philosophy.

When the Chinese invaded in 1959, Trungpa left Tibet and went to study at Oxford. He later renounced monastic life and founded the Samye-

Ling meditation center in Scotland in 1967. Chogyam Trungpa's lifestyle challenged and frequently shocked followers and Western Buddhists until his death in 1987. Trungpa refused to conform to stereotypical ideas of what a religious teacher should be, often blending Asian and American culture in a creative mix.

In 1970, Trungpa received a visa to enter the United States and began to found Dharma centers in many urban areas. In 1973, he established the Vajradhatu, an international organization to consolidate the educational and meditative activities of the Dharma centers. The Vajradhatu centers became the conduit from which Trungpa Rinpoche passed his Kagyu practice lineage and later his Shambhala teachings. It would become the ecclesiastical branch of the Trungpa movement.

Naropa was founded in 1974 in Boulder, Colorado, by Chogyam Trungpa Rinpoche as a summer institute. Its faculty included Trungpa, Allen Ginsberg, Ann Waldman, John Cage, Gregory Bateson, Ram Dass, Herbert Guenther, and Agehananda Bharati. There were courses on meditation, t'ai chi, *thangka* painting, tea ceremony, Tibetan and Sanskrit, Madhyamika philosophy, physics, and psychology. There were nightly readings of poetry, performances, debates, colloquiums, and informal round table discussions.[8] Naropa Institute expected two hundred students, yet two thousand students came to Boulder for what writer Rick Fields described as a "summer Woodstock of Consciousness."[9] Two years later the school became a year-round institute offering a contemplative education curriculum and academic studies in spiritual practice. Nearly twenty-three years later, Naropa has evolved into a fully accredited school with degree programs on the undergraduate and graduate levels, an internationally renowned summer writing program, and on-going continuing education programs. Notwithstanding its place as the first accredited, Buddhist-inspired college in America, Naropa is nonsectarian and open to all who want a liberal arts education with a contemplative slant.

The Shambhala Teaching

The key to Chogyam Trungpa's transmission of Tibetan education to the West was his stress on the *non-Buddhist* tradition of Shambhala training. Shambhala training arises from treasure texts *(terma)* revealed to him in a series of visions.[10] Along with the Nyingmapa sect, the Kagyupa have had a long tradition of treasure texts discovered and recorded centuries later, or revealed in visions or dreams. When Trungpa received these texts in visions, he recorded them in Tibetan, translated them, and wrote commentaries on their meaning. These commentaries became the basis for the five levels of

Shambhala training, a meditation curriculum based on a nonsectarian approach to "warriorship."

The antecedents for the Shambhala lineage can be found in the nineteenth century in the Rime movement of eastern Tibet.[11] The Rimé movement attempted to integrate indigenous elements within Tibetan culture—popular traditions, Bon, Taoist, and even Neo-Confucian traditions—into the fabric of Buddhist practice. The term *rimé* (Tibetan: *ris med*) is frequently translated as "eclectic," but "universal" would be closer to its original meaning.[12] Students of Trungpa construe *rimé* as "nonsectarian" and "ecumenical."

The Rimé movement helped to break down sectarian rivalry among the Nyingmapa, Kagyupa, and Bonpo traditions—representing a synthesis quite different from the Gelukpa, who follow the synthesis of the path proposed by the fourteenth-century scholar-monk Tsongkhapa.[13] Both the Gelukpa and Rimé contain shamanic and monastic emphases, but the Rimé stress the shamanic and tantric far more.[14] The Rimé was not simply an academic movement, but also a popular ecumenical movement that made esoteric teachings available to the masses. Rimé lamas were often less committed to their particular formal practice lineages and sectarian rivalry, for they were willing to cross lineage lines to receive teachings from the most famous teachers.

Chogyam Trungpa's Shambhala treasure teachings interpret the millenarian Shambhala myth to represent an ideal of a secular enlightenment.[15] According to the Kalachakra Tantra, Shambhala is a harmonious society, governed by a lineage of enlightened rulers. At a future date, the Shambhala king Rigden will lead a peaceful army to save the world from destruction and establish an enlightened society. The Shambhala kingdom became for Trungpa a metaphoric vision of "the ideal of secular enlightenment, that is, the possibility of uplifting our personal existence and that of others without the help of any religious outlook."[16]

Trungpa Rinpoche's Shambhala teachings promote a path of social action that confronts the politics of domination with clarity, gentleness, love, and sanity. It is founded on three premises: the basic goodness of human nature, the sacredness of the world, and resources of the world's religious traditions to address social problems. Trungpa's Shambhala training program fulfilled his long-held dream of making contemplative practices accessible to those who were not interested in studying Buddhism. Some faculty I interviewed eventually became interested in Buddhist practice through the nonsectarian gate of the Shambhala teachings. Trungpa taught many of his students, now faculty at Naropa, to pursue a spiritual path within the world and to incorporate the secular world as part of that sacred path. Shambhala training is an ecumenical path that harnesses shamanic methods of envisioning the ordinary world as sacred, and yoking natural energies for personal and social transformation. It serves as a corrective to religiosity, the tendency to embrace meditative practice to the exclusion of involvement in the world. The Shambhala teachings act as an antidote to quietistic tendencies inherent in traditional Buddhist practice.

The Shambhala training envisions a path of "sacred warriorship" that develops awareness of basic goodness, gentleness, fearlessness, nonaggression, letting go, authentic action, leadership skills, and genuine love of the sacred world to create an enlightened society.[17] Warriorship is an awakening to authentic presence and genuine action within the world.[18] Trungpa's Shambhala teachings incorporate calligraphy, flower-arranging, poetry, theater, dance, fine arts, and martial arts to develop these innate qualities. His fundamental vision is to bring "art to everyday life," to integrate the sacred and the secular, and to transform the world into an enlightened society. Naropa Institute religious studies professor Judith Simmer-Brown observes,

> The Shambhala teachings are Trungpa's engaged Buddhist philosophy. It is how you approach the world, through whatever work you have: a chance to uplift society, to make it a more enlightened world. Trungpa Rinpoche's Shambhala teachings put a lot of emphasis on engagement, politics, and social service. He also put a lot emphasis on how Naropa can make a difference, by bringing gentleness and order—a noncombative, nonadversarial warriorship to whatever you encounter.[19]

When Naropa's publications describe a "Buddhist inspired, nonsectarian liberal arts college," "nonsectarian" translates the Tibetan *rimé*. Nonsectarian does not mean "secular" as it is commonly used in higher education but is perhaps understood as the ecumenical openness to contemplative practices and arts of the world's religious traditions that foster precision, gentleness, and spontaneity. Naropa's 1995 institutional self-study opens with a quote from Trungpa, expressing the Shambhala vision as the core of its institutional philosophy of education:

> When human beings lose their connection to nature, heaven and earth, then they do not know how to nurture their environment or how to rule their world. Human beings destroy their ecology and, at the same time, destroy one another. From this perspective, healing our society goes hand-in-hand with healing our personal, elemental connection with the phenomenal world.[20]

From 1974 to 1986, Trungpa taught and worked with faculty and administration at Naropa to shape its pedagogical orientation in contemplative learning and social engagement of the world. He mentored Naropa in a bold experiment of blending an American liberal arts curriculum with awareness practices and disciplines from Buddhist traditions.

In its Shambhala and Buddhist heritages, Naropa developed an educational practice that can truly be characterized as "engaged Buddhism."

CONTEMPLATIVE EDUCATION

In 1994, the institute's board of trustees adopted the following revised mission statement to elaborate Naropa's vision of contemplative education:

> To offer educational programs that cultivate awareness of the present moment through intellectual, artistic, and meditative disciplines;
>
> To foster a learning community that uncovers wisdom and heart;
>
> To cultivate openness and communication, sharpen critical intellect;
>
> To exemplify the principles of the Naropa Institute's Buddhist educational heritage:
>
> To encourage the integration of world wisdom traditions with modern culture; and
>
> To offer nonsectarian community open to all.[21]

Naropa claims to be a learning community characterized by its particular emphasis on contemplative education and its focus on transforming society:

> In the Buddhist tradition, it is said that the mark of learning is gentleness. Gentleness manifests as clear but unbiased perception, out of which sensitivity and concern for others naturally arises. The goal of the Institute is to provide an environment of gentleness and discipline in which to cultivate "discoverers" and innovators who will actively work in the world for the benefit of others. [22]

Contemplative education involves more than academic content by including practices that promote equanimity, mindfulness, and letting go. One Tuesday each semester is reserved as a "practice day" when students, faculty, and administrative staff engage in some form of meditation, whether it is sitting practice, t'ai chi, Hasidic prayer, Christian contemplation, or yoga. Much of the meditation taught at Naropa has its foundation in traditional Buddhism. All degree programs and some individual classes require students to practice meditation. Some faculty begin their classes with a few moments of silence. Naropa has a meditation practice coordinator (MPC), who is available to lead and instruct students in meditation. The MPC has the responsibility for connecting students with a meditation instructor. Eighty-five percent of the students have found this relationship to be beneficial. There are no additional charges for meditation instruction at Naropa. As the curriculum has grown and included more meditation-based classes, there has been a need for increasing numbers of meditation instructors to serve as teaching assistants. The MPC has recruited with other local religious organizations and traditions to serve as a referral base for students. As many universities and colleges have chapels, Naropa has a permanent meditation hall large enough to accommodate fifty to sixty practitioners and several other halls that accommodate up to three hundred practitioners.

Each semester the institute holds a "practice week" when classes are suspended for meditational practice, instruction, and creative workshops. I happened to visit Naropa during such a period. Dr. Reginald Ray gave instruction on mindfulness and led some three hundred students, staff, and faculty in sitting practice. That afternoon, I listened to a panel of faculty from the visual arts, the performing arts, and the writing program discuss how mindfulness fine-tuned their performance, creativity, and attentiveness. Contemplative learning infuses mindfulness, insight, and friendliness into the curriculum. It sets up an environment where students come to know themselves and learn to deal with their confusion and emotional problems.

Educational Programs

Naropa offers bachelor degrees in contemplative psychology, interarts (dance, music, theater), visual arts, creative writing and literature, environmental studies, early childhood education, traditional eastern arts (t'ai chi chuan, aikido, and yoga), comparative religion, and interdisciplinary studies. Graduate degree programs are offered on the masters level in Buddhist studies, creative writing and poetics, gerontology, engaged Buddhism, contemplative psychotherapy, somatic psychology, and transpersonal counseling psychology. Naropa has developed experiential learning in residential community settings in Nepal and Bali, and is now developing a program in Bhutan.[23] These study abroad programs provide students from both Naropa and other institutions of higher education the opportunity to experience contemplative education within traditional cultural settings with local faculty and artisans.

The Jack Kerouac School of Disembodied Poetics, founded by Allen Ginsberg and Anne Waldman, has been an integral part of Naropa degree programs and the Summer Institute. The school has developed an internationally renowned writing program attracting numerous students, visiting scholars, poets, fiction writers, artists, and religious teachers. The poets of the Kerouac school have pioneered a style of poetics, often rebellious and blending Buddhism with a postmodern perspective.[24]

Each program's curriculum and pedagogy reflect some aspect of the institute's vision of contemplative education. Perhaps Naropa's unique educational vision can be illustrated by a discussion of a few of its M.A. programs. Information on other undergraduate and graduate programs can be found on the Naropa website (<http://www.naropa.edu/>). The M.A. in Buddhist Studies builds on its undergraduate program in Religious Studies, offering three areas of concentration: a comparative religion concentration, a language concentration, and, more recently, an engaged Buddhism concentration. All three Buddhist tracks share a basic core curriculum: (1) five courses in the histories, cultural contexts, and institutions of various Buddhist traditions; (2) four courses in reading Buddhist texts; (3) Buddhist meditation practicums; and (4) the living tradition of Buddhist teachers and masters. The comparative religions track requires study of a variety of traditions, placing their contemplative practices in the contexts of history and religious philosophy. These courses are taught by scholar-practitioners of the respective traditions, such as Jewish Renewal rabbi Zalman Schachter-Shalomi. The language track is limited to the Buddhist canonical languages of Sanskrit and Classical Tibetan.

The M.A. in Contemplative Psychology blends Buddhist psychology and mindfulness/awareness meditation with Western humanistic psychology. The program includes a course on Buddhist *abhidharma* or systematization of psychology. At the heart of the program is a ten-week *maitri* ("friendliness") retreat in a scenic setting. It is an intensive residential, community retreat in which students combine sitting practice, study, and group living. Students are introduced to the Mahayana meditative practice of *tonglen* ("sending and taking") to cultivate compassion. A distinctive feature is the "maitri space awareness" which involves the five maitri rooms, each with distinctive colors and lights. These rooms are designed to evoke basic emotional states of relating to oneself and others. This maitri program provides an experiential ground for understanding confused states of mind and developing compassion for others. It also develops a learning community that intends to provide student support and feedback for each other. Like many other M.A. programs in psychotherapy, students intern in community agencies and mental health facilities.

The M.A. in Gerontology and Long-term Care Management attempts to train licensed administrators and caregivers who are interest-

Dr. Judith Simmer-Brown, director of the Engaged
Buddhism degree program, addressing students, Naropa
Institute, Boulder, Colorado. Courtesy Naropa Institute.

ed in improving the quality of living and dying. Like the Contemplative
Psychology program, the Gerontology program trains students in mindfulness, body-awareness disciplines, and compassion. These components of
the program are considered foundational for working with people who are
aging and dying; they are integrated into a series of practical courses. The
program's philosophy is rooted in the core value of providing a supportive
community of care for residents that recognizes the psychological
and physical needs of the elderly and terminally ill as they become frail
and challenged.

For example, Lucien Wulsin, the former president of the board of
trustees and himself a retired senior citizen, has worked with students in
the introduction of dance and performing arts into long-term care facilities with remarkable success. Other graduate students in the program
spoke enthusiastically of applying Buddhist principles to long-term care
facilities to combat the warehouse mentality, improve the quality of care
for the elderly, and to deal with both staff and resident's issues on death
and dying. Internships allow students practice in integrating Buddhist

principles of mindfulness, attentiveness, and compassion in real long-term facilities.

The M.A. in Environmental Leadership combines the study of ecosystems and human systems with the path of personal and social transformation. The core training of the environmental leadership program introduces systems theory, and applies these systems to an understanding of ecology, human culture, and political systems. Under the Buddhist understanding of interdependence, students are trained in leadership methods that can reverse the pattern of environmental degradation gripping the planet. During the academic year, visiting guests lead four-day intensives on particular topics. Thai Buddhist social activist, Sulak Sivaraksa, has been a regular guest. The uniqueness of the program is its attempt to combine contemplative awareness and practical training in the field.

The M.F.A. in Writing and Poetics grew out of the Jack Kerouac School of Disembodied Poetics. The curriculum is designed for students who wish to pursue creative writing within a contemplative environment. The full program consists of two summer institutes and three semesters of courses, and a final semester in which candidates prepare a creative manuscript and a critical thesis. Bombay Gin, Naropa's literary magazine, is edited by M.F.A. students. What is unique about this program is not only the contemplative practice but also a community outreach project. This places M.F.A. students in prisons, schools, homeless shelters, retirement homes, and hospitals, where they may instruct and inspire these communities in imaginative exercises of language and poetics, and learn social awareness and creative engagement. In the final semester, students may apply for a residency at Zen Mountain Monastery outside Woodstock, New York, where they can work on their manuscripts in a contemplative environment or where they can train in editing and publishing at the monastery's Dharma Communications.

In these graduate programs, Naropa is consciously seeking to build bridges between the sacred and the secular in American education, fostering a vision of the liberal arts that again connects contemplative practice to morality and public service.

NAROPA'S ENGAGED BUDDHISM PROGRAM

One of the newest programs is the Engaged Buddhism program. It is a sixty-credit degree program designed for social action work and was a natural expansion of the existing M.A. programs in Buddhist Studies with either a language track or a comparative religion track. The program evolved out of faculty experience of mentoring people to become engaged Buddhists.

The Engaged Buddhism program requires academic study of Buddhist philosophy, meditation practice, and experience-based learning in community settings. There are four areas of study and training in this degree program:

1. Spiritual Transformation and the Human Condition (primarily from a Buddhist perspective) introduces the student to a basic contemplative understanding of working with the mind, intellect, and emotions;

2. Meditation Training includes basic serenity and insight practice *(shamatha and vipassana)*, sending and taking practice *(tonglen),* and *maitri* space awareness practice;

3. Basic Engaged Buddhism focuses on the principles and issues of engaged spirituality as manifested in the social sphere; and

4. Process skills, which provide the training necessary to skillfully engage the world, focus on pastoral counseling, leadership skills, and community and organizational development.[25]

The Engaged Buddhism track shares some of the core courses and practicums with the M.A.s in Buddhist Language and Contemplative tracks: several courses that survey Buddhist history and culture, two Buddhist text courses, as well as the four meditation practicums, one each semester. On the other hand, the Engaged Buddhism track differs from the other two tracks: it is an experiential track with an academic thread, while the other two degree programs are academic tracks with an experiential thread. The program director, Roger Dorris, characterizes Naropa's Engaged Buddhism program as "blue-collar Dharma" as opposed to the academic study of Buddhism.

The Engaged Buddhism program exposes students to social activism from the time of the Buddha to modern Buddhist movements in Asia and the West. The program stresses alternative models of society (monasteries, practice communities), radical activism, changing social institutions and values (social activism), and social service work. The program is comparable to the pastoral care programs in Christian divinity schools; it includes training in the theory of counseling, clinical pastoral education (CPE), and internships in hospitals, prisons, hospices, and homeless shelters. Students also train in community organizing, leadership, and conflict resolution.

Built into the program is a commitment to meditation practice. The recruitment brochure for the program states: "Buddhism recognizes that social work entails inner work, and that social change and inner change are inseparable. It does not refer to a sectarian, religious view. Sitting meditation is the basis for such inner work, and we invite students from all spiritual traditions to train with us in this way."[26] Drawing from Trungpa's Shambhala teachings and from Tibetan Buddhism, mindfulness opens up raw emotions as a basis for authentic presence and action in the world. Meditation training includes four meditation courses, one per semester, in which students study contemporary meditation manuals, receive instruction, practice, and discuss their evolving understanding. A *dathun*, or month-long intensive group retreat of sitting meditation, is a prerequisite for the program. Naropa understands the commitment to meditation practice as essential for self-discovery and engagement of the world. Dorris stresses the relationship of meditation to experience by stating that one of the things he tries to get across to students is that for the purpose of our own practice and work with our minds, the phenomenal world is our teacher.[27]

The program requires a four-hundred-hour internship, usually in an accredited Clinical Pastoral Education (CPE) setting. This may lead to an additional one-year residency for chaplaincy certification in hospitals, long-term care facilities, hospices, or prisons. The Engaged Buddhism program is in the process of developing a program for hospice-caregivers. In time, the program will develop further specializations in various kinds of community organization.

In addition to program director Roger Dorris, the Engaged Buddhism adjunct faculty includes Roshi Bernard Glassman, Dr. Vincent Harding of Illif School of Theology, Sulak Sivaraksa of the International Network of Engaged Buddhists, Joan Halifax of the Peacemaker Order, and other politically active Buddhists. Each semester, workshops are offered on topics of engaged Buddhist social action or pastoral care.

Much of the program's goal is to understand and analyze human suffering. The Engaged Buddhism recruitment brochure states,

> The program trains the student to work with suffering from the contemplative ground of nonviolence and compassionate presence. It provides the student with leadership skills, including personal awareness, group process, conflict resolution, and community development.[28]

Courses, meditation practicums, and field placements stress the Mahayana principle that the suffering of others is also one's own suffering and that the violence of others is also one's own violence. Engaged Buddhists do not turn away from suffering but learn from suffering in order to transform it. By integrating meditative practice with Mahayana principles, the program seeks a grassroots contemplative activism, or what Ken Jones describes as "transcendental activism."[29] The goal is not to promote a quietist

Buddhism or a privatized practice, but to provide students with learning opportunities to engage the world before enlightenment, and to integrate meditative practice and social activism. Dorris reiterates that the program attempts to place students into the world before attaining enlightenment:

> It is by working with the world that we learn how to wake up personally, and by waking up personally we learn how to work with the world. Even the Buddha said that enlightenment would never be complete until it included others.[30]

Like many of other degree programs at Naropa, the Engaged Buddhism program embodies Shambhala teachings. The secular becomes the sacred ground for awareness and transformation. It does not matter if students are arranging flowers, writing a poem, sculpting, counseling, protesting toxic waste dumps, providing a hospice, or feeding the homeless, as long as they bring awareness, gentleness, nonaggression, compassion, and genuine action to transform society, culture, and the world.[31] Naropa prepares students to encounter and challenge a wide range of social and cultural issues: aging and dying, rapid global secularization, economic development, rampant materialism, and social and environmental problems.

Engaged Learning: An Epistemic Shift

Naropa advertises its unique stress on contemplative education: "The goals of contemplative education are to deepen students' knowledge of themselves and their place in the contemporary world, to develop and strengthen personal discipline within a specific field of study, and to nurture a desire to contribute to the world with understanding and compassion."[32] Naropa's curriculum of contemplative education develops Buddhist virtues of openness, pluralism, and eschewing dogmatism. It has included other contemplative religious traditions while remaining Buddhist to the core, attempting to integrate contemplative education and its liberal arts programs.

Naropa's contemplative education reflects an epistemic shift in higher education toward what may be called a holistic paradigm of knowledge. Through meditation, practitioners can come to greater self-understanding, and learn how they can change themselves and their situations. Naropa envisions education as a means to learn about self and the world, while developing contemplative practice and developing an ethic of compassion. The 1997 Spirituality in Education Conference at Naropa brought together participants with an educational vision congruent with the goals of contemplative education. Many of the keynote speakers share an educational vision congruent with Naropa's contemplative learning philosophy. The faculty included Tenzin Gyatso, the fourteenth Dalai Lama, who "represents the sanity and the articulation of engaged spirituality within the context of general, non-sectarian culture," according to the conference press release. "'Kindness is my religion' the Dalai Lama states, and his teachings of awareness, compassion, and interdependence go directly to the heart of the conference's purpose."[33]

Each day the conference was organized around a particular theme: "Sacredness: The Ground of Learning," "Pluralism and Identity," "Relationship and Community," and "Tradition and Innovation." The purpose was to bring together scholars, students, and spiritual and community leaders to reassess the place of spirituality within contemporary education. The conference listed recommended readings online that provide a vision of holistic education. These suggested readings all imagine holistic models of education based on an epistemological model that unites reflection and practice for social engagement. One of the conference speakers, Parker Palmer, wrote that people "have been schooled in a way of knowing that treats the world as dissected and manipulated, a way of knowing that gives us power over the world."[34] Students are taught to keep their distance, to be objective, and to compete. For Palmer, a spiritual learning environment makes connections between self and the world, allowing space for personal development.

> The goal of knowledge arising from love is the reunification and reconstruction of broken selves and worlds. A knowledge born of compassion aims not at exploiting and manipulating creation but at reconciling the world to itself. The mind motivated by compassion reaches out to know as the heart reaches out to love. Here the act of knowing is an act of love, the act of entering and embracing the reality of the other, of allowing the other to enter and embrace our own. In such knowing we know and are known as members of one community, and our knowing becomes a way of reweaving that community's bonds.[35]

In her keynote speech, Buddhist practitioner and anthropologist Joan Halifax compared learning to a process of initiation with three phases: severance, threshold, and return. Students ideally separate from the familiar, enter into the threshold where boundaries of self are tested and broken, and return to the world with a spirit of engagement. Halifax envisioned a model of education that includes the individual and the community:

> We have to ask of our educational system, What does it means to develop an ethic of love, of compassion? How can we educate our people so they return to the community with their love and compassion renewed? How

can we open our young to the unknown? Our education in this time needs to be fundamentally about redemption. It must teach us how to selflessly offer ourselves for the well being of others. We need to revision education in the West in the twenty-first century as a way to enter the unknown, bear witness to joy and suffering, and heal ourselves and the world.[36]

Palmer, Halifax, and other conference faculty challenged the spiritual aridness of academic institutions, including departments of religious studies, which focus on historical and scientific research while forgetting the transformational value of learning and teaching.

ENGAGED EDUCATION AND
CONTEMPLATIVE SOCIAL ACTION

The Naropa Institute promotes a bold pedagogy of "grassroots Dharma." Its programs aim to unite theory and practice for personal, social, cultural, and environmental transformation. It is difficult to teach compassion in the classroom, but Naropa attempts to provide a learning environment whereby students may experience or discover compassion through contemplative self-awareness, personal mentoring, and experiential attempts to integrate the Shambhala vision of discovering the sacred in the everyday. Compassion is an experience of profound connectedness that breaks down the barriers between self, other human beings, the social world, and the ecosphere.

Naropa is currently exploring ways in which Buddhist practices and principles can be applied in the search for new global paradigms for social, cultural, and ecological transformation. How may we judge and evaluate the grass roots initiatives of Naropa's contemplative education? Ignatius Loyola, founder of the Jesuit Order, taught that practitioners could judge the validity of contemplative experience by an analytic method that he called "discernment of spirits." Discernment of spirits judges contemplative experience by the fruits that it produces—a principle with which many Mahayana Buddhists would agree. Let me briefly apply such a criterion to Naropa's contemplative education programs as socially engaged learning.

In its institutional self-study, Naropa enumerates a set of goals that can be applied as criteria for evaluating the performance of engaged education:

1. To enrich the intellectual and cultural life of Boulder/Denver by offering classes, lectures, concerts, workshops, exhibitions, symposia, conferences, and other special events to the general public;

2. To communicate our educational process, development, and models to relevant outside communities, through such activities as the publication of articles, magazines, journals and books by faculty, staff and students;

cultivation of relationships with peers at other institutions; participation in professional conferences; and the development of new association and organizations relevant to the institute's work; and

3. To foster and maintain communication and dialogue with individuals, groups, and associations who share similar interests, as essential to the vitality and freshness of the intellectual and artistic life of the institute.[37]

Institutionally, Naropa is an integral part of the cultural and educational life of the Boulder community through ongoing theater performances, the continuing education program, and its summer institute. It has carved out a unique niche in the continuing education market, offering more than one hundred courses and weekend workshops that focus on personal enrichment, spirituality, and creativity. It differs from the University of Colorado's continuing education program by concentrating not on vocational skills but on a range of courses from creative writing to environmental issues and holistic health. In addition to the Spirituality in Education Conference, Naropa also hosted the Body and Soul Conference, the Sixth Annual Somatic Psychology Symposium, the Fourth Annual Transpersonal Counseling Conference, and the five-week summer writing program. Naropa has a high cultural and educational profile in the Boulder community.

Many Naropa graduates work in the arts, academia, social services, and the healing disciplines such as psychotherapy and massage. If Naropa's contemplative curriculum is education for the development of personal compassion, then the results will be measurable in the present and future. Here I will note some of the successes of Naropa education.

Connie Holden, the executive director of the Boulder County Hospice program, describes how important Naropa volunteers are for carrying out everyday hospice services. Naropa graduates are prominent in staffing the Boulder AIDS programs, long-term care facilities, home care management programs such as Copper Mountain, pre-schools, and mental health facilities. Clinical Pastoral Education certification has enabled Naropa students to work in hospitals, hospices, prisons, and homeless shelters. Moreover, Naropa is producing environmental leaders who are trained in the natural and social sciences with leadership skills in conflict management, diversity training, dialogue training and ethics.

Further assessment of Naropa's contemplative education programs would require periodic impact studies on Boulder County's social services, long-term facilities, the performing and fine arts, and mental health facilities. Perhaps alumni tracking will provide data for follow-up studies of Naropa graduates in these areas.

Socially engaged Buddhism at Naropa is best practiced in some degree of association with fellow Buddhists. Naropa has consciously built linkages with other Buddhist socially engaged and educational networks. It has made connections with the Thai Spirit in Education Movement, the Buddhist Peace Fellowship, and the International Network of Engaged Buddhists (INEB), and continues to collaborate with non-Buddhist activists from other contemplative traditions who are working to address social, economic, political, and ecological issues.

Engaged education, Naropa style, involves bringing together Buddhists of all persuasions and students of many other contemplative traditions in a learning community to educate themselves to respond to global, political, and environmental problems. Naropa engages American culture, addressing its social problems, and its educational philosophy recognizes that social transformation of structures entails inner or contemplative work. Social change and personal change are inseparable, and Naropa's contemplative educational programs aim to unite theory and practice for personal and social transformation.

NOTES

1. The Naropa Institute, *Engaged Buddhism: Master of Arts in Buddhist Studies* (recruitment brochure, n.d.).

2. Webster's *New Collegiate Dictionary* (Springfield, MA: A. Merriam-Webster, 1975) relates the verb *engage* to the French *engagé,* "being actively involved in or committed especially to political concerns."

3. Rita Gross, *Buddhism After Patriarchy* (Albany: State University of New York Press, 1993), pp. 17–54.

4. Christopher S. Queen and Sallie B. King, eds., *Engaged Buddhism: Buddhist Liberation Movements in Asia* (Albany: State University of New York Press, 1996).

5. See these websites for information on the Spirit in Education Movement and the International Network of Engaged Buddhists: <http://www.bpf/ineb. html>, Buddhist Peace Fellowship <http://www.igc.org/bpf/>, Nyingmapa Institute <http://www.nyingma.org/inst.html>, Dharma Realm Buddhist University <http://www.drba.org/>.

6. Robert E. Goss, "Buddhist Studies at Naropa: Sectarian or Academic?" in *American Buddhism: Methods and Findings in Recent Scholarship*, ed. Duncan Ryuken Williams and Christopher S. Queen (Surrey, U.K.: Curzon Press, 1999).

7. Christopher S. Queen, introduction, *Engaged Buddhism: Buddhist Liberation Movements in Asia*, p. 23.

8. Rick Fields, *How the Swans Came to the Lake* (Boston: Shambhala Publications, 1992), pp. 316–18.

9. Rick Fields, "Mindstreaming," *Yoga Journal* 121 (April 1995): 4.

10. Chogyam Trungpa, *Shambhala: The Sacred Path of the Warrior* (Boston: Shambhala Publications, 1984). See also Jeremy Hayward, *Sacred World: A Guide to Shambhala Warriorship in Daily Life* (New York: Bantam Books, 1995). On treasure texts, see Janet R. Gyatso, "Drawn from the Tibetan Treasury: The gTer ma Literature," in *Tibetan Literature: Studies in Genre*, ed. José Ignacio Cabezón and Roger R. Jackson (Ithaca, NY: Snow Lion Publications, 1996), pp. 146–69.

11. Geoffrey Samuel, *Civilized Shamans: Buddhism in Tibetan Societies* (Washington, D.C.: Smithsonian Institute, 1993), pp. 346–49 and 537–43. In personal conversation, both Judith Simmer-Brown and Reginald Ray placed Trungpa in the Rimé tradition of nineteenth-century Tibet. The Vajradhatu does likewise: see "Shambhala Vision" on the Vajradhatu website <http://www.shambhala.org/int/vision.html>.

12. Tibetan scholar David Seyfort Ruegg has argued that this rendering is inadequate: "In fact this Rimé movement was not exactly eclectic but universalistic (and encyclopedic), *rimé (pa)* (the antonym of *risu ch'ed-pa*) meaning unbounded, all-embracing, unlimited, and also impartial." D. Seyfort Ruegg, "A Tibetan Odyssey: A Review Article," *Journal of the Royal Asiatic Society* 2 (1989): 310.

13. See Samuel, *Civilized Shamans*, pp. 546–51.

14. Ibid, pp. 344–49.

15. See Edwin Bernbaum, *The Way to Shambhala* (New York: Anchor, 1980).

16. Trungpa, *The Sacred Path of the Warrior*, p. 27.

17. Trungpa expands on his usage of warriorship: "Warriorship here does not refer to making war on others....Here the word warrior is taken from the Tibetan *pawo*, which means 'one who is brave.' Warriorship in this context is the tradition of human bravery or the tradition of fearlessness." Ibid., p. 28.

18. Hayward describes the practice of warriorship, *Sacred Worlds*, pp. 49–189. He characterizes the application of warriorship as authentic action in the world, ibid., pp. 195–244.

19. Taped interview with Judith Simmer-Brown, March 15, 1997.

20. The Naropa Institute, *Institutional Self-Study Report*, March 1995, p. 3.

21. Ibid., p. 25.

22. Ibid., p. 8.

23. Naropa's study abroad programs are similar to Antioch College's semester in Bodh Gaya. Naropa has recently added a new overseas program in Bhutan.

24. See, for example, Anne Waldman and Andrew Schelling, *Disembodied Poetics* (Santa Fe: University of New Mexico Press, 1995).

25. The Naropa Institute, *Engaged Buddhism*, recruitment brochure, p. 2.

26. Ibid., p. 2.

27. Taped interview with Roger Dorris, March 10, 1997.

28. The Naropa Institute, *Engaged Buddhism*, recruitment brochure, p. 2.

29. Ken Jones, *The Social Face of Buddhism* (London: Wisdom Publications, 1989), p. 169.

30. Taped interview with Roger Dorris, March 10, 1997.

31. In a number of interviews, when I suggested the term "contemplative in action" from Jesuit spirituality, most interviewees concurred that term aptly described the orientation of Naropa's educational philosophy.

32. 1996 Peterson's Report, Princeton, New Jersey.

33. Lisa Trank, Press Release, Spirituality in Education Conference.

34. Parker J. Palmer, *To Know as We Are Known* (New York: HarperCollins, 1993), p. 2.

35. Ibid., p. 8.

36. *Spirituality in Education Online*,<http://csf.Colorado.edu/sine/sat/halifax2.html>.

37. The Naropa Institute, *Institutional Self-Study Report*, March 1995, p. 31.

THE ANGULIMALA LINEAGE:
BUDDHIST PRISON MINISTRIES

Virginia Cohn Parkum and J. Anthony Stultz

SOCIALLY ENGAGED BUDDHISM IN THE WEST has taken many paths as Buddhists seek "to apply the ancient teachings to the challenges of modern life."[1] One such path, chaplaincy services and related ministries in the criminal justice system, has its roots in the canonical and historical foundations of the Buddhist tradition.

Early texts and later commentaries are replete with references to the efficacy of the Dharma (the teachings of the Buddha) in overcoming harmful behavior rooted in the three poisons of greed, hatred, and delusion. Indeed, the greatest Buddhist saints are often those who began with the greatest defilements.[2]

The criminal justice systems of the West, with their huge bureaucracies and complex regulations, present great challenges to those on the inside: inmates, staff, and volunteers; and those on the outside: society members in general.[3] Buddhist ministries in the criminal justice system have been extensive and at times very effective. Virtually all the major traditions are currently involved. Buddhist challenges to prison policies have gone all the way to the U.S. Supreme Court. Inmate programs range from providing traditional teachings, creating zendos and Buddha groves (outdoor meditation areas), to giving courses in meditative techniques. Pressure groups have been created and protest actions carried out. Networks are forming in attempts to coordinate activities and share resources and information. Yet this has largely been hidden from sight, like the danger-filled jungle trail along which these activities originated—in Shakyamuni Buddha's conversion of the serial killer Angulimala, "Necklace of Severed Fingers."

CANON, COMMENTARY, AND HISTORY

He walked slowly down a quiet road. The day was coming to an end. Shepherds and plowmen who crossed his path earlier in the day had told him

347

of the danger he might encounter on this dusty highway. He did not deny what they said, or even pause to argue. He simply bowed and continued silently on his way.

Night was falling and the killer spotted his prey. He followed the traveler just yards away, hidden by the trees and brush. His pulse raced and his fevered brain squirmed in his skull like a toad. He needed but one more finger to complete the necklace he would present to his evil teacher to get back in his good graces, having been betrayed by jealous fellow students. He would have killed his own mother, on her way to visit him, had not this stranger come along.

The pace began to quicken. Perhaps the traveler had sensed that he was being stalked. The dried remains of severed fingers swung about the neck of the killer in a macabre necklace as he broke into a run. Sweat dripped into his sunken eyes as he became enraged by the evasion of the traveler. Perhaps it was the heat, or the glare of the moon, but with each step he took, the traveler seemed to retreat farther away. Violent thoughts and chaotic emotions raced through his mind as he drew his sword to decapitate the traveler. He ran even faster and then in frustrated desperation he screamed at the robed figure that eluded him, "Stop, monk! Stop!"

The world came to a halt. The silent traveler stopped, turned slowly and, like a compassionate father to this prodigal son, spoke, "I have stopped, Angulimala, you stop too."[4]

Thus begins the story of the Buddha's disciple Angulimala. He is converted to the Dharma by the simple words and powerful presence of the Holy One. He awakens to the interdependent nature of reality. Angulimala repents, grows in wisdom, and reaps the fruit of his karma. He is steadfast and finally attains the Way.

This tale from Buddhist scriptures is the first evidence of a relationship between the Dharma and those who commit offenses against society. Angulimala was later instructed by the Buddha to save a woman in painful childbirth, for whom Angulimala had felt great compassion, by telling the truth about his Noble Birth (ordination). The woman and child lived, and henceforth Angulimala had less difficulty in his alms-rounds collecting food from a still-wary populace.[5] He was pelted with stones but was told by the Blessed One to bear it, as he was experiencing here and now the ripening of karma that he might otherwise have experienced in millennia in hell.[6] He became an *arahant*, a noble one assured of enlightenment. His story inspires both prisoners and Buddhists involved in the criminal justice system today, as exemplified by the British organization Angulimala discussed below.[7]

Angulimala's tale was taken from an early source in the Pali scriptures known as the *Middle Length Sayings*. Elsewhere Shakyamuni points to poverty as one of the causes of immorality and crime.[8] He teaches that trying to suppress crime through punishment alone was ultimately futile, like trying to hold back water with a dam. The barrier may temporarily hold back the water, but there is always the threat that the waters will rise and the dam will break. Shakyamuni teaches that in order to eradicate crime, the economic conditions that cause it should be removed.[9]

Many of the verses in the *Dhammapada* (The Path of Morality) contain admonitions against killing and anger: "All beings tremble before danger, all fear death. When a man considers this, he does not kill or cause to kill" (v. 129); "Watch for anger of the body: let the body be self-controlled. Hurt not with the body, but use your body well" (v. 231).[10] Anger and killing remain central themes in Buddhist ethical texts up to the most recent writings today.

The edicts of the Indian Buddhist emperor Ashoka (third century B.C.E.) contain specific instructions for reducing violence and revenge against humans and animals, possibly a reaction to his own remorse at causing the slaughter of over one hundred thousand in the battle of Kalinga. Legend has it that a beggar, stepping out of a blood-red river while holding a dead child asks, "Mighty king, you are able to take so many thousands of lives. Surely you can give back one life—to this dead child?"[11] Capital punishment was not abolished in Ashoka's edicts, though the condemned were granted three days to meditate in order to gain the next world and for relatives to appeal the sentence, an unprecedented procedure (Pillar Inscription, Edict IV).[12]

The great Indian Buddhist philosopher Nagarjuna (second century C.E.) wrote in his *Jewel Garland of Royal Councils* specific instructions to his student, King Udayi, on how to deal with the problem of crime.[13] He exhorted the king to institute the following mandates: a compassionate social welfare system to keep people from being driven to crimes of desperation; a reasonable, well-educated, virtuous, and experienced justice system; and the abolition of capital punishment, as the taking of one life should not be followed by taking another. Banishment is recommended even for "those murderers, whose sins are horrible"; criminals should be treated nonviolently, like wayward sons who may eventually be rehabilitated.[14]

Ashvaghosha discusses the means for overcoming lures to criminal or harmful behavior, mindfulness meditation: "He who has established mindfulness as a guard at the doors of his mind cannot be overpowered by the passions, as a well-guarded city cannot be conquered by the enemy....Attracted by evil are men, and upon their own true weal they turn their back; regarding the perils that are so close to them, they feel no apprehension. All that is due to lack of mindfulness."[15]

The *Bodhicharyavatara (Guide to the Bodhisattva Way of Life)* of Shantideva, a Buddhist master at the monastic university of Nalanda, India, in the eighth century, contains these thoughts: "Abandon evildoing, practice virtue, subdue your mind."[16] Anger and the results of anger are also touched on: "No evil is there similar to hatred..." In his commentary the Dalai Lama notes, "As a destructive force there is nothing as strong as anger."[17]

The Vajrayana tradition of Tibet includes stories of the conversion of humans and transcendental beings, helpers on the higher path to tantric realization. The famous saint Milarepa (1040-1123) had been a sorcerer but sought the transformative teachings of the Dharma after his magic killed thirty-five of his own relatives. After many ordeals he became a perfectly enlightened adept, travelling and teaching thousands of people.[18]

Mahakala, the meditation deity, was converted from the demonic realm by the enlightened personifications of wisdom and compassion, and was then called into service as a protector of the Dharma.[19] The fierce Lhamo, also originally a hostile demon, is the female aspect of Mahakala and likewise a guardian of the Dharma. She is also a special protectress of the Dalai Lamas.[20]

The Zen tradition, whose masters were often reformers, is filled with records and stories of criminal behavior.[21] Sengai (1750-1838) deliberately committed an offense for which a gardener had just been condemned to death—damaging the lord's prized chrysanthemums. Appearing at the castle the next day Sengai declared: "I have cut down all the plants, so please have me killed. But which is more important, the lives of humans or flowers?" Upon reflecting on this the lord released Sengai, took measurers to help local farmers, and also gave him a favorite plum tree.[22]

The following few simple tales told by famous masters illustrate the general attitude of the historical Zen community toward those who commit crimes.

Shichiri: A criminal sneaks into a temple and threatens the master Shichiri. The master does not resist but instead offers the thief all that he has. He points out to the thief that he should say "thank you" for the gifts he has been given. A little later the thief is apprehended and when they confront him with the master, Shichiri says that no crime has been committed and that the items taken were given freely as gifts. "Laying down his butcher's knife, the thief became a Buddha." After he had finished his prison term, the man went to Shichiri and became his disciple.[23]

Bankei: A criminal is taken into the sangha. Items begin to disappear and the community appeals to the master to remove the thief. Bankei weeps and says that all may leave if they wish, but that he cannot turn the thief out. If he rejects him now, who will accept him? With that the thief confesses, suddenly understanding the nature of right and wrong.[24]

Rashomon: This story takes place at the great city gate of medieval Kyoto during a great famine. In this tale two crimes are compared showing that a crime of desperation is based on unjust circumstances, whereas a crime of cruelty is based solely on hatred.

Daigan: One night while the master is reading in his study, a thief enters the room and threatens him. Daigan gives the thief all that he has and as the thief beats a hasty retreat, the master stops him with a shout, "When you leave, please shut the door to keep out the crooks!" With these words the thief is awakened.

Ryokan: One day a thief entered the hut of the master, but he discovered that there was nothing of value to steal. Ryokan insists that he shouldn't go home empty-handed and offers him the coat off his back. The thief runs off into the night leaving the master to lament, "Poor man. If only I could offer him the moon as well."[25] Ryokan also wrote, in direct reflection on these events:

> My zazen platform, my cushion—they made off with both!
> Thieves break into my grass hut, but who dares stop them?
> All night I sit alone by the dark window,
> Soft rain pattering on the bamboo grove.[26]

The Shin tradition also contains directly relevant writings. It teaches self-acceptance and the "notion that we are saved as we are, warts and all."[27] Shinran had a response to those disciples who felt this allowed them to commit evil deliberately as they were saved by the vow of Amida Buddha: "Do not take a liking to poison just because there is an antidote."[28]

This brief compilation, while by no means exhaustive, is foundational to understanding the general attitude of the Buddhist community for the first two millennia. Crime was understood to be the result of the three poisons (delusion, hatred, and greed) manifested in social malaise. From an absolute view, criminals were no worse than anyone else blinded by delusion, hatred and, greed. However, a considerable amount of attention was paid to the relative nature of the crime, and it appears to be the general mind of the early sangha to teach socioeconomic inequities as the cause of most criminal activity.[29] Capital punishment and tortuous imprisonment were anathema to the first precept not to kill. A strong argument can be made that a compassionate attitude toward criminals was advocated. How this was actually embodied is more difficult to ascertain. Certainly Ashoka and Nagarjuna advised the banishment of violent criminals (one of course wonders how this was accepted by the neighboring kingdoms), while Zen communities of China mirrored the Christian monasteries of medieval Europe, often taking in the outcast and banished.[30]

Buddhist engagement in today's criminal justice system can be introduced by a story which, like the tale of Angulimala, sets a precedent for work with prison inmates and staff. Like Angulimala's ministry, it began in an atmosphere of anger and misunderstanding.

The Reverend Hogen Fujimoto teaching at the San Quentin State Prison.
Photo by Isao Tanaka, courtesy Anthony Stultz.

A SURVEY OF BUDDHIST PRISON MINISTRIES

Jodo-Shinshu and the Buddhist Churches of America

Formal Shin Buddhist temples were established in California in 1898/1899 by the sect headquarters in Kyoto, Japan, to serve the large Japanese American immigrant population.[31] In 1942, over 110,000 Japanese American citizens were evacuated from their homes and put in relocation camps in prison-like conditions, not to be released until December 1944. Most Buddhist priests were taken into custody by the Federal Bureau of Investigation on the night of December 7, 1941, immediately following the attack on Pearl Harbor. Released into the camps months later, they were allowed to conduct services and provide what help they could under conditions of extreme deprivation. As prison chaplains must do today, they shared facilities with other denominations, working together on building-use schedules. There are records of one Caucasian Buddhist priest visiting the camps, but that was virtually the only contact and support.[32] Upon release, Buddhists and non-Buddhists quietly rebuilt their shattered lives from the ground up, as so many prisoners must.

Out of this mud grew the lotus-like work of the Reverend Hogen Fujimoto, minister in the (Shin) Buddhist Churches of America (B.C.A.). Headquartered in San Francisco from 1963 through 1979, Fujimoto had been prevented by Japanese authorities from returning to the U.S. during the war, being an American citizen studying in Japan.[33]

The Reverend Fujimoto's work is almost a handbook for effective "lone chaplain" prison practice. From his office he corresponded with hundreds of inmates from all over the U.S. Most of the correspondents were neither Japanese Americans nor B.C.A. members. Inmates looking up Buddhism in directories of organizations came across "Buddhist Churches of America" right at the beginning, a name that sounded as if it represented all of Buddhism. He taught a course in Buddhism at the San Quentin State Prison School of Religions to a multiethnic class for three years until the school closed after an inmate riot. Dharma sessions were held at Soledad Prison, among other locations. Meeting with former inmates after they had been released, he offered emotional support and employment assistance.

The outcome of the Reverend Fujimoto's correspondence with an inmate in the Texas prison system has had wide influence on Buddhist inmates and volunteers ever since. In late 1967, inmate Fred A. Cruz wrote to Fujimoto requesting information on Buddhism. He received it, loved the teachings about Amida and the Pure Land and the Buddha and shared them with other inmates. For this he was placed in a totally dark isolation cell with only two slices of bread daily and a small meal every third day, on and off for several months. He filed a lawsuit, originally written on toilet paper in his solitary confinement cell, which six years later was decided in his favor by the U.S. Supreme Court *(Cruz v. Beto)*.[34] Cruz and Fujimoto corresponded during and after Cruz's release in 1973 and again when the case was won in 1977. Cruz wrote, "Your letters came—precious jewels that I will always treasure. You gave so much without knowing you had given."[35]

Prison Ashram Project

At the time the Texas case was working its way through the legal system, two other pioneers of Buddhist-oriented prison ministry, Bo and Sita Lozoff, were in the process of founding the Prison Ashram Project (1973) and the Human Kindness Foundation in North Carolina. Bo authored the very influential book, *We're All Doing Time*, that describes a threefold ministry dependent as much upon Hindu teachings as those of Buddhism.[36] This ministry includes letter-writing to as many as 18,000 inmates, speaking in the halfway house ashram, and making in-prison presentations, many of which are available as audio or video cassettes.[37] The Prison Ashram Project newsletter goes out to 35,000 families. The Dalai Lama has endorsed this work by letter and a personal visit with the Lozoffs, noting that "kindness and compassion are extremely important in every area of life, whether we are prisoners, prison guards or victims of crime."[38]

Angulimala Comes to Britain

While in the 1970s and 1980s Buddhist prisoners in the U.S. were struggling to establish legal rights to practice, and to receive books, ritual items, and visits from Buddhist ministers and lay persons, inmates in the United Kingdom already had access to these. The Prison Act of 1952 requires the prison service to make provision for prisoners to receive the services of the appropriate Church of England chaplains or visiting ministers of other faiths appointed by an agency of the state to deliver pastoral and religious care to prisoners and staff.[39] Prisoners also have recourse to the European prison rules, which include the statement: "The religious beliefs and moral precepts of the group to which a prisoner belongs shall be respected."[40] Like the U.S., Great Britain has an increasingly culturally diverse population.

In 1984 the Venerable Ajahn Khemadhammo, of the Wat Pah Santidhamma, after serving as a visiting minister for years in many different prisons, founded Angulimala. This has become the most formal organization for visiting ministers in the United Kingdom and a model for American Buddhists seeking to set up a similar organization in the U.S.[41]

This work is supported by Buddhists of all traditions and has made available facilities for the teaching and practice of the Dharma in Her Majesty's prisons. Specifically they recruit, train, and advise visiting chaplains, act in an advisory capacity and as a liaison to the national Prison Service Chaplaincy (a government organization in charge of Her Majesty's chaplaincies), provide aftercare and advisory services for prisoners after release, and publish *The Forest Hermitage Newsletter* in print and on the internet. There are some three hundred Buddhist prisoners in England and Wales served by about forty-five chaplains covering approximately 100 institutions. Women are being recruited to serve in women's prisons, and efforts are being made to extend Angulimala's activities to Scotland, Northern Ireland, and the Channel Islands, which are under separate administration.

Angulimala also trains prison visitors, develops and maintains Buddha groves and shrines in prisons, obtains and distributes reading matter, and offers, through the Buddhist Society and others, correspondence courses and the loan of tapes about Buddhism. Courses are also taught through the auspices of the prison education departments. Prisoners are linked with "pen friends."

The Venerable Ajahn Khemadhammo wrote the authors:

> I always point out that I do not believe in engaged Buddhism or anything like that. I have a responsibility to see that those teachings are available. Here at my monastery the opportunity to hear Buddhist teaching and to practice is available to anyone who cares to come here. Prisoners cannot come here. Prisoners cannot come to the monastery, so the monastery must go to the prisoners. As you will see from the website we aim to make Buddhist teaching and practice available to HM Prisons. If you practice Buddhism you practice mindfulness. If you are mindful you act appropriately—if an opportunity to do something helpful presents itself and you can do it, you do it.[42]

Zen Mountain Monastery

At the same time Buddhist prison involvement was being organized and formalized in England, activity by individual groups and monasteries was increasing in the U.S. Abbot John Daido Loori of the Zen Mountain Monastery, Mount Tremper, New York, received a to-whom-it-may-concern letter from an inmate in the state maximum security facility of Green Haven. The inmate wrote that he was presently incarcerated and had "no money to attain the information that I am asking for in this letter. I have never had the inner peace I have longed for all my life, until now, when I started studying Buddhism."[43]

Abbot Loori responded with a visit. A subsequent attempt to form a sitting group was refused by the prison authorities, who associated Buddhism with the martial arts (kung-fu) and felt it would be a disruptive influence, a misperception Buddhist groups may still encounter when first contacting prison administrators. The inmate pursued this through the New York court system and, when the case was settled a year later, the courts recognized Zen Buddhism as "an acceptable religion within the New York State Prison System," and the Lotus Flower Zendo was established in Green Haven. Zen Mountain Monastery's programs now include inmate correspondence, providing books and audiotapes, a video lending library, and regular trips to New York prisons for *zazen*, talks, services, Buddhist studies, *sesshins*, and annual Buddha's birthday and enlightenment celebrations.

Abbot Loori serves on the Religious Advisory Committee, a council of prison chaplains who meet regularly to discuss the prison system and religious practice. The monastery was requested to serve as an advisor on Buddhist matters to the New York Correctional system and has helped set up Buddhist practice groups in other prisons in the state. The fall 1998 issue of its journal *Mountain Record* was subtitled "Our Prisons."[44]

Upon their release, two Lotus Flower Zendo members have lived at ZMM for a year. This could be a prototype for the kind of post-release follow-up care that several of the prison chaplains interviewed for this study recommended as essential for re-integrating prisoners into society, helping them build new identities as members of a supportive, caring community, including continued meditation practice.

National Buddhist Prison Sangha

Recently the National Buddhist Prison Sangha (NBPS) has been established under the direction of Geoffrey Shugen Arnold Sensei. This networking organization is still in its formative stage, but it is also active. Based on a questionnaire sent to prisoners and sanghas of all denominations, a large database has been compiled. An attempt is made to match prisoners requesting help with someone living within two hundred miles of the facility. Sensei Arnold noted how rapidly word about this has spread through the (male) prisoners' own underground network. Volunteers living near ZMM are trained there, and an effort has been made to see that out-of-area volunteers have sufficient training, based on their responses to the questionnaire.

A retreat with other groups was planned, but insufficient interest led to its being cancelled. Arnold feels that the loose-knit structure of the NBPS is probably appropriate for the times, as each center throughout the U.S. has different resources, traditions, and ways of doing things.

Another NBPS project is publishing a *Training Manual for Zen Buddhist Practice*. Level 1 was issued in 1999. The looseleaf folder includes basic ideas for practicing in a cell, a brief introduction to Zen, and a copy of the Heart Sutra and the Four Great Vows as daily liturgy.

Sensei Arnold also noted that ZMM has no programs as yet in women's facilities, though he hoped to develop them eventually. A number of letters from women were received following the prison issue of *Mountain Record*.

Engaged Zen Foundation

Another prison support group, the Engaged Zen Foundation (EZF), was co-founded in 1994 by the Reverend Kobutsu Kevin Malone, a Rinzai Zen priest who has practiced Buddhism for thirty years. The EZF provides books, advice, Dharma instructors, and correspondence for Buddhist prison meditation groups and zendos.[45] In 1992 Malone, with Liz Potter, set up what became the Dharma Song Zendo in the New York maximum security prison facility at Sing Sing. While some inmates did try to "con" him for funds, and the administration was initially reluctant to accept Zen or any Buddhism, Malone and Potter learned lessons that prepared them to advise volunteers in the future. Since 1996 the Flowering Dogwood Zendo, also founded by Malone, has met in the Adult Diagnostic and Treatment Center in Avenel, New Jersey, a special state prison for sex offenders.

The Engaged Zen Foundation publishes the innovative *Gateway Journal*, dedicated exclusively to meditation practice in prisons. It has a print circulation of three thousand and is available on the internet. It includes the popular "Zen Karmics," a cartoon guide to sitting prison *zazen*, drawn by Duncan Eagleson. EZF is currently designing *A Prisoner's Common Book of Zen* to take the place of materials that the Reverend Malone feels are not really appropriate for beginning prison practitioners. Like Zen Mountain, the EZF material is oriented toward Zen practice. EZF is also involved in death penalty work, which has included Malone becoming the spiritual advisor of an inmate two months before his execution, which Malone attended at the inmate's request. The intense nature of this death row work, which included pleas to the governor and rounds of speaking engagements, left Malone drained at one point, and the regular EZF work suffered somewhat. This too became a lesson for volunteers, and Malone has been asked to write a book about the experience.[46] In May 1998 the Reverend. Malone and Liz Potter were granted a private interview with the Dalai Lama in New York City. His Holiness has since issued a formal declaration supporting a moratorium on the death penalty. Malone continues his very active death row ministry. Funding for the work is urgently needed, however.

Buddhist Peace Fellowship

The Buddhist Peace Fellowship (BPF), headquartered in Berkeley, California, is a nationwide and international umbrella group linking socially concerned members with chapters and activities compatible with their desire to serve. Its prison committee sponsors various criminal justice system activities under its mission statement:

> The Buddha taught one thing: freedom. The mission of the Buddhist Peace Fellowship Prison Project is to work with prisoners and their families, other faith-based organizations, and the public to address the systemic violence within the criminal justice system, and to engage in compassionate action through direct service, education, advocacy and networking.[47]

BPF's quarterly, *Turning Wheel*, is sent free to inmates. It often contains articles of interest to prison volunteers, such as the winter 1999 issue devoted to Buddhist perspectives on the death penalty, as well as news and contact information on Buddhist chaplaincy and other prison programs.

BPF also does issue-related advocacy, such as death penalty vigils and teach-ins. It provides legal advice about, for example, vegetarian questions. BPF's Prison Meditation Network includes over twenty people who work in jails or prisons. It meets monthly at the San Francisco Zen Center and provides training and support to the volunteers. A brochure to describe its program to prison administrators is being developed.[48] A Buddhist sangha at San Quentin is being established. There is already a secular stress reduction class there combining meditation and yoga, under the auspices of the Network.

The San Francisco Zen Center has been designated as an official BPF chapter to integrate the activities of its members with programs in the wider Buddhist community. The Zen Center has started a prisoner correspondence program to help the BPF with its overflow of requests. Some twenty-five volunteers currently write to inmates and send them the Buddhist books they request. They also teach mindfulness courses.[49]

BPF itself is in the process of establishing a prison BASE (Buddhist Alliance for Social Engagement) group. Each member will do direct contact prison work and also network with other community groups focusing on the criminal justice system.

Upaya Prison Program

The Upaya Prison Program is part of the Upaya Peace Institute (Zen Peacemaker Order) of Santa Fe, New Mexico. It sponsors a unique program of teaching mindfulness, peacemaking, and meditation practice in the maximum security penitentiary. It was developed by Laurel Carraher, a psychologist at the penitentiary, and her Zen teacher, Joan Halifax, with the support of the mental health staff. They now work with three prison units and are interested in beginning a program for the staff. The director of the mental health program reports a noticeable reduction in antisocial behavior. For example, one inmate refused to carry out his gang leader's command to kill someone.[50]

Prison Dharma Network/National Prison Hospice Association

Another inter-prison group is the Prison Dharma Network (PDN), founded and run by Fleet Maull, an inmate since 1985.[51] His varied Buddhist background includes a masters degree in Buddhist and Western Psychology, study with Vidyadhara Chogyam Trungpa Rinpoche, Vajrayogini empowerment, and ordination in Bernard Glassman's Zen Peacemaker Order. PDN was founded in 1989 as a nonsectarian Buddhist support network for prisoners and volunteers. Maull corresponds with people across the U.S. and counsels inmates at in his own prison. He writes for several publications and conducts a Dharma study group. PDN is now a Buddhist Peace Fellowship affiliate.

Fleet Maull also established the National Prison Hospice Association. He serves time in the U.S. Medical Center for Federal Prisoners, which is the major hospital for federal prisoners. The pilot program for visiting dying prisoners, many of whom are AIDS patients, has become a professionally authorized hospice training program that offers assistance to establish hospice programs in other prisons.[52]

Vipassana Groups

Vipassana meditation, as taught by the Indian teacher S.N. Goenka and his assistants, has been offered with great success in prisons in India since 1975. The programs, available to both inmates and staff, are movingly documented in the video *Doing Time, Doing Vipassana*.[53] Goenka's approach is nonsectarian, regarding the Dharma as a universal path to liberation.[54] The course is now being offered by the Northwest Vipassana Center, in the North Rehabilitation Facility, a minimum security jail in Seattle. Both a men's and a women's program have been given. The course was presented at the request of the facility's director, Lucia Meijer, who had attended the ten-day *vipassana* course. Results, though not documented in a formal study, have been very positive as reported by prison administrators and counselors. Trained volunteers conduct the program, free of charge. The video *Changing from Inside* shows the course and helps answer questions posed by security and administrative staff members. Sensei Arnold of the National Buddhist Prison Sangha discussed the *vipassana* programs in a February 1999 trip to New Zealand as part of his prison service outreach work.

Soka Gakkai International—USA

Soka Gakkai International—USA is quite active visiting and helping members in prison. Interestingly, its two founders themselves experienced incarceration in Japan during World War II for resisting the war effort and refusing to follow state Shinto worship. Tsunesaburo Makiguchi, imprisoned as a "thought criminal," died there in 1944. Josei Toda studied the *Lotus Sutra* in his cell, experiencing deep realization of buddhahood.[55]

Two SGI initiatives are worthy of particular note. One member, once a prisoner himself, runs a drug rehabilitation program for former inmates, funded by the state of Hawaii.[56] In another, SGI District Leader Janette Stewart responded to an appeal by the Chaplain of the Muncy Prison for Women in Pennsylvania to set up religious services for Buddhist prisoners there.[57] About fifteen women come to each weekly meeting, which includes chanting, study, and discussion. An older inmate who became a Buddhist in prison, learning about it from a short-term SGI prisoner, assists Stewart and is now "like a momma" to the group. The chaplain has seen a marked decrease in the anger level of the inmates who attend the sessions.

Also of interest is the growth of a communication network among women prisoners throughout the country. This resulted from an article about Muncy's SGI program written by the older prisoner for the SGI newsletter. Inmates in other prisons wrote back, replies were sent, and a support network now exists for women prisoners, reducing the sense of isolation unique to that smaller prison population.

Vajrayana Groups

Tibetan ministers like Tharchin Rinpoche and Chagdud Tulku Rinpoche have used empowerment ceremonies to strengthen inmates with a new sense of dignity and a new way of envisioning themselves in relation to their environment. The Vajrayana approach has inspired the death row inmate Jarvis Masters to write *Finding Freedom*, a book about his experiences at San Quentin Prison.[58] Visualization practices such as calling on Red or Green Tara are often mentioned by inmates as being a very potent technique.

The American branch of the international Foundation for the Preservation of the Mahayana Tradition (FPMT) is very active in prison correspondence and book distribution. Their newsletter *Mandala*, available online, features inmate letters and is sent to inmates without cost.[59] Lamas also have visited prisoners at such facilities as Pelican Bay, the maximum security prison in California, though prison regulations now prevent visits there.

Lama Yeshe Wangmo from the Vajrayana Foundation, Hawaii, works extensively with death row inmates on the mainland. As well as visiting them she is involved with publicity efforts, has organized a national prayer wheel, written to the Governor of Arkansas regarding prisoners there, and set up discussion groups in her sangha. Her own teacher, Lama Tharchin Rinpoche, urged her to do something in the social or political arena about the death penalty.[60]

Political Action: The Interfaith Prison Task Force of Boston

Many of the groups discussed above engage in activities to bring about direct changes in the criminal justice system, such as death penalty vigils and letter-writing campaigns. Since so much of what chaplains can do in prison depends upon the policies of the prison boards and on state and federal laws, more effort is needed to organize Buddhists to influence the public policy process. In 1996 Buddhists were instrumental in founding an ongoing lobbying group, the Interfaith Prison Task Force of Boston. The organization was developed under the auspices of the Boston City Mission Society by United Church of Christ Minister Laura Biddle and J. Anthony Stultz, co-author of this study.

Representatives of all faiths are invited to attend. One of the group's goals is to be a support network for members doing prison volunteer work, helping each other with such things as getting admitted to the prison system. Legitimization is very important for programs the prison staff may see as unimportant. The task force also lobbies for such policies as alternative sentencing.

A GROWING LITERATURE

Writing for publication may be seen as another form of social engagement. For activists it serves at least three purposes: spreading information about "skillful means" for carrying out the programs with which they are involved, reaching a broader public to enlist their active or passive support, and spreading knowledge of the Dharma. Scholarly studies of engaged Buddhism reach an interested but relatively self-selected audience. However, their potential for reaching a broader audience is enhanced by the likelihood that they are indexed in on-line research databases and other bibliographic reference tools. In this way they become available through interlibrary loan and form the basis of conference presentation and further scholarly studies.

Popular works are geared to a broader lay audience. An especially successful example is *Altars in the Street* by Melody Ermachild Chavis.[61] This story of the author's Buddhist practice, her heroic struggle against the drug culture in her neighborhood in Oakland, California, and her legal work as a private investigator for death sentence appeals such as that of Jarvis Masters became a featured selection of the Quality Paperback Book Club, receiving a special write-up in its widely distributed member sales monthly.

Various publishers such as Wisdom Publications, Parallax Press, and Snow Lion Publications provide materials to prisoners or prison libraries. This is a very important activity, as reading is the way most prisoners spend their free time.[62] Reading material is frequently requested by prisoners in their letters to the various Buddhist groups.

VOLUNTEER TRAINING

Training volunteers and employees is an important component of Buddhist prison work. Not all centers provide the quality training for its volunteers that Zen Mountain Monastery and Angulimala do. A major Buddhist effort in this direction is The Naropa Institute's Master of Arts Program in Engaged Buddhism. Sixty credits must be taken in such courses as Death and Loss, meditation techniques, Pastoral Care, and Buddhism and Social Action. The required "Engaged Buddhism: Working in the Community" is a four-hundred-hour internship supervised by the Association for Clinical Pastoral Education that can lead to chaplaincy certification. Internships can take place in local correctional settings, the National Prison Hospice Association, and the Shambhala Prison Community.

Many sanghas sponsor prison volunteer work. Only a brief survey can be given here. The Kwan Um School of Korean Zen has a history of providing prison ministry, particularly in Massachusetts, Indiana, and Florida. K.C. Walpole, as a member of the Cambridge Zen Center, began such a meditation ministry to area prisons. The center has practice groups at the medium and minimum facilities of the State Prison in Shirley, Massachusetts. The Toronto Buddhist Temple has a prison ministry. Robert Aitken Roshi, a BPF

International Advisory Board member, did prison visitations. Of special note is the Maitai Zendo in New Zealand, which runs an anger management program that people in the criminal justice system may attend by court order or by choice.

CONCLUSION

Engaged Buddhism provides for fresh applications of the Dharma to social problems, specifically an understanding of our socio-economic status as a part of the interdependent nature of existence. This approach understands the four noble truths (anguish and the release from anguish) and the four immeasurables (loving-kindness, compassion, unselfish joy, and equanimity) operating on the social as well as the personal levels.

The activities of Western Buddhists in the criminal justice system reflect this outlook and have contributed greatly to its development. These activities are based on a firm groundwork of Buddhist teachings and the inspiration of Buddhist figures throughout history. One prisoner wrote of a new prison study group: "We decided upon the name Milarepa Buddhist Community because the example of Je Mila is especially dear and relevant to us."[63]

Virtually all of the Asian lineages and traditions are actively represented in prison ministries and related work in locations throughout the Western world. A blending of practice techniques often occurs. Inmates may try different paths as these become known through readings, fellow inmates, and volunteers. This variety facilitates the acceptance and spread of Buddhism in the multicultural prison and societal environment. Cartoons from the 1950s and 60s show "White" Buddhists in Zen robes, floating off in meditation. Today's popular culture likewise is catching up with images of the "new" Buddhism. For example, Tina Turner, an SGI member, is shown chanting in a redemptive scene in the biographical film *What's Love Got to Do With It*.[64]

Meditation techniques are sometimes developed and presented in prisons as merely a stress reduction program. Yet in observations of prisoner behavior over time, meditation is most effective when linked with the precepts, vows, and "full practice" of a Buddhist tradition. Chaplains with lengthy prison or halfway house experience are in a good position to observe this. One stated flatly: "The vows are the glue that holds it all together." An inmate wrote Sensei Arnold: "Recently I found myself on the receiving end of a physical assault during which I chose not to fight back...and only block his blows. This is in no small part due to my vow not to harm anyone."[65] However, stress reduction education, even without Buddhist teachings, can reduce tension levels among prisoners and between prisoners and staff, an admirable goal in itself. Nonsectarian or even nonreligious approaches are often favored by prison staff as an acceptable way for Buddhists to offer their services. Organizations and volunteers must decide how to direct their efforts most effectively and efficiently, and which ways are acceptable to their tradition and belief structure.

Prisons are a unique place to practice. For the inmates, large blocks of time are available. The challenging environment of noise and threats can add an urgency to the practice not felt in the comforts of "civilian" life.

Likewise the reality of working in prisons has a profound effect on the chaplains and other Buddhist volunteers. FPMT's Venerable Thubten Kunsel writes of the inmates: "Without a doubt, every one of them has inspired me to practice more strongly, has helped me know there is no time to waste."[66] Another stated, remembering the eyes of an inmate staring back at him as he peered inside the small opening to the isolation room known as the hole: "Something inside me had changed. Something in those prison walls had gotten inside. Those eyes were not the eyes of a stranger, they were my own."[67]

The acceptance of voluntarism as a societal value in the United States and Great Britain greatly facilitates prison volunteer work once the need is known. It also fits well into Engaged Buddhist rhetoric.

Networking and support organizations are being founded and formalized. New communication technology not available at any other time in history greatly aids this. Whether this results in more cooperative and unified actions remains to be seen. There is an indication that groups may communicate, and some will remain committed to the proven ways of their traditions, while others experiment with innovative ideas and practices. Both ways may well continue to work side by side, each serving its own clientele.

A formal organization is useful in working with criminal justice institutions and is sometimes necessary for admission to and certification in the prison. Sitting around a conference table as well as in the meditation hall is a feature of socially engaged work in its most constructive form. Legitimization is vital for long-term results.

The effect of Buddhist ministries and other activities in the criminal justice system has been both subtle and profound. Legal cases involving prisoners' rights to practice as Buddhists, obtain implements for worship, and receive and share Buddhist literature are now cited as precedents by prisoners in other states and from other religious groups. Meditation practices are receiving wider acceptance as the positive results become known. This in turn may increase Buddhism's acceptance by the wider population.

All the activities in which Buddhists have been engaged in the criminal justice system—letter writing, material provision, zendo support, visitation and instruction, meditation courses, volunteer ministry, AIDS hospice work, and legal aid concerning freedom of religion—are likely to be of increasing importance. Meanwhile, funding for prison programs is decreasing. The legislative and rhetorical climate in the U.S. as the new century dawns continues to shift toward seeing prisons as warehouses rather than rehabilitation centers.[68] Repercussions of the repeal of the Religious Freedom Restoration Act of 1993 in 1997 may be seen in the decreased support for religious, social, and educational programs and in reduced compulsion for administrators to pay special attention to requests of inmates based on religious considerations.[69] Georgia has just severely limited all services to prisoners, including cutting the GED (high school equivalency exam) training programs and allowing religious services for only "major religions."

In such a climate, the need for voluntary provision of support to inmates presents Buddhist groups with both a challenge and an opportunity. The chance to provide, for free, programs the institutions can no longer provide themselves due to lack of funds or changing policies offers a potential opening for increased service both to the prisoners and staff of the institutions and to society at large. One development might be the creation of halfway homes that incorporate the elements of a traditional Buddhist monastery. This would help to provide a safe and empowering environment and would facilitate what is known by experts to be the highest deterrent to recidivism, new personal and interpersonal associations. The Engaged Zen Foundation is seeking funding for such a project.

Buddhists have a unique opportunity to present themselves and their teachings to societies hungry for a new point of view, particularly a religious view that is not alien to modern life but in fact is congruent with much of our scientific and psychological understanding of the world today. It is our hope that Buddhists of every stripe will join with other persons of good faith to serve those who suffer in prisons. For the promise of such work is nothing less than the peace and freedom offered by the Buddha to Angulimala:

> Who once lived in recklessness
> And then was reckless nevermore,
> He shall illuminate the world
> Like the full moon unveiled by a parting cloud.[70]

ACKNOWLEDGMENT

We wish to thank the reference, interlibrary loan, circulation, and technical services staff of the Heindel Library, Penn State Harrisburg, for their invaluable and unceasingly courteous help; Elson Snow, Buddhist Churches of

America, for his kind aid in recommending and locating difficult to obtain references; all the busy people who agreed to be interviewed; Terri Jansen for technological and other sustenance; Nancy Eichelberger for typing under deadline pressure; Rebecca Stultz for editing; and Jodie Nicotra for inspiration.

NOTES

1. Damien Keown, *Buddhism: A Very Short Introduction* (New York: Oxford University Press, 1996), p. 130.

2. Reginald A. Ray, "The Temptress and the Monk," in Samuel Bercholz and Sherab Chodzin Kohn, eds., *Entering the Stream: An Introduction to the Buddha and His Teachings* (New York: Oxford University Press, 1993), pp. 259–66.

3. For an overview of various Western criminal justice systems, see William L. Selke, *Prisons in Crisis* (Bloomington: Indiana University Press, 1993).

4. For a blend of story and scripture, see Hellmuth Hecker, *Angulimala: A Murderer's Road to Sainthood* (Kandy, Sri Lanka: Buddhist Publication Society, 1984); for scripture see the section on the *Angulimala Sutta* in Bhikku Bodhi, ed., *The Middle Length Discourses of the Buddha* (Boston: Wisdom Publications, 1996), pp. 710–17.

5. The stories are found in Hecker, *Angulimala,* pp. 16–17.

6. Ibid., p. 19.

7. Interestingly, the *Mahavagga*, part of the *Vinaya Pitaka* (monastic rule) texts, states that no robber after Angulimala who wears the emblems of his deeds can be a monk (I, 41), nor can robbers escaped from jail (I, 42), nor proclaimed robbers (I, 43), people punished by scourging or branding (I, 44, 45), debtors (I, 46), or runaway slaves (I, 47). T. W. Rhys Davids and Hermann Oldenberg, eds., *Vinaya Texts: Part I* (Delhi: Motilal Banarsidass, 1968), pp. 196–99. This would seem to preclude some of the prison work done by Buddhist groups today. However, with regard to the discipline for the Hinayana monastics, this collection of rules was composed for those who were leaving society and taking on a new identity as a community devoted to the path of the *arahant*. The Theravadin communities developed a canon law that was probably written in the second century B.C.E. This canon, which has largely fallen into disuse within contemporary Theravadin life, was very strict and replete with sectarian bias, a rejection of lay life, distortions, additions, and omissions. In time, a schism developed which eventually led to the creation of the Mahayana community, which had a more lay-oriented approach to the Dharma and was not obsessed with the keeping of monastic rules. See Richard H. Robinson and Willard L.

Johnson, *The Buddhist Religion* (Belmont, CA: Wadsworth, 1982), pp. 39–42 and 65–67.

8. John Daido Loori, *The Heart of Being* (Boston: Charles E. Tuttle, 1996), pp. 2–10.

9. Phillip K. Eidmann, *Young People's Introduction to Buddhism* (San Francisco, CA: Buddhist Churches of America, 1996), pp. 1–10.

10. *The Dhammapada*, trans. Juan Mascaro (New York: Penguin Books, 1973), pp. 54, 69.

11. Gita Mehta, "Ashoka, Beloved of the Gods," in *Tricycle* 8.2 (winter 1998): 22.

12. Vincent A. Smith, *Asoka: The Buddhist Emperor of India*, 2d ed. (Delhi: S. Chand & Co., 1964), p. 186.

13. Jeffrey Hopkins, *The Precious Garland* (London: Allen and Unwin, 1975).

14. For a more detailed discussion of sources dealing with the death penalty, see Damien Horigan, "A Buddhist Perspective on the Death Penalty," in *Turning Wheel* (winter 1999): 16–19.

15. Nyanaponika Thera, *The Heart of Buddhist Meditation: A Handbook of Mental Training Based on the Buddha's Way of Mindfulness* (New York: Citadel Press, 1962), p. 195. This book also contains an anthology of Pali and Sanskrit texts dealing with mindfulness as taught by the Buddha in the *Satipatthana Sutta*, the method for training the mind to handle life's routine problems as well as deliverance from greed, hatred, and delusion.

16. Tenzin Gyatso, the Fourteenth Dalai Lama, *A Flash of Lightening in the Dark Night: A Guide to the Bodhisattva's Way of Life* (Boston: Shambhala Publications, 1994), p. 3.

17. Ibid., p. 52.

18. Robert A. F. Thurman, *Essential Tibetan Buddhism* (Edison, NJ: Castle Books, 1997), pp. 28–31.

19. John Blofeld, *The Tantric Mysticism of Tibet* (New York: Arkana Press, 1992), pp. 40–43.

20. Thurman, *Essential Tibetan Buddhism*, p. 316. Lhamo was featured in the movie *Kundun* when the young Dalai Lama, frightened one night in his room, asks if the fierce figure on the wall is real and his monk companion replied that yes, she is.

21. Philip Kapleau, *Zen: Dawn in the West* (Garden City, NY: Anchor/Doubleday, 1979), p. 214.

22. Stephen Addis, *The Art of Zen* (New York: Harry N. Abrams, 1989), p. 178.

23. Paul Reps, ed., *Zen Flesh, Zen Bones: A Collection of Zen and Pre-Zen Writings* (New York: Anchor Books, n.d.), p. 41.

24. Ibid., pp. 41–42.

25. Ibid., p. 12.

26. Burton Watson, trans., *Ryokan: Zen Monk-Poet of Japan* (New York: Columbia

University Press, 1977), p. 84.

27. John Snelling, *The Elements of Buddhism* (Shaftesbury, U.K.: Element, 1990), p. 112.

28. Kenneth K. Tanaka, "Concern for Others in Pure Land Soteriological and Ethical Considerations: A Case of Jogyo daihi in Jodo Shinshu Buddhism" in Kenneth K. Tanaka and Eisho Nasu, eds., *Engaged Pure Land Buddhism: Challenges Facing Jodo Shinshu in the Contemporary World, Studies in Honor of Professor Albert Bloom* (Berkeley, CA: Wisdom Ocean Publications, 1998), p. 110.

29. Konchog Gyaltsen, *In Search of Stainless Ambrosia* (Ithaca, New York: Snow Lion Publications, 1989), p. 54.

30. Reps, *Zen Flesh,* pp. 36–27, and Tsai Chih Chung, ed., *Zen Speaks: Shouts of Nothingness* (New York: Doubleday, 1994), pp. 36–37.

31. Thomas A. Tweed, *The American Encounter with Buddhism, 1844–1912: Victorian Culture and the Limits of Dissent* (Bloomington: Indiana University Press, 1992), p. 36.

32. Lester Suzuki, *Ministry in the Assembly and Relocation Centers of World War II* (Berkeley: Yardbird Publishing Co., 1979), pp. 32–41, 73. Two major figures in American Zen were interned in these camps. Sokei-an, Alan Watts' teacher, suffered health problems in the badly heated facilities. See Rick Fields, *How the Swans Came to the Lake* (Boulder, CO: Shambhala Publications, 1981), p. 193. Nyogen Senzaki practiced *zazen* at the Heart Mountain Relocation Camp, Wyoming, chanting Buddhist sutras with fellow internees, giving Dharma talks, and sending monthly lectures to his students in Los Angeles. The "homeless mushroom" grew well even in this fetid soil. See Perle Besserman and Manfred Steger, *Crazy Clouds: Zen Radicals, Rebels, and Reformers* (Boston: Shambhala Publications, 1991), pp. 147–48.

33. The material about the Reverend Fujimoto comes from his book *Out of the Mud Grows the Lotus* (San Francisco: Lotus Press, 1980) and two phone interviews with B.C.A. staff member Elson Snow in January 1999. Mr. Snow took over the Reverend Fujimoto's prison correspondence when he left B.C.A. Headquarters. It is interesting to note that while the Reverend Fujimoto was at B.C.A. Headquarters he met Bishop Shinsho Hanayama. Hanayama was chaplain to the Japanese tried as war criminals in 1946, having volunteered for this Buddhist prison ministry while a professor at Tokyo University. See Shinsho Hanayama, *The Way of Deliverance: Three Years with Condemned Japanese War Criminals* (London: Victor Gollancz, 1955). As a further footnote to East-West-East encounters in the criminal justice system Roshi Philip Kapleau began his first phase of Zen study in 1948 when he met D.T. Suzuki while working as a court reporter for the International War Crimes Tribunal, at

which Dr. Hanayama served the condemned prisoners, as noted in Rick Fields, *How the Swans Came to the Lake,* p. 239.

34. *Cruz v. Beto,* 405 U.S. 319, 92 S. Ct. 1079, 31 L. Ed. 2d 263 (1972).

35. Fujimoto, *Out of the Mind,* p. 75. The case is cited in *The Encyclopedia of American Prisons* (1996) as one of the two landmark cases the Supreme Court has decided on inmates' rights to religious freedom, while *West's Encyclopedia of American Law* (1998) regards *Cruz v. Beto* as a precedent-setting case. See Marilyn D. McShane and Frank P. Williams III, eds., *Encyclopedia of American Prisons* (New York: Garland, 1996), p. 291, and *West's Encyclopedia of American Law,* vol. 8 (St. Paul, MN: West Group, 1998), p. 31. Yet neither scholars of Buddhism nor any of the groups or people interviewed, with the exception of Fujimoto's successor, mentioned this foundational criminal justice system work, confirming Baumann's observation that when studying Buddhism in the West, "ethnic" Asian Buddhists are often neglected or forgotten. See Martin Baumann, "The Dharma Has Come West: A Survey of Recent Studies and Sources, in *Journal of Buddhist Ethics* 4 (1997): 122 <http://jbe.la.psu.edu/baum2.html> (January 17, 1999). Taitetsu Unno, in his lead essay, "Shin Buddhism in the West," in Tanaka and Nasu, *Engaged Pure Land Buddhism,* pp. 3–27, notes the invisibility of Shin in studies of American Buddhism. Yet even in this insight-filled volume on Jodo Shinshu the Reverend Fujimoto's work was not mentioned.

36. Bo Lozoff, *We're All Doing Time* (Durham, N.C.: Human Kindness Foundation, 1985). The work received initial funding from Ram Dass of the Hanuman Foundation.

37. *Bo Lozoff at Twin Rivers Correction Center,* videotape, Human Kindness Foundation, 1995; Bo Lozoff, *Texas Prison Workshop: Texas Prison Tour— Diagnostic Unit, Huntsville, Texas, April 1997;* and *Prison Volunteers Discussion, Durham, N.C., April 13, 1997* (Human Kindness Foundation, 1997), audiocassettes.

38. Lozoff, *We're All Doing Time,* p. vii.

39. James A. Beckford and Sophie Gilliat, *Religion in Prison: Equal Rites in a Multi-Faith Society* (New York: Cambridge University Press, 1998), pp. 2–7.

40. Ibid. See also Alexandra Luini Del Russo, "Prisoners' Right to Access to the Courts: A Comparative Analysis of Human Rights Jurisprudence in Europe and the United States," in Geoffrey A. Alpert, ed., *Legal Rights of Prisoners* (Beverly Hills: Sage, 1980), pp. 129–71.

41. Beckford and Gilliat, *Religion in Prison,* p. 45; and *The Forest Hermitage Newsletter* <http://www.users.znet.co.uk/pharkhem/ang.htm> (January 11, 1999).

42. Personal e-mail from Venerable Ajahn Khemadhammo <phra.khem@

zetnet.co.uk>, "Operational philosophy of Angulimala," to Virginia Cohn Parkum (January 21, 1999).

43. Geoffrey Shugen Arnold and inmates of the National Buddhist Prison Sangha, "There Has to Be a Better Way to Live," in *The Mountain Record* 17.1 (1998): 20.

44. Ibid., pp. 20–29; and Geoffrey Shugen Arnold in a telephone interview by Virginia Cohn Parkum, February 16, 1999.

45. The Reverend Kobutsu Malone in a telephone interview by Virginia Cohn Parkum, January 22, 1999; see also issues of *Gateway* <http://www.engaged-zen.org> (April 18, 1999).

46. The Reverend Kobutsu Malone, "Prison Zen Practice in America: Life and Death on the Razor's Edge," in Brian D. Hotchkiss, ed., *Buddhism in America: Proceedings of the First Buddhism in America Conference* (Rutland, VT: Charles E. Tuttle Co., 1998).

47. *Turning Wheel: Journal of the Buddhist Peace Fellowship* (winter 1999), p. 44.

48. Ibid.

49. For further information, contact the San Francisco Zen Center, 300 Page St., San Francisco, CA 94102.

50. Upaya Peace Institute, *Summer Newsletter.* See also <http://www.peacemaker community.org/upaya/newsletter_sum_98.htm> (January 17, 1999).

51. Tashi Colman, "Dharma in Hell: Prison as Path," in *Shambhala Sun* <http://www.shambhalasun.com> (March 11, 1999).

52. See Fleet Maull, "Dying in Prison: Sociocultural and Psychosocial Dynamics," in *Hospice Journal* 7 (1991): 127–42; and "Hospice Care for Prisoners: Establishing an Inmate-Staffed Hospice Program in a Prison Medical Facility," in *Hospice Journal* 7 (1991): 43–55.

53. *Doing Time, Doing Vipassana,* videotape, produced and directed by Ayclet Menahemi and Eilona Ariel, Karuna Films, 1997; for the Seattle experience see *Changing from Inside,* videotape, David Donnenfield Productions (1998).

54. At <http://www.dhamma.org/geonka.htm> (January 11, 1999).

55. See SGI-USA's website <http://www.sgi-usa.org> (February 14, 1999).

56. Al Albergate, SGI-USA community relations director, in a telephone interview with Virginia Cohn Parkum, March 1, 1999.

57. Janette Stewart, SGI District Leader, telephone interview with Virginia Cohn Parkum, March 30, 1999.

58. Jarvis Jay Masters, *Finding Freedom: Writings from Death Row* (Junction City, CA: Padma Publishing, 1997).

59. Various issues of *Mandala,* <http://www.cuenet.com/~fpmt/Mandala> (February 16, 1999).

60. Doll Mathis, "Interview with Lama Yeshe Wangmo about Death Row"

<http://lehua.ihawaii.net/~vfh> (1999).

61. Melody Ermachild Chavis, *Altars in the Street: A Neighborhood Fights to Survive* (New York: Bell Tower, 1997).

62. Victoria R. DeRosia, *Living Inside Prison Walls: Adjustment Behavior* (Westport, CT: Praeger, 1998), pp. 96–98.

63. *Mandala* (Nov./Dec. 1997).

64. *What's Love Got to Do With It*, produced by Doug Chapin and Barry Krost, directed by Brian Gibson, Touchstone Pictures, 1993. The film begins with the printed words "The Lotus is a flower that grows in the mud. The thicker and deeper the mud, the more beautiful the lotus blooms. This thought is expressed in the Buddhist chant: *Nam-myoho-renge-kyo*."

65. Arnold, "There Has to Be a Better Way to Live," p. 27.

66. *Mandala*, (Nov./Dec. 1997).

67. In summary, my experience in the criminal justice system has taught me to especially value three teachings from the Dharma that continue to illuminate my practice: *Great Doubt*—As a prison chaplain I must go into every interview and each situation with a suspension of disbelief. I must trust my experience and my intuition and move into each relationship with an openness to the possibilities rather than an alertness to what may seem to be an impossible and hopeless situation. *Great Faith*—As a prison chaplain I must have great faith in the inherent buddha-nature within every inmate that I meet. The more repulsive his actions, the more I must acknowledge that poisonous reality within myself. I must go deep into my own darkness to touch the shining brilliance of my true nature so that I can be a spiritual midwife to the other's awakening of heart and mind. *Great Perseverance*—As a prison chaplain I must have great endurance and I must cultivate an attitude of patience. The inmates, the system, and society must be approached as an interrelated and interdependent whole. I cannot serve society without trying to transform the system. I cannot change the system without helping the inmates to transform themselves. I must work toward the goal of a more just society without desiring to see reward. I must find my compensation in the service itself. (J. Anthony Stultz, co-author.)

68. Selke, *Prisons in Crisis*, pp. 41–46; also Timothy Egan, "Hard Time: Less Crime, More Criminals," *New York Times*, March 7, 1999, sec. 4, pp. 1, 16.

69. McShane and Williams, *Encyclopedia*, p. 292.

70. Hecker, *Angulimala*, p. 20.

Work as Dharma Practice: Right Livelihood Cooperatives of the FWBO

Martin Baumann

THE FRIENDS OF THE WESTERN BUDDHIST ORDER (FWBO), founded in 1967 by the English Buddhist monk Sangharakshita, aspires to build a new society through a range of public programs and enterprises. Among these engaged Buddhist endeavors, the FWBO's entrepreneurial projects are both innovative and emblematic of their understanding of the Buddhist path. Right livelihood enterprises, as they are called, echoing the fifth step on the ancient eightfold path (*samma ajiva*, "right livelihood"), form a vital part in the FWBO's attempt to change existing sociopolitical structures of Western, industrial society. This critical stance toward prevalent conditions of power distribution, and social-cultural and religious ideals contrasts with the historical and contemporary position of most Buddhist institutions in Asia. These, to a large extent, have been affirmative and supportive of the dominant sociopolitical ideas and structures in their societies.[1] As Ken Jones has written with regard to Thailand, "the vulnerable dependence of the Asian sangha on the political and economic establishment for patronage and protection forces it, at best, into a kind of apolitical conservatism."[2]

In contrast to these traditional patterns, the stated purposes of the FWBO are "to encourage and facilitate the growth of real individuals," and to "create a New Society in the midst of the old."[3] Furthermore, senior Order member Subhuti declares that "the purpose of the FWBO is not to find a corner for Buddhists in the midst of the old society. It does not seek to give Buddhism a place in the Establishment so that Buddhists can carry out their own colorful practices and hold their own peculiar beliefs. The FBWO is, to this extent, revolutionary: it wishes to change society—to turn the old society into the new."[4] Subhuti's statement, style and content, mirrors the FWBO's origins in the countercultural movements of the 1960s and their rejection of the "establishment."

It remains to be seen whether these revolutionary ideals may still find resonance today. Repeatedly, criticism of sociopolitical conditions has been incorporated into mainstream institutions, as in the case of the environmental movement in the Western democracies. Similarly, the deliberately revolutionary position of the early FWBO has shifted to one of accommodation and transformation of existing structures. Engaged Buddhism has been said to target those sociopolitical and economic conditions that cause, in Buddhist terms, "suffering for living beings." This critical attitude takes an optimistic and activistic appearance, in contrast to early Western images of Buddhism as nihilistic, pessimistic, and sociopolitically non-engaged.

This paper concentrates on the economic pillar of the FWBO's "New Society." The other pillars are the public Buddhist centers and the residential communities of the FWBO. Our discussion will be contextualized within the broader discourse of the alleged "world-rejection" of Buddhist teachings and ethics, as most prominently voiced by the German sociologist, Max Weber. Our recapitulation of Buddhist ethics will be followed by a critique of Weber's image of Buddhist world-rejection, supposedly its total withdrawal from social and economic activities. Buddhist ethics, as portrayed by Weber, nowhere promote sociopolitical engagement and entrepreneurial activities.

BUDDHIST ETHICS AND THE PRINCIPLE OF RIGHT LIVELIHOOD[5]

Ethics and moral guidelines are defined as *sila* (Pali) in Buddhist tradition. The reference to ethics can be found in the fundamental teachings of Buddhism, the four noble truths. The fourth truth, the noble eightfold path (Pali: *atthangikamagga*), includes right (or perfect) view, right resolve, right speech, right action, right livelihood, right effort, right awareness, and right meditation. Traditionally, these eight factors are divided into three groups: right view and right resolve are seen as aspects of insight or wisdom *(pannya)*. Right speech, action, and livelihood comprise the range of virtue and ethics *(sila)*. The three remaining factors are seen as aspects of contemplation or meditation *(samadhi)*. Concentrating on the second of the three Buddhist pillars, right speech *(samma vacha)* comprises telling the truth and not lying to gain advantage. Right speech also means omitting meaningless and superfluous words and promoting a social unity and reconciliation. Right action or conduct *(samma kammanta)* is the avoidance of killing, stealing, and inappropriate sexual intercourse. Right action should encourage generosity *(dana)* and amicable social relations.

The teaching of right livelihood *(samma ajiva)*, the cultivation of a moral working life, is treated in comparatively few places in Buddhist literature. Typically enough, German-born Theravada monk Nyanaponika Thera, renowned for his translations and systematizations, omits this fifth item of the eightfold path in his exposition of the fourth noble truth.[6] The rare discussion in the commentaries is usually in the negative, pointing to occupations considered immoral and thus detrimental to the Buddhist path of enlightenment. The jobs of hangman, butcher, and thief are listed as "nonbeneficial" *(akusala)*. Likewise the professions of military men and hunters or fishermen are regarded as "nonsalutary" *(Majjhima Nikaya* 51). Equally, Buddhists should abstain from trading with weapons, living creatures, meat, intoxicating drinks, and poison *(Anguttara Nikaya* 5, 177). Lay Buddhists who happen to be tradesmen should not betray customers but treat them honestly.[7]

These ethical instructions are codified into the five resolutions or vows for lay Buddhists. A lay Buddhist pledges not to kill, not to steal, to avoid sexual misconduct, not to lie, and to refrain from intoxicants such as alcohol or drugs *(Anguttara Nikaya* 5, 174). There are additional vows for a monk or nun, including ten fundamental ones, and a further 217 to 240, depending upon the specific monastic traditions. Generosity *(dana)*, in the form of giving alms, is the other, possibly even more fundamental, Buddhist ethical orientation. Alms are usually given to members of the Buddhist monastic order in countries of Theravada Buddhism. Similarly, Mahayanists also give alms to support monks, nuns, and temples.

Traditional Buddhist ethics claim no direct involvement in social institutions or social reform. Rather, according to Heinz Bechert's interpretation, the "original aim (of the Buddha's teaching) was not to shape life in the world, but to teach liberation, release *from* the world."[8] In this sense, Buddhist ethics can be regarded as a means for approaching the final goal of liberation *(vimutti, nibbana)*. Ethical principles serve the members of the monastic order as preparation to achieve insight by means of meditation. Laymen and laywomen strive to observe ethical standards so as to achieve a better rebirth. This is the aim of Buddhist ethics, which can be called an ethics of intention.

Buddhist ethics originated in an Asiatic agricultural society. But how is it interpreted by contemporary Western Buddhists in modern, industrial societies? In the West, does the popular image of the 'withdrawn Buddhist' also apply, a Buddhist who supposedly does not take any direct action in the world so as not to get involved with suffering?

BUDDHIST WITHDRAWAL FROM THE WORLD

The image of the socially withdrawn Buddhist was popularized by Max Weber. As an "ideal type" in the history of religions, the "other-worldly asceticism" of Buddhist monks was contrasted with the "inner-worldly asceticism" of Protestant clergy and laity in Weber's comparative studies. This stereotyped image has dominated scientific studies in the history of religions and Buddhist studies to a very high degree.[9] In his *Studies on Hinduism* and *Buddhism*, Weber asks to what extent "Indian religiosity" was involved in the failure of re-investment capitalism in Asia.[10] Weber's study is situated within his global research about the economic ethics of the world's major religions *(Wirtschaftsethik der Weltreligionen)* that takes Protestant ethics as its point of comparison. According to Weber, only ascetic Protestantism has given rise to "the spirit of capitalism," in which active involvement in this world is a religious calling, and economic success is a sign of divine chosenness. "Holy worldliness" *(Weltheiligkeit)* and a "methodical, rational, innerworldly way of life" *(methodisch rationale innerweltliche Lebensfuhrung)* are key concepts of Weber.[11]

Just as these features are characteristics of Calvinism, they are uncharacteristic for early Buddhism, according to Weber. Weber describes early Buddhism as a "specific unpolitical and anti-political profession-religion," a "soteriology of intellectuals."[12] It has "not set up the slightest social-political aim" and has been "per se apolitical."[13] Weber characterizes Buddhist ethics as "ethics of not acting."[14] According to him, a "methodical ethics for the laity" are not provided.[15] Key words here are "indifference toward the world" *(Weltindifferenz),* "external world withdrawal" *(äusserliche Weltflucht),* and "world indifferent acting" *(weltindifferentes Handeln).*[16] Weber concludes that a religious legitimation of worldly action cannot be found in Asia: "An internal connection of service in the world with extra-worldly soteriology was not possible."[17] However, is such a combination possible in principle? And if so, what determinants and circumstances might contribute to the connection between inner-worldly action and extra-worldly liberation teachings— or, in Buddhist terms, suffering and the way leading to the termination of suffering?

Tentative starting points for such a combination and thus a move away from indifference to the world can be found in the development of Mahayana Buddhism and its ideal of the bodhisattva. A bodhisattva, whether nun/monk or lay woman/man, remains and acts in the world and nonetheless is not attached to it. According to Weber, the development of the Mahayana is "an adaptation to the economic conditions of existence in the world and to the needs of the laity looking for an auxiliary saint."[18] Nevertheless, even the Mahayana, similar to early Buddhism, does not account for a rational ethics of economy, according to Weber.[19]

Despite these considerations, it is possible to show that in a new social context, Buddhist teachings are able to bring forth an "economic rationalism" and a "rational method of life."[20] Accordingly, let us turn to a brief portrait of the The Friends of the Western Buddhist Order and its interpretation of Buddhist action in the world.

THE FRIENDS OF THE WESTERN BUDDHIST ORDER

The Friends of the Western Buddhist Order was founded early in Buddhism's rapid growth in the West, in 1967. In the decades since then Buddhism has experienced explosive growth in the number of practitioners and Buddhist centers established in North America, Australia, Europe, and South Africa.[21] FWBO's founder, the former Theravada monk Sangharakshita, was born Dennis Lingwood, to lower middle class parents near London in 1925. He was ordained as a *sramanera* (monk novice) in 1949 and as a *bhikkhu* (monk in the Theravada *sangha*) in 1950. Sangharakshita ("Protector of the Order") settled down in Kalimpong in the the Darjeeling district of northeast India. He became very active in publication activities, as co-editor of the *Maha Bodhi Journal*, enjoyed close contact with Tibetan refugees in the area, and began studying Vajrayana Buddhism with them and received initiations in its different traditions. Sangharakshita conducted preaching tours throughout India and became active in the conversion movement of the ex-Untouchables, initiated by B. R. Ambedkar in 1956.[22]

After more than twenty years of Buddhist life in India, Sangharakshita returned to England in 1967. There he started the Friends of the Western Buddhist Order, believing that "a new Buddhist movement was badly needed in Britain."[23] Sangharakshita conducted meditation classes, organized study groups, and "happily engaged with younger people themselves involved with the emerging hippie sub-culture."[24] He held that "the FWBO is a Western spiritual movement, a Western spiritual phenomenon. It seeks to practice Buddhism under the conditions of modern Western civilization, which is a secularized and industrialized civilization."[25] The FWBO seeks to give Buddhism "an up-to-date shape, fitting Western conditions."[26]

The new, Western Buddhism was to be built on a "core of the Buddhist tradition," which is interpreted as timeless and universal[27]. Even within the context of a highly industrialized and urbanized society "the Buddhist way of life, the spiritual life" is feasible.[28] In order to create such a "Western form," the FWBO utilizes methods and contents of various Buddhist schools and traditions.[29] Basic to the FWBO is its reference to "the spirit of the original teaching," or as Sangharakshita calls it, "a return to the spiritual roots of Buddhism."[30] The movement calls itself "a fully traditional Buddhist school."[31] As its central project, stated in a recent clarification by leading order members, this objective is called a kind of Buddhism "that is rooted in tradition yet is appropriate to the modern world; one that speaks the language of Western culture, just as Japanese Buddhism speaks the language of Japanese culture, and so on."[32] "Rather than to train students in an Eastern form," Sangharakshita, as "translator," aims to communicate the spirit and the core of the Dharma.[33] To this end, Western arts and literature—among others, William Blake, Goethe, and Nietzsche—are introduced "as a bridge to an understanding of the Dharma."[34]

The Order

The focal point of the FWBO is the Western Buddhist Order. Sangharakshita explicitly started an order because he felt that the personal engagement of the individual and the spiritual fellowship of the order members should be the basis of the new Buddhist movement that he envisaged. The personal commitment to the Buddha, Dharma, and Sangha are of prime importance. Thus, the FWBO places a major emphasis on the act of "going for refuge" *(saranagamana),* considered as a turning point in the life of an individual. "The Going for Refuge is really the central act of the Buddhist life. It is what makes you a Buddhist."[35]

Members of the Order are men and women, single, married, or those living in celibacy, some with full-time jobs and others who devote all of their energy to the further development of the FWBO. "The member of the Western Buddhist Order represents a new type of Buddhist, or rather a full-time committed Buddhist of the traditional kind working under the very different conditions of the 'global village' and 'post-industrial society.'"[36] Order members are ordained in a ceremony, taking the ten precepts, the title *Dharmachari* or *Dharmacharini* (male or female "Dharma-farer"), and a new name in Pali or Sanskrit. "In a sense they are neither monk nor lay."[37]

Many, although not all, order members live together in residential communities to enable the development of "spiritual friendship" amongst each other. Such communities, most often single-sex, are usually found near a center of the FWBO. Through the centers and their meditation and yoga courses, study days, *pujas* (devotional ceremonies), and the celebration of Buddhist festivals, members of the public come into contact with the FWBO.[38]

Development and Size

In the beginning the movement was restricted to England, where the first centers, shared flats, cooperatives, and projects came into being. As Vishvapani reports, many of the early members, coming to Buddhism through the hippie counterculture, "were defiantly at odds with conventional society and enthusiastically engaged in the process of starting co-ops and developing community life as a radical social experiment."[39] By the end of the 1970s, the movement started to gain a foothold in other countries of Europe and overseas. Among its overseas branches, the FWBO emphasizes its relation with the Buddhist conversion movement of Ambedkar. Since 1978 there have been European FWBO Buddhists living in western India as teachers and leaders of the neo-Buddhists there. FWBO members founded charities, that is, Karuna Trust and Bahuja Hitay, cooperatives, and craft businesses for the material and medical support of the former Untouchables. After Great Britain, most FWBO centers and order members can be found in India, where the number of Friends is estimated to be several tens of thousands.[40]

In addition to the strong Indian branch, FWBO centers and projects were founded during the 1980s and 1990s in Australia, New Zealand, Malaysia, Sri Lanka, Nepal, North and South America, and various countries in Europe. In the mid-1980s, there existed eleven centers, various FWBO groups, and ten cooperatives in Great Britain. Ten years later the movement had grown to about thirty centers and thirty-five groups in Great Britain alone (1997). On a global scale there are about fifty-five city centers, fifteen retreat centers, various local groups, and right livelihood cooperatives in 1998.[41]

Worldwide there were 187 order members in 1982; in 1988 the number was 345. Likewise, the increase continued during the following years. In 1991 the figure was about 450, and in spring 1999 the size of the order was approximately 800 members. The number of supporters and Friends is estimated to be approximately 100,000, the vast majority of them being Buddhists in India. The movement has established a highly productive publishing service, launching books by Sangharakshita and order members and also producing various journals of high standards. During the 1980s and 1990s the organization grew to become one of Great Britain's principal Buddhist movements.[42]

Since the mid-1990s, Sangharakshita has been handing over responsibilities to elder Order members. In the spring of 1997, the responsibility for ordination and spiritual leadership was conveyed to the Preceptor's College Council, formed by eleven men and two women based in Birmingham. In this way, a smooth transference of tasks and responsibilities from the founder of the movement to a group of experienced disciples should be ensured. Contrary to the experience of many newly created schools, the almost inevitable difficulties of succession and issues of power are being solved already during the lifetime of the movement's initiator. Only time will show whether this model will work out successfully, or whether the FWBO will be faced with controversies and splits after Sangharakshita's decease.[43]

RIGHT LIVELIHOOD ACCORDING TO THE FWBO

The FWBO understands itself as a "Western" Buddhist movement. *Western* is less a geographic label than a description of its contents: hinted at are the secular, industrial, and urban structures of society. According to Sangharakshita, present Western society makes it more difficult to lead a Buddhist life. The main causes of this are the higher standard of living, over-stimulation, and limited possibilities for the individual to develop spiritually due to societal constraints.[44] Within this less beneficial context, according to Sangharakshita, the order would provide the best environment to move and develop on the Buddhist path. In this way, considerations of the social context affect the interpretation of Buddhist norms and ethics. Thus, Buddhist ethics are reinterpreted according to the demands of the new social situation.

Sangharakshita aims to develop an alternative to the division between monks and lay people. This implies that ethical mandates traditionally applied to the monks (and nuns) now also apply to the whole Buddhist community. Similarly, economic standards previously applicable only to the laity, such as vocational and professional engagement, now apply to ordained order members as well. The aphorism "Commitment is primary, lifestyle secondary" is often cited as a bridge between monks, lay people, and their distinctive ways of life.[45] Sangharakshita and the emerging FWBO sought to apply this idea to the financial needs of the committed individuals and the FWBO collectively. Rather than aiming to get a mainstream job, members aspired to both "live the Dharma" and earn a living. As Dharmachari Vajraketu, managing director of FWBO's leading right livelihood venture, Windhorse Trading, recalls: "The main reason the FWBO has chosen to set up businesses is in order to create environments where we can live ethical lives to the fullest possible extent, with others who share our values and aspirations. We aim to make work as powerful a tool of personal transformation as formal sitting meditation. Indeed, if we understand meditation to be the systematic cultivation of positive states of mind, one might say that we aim to make our work an extension of our meditation."[46]

In what specific ways, then, does the FWBO translate the idea of right livelihood into action in a capitalist context? Ideally, FWBO members endeavor to take the ethical instruction of right livelihood as a challenge and guideline to adjust their lives to Buddhist principles regarding economic pursuits. Dharmachari Vajraketu sees it thus: "Through the hard grind of business one has many experiences of the impermanent, insubstantial and unsatisfactory nature of life, giving one the opportunity to align one's being more with these realities."[47] The members of the Order are not only careful in not taking up certain professions, but they also want to use their working time constructively for their own spiritual development.

The criterion for a morally pure profession is that the activity is wholesome, beneficial, and skillful *(kusala)* in a Buddhist sense, for both the individual and for society. Expanding the above-mentioned list of nonbeneficial professions, FWBO members consider the production and sale of superfluous goods and inferior products negatively. As Dharmachari Virachitta puts it: "It is easy to list jobs which are wrong livelihood, and which cannot possibly be transformed into right livelihood, but many jobs today are more subtly unethical. Examples would include the manufacture and sale of useless luxury goods, of shoddily-produced goods, or the advertising industry—

Moving the product at Windhorse Trading, Cambridge, England.
Courtesy Friends of the Western Buddhist Order.

surely at times blatantly 'insinuating' and 'dissembling.'"[48] Not only is a job's specific nature important, but also its contents and purpose. Accordingly, a job has to be ethical—it must not hurt, exploit, or cheat any living creature. Respect for nature and the environment is also of importance.[49] Expressed positively, it means that a piece of work should be meaningful and useful: it should be beneficial for the individual as regards his or her spiritual growth, and likewise useful for society, offering basic and useful goods or services. Dharmachari Virachitta emphasizes: "If we want to *perfect* our livelihood, then we must try to do something that makes a positive contribution to ourselves and to the society in which we live. Professions that spring to mind would include those of doctor, nurse, teacher, writer, or artist. Work undertaken to fund worthwhile projects (such as social and educational projects in the Third World, or Buddhist retreat centers) is another way of contributing."[50] The goods produced or services done are expected to be of a high standard. Good quality and honesty should aim to be an advertisement for the reliability of the FWBO cooperatives.

A further criterion for a justly applied right livelihood activity is that, if possible, an activity should be team-based: not carried out alone, but jointly with others. This feature provides the possibility of working together in a group with people who share the same ideals and thus encourage and inspire each other. At the same time, people who work together would be able to learn to act and manage without an authoritarian hierarchy, to take over responsibilities and to make decisions according to the principle of consent. Working in structures of a cooperative nature would also contribute to a positive working climate and, apart from the Buddhist ethical ideals, would offer further motivation to do even unpleasant tasks with a smile.

On the basis of these considerations, FWBO members founded team-based cooperatives and right livelihood cooperatives in the mid- to late 1970s. Dharmachari Tejamati, formerly involved with the London Buddhist Centre, remembers, "As far as I can ascertain, Windhorse Bookshop, established in Brighton in January 1975 by Buddhadasa, must claim the honor of being the first right livelihood venture in the FWBO. On the ground floor, books, incense, candles, crafts, and some Indian clothing were sold, whilst upstairs a room was offered for meditation classes. The shop made a modest profit and also helped to introduce people to the FWBO."[51] Needless to say, the structures and motives to a large extent mirrored those counter-cultural and alternative ideas that formed the personal background of most members. Ideas for further businesses were sought and turned into action, most often with rather less skill, experiences, and start-up and working capital. Dharmachari Tejamati takes a look at the spectrum of ventures initiated:

In 1977 and 1978 right livelihood projects were beginning to be formed throughout the Movement in the U.K. A vegetarian restaurant, Sunrise, opened in Brighton; two shop premises were acquired in Croydon and converted into a wholefood shop and café. Ink, a screen printing/design business, and Gardening Friends appeared in Glasgow. Oranges vegetarian restaurant in Norwich came into the Movement along with its founder, Kulananda; a transport and removals business was formed in West London; Spectrum painting/decorating service, and Kusa Cushions was started by the women's community in Wanstead.[52]

Rather than being a pure story of success, most businesses did not survive. "Many businesses were started in the 1970s and 1980s—without capital, skills or business experience; somewhat predictably, several barely managed to get by and, being essentially unprofitable, eventually closed."[53]

In the mid- to late 1980s, approximately half of the order members and many Friends worked in FWBO-related cooperatives and projects. During this time the cooperatives in Great Britain achieved an annual turnover of about two million pounds, employing eighty-five people full time.[54] During the 1990s, the FWBO's leading business has become Windhorse Trading in Cambridge (U.K.). Founded in 1980 as a market stall in East London, ten years later it runs a wholesale and retail gift business, importing handicrafts and gifts and selling them through a chain of Buddhist-run retail stores and wholesale outlets. The business was listed as one of the hundred fastest-growing companies in Britain in 1992, with annual growth of 37 percent. In 1996 sales were again up 37 percent to £7.5 million ($12 million) and profits were up 101 percent to £1.27 million. Half-a-million pounds of this was given away to Buddhist centers and charities. The turnover for 1997 was up 31 percent to £9.9 million. In 1997, Windhorse Trading has had eighteen "Evolution Gift Shops" in the U.K., Ireland, Spain, and Germany, employing some 190 Buddhists. Centers that wished to start a business often did so by opening a branch of Windhorse Trading. The Evolution shops are run by a small team of women and men, retailing the goods and products supplied by Windhorse Trading. As FWBO's right livelihood enterprises had become dominated by these franchise operations by 1997, Windhorse Trading decided that no new Evolution shops were to be opened for the time being.[55]

Acting as a retailer encompasses only one aspect of actual work done within Windhorse Trading. About half of the employees are based at the warehouse in Cambridge, doing the same kinds of things that are performed in any warehouse—bringing in stock from container trucks, storing it on pallets, and processing, picking, and dispatching orders. Work is organized in teams according to the specific work and task in question. There is a ware-house team, an accounts team, a sales team, several administrative teams, and customer teams. Emphasis is laid on joint work and practice of the Dharma. "Each team begins the day with some Buddhist ritual and chanting, followed by a short reporting-in, where there is a chance to tell the others what is happening in our lives and our experiences. Once a week there is a longer meeting where some aspect of work-as-spiritual-practice is discussed in greater depth."[56]

Apart from Windhorse Trading, there are other successful right liveli-hood businesses in the U.K., U.S., Germany, and India. At Windhorse Publications (Glasgow, U.K.), the work involves commissioning, editing, designing, and publishing books. At the Gallery Café and the Cherry Orchard Restaurant in London and the Indian restaurant Tipu's Tiger in Missoula, Montana, the teams cut vegetables, cook, wait on tables, and sell coffee. Tipu's opened in 1997 and soon won an award as Missoula's "Best New Restaurant." Friends Foods in London and the Wholefood Shop in Croydon, U.K. sell health foods, natural supplements, and cosmetics. At Bodywise, in London and Manchester, the team offers natural therapies and bodywork, including shiatsu, yoga, massage, and rolfing.[57]

Team-based, spiritual work is one side of the right livelihood coin for FWBO members. Of equal importance is that, in economic terms, the busi-ness is efficient and raises money for Buddhist projects. The work should not not wear out the workers, but should yield enough money for one's own liv-ing and for Buddhist welfare projects. "The work should serve some wider purpose, either in itself, or through the profits made, the spirit here being one of generosity."[58] In this way, the charitable work of Karuna Trust and Bahuja Hitay on behalf of the Indian FWBO branch, the Trailokya Bauddha Mahasangha Sahayak Gana (TBMSG), is largely funded by donations from right livelihood enterprises. Thus, working in the cooperatives enables mem-bers to practice the Buddhist virtue of generosity (dana). The fundamental principle dealing with donations and earnings within the FWBO runs, "Give what you can, take what you need."[59] As Dharmacharini Subhadramati, who worked nine years in the London Cherry Orchard restaurant, explains: "We all receive the same basic money each week (enough to live on but not to save) and a set number of weeks for retreats and time off. But if anyone needs more, they ask and the team discusses it. I used to view not asking for extras as a virtue."[60] Whether one judges such an attitude as naïve and credulous, or as a strong and strict position toward changing capitalistic society, Dharmacharini Subhadramati valued her years working in the right livelihood restaurant as "a situation in which I can be wholehearted."[61] The equality principal applies to all, regardless of the position, as Dharmachari Vajraketu, director of Windhorse Trading, explains: "Everybody receives the same basic financial support (or income), with extra money given where needed. As a single man with no special needs and no dependents, I receive the basic level of support; thus I can claim the distinction of perhaps being the only Managing Director of a U.K. limited company with a lower income than many staff in the shops, office or warehouse, who have dependents or other special needs."[62] In the cooperatives people aim to transform their work into a form and practice of giving. Generosity and conscious avoiding of exploitation are thus the basis of a Buddhist economy as the FWBO understands it.[63]

Second but last, the cooperatives and businesses are also a means to spread the Dharma and to establish contacts with the wider world. "Right Livelihood provides a significant interface with the non-Buddhist world. In the course of our business activities we meet people who might never come to a Buddhist center or read a Buddhist magazine. There is no doubt that some are influenced to consider alternative ways of living and working, when they see that these manifestly produce happier, more energetic people."[64] Ten years later Dharmachari Vajraketu underscores this feature of "bringing Buddha to the marketplace": "By engaging in economic activity we interact with non-Buddhists in ways we would not if we confined ourselves to monasteries, or even in Buddhist centers. Hundreds of people who might otherwise never meet a Buddhist—customers, suppliers, bank executives, lawyers—come into contact with us, and we consistently hear that this contact leaves them with a positive impression."[65]

Finally, leading a life according to right livelihood principles should be distinguished not only in its form and content but also by way of its objective. For members of the FWBO, to be a Buddhist does not entail only working on oneself individually through meditation and teachings. A *true* Going for Refuge for many also finds expression in activities that have broader social and political implications. The bodhisattva ideal of Mahayana Buddhism is explicitly referred to in this context. The selfless and altruistic attitude of a bodhisattva is interpreted as sociopolitical engagement to create better conditions for the practice of the Dharma in the Western world. As stated in the beginning, the aim of a right livelihood business is both to produce a financial surplus and to change existing society. Already today one should start creating the "new society," as the existing conditions are seen as detrimental to mental and spiritual growth.[66] In this sense the function of cooperatives to act as bridges between the spiritual world of the FWBO and the profane environment become vital. The businesses serve as a means to draw attention to Buddhist teachings and to advertise them. And last but not least, right livelihood businesses enable the FWBO to be financially self-supporting and thus not obliged to depend on the old society and its demands.

In the communities and cooperatives, possibilities of living jointly are organized in a practical way. The combination of a Buddhist center, residential community, and cooperative serves as a Buddhist society in miniature within the Western, industrialized world. This Buddhist society does not aim only to be a pattern and example of the ideal New Society, but also intends to criticize the existing structures and values of society by way of its attractiveness. As an advertisement of Windhorse Trading runs: "Some people dream of an alternative society. At Windhorse Trading we are helping build one."[67] All these activities are not only backed, but encouraged by Sangharakshita: "I do not want to see little pockets of Buddhism here and there with the remainder of society completely unchanged. I don't want there to be just little Buddhist oases in the midst of the desert of secular life. I want them to spread and to influence their surroundings in a positive way."[68]

A BUDDHIST REEVALUATION OF SOCIETY AND WORK

Shakyamuni Buddha, whom all Buddhist schools revere as founder and exemplar, never did regular work himself (in modern terms), either in a paying job or as a volunteer. Nevertheless, the exhortation for a right way of living is central to the Buddhist teachings. On the one hand, the historical Buddha attracted many lay followers who carried out occupations as merchants, blacksmiths, herdsmen, or farmers. On the other hand, manual and physical work was often assigned to India's lowest castes and thus enjoyed little prestige and respect. Even today it is difficult in India to live a religious life and to do manual work at the same time. Maybe that was a reason for including the right livelihood within the eightfold path—it offers lay people an opportunity to succeed in living a Buddhist life while rejecting the stigma of manual work.

In the modern West, the FWBO places right livelihood, relatively little emphasized in the Asian Buddhist texts, somewhere near the center of its movement. The updating of this ethical teaching goes beyond the activity of the individual and lays the groundwork for a new society. Next to this sociopolitical component, a reevaluation of work becomes evident. Work is valued as positive and beneficial. Parallels between this Buddhist work ethic and the notion of the "calling" in the Protestant work ethic become evident. Both English FWBO Buddhists and members of American Puritan sects of the seventeenth century followed *religious* goals in their professional and social activities. By way of these religious ideals, both have been motivated to work industriously and to do work of high quality. As regards social reputation, being a member of a specific religious group vouches for quality, sincerity and honesty. Members of the FWBO are still striving for that reputation. We see, then, that Weber's "economic rationalism" is present in this Buddhist movement.[69]

Though it seems that the FWBO work ethic and the Calvinist ethic of a religious-vocational calling are structurally similar, they diverge totally as regards religious motivation and goals. The Puritan, led by the doctrine of predestination, attempts to identify a *sign* of his own state of grace, as being either chosen or damned by God. Success in one's work is interpreted as a sign of chosenness. Specifically, profit in business is valued as a tangible indication of God's blessing and thus serves both as a sign and a confirmation of "the only just way: to work for God's glory."[70]

In contrast, a person jointly working in an FWBO cooperative seems to be motivated by the opportunity of personal, spiritual growth with co-followers. He or she contributes to the spread of the Dharma and helps, bit by bit, to change existing society in the direction of the new society. Nevertheless, the driving force appears to be to gain insight and wisdom in a Buddhist sense, and to help others to achieve this. The rules of morality outlined in the eightfold path serve that purpose: not until excellence in one's own speech, action, and livelihood is realized can one hope to gain insight through meditation.

Returning to the point raised by Weber, in a changed social context, "an inner connection of achievements in the world with an extra-worldly soteriology" seems to match the pattern of the new Buddhism.[71] Whether one agrees with Weber's stereotyped analysis or not, the case of the FWBO points to a more general feature. Under new sociocultural conditions, Buddhist teachings prove to be highly adaptable and flexible. The example of the FWBO makes evident that Western concepts, such as a capitalist work ethic, ecological considerations, and a social-reformist perspective, can be integrated into the Buddhist tradition. These features must be acknowledged as one of many accommodations of the Buddhist religion to modern conditions.

Earlier in this chapter, I described Buddhist ethics as an ethics of intention. Buddhist teachings are fine-tuned, practical means only for reaching a specific goal. In the *Alagaddupama Sutta* (*Majjhima Nikaya* 22) the Dharma is compared to a raft that brings the person striving for insight across the stream of suffering. In the modern context, the scope of the teaching is widened from the sole individual to society at large. In this way, engaged Buddhism recognizes the collective nature of a human existence and its susceptibility to collective intervention. The right livelihood enterprises of the Friends of the Western Buddhist Order stand as a successful instance of this recognition.

NOTES

1. A striking example is presented by Brian Daizen A. Victoria, *Zen at War* (New York, Tokyo: Weatherhill, 1997). See, however, the account of Buddhist liberation movements in Asia by Christopher S. Queen and Sallie B. King, eds., *Engaged Buddhism: Buddhist Liberation Movements in Asia* (Albany: State University of New York Press, 1996).

2. Ken Jones, *The Social Face of Buddhism: An Approach to Political and Social Activism* (London: Wisdom Publications, 1989), p. 213.

3. Dharmachari Subhuti (Alex Kennedy), *Buddhism for Today: A Portrait of a New Buddhist Movement*, 2d enlarged ed. (Glasgow: Windhorse, 1988), p. 174. Capitalization by Subhuti.

4. Subhuti, *Buddhism for Today*, p. 174. Capitalization by Subhuti. See in more detail also Subhuti, *Sangharakshita, A New Voice in the Buddhist Tradition* (Birmingham: Windhorse, 1994), pp. 219–63.

5. Most of the following sections are based on the article "Working in the Right Spirit: The Application of Buddhist Right Livelihood in the Friends of the Western Buddhist Order," *Journal of Buddhist Ethics* 5 (1998): 120–43, <http://jbe.la.psu.edu/5/baum1.html>. Quite a number of parts, points, and issues have been updated and enlarged. Many thanks for most helpful comments by order members Vishvapani and Ian Tromp.

6. Nyanaponika, *Der Weg zur Erlösung*, 2d rev. ed. (Konstanz: Christiani, 1981), pp. 53–71. In his *Das Wort des Buddha*, 5th ed. (Konstanz: Christiani, 1989), however, he gives some relevant canonical passages, see pp. 70–71.

7. A reference to right livelihood also can be found in the "four kinds of virtue based on purity" *(catuparisuddhisila)*. These, however, relate to the monastic order only and comprise: (1) restraint with regard to the monastic obligations, (2) control of the senses, (3) purity in one's means of livelihood, and (4) virtue in respect of the four monastic requisites (dress, food, shelter, and medicine); see, among others, Nyanatiloka, *Buddhistisches Wörterbuch*, 4th ed. (Konstanz: Christiani, 1989), pp. 162, 210, and Sangharakshita, *A Survey of Buddhism*, 6th ed. (London: Tharpa, 1987), p. 168. Additionally, see Russell F. Sizemore and Donald K. Swearer, eds., *Ethics, Wealth and Salvation: A Study in Buddhist Social Ethics* (Columbia: University of South Carolina Press, 1990); P. A Payutta, *Buddhist Economics: A Middle Way for the Market Place*, 2d enl. ed. (Bangkok: Buddhadhamma

Foundation, 1994), and Claud Whitmyer, ed., *Mindfulness and Meaningful Work: Explorations in Right Livelihood* (Berkeley, CA: Parallax Press, 1994).

8. Heinz Bechert, foreword in Heinz Bechert and Richard Gombrich, eds., *The World of Buddhism* (London: Thames and Hudson, 1984), p. 7, italics by Bechert. In contrast, however, Walpola Rahula, in his famous *What the Buddha Taught* (Bedford: Gordon Fraser, 1959), emphatically pointed to the teaching's applicability in economic and political life, pp. 76–89. See also Perry Schmidt-Leukel, "Die gesellschaftspolitisch Dimension des Buddhismus," *Zeitschrift für Missionswissenschaft und Religionswissenschaft* 81.4 (1997): 289–305.

9. Weber's image of early Buddhism is valued by leading scholars in Buddhist studies as to a large degree correct, see Heinz Bechert, "Max Webers Darstellung der Geschichte des Buddhismus in Süd- und Südostasien," in Wolfgang Schluchter, ed., *Max Webers Studie über Hinduismus und Buddhismus* (Frankfurt: Suhrkamp, 1984), pp. 274–92, especially p. 274; and Etienne Lamotte, "The Buddha, His Teachings and His Sangha," in: Bechert and Gombrich, eds., *The World of Buddhism*, pp. 41–58. Evers, scholar in the sociology of religion, confirms Weber's division of world-involvement and world-withdrawal, see Hans-Dieter Evers, *Monks, Priests and Peasants* (Leiden: Brill, 1972), especially p. 104. On the other hand, Tambiah criticizes Weber's interpretation as exaggerated and narrow minded; see Stanley J. Tambiah, "Max Webers Untersuchung des frühen Buddhismus. Eine Kritik," in Schluchter, *Max Webers Studie über Hinduismus und Buddhismus*, pp. 202–46, especially p. 207. With regard to the sources Weber used, see Bechert's above-mentioned contribution in the Schluchter volume, p. 277; and Karl-Heinz Golzio, "Zur Verwendung indologischer Literatur in Max Webers Studie über Hinduismus und Buddhismus," in Schluchter, *Max Webers Studie über Hinduismus und Buddhismus*, pp. 363–73.

10. Max Weber, *Gesammelte Aufsätze zur Religionssoziologie*, vol. II, 5th ed. (Tübingen: Mohr, 1972), p. 4. Here and following, the German expressions were translated by the author.

11. Ibid., p. 371, the German expression runs: "methodisch rationale innerweltliche Lebensführung."

12. Ibid., p. 218.

13. Ibid., pp. 245 and 256.

14. Ibid., p. 235.

15. Ibid., p. 236.

16. Ibid., p. 367.

17. Weber's key sentence in German is: *"Eine innere Verbindung der Leistung in der Welt mit der ausserweltlichen Soteriologie war nicht möglich,"* Weber, *Gesammelte Aufsätze zur Religionssoziologie*, vol. II, p. 367. The accuracy of

Weber's claims cannot be discussed here, but their appropriateness seems questionable in light of the Buddhist teachings to lay people, the concept of the *chakkavatti* king, and the activities of a bodhisattva; see also Queen and King, eds., *Engaged Buddhism;* Sulak Sivaraksa, *A Buddhist Vision for Renewing Society* (Bangkok, 1981); and, as basic reading, Damien Keown, *The Nature of Buddhist Ethics* (London: Macmillan 1992). See also the references to Rahula, *What the Buddha Taught,* and Schmidt-Leukel, "Die gesellschaftspolitisch Dimension des Buddhismus," note 8. There is a vast amount of secondary literature on Weber, his Protestant-capitalism thesis, and whether similar features are traceable in Asia. Among these, see Robert N. Bellah, *Tokugawa Religion* (Glencoe, IL: Free Press, 1957); the collection of papers in Constans Seyfarth and Walter M. Sprondel, eds., *Seminar: Religion und gesellschaftliche Entwicklung. Studien zur Protestantismus-Kapitalismus-These Max Webers* (Frankfurt am Main: Suhrkamp, 1973); and Andreas Buss, "Buddhism and Rational Activity," in *Internationales Asienforum* 13.3–4 (1982): 211–30.

18. Weber, *Gesammelte Aufsätze zur Religionssoziologie,* vol. II, p. 271.

19. Ibid., pp. 234 and 277.

20. Ibid., p. 375.

21. Charles S. Prebish, "Ethics and Integration in American Buddhism," *Journal of Buddhist Ethics* 2 (1995): 125–39, <http://jbe.la.psu.edu/2/prebish3.html>, p. 126. Buddhism's development outside Asia has been documented and analyzed in Stephen Batchelor, *The Awakening of the West: The Encounter of Buddhism and Western Culture* (Berkeley, CA: Parallax Press, 1994); Martin Baumann, "Buddhism in the West: Phases, Orders and the Creation of an Integrative Buddhism," *Internationales Asienforum* 27.3–4 (1996): 345–62; and Baumann, "The Dharma Has Come West: A Survey of Recent Studies and Sources," *Journal of Buddhist Ethics* 4 (1997): 194–211, <http://jbe.la.psu.edu/4/baum2.html>, reprinted in *Critical Review of Books in Religion* 10 (1997): 1–14.

22. There is a rapidly growing amount of literature by Sangharakshita and the FWBO, see Sangharakshita's memoirs, *Facing Mount Kanchenjunga* (Birmingham: Windhorse, 1991); and *The Rainbow Road* (Birmingham: Windhorse, 1997), incorporating *The Thousand-Petalled Lotus* (Gloucester: Alan Sutton, 1976). See also Sangharakshita's autobiographical records *The History of My Going For Refuge* (Glasgow: Windhorse, 1988) and *Forty-Three Years Ago: Reflections on My Bhikkhu Ordination* (Glasgow: Windhorse, 1993). An authorized biography was written by Dharmachari Subhuti, *Bringing Buddhism to the West: A Life of Sangharakshita* (Birmingham: Windhorse, 1995). In 1957, Sangharakshita presented his own overview of Buddhism in *A Survey of Buddhism,* 6th ed. (London: Tharpa, 1987).

23. Sangharakshita, *The History of My Going For Refuge*, p. 83.

24. FWBO Communications Office, *The FWBO Files: A Response* (Birmingham: FWBO 1998), p. 17. See also Subhuti, *Buddhism for Today*, pp. 30–31.

25. Sangharakshita, *New Currents in Western Buddhism* (Glasgow: Windhorse, 1990), p. 54.

26. Quoted from the program of the Buddhist Centre Essen (Germany).

27. FWBO Communications Office, *The FWBO Files: A Response,* 1998, quote p. 6; see also pp. 22–23.

28. Sangharakshita, *New Currents in Western Buddhism*, p. 19.

29. With regard to this synthetic approach see the *FWBO-Newsletter* 68 (1984), characterizing the three Buddhist vehicles *(yanas)* from an FWBO point of view.

30. Sangharakshita, *Survey of Buddhism*, p. 97, capitalization by Sangharakshita. Second quote: Sangharakshita, *The FWBO and "Protestant Buddhism": An Affirmation and a Protest* (Glasgow: Windhorse, 1992), p. 93.

31. Dharmacharini Vessantara, *The Friends of the Western Buddhist Order: An Introduction* (Glasgow: Windhorse, 1988), p. 9. See, likewise, FWBO Communications Office, *The FWBO Files: A Response*, 1998, p. 6.

32. FWBO Communications Office, *The FWBO Files: A Response*, p. 45.

33. Ibid., p. 5.

34. Dharmacharini Vessantara, *The Friends*, p. 9. For this point, see in detail Sangharakshita, *Alternative Traditions* (Glasgow: Windhorse, 1986) and *The Religion of Art* (Glasgow: Windhorse, 1986), as well as Subhuti, *Buddhism for Today*, pp. 94–101; for the forms of Buddhist meditation practiced see pp. 48–60.

35. Sangharakshita, *New Currents in Western Buddhism*, p. 85. Likewise, see Subhuti, "Buddham saranam gacchami," *Golden Drum* 1 (1986): 12–13 and Subhuti, *Buddhism for Today*, pp. 140–44.

36. Subhuti, *Buddhism for Today*, p. 140. For the importance of the order see pp. 129–73.

37. Ibid., p. 140. On the ten precepts, i.e., "the ten *akusala-dharmas* from which one undertakes to refrain, and the ten *kusala-dharmas* which one undertakes to observe," see Sangharakshita, *The Ten Pillars of Buddhism* (Glasgow: Windhorse, 1984), p. 6.

38. For nonmembers' accounts of the FWBO, see Batchelor, *Awakening of the West*, pp. 323–40; Martin Baumann, *Deutsche Buddhisten. Geschichte und Gemeinschaften*, 2d enl. ed. (Marburg: Diagonal, 1995), pp. 164–81; Sandra Bell, "Change and Identity in the Friends of the Western Buddhist Order," *Scottish Journal of Religious Studies* 17. 2 (1996): 87–107; and Andrew Rawlinson, *The Book of Enlightened Masters: Western Teachers in Eastern Traditions* (Chicago, La Salle, IL: Open Court, 1997), pp. 501–8. The account by Philip Mellor,

"Protestant Buddhism? The Cultural Translation of Buddhism to England," *Religion* 21.2 (1991): 73–92, despite interesting ideas, lacks accuracy and is based on too few primary sources. Lifestyles in FWBO communities was publicly addressed in one of Britain's leading national newspapers, *The Guardian,* Supplement, October 27, 1997. It accused Sangharakshita of homosexual abuse and a center's chairman of exerting control and power over members. *The FWBO Files: A Response* (autumn 1998) is a reply to these anonymously distributed allegations. This "sex and suicide scandal," as it was entitled by *The Guardian,* will not be treated here, since right livelihood ventures, and not the lifestyle of FWBO members, is of interest here.

39. Dharmachari Vishvapani, "Still Building the New Society," *Golden Drum* 36 (1995): 24.

40. See Sangharakshita, *Ambedkar and Buddhism* (Glasgow: Windhorse, 1986); Dharmachari Nagabodhi (Terry Pilchick), *Jai Bhim! Dispatches from a Peaceful Revolution* (Glasgow: Windhorse, 1988); and the issues of the FBWO magazine *Golden Drum* 10 (1988), 25 (1992), and 31 (1994). For a general and scholarly, non-FWBO-biased account of the neo-Buddhist movement, see Timothy Fitzgerald, "Buddhism in Maharashtra: A Tri-partite Analysis—A Research Report," in A.K. Narain and D.C. Ahir, eds., *Dr. Ambedkar, Buddhism and Social Change* (New Delhi: D.K. Publishing, 1994), pp. 17–34; and Alan Sponberg, "TBMSG: A Dhamma Revolution in Contemporary India," in Queen and King, eds., *Engaged Buddhism. Buddhist Liberation Movements in Asia,* pp. 73–120. For a comparison of the reformist interpretations of Ambedkar and those of Sangharakshita, see Martin Baumann, "Neo-Buddhistische Konzeptionen in Indien und England," *Zeitschrift für Religions- und Geistesgeschichte* 43.2 (1991): 97–116.

41. For the figures relating to Great Britain, see *The Buddhist Directory,* ed. the Buddhist Society London, 7th ed. (London: The Buddhist Society, 1997), pp. 121–22. For current information, see the movement's website at <http://www.fwbo.org/>. A four-part video series of the history of the FWBO (1964–1979) is also available.

42. Numbers according to Subhuti, *Buddhism for Today,* p. 199; Sangharakshita, *The FWBO and "Protestant Buddhism,"* pp. 24, 140; *Golden Drum* 29 (1993) ("The Western Buddhist Order in Its Twenty-Fifth Year"), and personal communication with Vishvapani and Ian Tromp in May 1999.

43. For the Preceptor's College Council, see Dharmachari Guhyapati, "Vital Connections," *Dharma Life* 5 (1997): 60–61. Some previous internal problems as regards exerting control and power as a center's chairman were quite openly discussed in *Dharma Life* 7 (1998): 8–9 and 56–61. This was, however, also done in response to the above-mentioned article in *The Guardian,* 27.10.1997 (see footnote 38).

44. Sangharakshita, *New Currents in Western Buddhism*, pp. 26–33.

45. Sangharakshita, *The Ten Pillars of Buddhism*, p. 49.

46. Dharmachari Vajraketu, "Marketing Values," *Dharma Life* 6 (1997): 25.

47. Vajraketu, "Marketing Values," p. 27.

48. Dharmachari Virachitta, "The Practice of Right Livelihood," *Golden Drum* 12 (1989): 5.

49. See *Golden Drum* 16 (1990): "Buddhism and the Environment," and Dharmachari Saramati, "How Green Is the Path?" *Dharma Life* 2 (1996): 16–22. With regard to a correspondence between a profession and the five ethical principles of a lay Buddhist, see Dharmachari Sanghaloka, "The Modern Context," *Golden Drum* (1989): 6–7, and Subhuti, *Buddhism for Today*, pp. 74–88.

50. Dharmachari Virachitta, "The Practice of Right Livelihood," p. 5, emphasis in the text.

51. Dharmachari Tejamati, "Working Inside the Movement," *Golden Drum* 12 (1989): 8.

52. Ibid., p. 9, capitalization in the text. The list continues, enumerating gardening and candle-making businesses, a cleaning service, and a design studio. Dharmachari Kulananda, mentioned in the quote, has been founder of Windhorse Trading and became one of the leading Order members, now being a member of the Preceptor's College Council.

53. FWBO Communications Office, *The FWBO Files: A Response*, p. 41.

54. Tejamati, "Working Inside the Movement," p. 9.

55. Figures according to Vajraketu, "Marketing Values," p. 24, and information by Ian Tromp, a member involved in Windhorse Trading, in his e-mail messages from May 5, 1998 and July 8, 1998. For Windhorse Trading see also "Transforming Work," *Golden Drum* 39 (1995): 13, and Dharmachari Vajraketu, "The Dana Economy," *Golden Drum* 22 (1991): 6–7.

56. Vajraketu, "Marketing Values," p. 25.

57. For example, see the description of duties as a team-member in a restaurant by Dharmacharini Subhadramati, "Working Wonders," *Dharma Life* 5 (1997): 38–41; likewise the experiences of work in Jambala, a gift and book shop in London, by Dharmcharini Dhammadinna, "In the Town But Not of It," *Golden Drum* 11 (1988/89): 9. Thanks also to Ian Tromp for further explanations in his e-mail messages from May 1999.

58. Tejamati, "Working Inside the Movement," p. 9.

59. Subhuti, *Buddhism for Today*, p. 77. Likewise, Dharmachari Vajraketu, "Working for the World," *Golden Drum* 4 (1987): 7. See also "The Art of Generosity," *Golden Drum* 22 (1991).

60. Subhadramati, "Working Wonders," p. 41.

61. Ibid., p. 41.

62. Vajraketu, "Marketing Values," p. 26.

63. See also Dharmacharini Jayachitta, "Die Dana-Gesellschaft," *Lotusblätter* 4 (1996): 29–31.

64. Vajraketu, "Working for the World," p. 7.

65. Vajraketu, "Marketing Values," p. 26.

66. See Subhuti, *Buddhism for Today*, p. 129, and Subhuti, *Sangharakshita*, pp. 219–63. Apparently, the FWBO website contains a hyperlink "Creating a New Society." The page is based on Dharmacharini Vessantara, *The Friends*. However, striving to "create the new society" has slipped out of usage during the 1990s, as Vishvapani self-critically asserts; see Vishvapani, "Still Building the New Society," p. 24.

67. Inside page of the back cover of *Dharma Life* 5 (1997).

68. "Den Westen Integrieren. Interview mit Sangharakshita," interview done by Martin Baumann and Christian von Somm, in German translation in *Spirita-Zeitschrift für Religionswissenschaft* 1 (1992): 58–61, quote p. 60; quoted also in Subhuti, *Sangharakshita*, p. 253.

69. Weber, *Gesammelte*, p. 375.

70. Max Weber, *Die Protestantische Ethik*, ed. by J. Winckelmann, 7th ed. (Gütersloh: Mohn, 1984), p. 347.

71. Weber, *Gesammelte*, p. 367.

ENGAGED BUDDHISM
IN EUROPE, AFRICA,
AND AUSTRALIA

Sensei Claude AnShin Thomas leads a street retreat in Berlin, 1997.
Courtesy Franz-Johannes Litsch.

A Survey of
Engaged Buddhism in Britain

Sandra Bell

During the past twenty years Buddhism in Britain has enjoyed a
rapid rate of expansion. Evidence for this is to be found mainly in the number of Buddhist centers and groups recorded in the *Buddhist Directory* for
Britain maintained by the Buddhist Society in London.[1] When it comes to
accounting individual numbers of Buddhists in Britain the matter is less
clear, as the census forms for the United Kingdom do not require people
from outside Northern Ireland to enter a religious affiliation. Martin
Baumann gives a rough estimate of 50,000 Buddhists of European and
North American origin in Britain together with 130,00 Buddhists of Asian
descent.[2] It is also necessary to employ the term "British" with some caution. For example, a group of indigenous Theravada monasteries in Britain
style themselves as belonging to the British Forest Sangha, yet the chief
abbot hails from North America, as do some of the other monks, and among
its numbers the BFS can count Australians, New Zealanders, and representatives from several European countries. A further complication arises from the
fact that many Buddhists who have immigrated from Asia to the United
Kingdom have full British citizenship. It is entirely up to individuals to
declare themselves on the census form as belonging to an ethnic group.[3] Very
little research on Buddhism in Britain was conducted prior to the 1980s, and
the small band of researchers whose work has appeared during the past ten
years have confined themselves to groups with a membership predominantly composed of Buddhists of European origin.

It would be convenient, but ultimately inappropriate, to adopt a distinction between "ethnic Buddhism" and "export Buddhism." This last term was
first postulated by Winston King to identify forms of Buddhism in South and
Southeast Asia that were influenced by contact with Western practices and
systems of thought during the nineteenth century and transposed to the West

by returning colonial officials or academics.[4] However, I have argued else-where that the concept of export Buddhism fails to take account of the role that Asian Buddhists played in this process.[5] In a similar vein Kay[6] has point-ed to what he describes as a "Western theoretical bias" in the treatment of Tibetan Buddhism in Britain by scholars, and to a more general tendency among Western Buddhist practitioners "whose understanding of the tradi-tions they espouse is often simplistic, idealistic and uninformed about how broader historical and oriental contexts continue to exert a normative influ-ence on their development in the Occident."[7] It should be understood that Asian Buddhists continue to play an important part in the development of Buddhism in Britain. Some organizations have Asian founders and leaders who remain embedded within spiritual lineages in Asia. Others have Western leaders who received training in Asia and maintain important links with ecclesiastical authorities and teachers in Asia.

The forms of Buddhism represented range from comparatively rare forms of Chinese Buddhism to various Tibetan groups, Zen and other Japanese traditions, Theravada monasteries and nonmonastic groups employ-ing *vipassana* meditation techniques, as well as syncretistic movements such as the Friends of the Western Buddhist Order.[8] Buddhism in Britain is thus extremely diverse and prone to sectarianism. There are also a significant number of small groups that do not subscribe to a particular tradition.[9] Most of those who join groups of one kind or another emphasize the need for "community," which is usually expressed by the term "sangha." In Britain the term "sangha" is used in a variety of ways, from the most restricted sense, meaning members of a monastic community, to a rather vague notion of friendly association. For others the notion of sangha is less significant. Some individuals identify themselves as Buddhist practitioners, but reject the idea of belonging to institutions, regarding them as obstacles to personal spiritual development.

The three largest Buddhist organizations in Britain are the Friends of the Western Buddhist Order (FWBO), the New Kadampa Movement (NKT), and Soka Gakkai International—United Kingdom (SGI-UK). All three are closely bounded, hierarchical organizations with clearly delineated institu-tional structures and forms of membership and an undisguised commitment to recruitment and expansion. These types of movements have sprung up during the past three decades, and may indicate a new direction in British Buddhism, though, as we shall see, this trend has opponents who wish to stem the tide.

The history of Buddhism in Britain dates back to the nineteenth centu-ry. The middle classes in Victorian England displayed a fascination with

Buddhism that has been ably charted by Philip Almond, but even those who took the lead in promoting Buddhism at this time did not claim to be adherents.[10] There was speculation about the true religious allegiance of important figures such as Edwin Arnold and Professor Rhys-Davids, who were suspected of being crypto-Buddhists, but both men hedged the question and stopped short of proclaiming themselves to be actual Buddhists.[11] The major change initiated at the beginning of the twentieth century was a shift from scholarly interest to practice. Initially practice consisted of the adoption of lay precepts, together with the interpretation and promotion of Buddhist teachings, but meditation became a major focus after the Second World War. By the 1980s the teaching and practice of meditation in both lay and monastic organizations was absolutely central. As Sharf observes, a popular exegetical strategy led to the view that "Buddhist ethics, doctrine, art and ritual ultimately emerge from, and revert to, a mode of meditative experience."[12] This perspective is closely related to a much-vaunted image of Buddhism as an enlightened spirituality "based on experience rather than faith."[13]

As with the lay meditation practitioners in Sri Lanka described by Gombrich, British practitioners ascribed instrumental as well as spiritual benefits to the practice of meditation so that Buddhism came to be seen as a religion of self-help.[14] This is not the place to embark on an analysis of the long and complex history of the self in Western culture. It is sufficient to note the observations of one well-known contributor to the field. The British sociologist Anthony Giddens asserts that "in the context of a post-traditional order, the self becomes a *reflexive project*."[15] Giddens argues that in the more stable conditions of "traditional society" changes in identity inherent in the human life cycle were marked and achieved through well-worn *rites de passage*. In the contemporary setting—for which Giddens coins the term "high modernity"—this is no longer the case. Instead of redefining itself according to clear and well-defined collective principles, the altered self "has to be explored and constructed as part of a reflexive process of connecting personal and social change."[16] According to Giddens, in these circumstances the self must pursue its own identity, frequently through some form of therapy that "involves the individual in systematic reflection about the course of her or his life's development."[17] Meditation, together with discussions based on the experience of meditation with teachers and fellow practitioners, constitutes just such a form of "systematic reflection."

There are, however, small signs that in Britain what Prebish observes in North America as "the mad dash to meditation" is mitigated by other concerns, which brings us closer to the topic of engaged Buddhism.[18] After decades dedicated to inward-looking efforts to establish Buddhism in Britain through the founding of groups and organizations that stress the practice of meditation, there are indications that some Buddhists want to reach outward to establish their position within the wider religious landscape. This will entail two new adaptations. Firstly, Buddhists will need to demonstrate a prepared-ness to extend their concerns with personal spirituality toward involvement with public issues. Second, they will need to overcome a preoccupation with institution-building and its inherent dangers of division through sectarianism.

THE ANATOMY OF ENGAGED BUDDHISM IN BRITAIN

Among Buddhist circles in Britain there is disagreement about the precise meaning and implications of the term "engaged Buddhism." Sallie King's assertion that Buddhist social reformers, though distinct from one another in many respects, begin from the same premise that "the basic teachings of Buddhism can profitably be read with the *intention* of determining their impli-cations for social ethics, and for social and political theory"[19] is strongly sup-ported by some commentators and a small number of activists in Britain. Others dismiss such a statement as tautology. The Theravada monk Venerable Khemadhammo, founder and spiritual leader of the Buddhist prison chap-laincy and aftercare service Angulimala, is one example of those who eschew the term for that reason.

In all respects Khemadhammo exemplifies Christopher Queen's descrip-tion of socially engaged Buddhists who "direct their energies towards social conditions over which the state has legal authority" but whose objective is "to influence the exercise of temporal power, not to wield it."[20] As a monk who visits and attends to the welfare of prisoners and who, in his work since 1985, aims to secure a nonsectarian Buddhist chaplaincy service to cover all of Britain's penal institutions, Khemadhammo is "engaged" on two fronts. He is bringing direct comfort to prisoners while tackling imbalances and prejudices in the British penal system. One moment he may be face to face with a pris-oner, in the next he may be tackling the civil servants of the British govern-ment's Home Office over issues that affect the quality of life of prisoners. Angulimala is also a rare example of an organization where Buddhists of dif-ferent persuasions work together. Currently there are forty chaplains working in two-thirds of the penal institutions in England and Wales. In 1996 there were 230 inmates registered as Buddhists in British prison establishments, including young offenders' institutions. However, chaplains often find them-selves encountering those who are not officially registered as Buddhists, so that the numbers served are greater than those represented by official figures. Four training workshops for chaplains are held each year at Khemadhammo's Wat Pah Santidhamma in the Warwickshire countryside.

Despite his proximity to Queen's model of an engaged Buddhist, Khemadhammo dismisses the notion as something apart and different from everyday Buddhist practice:

> I do not consider myself working in some separate category of Buddhism. To me Buddhism is Buddhism and it is about the practice of the Noble Eightfold Path. I consider myself doing in the jails what I do out of the jails. The difference being that while I can make Buddhism available round here just by being here and letting people come to me if they will. People in jail cannot come to me and so I have to go to them and take the monastery to them. And just as I have had to make an effort to establish this monastery and I continue to make an effort to maintain and improve it, so I have to make an effort to establish Angulimala and continue to make an effort to maintain it and improve the service we offer. Unfortunately, it seems to me that engaged Buddhism is a bit precious.[21]

At the other end of the scale are people who identify themselves as engaged Buddhists by joining an organization that incorporates the term in its title, but who do not themselves necessarily participate in overt forms of political or social activism beyond writing occasional letters, or collecting signatures for petitions in support of humanitarian, animal welfare, or environmental causes. A high proportion of members of the Leeds Network for Engaged Buddhists (LNEB) fall into this category. But here too the concept of engaged Buddhism is contested.

Alex White is editor of the LNEB journal *Interbeing* and plays an important role in coordinating the network's membership of 237 people,[22] all of whom receive the journal, which is also available in shops and Buddhist centers around Britain.[23] It is also delivered to prisoners through the auspices of Angulimala. Even though most of Alex White's spare time is taken up with editing and distributing the journal of an organization that is in name at least dedicated to engaged Buddhism, she nevertheless reveals similar reservations about the term to those expressed by Khemadhammo.

> Wherever I turn I find myself engaged—enmeshed in, creating and created by innumerable relationships and the play of cause and effect. How can I opt out? Whoever, whatever, wherever would I be if I did? When people ask me—as they quite often do—What is an engaged Buddhist? I am embarrassed. The phrase seems to imply that there are, can be, disengaged Buddhists. That is not something I feel it is polite, or politic, to admit. This becomes clearer if we use the Dalai Lama's alternative expression, *universal responsibility*. Would it sound okay to say, "We are the responsible Buddhists, they are the irresponsible ones"?[24]

It is apparent from the pages of *Interbeing*, and from the *Members Only Newsheet*, that participants share Alex White's ambivalence about the range of meanings attached to the concept of engaged Buddhism, though they are prepared to belong to an organization that features the problematic term in its title. The Leeds Network does not organize activities. The majority of members are looking for like-minded contacts and an exchange of ideas rather than collective action, though on occasions concerted effort arises over a specific issue. For example, when one member brought the campaign for a re-trial for Brandon Astor Jones, who was awaiting execution in Georgia State Prison, to the attention of the network, others joined in. Support consists of letters to Astor Jones, appeals to the state authorities, and canvassing for donations to his campaign fund.

The employment of networks as alternatives to, or in conjunction with, more formally constituted organizations is a feature of engaged Buddhism in Britain and elsewhere. Networks connect people who share a common interest, but who are otherwise dispersed, either geographically or because they are embedded within separate institutions. Networks consist of a constellation of interpersonal relationships and linkages that overlap and cross-cut organizational boundaries to embrace a wide, but relatively fluid, constituency. The cultivation of networks for the achievement of social purposes is not new, but the potential for their effectiveness has been advanced by relatively recent developments in information and communication technology. Because of the growth of e-mail and other forms of electronic communication in many sectors of commerce and government "the dominant image for human organization is now the network."[25]

In Britain the use of networks among engaged Buddhists is attractive for a number of other reasons. Firstly, it keeps individuals informed and in touch while enabling them to maintain their major focus of activity elsewhere. Secondly, as engaged Buddhism in Britain is still in its infancy, networks provide a forum for ongoing discussion and argument. This is because networks are less constrained by requirements to produce officially sanctioned policies and actions than are formally constituted organizations. Thirdly, the metaphor of the network is widely deployed in the discourse of engaged Buddhism to evoke Buddhist ideas about the relatedness of all phenomena. The network is therefore viewed as an organizational parallel of the central insight that has ideally led each member to join. On the title page of recent editions of *Indra's Network*, the journal of the Network of Engaged Buddhists—UK, is the explanation "At each intersection of the net is a light revealing jewel. Each and all exist only in their mutuality."[26]

Because of their loosely federated form networks can spawn other networks with little disruption or acrimony. The Leeds Network began as a local branch of the Network of Engaged Buddhists (NEB), originally known as the Buddhist Peace Fellowship and based in London, but it has since evolved in size and character to become distinct from the parent body. Views expressed within the LNEB are not as directly and exclusively concerned with the shaping of political opinion as are those expressed within the NEB. *Interbeing* was for a while the journal of the NEB, replacing a previous journal *Indra's Net*. However, leading members of NEB in favor of a more overtly political stance than that adopted by Alex White founded a new journal, *Indra's Network*, while *Interbeing* became the journal of the Leed's Network.

In 1991 members of the NEB living in and around Leeds wanted to increase communication amongst members of the six separate, local Buddhist groups. True to the sectarian tendencies that afflict British Buddhism, the inaugural meeting revealed tension between the groups. It was clear that aspirations for closer local cooperation between groups was not to be met, though there were enough individuals prepared to support the principle of loose affiliation. After two months the network had a chairperson, a secretary, a newsletter, and twenty-one members, several of whom were not attached to local groups. The network has proved to be particularly attractive to isolated self-ascribed Buddhists who eschewed joining a group, indicating that for some, engaged Buddhism denotes a form of Buddhism that is attractive more for its ecumenical approach than for its social engagement.

The NEB was formed in 1983 by a group of Buddhists who were active as individuals in the British Green Party and other peace and environmental groups. The wider social context was one of growing support for the British peace movement's anti-nuclear campaign, which had reached new heights in response to the installation of nuclear Cruise missiles at U.S. bases in Britain and other parts of Europe. The declared aim was to provide an affinity group and a pressure group to provide an opportunity for personal and social transformation. As such the British NEB was modeled on the American Buddhist Peace Fellowship whose name it originally bore and to which it became affiliated.[27] The problem with the BPF was that it required people to attend meetings. But supporters were also occupied in other campaigning groups and it was difficult to get more than twenty people together at any one time. It was agreed that a Buddhist version of groups that were already flourishing represented a reduplication of effort and resources. Consequently, the organization transformed itself into a network of concerned Buddhists whose activism could continue to be expressed within existing organizations, such as local and national peace groups. The network became a focus for thinking about Buddhist perspective on social issues through exchanges in the pages of its journal, attendance at occasional retreats or workshops, and interpersonal contacts established through the circulation of a list of members and their interests.

The larger network was to comprise smaller networks of individuals and groups living in the same area or interested in the same types of activities. The organizational design was intended to address the geographical dispersion of the membership while providing a forum for the development of a Buddhist approach to social and political issues. This worked to an extent, though numbers did not reach more than several hundred and currently stand at less than two hundred. In the early days Thich Nhat Hanh was invited to lead retreats organized by the NEB, which offered discounted rates to members, thus attracting followers of Thich Nhat Hanh to take up membership. However, preparations for the founding of a U.K. branch of Thich Nhat Hanh's Community of Interbeing in 1996 focused the attention of his followers away from the NEB and into organizing their own retreats and raising money for a U.K. retreat center. For some NEB members these events confirm a view that the institutionalization of Buddhism in Britain has resulted in the creation of too many competing organizations, creating diversions and divisions that are counterproductive. In 1990 John Snelling, a figure well known within British Buddhist circles through his writings, voiced these criticisms in an article in *Indra's Net.*[28]

Snelling aired his anxieties about how opportunities for the accumulation of wealth and power increase as Buddhism grows and becomes more fashionable in Britain.

> Competition to control that wealth and power is growing. We see at the same time the whole infrastructure of organised religion beginning to emerge: temples and monasteries and centres and new professional functionaries of various sorts. A great deal of sectarianism has also meanwhile crept in by the back door. I have seen at first-hand the liberal spirit, which I feel is axiomatic to Buddhism, undermined in Western Buddhist institutions.[29]

Ken Jones, a prominent member of NEB and writer on engaged Buddhist social theory—which he terms "engaged Buddhology"—has recently spoken in a similar vein to Snelling. Jones has lived a political life first as a Marxist and later as a member of the Green Party in Wales, and has been a practicing Buddhist for the past fourteen years. His biography is not so unusual for a British Buddhist. In ten years of research I have met others who had been active in left-wing organizations, in the green movement, and in trade unions. Unlike Ken Jones, however, several other of my informants had come to Buddhism through despair over politics and wished to avoid further entanglement in political processes.

In an article for the British journal *New Ch'an Forum*,[30] Ken Jones complains of the "dominance" in British Buddhism of the three large groups mentioned earlier—the FWBO, NKT, and SGI-UK. Jones is wary of the degree of uniformity that he perceives in each of the organizations and suspicious that it is maintained through "a process of socialization." Jones asserts that such movements "satisfy belongingness and identity needs and offer an assured belief system, free of ambivalence, choice, uncertainty and other disturbing challenges encountered on more exposed spiritual paths."[31] As we shall see, Jones has his own agenda to pursue, but his idea that these organizations constitute important sources of identity and community for their membership does receive support from recent academic research on the FWBO, NKT, and SGI-UK.[32]

Jones suggests a scheme for the taxonomy of engaged Buddhism in Britain based on a continuum running from a "hard end" to a "soft end." Jones places himself and the British NEB, of which he is a leading member, at the hard end.

> At the soft end are individuals and organizations who see Engaged Buddhism as ranging from being kind to your neighbors to promoting a society based on the principles of the Dharma. The hard enders do not deny the irrefutable logic of this, but claim that it robs Engaged Buddhism of a sufficiently clear definition. So at the hard end they tend to draw the line to include service and welfare initiatives but exclude personal, every day acts of kindness and the like. These positions are not only about the differing areas of concern. Hard enders believe governments and other institutions should be included in the active concerns of Buddhist morality; soft enders tend to urge only personal responsibility. Soft enders tend to be less keen on Buddhist social analysis and more on personal experience and mindfulness.[33]

The continuum model was developed within the NEB. It is therefore an illustration of how people involved in the engaged Buddhism debate model themselves. The model was generated within the most active section of the NEB, that is by the self-designated "hard" end. For them engagement has to entail a wholesale critique of current social and political realities using Buddhist concepts and teachings as exemplified in the writings of Jones and also those of Green Party activist and former Theravada monk, Christopher Titmuss. Hard enders regard themselves as ecumenical in the sense that they want to involve Buddhists of all persuasions and are prepared to cooperate with like-minded folk from other faiths. They do not deny that the personal is the political, indeed this is an important part of their argument. Nor do they accept that the term "engaged Buddhism" is redundant in the manner of Khemadhammo and Alex White.

The hard end/soft end model is not so much a sociological tool of analysis as a critique of British Buddhism by those who see themselves as engaged Buddhists. As a model from within it places the proponents in a relation to others—there are those who talk, and those who act, those who build institutions, and those who look outwards. The model therefore challenges others to think metaphorically about their own position across a spectrum of priorities. It cannot however act as a social scientific model as it does not accommodate the full sweep of the disparate British Buddhist scene.

During the past two years a new and somewhat younger grouping has begun to emerge known as the Buddhist Social Activist Network (BSAN). The network is coordinated by Guhyapati, a member of the FWBO, and around half of the forty or so people involved in the network are also members of the FWBO (four of whom are Order Members). The intention is for the BSAN to operate separately and its activities are not formally sanctioned by senior Order Members.

BSAN seeks to bring Buddhism to social activism as well as bringing social activism to Buddhism. One project has been to introduce Buddhist perspectives to those who are already working as activists and to this end workshops were held during the British Green Party Autumn Conference in 1995. This was followed up by what Guhyapati describes as "a kind of Buddhist activist road-show" that traveled during the summer months of 1996 and 1997 around activist gatherings and protest camps. The workshops are designed to introduce Buddhist principles into issues such as conflict management and communication, and to introduce activists to meditation as a tool for "purifying motives and managing burn-out." Members of the network also operate as affinity groups during particular actions, especially those centering on protests against the arms trade. For example, members joined a blockade of the Covert Operations and Procurement Exhibition held at Farnborough Airbase in 1997 and have coordinated actions directed at Britain's twelve most prominent arms companies. The BSAN is not at odds with the NEB and there have been explorations toward affiliation. However, the emergence of BSAN does represent a new generation who have strong connections with numbers of other pressure groups. Several members of

BSAN are also members of high profile activist groups such as Earth First! and Radical Roots, who have received massive publicity in Britain through daring and tenacious exploits in protesting against new roads and the expansion of Manchester Airport. BSAN is therefore operating within a wider movement that adopts an uncompromising stance against authority. At present their activities are not well known among British Buddhist circles and the question of whether or not they will gain a measure of support remains to be tested. As will be demonstrated in the following section, many other Buddhist projects in the fields of health, welfare, and education and are currently in the early stages of development and seeking to be taken seriously by a general public divided over the legitimacy of the self-styled eco-warriors whose daring, but contentious, tactics and anti-establishment life styles are periodically plastered across newspapers and television screens.

PSYCHOTHERAPY

One of the most notable features of the translation of Buddhism in the West is its association with psychotherapy. In Britain this aspect of Buddhism has not kept pace with developments in the United States, but there are signs that this is changing. For example, a three-day conference on Buddhism, science, and psychotherapy entitled "The Psychology of Awakening" held at Dartington Hall in Devon during the summer of 1997 was so heavily oversubscribed that places could have been filled three times over.

The numbers of psychotherapists and counselors whose work is informed by Buddhist psychology are increasing as pioneers in the field turn their attention to training students in Britain. Maura and Franklyn Sills are founders of the Karuna Institute in Devon where they run a program of courses and professional training in what they term Core Process Psychotherapy. This form of therapy stresses the joint relationship between therapist and client. It draws heavily upon Buddhist psychological theory in relation to the *skandhas* attempting to show "how the person continues to re-embody the past situation or condition and is stuck in the problem."[34] The four-year training course begins with an introduction to Buddhist theories of personality and students are introduced to contemplative practices to support their learning. In the second year Western models of personality are introduced and set within a Buddhist context. During the third and final year students continue to study Buddhist teachings while drawing on mythical and symbolic materials from oriental and occidental traditions. Students engage with the ethical issues surrounding psychotherapy and learn practical skills such as the compilation of case notes. Courses are also offered to experienced and accredited psychotherapists who want to gain a Buddhist perspective on their work.

Developments such as this have to be seen within the context of a more general concern for the contemporary "reflexive project of the self" identified by Giddens and discussed earlier in relation to meditation. In Britain it was not until the latter half of the twentieth century that techniques and theories concerning self-awareness and self-cultivation originating in academic and clinical psychology, especially in the U.S., began to assume an impact. By the 1970s the notion of "consciousness raising" became associated with questions of personal morality, creating a connection between collective responsibility and the idea of "personal politics" that has been shown to play an important part in the debate about the nature and scope of engaged Buddhism. Ideas and techniques for self-improvement exploded at a popular level and have continued to grow in range and availability during the past two and a half decades. Counseling evolved as a profession to cater for the rise of interest in the self, providing a new form of mental health care as well as creating a burgeoning area of employment within the private and public sectors.

It is becoming increasingly likely that in Britain a person's first encounter with Western Buddhism may take place during consultation with a psychotherapist, or through reading the published work of practicing Buddhist therapists, such as David Brazier's book *Zen Therapy*.[35] Although the title of the book refers to Zen, Brazier's ideas are keenly influence by his reading of the *Abhidhamma* and by his personal history. Brazier first began practicing in the Zen tradition in 1967, when his teacher was Jiyu Kennett Roshi. He spent a year as a monk at Kennett Roshi's British center, Throssel Hole in Northumberland. Afterwards Brazier was in search of a career that would measure up to his ideals of "right livelihood" and trained as a psychiatric social worker. By the early 1980s he began seeing clients independently and working out the foundations for a therapeutic relationship based on a dialectic between Buddhist teaching on the nature of personality and the humanistic approach of Carl Rogers, with the aim of "achieving something new that goes beyond both."[36]

A central theme in *Zen Therapy* is the influence of Buddhist ideas and practice on the therapist and how that influence might benefit the therapeutic relationship with clients. The idea that therapists who practice meditation are likely to become more effective in facilitating a healing process in the client had already been suggested by the British academic, therapist, and meditation teacher, Guy Claxton.[37] Claxton does not advocate meditation for clients because in some cases it might "push them further than they are ready, willing or able to go," but Claxton does advocate meditation as something "that ought to be a part of every therapist's initial and on-going training."[38] Brazier suggests that therapists can also support clients by adopting the Zen principle of *roshin,* which he translates as "parental mind." According to Brazier, the principle of roshin requires "that we should view all beings as though they were our only child."[39] Western psychotherapy problematizes the tendency of the client to view the therapist as a parent through the processes of "transference." As Brazier has it "psychoanalysts attempt to 'analyse' transference, thus standing above it, while humanistic therapists try to avoid transference arising, by acting congruently."[40] By contrast, the Zen therapist is encouraged to adopt the attitude of a parent.

> But here, we are not talking about the kind of parents who insists on superiority. Rather, we are talking about the fact that the person with real parental mind, loves, understands and feels kindly disposed towards the person no matter what they do or have done or have become.[41]

David Brazier and his wife Caroline, who specializes in the treatment of eating disorders in women, are based in Newcastle-upon-Tyne, in the northeast of England. Together they have developed a number of courses in Buddhist psychotherapy that are taught under the auspices of the Amida Trust. The Amida Trust is a nonsectarian organization, formally registered as a charity in January 1997. The trust has built up a network of individuals known as the Amida Sangha. Through the medium of the network, members of the Amida Sangha have recently taken the first exploratory steps toward involvement with peace and reconciliation work in Bosnia.

An hour's drive away from Newcastle, over the border in the Dumfries and Galloway region of Scotland, is the only Buddhist therapeutic community in Britain. The community inhabits the largest log house in Britain, named Lothlorien. The original owners of Lothlorien donated the property to the Rokpa Trust in 1989. Rokpa is a charitable trust, founded in 1982, that developed from work at Samye Ling Tibetan Buddhist Centre in the Galloway Hills. It was founded in the 1960s by two exiled lamas, Chogyam Trungpa Rinpoche and Akong Rinpoche, though Chogyam Trungpa departed for the United States in 1970. Samye Ling has a long history of assisting distressed people. Akong Rinpoche and his senior disciples realized that many visitors who arrived in search of a haven were often in need of specialized care. The result was Lothlorien, which functions as a supportive community for people experiencing mental health problems. The project was developed by Nick Jennings, a mental health worker with twenty-five years involvement with Samye Ling. The community consists of eight residents and four volunteers who together maintain seventeen acres of vegetable gardens, woodland, and pasture land. Training is provided in organic horticulture and other practical skills to improve community members' future job and training prospects. There are also three nonresident members of staff to provide individual support and to facilitate the meditation sessions and art work that are offered on an optional basis. Lothlorien is now sufficiently well recognized to receive contributions for its funding from the Scottish Office and from Dumfries and Galloway Regional Council on the grounds of its proven effectiveness and the service it offers to local people.

Another example of service provision in the field of mental health established by disciples of Akong Rinpoche is Tara Associates, specializing in personal development for people at work, located in Warrington in northwest England. Tara Associates' promotional literature uses a lotus flower as its emblem and declares the methods used to "have been well tried over the centuries in Tibetan Buddhist training." There is also a photograph of Akong Rinpoche, who is described as Tara Associates' patron and advisor and "a master within an ancient spiritual tradition."[42]

These kinds of ventures whereby Buddhist practitioners explicitly draw upon Dharma teaching to provide management consultancy and skills training is very new in Britain, and it is especially interesting to note that conventional public organizations, such as local government councils, are prepared to hire them. Pertinent questions for the future are whether Tara Associates will prosper and grow in influence and whether we might expect to see further initiatives in the fields of human resource management and management training.

In Britain Buddhists are well represented in the caring professions, which provide favorable locations for Buddhist ideas to intersect with mainstream policy and practice. The climate in Britain is receptive to new ideas in areas of mental health provision, welfare, and employment, as the country's welfare state is currently under review. At the same time the labor market and employment patterns are changing rapidly in response to globalization and new technologies.

SOCIAL AND ENVIRONMENTAL PROJECTS

Although Akong Rinpoche's center at Samye Ling is one of the most geographically isolated Buddhist establishments in Britain, its development over the past thirty years has become ever more outward-looking. Presently, Samye Ling is the hub of several ventures, other than those discussed above, seeking to serve a variety of constituencies and purposes. Akong Rinpoche spends a large proportion of his time in Tibet overseeing Rokpa's work there. Rokpa currently supports over fifty aid projects at the local level in Tibet. The projects include the provision of schools and clinics and training centers in some of the most remote rural areas. Rokpa funds cultural projects, such as the woodblock printing of Tibetan texts, as well as environmental projects, such as tree nurseries, reserves, reforestation projects, and the promotion of solar-powered energy sources. Rokpa also undertakes work in Britain, but so far its activities have not reached the scale of the work carried out in Tibet. Volunteers in Glasgow, Birmingham, and London have concentrated on working with homeless people living on the streets. This work has sometimes been undertaken in association with existing charities for the homeless, but since 1988 Rokpa volunteers have managed programs to distribute food, clothing, and blankets to the homeless in three London boroughs.

The most celebrated scheme emerging from Samye Ling is the Holy Island project. In 1992 Samye Ling purchased a small island in the Firth of Clyde off the west coast of Scotland. The island has a strong religious history. The origin of its name goes back to the sixth century when the island sheltered a saint of the Celtic church, Saint Molaise. Through its association with Saint Molaise, the island became a pilgrimage site and during the thirteenth century a small monastic community was located there. Lama Yeshe Losal, Samye Ling's resident meditation instructor, oversees a project that seeks to draw on the island's historical association with contemplative Christianity by the foundation of an inter-faith center. This has brought Yeshe Losal into a close working relationship with some Christian leaders in Scotland, including the Bishop of Edinburgh, who is an ardent supporter and patron of the project. Tree planting and nature conservation form another aspect of the project that requires the cooperation of the Scottish Office, the Forestry Commission, and the Farming and Wildlife Advisory Group with Samye Ling. Already volunteers have planted 27,000 trees. Plans for a self-sustaining retreat center, designed by architect Andrew Wright, won the main prize in the AJ/Bovis Royal Academy Summer Show in 1994, and aspects of work on the project have attracted grant funding from the British government's Department of the Environment These events have given the project a very high profile among British landscape designers and architects with an interest in sustainable environments. Lord Richard Rogers, famous for his design of the Lloyds' building in London and the Pompidou Center in Paris, has become a patron of the project, as has Jonathan Porrit, a former director of the environmental campaign, Friends of the Earth, and an advisor to Prince Charles. Success in forging these kinds of public links with influential figures from within the British establishment have contributed considerably to Samye Ling's growing reputation as the center of a Buddhist organization intent on forging alliances with non-Buddhist institutions and individuals.

Another Tibetan Buddhist movement in Britain with an agenda for social service is Rigpa, whose spiritual leader is Sogyal Rinpoche. Rigpa has centers in London, Norwich, and Birmingham. At the London center the Tibetan ritual known as *ts'og* has been adapted to meet urban conditions and Western sensibilities. The ritual involves tantric practitioners making offerings of food and alcohol to divine and semi-divine beings. After the offering practitioners consume the food and drink. In the Tibetan context surplus sacralized food is put outside to be consumed by wild birds and animals. This is also the practice adopted by members of some Western Tibetan Buddhists groups such as the New Kadampa Tradition. Sogyal Rinpoche, however, advises his followers in London to donate the remains of the fortnightly *ts'og* ritual offerings to a center for homeless people in the Kings Cross area of the city.

Rigpa's major social platform is the provision of education on aspects of emotional and spiritual care for the dying and bereaved through a spiritual care education and training program. Seminars and workshops are based on the principles expounded by Sogyal Rinpoche's book, *The Tibetan Book of Living and Dying,* and are attended by members of the medical profession, hospice workers, those who are dying, and family members caring for the dying. The long-term aim is to establish a service for people from all walks of life and religious backgrounds who are facing death, to expand existing training and public education programs to reach more people within the health and caring professions, and to establish centers that offer care to the dying. The first of these centers is the Copper Mountain Living With Dying Project at Bantry Bay in southwest Ireland designed to offer spiritual care together with appropriate modern nursing and medical support. Fund-raising is in progress for a facility to be operating by the year 2000.

One means by which the fund-raising program for the Copper Mountain project has been able to appeal to other British Buddhists interested in care for the dying is through *Raft*, the bi-annual journal of a national organization, Buddhist Hospice Trust, established in 1986. The Trust operates the Ananda Network, a nationwide network of volunteers willing to visit and offer spiritual friendship to those who are seriously ill, dying, or bereaved. Most requests for support come from Buddhists who are not aligned to particular groups or organizations. The trust also runs seminars, study days, and retreats, which are usually held in London. Members have access to information and resources, including free use of an audiocassette library. A future objective is the provision of residential care for the dying.

EDUCATION

Buddhist educational institutions in Britain are scarce. The seeds for future developments in this field exist in some recent projects. In 1994, after two years of fund-raising and preparation, the Dharma School was opened near the town of Brighton on the south coast. The school caters to boys and girls aged between three and eleven years old. It is a fee-paying school, but the fees of £2,500 per year are insufficient to cover costs, and the school is also supported by parents and other volunteers who contribute to school activities and money-raising events. At the other end of the age range is Sharpham College for Buddhist Studies and Contemporary Enquiry, located in Devon, which offers a yearlong residential program for adults. In 1997 twelve students from six countries were registered for the course

The director of studies is author and teacher Stephen Batchelor. Other teachers, including Christopher Titmuss and Christina Feldman, are drawn from the area around the market town of Totnes, which is fast becoming a major center for Buddhist activities in Britain.[43] The course is divided into two sections—Buddhist Studies deals with the various schools of Buddhism, Buddhist history, philosophy, and psychology; and Contemporary Enquiry explores the relationship between Buddhism and society through topics such as right livelihood, ecology and the environment, Western philosophy, psychology, science, art, and culture. The students live as a community sharing cooking, cleaning, and gardening, and undertake voluntary work in the locality.

Stephen Batchelor has reservations about detaching the notion of engaged Buddhism from other aspects of Buddhist practice:

> Leaving aside language of engagement—or its opposite—Buddhist practice, in essence, is one in which a person tries to seek and balance qualities such as wisdom, tolerance and understanding with compassion and love. Traditionally these have been seen as the two wings of a bird. In many different schools practice has been seen as operating within a tension between insight and understanding on the one hand and a compassionate response to the world on the other. That is a classic tension. If one starts from there the whole notion of making an issue out of engagement becomes somewhat superfluous.[44]

Batchelor maintains that authentic Buddhist practice leads necessarily to some engagement with the world. He is concerned that Western Buddhists may be responding with a knee-jerk reaction to criticisms that their practice is inward looking. He stresses the danger in Western Buddhists looking for self-justification according to the values of the societies in which they live:

> Most Buddhist practitioners have been asked at one time or another—"Why do you go off on these retreats? Isn't it selfish? Why don't you go out and do something useful in the world?" Engaged Buddhism is, in a way, counter to that objection. The question is what motivates a person to adopt engaged Buddhism? Is it because they feel they have to somehow justify themselves in the light of Western criticism of Buddhism? Or is it a spontaneous and genuine outflow of their Buddhist practice?[45]

Batchelor maintains that it is dangerous to privilege one dimension of practice over another because the ultimate effect is to reduce Buddhism to one aspect of the whole.

This is perhaps also the place to mention the many external activities of Soka Gakkai International, whose branches are encouraged to sponsor causes that promote international cooperation. From the perspective of the general public SGI may be the best-known Buddhist movement in Britain, though it often receives harsh criticism from other Buddhists. According to Dobbelaere and Wilson's study of SGI in Britain, "Its sponsorship of international peace; its promotion of ecological concerns; its educational commitments and benefactions and its cultural promotion of music and dance, ensure that it enjoys conspicuous public recognition."[46] Certainly the pages of SGI's English language publications are full of references to fund-raising efforts by local groups for the United Nations High Commission for Refugees. SGI's national headquarters at Taplow Court in Buckinghamshire has been host to a number of very high profile events, including the 1992 consultative conference on sustainable development through cultural dialogue, which was designed to precede and influence the United Nations conference on environment and development. The conference was organized jointly with the Commonwealth Human Ecology Council. It was attended by an international gathering of academics and diplomats, with the proceedings being initiated by a personal message from the queen. Few Buddhist organizations in Britain could muster such a glittering display of concern for social and environmental issues. It is therefore curious to note that according to Dobbelaere and Wilson only a small proportion of their informants "ascribed the appeal of the movement to ethical considerations," while "taking control of one's life was a widely diffused desideratum for members."[47] It is this kind of discrepancy between the public face of SGI and views expressed by individual members that may account for some of the caution with which the organization is treated by other Buddhist groups.

WHERE ANGELS FEAR TO TREAD

The most substantive texts on the theory of engaged Buddhism produced by British authors are *The Social Face of Buddhism* and *Beyond Optimism: A Buddhist Political Ecology* by Ken Jones and *The Green Buddha* by Christopher Titmuss.[48] Both men know and respect one another well. Speaking of their relationship and their approach Christopher Titmuss told me: "We have a political aspect and sometimes Buddhism has been apolitical. We go where angels fear to tread. Green politics, door-knocking and protest are part and parcel of what we stand for."

Something has already been said about Jones' background. Christopher Titmuss began his political life at the age of fourteen when he campaigned on behalf of the British Labour Party. In 1967 he left Britain to take the hip-

Buddhist writer-activist Christopher Titmuss addressing students at the Inter-Faith School he co-founded for village children in Bodh Gaya, India. Courtesy Christopher Titmuss.

pie trail to Asia and three years later became a Buddhist monk in Thailand, during which time he spent a period in residence at Buddhadasa Bhikkhu's retreat center Suan Mokkhabalarama ("Garden of the Power of Liberation"). Titmuss disrobed in 1976—"I felt that when the fruit is ripe it has to leave the tree"—and returned to Britain, where he became interested in the fledgling Green Party. After the notorious accident at the Soviet nuclear power station at Chernobyl in 1986 Titmuss became more involved in green politics in Britain, partly because he was so shocked by the British complacency over the ramifications of the accident. In 1987 and 1992 he stood as parliamentary candidate for the Green Party in his home constituency in Devon.

There is insufficient space here to discuss and compare the detailed arguments contained in the work of these authors, each of whom has a distinctive analytical style, while agreeing in broad terms about the relationship between Buddhist spirituality and political engagement. Behind the problems of survival and sustainability that preoccupy Jones and Titmuss is the felt need for an anthropology with which to anchor political discourse and action. Titmuss expresses it thus: "The central issue today is more than the survival of the earth, or the human species; it is what it actually means to be homo sapiens."[49] Our humanity cannot be taken for granted by virtue of belonging to the human species. It has to be achieved through what Jones refers to as "the way of liberation" and demands a political philosophy that connects economic and social justice to ecological factors across the global system. The possibility of reaching "a more complete humanity" can be impeded or assisted according to "whether the social climate helps us to become more human or whether it stokes up the fires of delusion."[50] The social context cannot be a matter of indifference to those who seek spiritual insight through gnosis, for two reasons: first, because social context is a factor that impinges upon an individual's spiritual progress; and second, because it is inevitable that an individual who makes progress realizes that "the notion of self-liberation has become delusive because there is no longer a sense of separate selfhood from which to be liberated."[51]

A Buddhist anthropology thus conceives of human beings as wholly interdependent creatures whose humanity can be compromised by a false or deluded consciousness that separates and divides self from other. For Titmuss the reification of the self and other is the basis for an obsession with profit and a charter for individuals and groups to exploit one another. "The teachings of nonself challenge the basis of contemporary politics, rooted in the market place, and that people exist independently and in competition with each other for control and access to goods and the environment."[52] The essential message conveyed by the writings of Titmuss and Jones is that a paradigm shift in the way people regard themselves and others can result in concrete changes in the world they inhabit. A Buddhist anthropology is inseparable from the development of a Buddhist theory of political economy.

Simon Zadek is an economist and a Buddhist. He is an associate and former research director of the New Economics Foundation in London, the leading research, consultancy, and policy organization for radical economics in Britain. NEF, while not a Buddhist organization, promotes the creation of a just and sustainable economy that puts people and the environment first. Simon Zadek is interested in exploring the bridge between Buddhist ideas and economic theory. He points out that to date there are two dominant trains of thought regarding this relationship. One is connected to E.F. Schumacher's utopian ideas, which are not exclusively inspired by Buddhist sources, though they resonate fairly closely with ideals held by Buddhist radicals in Asian and North Atlantic societies. According to Zadek, "Schumacher's vision was, quite simply, that the economy should exist to serve people, not vice versa, and that it should be in harmony with, rather than exploitive of, nature."[53] The other view originates in the writings of Max Weber, who suggests that value-systems such as Buddhism "constrain progress towards modernization by preventing the rationalization of productive forces."[54] Zadek sees these two interpretations as the opposite sides of the same argument:

> What Weber described as a constraining influence on a certain type of progress, Schumacher depicted as an alternative development model. What Weber saw as the restrictive and embedded social structure of Buddhism, Schumacher saw as the potential for an invigorated human economics. The quintessential sociologist meets the unequivocal utopian.[55]

Zadek asserts that Schumacher's utopia has "clear links with Buddhist principles," but raises the issue of whether it can be applied only to small-scale contexts where schemes based on such principles can enable marginalized people merely to cope with their structural position of exclusion. The question is "Must Buddhist economics be able to penetrate the modern economy to prevent it from driving us along a materially unsustainable path, and to uproot its growing hold on our psychological conditions?"[56] Zadek's answer is a cautiously affirmative. He nominates certain ongoing activities and perspectives as concrete moves toward a Buddhist economics. These include the growth of the "fair-trade" movement, the development of social auditing in the commercial, government, and voluntary sectors, and the notion of sustainable consumption. It is these kinds of initiatives that Zadek thinks that Buddhists "need to identify, acknowledge and support. It is these we must name as moves towards a Buddhist Economics."[57]

Jones, Titmuss, and Zadek all stress the dangers that overconsumption holds for the future in terms of depletion of resources and environmental degradation, but they also emphasize the psychological implications of its impact on individuals and societies. They maintain that in Buddhist terms the drive to consume and the almost complete commoditization of the world is ultimately alienating, and therefore a source of suffering, as much for the have-lots as for the have-nots. Despite the many differences among British Buddhists, the great majority of British Buddhists would agree with this analysis, even if they remain unsure what to do about it. One of the reasons why Soka Gakkai is unpopular with other British Buddhists is because it is perceived as adopting a favorable attitude to the acquisition of worldly goods.

CONCLUSION

The material discussed in this chapter, though covering a wide and varied range of enterprises and ideas, suggests that Buddhism in Britain has moved beyond the initial stages of transmission and institutionalization. Engagement with social and political realities reflects a new confidence and maturity. There is a determined will to integrate Buddhism further into the mainstream of British society and to establish its presence as a moral force in the nation. It is, however, too early to assess how successful this project will be in the long term, as much depends on the extent to which a fragmentation of effort might weaken its ultimate effectiveness. In the short term, social engagement presents Buddhists with important channels of access to the wider society. In this respect the kinds of initiatives described here are likely to have a significant impact on the domestication of Buddhism in Britain.

NOTES

1. *The Buddhist Directory*, 7th ed. (London: The Buddhist Society, 1997). The 1983 *Buddhist Directory* lists 107 societies, groups, public centers, and residential communities. By 1987 there were 44 centers, 105 societies and groups, and 16 monasteries and temples. The 1994 *Directory* has 270 entries and the 1997 *Directory* lists 340 entries.

2. Martin Baumann, "The Dharma Has Come to the West: A Survey of Recent Studies and Sources" *Journal of Buddhist Ethics* 4 (1997).

3. For the 1991 Census for England and Wales, residents were required to fill in

their country of birth and their ethnic group. Here are the results: 29,474 gave Sri Lanka as their country of birth and Asian as their ethnic group; 2,322 gave Burma as their country of birth and Asian as their ethnic group; 4,882 gave Thailand as their country of birth and Asian as their ethnic group; 9,561 gave Vietnam as their country of birth and Asian as their ethnic group. U.K. residents originating in Cambodia, Laos, or Tibet are subsumed under the category "Other Asia," which totals 9,890. A fairly small proportion of the 309,610 residents of the U.K. who were born in India and give Indian as their ethnic group represent the British followers of Dr. Ambedkar. Scott (1995) suggests a figure of 45,000 Ambedkarite Buddhists in Britain. Buddhists are likely to be found among the 53,473 people who report their place of birth as Hong Kong and who give their ethnic group as Chinese, and among the 4,858 who report their place of birth as Singapore and their ethnic group as Chinese.

4. Winston King, *A Thousand Lives Away* (Oxford: Bruno Cassirer, 1964).

5. Sandra Bell, "Buddhism in Britain: Development and Adaptation" (Ph.D. diss., University of Durham, 1991).

6. David Kay, "The New Kadampa Tradition and the Continuity of Tibetan Buddhism in Britain" *Journal of Contemporary Religion* 12 (1997): 277–93.

7. Ibid., p. 278.

8. See Baumann, this volume.

9. For a description of one such group in the city of Bath see Helen Waterhouse, *Buddhism in Bath: Authority and Adaptation* (Leeds: Monograph Series Community Religions Project, Dept. of Theology and Religious Studies, University of Leeds, 1997).

10. Philip Almond, *The British Discovery of Buddhism* (Cambridge: Cambridge University Press, 1988).

11. Bell, "Buddhism in Britain," p. 35.

12. Robert H. Sharf, "Buddhist Modernism and the Rhetoric of Meditative Experience," *Numen* 42 (1995): 228–83.

13. Ibid., p. 233.

14. Richard Gombrich, "From Monastery to Meditation Centre: Lay Meditation in Modern Sri Lanka," in P. Denwood and A. Piatogorsky, eds., *Buddhist Studies Ancient and Modern* (London: Curzon, 1981), pp. 20–34.

15. Anthony Giddens, *Modernity and Self-identity: Self and Society in the Late Modern Age* (Stanford, CA: Stanford University Press, 1991), p. 32. Author's italics.

16. Ibid.

17. Ibid., p. 71.

18. Charles Prebish, "Ethics and Integration in American Buddhism," *Journal of Buddhist Ethics* 2 (1995): 125–39.

19. Sallie King, "Conclusion: Buddhist Social Activism," in Christopher Queen and Sallie King, eds., *Engaged Buddhism: Liberation Movements in Asia* (Albany: State University of New York Press, 1996), pp. 401–36. Author's italics.

20. Christopher Queen, "Introduction: The Shapes and Sources of Engaged Buddhism," in Queen and King, *Engaged Buddhism,* pp. 1–44.

21. All quotations without citations are taken from personal communications in writing or from the transcription of taped interviews held during the period of research for this paper during the summer of 1997.

22. Two-thirds of the membership of the network are drawn from outside of Yorkshire, but its title continues to refer to the west Yorkshire city of Leeds where it was founded. In June 1998 Alex White announced that she was taking a sabbatical of eighteen months.

23. *Interbeing* currently has a print run of 1,000 copies.

24. Personal communication, 1997.

25. Martin Albrow, *The Global Age* (Cambridge: Polity Press, 1996).

26. For example see *Indra's Network* 8 (May 1997).

27. The British NEB is nowadays also affiliated to the International Network of Engaged Buddhists, whose headquarters are in Bangkok, and the International Fellowship for Reconciliation, an interfaith organization.

28. The Community of Interbeing U.K. became a registered charity in November 1996. John Snelling is author of *The Buddhist Handbook: A Complete Guide to Buddhist Teaching, Practice, History and Schools* (London: Rider, 1987). The article "Do We Need a Buddhist Church?" appeared in *Indra's Net* 4.2 (1990).

29. John Snelling, "Do We Need a Buddhist Church?"

30. *New Ch'an Forum* 13 (spring 1996).

31. Ibid.

32. Sandra Bell, "Change and Identity in the Friends of the Western Buddhist Order," *Scottish Journal of Religious Studies* 17 (1996): 87–107; David Kay, "The New Kadampa Tradition and the Continuity of Tibetan Buddhism in Britain," *Journal of Contemporary Religion* 12 (1997): 277–93; Helen Waterhouse, *Buddhism in Bath: Adaptation and Authority* (Leeds: Monograph Series Community Religions Project, Dept. of Theology and Religious Studies, University of Leeds, 1997); Bryan Wilson and Karel Dobbelaere, *A Time to Chant: The Soka Gakkai Buddhists in Britain* (Oxford: Clarendon Press, 1994).

33. Personal communication.

34. Rosamund Oliver, "Psychotherapy as a Spiritual Journey—Rosamund Oliver Interviews Maura Sills," *Self and Society* 24 (1996): 7–14.

35. David Brazier, *Zen Therapy* (London: Constable, 1995).

36. Personal communication.

37. Guy Claxton, "Therapy and Beyond: Concluding Thoughts," in Guy Claxton,

ed., *Beyond Therapy: The Impact of Eastern Religions on Psychological Theory and Practice* (London: Wisdom Publications, 1986), pp. 311–25.

38. Ibid., p 320.

39. Brazier, *Zen Therapy*, p. 152.

40. Ibid.

41. Ibid., p. 153.

42. Information booklet published by Tara Associates, n.d.

43. There is no space in this article for a full explanation of why South Devon has become a focus for Buddhism in Britain. Such an explanation requires reference to the history of the activities of the Dartington Hall Trust, founded by Leonard Elmhurst and his American heiress wife, Dorothy, who were influenced by the ideas of the Indian poet and educationalist Rabinranath Tagore. Despite this influence the school and other institutions connected with the Dartington Hall Trust were essentially secular in orientation. In the mid-1980s, Maurice Ash, a former chairman of the Trust and son-in-law of the Elmhursts, wanted to establish a second trust that would be directly informed by a spiritual tradition. Through their association with American heiress and writer, Nancy Wilson Ross, Maurice and Ruth Ash were introduced to the San Francisco Zen Centre and invited the monks there to set up a community at Sharpham. However, these plans were upset by a crisis that followed revelations about the behavior of the Center's leader Richard Baker Roshi. Instead, in late 1983, a community of English Buddhists was established at Sharpham, including teachers and writers such as Christopher Titmuss, Christina Feldman, Martine Batchelor, and Stephen Batchelor. In 1995 the community was reformed into Sharpham College.

44. Personal communication, September, 1997.

45. Personal communication, September, 1997.

46. Wilson and Dobbelaere, *A Time to Chant,* pp. 1–2.

47. Ibid., p. 59.

48. Ken Jones, *The Social Face of Buddhism* (London: Wisdom Publications, 1989); Ken Jones, *Beyond Optimism: A Buddhist Political Ecology* (Oxford: Carpenter, 1993); Christopher Titmuss, *The Green Buddha* (Totnes: Insight Books, 1995).

49. Ibid., p. 5.

50. Ken Jones, *The Social Face of Buddhism*, p. 126.

51. Ibid., p. 127.

52. Titmuss, *The Green Buddha*, p. 167.

53. Simon Zadek, "Towards a Progressive Buddhist Economics," in J. Watts et al., eds., *Entering the Realm of Reality: Towards Dhammic Societies* (Bangkok: International Network of Engaged Buddhists, 1997), pp. 241–73.

54. Ibid., p. 261.

55. Ibid.
56. Ibid., p. 258.
57. Ibid., pp. 268–69.

Engaged Buddhism in German-Speaking Europe

Franz-Johannes Litsch

ENGAGED BUDDHISM IS A MOVEMENT to restore a spiritual dimension to the practical concerns of daily life. Engaged Buddhists attempt to apply the wisdom and strength of an ancient tradition to the task of overcoming the manifold sufferings of our world. To practice engaged Buddhism is to unlock the deepest potential of persons, to serve others, and to become enlightened. Because the interlocking crises threatening the world today are global manifestations, engaged Buddhism is a global movement. Encompassing all schools, cultures, ethnic groups, genders, and ecosystems, engaged Buddhism invokes a slogan of the late Thai Buddhist philosopher, Buddhadasa Bhikkhu: "The Dharma protects the world."[1]

Engaged Buddhism is responsible Buddhism. It is rooted in an insight into the reciprocal interconnectedness of all existence. It recognizes that everything is "myself," nothing is unfamiliar to me, nothing is separate from me. It recognizes that the way of the Buddha consists in assuming "universal responsibility," as the Dalai Lama has taught. Given the scope of engaged Buddhism as a universalizing perspective, it is possible that an historic and unprecedented phase of the tradition is emerging. We might call this development of Buddhism a new turning of the Dharma wheel.

The content of this new understanding of Buddhism is based on new insights into the Dharma, particularly the teachings of *paticcasamupadda*, *anatta*, and *emptiness*. These have come to be understood, in the term coined by Thich Nhat Hanh, as *interbeing*, a global network of all being and phenomena, mutually connected and contained. A new understanding of buddhahood arises as well. The Buddha's path to liberation begins with oneself and consists in the liberation of the self. This path cannot end with oneself, however. Rather, it recognizes the self in everything, and everything in the self. Buddhahood can no longer be an individual way to liberation and realization; it must expand into a common human realization. This is the immense vision of engaged Buddhism.

Finally, engaged Buddhism imparts a new and deeper meaning to the term "sangha." The sangha, as the community of those who proceed on the way to Buddhahood, becomes the community of all beings, all life, and all evolving processes on our planet. Thich Nhat Hanh can thus speak about the coming buddha, Maitreya, appearing on the earth not in the form of a single person, but in the form of a great spiritual community. Such an expanded vision of liberation suggests that in the encounter between Buddhism and Christianity—in which Christianity has thus far appeared as the exclusive beneficiary—Buddhism may be enriched by many traditional teachings of Christian theology: a divine history of salvation, the message of the coming kingdom of God, the mystical body of the church, the heavenly Jerusalem, and the universal dimension of the one, cosmic Christ. Such conceptions may open up new encounters with Judaism and Islam.

EARLY GERMAN PERCEPTIONS OF BUDDHISM

Germany's interest in Buddhism first emerged among philosophers. Gottfried Wilhelm Leibniz (1646–1716), drawing from the texts of Jesuit missionaries, was possibly the first European to develop a serious interest in the teachings of the Buddha. As an enlightened rationalist, he was fascinated by the Buddha's idea that the world was reduced not to God, but to pure phenomena. His doctrine of monads has a certain rough similarity to the teaching of the *dharmas* in the Abhidharma tradition.[2]

It took another 150 years, however, until another great German philosopher approached the spiritual world of Buddhism. Arthur Schopenhauer (1788–1860) studied the first European translations of Buddhist texts. He eventually called his own philosophy, which developed out of the study of these texts, European Buddhism. In Schopenhauer's writings, Buddhism received its first attention in the hermetically sealed citadels of the Western academy. Schopenhauer's view, however, was marked by a fundamentally pessimistic attitude toward the world and life. As such, his philosophy had much more in common with the tradition of Christian asceticism than with that of the Buddha. For this reason, the effect of his views was all the stronger in the Christian world.

His characterization of Buddhism as a teaching of negation of the will, of the world, and of life not only had a great influence on the people of his own time, but has had a sustained impact on the interpretation of Buddhism in the entire Western world. In the German-speaking areas of

Europe, non-practitioners continue even today to describe and interpret Buddhism in the same manner as Schopenhauer did 150 years ago.

These misinterpretations were deepened further through the contribution of the German sociologist Max Weber (1864–1930). In his famous investigation of the influence of religion on the social development of various cultures, Weber described Buddhism as a world-renouncing and world-denying religion.[3] From this, he claimed, no modern, innovative, and world-changing impulses for society, economics, and scholarship could arise. Ignoring the powerful historical influence of the Buddha on the Brahmanical cultures of South and Southeast Asia, Weber even claimed that Buddhism had never been associated with any social movement whatsoever, and that Buddhism failed to influence the lives of the laity. As insufficient as Weber's knowledge of Buddhism was, his claims have exerted a considerable influence on European scholarship. One of his stereotypes continues to reign: Buddhism is a life-denying tradition incompatible with the requirements of engagement in society.

Up to the First World War, this interpretation of Buddhism intensified. This development was fueled by Christian and Eurocentric apologists, for whom Buddhism became the embodiment of a nihilistic, life-denying threat from the East. In some versions, Buddhism was represented as a religion of spiritual and bodily apathy, resulting from the humidity of South Asia—the religion of an inferior people. In a sketch prepared by the German emperor Wilhelm II, in which he expressed his vision of the "yellow plague" surging against the Occident, the seated Buddha eventually appears as the embodiment of the approaching decline of the world.

Even today, ninety years later, the present pope, John Paul II, writes in his latest book—after numerous personal encounters with representatives of Buddhists of every school—that Buddhism is a pessimistic, life-denying, world-renouncing religion. Indeed, he writes that Buddhism is in fact no religion at all, since it offers not salvation but only renunciation of life, as opposed to Christianity, which is full of affirmation and joy.[4]

The First Buddhists in Germany

The first convert to Buddhism in German-speaking Europe was the great translator Karl Eugen Neumann (1865–1915).[5] Neumann came to Buddhism through Schopenhauer, and subsequently decided to engage in a thorough study of Indology. He devoted his life to translating the Pali canon into German. While this translation is linguistically and aesthetically refined, from today's vantage point it appears to be so full of Christian terminology and interpretations—as well as of Schopenhauerian pessimism—that it has contributed to perpetuating a one-sided, reductive view of the teaching of the Buddha that is embraced even by many Buddhists today.

In the twentieth century, Buddhism has emerged for the first time in the West as a spiritual movement. Intellectuals, artists, and scholars have been attracted to this "religion of reason." Many of these were searching not only for an alternative to Christianity and an academic world that had become removed from real life, but also for new approaches to society. It was for this reason that a very lively, if somewhat comical, encounter began between the budding counterculture of the 1960s and the new wisdom teachings from Asia. Pacifists, vegetarians, and animal rights advocates in particular found in Buddhism a new religious home that corresponded to their values. Conversely, those who arrived at Buddhism in search of a religion found in it the same ethical teachings and life values as did the counterculturists.

This movement ultimately found its most concrete expression in Hermann Hesse's novel, *Siddhartha*. Yet, just as Hesse's Siddhartha left the Buddha in order to go his own way, two currents in German society separated without being enriched or transformed by the other. The youth movement became reactionary and finally fascist, while Buddhism remained renunciatory and intellectual.

A real convergence of those two currents would have to await an authentic and personal encounter with practitioners in Asia. Paul Dahlke, a physician living in Berlin, took the first step in that direction. In 1924 Dahlke, who had taken several trips to Sri Lanka, founded one of the first Buddhist viharas in Europe. This beautiful temple complex still stands in the north of Berlin, and a small, rotating group of monks from Sri Lanka still lives and teaches there. The temple was an important Buddhist center in Germany for several decades. However, the Dharma taught there was more a world view than a practice. The students examined the teaching, not themselves.

The tendency in German-speaking Europe to see Buddhism mainly as a rational, philosophical world view characterized the understanding of the first generation of Buddhist teachers such as Paul Dahlke, Georg Grimm, and Martin Steinke (Tao Chuen). It was this view, too, that brought renowned German philosophers—for the third time—to engage in an intensive study of the Buddha's teaching. The phenomenologist Edmund Husserl (1859-1938) was deeply impressed by the teachings of Buddhism after reading Eugen Neumann's translations of the Pali canon, claiming that they provided new standards during a period of disorientation. At the same time, Husserl attracted an entire generation of Japanese students of German philosophy to the University of Freiburg. These students would go on to exert a great influence on twentieth-century Japanese philosophy, in particular on the Zen-oriented Kyoto School of philosophy.

Husserl's student Martin Heidegger (1889–1976) engaged in an intensive study of Japanese Zen late in his career. Heidegger invited several important Zen masters to his refuge (which resembled a Japanese teahouse) in the Black Forest. One result of this was that Heidegger was admired in Japan to a degree that was denied him in Germany.[6]

The most important impulses that allowed Buddhism to become a complete life praxis in this region were set in motion by the political, social, and ideological catastrophe that came about—first in Germany and eventually throughout Europe—in 1933.

From Philosophy to Practice

The original, monastic way of the Buddha was first pursued in German-speaking cultural regions by three great personalities. In 1903, the talented musician Anton W. F. Gueth donned the robe of a *bhikkhu* in Burma and assumed the name Nyanatiloka. With his thorough knowledge of Buddhist literature, Nyanatiloka achieved such great renown in the Theravadan countries of Asia that, upon his death in 1957, he was honored with a state funeral in Sri Lanka.[7]

Another artist, the painter and poet Ernst Lothar Hoffmann, later became the world-famous Lama Anagarika Govinda. In 1928, at the age of thirty, he became a *bhikkhu* and a disciple of Nyanatiloka. While on a trip to Sikkhim, he came into contact with Tibetan Buddhism. He was so taken by this form of Buddhism that he changed traditions and became a disciple of a Tibetan master, Tomo Geshe Rinpoche. He wandered around Tibet for many years. After the end of the war he founded the first Western order of Tibetan Buddhism, wrote numerous works, and preached the Dharma throughout Germany during the 60s and 70s. Lama Anagarika Govinda died at an advanced age in the late 1980s in California.[8]

The third great German monk of this early period was the renowned Nyanaponika Mahathera. Born Siegmund Feniger of Jewish parents, Nyanaponika initiated in Germany what we today call engaged Buddhism.[9] Even though he donned the monk's robe in Sri Lanka, Nyanaponika saw it as his mission to extend whatever help he could to the increasingly persecuted and terrorized Jewish community in Germany. For several years, he worked in this manner in the midst of Nazi Germany for the Central Jewish Committee for Reconstruction and Aid.[10] In 1936, when this became impossible, he immigrated to Sri Lanka, and later managed to save his mother. He produced classic works of modern Buddhism through his thorough translations and interpretations. Later in his life, Nyanaponika would often cite a statement of the Buddha's from his favorite scripture, the *Satipatthana Sutta*, that has become the motto of the contemporary Network of Engaged Buddhists in Germany: "Protecting oneself, one protects others; protecting others, one protects oneself."[11] Nyanaponika visited Germany and Switzerland often during the 1960s and 70s.

The German nun Ayya Khema, also a Jew forced to flee Berlin in the 1930s, eventually become a disciple of Nyanaponika's in Sri Lanka. Before she died in 1997 Ayya Khema founded a Theravadan monastery of the forest tradition on German soil.

The Viennese professor Fritz Hungerleider, also of Jewish descent and living in Shanghai exile at the same time as Ayya Khema, became acquainted with Buddhism there and brought back the teaching of the Buddha to his homeland after the war. In the early 1960s he led the first Zen *sesshins* in Germany.[12]

During the 1930s, three German professors went to Japan for an extended visit and became unexpectedly engaged in Zen meditation. One of them, Eugen Herrigel, a philosophy professor, was the first European to study Zen and the art of archery. His book by this title became a classic for an entire generation of Zen students. Karlfried Graf Dürckheim, a psychology professor and co-founder of Gestalt psychology, studied *zazen* under Master Yuho Seki Roshi. After World War II, he brought his practical experience in Buddhist meditation to Germany, where he opened the Psycho-Physical Therapy Center in the Black Forest.[13]

The third was Eugen Enomiya Lassalle, a Jesuit teaching at the Catholic university in Kyoto. Miraculously surviving the atom bombing of Hiroshima in 1945, he opened a monastery of "Christian Zen" near Tokyo. Lassalle continuously deepened his study of Japanese Buddhism and, after several decades, completed the traditional training of Soto Zen under the tutelage of Yamada Roshi, who authorized him to teach Zen. In the 1960s, he led Zen *sesshins* in Germany. Meanwhile, Lassalle's colleague at the University of Tokyo, the German Jesuit Heinrich Dumoulin, emerged as one of the foremost historians of Zen, writing several comprehensive works on the subject.

One of the first Germans to become an ordained Buddhist while living in Germany may also be considered an early practitioner of socially engaged Buddhism. This was the former communist leader Wilhelm Müller, also known as Anagarika Subhuti.[14] Subhuti came from a working class family in the Lower Rhineland. As a young man, he fought against the ascendancy of the Nazis, was arrested in 1933 for high treason, and served several years in prison. In prison, he came across some Buddhist literature and, after the war, began to transmit the teaching of the Buddha by lectures, workshops, and the publication of a journal. His primary audience was the simple worker. As a member of the order that had been founded by Lama Govinda, the Arya Maitreya Mandala, he established programs for emotionally disturbed youths, drug abusers, and conscientious objectors, and to provide protection for animals. He saw these activities as the fulfillment of his bodhisattva vows to help all living beings in the world. Wilhelm Müller died in 1990 at the age of seventy-eight, believing that a Buddhist cannot achieve salvation without working for the welfare of others.

The rise of Buddhism in German-speaking Europe was greatly accelerated with the youth and student movements of the 1960s. Underlying this movement was a sense of guilt over war crimes perpetuated by Germans against the Jews. Many Germans also agonized over their role as an ally of the United States in the war in Southeast Asia. At the same time, a creative and liberating message came from the youth movement in the West: make love, not war. This was accompanied by an unprecedented interest in the expansion of consciousness, spiritual experience, and millennia-old Asian methods of self-realization. Precisely at this time, the first courses on Zen meditation were being offered in Germany. No longer was it the idea but rather the practice of meditation that attracted young Germans.

The countercultural revolution of the 1960s was carried on in numerous movements in the 1970s: neo-Marxist groups, third-world solidarity movements, the commune movement, the women's movement, the ecology movement; and, in the 1980s, the peace movement, the therapy movement, New Age religions, esotericism, and finally, the enormous growth of Buddhism. Some of these movements developed, however, as countercurrents to the earlier activism. They saw themselves as teaching a way to the inside, in contrast to the way to the outside. Many had experienced the earlier political movements as dominated by intolerance, dogmatism, and violence. No longer were they willing to place their hopes in distant promises of happiness and peace, but instead desired that these be realized here and now. They sought methods that would enable the individual to overcome the lack of peace and freedom in oneself, before presuming to be able to bestow these on others. In this way, psychotherapy, self-awareness, meditation, and spiritual exploration enjoyed a sudden boost. Within this broad and colorful spectrum, Buddhism achieved a level of strength, significance, and popularity not previously seen in the Christian West.

THE RISE OF ENGAGED BUDDHISM

The social and humanitarian engagement of Buddhism in German-speaking regions arose with the appearance of Tibetan Buddhist teachers in the West. As refugees of an occupied country and of a persecuted religion, these teachers awoke in many of their followers the willingness to help the Tibetan people, and to devote themselves to the preservation of Tibetan culture and religion. In particular, the intellectual openness and personal charisma of the Dalai Lama has contributed to this interest. In speaking of our "universal responsibility," rather than limiting himself to the theme of the suffering of Tibet, the Dalai Lama has been instrumental in opening countless Buddhists to an awareness of contemporary global problems.[15]

A second impetus likewise originated with an exiled Asian Buddhist tradition—namely, that of Thich Nhat Hanh and the monks and nuns from Vietnam. Here, too, the initial concern was practical aid for Vietnam after a war that plunged the country into deep poverty. Through Thich Nhat Hanh's distinctive and exemplary teachings in Vietnam and the West, engaged Buddhism finally gained currency and became widespread as an independent impulse.[16]

North American culture is founded upon the cultures and the peoples of Europe. Today, however, Europe is becoming increasingly influenced by developments that arise in the United States and spread throughout the world. This also applies to Western Buddhism. Engaged Buddhism comes to Europe as a typically American form of the Dharma. The characteristically practical and pragmatic nature of American civilization can be recognized in this form of the Dharma. American representatives, teachers, and authors of engaged Buddhism—particularly those involved in the Buddhist Peace Fellowship—have provided a strong impulse for the development of engaged Buddhism in Europe. The paths and practices of Asian Buddhists teaching in North America have also been important. They include Chogyam Trungpa, Tarthang Tulku, and Sogyal Rinpoche. The teaching of the latter, for instance, has addressed the peculiar culture of death and dying in the West, and the need for a Buddhist contribution.

Most recently, Bernard Tetsugen Glassman Roshi and Claude AnShin Thomas, representing the Zen Peacemaker Order in the United States, have held meditation retreats in the former German concentration camp sites of Auschwitz and Sachsenhausen, and street retreats in the larger German cities.[17]

A decisive impulse for the formation of engaged Buddhism in the West has been the cultural crisis in Asian Buddhist countries in the twentieth century. As the result of centuries of colonial domination by the West and the postcolonial onset of rampant materialism and information saturation today, many countries are trapped in totalitarian ideological systems. Out of this crisis a new generation of socially critical monks, nuns, teachers, and authors has emerged, including Sulak Sivaraksa, Phra Payutto, Chatsumarn Kabilsingh, and the late Buddhadasa Bhikkhu of Thailand; Maha Ghosananda of Cambodia; Aung San Suu Kyi and Rewatta Dhamma Sayadaw of Burma; Walpola Rahula and A. T. Aryaratne of Sri Lanka; Samdhong Rinpoche, Dagyab Kyabgon Rinpoche, and Akong Rinpoche of Tibet; and Hozumi Roshi, Sasaki Genso Roshi, and Fumon Nakagawa Roshi of Japan.

One expression of this current renewal was the founding of the International Network of Engaged Buddhists (INEB) in Thailand in January 1989.[18] This organization has become an important progressive force in South and Southeast Asia, a force that has begun to influence the West and to create a completely new emphasis for the development of Buddhism there.

The German Network of Engaged Buddhists was founded in 1993 as a branch of INEB and as a member of the German Buddhist Union (Deutsche Buddhistische Union or DBU).[19] In 1993 at the Fifth Annual Conference of INEB in a Thai monastery, a small circle of Dharma students from German-speaking countries took the initiative to found a German-speaking network of engaged Buddhists. A journal was initiated, an office for coordination and information set up, and nationwide network meetings held. A wealth of contacts, exchanges, activities, and projects has developed since then. At first, the emphasis was on the support of engaged Buddhists in Asia. Increasingly, however, efforts were initiated to apply the principles of engaged Buddhism in our own areas.[20]

The primary motive for the network's activities is a desire to give something back to those Asians for their gift of the Dharma. What we can give is, of course, financial and material support, and scientific and technological training. In this manner, some of us have been engaged for several years in numerous projects involving direct emergency and construction aid in Southeast Asia.

Emergency Aid to Asia

German-speaking Buddhists have been eager to help the victims of the Burmese military regime's war against minorities who have fled to Thailand or Bangladesh. In the countless refugee camps along the Thai-Burmese bor-

Members of the Netzwerk engagierter Buddhisten (German Network of
Engaged Buddhists). Founder Franz-Johannes Litsch is second from left.
Courtesy Franz-Johannes Litsch.

der, tens of thousands are leading a miserable existence devoid of hope. They
were forced out of Burma, merely tolerated in Thailand, and overseen and
forgotten by the large aid organizations. The numerous ethnic minorities of
Burma can be found in these camps—the Karen, Kachin, Shan, Mon, Pao,
and many others—peoples who are among the oldest and most creative bearers of Buddhist high culture in Southeast Asia. Yet, their only hope of survival
is to participate in the economic exploitation of their respective homelands,
in the sale of girls, for example, or in the drug trade.

The health conditions in the refugee camps is particularly catastrophic. It
is here that the members of the Network have provided many forms of direct
help. Medicines and medical instruments have been brought to Thailand from
Germany; monetary donations have made it possible to buy inexpensive
indigenous medicine or to set up small medical stations; and young people
from the refugee camps have been trained as medical aids. This has made it
possible to bring basic treatment to remote jungle villages. Because the major
cause of numerous contagious diseases is contaminated water, the introduction of wells, water pumps, and toilets has been a priority. Women have been
provided with information about birth control, family planning, and measures for improving general hygiene.

We have been able to support the construction and maintenance of schools, and to provide children with school supplies. We have also sent Buddhist and non-Buddhist reading materials and cassette recordings to Buddhist communities, both ordained and lay. Acknowledging and supporting individual cultures and communal identities is of central importance as external, material suffering is usually accompanied by a drying up of the inner, spiritual, and cultural life of a people.

The Buddhist Society of Munich (Buddhistische Gesellschaft München) has supported a number of villages, monasteries, schools, and homes for the elderly belonging to the Buddhist minority in Bangladesh. The fact that this country possesses a significant Buddhist culture and tradition is unknown even by Buddhists in the West. Similarly, the fact that this minority is subject to increasing persecution by the militant Islamic majority receives no attention. Yet the work and projects of the monks of Bangladesh can be held up as an exemplary model of engaged Buddhism in Asia.

German-speaking Buddhists have supported individuals and entire villages in overcoming initial difficulties and achieving self-sufficiency. It is hoped that these beneficiaries will, in turn, be able to help to others so that a snowball effect of improvement can be set in motion.

From the circle of Thich Nhat Hanh's disciples an organization devoted to the aid of Vietnam and Cambodia has emerged. Medical aid is of utmost urgency. Leprosy is once again a widespread disease in Vietnam. The Maitreya Fund offers broad support for the construction and maintenance of schools, orphanages, kindergartens, and homes for the elderly in central Vietnam, the area that continues to suffer the most from the consequences of the war. The farmers there are confronted with environmental conditions that still bear the marks of the war's destruction, such as land mines and chemical wastes. The elderly, the sick, and those crippled in the war are often without relatives, while the state offers no form of social security.

Similarly, the Maitri Project treats leprosy in the most holy of Buddhist sites in northern India: the town of Bodh Gaya. The hospital was initiated by the Tibetan Lama Thubten Zopa Rinpoche, and is led today primarily by the Foundation for the Preservation of the Mahayana Tradition (FPMT). The Italian director, Dr. Adriani Ferranti, is accomplishing excellent work there. Although leprosy is a terrible disease, it can be brought into remission within six months to two years. Because of the high risk of contagion, all those affected by the disease must suffer additionally from social quarantine. Furthermore, Bihar, the state in which Bodh Gaya is located, is one of the poorest areas of India. Someone suffering from leprosy there is condemned to a slow, painful death. In the leprosy clinic, the afflicted receive medical and social care, treatment, and rehabilitation. In addition to this, the project has developed a far-reaching preventive treatment program for the entire surrounding area. Because of the success of leprosy treatments, it has recently become possible to extend assistance to those suffering from tuberculosis. Through the offering of donations, and the dissemination of information to the many Western Buddhist visitors to Bodh Gaya, the Network is making an effort to support the valuable work of the clinic.

The majority of humanitarian efforts among engaged Buddhists in German-speaking regions consists of those offered by Tibetan teachers or Tibetan Buddhist organizations for Tibet. Approximately twenty different aid organizations and project initiatives are active here. The financial and managerial scope of these activities is quite considerable, being in the range of several million deutschemarks. The emphasis is on daycare centers for children, schools, orphanages, training centers, and medical stations, as well as individual sponsorships and stipends for children, monks, and nuns. With the founding of her German Tibet-Aid (Deutsche Tibet-Hilfe), a single woman, Ingrid Waeger, has carried out extraordinarily effective work, working tirelessly for decades. The Dalai Lama regards her as one of his closest friends and as one of the most important benefactors of Tibet.

Similar to the Maitri Project in Bodh Gaya, several of these Tibetan establishments in Asia offer direct emergency aid. An example of this is Rokpa, which sends food to Nepal with support from groups in Germany, Switzerland, and Austria. Another example is the Dagyab Association. Founded by the Tibetan teacher Dagyab Kyabgon Rinpoche, who has been residing in Germany for thirty years, this organization is even planning a development and construction program for an entire Tibetan province, Kyabgon, in eastern Tibet.

Human Rights

Like the International Network of Engaged Buddhists, the German-speaking network particularly emphasizes efforts on behalf of human rights. It is widely overlooked in the West that Buddhism is among those religions that have suffered great persecution and destruction in the twentieth century. Such persecution was practiced in Russia, Mongolia, China, North Korea, Tibet, Thailand, Laos, Cambodia, and Bangladesh. Even in Buddhist countries such as Burma, Thailand, and Sri Lanka, Buddhist monks are not free from political persecution when they challenge the interests of the ruling authorities.

Particularly in Burma, since the coup of the military junta against the democracy movement of Aung San Suu Kyi, thousands of members of the sangha have been imprisoned, tortured, and sentenced to forced labor, not to mention the many thousands of lay Buddhists who have been imprisoned and pressed into forced labor. Immediately upon its founding, our Network, together with the Japanese Buddhist Relief Mission, began a widespread letter-writing campaign for the release of the monks imprisoned in Burma. We have demonstrated that the military has not only imprisoned the most worthy bearers of the Dharma, but has for years carried off some of the most prominent monks to unknown places. Taking Amnesty International as its model, the letter-writing campaign was directed toward prominent politicians and religious leaders throughout the world. It has received positive response from numerous Buddhists. It nonetheless came as a great surprise to us when we began to achieve success with the campaign.

Six months after we began, the United Nations Human Rights Commission in Geneva received a letter from the Burmese government announcing that, in response to our letters, it was releasing eighty-four Burmese monks from prison. Among these monks was Tipitakadara, one of five monks worldwide who has mastered the memorization of the entire Tipitaka canon. Through subsequent investigations in Burma we could substantiate that the Burmese government's announcement was legitimate, at least regarding this monk. This showed us that, in the countries in which Buddhism has a high cultural significance, the voice of Western Buddhists has some influence.

Western Buddhists have been less successful in their efforts to support Nobel Peace Prize winner Aung San Suu Kyi and countless other representatives of the democracy movement and ethnic minorities in Burma.[21] We are working closely with various non-Buddhist human rights groups in Germany in order to keep government and business leaders abreast of the situation.

Our efforts to have the highest representatives of Vietnamese Buddhism freed after years of incarceration by means of a similar letter-writing campaign has had no success whatsoever. Many of these are the Dharma brothers of Thich Nhat Hanh who were leaders of the non-partisan Buddhist peace movement in Vietnam in the 1960s. Some of these monks were recently released from long prison terms, only to be reincarcerated for helping the victims of a catastrophic flood in southern Vietnam. There is apparently nothing that the present Vietnamese government fears more than the great tradition of engaged Buddhism in its own country.

Engagement for human rights in Tibet and for exiled Tibetans has found particularly strong supporters among both Buddhists and non-Buddhists in Western Europe. The Dalai Lama's popularity in Germany is great; and even people who normally exhibit neither political nor religious interests have been demanding freedom for Tibet. However, German foreign policy is so concerned with trade with China that it took years of great effort for the Dalai Lama to be received by a representative of the German government. When the German parliament (Bundestag) eventually passed, with a large majority, a resolution against China's repression in Tibet, a serious crisis arose in German-Chinese relations, and an acrimonious debate in German politics was sparked. Since then, the subject of human rights in Tibet has been a matter of central concern for certain political parties in Germany.

Remaining in the shadows of world attention is the persecution of the Buddhist minority in Bangladesh by fundamentalist Muslims. The people there live in constant fear. Villages are attacked, young girls raped or abducted, and significant, centuries-old temples destroyed, heads from statues of the Buddha are cut off, and cemeteries are desecrated. Because the consequences of resistance are even harsher, the victims have no choice but to acquiesce helplessly. Friends of our Network who have travelled to these areas in order to get an impression of the situation were celebrated by thousands of people as high ranking representatives of a liberating force. They were disturbed to learn just how abandoned by the rest of the world these people feel, and how grateful they were for the attention being given them. Because of its extremely threatening ecological situation, its overpopulation, and its massive poverty, however, Bangladesh apparently belongs to the group of countries that the world has written off as destined to decline.

Women's Liberation

There can be no religious or social liberation without the liberation of women. Therefore, in founding our Network, we turned our attention to improving the situation of Asian women and nuns. Men from Europe participate to a considerable degree in sex tourism and in the trade of girls, while the traditional repression of women in Asia makes it difficult for Western women to gain access to Dharma practice to the same degree enjoyed by men. In some Theravadan countries, such as Thailand, it is not possible to receive ordination as a nun; and in others, such as Burma and Sri Lanka (as also in Tibetan Buddhism and Japanese Zen), ordination is limited in various ways. Only in Vietnam, Taiwan, and Korea has the ordination of nuns been preserved.

The Heinrich Böll Foundation has been single-mindedly engaged in these issues for years. The Heinrich Böll Foundation is an alternative NGO that generously supports Buddhist projects in Cambodia and Thailand devoted specifically to women and nuns. By working closely with INEB it has been possible to organize numerous international meetings, workshops, and developmental projects for the benefit of women in Asia. Through such education and exchange, the conditions for the re-establishment of the ordination of nuns in these countries are being created. At the same time, these women are motivated to reawaken the ethnic and spiritual energy that will lead to social renewal in their respective areas.

This work is being carried out worldwide by Sakyadhita, an international Buddhist women's network. As with INEB and our own German network, the connection and coordinated work with this international movement is of utmost importance, for the Buddhism of the future must fully recognize and foster the particular capabilities and power of women.

Since its founding, the German Network of Engaged Buddhists has taken on the problems of sex tourism, trafficking of women, and the spread of AIDS in traditional Buddhist countries such as Thailand, Burma, Vietnam, and Sri Lanka. The emergence and spread of these problems stem largely from the actions of irresponsible travellers and unscrupulous businessmen from wealthy European countries. Until now, however, we have been unable to do more than support the activities of other NGOs engaged in this work. Recently, members of the Network have taken up the struggle against child pornography and prostitution on the Internet—a phenomenon that, because of its considerable dimension of criminal profiteering, has recently shaken and unsettled many Europeans.

Peace Work

Our world is plagued by war—from small wars in the family, at work, at school, in the streets, between political parties, interest groups, businesses, corporations, monopolies, and economic blocks, to large wars between countries, peoples, races, ideologies, and religions. The teaching of the Buddha is, at its core, a teaching of nonviolence and peace. To be a Buddhist means first of all to be a peacemaker. Overcoming violence and belligerence is therefore one of the central features of engaged Buddhism. For this reason, a basic orientation of the Buddha's teaching is that peace must begin with the practitioner, if it is to have an effect on others and to radiate out to the world.

The possibilities open to us for having an impact in the area of large-scale wars are, unfortunately, extremely limited. We can nonetheless have some effect by demanding the cessation of support of these wars by our own countries. For example, our work in Burma and Cambodia revealed the horrible fact that millions of mines are buried throughout those countries. Some of us became engaged in the anti-landmine campaign, in which Germany became one of the first countries to renounce the deployment and export of this means of terror. In the meantime, this subject has received attention worldwide. The first international accord prohibiting landmines was signed, and the Nobel Peace Prize was awarded to the movement for the abolition of landmines—an extraordinary success considering that it was achieved within a few years through a worldwide grassroots movement. The contributions of engaged Buddhists to this campaign were considerable.

The German Network has also supported Maha Ghosananda's peace work in Cambodia, most notably the annual Dhamma Yetra peace march through strife-torn Cambodia.[22] This march is joined by thousands of participants. In Sri Lanka, a cruel and senseless civil war between Singhalese and Tamils has been raging for nearly twenty years, as small wars are fought by opposing splinter groups. Some Buddhist monks and lay people are making courageous and persistent efforts to overcome the seemingly irresolvable situation. One of these monks, a leader of a large reconciliation project in southern Sri Lanka, works closely with a center for nonviolence in Germany. There, he participated in training programs in the anti-nuclear movement.

The civil war in the former Yugoslavia was a great shock to all of us after forty-five years of peace in Europe. True, the rest of the world was not free from war; but those conflicts seemed so distant. Once again, we saw European villages and cities riddled with bullets, mutilated bodies lying in marketplaces, massacres, concentration camps, and ethnic extermination. Many were deeply shaken by this; some were able to find ways to initiate limited though direct help, or to care for the refugees from the war-torn areas.

A few were even willing, at the risk of their own lives, to intervene directly in the war in order to create momentum for peace and reconciliation. Approximately seventy-five participants of the international, interfaith initiative called Sjeme Mira (Seeds of Peace) found their way through the Bosnian war zone in order to show the inhabitants through their presence that there exist peaceful and friendly ways of living together.

In honor of the fiftieth anniversary of the end of the Second World War, a commune that runs a large meditation center in the south of Germany initiated a meditation network with the goal of creating Europe-wide gatherings for silent reflection during the memorial week. Our Network embraced this initiative and spread the idea to numerous Buddhists.

In December of 1994, fifty years after the liberation of the concentration camp in Auschwitz, approximately two hundred people from several countries and different religions gathered in that place of immeasurable suffering. The meeting was initiated by monks of the Japanese order Nipponzan Myohoji. At the end of the meeting, many participants from around the world began a peace march that was to commence in Auschwitz, continue through Poland, Yugoslavia, Israel, India, Cambodia, and Vietnam, and end in Hiroshima.

In fact the march began several weeks earlier in Berlin, at the Brandenburg Gate, where, just five years earlier, the division of Germany and the West had ended through the fall of the Berlin Wall. Together with Buddhists from Berlin, the Japanese monks then began the peace march through Berlin and the formerly socialist Germany. They followed in part the routes that thousands of prisoners from the concentration camps were forced to take at the end of the Second World War because the Nazis did not want them to fall into the hands of the approaching Soviet army. Many of the prisoners, already suffering from sickness, died underway.

The former Vietnam veteran and now Zen monk Claude AnShin Thomas played a crucial role in the leadership of the peace march. After many difficult and painful years of internal and external struggle following the war, Claude had an experience of healing and profound conversion upon coming into contact with Thich Nhat Hanh and his monastic community in Plum Village, in the south of France. He has now dedicated his life to overcoming violence and war throughout the world.

The Berlin branch of Thich Nhat Hanh's sangha has maintained a close relationship with Claude for several years now. Inspired by him, and in conjunction with Buddhists from other countries, they dared to hold the first meditation and mourning retreat in a German concentration camp. The retreat took place in Sachsenhausen, near Berlin, in which tens of thousands of political prisoners from Berlin—and later from all of Europe—met their deaths. The experience of the retreatants was deeply moving and lasting. Numerous German Buddhists and friends of the Network also participated in the gathering at Auschwitz and the subsequent peace march through Europe.

For German Buddhists, these activities involved a completely new form of Dharma practice, one that allowed us directly to confront suffering, the cause of suffering, and our own history. Since then, this new approach has continued, and has become accepted. In the winter of 1996, Bernard Tetsugen Glassman announced an international and interreligious week of meditation to be held at Auschwitz. One hundred and fifty people from around the world responded to his invitation. Among them were Buddhists and Christians from Germany, Switzerland, and Austria. For one week, they endured the terror, coldness, and pain of this place. To everyone's surprise, however, they experienced not only unsettling sadness and, for us Germans especially, a feeling of collective guilt, but also a deep and liberating openness, joy, and friendship. They experienced directly the boundless power of the Dharma.[23]

Social Work

Some Buddhists interested in the work of the German Network have found fault with what they perceive to be our overemphasis on engagement in Asia. It is a fact that involvement in this area dominated our first years. The reason for this is simply that our initial concern was to become integrated in the international activities of engaged Buddhism. However, an important and obvious matter of concern to us was to become involved in our own social and ecological world.

Today there is a particularly high percentage of German Buddhists involved in social, therapeutic, healing, and educational occupations. Many of these people are social workers, teachers, psychotherapists, or physicians who see their Dharma practice as integral to their professional work. For this reason, the Austrian Buddhist Religious Community (ÖBR: Österreichische Buddhistische Religionsgemeinschaft) resolved to create a psychosocial network that would both bring all those who were involved in this type of work into contact with one another, and make their services more accessible to interested Buddhists. The Network took over this initiative for Germany and Switzerland. After a year's effort, the first psychosocial directory was published to advertise their specialties and services, and to present their projects and ideas. The initiative met with less success than was expected, however. Offerings rarely met demand, the distance between regions covered was too great, those involved took little initiative on their own, interests changed rapidly, and addresses and phone numbers became quickly outdated.

Work with the dying has seen increased interest among Dharma practitioners in recent years. This is no doubt due to the efforts of Sogyal Rinpoche and his Rigpa Foundation, with support from teachers in the United States such as Christine Longaker and Frank Ostaseski of the Zen Hospice Project of San Francisco. Rigpa teamed up with different hospices to sponsor a conference on death and dying. This conference brought together over one thousand guests and speakers from the most varied fields. The conference was therefore not directed, as was usually the case, to a Buddhist audience, but to people who are confronted daily with death and dying in hospitals, homes for the elderly, hospices, and emergency medical teams. Certainly, the conference offered no new knowledge in the various areas of specialty of the participants. But the spiritual teachings on death offered by Buddhist teachers and practitioners, as well as Christian monks and practitioners of meditation, offered to countless visitors a completely new horizon for their daily work and personal life. It also provided a fascinating encounter between people of the most varied backgrounds.

A new dimension of Buddhist practice and social engagement was opened through our encounter with the American Zen master, Bernard Tetsugen Glassman Roshi. In the early 1980s, Glassman Roshi constructed a mandala of Buddhist social services in Yonkers, New York. Bordering New York City, Yonkers has a particularly high rate of unemployment, and is laden with severe ethnic conflict.[24] By its comprehensiveness, Glassman Roshi's organization serves as a model for future social development. Glassman Roshi's approach has nothing to do with the projects and solutions themselves. Rather, his approach involves "bearing witness" to the suffering—a fundamental removal of all barriers between the helper and the receiver of help, barriers that are inherent in conventional aid projects and organizations. His students place themselves in the situation of the person in need of help in order to perceive directly what type of help is necessary and appropriate. It is thus on the basis of the Buddhist notion of nonduality that Glassman Roshi finds the most appropriate solutions for his social, economic, organizational, and therapeutic engagements.

In the fall of 1997, Bernie Glassman undertook an extensive lecture tour of several German and Swiss cities. In the old cathedral city of Cologne, assuming the state of a homeless person, he led a group of German Zen practitioners in a street retreat. Just two weeks later, the Thich Nhat Hanh sangha together with Claude AnShin Thomas led a weeklong street retreat in Berlin. After his return from military service in Vietnam, Claude himself had been homeless for several years. Experiencing the insecurity, helplessness, and rejection confronting the homeless had a profound and lasting effect on the participants and the entire sangha.

On the last day of the retreat, the participants and the Buddhist community organized a feast for homeless people. This event was held in a church that has been working with the homeless for several years. On this day, a considerable donation was offered to several homeless organizations. The funds were solicited from friends and acquaintances as a condition for participation. Since then, some sangha members have been assisting Protestant churches in their work with the homeless—an exercise in interfaith dialogue. Claude AnShin Thomas was an early member of the Zen Peacemaker Order, founded by Glassman Roshi and his late wife, Sensei Sandra Jishu Holmes. The German branch of the order was made official at a conference at the end of 1997, in which Tetsugen, Jishu, and Joan Halifax participated. The German order is now run by a Zen priest and his community of Soto Zen students from the Rhineland.

Environmental Protection

A considerable number of Germans came to Buddhism through the ecology movement of the 1970s and 1980s. Such people found Buddhism after years of disappointment with the lack of success and inner hardening that characterized this movement. They were active in the anti-nuclear movement, fought for the protection of the forests, and opposed the polluting of water, air, and food. For years they supported organizations devoted to the protection of the environment, contributed to the founding of the Green Party, and stood for election in parliaments and city councils. Some attempted to remove themselves completely from the customary relationship to production and consumption, which is damaging to nature, and to develop small islands of alternative lifestyle and work. They saw the teaching of the Buddha as a way to reconcile their outward-oriented efforts to heal our destructive way of life, with the inner-oriented efforts for healing oneself. While many of them gave up their former activities, many nonetheless found their way back to their earlier careers and engagements.

Because of its compatibility with ecological thought, Buddhism has contributed to the development of a new philosophy of interdependence. Several teachers from the Tibetan Buddhist tradition in particular have been making efforts for years to foster an ecological consciousness deepened by Buddhist teachings. Traditional meditation and awareness exercises such as the Tibetan *tonglen* practice ("taking and giving") can effectively train our perception of the connections among all sentient beings. Such forms of meditation practice, applied to concrete contemporary problems, often appeal to people who had no former interest in applied spirituality.

More and more people in western Europe today are turning away from the excessive meat consumption that has become normal in the modern industrial societies. There are many reasons for this change, such as heightened health consciousness, increased sympathy for the suffering of animals, a greater commitment to end violence, and respect for all of life. Here, the fundamental nonviolent and benevolent attitude of Buddhism toward all living beings benevolently connects with the thinking of many people today who are prepared to assume increasing personal responsibility.

Buddhist activists, in cooperation with other religious groups, have called for the abolition of concentration-camp-style animal factories. They have thus been leading "animal protection pilgrimages" to animal factories that are particularly contemptuous toward life. In these high-profile media events, they often perform Buddhist rituals such as prostrations to the sacredness of all sentient beings, and participate in Christian worship.

Living Communities

Twentieth-century European history is filled with rich and varied examples of people making efforts to drop out of existing social environments that they see as hostile to life and detached from nature, and to find simpler forms of communal life. In Germany, each decade in the past thirty years has seen a wave of communal experiments. The first was the commune movement inspired by California's hippie culture and the student movement of 1968. This movement was strongly influenced by anarchist ideals. The return-to-the-country movement paralleled the powerful ecology movement toward the end of the 1970s. The third wave, presently gaining momentum, is no longer as spectacular, romantic, or exotic, and is less opposed to technology. It has a marked social character and therefore constitutes an answer to the increasing unemployment and loss of confidence among young, well-trained men and women of Europe. It is characterized by great openness and willingness to overcome the old dualistic divisions between life and work, private life and public responsibility, daily reality and spirituality.

All of these initiatives for ecological villages are bound together internationally, and are committed to a vision of the "global village." The structure of the Buddhist sangha has always followed this egalitarian, decentralized, self-providing, and interconnected principle of social order. And the more the Dharma is integrated into our Western societies through the practice of "engaged Buddhism," the more will such forms of social unity in diversity come forth. This is a great experiment in social transformation, in which Buddhism in the West becomes a distinctive Western Buddhism, and, conversely, in which Western society can become a new society, molded in part by Buddhism.

AN INTERFAITH VISION FOR THE FUTURE

A new pattern of ecumenical cooperation between Buddhists and non-Buddhists has also emerged in the movement for alternative living and working communities. In many of the movements we have surveyed, inter-religious or inter-world view dialogue has emerged as an important aspect of engaged Buddhist practice. At the World Parliament of Religions held in Chicago in 1993, the Catholic theologian Hans Küng coined the slogan "No world peace without peace among religions."[25] The present essay puts forth the following slogan, "No healing of the earth without the healing of religions." This healing of the religions must come from within—that is, from each religion itself, as well as from the hearts of men and women. The external impulse, however, can be decisive for setting internal healing in motion. For this reason, genuine and serious interreligious dialogue is crucial not only for the survival of the various religions, but also for all of humanity. It opens up the vision of an all-encompassing, limitless, and inexhaustible wholeness of reality, and of the truth that we may never possess the whole truth.

Interest in this dialogue is considerable among Buddhists in the German-speaking world, and activities and participants in the dialogue are numerous. Such a concern goes hand in hand with confronting ourselves with ourselves, with our own historical or biographical roots and origins. It is here that the majority of Buddhist communities have, for many years, been seriously engaged and interested, and willing to move toward increasing closeness, cooperation, and understanding. Some see in this a danger that Christianity will attempt to salvage its claims to absoluteness by appropriating Buddhist meditative techniques. Others see a danger that Buddhists, through widespread opportunism, will compromise themselves to attract a wider following. These dangers do exist, and must be kept in mind. As this essay has attempted to show, however, the importance of religion to humanity and to the future of the earth is too great to abandon our quest for a more activist spirituality.

Religion, from the Latin *religio*, means "to tie back, return." Religion is religion when it reconnects us to a perfect and liberating source of nature and society. If this original wholeness and sacredness were already manifested in our living reality, then we would not need engaged Buddhism or any other activist faith. Meanwhile, as we enter a new millennium, we shall continue to find new ways of walking the ancient path of the Buddha in a world presently marred by discord and suffering.

NOTES

1. Buddhadasa Bhikkhu, *Zwei Arten der Sprache* (Zurich: Theseus-Verlag, 1979), p. 122.
2. Volker Zotz, *Geschichte der buddhistischen Philosophie* (Hamburg: Rowohlt, 1996), p. 266.
3. Max Weber, *Gesammelte Aufsätze zur Religionssoziologie* (1920–21).
4. Johannes Paul II, *Die Schwelle der Hoffnung überschreiten* (Hamburg: Hoffmann & Campe, 1994).

5. Martin Baumann, *Deutsche Buddhisten: Geschichte und Gemeinschaften* (Marburg: Diagonal-Verlag, 1993), p. 50.

6. Willi Hartig, *Die Lehre des Buddha und Heidegger: Beiträge zum Ost-West-Dialog des Denkens im 20. Jahrhundert* (Konstanz: Universität Konstanz, Forschungsberichte 15, 1997).

7. Hellmuth Hecker, *Der erste deutsche Bhikkhu: Das bewegte Leben des Ehrwürdigen Nyanatiloka und seine Schüler* (Konstanz: Universität Konstanz, Forschungsberichte 10, 1995).

8. Detlef Kantowsky, ed., *Der Weg der Weissen Wolken: Texte, Bilder und Dokumente aus dem Leben von Lama Anagarika Govinda* (Konstanz: Universität Konstanz, Forschungsberichte 12, 1996).

9. Helmut Hecker, ed., "Nicht derselbe und nicht ein anderer," *Beschreibungen und Gespräche: Texte, Bilder und Dokumente zum 90, Geburtstag des Ehrwürdigen Nyanaponika Mahathera* (Konstanz: Universität Konstanz, Forschungsberichte 3, 1991).

10. "Zentralausschuss der Juden für Aufbau und Hilfe."

11. *Satipatthana Sutta, Samyutta Nikaya,* 19.

12. Fritz Hungerleider, *Mein Weg zur Mystik, Eine religiöse Autobiographie* (Freiburg: Herder-Verlag, 1988).

13. *Existential-psychologische Bildungs-und Begegnungsstätte Todtmoos Rütte.*

14. Baumann, *Deutsche Buddhisten*, p. 129.

15. The Dalai Lama, *Eine Politik der Güte* (Olten/Freiburg: Walter-Verlag, 1992), p. 111.

16. Thich Nhat Hanh, *Vietnam: Lotus in a Sea of Fire* (New York: Hill and Wang, 1967); and Chan Khong, *Learning True Love* (Berkeley, CA: Parallax Press, 1993).

17. Bernard Glassman, *Bearing Witness* (New York: Bell Tower, 1998).

18. See INEB at <www.igc.apc.org/bpf/ineb.html>.

19. See DBU at <www.dharma.de/dbu>.

20. See Netzwerk engagierter Buddhisten at <www.buddhanetz.net>.

21. Aung San Suu Kyi and Alan Clements, *The Voice of Hope* (London: Penguin Books, 1998).

22. Maha Ghosananda, *Step by Step: Meditation on Wisdom and Compassion* (Berkeley, CA: Parallax Press, 1992).

23. Glassman, *Bearing Witness.*

24. Bernard Glassman and Rick Fields, *Instructions to the Cook* (New York: Bell Tower, 1996).

25. Hans Küng and Karl-Josef Kuschel, eds., *Weltfrieden durch Religionsfrieden, Antworten aus den Religionen* (München: Piper, 1993).

ENGAGED BUDDHISM IN SOUTH AFRICA

Darrel Wratten

To live in South Africa is to live in a country in which injustice, exploitation, and hierarchic dualism in the name of "separate development" was not only pervasive but formally legislated. As several South African Buddhists document, however, to reside in a land governed by the punishment of difference under *apartheid* (an Afrikaans term meaning "separateness") is to reside in a land conditioned by "national karma." Not unreasonably, a Zen teacher in the northern Cape Karoo town of Colesberg asks, "Was there ever a better place for practice?" South Africa can teach Buddhists about the truth of suffering and its causation, he concludes, because South Africans are inevitably caught up in the peculiar and institutionalized manifestations of *dukkha*, or unsatisfactoriness, in this country.[1]

South Africa provides an insightful lens through which to examine central Buddhist concepts. Conversely, Buddhist concepts suggest the causes of discrimination and shape responses to inequity and injustice in this country. In a brief review of the beginnings of Buddhism in a place Afrikaans poet Breyten Breytenbach once designated the "last lip of annihilation," Stephen Batchelor reminds us that the Buddhist critique of unchanging essences helps free the minds of South Africans from the "lingering web of suspicion and reification that underpinned the psychology of apartheid." Buddhist insight into the transparent, dependently emergent nature of things dispels "perceptions of people as endowed with inherent traits of character."[2]

Several South African commentators and teachers note that the Buddhist teachings of *anatta* (no-self), *anicca* (impermanence), and *pratityasamutpada* (dependent co-arising) provide a penetrating critique of race, class, and gender associations, and that these teachings outline how to overcome duality and discrimination. Buddhism counsels how to transcend "the sociopolitical impasse to which egoistic, individualistic, and racist consciousness lead." Buddhism encourages "a feeling of interconnectedness, thus clearing the mind for appropriate and engaged action." More specifically, Buddhist teachings on nondualism reveal to what extent the vision of a just society cannot be "multi-racial," but that the new South Africa requires "*non*racism, and *non*sexism."[3]

Many South African Buddhists argue, therefore, that Buddhism can make a practical contribution in support of the country's transition to a more equitable political dispensation. That contribution, they acknowledge, must be premised on a particular and contextual reading of the meaning of Buddhism, one in which South African Buddhists have to confront racism, sexism, and manifold forms of daily discrimination in the light of what might be termed a South African Buddhist hermeneutic. Three recent examples of an incipient South African Buddhist hermeneutic and an emerging engaged Buddhist ethic are instructive.

First, in April 1994, a Sowetan *bhikkhu*, Reverend Shoji Sawaguchi, together with nine monks from the Nipponzan Myohoji Buddhist Order, undertook a "pilgrimage for peace" in South Africa. Led by Reverend Sawaguchi, the Buddhist monks walked three hundred miles from Phoenix,

Buddhist nun Nara Greenway begins a forty-day fast for the release of detained children, St. George's Cathedral, Cape Town, 1987. Courtesy Darrell Wratten.

Durban, through a region covering some of the most serious areas of violence in South Africa, including Thokoza and Katlehong, to Orlando West, Soweto. The pilgrimage was organized in support of nonracism and to celebrate the first free and fair democratic elections in the country. Inviting people to participate in the pilgrimage and in chanting the *namu myoho renge kyo* mantra, however, Reverend Sawaguchi also hoped that this engaged Buddhist practice would "console the spirit of the victims of the apartheid system and encourage living together peacefully on the land no matter what race, creed, or religion." The pilgrimage, which ended with a fast and prayer for peace at the memorial to Hector Peterson, whose death symbolized the concerns of the Soweto riots in 1976, was thus undertaken, as the Founder and Preceptor of the Japanese Order, the Most Venerable Nichidatsu Fujii indicated, "with the hope of modeling a community coexisting in peace." That community, like the pilgrimage itself, suggested Reverend Sawaguchi, recalled Mohandas Karamchand Gandhi's campaign for Sarvodaya (the well-being of all) in India and the pursuit of *satyagraha* (keep to the truth) in the province of KwaZulu Natal, South Africa, in the earlier part of the century.[4]

Second, in April 1987 a Buddhist *bhikkhuni*, Nara Greenway, undertook a forty-day fast in Cape Town in which she prayed for the release of children from detention without trial. Her vigil of prayer, chanting, and drumming in support of the "Free the Children Campaign" elicited contrasting responses. Several pedestrians passing her small shrine on Government Avenue acknowledged that the Buddha's teachings on compassion for all sentient beings demanded that the nun oppose injustice; other onlookers ironically accused the *bhikkhuni* of sanctioning lawlessness in her opposition to the legislated violation of human rights in South Africa. People "shouted out blasphemies and the police continually disturbed her," one person recalled, whilst in a distinctively South African inquiry another questioned whether it was plausible for Europeans (white South Africans) to be members of an Asian Buddhist order. For Nara Greenway, however, the vigil was exemplary of a Buddhist commitment to nonviolent, peaceful, and symbolic protest; her fast, and the proposal to build a peace pagoda in Alexandra township, emerged as a Buddhist attempt to ameliorate suffering and creatively respond to the social and political crisis in South Africa.[5]

Third, in November 1984, David Hartman, a Buddhist war resister, appeared before the Board for Religious Objection to register his opposition to conscription into the South African Defense Force. As the first of several Buddhist war resisters in South Africa, Hartman succeeded in challenging the imposition of an ethnocentric, theistic definition of religion for the legislation of moral conscience. Premising his objection on passages from the

Anguttara Nikaya, Hartman held that the Buddhist teachings, when applied to the South African situation, instructed people to live a life of compassion and nonviolence. Distinctive from forms of Christian compassion that motivated antecedent just war theorists and resisters, Hartman argued, the Buddhists' commitment to peace in South Africa was based on detachment: "it is only when truly freed from desire, passion, and attachment that Buddhists avoid self-interest." After a three-year-long legal battle, the Supreme Court of South Africa ruled, principally, that Hartman would not serve an impending and severe jail term for resisting conscription, and, subsequently, that Buddhism could for the first time be considered a South African religion, or *godsdiens* (service to god).[6]

It is clear that the voices of politically engaged Buddhists in South Africa resonate as poignant reminders that political and judicial authorities in this country have had to adapt to a plurality of religious beliefs, rather than define faith within the exclusive constraints of Christian nationalism. In this sense, as David Chidester notes, "Buddhism represents an implicit challenge to any hegemonic closure of the political order under the sacred canopy of a transcendent, legitimating god" in South Africa.[7]

It is less clear, however, to what extent Reverend Shoji Sawaguchi's peace pilgrimage in celebration of democracy in Soweto, Nara Greenway's forty-day vigil and fast against injustice in Cape Town, and David Hartman's pioneering objection to conscription in the South African courts are *distinctively Buddhist* examples of socially engaged practice. The actions of each were inspired by a critical and contextual reading of general Buddhist precepts, but their symbolic acts of opposition—a peace march, a vigil, and a fast—were not essentially incongruous with Christian Catholic or Protestant, or Muslim anti-apartheid activities employed in the struggle for a nonracist, nonsexist, and democratic South Africa. In these terms, the emerging history of an engaged Buddhist ethic in South Africa contests the very definition of religion in the country, rather than the particular authenticity or meaning of Buddhist-inspired conventions of social engagement.

INDIAN AND CHINESE BUDDHISTS IN SOUTH AFRICA

Although the first Buddhist society in South Africa, the Overport Sakya Buddhist Society (later Natal Indian Buddhist Society) was formed in Durban, KwaZulu Natal, in 1917, South Africans have demonstrated an interest in Buddhism and its origins since the early nineteenth century. Romantic and Orientalist preconceptions proliferated local publications that endeavored to locate and represent the tradition in an emerging science of comparative religion: Buddhism was "a creed more primitive and more original than Christianity," contested the *Cape Monthly Magazine* in 1846. Conversely, Buddhism was "handed down from the immediate descendants of Noah," argued the *Christian Express*. By 1874 the ill-named Cape Christian journal, the *Kaffir Express*, conceded that Buddhism arose as a "reaction against Brahmanism" in India, thereby discounting William Jones, William Francklin, and others who earlier promoted an unlikely African etiology—although as the writings of the South African traveler James McKay reveal, allegations of an African genealogy, and reverse arguments for a Buddhist origin among indigenous African religions, were never quite concluded: Bushmen cave paintings in the northern Cape, argued McKay, were "inherited from Buddhist ancestors in East Africa."[8]

With this interest in Buddhist origins in South Africa came an inquiry into the central tenets of the Buddhist tradition. Consonant with salient Victorian social mores, most South Africans regarded Buddhism as nihilist. James Stuart suggested to his Zulu-speaking informant Mabaso in the 1890s, for example, that "Buddhism was annihilation." The African Bookman's *Religion in Many Lands* concluded that Buddhism was "quietist." Confirming that the *dharma* was a "law very like in some points the ten commandments," and that *nirvana* was a "passive rather than active good," Arnold Watkins in an 1891 edition of *The Cape Illustrated Magazine* adduced that "Buddhism was the first religion that recognized the universal brotherhood of man."[9]

Conflicting interpretations of a nascent tension between quietism and social activism in nineteenth-century South African accounts of Buddhism were prominent. Unitarians, in particular, viewed Buddhism to be a positive social force. In 1882, David Pieter Faure, the founder of the South African Free Protestant (Unitarian) Church, declared the Buddha a remarkable illustration of social reformism who, "seeing the evils and miseries caused by the religious creed by which India was enslaved," confirmed the reality of Buddhism as a "practical theology." In these terms, Faure's successor Ramsden Balmforth proposed that a League of Peace be established in South Africa to "encourage the views of the Buddha," arguing that Buddhism provided South Africans with an example of how anti-racism and peace could be promoted. Olive Schreiner's *Buddhist Priest's Wife*, published in the Cape in 1891, praised Buddhism for its nondiscriminatory attitude toward women. Further writings on gender inequity and unjust economics in South African Unitarian circles fueled local interest in Buddhism as an exemplary representative of nonsexism and an alternative to Christian "materialism" and the Victorian "cult of domesticity." South African Theosophists "concerned with the elimination of disturbances and wars, all of which Buddhism teaches in an eminent degree," likewise acknowledged that Buddhism promised to "solve most of our present-day perplexing problems and thus bring to [South Africa] that peace it so greatly needs."[10]

Bound to Christian theism and evasive of any fundamental teaching of the Buddhist tradition that conflicted with Christian doctrine, nineteenth-century South African Unitarians and Theosophists were undoubtedly drawn to Buddhism because they perceived that it promoted social welfare. Interest rarely translated into practice, however. In any event, politically engaged practice at the time was initiated in agreement with a Protestant Christian, not a nineteenth-century "Protestant Buddhist" perspective.

The advent of the Natal Indian Buddhist Society in KwaZulu Natal in the 1920s did little to alter this position. The community comprised predominantly low-caste Tamil-speaking Indian indentured laborers marginalized by racist legislation and economic deprivation. They converted to Buddhism in the wake of anti-Brahmanist and anti-caste revolts in India, led by among others Jotirao Phule and his *Satyashodak Samaj* (Society for the Search of Truth), E. V. Ramaswamy and the Self Respect Movement, and Pandit Iyodhi Dass, who constructed in Madras in 1906 one of the first modern Buddhist *vihara* and whose son, Rajaram, founded the Overport Sakya Buddhist Society a decade later. Subsequent converts were drawn to the society as a result of Bhimrao Ramji Ambedkar's *Bahishkrit Hitakarini Sabha* (Society for the Benefit of the Excluded Classes). While no direct evidence of Ambedkar's preoccupation with the religious meaning of social oppression is documented, an indication of his influence on Indian Buddhists in South Africa is reflected in the Natal Buddhist Society's formation of a "Mother's Union"—established with the aim of promoting social welfare among the poor in KwaZulu Natal. However, the attempt to translate a Buddhist ethic into sustained socially engaged practice was curtailed. As census returns suggest, the number of Asian Buddhists in South Africa declined from more than twelve thousand in 1921 to just over five hundred in 1951. By the 1990s only a handful of families registered their commitment to Buddhist principles. Occupied with preserving the ritual observance of their imported faith in the context of social and political marginalization and economic deprivation, Buddhist practice in South Africa remained more introspective than socially active.[11]

The recent emergence of a more prosperous, immigrant Chinese Buddhist community in South Africa has not significantly advanced a politically engaged Buddhist ethic. For example, the construction in 1993 near Pretoria of the Fo Kuang Shan Nan Hua (Africa China) Temple complex, which now comprises an African Buddhist College, is dedicated to "promoting humanitarian Buddhism, fostering talent through education and creating a Pure Land on earth." A social relief program comprising the distribution of food, clothing, and books among the disabled, orphaned, and aged is in its beginning stages. Therefore, although founding Master Venerable Hsing Yun, Fo Kuang Shan teachers, and the Congolese, Tanzanian, and South African students of the African Buddhist College are committed to "participate in healing the wounds of the past in this country, in eliminating all remaining national, religious and racial barriers, in building a strong moral foundation among the youth of this continent and in promoting international peace," it is too early to tell in what ways commitment will translate into practice, or indeed in what ways social engagement will be distinctively Buddhist. As one teacher indicated, however, the failure of Chinese Buddhists to accommodate African customary practice in its monastic institutions may even frustrate attempts to develop an engaged Buddhist principle in African communities: prescriptions associated with a life of celibacy central to Buddhist monastic precepts relegate African Buddhist converts to the status of minors in a society that values marriage. Perceived to have abrogated ancestral duties, African Buddhist monks are viewed by indigenous communities as irresponsible and not socially accountable.[12]

By the late 1960s and early 1970s, however, an interest in Buddhism in South Africa developed beyond the confines of Indian and Chinese immigrant communities. Several Tibetan, Theravadin, and Zen centers and groups formed to promote Buddhism in the country. Each contributed to a widening debate on the relationship between inner spiritual practice and politically engaged Buddhist activism in South Africa.

TIBETAN AND NICHIREN BUDDHISTS IN SOUTH AFRICA

In 1969 the English-born Tibetan Buddhist nun Karma Tsultim Khechog Palmo established in Cape Town the first South African Tibetan Friendship Group. The group aimed to provide material assistance to Tibetan refugees in India. A fund was established in support of a hospital for tuberculosis sufferers in Himachal Pradesh. Sister Palmo, who in the early 1960s was appointed by the Dalai Lama to teach Western metaphysics to, among others, Chogyam Trungpa, also began to teach Buddhism to South Africans, establishing a Tibetan Buddhist group in Cape Town so that "all who seek a solution to the problem of suffering, its cause and the way to eliminate it may be satisfied."[13]

By the 1970s several Tibetan Buddhist groups were active, notably in Cape Town, Port Elizabeth, Durban, and Johannesburg. A Johannesburg member recalled that several groups, including the Johannesburg Karma

Rigdor Chakra, were discriminated against by the National Party govern-ment. In an article for *Middle Way* published in 1972, he argued that South Africans had a "blueprint" for the practice of Buddhism in this apparent con-text of statutory discrimination: South African Buddhists would "lay down [their] lives for the *dharma*."[14]

In spite of conspicuous accusations of prejudice, tantric Buddhist prac-tices in South Africa evolved and indigenous forms of Buddhism began to develop. Tibetan Buddhism, suggested poet and novelist Sheila Fugard, had "mingled with the archetypal images of Africa." Tantric Buddhist visualiza-tions and the practice of Amitabha *puja* at the Karma Rigdor meditation group in Cape Town had also provided relief to the "dark and twisted roots of racism that proliferated the country." "In a land darkened by political unrest," she recalled, "the principle of enlightenment was surely manifest to countless suffering beings, for the cessation of that suffering." After meeting the Karmapa with the Beat poets Allen Ginsberg and Lawrence Ferlinghetti in 1973, Fugard concluded, "the idea of Black powerful yogis in South African was close to a reality."[15]

By 1981 a center affiliated with the Tibetan Kagyu tradition was inau-gurated as a full-time Tibetan Buddhist retreat center in the rural northern Cape Karoo village of Nieu Bethesda. The Samye Ling Center, formed by Rob Nairn under the guiding direction of Akong Rinpoche, "harnessed and focused some of the raw and potent power of Africa." Alongside meditation retreats and rain and medicine *pujas*, the formation of a soup kitchen, karma shop, needlework center, and pottery at Samye Ling were examples of how Buddhist residents at the center also "worked towards social reconstruction" in the region.[16]

In these terms, Tibetan Buddhist communities in South Africa married the dual Mahayana concerns of insight and compassion. As Sheila Fugard recalled, "as Western Buddhists, we cannot just go into retreat. We have also got to deal with the very real problems of South Africa—hunger, poverty, unequal education. Buddhism demands social activism, otherwise it will be a very arid Buddhism." In what Sarah Christie and others argue is a novel with the "status of *koan*," a "Buddhist allegory," and "a meditation on spiri-tual and political power" in South Africa, Fugard wrote, in *The Castaways*, that South Africans needed to "seek *satori* through action."[17]

Principally, however, as the formation of The Tibet Society of South Africa, the South African Dewachen Tibetan Cultural Center, and a South African branch of Akong Rinpoche's Rokpa Foundation attest, social and politically engaged practice among Tibetan Buddhist traditions in South Africa is focused on support of the international Free Tibet campaign. For example, on the anniversary of His Holiness's Nobel Peace Prize Award many groups—among them Kagyu, Lam Rim, and Dzogchen centers established in Gauteng, KwaZulu Natal, and the Cape provinces in the 1980s and 1990s—participated in the Ten Thousand Lamp Mandala for Peace in Tibet, organized by the Tibet Society of South Africa. The society actively campaigned for state support of the Tibetan cause and the Dalai Lama's Five Point Peace Plan in Tibet.[18]

Similarly, the Dewachen Tibetan Cultural Center, founded in 1996 prior to the Dalai Lama's World Conference on Religion and Peace (WCRP) visit to South Africa for the Desmond Tutu Peace Lecture, lobbied government ministers, organized public nonviolent demonstrations, and, with the aid of its website "Dewachen South Africa Online," promoted media awareness of the Tibetan crisis. The common experiences of totalitarianism in South Africa and Tibet led to the formation of the center's Afro-Tibetan Friendship Forum. In April 1997 the forum sponsored the visit of Professor Samdhong Rinpoche of the Tibetan government-in-exile, and, with The Tibet Society of South Africa, initiated a meeting between Tashi Phuntsok, His Holiness's resident Representative for Africa at the Office of Tibet (South Africa), and the African National Congress's Chief Director of Human Rights and Social Affairs. More recently, an initiative allowing for young black South Africans and their Tibetan compatriots in exile to participate in an exchange program was promoted by the center.[19]

While these politically engaged initiatives receive the support of South African Buddhists and are informed by Buddhist principles—notably, as the founder of the Dewachen Tibetan Cultural Center suggests, that "all sentient beings deserve compassion"—the societies and centers are not distinctively Buddhist and their campaigns are not different from, for example, politically engaged Christian, Hindu, or Muslim efforts in aid of social and political liberation in South Africa and internationally. The Buddhist organizer of a long-standing Free Tibet campaign in South Africa noted, for example, that "it could just as easily be said that I'm trying to be a good Jew." Therefore, insofar as the Dalai Lama characteristically suggested, following a meeting with President Mandela in Cape Town in 1996, that he had come to South Africa to talk with "Gandhi's successor" and "learn from your country's peaceful transition," it was the historical context of South African oppression and liberation that taught Tibetan Buddhists in South Africa about suffering, its cause, and the creation of a society based on *ahimsa*—not Buddhism in South Africa.[20]

The reformation in the early 1990s of several chapters of Soka Gakkai South Africa, following their break from the Nichiren Shoshu priesthood at

Taiseki-ji in Japan, reflects a similar situation. *Kosen rufu* (propagation) of the beliefs of Soka Gakkai International (SGI), and consequently the reconstruction of society through religious practice, are central concerns. Daily *gongyo* (prayer), *daimoku* (recitation of the *namu myoho renge kyo* mantra), and meditation on the *gohonzon* mandala aim to develop not only personal, material, and spiritual benefit, but create collective value, peace, harmony, and democracy in society. To this end formal *gongyo* and *daimoku* for peace in South Africa are promoted. In understanding that socioeconomic security, peace, and the promotion of human rights are achieved principally through the pursuit of education and culture, recent SGI initiatives in South Africa also led to the institution of education bursaries for disadvantaged African students. For his role in promoting opportunities for South African students, President Daisaku Ikeda was in 1995 awarded an honorary doctorate from the University of the North at which President Nelson Mandela acknowledged Ikeda's philosophy, stating that "when applied to my own country…education is the basic cause of a nation's growth." However, as one member of SGI South Africa indicated, Ikeda's humanistic education, like her own involvement in monitoring political violence prior to the country's first democratic elections in 1994, was not a uniquely engaged Buddhist response. Rather, activities that SGI South Africa promoted, including an anti-apartheid and world peace art exhibition in Cape Town, were "philanthropic" acts aimed at creating human value in an age of *mappo*, or degenerate Dharma.[21]

THERAVADIN BUDDHISTS IN SOUTH AFRICA

Established in 1972 in the war-torn Umkomaas Valley region of Ixopo, KwaZulu Natal province, the construction of an ostensibly Theravadin-oriented Buddhist Retreat Center may have marked the beginning of a more sustained engaged Buddhist presence in South Africa. Built "in spite of the turmoil and agony" that South Africans experienced, "simultaneously with this *dukkha*," the center was an indication, co-founder Louis van Loon suggested, that the Buddhadharma was successfully "unfolding for the first time in the history of the [African] continent."[22]

The Buddhist Retreat Center at Ixopo hosted visitors and teachers from many traditions, among them Stephen and Martine Batchelor, Joseph Goldstein, Lama Anagarika Govinda, Gavin Harrison, Ayya Khema, Rob Nairn, Master Seung Sahn, Louis van Loon, Geshe Damcho Yonten, and, from 1995, the resident Theravadin teachers Kittisaro and Thanissara. Basic Buddhism, intensive meditation, and noble silence retreats run throughout the year, and although one commentator wrote that the center's perimeter fence marked "the border between white and black South Africa," attempts to develop a specifically engaged and community-based social welfare program at the center progress.[23]

Funds for a local school were collected and proposals to address unemployment by financing a training center to improve basic construction skills were discussed. These initiatives evolved in part from several "meditation and social action retreats," among them one held by the Vipassana teacher Godwin Samararatne, who demonstrated that meditation did not imply a withdrawal from the world but the development of an "ever-deepening clarity, openness and calmness of awareness in which we see things as they are." In 1995 Stephen and Martine Batchelor inaugurated an "Engaged Buddhist Retreat" to redress the "imbalanced perception" that Buddhism was a "passive and introverted tradition with little interest in social and political issues." Participants attempted to "find an equilibrium between the demands of spiritual and psychological well-being, on the one hand, and those of the world's suffering and injustice, on the other." In the light of these retreats, and, in particular, as a result of the personal experiences and writings of local Vipassana teacher Gavin Harrison, the intention to develop an AIDS awareness and outreach program also emerged.[24]

Primarily, however, the Buddhist Retreat Center channeled its energies into developing a sustained program of environmental and ecological awareness. In 1996 it was recognized as a natural heritage site because of its contribution to developing the Umkomaas Valley as an ecologically sustainable bioregion, eliminating invasive alien plants, promoting indigenous forestation, and protecting the endangered Blue Swallow. Acknowledging that the Buddhist concept of interdependence "encourages an active engagement," deep ecology "Being Human, Being Earth" retreats focused on workshops encouraging South African Buddhists to "radically transform our everyday lives and activist engagements." Residents, however, spoke of how environmental activism "keeps us alive to the opportunities of understanding and penetrating the great teachings of Dharma. The impermanence and interdependence of all things is revealed [in nature] each day." In these terms, the natural environment in South Africa provided an opportunity to reflect on central Buddhist concepts. In turn, Buddhism encouraged South African Buddhists to be mindful of their interconnectedness with the wild and each other.[25]

Satellite Theravadin centers established in the 1980s in Pretoria and Cape Town were perhaps more active in their pursuit of local responses to social and political deprivation and discrimination. For example, Alison Smith of the Cape Town Buddhist Group participated in an Institute for Democracy in South Africa (IDASA) workshop on identity and "nation building" in South Africa. And in 1991 Michel Clasquin of the Pretoria Buddhist Group drew up the group's submission to the Declaration on Religious Rights and Responsibilities at the local chapter of the WCRP. Recognizing that "the emergence of a social conscience" would be one of the "cardinal features of twentieth-century Buddhism," the group contributed to the charter and the Draft Declaration on Human Rights by committing itself to "reconciliation between the people of South Africa" and pledging to "work towards democracy, tolerance and peace."[26]

Attempts to integrate human rights theory with the Buddhist doctrine of *anatta* were discussed. Van Loon asserted in the Afrikaans weekly *Vrye Weekblad* that because Buddhism is a nontheistic religion, and its central teachings repudiate any possibility of a lasting or substantial self, the promotion of "god-ordained" human rights was a necessary contradiction—although it did not follow that Buddhism was opposed to human rights. Similarly, Clasquin contested that "Buddhism has little to say about the human rights concept in its original legal and political context," and that the "outcome of all this is that Buddhists cannot logically use the term 'human rights' without involving themselves in a contradiction in terms of their own religio-philosophical system." However, the leader of the Pretoria Buddhist Group developed the relevance of the debate for a socially engaged Buddhist ethic in South Africa. In a reading of the *Sigalovada Suttanta*, Clasquin asserted that ethical injunctions were "subject to change *(anicca)*, have no substantial existence independent of the circumstances that brought them about *(anatta)*, and are forever unsatisfactory and subject to revision *(dukkha)*." Thus, whilst it was important that South African Buddhists be engaged in drawing up "constitutional blueprints to protect human rights" in the reconstruction of a more equitable and just South African society, it was not from "a rigid adherence to a set of rules that a 'kinder, gentler' South Africa" would emerge.[27]

Further theoretical issues concerning Buddhism and its relevance to the reconstruction of South African society were enunciated in Theravadin-oriented Buddhist communities in the country. To cite two examples: questions were formulated concerning Buddhism and bioethics and Buddhist responses to economic deprivation in South Africa. In 1978 van Loon published a pioneering but, as Damien Keown notes, imperfect paper on Buddhist responses to euthanasia. More recently Clasquin argued that although "Buddhism is not, and perhaps never has been, a strongly socially committed tradition," the engaged activism of Buddhadasa Bhikkhu, among others, counseled the development of a "spiritualized, humanized socialism" that moved away from an "excessive emphasis on economic aspects of life." Designating this form of Buddhism "*ubuntu Dharma*," or Dharma committed to what indigenous African religion refers to as *ubuntu*, or "community," Clasquin encouraged Buddhists in South Africa to advocate "the establishment of a social structure that would be something like the Buddhist *sangha*."[28]

ZEN BUDDHISTS IN SOUTH AFRICA

The first Zen center in South Africa, the Dojo Marisan Nariji, was founded in 1979 by Taicho Kyogen, a student of the Soto Zen teacher Taisen Deshimaru. Other South African students included Breyten Breytenbach, who in 1975 was sentenced to nine years imprisonment at Pretoria Maximum Security on terrorism charges. In a section of his novel *The True Confessions of an Albino Terrorist* entitled "Zen in the Way of Being a Prisoner," he recalled how he practiced *zazen* and, inescapably, Bodhidharma's *pi kuan* (wall gazing).[29]

More recently, several Kwan Um School of Zen centers were established under the direction of the Korean Zen master Seung Sahn and local Dharma master Heila Downey (Ji Do Poep Sa Nim). Satellite centers in Grahamstown and Colesberg support the work of the head temple at the Dharma Center in Robertson, Western Cape Province. Meditation, chanting, bowing, and *kyol che* (intensive practice) retreats aimed to develop insight "freed from intellectual attachment," and compassion for the suffering of all sentient beings, "not just as a logical consequence but an unavoidable inner exigency."[30]

Opportunities to increase insight and compassion also occurred as a direct result of living in the distinctive conditions of South African society. Charlotte Jefferay of the Bamboo Grove Zen Center in Grahamstown stressed, for example, that the polarity entrenched by an apartheid ideology of "separate development" provided a profound example of why Buddhists should work to oppose "polarized thinking." Similarly, in an essay on Buddhism in a new South Africa, Antony Osler of the Poplar Grove Zen Center in Colesberg noted that "the pain all around us—the pain of poverty, prejudice, a million daily humiliations, guilt and greed, fear and ignorance, and of the separation we all seem to have in common—[impels South African Buddhists] to participate in the changing human world." Examples of politically engaged Zen participation in South Africa are evident: In the late 1980s Downey and Osler provided pastoral advise to Buddhist war resisters; in 1991 the Dharma Center contributed to drafting the WCRP-SA document on Religious Rights and Responsibilities for the Draft Declaration on Human Rights; and on the eve of the first democratic elections in South Africa, its members participated as monitors for the Independent Electoral Commission.[31]

More recently, members of the Kwan Um School of Zen in South Africa trained as counselors for the Truth and Reconciliation (TRC) hearings on gross human rights violations. The school also provided a submission to the TRC Human Rights Violations Committee, recording first that Buddhism was "strongly motivated by human rights and the rights of everything that exists," and second, that "in recognizing the interdependency of all forms of life and reciprocal obligations which arise from it," the school's belief in mutual dependency required that "whatever can be done to reduce suffering in the world should be done." Committing itself to cultivating understanding and compassion, and to participate in the process of bringing about reconciliation, however, the school apologized for not doing more to alleviate suffering under apartheid. In a tacit assessment of the failure of South African Buddhists to promote nonracism and actively contribute to the constitution of human rights in South Africa, the Dharma Center reported that "our voice has been small and often silent by the *very nature of our tradition* and belief in non-violence."[32]

In these terms, although the notion of "engaged Buddhism," as Stephen Batchelor points out, "strikes a particularly resonant chord with many South Africans," the Buddhist tradition, in some estimates, is viewed as an impediment to the promotion of politically engaged practice in South Africa. Where South African Buddhists did mount initiatives to ameliorate suffering and the violation of human rights, for example, these did not specifically or definitively translate Buddhist values into an engaged social ethic.

THE CAPE TOWN ECO-PROGRAM

The formation in Cape Town of an ecological awareness group, the Cape Town Eco-Program, is one exception to the general absence of any sustained engaged Buddhist practice in South Africa. Inspired by, among others, Thich Nhat Hanh's writings on "interbeing," Ken Jones's "social face of Buddhism," Joanna Macy's "despair work," and Gary Snyder's thoughts on ecology and bioregionalism, the program is involved in what co-founder Julia Martin calls political, cultural, and critical literacy: "Engaged in dialogue and actions with people in community organizations," the program is committed to "identifying correspondences between environmental degradation and social inequality" that are "shaped by a practical and research-related interest in Buddhism."[33]

In particular, Martin suggested, the Madhyamika concepts of nondualism, interconnectedness, and *pratityasamutpada*, translated following Thich

Nhat Hanh as "emptiness-interbeing," contributes in theory and practice to identifying the causes of suffering and defeating "the diseases" of racism, sexism, and environmental degradation in South Africa. The concepts also provided a theoretical framework for analyzing and identifying problems of dualistic epistemology; they offer an alternative to human rights campaigners, feminists, and social and environmental activists in South Africa disenchanted with postmodern and deconstructive propositions that failed to advance social transformation; and they develop an alternate vision and practical method for empowering South Africans to see neither their environment as "other," "nor our fellow beings as such." In these terms, recalled Martin, Buddhism avoids the dichotomy between theory and practice and advances the promotion of human reconciliation and ecological transformation, principally, she argues, because it is informed by the "politics of *shunyata*"—a paradoxical commitment to "passionate detachment."[34]

In an editorial introduction to the proceedings of a conference entitled "Ecological Responsibility: A Dialogue with Buddhism," Martin writes that the "Buddhist realization of *pratityasamutpada* brings dimensions of consciousness and Mind to the ecologist's picture of the interrelations of organism and environment."

> It also gives an image of the universe as a jeweled network of interdependence. But this awareness, and the compassionate commitment to relieve suffering, are discovered and made real in practice.[35]

Members of the Eco-Program, affectionately called "Nagarjuna for Beginners," responded creatively and compassionately to the suffering of this "jeweled universe of interdependence" in South Africa in several ways. They held ecological workshops for nongovernment organizations; they produced a fact sheet on nuclear power as part of the Koeberg Alert initiative campaigning against the Cape Koeberg nuclear energy site; and their booklet, *Interconnectedness*, promotes an awareness among political, religious, and environmental activists in South Africa on issues related to pollution, desertification, deforestation, unequal land distribution, and the ideologies of consumption and profit that encourage exploitation and discrimination in South Africa. Failure to recognize "interbeing in the region," the booklet suggests, led to the unique history of economic and political destitution among South African "sky-breathers." Such patterns of exploitation, in which South Africans had failed to observe the complex interconnectedness of society, were merely made explicit under apartheid. Coopting the popular South African political slogan "an injury to one is an injury to all," the Buddhist concepts of interconnectedness and emptiness, suggested one member of the program, offer a practical alternative to these manifestations of apartheid separation. The Buddhist concept of co-dependent arising, moreover, makes possible "tiny interventions" that help South Africans understand the role of "the individual," "nature," and "women" in a way that was "usefully different from that which the international networks of business, money and power are interested in promoting."[36]

By locating the truth, cause, and cessation of ecological and human suffering in its reading of a South African desire for separate selfhood and the oppressive social, political, and economic formations of apartheid policies, the Eco-Program is developing a distinctively engaged Buddhist practice in South Africa. Activism, in turn, occasions small but significant consequences for an understanding of Buddhism. As Martin points out, the transformation of language is a common feature of the program. For example, ecological terms like "pollution" give new meaning to Buddhist explanations of body-mind states. Conversely, Buddhist terms like "defilement" clarify assessments of various environmental conditions.[37]

Informed to a large extent by the philosophy and practice of engaged Buddhism, a recycling project of the Khayalitsha Environmental Action Group, founded by the Program in the sprawling township outside Cape Town, reflects this transfer of language. Martin's environmental literacy course, "Interbeing and the 'I' Habit," further suggested an interrelationship between Buddhism and environmentalism in South Africa: participants were asked to read Thurman's account of Nagarjuna's guidelines for social practice and Macy's listing of the Sarvodaya movement's "ten basic human needs," adapting these texts of Buddhist social engagement to the South African situation.[38]

Notwithstanding these initiatives, and the belief that the "gift of mindfulness and meditation practice may be the most powerful contribution Buddhism can make to eco-social activism," the Cape Town Eco-Program concedes that the tiny, ostensibly white, middle class Buddhist community in South Africa reveals an inappreciable interest in the field of social liberation. "Perhaps," they suggest, the "concern for 'ecology' seems more attractive because it sounds less 'political.'"[39]

CONCLUSION

South African Buddhists understand that South Africa provides a penetrating example of the consequences of polarized thinking. The entrenched ideology of apartheid is accepted by Buddhists to be a benchmark against which the meaning of *dukkha* and the consequences of clinging to legislated dualism in the name of "separate development" can be measured. Constituted from at least the late nineteenth century, how-ever, the Buddhist community in this country has seldom succeeded in translating awareness into sustained or distinctively Buddhist patterns of social or political praxis.

Infrequent incidents of an engaged Buddhist hermeneutic have occurred. Initiatives have failed, notably Gavin Harrison's attempt in 1987 to form a local chapter of the Buddhist Peace Fellowship that was to "transcend the vacuous mountaintops and deserts of *dharma* in South Africa and bring it into the Sowetos, Crossroads, and resettlement areas of the country." A proposed Buddhist response to the South African Christian Kairos document involving a "dialogue between South African Christian liberation theologies and the precepts of the Tiep Hien Order of Thich Nhat Hanh" also miscarried.[40]

For the most part, therefore, engaged Buddhism in South Africa has registered as a remarkable absence. Indeed, whereas in the 1970s and 1980s South African Christian and Muslim theologies of liberation developed a sustained theoretical critique of apartheid—a critique emanating from socially engaged practice—there has been almost no attempt to formulate an indigenous South African Buddhist response to what has become an international synonym for institutionalized discrimination and suffering.

What are the reasons for this omission? There are many, foremost among them the demographic status of the small, white, middle class, and generally conservative Buddhist community in the country. More impor-tantly, what do these South African experiences and omissions tell us about the position of an engaged Buddhist ethic in the West? Two recent observations about the role of Buddhism in South Africa's transition to a nonracist, nonsexist, and democratic South Africa offer instructive insights.

First, as the submission to the TRC hearings on gross human rights violations by the Kwan Um School of Zen in South Africa suggests, socially engaged practice continues to be restrained, in part, "*by the very nature of our tradition.*" One member of the school noted, in this regard, that a concept "like karma," which she used "to make sense of the world," caused her to "remain on the fringe of political activity," "relinquishing most of my own responsibilities to the socio-political powers that be."[41]

Similarly, in defining the role of Buddhists in the "New South Africa," Michel Clasquin argued that South African Buddhists had to "take the Buddhist teaching of the impermanence of all conditioned things seriously." However, Buddhists would "always keep in mind that our efforts will come to naught in the long run [because] decay is inherent in all compounded things." Along these lines, Antony Osler inquired if the Buddhist injunction to avoid grasping made the task of resolving violence and attaining a lasting peace possible.[42]

Questions regarding an engaged Buddhist ethic in South Africa, therefore, are moderated by the perception, however specious, that Buddhist concepts like karma, impermanence, and attachment may prove impediments to Buddhist-inspired activism. The Cape Town Eco-Program offers an alternate reading of the benefit of these concepts as vehicles for social engagement in the South African context. Generally, however, central Buddhist teachings have failed to inspire either opposition to apartheid or the emergence in South Africa of an alternate and engaged Buddhist yana.

Second, whilst recent efforts to develop responses to social injustice, suffering, and discriminatory legislation have been informed by a general Buddhist ideal—namely that insight and wisdom is most meaningfully developed in compassionate action—few initiatives have succeeded in formulating distinctively Buddhist responses to South Africa's crises. As several South African Buddhists have commented, the exercise of Buddhist-inspired activism in South Africa is not explicitly distinct from any other socially engaged ethic. In addition, it has been the political context in South Africa that has inspired South African Buddhists to oppose suffering and the danger of attachment to polarized thinking, not, fundamentally, a commitment to Buddhist precepts or practices.

In these terms, more evidence and more time is required before the authenticity or distinctively Buddhist aspect of an engaged Buddhist ethic in South Africa can be demonstrated conclusively.

NOTES

1. Julia Martin, "All the Cries of the World: Notes and Questions for an Eco-Buddhist Practice," in *Ecological Responsibility: A Dialogue with Buddhism,* ed. Julia Martin (Delhi: Tibet House and Sri Satguru Publications, Sambhota Series V, 1997), p. 138; "Confronting Apartheid with Compassion: A Talk by Gavin Harrison," in *Karuna: A Journal of Buddhist Meditation* 5.3 (1988): 11; and Antony Osler, "Buddhism in a New South Africa," *Shuza: The Dharma Center Newsletter* 5 (1991): 2.

2. Stephen Batchelor, "No Man's Land: A Letter from South Africa," *Tricycle: The Buddhist Review* 11.4 (1993): 68–69.

3. Felicity Souter Edwards, "Vipassana Meditation and Transcultural Consciousness," *Journal for the Study of Religion* 1.2 (1988): 49; Antony Osler,

"Buddhism in a New South Africa"; Michel Clasquin, "Buddhism and the New South Africa," *Shuza: The Dharma Center Newsletter* 6 (1992): 2–3; and Julia Martin, "On Healing Self/Nature," in *Between Monsters, Goddesses and Cyborgs: Feminist Confrontations with Science, Medicine, and Cyberspace,* eds. Nina Lykke and Rosi Braidotti (London and Atlantic Highlands, NJ: Zed Books, 1996), p. 104.

4. Bhikkhu Shoji Sawaguchi, *South Africa: Interfaith Pilgrimage for Peace and Life, Durban-Johannesburg,* 1994. Unpublished and undated pamphlet. For newspaper reports see "Japanese Buddhists to Lead Peace Pilgrimage through South Africa," *Natal Witness,* March 30, 1994; and "A Long Haul for Peace," *The Star,* April 21, 1994.

5. For newspaper reports see "Buddhist Nun to Fast and Pray for Detainees," *Cape Argus,* April 18, 1987; "Police Tell Fasting Nun: You Need Permission," *Cape Argus,* May 12, 1987; "Nun's Forty-Day Fast Comes to an End," *Cape Times,* June 20, 1987.

6. Chairman, Board for Religious Objection, *Hartman vs. Chairman, Board for Religious Objection and Others,* Case No: 3770/85 (Bloemfontein: Supreme Court of South Africa, Orange Free State Provincial Division, November 8, 1984); "Hartman vs. Chairman, Board for Religious Objection, and Others," *South African Law Reports* 1, (1987): 922–35; and W. A. Saayman, "Religious Freedom in Apartheid South Africa," in *Religious Freedom in South Africa,* ed. J. Kilian (Pretoria: University of South Africa, 1993), p. 42.

7. David Chidester, "Review Article: Christians, Buddhists, Muslims and Others," *Journal of Theology for Southern Africa* 60 (1987): 82.

8. For a general overview of the history of Buddhism in South Africa see Louis H. van Loon, "Buddhism in South Africa," in *Living Faiths in South Africa,* ed. Martin Prozesky and John de Gruchy (Cape Town and Johannesburg: David Philip, 1995), pp. 209–16; Darrel Wratten, "Buddhism in South Africa: From Textual Imagination to Contextual Innovation" (Ph.D. diss., University of Cape Town, 1995). On early nineteenth-century perceptions, see *Cape Monthly Magazine* 12.69 (1846): 145; *Christian Express* 12.124 (1880): 8; and *The Kaffir Express* 4.42 (1874): 1. On the African origins of Buddhism see William Jones, "A Supplement to the Essay on Indian Chronology," *Asiatic Researches* 2 (1800): 401; and William Francklin, *Researches on the Tenets of the Jeyns and Buddhists Conjectures to the Brahmins of Ancient India, with Discussion of Serpent Worship* (London: Francklin, 1827), p. 72. For a local account of Buddhist origins among African religions see James McKay, *The Origin of the Xosas and Others* (Cape Town: Juta, 1911), p. 41.

9. Colin de B. Webb and J. B. Wright, eds., *The James Stuart Archive of Recorded Evidence Relating to the History of the Zulus and Neighbouring Peoples*

(Pietermaritzburg: University of Natal Press, 1976), p. 281; J. D. Mackin, *Religion in Many Lands* (Cape Town: The African Bookman, 1944), p. 11; and Arnold H. Watkins, "Buddhism," *The Cape Illustrated Magazine* 1 (1891): 253–58.

10. David Pieter Faure, *Reasonable Religion* (Cape Town: Van de Sandt de Villiers, 1882), p. 27; Ramsden Balmforth, "Proposals for a League of Peace," *Report of the South African Association for the Advancement of Science* (Cape Town: The Association, 1918), p. 292; Balmforth, *Where Saint Paul Went Wrong: Teaching in Women's Sphere Examined* (Cape Town: South African News, 1911); Balmforth, *Unjust Economics* (Cape Town: Cape Town Unitarian Church, 1923); and F. Blanning-Pooley, "The Ability of Buddhism to Solve Present Day Problems," *The South African Theosophist* 6.11 (1923): 11–12.

11. Louis H. van Loon, "The Indian Buddhist Community in South Africa: Its Historical Origins and Socio-Religious Attitudes and Practices," *Religion in Southern Africa* 1.2 (1980): 3–18. On census returns see *Census of the Union of South Africa, Religions of the People* (Pretoria: Government Printer, 1911); and *Census of the Republic of South Africa: Marital Status, Religions, and Birthplace of the of the Coloured, Asiatics, and Natives* (Pretoria: Government Printer, 1951).

12. Master Hue Lee, "Buddhist College Now Open to English Students," *Buddha's Light South Africa* 18 (1996): 19. Also Ivan Frimmel, "About Fo Kuang Shan," *Dharma News: The Bi-Monthly Newsletter for all Buddhists and Buddhist Groups in South Africa* 1.1 (1997): 2.

13. Sister Palmo, "The Aims of the Tibetan Buddhist Friendship Group in South Africa," *Tibetan Friendship Group Newsletter* 1 (1969): 3.

14. Cyril Silberbauer, "Blue-Print for the Dharma?" *Middle Way* (May 1972): 17–20.

15. Sheila Fugard, *Lady of Realization* (Cape Town: Maitri Press, 1984), p. 9. Also Sheila Fugard, "Buddhism in the West," *Maitri: The South African Buddhist Quarterly* 6 (1978): 13.

16. Rob Nairn, "Nieu Bethesda Samye Ling," *Odyssey* 11.4 (1987): 37; and Katrin Auf der Heyde, "The Buddhist Impact on Nieu Bethesda" (B.A. thesis, University of Cape Town, 1986).

17. Sheila Fugard, *The Castaway* (Johannesburg: Macmillan, 1972); and Sarah Christie, Geoffrey Hutchings, and Don Maclennan, "Sheila Fugard: *The Castaways*," in *Perspectives on South African Fiction* (Cape Town: A.D. Donker, 1980), pp. 164–73.

18. *The Tibet Society of South Africa Newsletter* (November 1997): 1–4.

19. See *Dewachen Online* <http://www.dewachen.co.za> for information on the aims, objectives, and activities of the Dewachen Tibetan Cultural Center and Afro-Tibetan Friendship Forum.

20. "Dalai Lama says Mandela is Worthy Successor to Gandhi," *The Star*, August

30, 1996; and "Tibetan Spiritual Leader Arrives in South African to Low-Key Reception," *The Star*, August 30, 1996.

21. "SGI President Receives Honorary Doctorate from South Africa's University of the North," *Soka Gakkai Newsletter* 2392 (October 1995): 1–5.

22. Louis H. van Loon, "Africa: The Buddhist Institute of South Africa," *Middle Way* 54.1 (1979): 49.

23. Stephen Batchelor, "No Man's Land: A Letter from South Africa," *Tricycle: The Buddhist Review* 11.4 (1993): 64.

24. *Buddhist Retreat Center Newsletter* (August 1995): 1–5. See also Gavin Harrison, *In the Lap of the Buddha* (Boston and London: Shambhala Publications, 1994).

25. *Buddhist Retreat Center Newsletter* (November 1997): 1–4.

26. Michel Clasquin, "Religion, Ethics and Communal Interaction in the New South Africa: The Case of the Declaration on Religious Rights and Responsibilities," *Missionalia* 22.1 (1994): 13–35. Also, World Conference on Religion and Peace—South Africa, *Believers in the Future: Proceedings of the National Inter-Faith Conference on Religion-State Relations* (Cape Town: WCRP-SA, 1991); and *Declaration on Religious Rights and Responsibilities* (Krugersdorp: WCRP-SA, 1992).

27. Louis H. van Loon, "Mense is Edel en Waardig, se die Boeddhis," *Vrye Weekblad*, October 12, 1990; Michel Clasquin, "Buddhism and Human Rights," *Journal for the Study of Religion* 6.2 (1993): p. 98; "Early Buddhist Interpersonal Ethics: A Study of the *Sigalovada Suttanta* and its Contemporary Relevance" (M.A. thesis, University of South Africa, 1993); "Buddhist Ethics and the South African Situation," in *Religion and the Reconstruction of Society, Papers from the Founding Congress of the South African Academy of Religion*, ed. John W. de Gruchy and Steve Martin (Pretoria: University of South Africa Press, 1994), p. 330.

28. Louis H. van Loon, "Euthanasia: A Buddhist Viewpoint" in *Euthanasia*, ed. G. C. Oosthuizen, et al. (Pretoria: Oxford University Press, 1978), pp. 71–79. For a critique of van Loon's position, see Damien Keown, *Buddhism and Bioethics* (London: St. Martin's Press, 1995), pp. 180ff. On economic injustice and Buddhism in South Africa see Michel Clasquin, "Buddhism and Unemployment: A Conceptual Reappraisal of Social Classification Systems," in *On Being Unemployed and Religious, Papers Presented at the 16th Symposium of the Institute for Theological Research*, ed. W. S. Vorster (Pretoria: University of South Africa Press, 1992), pp. 96–105; and *Buddhist Retreat Center Newsletter* (September 1993): 1–4, and (August 1995): 1–4.

29. Breyten Breytenbach, *The True Confessions of an Albino Terrorist* (London: Faber and Faber, 1984).

30. Rodney and Heila Downey, "Zen: Seeing Things the Way They Are," *Odyssey*

11.2 (1987): 36.

31. Antony Osler, "Buddhism in a New South Africa," *Shuza: The Dharma Center Newsletter* 5 (1991): 2–3. Also, *Bamboo Grove Meditation Center Newsletter* (January 1995): 1–3. And *Shuza: The Dharma Center Newsletter* 2 (1990): 1–4; 9 (1993): 1–4; 15 (1995): 1–4.

32. Unpublished submission to the Chairperson of the Human Rights Violations Committee, Truth and Reconciliation Commission, June 25, 1997. Emphasis added.

33. Martin, "On Healing Self/Nature," p. 105; "To See the World in its Thusness: A Reading of Gary Snyder's Later Poetry" (M.A. thesis, University of Cape Town, 1985); "Coyote-Mind: An Interview with Gary Snyder," *Tricycle: The Buddhist Review* 79.3 (1990): 148–72; and "Practicing Emptiness: Gary Snyder's Playful Ecological Work," *Western American Literature* 27.1 (1992): 3–19.

34. Martin, "On Healing Self/Nature," p. 104; and "The Snake Person Takes on the Cock-Sure Boys: Buddhism/Postmodernism/South African Eco-Politics," in *Liminal Postmodernism: The Postmodern, the (Post-)Colonial, and the (Post-)Feminist,* ed. Theo D'haene and Hans Bertens (Amsterdam: Rodopi, 1994), p. 353.

35. Martin, "Introduction," *Ecological Responsibility*, p. xvii.

36. Michael Cope, *Interconnectedness* (Cape Town: Eco-Program, 1993); Martin, "All the Cries of the World," p. 139; and "On Healing Self/Nature," p. 116.

37. Martin, "Introduction," *Ecological Responsibility*, p. xv.

38. Martin, "Interbeing and the 'I' Habit: An Experimentation in Environmental Literacy," in *Feminist Perspectives on Sustainable Development*, ed. Wendy Harcourt (London and Atlantic Heights, NJ: Zed Books, 1994), pp. 156–75; and "Reading and Writing the Ecosocial Environment," *Agenda* 29 (1996): 31–36.

39. Martin, "All the Cries of the World," p. 140.

40. Private communication, cited in Darrel Wratten, "Buddhism in South Africa: From Textual Imagination to Contextual Innovation" (Ph.D. diss., University of Cape Town, 1995), p. 240.

41. Katrin Auf der Heyde, "About Our Role in a New South Africa," *Shuza: The Dharma Center Newsletter* 5 (1991): 2.

42. Michel Clasquin, "Buddhism and the New South Africa," *Shuza: The Dharma Center Newsletter* 6 (1992): 2. Also, Antony Osler, cited in "What is World Peace" 7.3 (1990): 12.

ENGAGED BUDDHISM IN AUSTRALIA

Roderick S. Bucknell

ENGAGED BUDDHISM IN AUSTRALIA is barely ten years old. It is correspondingly inconspicuous and little noticed, but is nonetheless deserving of attention and recognition.[1] The particular characteristics of engaged Buddhism in this country are naturally best appreciated when viewed against the background of Australian Buddhism in general.[2]

The presence of Buddhism in Australia dates from the 1850s, when Chinese gold-seekers began arriving in large numbers. Not long after the Chinese came Sri Lankans, most of whom were Buddhists, seeking work in the Queensland sugarcane fields. From that beginning a large-scale introduction of Buddhism from Asian sources might well have developed. However, the movement was effectively blocked in 1901, when the newly constituted federal government passed the Immigration Restriction Act and began formally implementing the infamous "White Australia Policy." This block on Asian migration would remain firmly in place until 1958, and would not be entirely removed until as late as 1975.

In the meantime, Buddhism slowly filtered into Australia by another route. During the early decades of the twentieth century a handful of Anglo-Australians acquired some knowledge of Buddhism through reading and travel, and gradually formed themselves into organized Buddhist groups. The first such group was established in Melbourne in 1925, and by the early 1950s there were Buddhist groups throughout the country. Most were Theravadin in orientation; a few identified with Japanese Zen. By the early 1970s some of these groups had established simple monasteries and invited Theravadin monks to take up residence. Some of the monks who came to practice and teach were Asians; others were local people who had trained and taken ordination in Sri Lanka, Burma, or Thailand.

The mid-1970s saw a major transition in the development of Buddhism in Australia. This stemmed from the abolition of racially discriminatory criteria in Australia's immigration policies, followed by a gradual shift in approach toward the wide variety of migrants who arrived as a result. Exclusion gave way to assimilation, then to integration, and finally to advocacy of cultural pluralism, as expressed in the term "multiculturalism." In theory, if not always in practice, government policy was to affirm and support the cultural and linguistic diversity that was rapidly becoming a hallmark of Australian society.

These changes in policy and attitude were already under way when large numbers of Vietnamese, Laotian, and Kampuchean refugees from the Indochina war began arriving in Australia. Most of the refugees were Buddhists, and this had varying implications for their settlement in their new home. The Laotians and Kampucheans were Theravadins, so were fairly well able to associate themselves with the Theravada-oriented groups that already existed in most Australian cities. Groups subsequently formed that were composed almost exclusively of ethnic Laotian or Kampuchean Buddhists, but many of these retained their association with existing Theravadin groups. This process facilitated the establishment of several large Theravadin monasteries, more or less on the Southeast Asian model but with non-Asian monks predominating. One such center, Bodhinyana Monastery (outside Perth, Western Australia), would become the location for the first Buddhist ordination on Australian soil in November 1987.[3]

For the Vietnamese Buddhists the situation was very different. Being in most cases followers of the Mahayana Pure Land School, they could not readily fit in with the existing Theravadin groups. Consequently, the Vietnamese soon formed their own independent Buddhist societies, many of which have since established temples and installed monks and nuns to minister to their needs.

Another group of refugee Asian Buddhists to come to Australia during the 1970s were the Tibetans. Though few in number, they had a strong and immediate influence. The arrival of the first Tibetan monks was soon followed by the establishment of several institutes for the study and practice of Tibetan Buddhism, mostly in the Geluk tradition. These have since developed into large, active organizations with substantial non-Tibetan memberships.

The most recent influx of Asian Buddhism has been associated with the arrival of many Chinese "business migrants" from Taiwan and Hong Kong. The Buddhists among them have contributed generously to the establishment of large temples supporting sizable communities of nuns and monks. The most conspicuous example is the Nan Tien temple in

Wollongong, south of Sydney, completed in 1995 at a cost of more than $30 million (U.S.) dollars.[4] In these Chinese groups the style of Buddhism taught is usually Pure Land or a syncretic blend of Pure Land and Chan.

As a result of these developments, the number of Buddhists in Australia has grown rapidly. It currently stands at about 200,000, which is slightly less than one percent of the total population.[5] There are about 170 Buddhist groups, representing all the major schools of Buddhism.[6] In most cases these Buddhist groups are "ethnic," in the sense that the members of any particular group are predominantly from one particular ethnic community: Laotian, Vietnamese, Taiwanese, etc. However, there also exist groups whose members are predominantly Anglo-Australian and are more interested in Buddhism in general than in some particular variety of Buddhism.

COMMUNITY INVOLVEMENT

Most of the ethnic Buddhist societies and temples perform more than a religious function. They double as welfare and cultural centers. During the years when the influx of refugees from the Vietnam war was at its peak, some Vietnamese Buddhist groups took upon themselves the task of meeting new arrivals and helping them to settle in. The need for that service has since diminished, but Vietnamese groups continue to serve their communities in other ways, for example by giving assistance to needy families and providing child-care services for working mothers. As their communities age, some groups are making plans to meet the coming need for retirement homes for the elderly. In Perth, for example, both the Congregation of Vietnamese Buddhists and the Vietnamese Buddhist Association plan to build retirement homes within their temple precincts, though they have made little progress in implementing these plans because hoped-for government subsidies have not materialized.

Alongside the more visible examples of service to their communities, Australia's ethnic Buddhist groups fulfill another important function, that of preserving community languages and customs. The mere existence of an ethnically based Buddhist group ensures that the members of the community have a place where they can meet their kind and follow their familiar patterns of language and custom. This role is particularly significant for the younger members of the community, who might otherwise become increasingly distanced from their cultural roots. In some groups formal language classes are available. An outstanding example is the Chinese language curriculum provided by the Fo Kuang temple in Brisbane.[7] Children attend regular weekend Chinese classes in well-equipped classrooms at the temple, and in some cases also receive instruction provided by volunteer Fo Kuang teachers at school during the week. The nuns at the temple point out that the children of Chinese parents will probably be fluent in spoken Chinese simply because the language is used at home, but will possibly never learn the written language unless given formal instruction. They see the preservation of such aspects of Chinese culture as an important aspect of their role as Buddhist monastics.

The "non-ethnic" Buddhist groups, in particular the groups that were established by Anglo-Australians in the years before the large-scale Asian migration began, generally show little inclination to become involved in socially relevant activities. In most cases their emphasis is on the study of the Dharma (particularly from a Theravadin perspective) or on the practice of meditation. But there are some significant exceptions. One example is the Buddhist Society of Western Australia, a Theravadin group whose membership includes a minority of people originating from Sri Lanka, Thailand, and other Asian countries. While appropriately dedicated to Dharma study and meditation practice, they are also engaged in social work. Since 1990 they have employed a full-time or part-time social welfare and community development worker.[8] The role of this worker is to help all local Buddhists to become aware of, and gain access to, relevant services that are available through government agencies—legal aid, job counseling, invalid pension, and so on—services that many people, particularly those from non-English-speaking backgrounds, might not otherwise know about. From its inception this work was funded by an annual grant from the Department of Immigration and Ethnic Affairs, and the society therefore spoke of "our grant-in-aid worker." Sadly, it seems likely that this funding will no longer be available as from 1998, so that the service may have to be drastically curtailed or even terminated.

The socially engaged activities described above are, for the most part, incidental to the main functions of the Buddhist groups in question and are directed toward the members of those groups themselves, or at least toward other Buddhists. However, there also exist in Australia several cases of Buddhist groups working for the benefit of a wider target population, cases that therefore probably fit more closely the notion expressed in the term "engaged Buddhism." These instances of engaged Buddhism are found to be of two main types. The first type comprises hospice centers providing palliative care for terminally ill people in their immediate communities. The second comprises groups supporting overseas projects, such as schools for deprived communities in India and elsewhere. These two types will now be discussed in turn. In each case one prominent example will first be described as representative of the type, and other similar instances will then be dealt with more briefly.

HOSPICE SERVICES

The prime example of this type is the Karuna Hospice Service.[9] Karuna is an organization dedicated to providing compassionate caring support at home for terminally ill patients and their caregivers. It began its work in 1992, following its founding a year earlier by the Venerable Pende Hawter.[10] Pende is an Australian-born Buddhist monk, trained as a physiotherapist and later ordained in the Tibetan Geluk tradition. He was encouraged to establish such a service by Lama Zopa, the Spiritual Director of the FPMT (Foundation for the Preservation of the Mahayana Tradition), of which Karuna became a member. From small beginnings Karuna has grown into an organization with eighteen professional staff and about seventy active part-time volunteers. It is based in Brisbane, Queensland, and services the Brisbane North region.

The people directly served by Karuna are terminally ill patients with a life expectancy of six months or less. Most are non-Buddhists. Karuna's first objective is to provide material, emotional, and spiritual support for such people in their own homes, as well as their caregivers, relatives, and friends. The emphasis on caring for patients in their own homes, rather than in the impersonal and unfamiliar environment of a hospital or other institution, is expressed in the slogan: "I'd rather be at home with Karuna."[11]

The inspiration for Karuna's work derives from the cardinal Buddhist ideals of compassion, selfless giving, and respect for life (*karuna* is Sanskrit for "compassion"). However, the spiritual component of the support itself is not explicitly Buddhist, unless the patient so desires. Counselors take due account of their patient's own world view and religious orientation.

Karuna's eighteen professional workers are trained nurses, qualified in all aspects of palliative care provision, and are paid accordingly. Working either full time or part time, they meet patients' varied needs, from symptom relief to psychological counseling. The seventy-odd part-time volunteers acquire the relevant skills through a six-week training course, provided by Karuna, before they begin work. Volunteers usually contribute one day per week, and commit themselves to maintaining this level of contribution for a year at a time. They mainly provide companionship for patients and respite for caregivers. With this workforce of professionals and volunteers, Karuna is able to serve about 120 families in the course of a year. Of that number, many have already lost the family member and are receiving bereavement counseling, a service that continues for up to a year following the death.

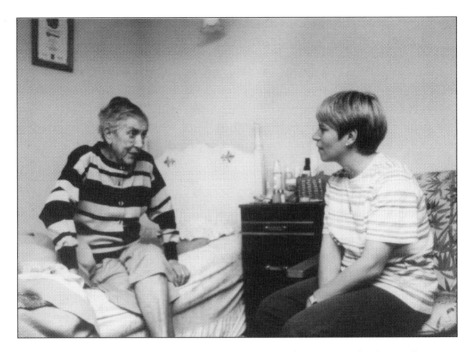

Karuna Hospice Service patient and volunteer, Brisbane, Queensland, Australia.
Photo by Lyn Moorfoot, courtesy Roderick Bucknell.

Karuna receives funding and some material support from the Health Department of the Queensland state government, a fitting recognition of its considerable contribution to the provision of hospice care in the state. This government funding covers about sixty percent of Karuna's costs; the remaining forty percent comes from private donors, trusts, service clubs, and similar sources. Some donations are made in kind, for example in the form of a piece of home nursing equipment or a car for Karuna's fleet. Funding is the major determinant of the amount of work the service can take on. At present, limitation of financial resources means that about 40 percent of patient referrals have to be turned away.

Karuna's members naturally hope that the present limitations on its services will eventually be overcome through future modest expansion. The Venerable Yeshe Khadro, who recently took over as director from Pende Hawter, shares the view of her predecessor that Karuna should ultimately acquire an adequately equipped building of its own, rather than relying, as at present, on temporary and minimal accommodation provided by the state Health Department. With such a building Karuna would be in a position to run a day hospice and provide in-patient accommodation. Such plans are always tempered, however, by the belief that "*hospice* is a concept of care, rather than a place."[12] Also, Karuna members recognize that their ideals can to some extent be realized indirectly, by convincing others about the value of home-based palliative care. The five hundred or more families that have been helped by Karuna since its inception need no such convincing. However, it is considered that the mainstream medical profession is not adequately equipped for dealing with the needs of dying people. Medical doctors, and indeed the general public, need to be educated to the idea that palliative care entails much more than relief of physical pain. Accordingly, Karuna has as one of its objectives "to provide education, for health professionals and others, about caring for the dying and bereaved."[13] Pende Hawter has been particularly active in this area. He has given many talks and courses on the subject; for example, in 1996 he went on a teaching tour in Europe and Taiwan, lecturing mainly at FPMT centers but also at hospitals.[14]

Another of Karuna's objectives is "to undertake research into all aspects of death, dying, and bereavement."[15] This is a longer-term task, made difficult by limited resources. Nevertheless, a substantial body of data is accumulating. Also, Karuna's approach and methods have been the subject of a Ph.D. thesis, completed in 1996.[16]

A gratifying development for Karuna and its supporters has been the recent successful establishment of a branch service, Cittamani Hospice, near the town of Nambour, a two-hour drive north of Brisbane.[17] Though only in its second year of operation, Cittamani, under the directorship of Hilary Clarke (one of Karuna's three founding members), is already firmly established as an outpost of Karuna.

Other hospice services, modeled more or less closely on Karuna but operating independently of it, have developed in centers more remote from Brisbane. These include the Hospice of Mother Tara in Bunbury, Western Australia; the Karuna Hospice Group in Bendigo, Victoria; the Tara Institute in Melbourne, Victoria; and the Amitayus Hospice Service in Mullumbimby, New South Wales.[18]

Broadly similar in approach to the above groups, though independent of them in every respect, are the Australian branches of the Buddhist Compassion Relief Foundation, or Tzu Chi. Since its establishment in Taiwan in 1966, Tzu Chi has grown into a worldwide organization providing relief as needed, particularly in fields relating to health care. Of Tzu Chi's three Australian offshoots (in Sydney, Melbourne, and Brisbane), the Brisbane branch claims attention for having established a particularly active youth group.[19] Its one hundred or so members, mostly recent arrivals from Taiwan, have been involved since 1994 in various small-scale projects at the large Mater Misericordiae Hospital in Brisbane. They work on a part-time, voluntary basis and in collaboration with the Catholic Sisters of Mercy, who run the hospital. Their work includes relieving the regular nursing staff of certain simple but time-consuming duties with feeble elderly patients, such as feeding them or simply providing them with conversation and companionship. They also maintain a program of regular visits to elderly patients in a number of nursing homes in the Brisbane area. Tzu Chi's work at the Mater Hospital well illustrates the organization's secondary aim of using its relief work to build bridges between Buddhism and other religions.

OVERSEAS PROJECTS

This style of engaged Buddhism is well illustrated by the group called BODHI, the Benevolent Organization for Development, Health, and Insight.[20] BODHI was founded in 1989 by Dr. Colin Butler and his wife Susan. The Dalai Lama became its founding patron later the same year. Based in Campbell Town, Tasmania, BODHI works primarily at raising funds to support development projects in developing countries. To date, it has mainly been involved in primary health and educational projects in India.

BODHI's founders derived their initial inspiration from the ideals of Tibetan Buddhism, particularly as expressed by the Dalai Lama (*bodhi* is Sanskrit for "enlightenment"). Consequently, much of the organization's work has been among Tibetan refugees. But BODHI also has non-Buddhists among its small team of dedicated supporters and advisors, and its target population is far from being exclusively Buddhist. For example, one of the most successful projects supported by BODHI benefits mainly low-caste Hindus in India's Bihar state. The driving force behind that project is Sister Jessie, a Roman Catholic nun originally from Kerala State, who became concerned with the plight of poverty-stricken families in the area around Bodh Gaya. She aims to provide low-cost primary education for the children of the area, and encourages their parents to augment their income—and their diet—by raising chickens.[21] Sister Jessie's work is a typical example of the very practical, down-to-earth projects that BODHI supports. Other examples, mainly from India, include: a large-scale program of vaccinating or sterilizing stray dogs to help eradicate rabies; organizing "tidy village" competitions to encourage communal cleanliness and healthy living habits; training Tibetan monks and nuns as community health workers; providing water pumps and water purification systems for refugee centers; and teaching handicraft skills to young hill-tribe women in Thailand, to help them avoid being drawn into prostitution.

The need to initiate a project—or the need to support an existing project—is identified by BODHI members during field trips to likely areas in developing countries. A crucial factor in evaluating such cases is the presence of a competent local worker who can be relied on to commit him- or herself to the project and become its prime mover. Once BODHI has identified a worthy project and taken on the task of supporting it financially or materially, its future is assured.

The main source of BODHI's funding is donations and bequests. Consequently, a large part of the organization's work consists in raising awareness, among potential Australian and overseas donors, of the problems that exist in developing countries and of the possibilities for solving them. Through its biennial newsletter, *Bodhi Times*, and other outlets, BODHI draws attention to the large-scale problems that beset the developing world, such as overpopulation, child labor, illiteracy among women, inadequate or unsafe water supply, and environmental abuse by multinationals. It also introduces the projects it is sponsoring as specific instances where the broad problems identified are being addressed on a modest scale. Stress is laid on the ability of affected populations to better their lot through self-help projects requiring only minimal outside financial or material support and guidance. BODHI's message is being heard by a growing number of supporters. The donations come in and the projects go ahead.

Another Buddhist organization that supports humanitarian development projects overseas is the Bodhgaya Development Foundation, based in Brisbane.[22] The BDF follows BODHI in providing substantial financial support for Sister Jessie's work. It also runs its own school, Pragya Vihar, for children of poor families in Bodh Gaya. The school began in 1993, with a few dedicated Buddhists teaching in a small mud brick house. It now has a teaching staff of twelve (of all religious persuasions) and an enrollment of some four hundred students, and is housed in a well equipped two-story building on land purchased by the BDF.

Provision of basic education in India is also a concern of the Tara Project Australia Inc., based in Sydney.[23] A recently formed affiliate of the Karuna Foundation of India, the Tara Project identifies itself as "an independent, nonprofit, non-sectarian organization based on the living principles of Mahayana Buddhism...dedicated to reconciliation on all levels through universal humanitarianism."[24] It funds its activities by donations and institutional sponsorship. In collaboration with Caretrain Inc. (an Australian support group for Tibetan refugees), the Tara Project is currently involved in a scheme to train Tibetan nuns in Himachal Pradesh,

India, as health care workers, particularly in the area of women's hygiene and midwifery. It is also supporting the Karuna Foundation in establishing a modern eye clinic in north India. But the Tara Project is also active on the home front, where it "promotes and supports responsible ethics in community, business and environmentalism."[25] To this end it has instituted a program whereby Australian companies and organizations that support the Tara Project's manifesto on business ethics are invited to declare this on their documentation. They also become part of a network of such businesses, which the Tara Project invites to participate in forums and meetings dedicated to reinforcing the ethical objectives of the program.

GENERAL REFLECTIONS

The above outline is based on a recognition that engaged Buddhism in Australia manifests in two main types of activity: provision of hospice care and related services, and promotion of development projects in overseas countries, particularly India. Arguments could no doubt be advanced for recognizing further types. Some might wish to recognize political activity, as exemplified in the Free Tibet campaign pursued by the Australia Tibet Council, but the ATC is not an overtly Buddhist organization, so does not meet the implied criteria for inclusion here. Again, it may well be that other candidates for inclusion—groups that might find a place in some more thorough study in the future—have simply escaped the attention of this preliminary survey. On the present evidence, however, engaged Buddhism in Australia is represented in the two broad types identified above.

It is instructive to reflect, however speculatively, on possible reasons why engaged Buddhism in Australia has manifested in this particular way. Likely explanations are not difficult to find. Promotion of development projects among economically disadvantaged fellow human beings, particularly fellow Buddhists, is a natural way for Buddhist compassion to manifest on a practical level. Australia, though by no means devoid of economically disadvantaged groups, offers comparatively little opportunity—and demand—for practical aid work. When assessed in terms of truly pressing need, the countries of South and Southeast Asia, Australia's nearest "developing" neighbors, are far more deserving beneficiaries of such activity. The principal target is India, particularly Bodh Gaya and surrounding areas in Bihar state. This clearly has a lot to do with the fact that this is the region most visited by Buddhist pilgrims. Australian Buddhists, bent on seeing the site of the Buddha's enlightenment, encounter one of the most poverty-stricken populations in Asia in the process. It is beside the point that the people thus identified as most in need are not Buddhists.

The relative lack of pressing need for material aid in Australia also suffices to explain the pattern of engagement displayed by Buddhist groups whose headquarters are located outside the country. For example, Fo Kuang Buddhism in Australia, as represented by the large temples at Wollongong and Brisbane, does not appear to be a prominent example of engaged Buddhism. Yet the parent organization in Taiwan has a fine record of hands-on engagement in projects in developing countries and in Taiwan itself.[26] Finding relatively little need for such work in Australia, the Fo Kuang organization channels its resources here into the less tangible things demanded by its local supporters, such as language instruction.

Also not difficult to account for is the emphasis on hospice care as the preferred way for Australian Buddhist groups to serve the local population. Most basic community needs, in the fields of education, health, and so on, are already met fairly adequately by the relevant government departments. Hospice care, however, is an area in which, as is freely recognized by all concerned, government services are seriously inadequate. But there do exist other areas of need that the Buddhist groups in question could equally well have identified as deserving their attention. It is likely, therefore, that another influence is operating here, namely the Buddhist concern with the phenomenon of death.

The Buddhist notion of rebirth makes death appear as the gateway to a new beginning rather than as the end of the road. Buddhists attach much importance to the dying person's state of mind as a factor determining the next life. This is particularly so in Tibetan traditions, where detailed instructions are provided on how to guide the dying person through the transition. A traditional example of such a set of instructions is the *Tibetan Book of the Dead;* a modern version is Sogyal Rinpoche's *Tibetan Book of Living and Dying.*[27] Such ideas are perhaps not a big factor in the motivations or practices of the lay workers in organizations like the Karuna Hospice Service, but they would certainly have figured prominently in the thinking of those who planned and set up such organizations. And as is often the case with Buddhist teachings, the practical outcome is not dependent on acceptance of the underlying doctrine. A peaceful state of mind in the period leading up to death is desirable in its own right, regardless of whether death will indeed be followed by rebirth.

A link with Tibetan traditions is a conspicuous feature shared by most of the examples of engaged Buddhism identified in this survey. BODHI, the Karuna Hospice Service, the Tara Project, and many others identify, directly or indirectly, with one Tibetan Buddhist school or another, in some cases recognizing some particular Tibetan lama as the source of their inspiration. Tibetan ideas about the process of dying may explain some but not all of these cases. More to the point is probably the Tibetan emphasis on the ideal of compassion *(karuna)* and its practical correlate, skillful means *(upaya)*. While these ideals are important in all forms of Buddhism, they receive emphasis in certain Mahayana Schools, and are particularly stressed in Tibetan Buddhism. Also significant, and probably as a correlate of the point just made, is the prominence in Tibetan Buddhism of active, energetic teacher-leaders, the Dalai Lama himself being the most outstanding example. Many workers in the projects surveyed here identify such figures as providing ongoing inspiration for their work.

The factors tentatively identified here as responsible for the particular form taken by engaged Buddhism in Australia would probably be found to apply equally in many other Western contexts. There is perhaps nothing particularly Australian about them. The exact nature of the underlying forces at work in the Australian situation will, no doubt, become more evident as time passes and this still very recent phenomenon develops. What is certain is that engaged Buddhism has, during the decade since it first appeared in Australia, put down enough healthy roots to ensure that it will grow abundantly in the decade to come, and beyond.

Notes

1. In preparing this account I may well have overlooked or underrated some of the less well publicized instances of engaged Buddhism in Australia, in which case I trust the groups concerned will accept that this was unintentional. To those people and groups that provided relevant information and material I here acknowledge my indebtedness and express my gratitude.

2. Sources drawn on for this section include: Terrance McDonnell and Roderick S. Bucknell, "Buddhists," in Ian Gillman, ed., *Many Faiths, One Nation: A Guide to the Major Faiths and Denominations in Australia* (Sydney: Collins, 1988), pp. 318–31; Paul Croucher, *A History of Buddhism in Australia 1848–1988* (Sydney: New South Wales University Press, 1989); Roderick S. Bucknell, "The Buddhist Experience in Australia," in Norman Habel, ed., *Religion and Multiculturalism in Australia* (Adelaide: AASR, 1992), pp. 214–24; Enid Adam, *Buddhism in Western Australia* (Perth: Enid Adam, 1995); Enid Adam and Philip J. Hughes, *The Buddhists in Australia* (Canberra: Australian Government Publishing Service, 1996).

3. Adam, *Buddhism*, pp. 29–30.

4. This remarkable structure, said to be the largest Buddhist temple in the southern hemisphere, is described and abundantly illustrated in *Nan Tien: Paradise of the Southern Hemisphere* (Balmain, Australia: Rala International, 1995).

5. Adam and Hughes cite the 1991 census figure of 139,795, *Buddhists*, p. 41. By the 1996 census the figure had risen to 199,812.

6. Adam and Hughes, *Buddhists*, p. 61.

7. Briefly introduced in Bret Malinas, *Master Hsing Yun of Fo Kuang Shan: A Study of a Successful Buddhist Reformer* (M.A. thesis, Department of Asian Languages and Studies, University of Queensland, 1997), pp. 1–3.

8. *The Buddhist Society of W.A. Newsletter*, section on "Community Services" in various issues from 1990 to 1997.

9. Karuna Hospice Service, PO Box 2020, Windsor 4030, Australia. Tel: (61)(7)38578555; Fax: (61)(7)38578040; E-mail: 100251.1722@compuserve.com.

10. Most information in this section is from: The Karuna Hospice Service Ltd, 1996 *Annual Report*; Vicki Mackenzie, "We Die as We Live," *Mandala*, Sept.–Oct. 1997, pp. 42–43; and interviews with Yeshe Khadro and Hilary Clarke, October 1997.

11. *1996 Annual Report*, front cover.

12. *1996 Annual Report*, p. 6.

13. Ibid.

14. Mackenzie, "We Die," p. 43.

15. *1996 Annual Report*, p. 6.

16. Pamela McGrath, *A Question of Choice: Bioethical Reflections on a Spiritual Response to the Technological Imperative* (Ph.D. thesis, Department of Social Work, University of Queensland, 1996).

17. Cittamani Hospice Service, PO Box 2535, Nambour West, QLD 4560, Australia. Tel: (61)(754)411555; Fax: (61)(754)411311; E-mail: 100251.1722@compuserve.com.

18. Amitayus Hospice Service, PO Box 696, Mullumbimby, NSW 2482, Australia. Tel: (61)(66)843808; Fax: (61)(66)341690.

19. Brisbane Tzu Chi Youth Group. Tel: (61)(7)33456124; Fax: (61)(7)33454867; E-mail: s321169@student.uq.edu.au.

20. BODHI, 4 Queen St., Campbell Town, TA 7210, Australia. Tel: (61)(03)811133; Fax: (61)(03)811675; Email: csbutler@peg.apc.org. Most information in this section is from Colin Butler, personal communication, October 1997; and various issues of *Bodhi Times* from 1993 to 1997.

21. *Bodhi Times* 10 (June 1996): 2–3.

22. Bodhgaya Development Foundation, 147 Richmond Road, Morningside, QLD 4170, Australia. Tel: (61)(7)33992017.

23. The Tara Project Australia Inc., 6 Walter Street, Leichhardt, NSW 2040, Australia. Tel/Fax: (61)(2)95600302; Email: 100017.3253@compuserve.com.
24. "Background to the organization," Tara Project information sheet.
25. Personal communication, December 1997.
26. A Fo Kuang project among refugees in Thailand is described in Malinas, *Master Hsing Yun*, pp. 57–58.
27. Francesca Fremantle and Chogyam Trungpa, trans. and eds., *The Tibetan Book of the Dead* (Berkeley: Shambhala Publications, 1975); Sogyal Rinpoche, *The Tibetan Book of Living and Dying* (London: Rider, 1992).

LOOKING AHEAD

His Holiness the Dalai Lama and members of the government-in-exile of Burma (Myanmar) at a German Buddhist Union sponsored rally, City Hall, Osnagrueck, Germany. Courtesy Franz-Johannes Litsch.

NEW VOICES IN ENGAGED
BUDDHIST STUDIES

Kenneth Kraft

AN AMERICAN BUDDHIST MAGAZINE RECENTLY RAN the following classified ad:

> The Greyston Mandala, an innovative Buddhist-inspired community development organization in Yonkers, New York, is creating a new position of Director of Path Maker Services. With 120 employees, Greyston serves economically disenfranchised families and individuals through housing development, enterprise creation, jobs....Masters degree preferred, with professional experience in human resource/organizational development, counseling, popular education, engaged Buddhism or other socially engaged spiritual tradition, or related field. Excellent salary and benefits...[1]

Professional experience in engaged Buddhism as a job qualification? The placement of "engaged Buddhism," "masters degree," and "salary and benefits" in such close conjunction is surely a first, and may indeed have caught the eye of an unusual group of job-seekers.

The Greyston ad heralds an emerging field: engaged Buddhist studies. Other evidence abounds. In 1995 the Naropa Institute of Boulder, Colorado, "a fully accredited Buddhist university," introduced a program leading to a masters degree in engaged Buddhism. Judith Simmer-Brown accordingly refers to a colleague as "engaged Buddhism faculty at the Naropa Institute."[2] The Boston Research Center for the 21st Century, in Cambridge, Massachusetts, has pioneered an engaged Buddhist research center based outside academia. Created in 1994 by Soka Gakkai International and administered in a nonsectarian spirit, the center supports an ambitious roster of activities and publications. In 1996 Harvard University's Center for the Study of World Religions hosted a major conference on Buddhism and ecology. Over a dozen recent books qualify as initiatives in engaged Buddhist studies.[3] Three very different journals, the *Journal of Buddhist Ethics, Seeds of Peace*, and *Turning Wheel*, are extending the conversation.[4] A first-of-its-kind electronic conference on engaged Buddhism, featuring peer-reviewed papers and free public access, will take place in the spring of 2000, coordinated by the *Journal of Buddhist Ethics*.

This volume builds on these developments and advances the field. The contributors have backgrounds in academia, Buddhist practice, political activism, the environmental movement, and international relief work, often in combination. Because this is the first collection of essays to focus on engaged Buddhism in the West, the collaboration is unprecedented for the writers as well as for readers. In many cases, engaged Buddhist scholars and thinkers are learning about one another's work for the first time, having yet to meet in person.

PARAMETERS OF ENGAGED BUDDHIST STUDIES

The subject matter of engaged Buddhist studies is engaged Buddhism, but the meaning of "engaged Buddhism" is far from settled. The title of the first chapter asserts that "all Buddhism is engaged." Paula Green declares in her essay, "Every moment of life is engagement; every moment of life is Buddhist." Franz-Johannes Litsch goes on in this expansive mode: "Engaged Buddhism...encompasses all schools, all cultures and ethnic groups, both genders, and...the totality of life on our planet." Although such inclusive definitions are appealing in some situations, more precise definitions are needed in others.

For example, it is important to be able to say what is *not* engaged Buddhism. Aum Shinrikyo, the "new-new religion" in Japan whose members released lethal sarin gas on Tokyo subways, uses Buddhist terminology and has definite ideas about changing the world for the better. There is even a photograph of the group's founder, Asahara Shoko, being greeted warmly by the Dalai Lama. Yet Aum Shinrikyo hardly qualifies as a form of engaged Buddhism. Why do we believe it does not? How would we compose an explanation?[5]

Any living religion or vital social movement changes constantly. Today, the Dalai Lama is widely regarded as the quintessence of engaged Buddhism, while a figure such as Jon Kabat-Zinn, who uses meditation techniques in pain-relief therapy, seems to occupy a more marginal position. Yet one can also imagine the reverse, say twenty years from now: the movement for Tibetan autonomy fails, the succession of Dalai Lamas is disrupted, and Buddhism becomes a force in Western culture through its impact on psychology and medicine. However serviceable, designations such as "engaged Buddhism" or "Buddhism" are constructions, limited and ultimately insubstantial. Even the most apparently detached and descriptive forms of historical research and writing are actually acts of dividing and shaping reality, a process that is considerably more creative than one might assume. As efforts to define engaged Buddhism continue, the indeterminate and contested aspects of the subject can function fruitfully as stimuli rather than impediments.

Buddhist Studies in Transition

Engaged Buddhist studies has arisen through the confluence of two factors: the vitality of engaged Buddhism itself and the increasing maturity and openness of mainstream Buddhist studies. For generations, Buddhist studies has been grounded in an empirical approach that emphasizes the mastery of Asian Buddhist languages and the critical, philological study of Buddhist texts. Ph.D. candidates typically demonstrate their competence by translating canonical works.

While the rigorous scrutiny of texts still prevails in European and Japanese Buddhology, Buddhist studies in North America has become a broader enterprise, embracing a range of multidisciplinary and comparative methods. Often situated within departments of religion or Asian studies programs, American Buddhist scholars are likely to look beyond texts to contexts, treating daily practice, rituals, gender-related matters, and other aspects of lived tradition as suitable objects of study.[6] In recent decades, confidence in "value-free" empiricism has waned, and texts are no longer seen as stable artifacts. Bernard Faure, a Buddhist scholar equally versed in textual analysis and postmodern thought, observes, "All this makes it rather difficult to know where the tradition (here the Chan/Zen tradition) ends and where scholarship begins—let alone where scholarship ends and I begin."[7]

Topics that were formerly out-of-bounds are taken up by senior scholars, and forms of discourse once shunned—normative, prescriptive, pastoral, confessional—are increasingly tolerated.[8] Richard Hayes, a scholar of systematic Buddhist philosophy, has written *Land of No Buddha: Reflections of a Sceptical Buddhist* (maintaining that it is "not intended to be a 'professional' monograph").[9] A similarly subtitled book by Tibetan Buddhist scholar Jeffrey Hopkins, *The Tantric Distinction: A Buddhist's Reflections on Compassion and Emptiness,* is advertised as his "personal, individual experience with Buddhism."[10]

Until recently it was taken for granted that the study of Buddhism was the study of *other* cultures. "Buddhist Studies continues to be a Western enterprise about a non-Western cultural product," wrote Luis Gomez in

1995.[11] Suddenly there are demands from scholars and students that the study of American Buddhism be given greater weight. "I have the feeling that—at long last—Buddhist studies has awakened to the reality of the historic transmission and transformation of Buddhism going on right before its eyes," Franz Aubrey Metcalf contends.[12] Using phrases such as "the American Buddhist movement" and "the American Buddhist tradition," Charles Prebish and others go so far as to argue that a doctoral degree in Buddhist studies should now include "proper attention" to American Buddhism.[13] If American Buddhist studies and engaged Buddhist studies continue to develop, the two fields will have areas that overlap. However, engaged Buddhism is not just American, and American Buddhism is not always engaged, so the two disciplines will also differ.

A Variety of Voices

The term "engaged Buddhist studies" contains a potential ambiguity, but perhaps it is a welcome one. As *engaged Buddhist* studies, it refers to the study of engaged Buddhism. This primary meaning is sufficient in most instances. As *engaged* Buddhist studies, the term suggests approaches that incorporate personal religious beliefs, political commitments, or other forms of involvement. Though secondary, this meaning is also pertinent at times. A defense of engaged Buddhist studies (a task beyond our present scope) would bring into view an abiding tension in modern religious studies: the study versus the practice of religion.

In order to identify some of the representative stances within the field, it may be helpful to imagine a large round table, with different groups clustered at different points. (King Ashoka's Round Table?) The three largest groups are scholars of engaged Buddhism, Buddhist scholars who are engaged, and nonacademic engaged Buddhist thinkers. There is no need to affix a permanent label on anyone cited below as an example of a position; at a lively gathering people move around freely.

On one side of the table are the scholars who objectify engaged Buddhism as a subject of study. The concerns of this approach include the command of pertinent sources and languages, the establishment of definitions and criteria, and the application of suitable theoretical frameworks. Those who work in this mode strive to uphold an established set of academic standards, avoiding personal views, citing sources carefully, not prejudging results, and so on. David Chappell's essay in this volume is a good example of this approach. On this same side of the table one also finds scholars of traditional bent who acknowledge some degree of personal involvement in Buddhism but choose not to write as Buddhists. Recent surveys of Buddhist scholars in

North America indicate that about a quarter identify themselves as scholar-practitioners; it is estimated that another quarter are privately Buddhist.[14]

The second large group at the table consists of Buddhist scholars who are somehow engaged. Among them are academics actively involved in a Buddhist-related political cause, such as the Free Tibet movement. "Tibet has been the prime source for the teachings that constitute my own practice of Buddhism," Jeffrey Hopkins says in these pages, "so I think that I'm obligated to help [Tibet] in whatever way I can." Here too are scholars who are closely affiliated with a Buddhist community. Contributor Andrew Olendzki, a Ph.D. in religious studies, directs a Buddhist studies center created by the Insight Meditation Society, a practice community in Barre, Massachusetts. Kenneth Tanaka, a professor at the Graduate Theological Union in Berkeley, is also a spokesperson for Pure Land Buddhists in North America.

The role of participant-observer often suits this group, as exemplified by Roger Corless's essay on the Gay Buddhist Fellowship of San Francisco. According to Corless, "The appropriateness of this [participant-observer approach] as a way of deconstructing the pseudo-objectivity of academic method, especially in discussions about sexuality, is now generally accepted."[15] A different kind of participant-observation is demonstrated by Paula Green, who concludes her essay with an expression of respect for the subjects of her study:

> I wish to express my enduring appreciation to Kato Shonin and Sister Clare of the Leverett Peace Pagoda, not only for their essential contributions to this chapter…but for the blessings of their presence in my life…. I bow deeply with thanks and gratitude for the moral vision of all the monks and nuns of Nipponzan Myohoji, both in the U.S. and abroad.

Some of the Buddhist scholars who are engaged address the question "What does it mean to be both a scholar of Buddhism and an engaged Buddhist?" Here academia offers precedents in the self-critical reflections of Christians who teach Christianity, or Jews who teach Judaism. Increasing numbers of academically credentialed thinkers do not hesitate to challenge or reconstruct Buddhism from within the Buddhist tradition. For example, Sallie King writes in this mode when she assesses the self-immolation of Buddhist monks and nuns during the Vietnam War:

> Let me state my own conclusions, as an American Buddhist and as a Buddhist scholar, as clearly as possible. At the end of the day, the actions of [self-immolators] Thich Quang Duc and Nhat Chi Mai remain profound-

ly challenging. Like others, I am in awe of their courage, selflessness, and capacity to love. But I remain troubled by the lingering moral issues which, to my mind, remain unresolved....Buddhist institutions have a duty as far as possible to prevent these actions which in many ways embody the Buddhist religion at its best.[16]

Another side of our round table is occupied by Buddhist practitioner-activist-thinkers who do not have formal ties to academia. This group demonstrates that engaged Buddhist studies can be pursued seriously and creatively from within the movement as well as from an outside perspective. Human rights, gender issues, education, and the nature of desirable societies are topics of particular concern. Several leading figures are identified in these pages: Sulak Sivaraksa, Thai activist and Nobel Peace Prize nominee; Robert Aitken, Zen teacher and Buddhist Peace Fellowship cofounder; Ken Jones, author of two books on Buddhism and society; Alan Senauke, director of the Buddhist Peace Fellowship; and Santikaro Bhikkhu, a senior disciple of the Thai scholar-monk Buddhadasa.

Individually and collectively, the members of this group are interested in developing "engaged Buddhist social theory." Jones offers a definition:

> an explication of social, economic, and political processes and their ecological implications, derived from a Buddhist diagnosis of the existential human condition.[17]

For example, engaged Buddhist social theory (even in outline form) holds that the traditional "three poisons"—greed, anger, and ignorance—do not apply only to individuals; these behavior patterns must also be analyzed and combatted as large-scale social and economic forces.

Of course, the same person can represent different stances at different times, depending on the intended audience or other conditions. Jeffrey Hopkins published two books in 1999: the personal reflections noted above and *Emptiness in the Mind-Only School of Buddhism*, a learned treatise of more than five hundred pages. Robert Thurman's translations of sutras and other classic texts are replete with annotation and other scholarly apparatus; his most recent book, *Inner Revolution*, has just two footnotes. Joanna Macy's *Mutual Causality in Buddhism and General Systems Theory* is published by an academic press; her *Coming Back to Life: Practices to Reconnect Our Lives, Our World* was published by an alternative press specializing in social change.

Robert Aitken, commenting on the shift from Asian Buddhist monasticism to lay practice in the West, has said, "The monastery walls are down."[18] In some respects, Aitken's remark also pertains to Buddhist studies in the academy. Fresh voices are entering the discussion, cherished suppositions are being called into question, and brand new subfields are proliferating. How will engaged Buddhist studies affect mainstream Buddhist studies? At this point such speculation may be premature. But if the question can be taken seriously, the landscape has already changed.

ISSUES TO EXPLORE

In recent years, Buddhists in Asia and the West have tackled a daunting array of issues. As this book demonstrates, the roster of concerns currently includes war resistance, liberation movements, human rights, the environment, education, commerce, race, prison systems, ethnicity, and gender. Any issue of engaged Buddhism is also, by definition, a concordant subject for engaged Buddhist studies.

Opposition to War as a Characteristic Issue

Consider, as an example, resistance to war. The primacy of this theme is evident in the first four chapters, grouped under the heading "Engaged Buddhism as Peacemaking." The first Buddhist precept, "Do not kill," seems to lead directly to pacifism, and many engaged Buddhists indeed regard themselves as pacifists. Prominent Buddhist leaders have become exemplars of nonviolence. The Dalai Lama refuses to fight with the Chinese. Thich Nhat Hanh unambiguously declares, "I am determined not to kill, not to let others kill, and not to condone any act of killing in the world, in my thinking, and in my way of life." The influential Japanese monk Nichidatsu Fujii (1885–1985) made absolute pacifism the touchstone of his thinking and acting. Claude Thomas, Vietnam veteran and a Peacemaker priest since 1995, says, "I'm convinced that we *do not need* to fight. It is an insane proposition that because we are human beings it is natural for us to fight and kill. Through mindfulness there are ways to resolve conflicts without violence."[19] Members of the Order of Interbeing accordingly seek to end war "without taking sides."

The Kosovo crisis in the spring of 1999 posed painful questions for all concerned. The NATO decision to bomb Serbia was intended to halt well-documented genocidal acts that had culminated in thousands of deaths and hundreds of thousands of refugees. Yet this "humanitarian intervention" itself caused additional civilian casualties and dramatically increased the flood of refugees. Western Buddhists, in common with other concerned citizens of NATO countries, felt compelled to seek answers to the crisis. Alan Senauke spoke for many when he said, "I wonder right at this moment how to respond to American bombs in Serbia and Kosovo when I really have no practical alternative in mind."[20] Paula Green, whose grassroots reconciliation work in the former Yugoslavia gave her firsthand knowledge of the region, held firmly to a pacifist position. She wrote:

> Our current crisis represents American and NATO faith in military might, an unimaginative and misplaced method of responding to conflict. There have been warnings for years that Kosovo would explode....Violence and revenge in the Balkans have never achieved peace. In fact we should question the premise of using violence to achieve peace anywhere. We failed to make alliances with the sizable, well-organized movement for nonviolent social change in Kosovo.[21]

Other Buddhists, equally earnest, reached different conclusions. Bodhin Kjolhede, abbot of the Rochester Zen Center, argued that nonviolent means had failed to halt Serbian atrocities. He insisted:

> We have a responsibility to respond. That's what responsibility means in Zen: responsiveness. If there is such a thing as a justifiable war, then this would appear to be it. What else could NATO have done under these circumstances, when Milosevic would not cease and desist from his ethnic atrocities, in spite of what many would argue were extraordinarily patient efforts to find a nonviolent resolution? I am willing to come out and say that we needed to intervene militarily.[22]

Such divergent positions suggest that Buddhist resistance to war merits closer examination. Does sustained Buddhist practice engender special insight into complex worldly issues? Not necessarily. Does a commitment to engaged Buddhism yield ready-made answers in times of crisis? Apparently not.

In the West, strategists and theologians alike have turned to just-war theories, which go back at least as far as Aristotle. Here is one definition:"A just war is a morally justifiable war after justice, human rights, the common good, and all other relevant moral concepts have been consulted and weighed against the facts and against each other."[23] Just-war thinking is evident in Kjolhede's statement. Helen Tworkov, editor of *Tricycle: The Buddhist Review*, is similarly explicit:

> [Pacifism] is a position for which I have enormous respect, but it's not one that I share. I am drawn to those schools of Buddhism in which "killing" becomes part of a more complex conversation; in the Balkans, the alleviation of suffering emerges as the prime motive for war, and the strategies accommodate paradox and contradiction.[24]

Just-war statecraft not only addresses permissible conditions for beginning a war; it also considers how a war should be fought once it has begun. Yet the principled pragmatism of just-war theory can be a slippery slope, leading to purported justifications that have little or no moral validity. In the long sweep of Buddhist history, it is not hard to find abuses: a twentieth-century example is the fervent embrace of militarism by many Japanese Buddhists during World War II.

If this is an opportune time to undertake a fresh critique of Buddhist pacifism, a pertinent model might be the work of the late Christian theologian John H. Yoder. A forceful advocate of nonviolence, Yoder nonetheless criticized certain varieties of religious pacifism as naive, sentimental, and dependent on utopian views of human nature. "That innocent suffering is powerful is not easy to believe," Yoder wrote. "Specifically, the bearers of power in our societies do not believe in that view, or they would not oppress as they do."[25] Can it be that pacifism and just-war reasoning are *equally valid* options for present-day Buddhists? The question deserves more attention than it has yet received.

Peacemaking is a domain-specific issue (however vast the domain), along with human rights, the environment, and so on. These issues are *characteristic* of engaged Buddhism. All could be examined in the above manner, but for now we must let one example suffice. There are other engaged Buddhist concerns, no more or less important, that cut across specific domains. For example: What is the relation between wisdom and compassionate action? Let's call this second group common issues. Four are presented below in the form of questions.

What Constitutes Engagement?

This basic question is a central motif of the present volume, eliciting a range of responses. As noted above, Patricia Hunt-Perry and Lyn Fine believe that "all Buddhism is engaged," and Paula Green asserts that "every moment of life is engagement." Others seek sharper-edged definitions. Christopher Queen, interviewing Zen teacher Bernard Glassman, asks, "What about a woman who stays home and cares for her family? Does one have to be involved in politics [to be engaged]?" David Chappell asks if Soka Gakkai International—USA is socially engaged, and, citing SGI-USA's demonstrable success in fighting racism, he concludes that it is. Roger Corless considers whether the activities of the Gay Buddhist Fellowship qualify as engagement. He too answers affirmatively, citing as criteria "the healing of homophobia" and "liberation from suffering." When Robert Aitken was asked, "Would you accept *zazen* [meditation] as a form of social action?" he gave a deceptively informal reply: "Probably not generally, but it could be."[26] One can see how meditating in protest alongside the tracks of weapons-bearing trains constitutes social action (a group in California does this). Might there also be situations when meditating quietly in one's room could count as a form of engagement? The issue invites continued scrutiny.

What Becomes of the Quest for Enlightenment?

Again, a variety of stances can be identified. Bernard Glassman, reflecting on his own experience, writes:

> In the beginning I believed that a diligent meditation practice was the answer. In fact, I was a fanatic about meditation and retreats. I thought that if I persevered I would become enlightened, like Shakyamuni Buddha 2,500 years ago. If I concentrated hard enough, I would experience what he experienced. And then I would go out and take action. It took me a long time to understand that I couldn't wait till then to take action.[27]

Some fear that in less capable hands such retrospection could give way to laxity or self-deception. Engaged Buddhism would then become a cop-out for frustrated meditators, a kind of Buddhism Lite. Toni Packer, a teacher originally trained in Zen, maintains that inwardly focused spiritual practice still takes precedence:

> Am I driven to do something helpful for humanity or the endangered planet because I feel deeply, achingly, apart from it all?...Can we wake up to the fact that separateness isn't real at all—that it exists only in thoughts, images, feelings? Are we interested in finding out the truth of this?[28]

Packer's line of questioning infers that unless one has achieved at least some degree of spiritual insight, engagement is little more than a misguided attempt to salve unrecognized inner needs. Others perceive engagement as worthwhile but properly subsumed by the process of awakening. For Stephen Batchelor, cited by Sandra Bell, the ideal of wisdom has long been in "classic tension" with the ideal of compassion, which corresponds to engagement. From this perspective, a deepening of wisdom is accompanied naturally by a deepening of compassion, so "the whole notion of making an issue out of engagement becomes somewhat superfluous."

A nondualistic understanding of the relation between enlightenment and engagement honors both "inner" work and "outer" work as mutually reinforcing and ultimately inseparable. While enlightenment remains a matchless goal, pursuit of that goal in isolation has limited value. As Batchelor concludes, "We cannot awaken for ourselves: we can only participate in the awakening of life."[29] In this spirit, some engaged Buddhists are investigating the proposition that social engagement can serve explicitly as a practice that leads to and expands awakening. To give this path a name requires a string of adjectives, such as "socially engaged Buddhist spiritual practices." Advocates of engagement as a road to awakening readily concede that further exploration is needed: "The question is whether...socially engaged practice in the world can approximate the depth and focus of traditional training."[30]

Personal Transformation and Social Change?

When classic Buddhist texts address the practitioner's potential effect on others, the language tends to be abstract and even paradoxical. A well-known passage in the *Diamond Sutra* states, "As many beings as there are in the universe of beings...all these I must lead to Nirvana....And yet, although innumerable beings have thus been led to Nirvana, no being at all has been led to Nirvana."[31] The *Avatamsaka Sutra* declares, "The bodhisattva will not give up one single living being for the sake of all beings, nor will he give up all beings for the sake of one living being."[32]

Without rejecting such formulations, contemporary Buddhists are framing a parallel set of concerns in more nitty-gritty terms. Does traditional Buddhist practice prepare people adequately for engaging in the world? What are the links, on a practical level, between spiritual insight and improved social conditions? Does the practice of right livelihood contribute meaningfully to the creation of a new society? It is often assumed that compassion almost automatically leads to the alleviation of others' suffering. Yet ethicist Lee Yearley, in a conversation with the Dalai Lama, cautions against oversimplification:

> Many modern Westerners believe compassion provides an insufficient basis for an ethical system—although all would agree that compassion is an important personal trait. These critics of compassion point to the fact that in spite of the ideal of compassion, Christianity and other traditions have tolerated many kinds of injustice. Most important, they believe that this fact is not simply a matter of chance, but shows the problems inherent in the idea of basing ethics on compassion....
>
> Most people normally feel compassion only at some times or toward some people....Compassion can tell me how to react to a suffering person I encounter on the street, but it alone cannot tell me what I should do to make sure that person, and others like that person, do not suffer any more.[33]

Are Engaged Buddhist Activities Distinctively Buddhist?

Darrell Wratten, in his essay on South Africa, tells of one Buddhist who led a peace pilgrimage in celebration of democracy, another who undertook a forty-day vigil and fast against the detention of children, and a third who established a precedent for conscientious objection to the military draft. Wratten then remarks:

> It is less clear to what extent [these activities] are *distinctively Buddhist* examples of socially engaged practice. The actions of each were inspired by a critical and contextual reading of general Buddhist precepts, but their symbolic acts of opposition—a peace march, a vigil, a fast—were not essentially incongruous with Christian Catholic, Protestant, or Muslim anti-apartheid activities.

In recent years this issue has been raised by Helen Tworkov, who asks point-blank, "What makes engaged Buddhism Buddhist?"[34] Several possible answers can be glimpsed in these pages and kindred sources, as follows.

(1) Current activities of engaged Buddhists are *not* distinctively Buddhist. In 1994 Tworkov wrote:

> If the essential emptiness of one's own Buddha-nature is not plumbed as the source for ethical action and compassion, and if ethics is separated from realization, then what is called "Buddhist ethics" offers nothing new to a predominantly Christian society.[35]

Five years later, Tworkov remains unconvinced that there is anything distinctively Buddhist about engaged Buddhism: "Social action, as distinct from radical political action, is sanctioned—even, shall we say, favored—by the Protestant ethic that continues to dominate this culture....Is it possible to have anything but Protestant Buddhism?"[36]

(2) Granted, engaged Buddhism is not yet distinctively Buddhist, but superficiality and hybridity are natural, necessary stages of a religious movement's development, especially in a new culture. In Bell's essay on Britain we learn that disciples of Akong Rinpoche have established a small business, Tara Associates, specializing in "personal development for people at work." Buddhist management consultants? At first one may be inclined to scoff. But what if a decade of experimentation yields new ways to actualize right livelihood in the workplace?

(3) Yes, contemporary engaged Buddhism *is* distinctively Buddhist. In this view, engaged Buddhism is a genuine expression of cardinal Buddhist teachings such as compassion and the way of the bodhisattva. Further,

engaged Buddhists' insistence on linking inner and outer transformation differs from the forms of social activism that have predominated in the West. Thus Janet McLellan declares in her essay on Toronto, "Buddhists do not become Protestants (or even Protestant Buddhists) when they embrace engaged practices."

(4) It does not matter: engaged Buddhism does not have to be distinctively Buddhist. For instance, leaders such as Thich Nhat Hanh and Sulak Sivaraksa speak of "buddhism with a small 'b,'" a reminder not to become sectarian. It might be possible to be a Buddhist and an activist without seeking to fuse the two roles. Some representatives of this stance are unfazed by prospective influences from other traditions: Litsch, writing in Germany, entertains the idea that "Buddhism could experience an expansion by means of a central teaching of Christianity and thereby become 'more Christian.'"

SKILLFUL MEANS

An emerging field must clarify its methods as well as its subject matter. Method has always been crucial in Buddhism as well. "The Compassionate Teacher is said to have guided beings to penetrate reality through many methods and doors of reasoning," wrote the fifteenth-century Tibetan master Tsongkhapa.[37] The use of "skillful means" (*upaya* in Sanskrit) is above all a matter of communicating truth, especially in the service of bringing others to awakening.[38] Method as a liberative art is where real Buddhist masters—Tibetan, Zen, all stripes—shine. The spirit of skillful means may also serve as a guide in the development of methodologies suitable to engaged Buddhist studies.

There are two broad areas to consider: social scientific modes and doctrinal modes. Social science is an umbrella term for history, sociology, psychology, and related fields. Although it is not possible to elaborate here, each field has distinctive ways of gathering data, constructing arguments, and justifying conclusions. Many of those same methods are applicable to the study of engaged Buddhism.

As in mainstream Buddhist studies, history is a good place to start. Westerners embracing Asian religions have tended to give short shrift to the cultural roots of their spiritual traditions. The perils of shallow historical understanding become evident, for example, when unwelcome realities of a tradition's past are belatedly brought to light. Most of the essays in this book conscientiously trace the history, however recent, of the group or activity under consideration. In the process, the authors demonstrate that such information is not merely informative; it also sparks insight.

The value of a sociological approach can be seen in David Chappell's study. To determine the racial composition of Soka Gakkai International—USA, he sampled 2,500 SGI-USA leaders from nine cities. Although statistical analysis may initially seem far removed from the spirit of religious life, Chappell uses his data to show how SGI-USA's sustained opposition to racism is indeed an expression of Buddhist spirituality and engagement. His findings thereby rebut old stereotypes.

Psychological studies focused on engaged Buddhism might strengthen our understanding of mindfulness, Buddhist-related approaches to healing, the roots of altruism, and comparable topics. For example, Batchelor raises provocative questions about motivation:

> What motivates a person to adopt engaged Buddhism? Is it because they feel they have to somehow justify themselves in the light of Western criticism of Buddhism? Or is it a spontaneous and genuine outflow of their Buddhist practice?

The second general mode of engaged Buddhist studies methodology is doctrinal thinking. Most of the characteristic and common issues noted above can be considered doctrinally. In the area of Buddhism and ecology, for example, there have been several rounds of stimulating exchanges. The pioneering 1997 book *Buddhism and Ecology: The Interconnection of Dharma and Deeds*, edited by Mary Evelyn Tucker and Duncan Williams, presents a number of essays in a doctrinal mode, such as "Is There a Buddhist Philosophy of Nature?" and "The Hermeneutics of Buddhist Ecology in Contemporary Thailand." Alan Sponberg, addressing "green Buddhism and the hierarchy of compassion," integrates Western ethical theory, Buddhist spirituality, and an urgent issue:

> A Buddhist environmental ethic is hence a "virtue ethic," one that asks not just which specific actions are necessary to preserve the environment but, more deeply, what are the virtues (that is, the precepts and perfections) we must cultivate in order to be able to act in such a way.[39]

The possible affinities between Buddhism and principles of human rights have generated another spirited discussion. Kenneth Inada sees a basis for a concept of human rights in Buddhist teachings about relational origination, which promote the "mutual respect of fellow beings."[40] Damien Keown points instead to a sense of human dignity derived from a universally shared potential for enlightenment.[41] However, others are not satisfied that lingering inconsistencies have been resolved. There is little in premodern Buddhism that corresponds to the well-grounded Western idea of rights. As for humans, Buddhism goes to great lengths to deconstruct the usual notions of self. Thus Michel Clasquin, a South African Buddhist, argues, "Buddhists cannot logically use the term 'human rights' without involving themselves in a contradiction in terms of their own religio-philosophical system." For the first time, such questions are receiving book-length treatment, as in the 1998 volume *Buddhism and Human Rights.*

Some doctrinal ruminations are similar to aspects of modern Western theology. It may already be possible to identify a cluster of foundational tenets as the rudiments of "engaged Buddhist doctrine." Is there agreement that acceptance of X idea, or access to Y experience, or adherence to Z teacher is an essential element of being an engaged Buddhist? This is also where discussions of applied ethics can be found. Concerned Buddhists are beginning to weigh in on some of the knotty and controversial issues of the day: abortion, euthanasia, biomedical research, genetic engineering, and so on. Rita Gross's agenda is candidly constructivist:

> [We] wish to use the wisdom and compassion we have learned from our study and practice of Buddhism to construct religious thought that speaks to contemporary issues and problems.[42]

It will not be long before engaged Buddhist studies will have its own store of texts to evaluate, just as texts play an important role in mainstream Buddhist studies. Among the many possibilities, two candidates are cited by Virginia Cohn Parkum and Anthony Stultz in their essay. *The Training Manual for Zen Buddhist Practice,* published in looseleaf form by the National Buddhist Prison Sangha, includes the *Heart Sutra,* the four bodhisattva vows, and guidelines for meditating in a cell. The magazine *Gateway Journal,* published by the Engaged Zen Foundation and dedicated exclusively to prison practice, has a circulation of three thousand and is available over the internet. Other possibilities include collections of mindfulness verses for daily practice, pledges taken by participants in nonviolent demonstrations, and passages recited in ecologically oriented ceremonies.

It may also be appropriate to apply some of the tools of philology, long favored in Buddhist studies, to the texts of engaged Buddhism. We have already seen how "engagement," "compassion," and other pivotal words are being problematized. Is there an emerging core of key terms? What do they mean in theory and in practice? At least three types merit attention: classic terms undergoing reinterpretation, Western-language terms crucial to engaged Buddhist vocabulary, and neologisms.

"Karma" is an example of a classic term that is being reinterpreted. When Wratten refers in his essay to the "national karma" of South Africa, most readers probably intuit what he means, even though we would have to search the sutras a long time before finding a locus classicus for such an expression. Another term being put to new uses is "right livelihood" (Pali: *samma kammanta*), as Claude Whitmyer shows:

> Whether right livelihood is actually possible, given the complexities of life in the modern world, is a question that many people ask. It seems clear, upon close examination, that most of the work we do today fails in one way or another to meet all of the criteria, especially the social criteria of responsibility for the long-term consequences of our work.[43]

Robert Aitken's philological sensitivity is evident in his reexamination of the classic Buddhist concepts of *karuna, metta,* and *mudita,* usually translated as compassion, loving-kindness, and sympathetic joy. Aitken reflects:

> Whether or not *karuna* is as intimate in sentiment as "compassion," and however enriching the English term "compassion" can be for our practice, the fact remains that both "compassion" and *karuna* are limited to the realm of sadness. To be as inclusive as the northern European words, we must combine the first two abodes, *metta* and *karuna,* with the third abode, *mudita.* Usually translated "sympathetic joy," *mudita* is the delight one feels when someone else finds liberation on the path. Perhaps *karuna* and *mudita* could be hyphenated to coin an encompassing term.[44]

A number of Western words are beginning to play the role of technical terms. Often they lack precise Buddhist equivalents. An example is "universal responsibility," an expression embraced by the Dalai Lama; although there are comparable notions in Buddhism, the phrase has a distinctly Western ring. In the context of engaged Buddhism its meaning is still being clarified, as the Dalai Lama himself observes:

> Universal responsibility is the best foundation for our personal happiness, and for world peace, the equitable use of our natural resources, and, through a concern for future generations, the proper care for the environment. My own ideas about this are still evolving.[45]

"Activism," an important word/concept with many Western roots but few Asian ones, is another example. Joanna Macy's reflections, as cited by Susan Moon, are illustrative:

> "Activism" is a term I use with some discomfort, because it implies that it's different from ordinary life. If you rush to pull your kid from under the wheels of a truck, are you being an activist? I don't like the moral self-con-

sciousness of the word, or the moral self-righteousness. Is it activism to open your eyes and learn to see?

Neologisms constitute a third group of key terms. "Engaged Buddhism" is itself a new expression (since the 1960s). Some Buddhist environmental activists call themselves "ecosattvas," as Stephanie Kaza reports. When Thich Nhat Hanh coined the influential "interbeing," he intentionally distinguished it from a cognate term, interpenetration:

> When we realize our nature of interbeing, we will stop blaming and killing, because we know that we inter-are. Interpenetration is an important teaching, but it still suggests that things outside of one another penetrate into each other. Interbeing is a step forward. We are already inside, so we don't have to enter.[46]

Further coinages are bound to arise. In his introduction, Christopher Queen advances the idea of a "fourth *yana*" to characterize modern Buddhism's turn toward engagement. Its predecessors are Mahayana, Hinayana, and Vajrayana; *yana* literally means vehicle. If the notion of a fourth yana proves useful, it will need a name. How about *Terrayana?* As a prefix, the Latin word for Earth would suggest that engaged Buddhism is an encompassing, earthy spirituality rather than an otherworldly quest for private salvation. Buddhist environmentalism is already an important stream of contemporary Buddhism, and the striking photos of our blue planet in space remind us that Earth is indeed our common vehicle. Etymologically, Terrayana combines East and West, as global Buddhism now does; rhythmically, Terrayana maintains the syllable count of its predecessors.

A Test Case: The Monk Nichiren

To illustrate some of the methodological challenges of engaged Buddhist studies, let us consider the Japanese monk Nichiren (1222–1282), who has been cited as an exemplar of engaged Buddhism. Nichiren founded the Nichiren sect, and he is the spiritual ancestor of two engaged Buddhist groups that are active internationally, Soka Gakkai and Nipponzan Myohoji. Several essays in this book refer to his life and teachings.

Was Nichiren an engaged Buddhist? Briefly, here are the arguments for the affirmative. Nichiren called for sweeping spiritual and social reform, boldly defying religious and governmental authorities. He was part of a larger movement to popularize Buddhism: "It welcomed all men and women, rejected the exclusivity of the monastic life away from the

world, and questioned the relevance…of formal religious rules and regulations."[47] Nichiren had a vision of a universal Buddhism, and he saw himself
as a bodhisattva.

At the next level of inquiry, complexities arise. Nichiren's thought and
actions stemmed from his understanding of the *Lotus Sutra*. Jacqueline Stone,
a scholar of medieval Japanese Buddhism, writes:

> Nichiren seems to have believed that the spread of faith in the Lotus Sutra
> would bring about harmony with nature, long life, and just government….
> His thinking draws on some sophisticated Tendai teachings concerning the
> nonduality of the individual and the outer world, or subjective and objec-
> tive realms. Thus in his view the believer has an obligation to spread faith
> in the Lotus Sutra, out of compassion for others and because it has conse-
> quences for this world (and in the next).[48]

Nichiren's religious vision was strongly Japan-centered; what he recognized as universal Buddhism was a Japanese orthodoxy that subsumed Indian
and Chinese Buddhism. Commenting on the word "world" in the *Lotus
Sutra*, he wrote, "By 'world,' Japan is meant."[49] He was openly intolerant of
other Buddhist teachers and sects, and his stated concern for the status of
women had its limits.[50] Nichiren did not see himself as a bodhisattva in a
general sense, but as the specific bodhisattva Vishishtacharitra (Eminent
Conduct), uniquely ordained to save Japan: "In the present I am unmistakably the one who is realizing the Lotus of Truth." Rather than shunning militarism, he hoped that the Mongols (recently victorious in China) would
invade Japan to cleanse it of corruption, and he was depressed when the
Mongols' attempted invasions failed.[51]

Directing attention to the engagement of past Buddhist leaders brings
several benefits. At the least, such assessments help to dispel the oversimplification that Buddhism is world-denying. To call Nichiren—or Shakyamuni or
others—"engaged" often casts their lives in a new light, thereby enabling
fresh appreciation of their teachings. These steps fulfill another vital function
for today's engaged Buddhists: they serve to confer legitimacy on contemporary developments, reassuring participants that engaged Buddhism remains
authentically within the Buddhist tradition. In a general sense, then, continuities can certainly be acknowledged. Bardwell Smith writes:

> One wonders about the overly sharp distinction that is made between mod-
> ern forms of Buddhist engagement, however unprecedented many of their
> features may be, and those that have occurred over the centuries, almost

as if there were no prophetic or deeply engaged precursors in Buddhist history.[52]

However, there is a trade-off. If in order to accommodate cases from the past, the terms "engaged Buddhist" and "engaged Buddhism" are stretched beyond a certain point, they lose significant chunks of meaning. We have seen that Nichiren's conception of spiritual and social reform had one over-riding aim: to have everyone take refuge in the *Lotus Sutra*. The world view of a premodern figure and the world view of a present-day engaged Buddhist may differ so fundamentally that to lump the two together does justice to neither. This is the conclusion reached by Stone:

> Although Nichiren's teaching had both a strong social component and an element of social responsibility, he was not concerned with such issues as charitable acts or efforts in social improvement for their own sake....I don't see him as "socially engaged" in the more usual contemporary senses of the term.[53]

METHODOLOGICAL ISSUES

Methodological issues differ from characteristic issues (that is, war resistance) and common issues (that is, personal/social change). Three examples should suffice here: uses of Buddhist tradition, room for criticism, and openness to new methods. Each of these issues can again be framed as a question.

When Do Re-evaluations of Traditional Buddhism Go Too Far?

That is, when do fresh interpretations, often in the service of engagement, distort Buddhism's past inauthentically? The case of Nichiren is but one example. Another, "sangha," originally referred to the community of monks but is now being recast in various ways. For some, sangha represents a proto-democratic form of social organization. In Robert Goss's essay it becomes an "alternative educational community." Robert Thurman sees sangha as a "monastic army of peace."[54] Bill Devall proposes an "ecocentric sangha" dedicated to "self-realization for all beings, not just human beings."[55] Litsch writes:

> The sangha, as the community of those who proceed on the way to Buddhahood, becomes the community of all beings, all life, and all evolv-ing processes on our planet, which are bound up in this path. Thich Nhat Hanh can thus speak about the coming buddha, Maitreya, possibly appear-ing on the earth not in the form of a single person, but in the form of a great spiritual community.

Other elements of past Buddhism are also being appropriated in new ways. According to the sutras, Angulimala was a murderer who became a disciple of the Buddha. Is it acceptable to use Angulimala as the patron saint of a modern prison-reform movement? "Wall-gazing" initially specified the meditation practice of the semi-legendary sixth-century monk Bodhidharma. Is it permissible to use the term today to describe meditation in a prison cell? Wratten suggests that the Buddhist teachings of no self, impermanence, and dependent origination "provide a penetrating critique of race, class, and gender associations." Is that a justifiable application of those teachings? Andrew Olendzki draws extensively from the Pali canon in his discussion of Kabat-Zinn's stress-reduction work. He cites the following passage:

> To which the Buddha replied, "It is true, sir, that your body is weak and afflicted....Therefore, sir, you should train yourself: 'Though my body is sick, my mind shall not be sick.'"

For Olendzki, past and present converge seamlessly: "One can almost imagine this conversation occurring at the University of Massachusetts Medical Center in Worcester." All such uses of the past compel methodologically aware reflection. We must ask, without prejudging the answer: When is the stretch from traditional Buddhism to engaged Buddhism too big?

Are Assessments of Engaged Buddhist Leaders Too Restrained?

The Dalai Lama is so universally admired (outside China) that one seldom hears a discouraging word about him. Other leading Buddhists, if judged at all, are typically questioned in gentle asides. John Powers, in his essay on the Campaign for Tibet, at least raises an eyebrow when he notes the unusual career of action-movie star Steven Seagal, now recognized as a *tulku*, a reincarnate Tibetan lama:

> His Buddhist spirituality is on display in his movie *The Glimmer Man*, in which he wears Tibetan prayer beads around his neck and speaks of cultivating inner peace. In the following scene, however, someone insults his sissy beads and he kicks him through a glass door, indicating that he may still need to put in more quality time on the meditation cushion.

Respect does not obviate the need for constructive criticism. Bernard Glassman has been charged with (in his own words) "moving too much to social action and leaving Zen behind." It is a point worth discussing. Conversely, some activists are concerned that Thich Nhat Hanh's teachings increasingly emphasize individual calm and local sangha-building at the cost of confronting larger political realities. That too deserves debate. Sallie King, deeply disturbed by the practice of self-immolation, goes so far as to disagree with Nhat Hanh's claim that Buddhist leaders ordinarily try to prevent it. "I must point out," King writes, "that Nhat Hanh's statement…is not strictly true."[56]

Does Engaged Buddhist Studies Propose Any New Methods?

An emerging field may permit, or require, some new approaches. For example, Stephanie Kaza experiments with a traditional technique of Buddhist logic, the tetralemma, in an essay on human-nature relations. She asks, "Can we keep peace with nature?" and then shows how the question can be answered four ways: yes, no, yes-and-no, neither-yes-nor-no.[57] In a different vein, innovative praxis-linked methodologies might incorporate meditation or community-based learning.

"Not knowing" may even be a candidate for a new method. Queen, in his essay on Glassman's work, observes that a type of agnosticism is shared by Glassman, Nhat Hanh, Batchelor, and other leading engaged Buddhist figures. In Buddhism not knowing is quite different from an ordinary profession of ignorance. Two well-known examples are the Buddha's silence on certain existential questions, and Bodhidharma's enigmatic answer, "I don't know," in reply to the sixth-century Chinese emperor Wu. Not knowing is intimately related to learning and insight, which are valued in Buddhist practice and Buddhist studies alike. Queen asks Glassman, "Why are you attracted to places of great suffering—the inner city, Auschwitz, the notorious needle park called the Letten in Zurich…?" Glassman replies:

> I don't know. The words that come to me are *the desire to learn*. I don't know what it is, but it happens a lot to me when I encounter a situation I don't understand. It generally involves suffering. When I enter a situation that is too much for me and that I don't understand—I have a desire to sit there, to stay a while.

Doubt, in the sense of deep questioning, is an essential element of *koan* practice in Zen. This approach may contain the seeds of a method with fruitful applications in several areas, from social theory to the ecocrisis. Can the planet be saved? We don't know. And that uncertainty must be taken into consideration in environmental work. Because agnosticism is sometimes interpreted as a tepid or unwelcome doubt, and because it carries baggage from Christian theology and Western intellectual traditions, a distinctively Buddhist form may require a tag such as "deep agnosticism."

In 1977, when few Westerners were familiar with engaged Buddhism, political scientist William Ophuls wrote:

> A Buddhist philosopher works with the grain of history, respecting the actual situation: he has no grand designs, no inflexible ideologies, no particular set of institutions to peddle—only the principle of *upaya*, or "skillful means" that manifest wisdom in action.[58]

As engaged Buddhist thinkers continue to refine methodologies, the concept of skillful means will itself be subjected to new tests. On this, Western scholars and Buddhist practitioners agree: a good method must also be a self-reflective one.

CONCLUSION

The process of articulating a field is not only an avenue to understanding; it can also be a type of engagement. We are compelled to define terms, make distinctions, take stands, and accept the consequences of taking stands. It is of course possible to study Buddhist ethics from the outside, and that approach has its place. In engaged Buddhist studies, the ethical issues *within* the work are recognized as well. As the participants in the Sarvodaya movement have discovered, "We build the road, and the road builds us."

The next steps may be respectably deliberate or freely experimental. Eventually the field may support networks and other forms of organization that accommodate both sangha thinkers and academy scholars. I can imagine an Engaged Buddhist Forum or a Partnership for Research on Buddhist Engagement (which yields the acronym PROBE). Even if efforts in that direction come to naught, the underlying questions will not vary much. One of those questions is, How best to respond to the plight of the world? The twenty authors of this book concur unanimously on the first part of the answer:

We must be engaged.

Notes

I am grateful to Wes Borden, Stephanie Kaza, Trudy Kraft, Donald Swearer, and William Washburn for their thoughtful comments on a draft of this essay.

1. *Tricycle: The Buddhist Review* 8.3 (spring 1999): 117.
2. Citations without annotation are from the present volume.

3. Here is a far-from-definitive list of books published since 1989 that represent work in engaged Buddhist studies (see bibliography for full citations):

Beyond Optimism: A Buddhist Political Ecology, by Ken Jones *Buddhism and Bioethics*, by Damien Keown

Buddhism and Ecology: The Interconnection of Dharma and Deeds, edited by Mary Evelyn Tucker and Duncan Williams

Buddhism and Human Rights, edited by Damien Keown and others

Buddhism after Patriarchy: A Feminist History, Analysis, and Reconstruction of Buddhism, by Rita Gross

Dharma Rain: Sources of Buddhist Environmentalism, edited by Stephanie Kaza and Kenneth Kraft

Engaged Buddhism: Buddhist Liberation Movements in Asia, edited by Christopher Queen and Sallie King

Engaged Buddhist Reader, edited by Arnold Kotler

Entering the Realm of Reality: Towards Dhammic Societies, edited by Jonathan Watts and others

Inner Peace, World Peace: Essays on Buddhism and Nonviolence, edited by Kenneth Kraft

Inner Revolution: Life, Liberty, and the Pursuit of Real Happiness, by Robert Thurman

Luminous Passage: The Practice and Study of Buddhism in America, by Charles Prebish

Mindfulness and Meaningful Work: Explorations in Right Livelihood, edited by Claude Whitmyer

Mutual Causality in Buddhism and General Systems Theory: The Dharma of Natural Systems, by Joanna Macy

Soaring and Settling: Buddhist Perspectives on Contemporary Social and Religious Issues, by Rita Gross

The Social Face of Buddhism, by Ken Jones

Socially Engaged Buddhism for the New Millennium, edited by Sulak Sivaraksa and others

World as Lover, World as Self, by Joanna Macy

4. The scholarly *Journal of Buddhist Ethics*, inaugurated in 1994, is distributed online. *Seeds of Peace* (1985–) is edited in Thailand by the International Network of Engaged Buddhists. *Turning Wheel* (1991–) is published quarterly by the Buddhist Peace Fellowship.

5. For an insightful assessment of Aum Shinrikyo, see Robert Jay Lifton, "Reflections on Aum Shinrikyo," in Charles B. Strozier and Michael Flynn, eds., *The Year 2000: Essays on the End* (New York: New York University Press, 1997), pp. 112–20.

6. Donald Swearer kindly shared his observations of a 1997 conference on the field of Buddhist studies held at Chulalongkorn University in Bangkok, Thailand.

7. Bernard Faure, *The Rhetoric of Immediacy: A Cultural Critique of Chan/Zen Buddhism* (Princeton: Princeton University Press, 1991), p. 3.

8. "[F]rom a positivist point of view, normative forms of discourse…fall outside the scope of Buddhist Studies. From the interpretivist perspective, on the other hand, there does exist a place within the academy for these modes of analysis." José Ignacio Cabezón, "Buddhist Studies as a Discipline and the Role of Theory," *Journal of the International Association of Buddhist Studies* 18.2 (1995): 260.

9. Richard P. Hayes, *Land of No Buddha: Reflections of a Sceptical Buddhist* (Birmingham: Windhorse Publications, 1998), p. 8.

10. Jeffrey Hopkins, *The Tantric Distinction: A Buddhist's Reflections on Compassion and Emptiness* (Somerville, MA: Wisdom Publications, 1999). The blurb is from Wisdom's "Buddhist Studies 1999" catalogue.

11. Luis O. Gomez, "Unspoken Paradigms: Meanderings through the Metaphors of a Field," *Journal of the International Association of Buddhist Studies* 18.2 (1995): 190.

12. Franz Aubrey Metcalf, review of Charles S. Prebish and Kenneth K. Tanaka, eds., *The Faces of Buddhism in America* (Berkeley: University of California Press, 1998), in *Journal of Buddhist Ethics* 6 (1999); <http://jbe.la.psu.edu>.

13. Charles S. Prebish, *Luminous Passage: The Practice and Study of Buddhism in America* (Berkeley: University of California Press, 1999), p. 266.

14. Charles S. Prebish, "The Academic Study of Buddhism in America: A Silent Sangha," in Duncan Ryuken Williams and Christopher S. Queen, eds., *American Buddhism: Methods and Findings in Recent Scholarship* (Surrey, England: Curzon Press, 1999), pp. 183–214.

15. Roger Corless, "Coming Out in the Sangha: Queer Community in American Buddhism," in Prebish and Tanaka, *The Faces of Buddhism in America,* p. 331 n. 27.

16. Sallie B. King, "They Who Burn Themselves for Peace: Buddhist Self-Immolation," in Sulak Sivaraksa, et al., eds., *Socially Engaged Buddhism for the New Millennium* (Bangkok, Thailand: Sathirakoses—Nagapradipa Foundation and Foundation for Children, 1999), p. 295.

17. Personal correspondence from Ken Jones to Sandra Bell, January 25, 1997. Jones proposes to call engaged Buddhist social theory "engaged Buddhology."

18. Helen Tworkov, "Buddhism without Walls: An Interview with Robert Aitken Roshi," in *Tricycle: The Buddhist Review* 8.3 (spring 1999): 46.

19. Claude Thomas, "Finding Peace after a Lifetime of War," in Arnold Kotler, ed., *Engaged Buddhist Reader* (Berkeley, CA: Parallax Press, 1996), p. 99.

20. Alan Senauke, letter circulated on the internet, April 7, 1999.

21. Paula Green, letter to supporters of the Karuna Center for Peacebuilding, April 1999.

22. Bodhin Kjolhede, "Zen at War," Dharma talk at the Rochester Zen Center, Rochester, New York, April 11, 1999.

23. Douglas P. Lackey, "Just War Theory," in Larry May and Shari Collins Sharratt, eds., *Applied Ethics: A Multicultural Approach* (Englewood Cliffs, NJ: Prentice-Hall, 1994), p. 200.

24. Helen Tworkov, "The Karma of Words," in *Tricycle: The Buddhist Review* 8.4 (summer 1999): 4.

25. John Howard Yoder, *Nevertheless: A Meditation on the Varieties and Shortcomings of Religious Pacifism* (Scottdate, PA: Herald Press, 1971, 1992), p. 127.

26. Tworkov, "Buddhism without Walls," p. 47.

27. Bernard Glassman, *Bearing Witness: A Zen Master's Lessons in Making Peace* (New York: Bell Tower, 1998), p. 85.

28. Toni Packer, "What Is Right Livelihood?" in Claude Whitmyer, ed., *Mindfulness and Meaningful Work: Explorations in Right Livelihood* (Berkeley, CA: Parallax Press, 1994), pp. 58–59.

29. Stephen Batchelor, *Buddhism without Beliefs* (New York: Riverhead Books, 1997), p. 90.

30. Donald Rothberg, "Responding to the Cries of the World: Socially Engaged Buddhism in North America," in Prebish and Tanaka, *The Faces of Buddhism in America*, p. 285.

31. Edward Conze, trans., *Buddhist Wisdom Books* (New York: Harper & Row, 1972), p. 25.

32. Cited in Luis O. Gomez, "Nonviolence and the Self in Early Buddhism," in Kenneth Kraft, ed., *Inner Peace, World Peace: Essays on Buddhism and Nonviolence* (Albany: State University of New York Press, 1992), p. 46.

33. Lee Yearley, "Three Views of Virtue," in Daniel Goleman, ed., *Healing Emotions* (Boston: Shambhala Publications, 1997), pp. 15–16.

34. Tworkov, "Buddhism without Walls," p. 45.

35. Helen Tworkov, *Zen in America: Five Teachers and the Search for an American Buddhism*, rev. ed. (New York: Kodansha International, 1994), p. 263.

36. Tworkov, "Buddhism without Walls," p. 47.

37. Donald S. Lopez, Jr., "On the Interpretation of the Mahayana Sutras," in Donald S. Lopez, Jr., ed., *Buddhist Hermeneutics* (Honolulu: University of Hawaii Press, 1988), p. 66.

38. See Michael Pye, *Skillful Means* (London: Duckworth, 1978). Another English translation of *upaya* is "expedient means," which carries both positive and negative nuances. That rendering is justified by uses of the term in the *Lotus Sutra* and other texts.

39. Alan Sponberg, "Green Buddhism and the Hierarchy of Compassion," in Mary Evelyn Tucker and Duncan Ryuken Williams, eds., *Buddhism and Ecology: The*

Interconnection of Dharma and Deeds (Cambridge: Harvard University Press, 1997), p. 370.

40. Cited in Damien V. Keown, "Are There Human Rights in Buddhism?" in Damien V. Keown, Charles S. Prebish, and Wayne R. Husted, eds., *Buddhism and Human Rights* (Surrey, England: Curzon Press, 1998), pp. 26–27.

41. Keown, "Are There Human Rights in Buddhism?" pp. 15–41.

42. Rita M. Gross, *Soaring and Settling: Buddhist Perspectives on Contemporary Social and Religious Issues* (New York: Continuum, 1998), p. 155.

43. Claude Whitmyer, "Using Mindfulness to Find Meaningful Work," in Whitmyer, *Mindfulness and Meaningful Work*, pp. 262–63.

44. Robert Aitken, "Sorting the Wisdom of Words: Milan Kundera and the Four Noble Abodes," in Sivaraksa et al., *Socially Engaged Buddhism for the New Millennium,* p. 447.

45. The Dalai Lama, "The True Source of Political Success," in *Shambhala Sun* 6.3 (January 1998): 38.

46. Thich Nhat Hanh, "The Sun My Heart," in Kotler, *Engaged Buddhist Reader*, p. 169.

47. Martin Collcutt, *Five Mountains: The Rinzai Zen Monastic Institution in Medieval Japan* (Cambridge: Harvard University Press, 1981), p. 31.

48. Personal correspondence from Jacqueline Stone, May 24, 1999. Stone devotes a chapter to Nichiren in her forthcoming book *Original Enlightenment and the Transformation of Medieval Japanese Buddhism* (Honolulu: University of Hawaii Press).

49. H. Byron Earhart, *Religion in the Japanese Experience: Sources and Interpretations* (Belmont, CA: Wadsworth, 1997), p. 94; Hajime Nakamura, *Ways of Thinking of Eastern Peoples*, rev. ed. (Honolulu: University of Hawaii Press, 1985), p. 443.

50. Commenting on the work of the Buddhist teacher Honen (1133–1212), Nichiren wrote: "It can lead its author nowhere but to the lower hell." Ryusaku Tsunoda, Wm. Theodore de Bary, and Donald Keene, eds., *Sources of the Japanese Tradition*, vol. 1 (New York: Columbia University Press, 1969), p. 218. On attitudes toward women, see Helen Hardacre, *Lay Buddhism in Contemporary Japan: Reiyukai Kyodan* (Princeton: Princeton University Press, 1984), p. 205.

51. Daigan and Alicia Matsunaga, *Foundation of Japanese Buddhism*, vol. 2 (Tokyo: Buddhist Books International, 1976), p. 154.

52. Bardwell Smith, review of Christopher S. Queen and Sallie B. King, eds., *Engaged Buddhism: Buddhist Liberation Movements in Asia* (Albany: State University of New York Press, 1996), in *Journal of the American Academy of Religion* 67.2 (June 1999): 500–501.

53. Personal correspondence from Jacqueline Stone, May 24, 1999.

54. Robert Thurman, "Tibet and the Monastic Army of Peace," in Kraft, *Inner Peace, World Peace*, pp. 77–90.

55. Bill Devall, "Ecocentric Sangha," in Allan Hunt Badiner, ed., *Dharma Gaia: A Harvest of Essays in Buddhism and Ecology* (Berkeley, CA: Parallax Press, 1990), p. 158.

56. King, "They Who Burn Themselves for Peace: Buddhist Self-Immolation," p. 287.

57. Stephanie Kaza, "Can We Keep Peace with Nature?" in Leroy S. Rouner, ed., *Religion, Politics, and Peace* (Notre Dame: University of Notre Dame Press, 1999), pp. 165–84.

58. William Ophuls, "Buddhist Politics," in *The Ecologist* 7.3 (May/June 1977): 84.

SELECTIVE BIBLIOGRAPHY

Compiled by Stuart Chandler

Adam, Enid, and Philip J. Hughes. *The Buddhists in Australia*. Canberra: Australian Government Publishing Service, 1996.

Ahir, D. C. *Ambedkar on Buddhism*. Bombay: Siddhartha Publications, 1982.

Aitken, Robert. *Mind of Clover: Zen Ethics*. San Francisco: North Point Press, 1982.

Allendorf, Fred. "The Conservation Biologist as Zen Student." *Conservation Biology* 11.5 (October 1997): 1045–46.

Ambedkar, B. R. *The Buddha and His Dhamma*. Bombay: People's Education Society, 1984.

Aung San Suu Kyi. *Freedom from Fear*. Ed. Michael Aris. New York: Penguin Books, 1991.

———. *The Voice of Hope*. New York: Seven Stories Press, 1998.

Avedon, John F. *In Exile from the Land of Snows*. New York: Vintage Books, 1979.

Batchelor, Martine and Kerry Brown, eds. *Buddhism and Ecology*. London: Cassell Publishers, 1992.

Batchelor, Stephen. *The Awakening of the West: The Encounter of Buddhism and Western Culture*. Berkeley, CA: Parallax Press, 1994.

———. *Buddhism without Beliefs: A Contemporary Guide to Awakening*. New York: Riverhead Books, 1997.

Baumann, Martin. "Neo-Buddhistische Konzeptionen in Indien und England." *Zeitschrift für Religions- und Geistesgeschichte* 43.2 (1991): 97–116.

———. "Buddhism in the West: Phases, Orders and the Creation of an Integrative Buddhism." *Internationales Asienforum* 27, no. 3–4 (1996): 345–62.

———. "The Dharma Has Come West: A Survey of Recent Studies and Sources." *Journal of Buddhist Ethics* 4 (1997): 194–211.

———. "'Working in the Right Spirit': The Application of Buddhist Right Livelihood in the Friends of the Western Buddhist Order." *Journal of Buddhist Ethics* 5 (1998): 120–43.

Berrigan, Daniel, and Thich Nhat Hanh. *The Raft Is Not the Shore: Conversations Toward a Buddhist-Christian Awareness*. Boston: Beacon Press, 1975.

Bethel, Dayle M. *Makiguchi: The Value Creator.* Tokyo: Weatherhill, 1973.

———. *Education for Creative Living: Ideas and Proposals of Tsunesaburo Makiguchi.* Ames, Iowa: Iowa State University Press, 1989.

Bond, George. *The Buddhist Revival in Sri Lanka: Religious Tradition, Reinterpretation, and Response.* Columbia, SC: University of South Carolina Press, 1988.

Boucher, Sandy. *Turning the Wheel: American Women Creating the New Buddhism.* San Francisco: Harper and Row, 1988.

Brazier, David. *Zen Therapy.* London: Constable, 1995.

Buddhadasa Bhikkhu. *Dhammic Socialism.* Bangkok: Thai Inter-Religious Commission for Development, 1985.

Chapin, Doug and Barry Krost, producers. *What's Love Got to Do With It.* Videotape. Touchstone Pictures, 1993.

Chappell, David W. "Searching for a Mahayana Social Ethic." *Journal of Religious Ethics* 24, no. 2 (fall 1996): 351–75.

Chapple, Christopher Key. *Nonviolence to Animals, Earth, and Self in Asian Traditions.* Albany: State University of New York Press, 1993.

Chavis, Melody Ermachild. "Patience: A Prisoner Waits on Death Row." *Turning Wheel* (spring 1995).

———. "Gun Control." *Shambhala Sun* (November 1995).

———. *Altars in the Street.* New York: Belltower, 1997.

———. "Strong Roots: Teenagers Plant Seeds of Hope." *Sierra* (May/June 1997).

———. "Hope and Peace: Urban Playgrounds." *Land and People* (fall 1997).

Clasquin, Michel. "Buddhism and Unemployment: A Conceptual Reappraisal of Social Classification Systems." In *On Being Unemployed and Religious: Papers Presented at the 16th Symposium of the Institute for Theological Research,* edited by W. S. Vorster. Pretoria: University of South Africa Press (1992): 96–105.

———. "Buddhism and Human Rights." *Journal for the Study of Religion* 6.2 (1993): 91–101.

———. "Buddhist Ethics and the South African Situation." In *Religion and the Reconstruction of Society: Papers from the Founding Congress of the South African Academy of Religion,* edited by John W. de Gruchy and Steve Martin, eds., Pretoria: University of South Africa Press (1994): 316–33.

———. "Religion, Ethics and Communal Interaction in the New South Africa: The Case of the Declaration on Religious Rights and Responsibilities." *Missionalia* 22, no. 1 (1994): 13–35.

Cope, Michel. *Interconnectedness.* Cape Town: Eco-Program, 1993.

Corless, Roger. "Coming Out in the Sangha." In *Faces of Buddhism in America*, edited by Kenneth Tanaka and Charles Prebish. Berkeley: University of California Press, 1999.

Davis, Susan. "Working with Compassion: The Evolution of Buddhist Peace Fellowship." *Tricycle: The Buddhist Review* (spring 1993).

DeFina, Barbara, producer. *Kundun.* Videotape. Touchstone Pictures, 1997.

Dresser, Marianne, ed. *Buddhist Women on the Edge: Contemporary Perspectives from the Western Frontier.* Berkeley, CA: North Atlantic Books, 1996.

Eppsteiner, Fred, ed. *The Path of Compassion: Writings on Socially Engaged Buddhism.* Berkeley, CA: Parallax Press, 1988.

Fields, Rick. *How the Swans Came to the Lake: A Narrative History of Buddhism in America.* Boulder: Shambhala Publications, 1981.

Friedman, Lenore, and Susan Moon, eds. *Being Bodies: Buddhist Women on the Paradox of Enlightenment.* Boston: Shambhala Publications, 1997.

Fujii, Nichidatsu. *Buddhism for World Peace.* Yumiko Miyazaki, trans. Tokyo: Bharat Sarvodaya Mitrata Sangha, 1980.

———. *Beating Celestial Drums.* Yumiko Miyazaki, trans. Los Angeles: Peace Press, 1982.

———. *The Time Has Come.* Tokyo: Japan-Bharat Sarvodaya Mitrata Sangha, 1982.

Fujimoto, Hogen. *Out of the Mud Grows the Lotus.* San Francisco: Lotus Press, 1980.

Galland, China. *The Bond Between Women: A Journey to Fierce Compassion.* Riverhead Books, 1998.

Gay Buddhist Fellowship Newsletter. For information and to be put on the mailing list, write to GBF, 2261 Market Street #422, San Francisco, CA 94114, call (415) 974-9878, or log on to the GBF website at <www.planeteria.net/home/abaki/gbf>.

Glassman, Bernard. *Bearing Witness: A Zen Master's Lessons in Making Peace.* New York: Bell Tower, 1998.

Glassman, Bernard, and Rick Fields. *Instructions to the Cook: A Zen Master's Lessons in Living a Life That Matters.* New York: Bell Tower, 1996.

Goss, Robert E. "Buddhist Studies at Naropa: Sectarian or Academic?" In *American Buddhism: Methods and Findings in Recent Scholarship*, edited by Duncan Ryuken Williams and Christopher S. Queen. Surrey, U.K.: Curzon Press, 1999.

Gross, Rita. *Buddhism After Patriarchy: A Feminist History, Analysis, and Reconstruction of Buddhism.* Albany: State University of New York Press, 1993.

———. *Soaring and Settling: Buddhist Perspectives on Contemporary Social and Religious Issues.* New York: Continuum, 1998.

Habito, Reuben L.F. *Healing Breath: Zen Spirituality for a Wounded Earth*. Maryknoll, N.Y.: Orbis Books, 1993.

Harrison, Gavin. "Confronting Apartheid with Compassion: A Talk by Gavin Harrison." *Karuna: A Journal of Buddhist Meditation* 5, no. 1 (1988): 11–17.

———. *In the Lap of the Buddha*. Boston and London: Shambhala Publications, 1994.

Hecker, Hellmuth. *Angulimala: A Murderer's Road to Sainthood*. Kandy, Sri Lanka: Buddhist Publication Society, 1984.

Holt, John C. "Protestant Buddhism?" *Religious Studies Review* 17, no. 4 (October 1991).

Horigan, Damien. "A Buddhist Perspective on the Death Penalty." *Turning Wheel* (winter 1999): 16–19.

Hunt-Badiner, Allan, ed. *Dharma Gaia: A Harvest of Essays in Buddhism and Ecology*. Berkeley, CA: Parallax Press, 1990.

Ikeda, Daisaku. *Human Revolution*, vols. 1–5. Tokyo and New York: Weatherhill, 1972–1986.

———. *A Lasting Peace*. Tokyo: Weatherhill, 1981.

Ikeda, Daisaku, and Arnold Toynbee. *Choose Life: A Dialogue*. Oxford: Oxford University Press, 1989.

Ingram, Catherine. *In the Footsteps of Gandhi*. Berkeley, CA: Parallax Press, 1990.

Inoue, Shinichi. *Putting Buddhism to Work: A New Approach to Management and Business*. Duncan Ryuken Williams, trans. Tokyo and New York: Kodansha, 1997.

Johnson, Wendy. "Redwood Sangha." *The Mindfulness Bell* 18 (Jan.–April 1997): 7.

Jones, Ken. *The Social Face of Buddhism: An Approach to Political and Social Activism*. Boston: Wisdom Publications, 1992.

———. *Beyond Optimism: A Buddhist Political Ecology*. Oxford: Carpenter, 1993.

Joshi, Barbara R., ed. *Untouchable! Voices of the Dalit Liberation Movement*. London: Minority Rights Group and Atlantic Highlands, N.J.: Zed Books, 1986.

Kabat-Zinn, Jon. *Full Catastrophe Living: Using the Wisdom of Your Body and Mind to Face Stress, Pain, and Illness*. The Program of the Stress Reduction Clinic at the University of Massachusetts Medical Center. New York: Delta, 1990.

Kabilsingh, Chatsumarn. *Thai Women in Buddhism*. Berkeley, CA: Parallax Press, 1991.

Kapleau, Philip. *To Cherish All Life: A Buddhist Case for Becoming Vegetarian*. San Francisco: Harper and Row, 1982.

Karma Lekshe Tsomo, ed. *Sakyadhita: Daughters of the Buddha*. Ithaca, NY: Snow Lion Publications, 1988.

Kaza, Stephanie, and Kenneth Kraft. *Dharma Rain: Sources of Buddhist Environmentalism*. Boston: Shambhala Publications, 1999.

Keer, Khananjay. *Dr. Ambedkar: Life and Mission*. Bombay: Popular Prakashan, 1971.

Keown, Damien V. *Buddhism and Bioethics*. London: St. Martin's Press, 1995.

————. *The Nature of Buddhist Ethics*. London: Macmillan 1992.

Keown, Damien V., Charles S. Prebish, and Wayne R. Husted, eds. *Buddhism and Human Rights*. Surrey, U.K.: Curzon Press, 1998.

Khong, Chan. *Learning True Love: How I Learned and Practiced Social Change in Vietnam*. Berkeley, CA: Parallax Press, 1993.

Klein, Anne C. *Meeting the Great Bliss Queen: Buddhists, Feminists, and the Art of the Self*. Boston: Beacon Press, 1995.

Kleinman, Arthur, Veena Das, and Margaret Lock, eds. *Social Suffering*. Berkeley: University of California Press, 1997.

Kotler, Arnold. *Engaged Buddhist Reader*. Berkeley, CA: Parallax Press, 1996.

Kraft, Kenneth, ed. *Inner Peace, World Peace: Essays on Buddhism and Nonviolence*. Albany: State University of New York Press, 1992.

————. *The Wheel of Engaged Buddhism: A New Map of the Path*. New York: Weatherhill, 1999.

Ling, Trevor. *Buddhism, Imperialism, and War: Burma and Thailand in Modern History*. London: George Allen and Unwin, 1979.

Litsch, Franz-Johannes. "Anweisungen für den Koch—Bernhard Glassman." *Lotusblätter, Zeitschrift der Deutschen Buddhistischen Union (DBU)* 4 (1997).

————. "Engagierter Buddhismus im deutschsprachigen Raum—Grundlagen, Geschichte, Praxis." <www.buddhanetz.net/texte>, December 1997.

————. "Buddhismus und Ökologie." *Intersein, Zeitschrift der Gemeinschaften und Freunde von Thich Nhat Hanh* 12 (May 1998).

————. "Der engagierte Buddhismus." *Connection, das Magazin fürs Wesentliche* 9/10 (1998).

Litsch, Franz-Johannes, and Hans-Günter Wagner. "Globale Verantwortung, Bodhisattva-Ideal und engagierter Buddhismus." *Lotusblätter, Zeitschrift der Deutschen Buddhistischen Union (DBU)* 4 (1998).

Loori, John. *The Heart of Being*. Boston: Charles E. Tuttle, 1996.

Lozoff, Bo. *We're All Doing Time*. Durham, NC: Human Kindness Foundation, 1985.

————, producer. *Bo Lozoff at Twin Rivers Correction Center*. Videotape. Human Kindness Foundation, 1995.

Macy, Joanna. *Despair and Empowerment in the Nuclear Age*. Philadelphia: New Society Publishers, 1983.

———. *Dharma and Development: Religion as Resource in the Sarvodaya Self-Help Movement.* West Hartford, CT: Kumarian Pres, 1983.

———. *Mutual Causality in Buddhism and General Systems Theory: the Dharma of Natural Systems.* Albany: State University of New York Press, 1991.

———. *World as Lover, World As Self.* Berkeley, CA: Parallax Press, 1991.

Macy, Joanna, and Molly Young Brown. *Coming Back to Life: Practices to Reconnect Our Lives, Our World.* Gabriola Island, British Columbia: New Society Publishers, 1998.

Maha Ghosananda. *Step by Step: Meditation on Wisdom and Compassion.* Berkeley, CA: Parallax Press, 1992.

Malone, Kobutsu. "Prison Zen Practice in America: Life and Death on the Razor's Edge." In *Buddhism in America: Proceedings of the First Buddhism in America Conference,* edited by Brian D. Hotchkiss. Rutland, VT: Charles E. Tuttle, 1998.

Martin, Julia. "Practicing Emptiness: Gary Snyder's Playful Ecological Work." *Western American Literature* 27, no. 1 (1992): 3–19.

———. "The Snake Person Takes on the Cock-Sure Boys: Buddhism/ Postmodernism/South African Eco-Politics." In *Liminal Postmodernism: The Postmodern, the (Post-)Colonial, and the (Post-)Feminist,* edited by Theo D'haene and Hans Bertens. Amsterdam: Rodopi, 1994: 332–55.

———. "Interbeing and the 'I' Habit: An Experimentation in Environmental Literacy." In *Feminist Perspectives on Sustainable Development,* edited by Wendy Harcourt. Atlantic Highlands, New Jersey: Zed Books, 1994: 156–75.

———. "Introduction." *Ecological Responsibility: A Dialogue with Buddhism* (Sambhota Series V). Delhi: Tibet House and Sri Satguru Publications, 1997: xv–xx.

———, ed. *Ecological Responsibility: A Dialogue with Buddhism* (Sambhota Series V). Delhi: Sri Satguru Publications, 1997.

Masters, Jarvis Jay. *Finding Freedom: Writings from Death Row.* Junction City, CA: Padma Publishing, 1997.

Mathis, Doll. "Interview with Lama Yeshe Wangmo about Death Row." <http://lehua.ihawaii.net/~vfh> (1999).

Matthiessen, Peter. *Nine-Headed Dragon River: Zen Journals 1969–1982.* Boston: Shambhala Publications, 1986.

Maull, Fleet. "Dying in Prison: Sociocultural and Psychosocial Dynamics." *Hospice Journal* 7 (1991): 127–42.

———. "Hospice Care for Prisoners: Establishing an Inmate-Staffed Hospice Program in a Prison Medical Facility." *Hospice Journal* 7 (1999): 43–55.

McLellan, Janet. "Religion and Ethnicity: The Role of Buddhism in Maintaining Ethnic Identity Among Tibetans in Lindsay, Ontario." *Canadian Ethnic Studies* XIX, no. 1 (1987): 63–76.

———. "Hermit Crabs and Refugees: Adaptive Strategies of Vietnamese Buddhists in Toronto." In *The Quality of Life Southeast Asia*, edited by Bruce Matthews. CCSEAS xx, no. 1, 1992: 203–19.

Mellor, Philip. "Protestant Buddhism? The Cultural Translation of Buddhism to England." *Religion* 21, no. 2 (1991): 73–92.

Menahemi, Ayelet Menahemi, producer. *Doing Time, Doing Vipassana*. Videotape. Karuna Films, Ltd., 1997.

Metraux, Daniel. *The History and Theology of the Soka Gakkai*. Lewiston, NY: Edwin Mellen, 1988.

———. *The Lotus and the Maple Leaf*. New York: University Press of America, 1996.

Morgante, Amy, ed. *Buddhist Perspectives on the Earth Charter*. Boston: Boston Research Center for the 21st Century, 1997.

Morioka, H. et al. *The Legacy of Fujii Guruji*. Tokyo: Japan-Bharat Sarvodaya Mitrata Sangha, 1988.

Nagabodhi, Dharmachari (Terry Pilchick). *Jai Bhim! Dispatches from a Peaceful Revolution*. Glasgow: Windhorse, 1988.

Nhat Hanh, Thich. *Vietnam: Lotus in a Sea of Fire*. Foreword by Thomas Merton. Afterword by Alfred Hassler. New York: Hill and Wang, 1967.

———. *Being Peace*. Berkeley, CA: Parallax Press. 1987.

———. *Peace Is Every Step*. Berkeley, CA: Parallax Press, 1991.

———. *Touching Peace*. Berkeley, CA: Parallax Press, 1992.

———. *The Blooming of a Lotus*. Berkeley, CA: Parallax Press, 1993.

———. *Love in Action*. Berkeley, CA: Parallax Press, 1993.

———. *Please Call Me By My True Names*. Berkeley, CA: Parallax Press, 1993.

———. *A Joyful Path*. Berkeley, CA: Parallax Press, 1994.

———. *Teachings on Love*. Berkeley, CA: Parallax Press, 1997.

———. *Interbeing*. Berkeley, CA: Parallax Press, Third Edition, 1998.

Numrich, Paul David. *Old Wisdom in the New World: Americanization in Two Immigrant Theravada Buddhist Temples*. Knoxville: University of Tennessee Press, 1996.

Obeyesekere, Gananath, and Richard Gombrich. *Buddhism Transformed: Religious Change in Sri Lanka*. Princeton: Princeton University Press, 1988.

Olcott, Henry S. *Buddhist Catechism, According to the Canon of the Southern Church.* Boston: Estes and Lauriat, 1885.

Payutta, P.A. *Buddhist Economics: A Middle Way for the Market Place.* Bangkok: Buddhadhamma Foundation, 1994.

———. *Buddhist Solutions for the Twenty-First Century.* Bangkok: Buddhadhamma Foundation, 1994.

Prebish, Charles S. "Ethics and Integration in American Buddhism." *Journal of Buddhist Ethics* 2 (1995): 125–39. <http://jbe.la.psu.edu/2/prebish3.html>.

———. *Luminous Passage: The Practice and Study of Buddhism in America.* Berkeley: University of California Press, 1999.

Prebish, Charles, and Kenneth Tanaka, eds. *Faces of Buddhism in America.* Berkeley: University of California Press, 1998.

Prothero, Stephen R. *The White Buddhist: The Asian Odyssey of Henry Steel Olcott.* Bloomington and Indianapolis: Indiana University Press, 1996.

Queen, Christopher S. "Buddhism, Activism, and Unknowing: A Day with Bernie Glassman." *Tikkun* 13, no. 1 (January/February 1998): 66–68.

———. "The Peace Wheel: Nonviolent Activism in the Buddhist Tradition." In *Subverting Hatred: The Challenge of Nonviolence in Religious Traditions*, edited by Daniel L. Smith-Christopher. Cambridge, MA: Boston Research Center for the 21st Century, 1998: 25–48.

Queen, Christopher S., and Sallie B. King, eds. *Engaged Buddhism: Liberation Movements in Asia.* Albany: State University of New York Press, 1996.

Rahula, Walpola. *What the Buddha Taught.* Bedford: Gordon Fraser, 1959.

———. *The Heritage of the Bhikkhu: A Short History of the Bhikkhu in Educational, Cultural, Social and Political Life.* First published in 1946. New York: Grove Press, 1974.

Rapaport, Al, and Brian D. Hotchkiss, eds. *Buddhism in America: Proceedings of the First Buddhism in America Conference.* Rutland, VT: Charles E. Tuttle, 1998.

Roche, Lisa, and Dan Turner, eds. *Ashes and Light: Auschwitz to Hiroshima Interfaith Pilgrimage for Peace and Life.* Amherst, MA: H. Newell Printing, 1996.

Rothberg, Donald. "Responding to the Cries of the World: Socially Engaged Buddhism in North America." In *Faces of Buddhism in America*, edited by Charles Prebish and Kenneth Tanaka. Berkeley: University of California Press, 1998: 266–86.

Sangharakshita. *Ambedkar and Buddhism.* Glasgow: Windhorse, 1986.

———. *New Currents in Western Buddhism.* Glasgow: Windhorse, 1990.

———. *The FWBO and "Protestant Buddhism"—An Affirmation and a Protest.* Glasgow: Windhorse, 1992.

Saramati, Dharmachari. "How Green Is the Path?" *Dharma Life* 2 (1996): 16–22.

Schmidthausen, Lambert. "The Early Buddhist Tradition and Ecological Ethics." *Journal of Buddhist Ethics* 4 (1997): 1–42.

Schneider, David. *Street Zen: The Life and Work of Issan Dorsey*. Boston: Shambhala Publications, 1993.

Seed, John, Joanna Macy, Pat Fleming, and Arne Naess. *Thinking Like a Mountain: Towards a Council of All Beings*. Philadelphia, PA: New Society Publishers, 1988.

Sharf, Robert, H. "Buddhist Modernism and the Rhetoric of Meditative Experience." *Numen* 42 (1995): 228–83.

Silberbauer, Cyril. "Blue-Print for the Dharma?" *Middle Way* (May 1972): 17–20.

Sivaraksa, Sulak. *A Socially Engaged Buddhism*. Bangkok: Thai Inter-Religious Commission of Development, 1988.

———. *Seeds of Peace: A Buddhist Vision of Renewing Society*. Berkeley, CA: Parallax Press, 1992.

———. *Loyalty Demands Dissent: Autobiography of an Engaged Buddhist*. Berkeley, CA: Parallax Press, 1998.

———. *Global Healing: Essays and Interviews on Structural Violence, Social Development and Spiritual Transformation*. Bangkok: Thai Inter-Religious Commission for Development, Sathirakoses-Nagapradipa Foundation, 1999.

Sivaraksa, Sulak, et al., eds. *Socially Engaged Buddhism for the New Millennium: Essays in Honor of the Venerable Phra Dhammapitaka (Bhikkhu P.A. Payutto) on His 60th Birthday Anniversary*. Bankok: Sathiraksoses-Nagapradipa Foundation, 1999.

Sizemore, Russell F., and Donald K. Swearer, eds. *Ethics, Wealth and Salvation: A Study in Buddhist Social Ethics*. Columbia: University of South Carolina Press, 1990.

Smith, Bardwell L., ed. *The Two Wheels of Dhamma: Essays on the Theravada Tradition in India and Ceylon*. Chambersberg, PA: American Academy of Religion, 1972.

———. *Religion and Legitimation of Power in Sri Lanka*. Chambersberg, PA: ANIMA Books, 1978.

———. *Religion and Legitimation of Power in Thailand, Laos, and Burma*. Chambersberg, PA: ANIMA Books, 1978.

Smith, Vincent A. *Asoka: The Buddhist Emperor of India*. Delhi: S. Chand & Co., 1964.

Snyder, Gary. *The Practice of the Wild*. San Francisco: North Point Press, 1990.

Subhadramati, Dharmacharini. "Working Wonders: Subhadramati's Experience of Practising Right Livelihood in a Buddhist Restaurant." *Dharma Life* 5 (1997): 38–41.

Subhuti, Dharmacari. *Buddhism for Today: A Portrait of a New Buddhist Movement*. Glasgow: Windhorse, 1988.

————. *Sangharakshita, A New Voice in the Buddhist Tradition*. Birmingham: Windhorse, 1994.

————. *Bringing Buddhism to the West: A Life of Sangharakshita*. Birmingham: Windhorse, 1995.

Swearer, Donald K. *Buddhism in Transition*. Philadelphia: Westminster Press, 1970.

————, ed. *Toward the Truth*. Philadelphia: Westminster Press, 1971.

Tambiah, Stanley J. *Buddhism Betrayed? Religion, Politics, and Violence in Sri Lanka*. Chicago: University of Chicago Press, 1992.

Tanaka, Kenneth K., and Eisho Nasu, eds. *Engaged Pure Land Buddhism: The Challenges Facing Jodo Shinshu in the Contemporary World*. Berkeley, CA: Wisdom Ocean Publications, 1998.

Tenzin Gyatso, Dalai Lama XIV. *Kindness, Clarity, and Insight*. J. Hopkins and E. Napper, eds. Ithaca: Snow Lion Publications, 1984.

————. *Freedom in Exile: The Autobiography of the Dalai Lama*. New York: Harper Collins, 1990.

————. *A Policy of Kindness*. Sidney Piburn, ed. Ithaca, NY: Snow Lion Publications, 1990.

————. *Ethics for the New Millennium*. New York: Riverhead Books, 1999.

Thompson, Penelope. "Beach Cleaning Meditation." *Mindfulness Bell* 9 (autumn, 1993): 11.

Thurman, Robert. *Inner Revolution: Life, Liberty, and the Pursuit of Real Happiness*. New York: Riverhead Books, 1998.

Titmuss, Christopher. *The Green Buddha*. Totnes, U.K.: Insight Books, 1995.

Tsomo, Karma Lekshe, ed. *Buddhism Through American Women's Eyes*. Ithaca, NY: Snow Lion Publications, 1995.

Tucker, Evelyn, and Duncan Ryuken Williams, eds. *Buddhism and Ecology: The Interconnection of Dharma and Deeds*. Cambridge: Harvard Center for the Study of World Religions, 1998.

Turning Wheel: Journal of the Buddhist Peace Fellowship. Berkeley, CA.

Tweed, Thomas A. *The American Encounter with Buddhism, 1844–1912: Victorian Culture and the Limits of Dissent*. Bloomington: Indiana University Press, 1992.

Tweed, Thomas A., and Stephen Prothero. *Asian Religions in America: A Documentary History*. New York: Oxford University Press, 1999.

Tworkov, Helen. *Zen in America: Five Teachers and the Search for an American Buddhism*. New York: Kodansha International, 1994.

Vajraketu, Dharmachari. "Working for the World." *Golden Drum* 4 (1987): 7.

————. "The Dana Economy." *Golden Drum* 22 (1991): 6–7.

————. "Marketing Values." *Dharma Life* 6 (1997): 24–27.

van Loon, Louis H. "Euthanasia: A Buddhist Viewpoint." In *Euthanasia*, edited by G. C. Oosthuizen et al. Pretoria: Oxford University Press, 1978: 71–79.

Victoria, Brian Daizen A. *Zen at War.* New York: Weatherhill, 1997.

Virachitta, Dharmachari. "The Practice of Right Livelihood," *Golden Drum* 12 (1989): 5.

Vishvapani, Dharmachari. "Still Building the New Society." *Golden Drum* 36 (1995): 24.

Watts, Jon, Alan Senauke, and Santikaro Bhikkhu. *Entering the Realm of Reality: Towards Dhammic Societies.* Bangkok: International Network of Engaged Buddhists, 1997.

White, James. *The Soka Gakkai and Mass Society.* Stanford, CA: Stanford University Press, 1970.

Whitmyer, Claud, ed. *Mindfulness and Meaningful Work: Explorations in Right Livelihood.* Berkeley, CA: Parallax Press, 1994.

Williams, Duncan Ryuken, and Christopher S. Queen, eds. *American Buddhism: Methods and Findings in Recent Scholarship.* Surrey, U.K.: Curzon Press, 1999.

Williams, George M. *Freedom and Influence: The Role of Religion in American Society.* Santa Monica, CA: World Tribune Press, 1985.

Wilson, Brian, and Karel Dobbelaere. *A Time to Chant: The Soka Gakkai Buddhists in Britain.* Oxford: Oxford University Press, 1994.

Winston, Diana, and Donald Rothberg. *A Handbook for the Creation of the Buddhist Alliance for Social Engagement.* Privately published by the Buddhist Peace Fellowship, August 1997.

Zadek, Simon. "Towards a Progressive Buddhist Economics." In *Entering the Realm of Reality: Towards Dhammic Societies,* edited by Jon Watts, et al., 241–73. Bangkok: International Network of Engaged Buddhists, 1997.

Zelliot, Eleanor. *From Untouchable to Dalit: Essays on the Ambedkar Movement.* New Delhi: Manohar, 1991.

CONTRIBUTORS

MARTIN BAUMANN, born in 1960 in Swakopmund, Namibia, studied History of Religions at the universities of Marburg, London, Berlin, and Hannover. His Ph.D. dissertation treated the transmission and adaptation of Buddhism in Germany. A post-doctoral thesis in 1999 treated the Hindu diaspora in the Caribbean and Europe. The diffusion and adaptation of Buddhist and Hindu traditions outside of Asia form the main focus of his research. The author of many articles on contemporary Buddhism in Europe, he is currently associate professor in the History of Religions at the University of Bremen (Germany).

SANDRA BELL teaches in the Department of Anthropology at the University of Durham, U.K. She has published articles on Western Buddhism in academic journals in Britain and the United States. She is co-editor, with Elisa Sobo, of *Celibacy, Culture, and Society: The Anthropology of Sexual Abstinence* (University of Wisconsin Press, in press) and, with Simon Coleman, *The Anthropology of Friendship* (Berg, in press).

RODERICK S. BUCKNELL traveled widely in Asia and practiced for four years as a Buddhist monk in Thailand, before returning to Australia in 1971 to take up academic life. He is currently reader in Chinese Language and Buddhist Studies at the University of Queensland. His publications include *The Twilight Language* and *The Meditative Way*, as well as several articles on Buddhism in Australia.

STUART CHANDLER, bibliographer and indexer for this volume, is a Ph.D. candidate at Harvard University. He is writing his dissertation on Master Hsing Yun and Fo Kuang Buddhism. While at Harvard, he has served as a researcher with the Pluralism Project, tracking the emergence of Buddhist, Hindu, Sikh, Jain, Islamic, and other religious communities in the United States. His chapter, "Placing Palms Together: Religious and Cultural Dimensions of the Hsi Lai Temple Political Donations Controversy," appears in Duncan Ryuken Williams and Christopher S. Queen, eds., *American Buddhism: Methods and Findings in Recent Scholarship* (Surrey, U.K.: Curzon Press, 1999).

DAVID W. CHAPPELL is professor and graduate chair of the Department of Religion, University of Hawaii. His doctorate at Yale University was on *Tao-ch'o* (563-645), *A Pioneer of Pure Land Buddhism*, and his major publications include

T'ien T'ai Buddhism: An Outline of the Four-fold Teachings (1983) and *Buddhist and Taoist Studies* vols. 1 and 2 (editor). After initiating a series of Buddhist-Christian conferences in 1980, he became founding editor (1980-1995) of the academic journal *Buddhist-Christian Studies,* founding director of the Buddhist Studies Program, UH (1987), and a co-founder of the Society of Buddhist-Christian Studies (1988). After co-editing *Unity in Diversity: Hawaii's Buddhist Communities* (1997), he is focusing more on Buddhist roles in modern society.

ROGER CORLESS is professor of religion at Duke University. Born near Liverpool, England, he read Theology at King's College, University of London (B.D., 1961), emigrated to the U.S. in 1962, and studied Buddhism, specializing in Pure Land Buddhism, at the University of Wisconsin at Madison (Ph.D., 1973). He has recently begun to investigate the practice of Buddhism in the gay-lesbian-bisexual-trans-sexual community. In July 2000 he will retire and increase his involvement in the developing field of Buddhist-Christian Studies.

LYN FINE has been practicing in the tradition of Thich Nhat Hanh since 1985, and was ordained as a Dharma teacher at Plum Village, France, in 1994. She is one of the founders of the Community of Mindfulness/NY Metro, and leads meditation retreats in the United States and Israel. An educational consultant in mindful conflict resolution, multicultural education, and peace education, Lyn works with parents, teachers, students, and administrators in the public schools in New York City. Her doctoral dissertation, "Children of War Becoming Leaders for Peace" (1995, NYU) focuses on the development of youth leadership and the transformation of traumatic memories in teenagers from zones of socio-political violence around the world, through personal storytelling, public speaking, and multicultural peer group support.

ROBERT GOSS is chair of the Department of Religious Studies at Webster University and Managing Editor of the *Journal of Religion & Education.* He is the author of *Jesus Acted Up: A Gay and Lesbian Manifesto* (1993) and coeditor of *A Rainbow of Religious Diversity* (1996) and *Our Families, Our Values: Snapshots of Queer Kinship* (1997). He has contributed a number of articles and book chapters on Buddhism and comparative religious studies on grief. He currently is working on a book on Buddhism and the cross-cultural study of grief.

PAULA GREEN founded and directs the Karuna Center for Peacebuilding, which provides education and training in intercommunal dialogue and conflict transformation worldwide. In recent years she has led educational seminars in Asia, Africa, Eastern Europe, and the Middle East, as well as in the U.S. and Canada.

Paula serves on the faculty of the School for International Training in Vermont, lectures and publishes internationally, and is the co-editor of *Psychology and Social Responsibility: Facing Global Challenges* (NYU Press). She holds graduate degrees in Counseling Psychology and Intergroup Relations from Boston University and New York University. Her Buddhist activities include membership on the Boards of Directors of the Buddhist Peace Fellowship, the Insight Meditation Society, and the International Network of Engaged Buddhists, as well as close affiliation with the Nipponzan Myohoji community in Leverett, MA.

PATRICIA HUNT-PERRY is professor of social thought at Ramapo College of New Jersey. She was the host commentator of the PBS series, *Prospects for Humanity*, and has lectured widely in the United States and abroad. The author of numerous articles and book chapters, she attended a retreat with Thich Nhat Hanh in 1987 to write a book chapter, and became a member of the Order of Interbeing. She lives on the farm where she was born in the mid-Hudson valley.

STEPHANIE KAZA is associate professor of environmental studies at the University of Vermont, where she teaches religion and ecology, environmental philosophy, and nature writing. She is a longtime Soto Zen practitioner affiliated with Green Gulch Zen Center. Her book, *The Attentive Heart: Conversations with Trees* (1993), is a collection of meditative essays on West Coast trees.

KENNETH KRAFT is chair of the Department of Religious Studies at Lehigh University. In the area of engaged Buddhism, he is the author of *The Wheel of Engaged Buddhism* (1999) and the editor of two anthologies, *Inner Peace, World Peace* (1992) and *Dharma Rain* (forthcoming, with Stephanie Kaza). He is also the author of the award-winning *Eloquent Zen*. He has served on the board of directors of the Buddhist Peace Fellowship.

FRANZ-JOHANNES LITSCH studied architecture at Fachhochschule in Konstanz. A Buddhist since 1962, he has studied under Karlfried Graf Dürckheim, Gesshin Prabasha Roshi, Genro Roshi, Tenga Rinpoche, Nyanaponika Thera, and Buddhadasa Bhikkhu. A student of Thich Nhat Hanh since 1985, he is a member of the Tiep Hien Order, founder of the Netzwerk engagierter Buddhisten (Network of Engaged Buddhists), and, since 1995, a member of the Council of the German Buddhist Union (DBU).

JANET MCLELLAN received her Ph.D in Social Anthropology from York University, 1993. Her interest in Asian Buddhists began over twenty years ago. She has taught for several years at the Department for the Study of Religion,

University of Toronto, and is currently a sessional instructor at Trent University. Her most recent publication is *Many Petals of the Lotus: Five Asian Buddhist Communities in Toronto* (University of Toronto Press, 1999).

SUSAN MOON is the editor of *Turning Wheel*, the journal of the Buddhist Peace Fellowship. She lives in Berkeley, California, where she raised two sons. She is a longtime Zen practitioner both at the Berkeley Zen Center and Green Gulch Farm, which is part of the San Francisco Zen Center, and she currently serves on the Board of San Francisco Zen Center. She has published many short stories and essays, and is the author of *The Life and Letters of Tofu Roshi* (Shambhala Publications, 1988), and co-editor with Lenore Friedman of *Being Bodies: Buddhist Women on the Paradox of Enlightenment* (Shambhala Publications, 1997). Her activism includes participation in the civil rights movement, the women's movement, and the anti-nuclear movement, and she has been arrested numerous times for acts of civil disobedience. In recent years her activism has been much quieter, expressed chiefly through the pages of *Turning Wheel*.

ANDREW OLENDZKI is the executive director of the Barre Center for Buddhist Studies in Barre, Massachusetts. His Ph.D. in Religious Studies is from Lancaster University in England (1987), and he has studied at Harvard University and the University of Sri Lanka. He has been executive director of the Insight Meditation Society (1990-96) and visiting lecturer at Harvard Divinity School (1996-99).

VIRGINIA COHN PARKUM received her Ph.D. in political science, focusing on participatory democracy and voluntarism, from the University of Mannheim, Germany. She helped develop public sector courses for the Yale University School of Organization and Management. She is currently studying Buddhism with Anthony Stultz and completing several works combining art and poetry, including reflections on Buddhist practice.

JOHN POWERS was awarded an M.A. in Indian Philosophy from McMaster University in 1984 and a Ph.D. in Buddhist Studies from the University of Virginia in 1991. He is currently Senior Lecturer in the Asian History Centre, Faculty of Asian Studies, Australian National University. He is the author of eight books and fifty articles, mostly on Tibetan and Indian Buddhism, including *Introduction to Tibetan Buddhism* (Snow Lion Publications, 1995), which has sold over 20,000 copies worldwide. He has also written extensively on contemporary Tibetan Buddhism and the human rights situation in Tibet.

CHRISTOPHER S. QUEEN is dean of students for continuing education and lecturer on the study of religion in the Faculty of Arts and Sciences, Harvard University. A student of Buddhism since 1965 (at Oberlin College, Harvard, and Boston universities), he has practiced *vipassana* meditation since 1978. He is co-editor and contributor to *Engaged Buddhism: Buddhist Liberation Movements in Asia* (State University of New York Press, 1996), and *American Buddhism: Methods and Findings in Recent Scholarship* (Curzon Press, 1999).

JUDITH SIMMER-BROWN is chair of religious studies at The Naropa Institute, Boulder, Colorado (Indian and Tibetan Buddhism, Engaged Buddhism, women and the feminine in Buddhism). Ph.D. Walden University. Dr. Simmer-Brown has been involved in Buddhist-Christian dialogue for the past fifteen years and has been an active participant in the contemporary North American discussion surrounding Buddhism in the West. She designed and founded the Engaged Buddhism track of the Buddhist Studies M.A. program at the institute. She writes and lectures on Indian, Tibetan, and North American Buddhist traditions and is currently completing a book entitled *Dakini's Warm Breath: Feminine Principle in Tibetan Buddhism*.

J. ANTHONY STULTZ is spiritual director of the Blue Mountain Meditation Center. He received an M.A. in Pastoral Theology from the Episcopal Divinity School (Cambridge) and has served both prisons and hospitals as a Buddhist clinical chaplain.

DARREL WRATTEN is lecturer in religious studies and associate director of the Institute for Comparative Religion in Southern Africa at the University of Cape Town. He is co-author of *African Traditional Religion in South Africa, Christianity in South Africa, and Islam, Hinduism, and Judaism in South Africa*, all published by Greenwood Press.

INDEX

About Wisdom Publications

Wisdom Publications, a not-for-profit publisher, is dedicated to making available authentic Buddhist works for the benefit of all. We publish translations of the sutras and tantras, commentaries and teachings of past and contemporary Buddhist masters, and original works by the world's leading Buddhist scholars. We publish our titles with the appreciation of Buddhism as a living philosophy and with the special commitment to preserve and transmit important works from all the major Buddhist traditions.

If you would like more information or a copy of our mail-order catalogue, please contact us at:

Wisdom Publications
199 Elm Street, Somerville, Massachusetts 02144, USA
Telephone: (617) 776-7416 • Fax: (617) 776-7841
E-mail: info@wisdompubs.org • http://www.wisdompubs.org

THE WISDOM TRUST

As a not-for-profit publisher, Wisdom Publications is dedicated to the publication of fine Dharma books for the benefit of all sentient beings and dependent upon the kindness and generosity of sponsors in order to do so. If you would like to make a donation to Wisdom, please do so through our Somerville offce. If you would like to sponsor the publication of a book, please write or e-mail us for more information.

Thank you.

Wisdom Publications is a not-for-profit, charitable 501(c)(3) organization and a part of the Foundation for the Preservation of the Mahayana Tradition (FPMT).